Also in the Variorum Collected Studies Series:

MIROSLAV HROCH
Comparative Studies in Modern European History
Nation, Nationalism, Social Change

JACEK KOCHANOWICZ
Backwardness and Modernization: Poland and Eastern Europe in the 16th–20th Centuries

ANNA ZARNOWSKA
Workers, Women, and Social Change in Poland, 1870–1939

NICOLAS OIKONOMIDES (Ed. Elizabeth Zachariadou)
Society, Culture and Politics in Byzantium

NICOLAS OIKONOMIDES (ED. Elizabeth Zachariadou)
Social and Economic Life in Byzantium

PETER B. GOLDEN
Nomads and their Neighbours in the Russian Steppe
Turks, Khazars and Qipchaqs

SIMON FRANKLIN
Byzantium – Rus – Russia
Studies in the Translation of Christian Culture

FRANCIS J. THOMSON
The Reception of Byzantine Culture in Mediaeval Russia

C.A. MACARTNEY (Ed. László Péter & L.G. Czigány)
Studies on Early Hungarian and Pontic History

PETER F. SUGAR
East European Nationalism, Politics and Religion

NIKOLAI TODOROV
Society, the City and Industry in the Balkans, 15th–19th Centuries

THOMAS S. NOONAN
The Islamic World, Russia and the Vikings, 750–900
The Numismatic Evidence

VARIORUM COLLECTED STUDIES SERIES

Christian Russia in the Making

Andrzej Poppe

Christian Russia in the Making

ASHGATE
VARIORUM

Published in the Variorum Collected Studies Series by

Ashgate Publishing Limited
Gower House, Croft Road,
Aldershot, Hampshire
GU11 3HR
Great Britain

Ashgate Publishing Company
Suite 420
101 Cherry Street
Burlington, VT 05401–4405
USA

Ashgate website: http://www.ashgate.com

ISBN 978–0–7546–5911–2

British Library Cataloguing in Publication Data
Poppe, Andrzej
Christian Russia in the making. – (Variorum collected studies series ; no. 867)
1. Russia – Church history 2. Russia – History
I. Title
281.9'47

Library of Congress Cataloging-in-Publication Data
Poppe, Andrzej.
Christian Russia in the making / by Andrzej Poppe.
p. cm. – (Variorum collected studies series ; no. 867)
Includes bibliographical references and index.
ISBN 978–0–7546–5911–2 (alk. paper)
1. Kievan Rus – Church history. 2. Kievan Rus – History – To 1500.
I. Title.
BR934. P64 2007
274.7–dc22 2006020595

The paper used in this publication meets the minimum requirements of the American National Standard for Information Sciences – Permanence of Paper for Printed Library Materials, ANSI Z39.48–1984. ∞ ™

Printed by TJ International Ltd, Padstow, Cornwall

VARIORUM COLLECTED STUDIES SERIES CS867

CONTENTS

Preface vii–xii

Acknowledgements xiii

I The Rurikid dynasty or seven hundred years of shaping Eastern Europe
First publication in English 1–25

II Once again concerning the baptism of Olga, Archontissa of Rus' (with Addendum, pp. 278a–279a) 271–277
Dumbarton Oaks Papers 46. Washington, DC, 1992

III How the conversion of Rus' was understood in the eleventh century 287–302
Harvard Ukrainian Studies 11. Cambridge, MA, 1987

IV Two concepts of the conversion of Rus' in Kievan writings 488–504
Harvard Ukrainian Studies 12/13. Cambridge, MA, 1988/1989

V The Christianization and ecclesiastical structure of Kievan Rus' to 1300 311–392
Harvard Ukrainian Studies 21. Cambridge, MA, 1997

VI Leontios, Abbot of Patmos, candidate for the metropolitan See of Rus' 1–13
Chrysai Pylai: Essays Presented to Ihor Ševčenko on this Eightieth Birthday, ed. P. Schreiner and O. Strakhov (Palaeoslavica X/2). Cambridge, MA, 2002, pp. 60–70, first publication in English)

VII Losers on earth, winners from heaven. The assassinations of Boris and Gleb in the making of eleventh-century Rus' 133–168
Questiones Medii Aevi Novae 8. Warsaw, 2003

VIII The sainthood of Vladimir the Great: veneration in-the-making 1–52
First publication in English

IX Words that serve the authority: on the title of "Grand Prince" in Kievan Rus' (with Addendum, pp. 185a–191a) 159–184
Acta Poloniae Historica 60. Warsaw, 1989

X On the title of "Grand Prince" in the *Tale of Ihor's Campaign* 684–689
Harvard Ukrainian Studies 3/4. Cambridge, MA, 1979/1980

XI Some observations on the bronze doors of the St. Sophia in Novgorod (with Addendum, pp. 419a–420a) 407–418
Les Pays du Nord et Byzance (Figura NS 19 – Acta Univsitatis Upsaliensis). Uppsala, 1981

XII On the so-called Chersonian antiquities (with Addendum, p. 105) 71–104
Medieval Russian Culture, ed. by H. Birnbaum and M.S. Flier. Berkeley: University of California Press, 1984

Index 1–18

This volume contains xiv + 362 pages

PREFACE

It has now been fifty-seven years since I began my study of history at the University of Warsaw, more than fifty since the completion of those studies, and nearly as many that I have been active as a teacher of the subject. While I have always approached my university teaching with a full sense of the responsibility it imposes, I must confess that it has only rarely brought me into contact with students genuinely interested in study. Likewise, while I have been impressed by the encyclopaedic knowledge of many of my teachers and university colleagues, my true passion has always been for detailed research in the field of medieval studies, for the clarification of developments only poorly covered by the sources or the solution of unresolved questions.

Already at the very beginning of my student years I was fascinated by the analytical prowess and bold hypotheses of a particular researcher who, it was said, "could see like a cat in the medieval night".[1] At the same time, the simplicity of that scholar's presentation, the imperfection of his annotation, and the general difficulty of his style, in a short, a certain heaviness of the pen, from which I likewise suffered, raised in me the hope that I, too, despite the delays imposed by seven lost wartime years, could cross the threshold in my studies and set off a on research career of my own. As I was soon to realize, however, the only road to such a career lay through firmly grounded seminar training, built upon mastery of the auxiliary disciplines of medieval studies. Hence my lively opposition to the current tendency toward turning the university into a kind of upper-level professional school preparing its students largely for imitative work. Too often today, university seminars, which were originally designed to awaken the interests of the young scholar and carefully shape an understanding of research methods, have been transformed into lecture courses for small or even large groups of listeners, at which one student reads his or her report (basically portions of an eventual masters essay) to the others, accompanied by the commentary of the instructor.

As I set out to acquire the principles of the skills and tools of the craft of medieval studies, I looked for models in the works of scholars who could,

[1] Tadeusz Wojciechowski, *Szkice historyczne XI wieku*, 3rd ed. (Warsaw, 1950): 20, prepared for publication by Aleksander Gieysztor, my teacher and academic master.

regardless of their national affiliation, generally be considered heirs of the school of Leopold Ranke. My particular research interests quickly became focused on the history of the East Slavs, supplemented, of course, by the often wide-ranging problems of Byzantine and West European history that the study of East Slavic questions entails.[2] In pursuit of those interests, I have not hesitated to combine a well-developed caution in formulating hypotheses with an openness to working concepts, while always seeking to avoid, however, the kind of unchecked speculation that can lead to the utterly fantastic conceptualizations that are sadly so popular among many students of early medieval Eastern Europe today.[3] Overall, I have preferred a model much like that of combinatorial mathematics, with its method for confronting a set of known facts with various carefully weighed, verifiable hypotheses. While not ruling out a role for intuition, I have allowed it to serve as the raw material for my thinking, appreciating how far off the road it can sometimes lead us.[4]

After half a century of research subjected to the hard rigours of the medievalist's craft,[5] I believe I have succeeded in filling in several small and a few medium-sized gaps in our knowledge of medieval Rus'. In recent years, my attention has been focused on three sets of problems in the history of Rus' during the tenth and eleventh centuries that either have been the subject of controversy or, passed over in silence, have demanded a fundamental revision. All are connected with the early medieval transformation of Rus'ian society that has had, through the whole of the second millennium, a decisive impact on the history of Eastern Slavdom: 1) the political situation and circumstances of the "baptism of Rus'" (see my 1982 collection, especially chapter II); 2) the process by which Rus' became a Christian country in the eleventh century, an era marked by the emergence of indigenous saints in royal and monastic garb (chapters VII and

[2] For example, my study of the circumstances and date of the creation of the Romanesque doors that have been located since the mid-fifteenth century at the portal of the cathedral in Novgorod (ch. XI here), required consideration of the place of the archdiocese of Magdeburg in the relations of the papacy with Frederick Barbarossa. See A. Poppe, "Die Magdeburger Frage. Versuch einer Neubewertung", *Europa Slavica-Europa Orientalis. Festschrift Herbert Ludat* (Berlin–Giessen, 1980): 297–340

[3] Cf. Brian J. Boeck, "Stone of Contention: Medieval Tmutarakan' as a Measure of Soviet Archeology in the 1950s and 1960s", *Ruthenica* IV (Kiev, 2005): 32–46

[4] I have held to this principle particularly in connection with the unusually complicated political conditions that were the cause and result of the treacherous assassination of the sons of Vladimir the Great and Anna the Pophyrogenita. Research conducted in various essays and analytic studies comprising nearly 360 pages have been presented in the current collection (ch. VII) in condensed fashion, supplemented in a few places by additional analysis.

[5] I consider my frequent characterization in the English-speaking world as a Slavist to be based on a misunderstanding, since I lack the necessary philological qualifications for such a title.

VIII in this volume); and 3) the role played in the political life of Kievan Rus', as *consors regni,* by Gertrude (1054–1107), the great-granddaughter of Otto II and his Byzantine wife, a personage who has been almost completely ignored by historiography.[6]

* * *

A quarter of a century has passed since the publication of the previous collection of my works by Variorum Reprints, *The Rise of Christian Russia* (CS157, 1982). This new collection is, in a certain sense, a continuation of the earlier one (see, especially, chapters III, IV and V here). It also contains several works that have not, until now, been available in English (chapters I, VI and VIII). The republication of works first published some years ago has understandably required some effort to supplement them with comments on the current state of research and to note any important new literature on those subjects (chapters II, IX, XI, XII).

It still has not always proved easy to come to terms with English-language terminology. However, the latter has by now adopted such terms as "Rus'" and "Rus'ian", as a way of more clearly distinguishing the medieval East Slavs from the modern Russia and Russians. Likewise, current usage in English-language writing has been affected by the emergence of Ukraine as an independent state, a process reinforced by the appearance in English translation of the great work of Ukrainian historiography by Myhailo Hrushevsky.[7]

At the close of the past century there were already signs of greater craftsmanship in East European medieval historiography. Nonetheless, a high degree of tolerance for often unwitting dilettantism still remains. The changes have not been as fast nor as radical as one would like. At the same time, it is worth noting that, despite many limitations, even under a totalitarian government, the study of medieval Russia enjoyed far greater freedom in its research, and a far greater possibility for polemic and critical assessment than did the study of modern or contemporary history.

* * *

[6] Part 1 of my study of this problem is published in Russian as: A. Poppe, "Gertruda-Olisava, ruskaia kniagini: Peresmotr biograficheskikh dannykh", *Imenoslov* II (Moscow, 2007): 205–229

[7] M. Hrushevsky, *The History of Ukraine-Rus'*, vol. 1: *From Prehistory to the Eleventh Century* (Toronto, 1997), 602 pp.; see my Introduction, pp. XLIII–LIV and additions to Hrushevsky's historiographical notes.

The title of this collection may appear both too broad as well as too compact, but the others I considered would have suggested a more exclusively religious focus than is the case here.

My principal work (chapter VII) concerns the sainthood of Boris and Gleb, which has been researched in different ways and with different results by many other scholars. This study interweaves both the political and genuinely religious themes in their respecive cults and for the first time provides secular reasons for the assassination of both princes: an unsuccessful attempt to challenge the succession to the Kievan throne, given that Boris and Gleb were the only legal heirs of Vladimir the Great and Anna Porphyrogenita, this argument has important significance for the eleventh-century history of Rus' and Byzantium. The Rurikid dynasty was not ready to accept Vladimir and Anna's decision to "byzantinize" the Kievan throne, and dynastic resistance after Vladimir's death played out in civil war (1015–1026). My proposition alters matters of the first half of the eleventh century, not only in Rus' but also for the Byzantine Empire. My thesis has been several years in the making, published in stages, but now complete and setting out the proof. It invites a future debate.

The abortive "byzantinization" of the Kievan throne at the beginning of the eleventh century calls attention to the Rus'ian dynasty itself, which persisted for over seven hundred years (chapter I). In this light we may note that the extinction of the Halich-Wolhynian branch of the dynasty at the beginning of the fourteenth was unfavourable to the formation of an Ukrainian state or nation. The significance of the Rurikid dynasty is one of reasons why I open this volume with a short essay ("A concise history") on medieval Russia, incorporating my observations and interpretations. I see it as particularly relevant to English-language readers who very often start their acquaintance with Russian history no earlier than Peter the Great, or sometimes perhaps Ivan the Terrible.

Chapter II, on the baptism of Olga, an event traditionally dated to 954/5, with her second visit to Constantinople occuring in 957, altered the terms of the debate. In the 1990s it was brought totally into question, but is now defended (see addendum). Furthermore, for my consideration of Olga's unsuccessful attempts in 959–961 to win the support of Otto, I have strong primary evidence to back this up; so far, there have been no objections to my analysis.

Chapter V: "Christianization and ecclesiastical structure...", begun in the early 1990s but not completed till 1998, reflects the results of the research I started in the 1950s. It also highlights questions that remain open. Chapter IX, on the title of "Grand Prince" is completed by a polemic with Martin Dimnik, who tried to prove that the Rus' started to use this title in the mid-eleventh century, against my argument for the end of the twelfth century. I discuss his opinion in addendum I.

In 1987 the late John Meyendorff encouraged me to explore the paths which led to the recognition of Vladimir's sainthood. The results of this exploration, which took more time than I had anticipated, are presented here in a triptych (chapter VIII). This study on "The sainthood of Vladimir the Great: veneration in the making", unlike other quests for the date of his "canonisation", offers the new conclusion that his sainthood was reached without any official Church proclamation, but developed from "time immemorial". In the first part of this chapter, the image of Vladimir as Christian is considered, alongside the historiography.

Some aspects of Western European Christian art are reflected in chapters XI and XII. The question under consideration is why the Romanesque bronze doors, made in 1153 in Magdeburg for the Polish cathedral at Płock on the Vistula and used to decorate the entrance to the cathedral church of Sophia in Novgorod the Great since the mid-fifteenth century, were perceived as having been manufactured in Byzantium and brought as spoils of war to Rus', specifically to Kiev and Novgorod, before the end of the tenth century from the Byzantine city of Cherson along with other "Chersonian" icons (chapter XII). For what reason was this legend composed in the last third of the fifteenth century? If it is merely to certify the possession of truly Orthodox relics then it is not only the emissary of the Austrian Emperor Sigismund, Herberstein (who visited Novgorod in 1517), that gives credence to this report. In the fifteenth and sixteenth centuries Moscow questioned many times the orthodoxy of the Novgorodians, and Novgorod used such arguments to protect its independence from the Muscovite rulers. It is easy to write this statement here now, but to unravel the background to it needed plenty of space.

In chapter XI the case for two discoveries is presented: both the bronze figures of the above-mentioned Romanesque doors were not made in Russian Novgorod in the fifteenth, as many art historians were ready to believe, but in Magdeburg in 1153 (the Abraham and Nicodemus). Since 1981 the technology of the brass-work of the doors has been analysed, and the conclusions, which support my earlier observations, are presented as an addendum.

One other contribution, now translated into English, focuses on a remarkable figure in the Byzantine Church, Leontios of Patmos (chapter VI). This also brings into question the old but erroneous conclusion that the Greek hierarchs delegated to Russia during the tenth-fifteenth centuries were motivated more by mercenary motives than pastoral duties.

Lastly, in a measured contribution to the great debate on the *Tale of Ihor's Campaign* (dated to the twelfth or the eighteenth century) I demonstrate (chapter X) that the title of "Great Prince" was employed there in accordance with the reality of the situation in the twelfth century, but still could not be used in the historiography as a strong argument against forgery. I suppose that both sides of the debate have ignored it.

In closing, I would like to express my thanks for the invaluable help I have received on several fronts in assembling this collection. For polishing of the English-language text, and the translation of a number of sections of it, I am obliged to Robert Scott, whom I have known for several years as a student, editor, and friend. I am also grateful to Ms Elisabeth Strakhov for her translation from the Russian of my essay on Leontios of Patmos. Among the many who have provided me with friendly advice and critical comment, special mention must be made of the outstanding Harvard polyhistorian Ihor Ševčenko and the seasoned publisher John Smedley, who also offered me much valuable advice and many helpful suggestions in 1980 and 1981 when I was preparing my first collection of reprints for publication. I would also like to thank the original publishers for consenting to the reproduction of the present set of articles here.

Finally it is my greatest pleasure to express my gratitude to my wife Danuta, who for the past fifty years has made it her task to ensure that my text is intelligible to my readers, and who has compiled the index for this volume.

ANDRZEJ POPPE

Warsaw
2007

ACKNOWLEDGEMENTS

Grateful acknowledgement is made to the following institutions and publishers for their kind permission to reproduce the essays included in this volume: Dumbarton Oaks, Washington, DC (II); The President and Fellows of Harvard College, Cambridge, MA (III, IV, V, X); The Board of Editors of *Questiones Medii Aevi* (VII); The Board of Editors of *Acta Poloniae Historica* (IX); Uppsala Univerisity (XI); The University of California Press, Berkeley, CA (XII).

PUBLISHER'S NOTE

The articles in this volume, as in all others in the Variorum Collected Studies Series, have not been given a new, continuous pagination. In order to avoid confusion, and to facilitate their use where these same studies have been referred to elsewhere, the original pagination has been maintained wherever possible.

Each article has been given a Roman number in order of appearance, as listed in the Contents. This number is repeated on each page and is quoted in the index entries.

I

The Rurikid Dynasty or Seven Hundred Years of Shaping Eastern Europe

In the seventh through tenth centuries, following the great migration of peoples, the expansive presence on the East European Plain of the Slavic neighbours of the Balts, Ugro-Finns and mostly Turkic nomads of the Black Sea steppes became increasingly apparent. Although, in contrast to Western Europe, Eastern Europe of the ninth and tenth centuries had not yet become a melting pot of ethnic ingredients in which the origins of future nations could already be seen, some territorial and political entities beyond the clan or tribal level were beginning to take shape. When the Vikings, or Varangians, as they were called there, appeared in the ninth century on the great waterway linking Scandinavia with the East and Byzantium, they found a variety of Slavic political groupings, headed by indigenous clan or tribal elites. Allying themselves with some of these groups against others, the Varangians set in motion a process of change that ultimately disrupted the formation of local territorial power and resulted in the creation of a remarkably far-flung state — Rus', with its capital in Kiev, which has often been compared, on the basis of a number of similarities, to the Carolingian realm. The multi-ethnic Kievan state was admittedly but one episode in the history of the Eastern Slavs, but it was to an episode of fateful consequence. Three Eastern Slavic nations were destined to emerge from its womb — Belarusians, Russians and Ukrainians, all of them known for centuries to their Polish neighbours as Ruthenians (Rusiny).

At the turn of the tenth to eleventh century, the construction of the Rus'ian state would be crowned by the adoption of Christianity, offsetting separatist tendencies with an episcopal and confessional unity and a common Old Church Slavonic written language that contributed to a sense of shared community. Before that time, however, it was the princely dynasty, assimilating to the predominantly Slavic environment and supported by multi-ethnic clan elites, that provided the cornerstone for Rus.

The beginnings of the Rus'ian ruling dynasty are lost in the mists of the ninth century, although the need to legitimize its claims inspired the development, in the eleventh century, of a semi-legendary tradition about its origins, written down by a chronicler at the beginning of the twelfth. According to that tradition, intensifying raids of Northmen in search of booty and tribute from the settlements of Ilmenian (Novgorodian) and Krivichian Slavs and the Finnish Wepsians and Chud' (Ests) to the south of the Gulf of Finland and Lake of Ladoga gave rise to a military alliance between those peoples, which succeeded in driving back the invaders. After the expulsion of the latter, however, the chronicler records, inter-tribal conflicts in the absence of any legal order led to a continuous state of war. It was therefore decided "to find a prince to rule and judge us fairly", and to this end, a clan of Varangians, called the Rus', was invited to assume power. One of its leaders, Rurik (Hrorikr in Scandinavian), settled down in Novgorod, founding a dynasty, that would come to be known, much later, as the Rurikids. In the sources of the ninth through eleventh centuries, the ethnic name Rus' came to be applied as well to the ruling elites of the state as a whole and, shortly thereafter, to most of the land and society ruled by the Rus'ian princes of Kiev.

The intense Scandinavian expansion into Western Europe that began in the ninth century was paralleled throughout that period by a similar penetration of Eastern Europe. However, no detailed information about the period of Rurik's own active rule is known, and the dates given in the chronicle for his reign (862–879) cannot be reliably verified. We can only be sure that in the mid-eleventh century Rurik was considered to have been the prince (*kniaz'*) of Novgorod. The Scandinavian-Slavic settlement of Horodishche near Novgorod, already in existence in the ninth century, could conceivably have been his residence. The title "kniaz'", common (in varying forms) to all the Slavic peoples as a designation for "leader", "ruler", or "king", was borrowed before the fifth century from the proto-Germanic "kuningaz", or Gothic "kunnings" or "kuning". The term thus has the same source as German "könig", Swedish "konung", or English "king". In early mediaeval Europe it was equivalent to the Latin title of "rex". Russian princes are consistently referred to in medieval sources as "reges".

The Primary Chronicle's account of the invitation to the Varangians had a continuing relevance for its readers. Clearly rejecting any suggestion of conquest, it presented instead the image of a social contract. The choice of a foreign *konung* as their prince, to serve as moderator and guarantor of internal peace, demonstrates the role that tribal assemblies played in the process. The communities and their elders, gathered together in assembly, bestowed on the prince, who already possessed power in the retinue of warriors (*druzhina*) who accompanied him, the authority that legitimized his rule. The dynasty thus enjoyed social acceptance, even before, as a result of Christianization, it could be said to exercise power by divine ordination. The historiography has tended to underscore the folkloric motifs of this legend, but the form preserved by the chronicler betrays the marks of a literary structure, one that appears to derive from an indirect knowledge of the Platonic concept of social contract, with which Christian authors, including the Byzantines, were certainly acquainted. While we can only conjecture about the true beginnings of the Rurikid dynasty, we can admire the erudition of the writer who was able to compile this account to order for the ruling family two centuries later.

The first historically verifiable ruler of Kievan Rus', known in Italy as well as Byzantium, was Igor (Ingvar), purportedly the son of Rurik, who was raised by his kinsman and regent, the semi-legendary Oleg "the Seer". Oleg (Helgi) extended the Rurikids' realm to the central Dnieper basin with a capital in Kiev and earned renown for himself by his 907 attack on Constantinople (Tsargrad), an event confirmed by the treaty of 911. Igor himself attacked the capital of Byzantium in 941. He died not long after conclusion of the Byzantine peace treaty of 944, during an attempt to force payment of tribute from the Derevlianians, settled between the rivers Sluch and Pripiat. If one can believe the account of the Byzantine historian Leo the Deacon, the Derevlianians inflicted a cruel death on the Rus'ian prince, rending him asunder by tying him to two treetops that had been bent together. No less cruel was the revenge exacted by his widow, Olga. Olga's reprisals against the Derevlianians' elite also reflected a consistent dynastic policy, aimed at the elimination of all the local leaders, whether physically, when resistance was encountered, or politically, when they proved more pliable, by cutting their status down to that of princely ministerials. The clan elites, if they managed to accommodate themselves to the process in time, were thus incorporated into the ranks of princely clients alongside the boyars, and his senior and junior retinues. The title kniaz' now became the sole prerogative of members of the dynasty, and certain names were reserved for them alone as exclusively princely ones. In external relations as well, only a Rurikid could present himself as a "prince of Rus'", "archōn ton Rhōs", "archōn Rhōsias" or "rex Russiae", underlining the exclusive claim of their dynasty to rule this land. In theory, any Rurikid could attain the right to the Kievan throne in accordance with the principle of seniority, but as the family grew larger, succession came increasingly to be decided by cunning and ability, or even, when necessary naked force and violence. Nonetheless, the seniority principle remained in force as well, legitimizing the enforcement of a claim if it could be backed up with power. As a result, the history of the dynasty was filled with quarrels and feuds among the princes, in which the family did not hesitate to involve its closest neighbours — the Polish princes, the rulers of Hungary, and the khans of the peoples of the Black Sea steppe, first their Polovtsian (Cuman) kinsmen, and then, beginning in the thirteenth century, the Mongols and Tatars.

Rus' truly entered on the European scene under Olga, who ruled Kiev as its regent from around 945 to 961 on behalf of her juvenile son Sviatoslav. She visited Byzantium twice, in 954 and 957, receiving baptism on the first trip. In that sacramental act, she took the name Helena, and her godparents were the imperial couple Constantine VII Porphyrogenitus and his wife Helena. Olga was also granted the exalted title of *zoste* (i.e., "girdled patrikia"), first lady of the imperial court. In 959, she dispatched envoys to the court of Otto I at Ingelheim and Frankfurt, requesting that a bishop and priests be sent to Kiev to spread the Christian faith. She also played a role in the education of her grandson, Vladimir, in a new spirit, even if this failed to yield immediate results. Nor did she neglect the consolidation of the Kievan state, emphasizing the administration and supervision of dependent territories. Olga-Helena's efforts to set the course for change were recognized as early as the eleventh century, in works that characterized her as "the morning light" or harbinger of the Christianization of Rus'. By the fourteenth century, she was widely venerated as a saint.

Sviatoslav, son of Olga and Igor (born *c.* 938 – slain in 972) achieved fame through his military expeditions against the Volga Bulgars and his breaking of the power of the Khazars in a campaign that reached as far as the foothills of the Caucasus. In 967 he concluded a military alliance with the Byzantine emperor, Nicephorus Phocas, against the Danubian Bulgars. When the emperor was assassinated in December 968, Sviatoslav, faithful to his ally, turned against the conspirators, led by the new emperor John Tzimisces, and began pursuing his own policy in Bulgaria. However, following a series of failures, he was forced to conclude a peace treaty with the Empire in July 971. He was killed the next year by the Pechenegs on the rapids of the Dnieper, and the proud victors turned his skull into a wine cup.

Of Sviatoslav's three sons, the youngest, Vladimir, finally succeeded him on the Kievan throne around 980. It was Vladimir who led Rus' into the Christendom, and placed the house of Rurik among the foremost dynasties of Europe. His decision to baptize Rus' grew out of changes dating back more than a century, but the moment of its realization was determined by favourable political circumstances. The Byzantine Emperor Basil II, entangled in a struggle against usurpers, sent envoys to Kiev in the summer of 987 in an attempt to save his crown. The delegation asked for permanent military support, in exchange promising to strengthen the alliance by the marriage of a member of the imperial family to the Rus'ian prince as soon as he became a

Christian. On January 6, 988 Vladimir and his court were baptized, and the prince assumed the Christian name of Basil (Vasily). Then, on 27 May, the day of Pentecost, a mass baptism of the Kievans took place in the waters of the Dnieper. A Rus'ian ecclesiastical province was created to spread the faith, an archdiocese (metropolitanate) subject to the jurisdiction of the patriarch of Constantinople. In the summer of 988, the emperor's sister, the *porphyrogenita* Anna, arrived in Kiev. A Rus'ian force of several thousand moved down to the Bosphorus that summer and ensured the victory of Basil II in two open-field battles, at Chrysopolis in January and at Abydos on 3 April, 989. The Emperor's diplomatic initiative paved Vladimir's way into the family of Christian rulers, and the marriage to the *porphyrogenita* assigned the Kievan prince a significant place in the family. Throughout the eleventh century, Europe's ruling houses — Piasts, Arpads, Premyslids, Capetians, Salians, the Scandinavian and Anglo-Saxon royal families — would seek dynastic ties with the Rurikids.

The year 988 added a new dimension and quality to the dynasty's contacts with the Christian cultural world. The Rus'ian ruling house was particularly adept at adjusting quickly to the new conditions and opportunities, sparing neither effort nor means in acquiring the values and cultural goods of the Christendom, drawing them primarily from the Byzantine world, including Bulgaria, with its already substantial literature in Church Slavonic.

The new faith substantially bolstered the position of the ruling dynasty. From the very beginning, the Church accorded a sacred quality to monarchical authority. Now, sermons and other writings, whether original or in translation, cultivated the notion that the Rus'ian prince was God's anointed, like the Biblical David or the Byzantine emperor. Princely authority was said to come from God. As Metropolitan Nikifor of Kiev put it, writing around 1113, the prince, a terrestrial ruler, was an icon of Christ, an earthly reflection of the heavenly ruler: God had set the example for an ideal ruler, which every prince should follow. Assigning the dynasty a clear set of duties toward the faithful, the Church ascribed to the prince the role of shepherd of Christ's flock, guardian of confessional orthodoxy, teacher and tutor, and instructed all his subjects that "to show disrespect for authority is to show disrespect toward God". The rich array of adjectives added to the prince's title in Rus', borrowed from Byzantium, was dominated by Christian terminology expressing the charismatic character of the prince's authority and person: "pleasing to God", "Christ-loving", "beloved of Christ", "guarded by God", "orthodox in faith", "most pious", etc. The ritual of accession to the throne was immediately Christianized by the *porphyrogenita* Anna upon her arrival. As a result, the existing ceremony of princely enthronement, symbolizing the active assumption of authority, became in the eleventh century an ecclesiastical ceremony, and the princely throne was given a permanent place in the palatine and cathedral churches. Enthronement now took place on a Sunday or a holy day. It began with the ceremonial entry of the prince into the town, where he and his attendants were met by a procession led by the clergy in liturgical vestments bearing icons and relics of the saints and followed by nobles and commoners crying out their welcome and acclamation. The metropolitan or a bishop then bestowed his blessing on the prince, and the latter, probably even before entering the cathedral, swore to reign with justice and in accordance with tradition, confirming his oath by kissing a crucifix presented to him by a church dignitary. On completing this act, the prince entered the temple to take part in liturgy. First he prostrated himself in prayer (*proskynesis*) before Christ and the Virgin, as an invocation drawn from Biblical texts describing God as the source of all terrestrial power and the ruler as God's elect were intoned. This was followed by the enthronement itself, in which the prince was led to his seat and was no doubt then handed the sword that symbolized his authority. The enthroned prince was led by a member of the dynasty or a court dignitary. The ceremony ended with the homage of the congregation to the ruler in the form of "prostration and kiss of respect". It is not certain whether the ceremony included an act of anointment, and if so, it would probably have had a merely metaphorical character, as in Byzantium, since every member of the dynasty in Rus' was considered already to be anointed by God by virtue of his or her birth into that family.

Seen from the Byzantine perspective, the ruler of Rus' did not bear a royal title, since the term "basileus" was considered a title appropriate only for the emperor of Romans (i.e. Byzantines). Instead, the Rus'ian prince was referred to in Byzantium as an *archōn*, a general term applied to various categories of power-holders. Byzantine-style coins represent Vladimir the Great with a flowing moustache, sitting on his throne, wearing a crown similar to the Byzantine stemma and holding a sceptre in his hand. There are reasons to believe that these insignia were carried to Rus' from the Bosphorus with the aim of adding royal splendour to the authority of the Rus'ian prince by Anna, herself a *basilissa* and *porphyrogenita* (so-called because of her birth in the porphyry-covered room of the Constantinople palace), whom Gerbert of Aurillac (later Pope Silvester II) characterized as "the daughter of the holy Empire" (*filia sancti imperii*), when she was asked to marry Robert the Capetian. In the family of rulers one might expect a crowned prince. But a crown was ultimately not retained by the House of Rurik. We can still see it on the coins of Vladimir's immediate heir, his son Sviatopolk (1015–1016 and

1018–1019), although already he began minting silver coins on which his own "portrait" was replaced by an image of his patron saint Peter. All coins of the next Kievan prince, Vladimir's son Yaroslav, bear only the image of his patron, St George. The brief episode of the crown was later so thoroughly forgotten that the rulers of Moscow sought to justify their own coronation by reference to a legend that the early twelfth-century Kievan prince Vladimir Monomakh had received imperial regalia from his grandfather, the Byzantine emperor Constantine IX Monomakhos (d. 1055).

Special rules clearly regulated the personal names used by the princely family, even if all the details can no longer be determined from the sources. There was certainly a group of names which were used exclusively by the dynasty. It became customary after the introduction of Christianity and until as late as the seventeenth century for princes to have two names: a lay one, used in everyday life, and a more intimate, Christian name. The Christian name, also known as the prayer name, was kept secret in everyday life to protect its bearer from evil spells, so that prince's Christian names must in most cases be indirectly ascertained, from the portrait of a patron saint on the front side of a princely seal or from information about church foundations. For instance, a chronicle entry for 1070 records that a son Rostislav was born to prince Vsevolod, and that in that same year his father began the construction of the church of the Archangel Michael, indicating that Vsevolod's Christian name must have been Michael. Starting in the mid-eleventh century the set of princely regnal names came to include the Christian names of earlier members of the dynasty. For instance, Sviatoslav named a son born around 1050 David, and toward the end of the eleventh century, Vladimir Monomakh, gave one of his sons the baptismal name of his grandfather, Yaroslav-George, and another the Christian name of his father, Vsevolod-Andrew. In the thirteenth century this custom of choosing princely names based on the Christian names of dynastic forebears became standard. Throughout the fourteenth and fifteenth centuries, baptismal "prayer" names which were often revealed only after the ruler's death continued to exist alongside the princely ones, although it appears that their choice was no longer guided by dynastic principles. The selection of patron saints depended more on the date of birth or baptism, as can be seen in the case of the baptismal name of Ivan III, born on January 22 (1440), the day of his holy patron St Timothy. On the other hand, the stock of princely names narrowed down in each line of the family; among the descendants of Muscovite prince Daniel, for example, two names, Ivan (John) and Vasil (Basil), predominate among those given to the eldest sons, the intended heirs to the throne.

Within a hundred years of the baptism of Rus', the significance of Vladimir's act was correctly appreciated, and compared to that of Constantine the Great and the Apostles. The gradually evolving cult of this "apostle among the rulers" was recognized by the Church at the end of the thirteenth century. His veneration developed particularly among the elites and, in an atmosphere of deepening political religiosity in the fifteenth century, assumed the characteristics of a state cult. In the view of society, St Vladimir came to be seen as the true founder of the dynasty, a view formally expressed in the "Book of Degrees of Imperial Pedigree", compiled in 1560–1563, which placed him at the starting point, relegating the earlier Rurikids to dynastic prehistory.

Soon after the death of Vladimir the Great (in July 1015), the dynasty and hence the entire Kievan realm were shaken by a powerful crisis, caused by the actions of the late ruler. Most likely under the influence of Anna, he broke with the customary right of succession to the throne of all his sons in order of seniority, instead naming his heirs exclusively from among the sons born from his marriage to the *porphyrogenita*, which had been sanctified by the Church. The Kievan throne was thus to be inherited, in Byzantine fashion, by Boris-Roman along with the minor Gleb-David as a co-ruler. The other sons defied this decision, according to which they were to be allotted peripheral shares subordinated to the senior in Kiev. Boris and Gleb were secretly assassinated and a struggle over the Kievan seniority ensued among the elder brothers. Responsibility for killing the *porphyrogenita*'s sons and Emperor Basil II's nephews was laid on the eldest son of Vladimir, Sviatopolk, the son-in-law of Boleslaw the Bold, who was most interested in overhauling the attempt to "byzantinize" the order of succession to the Kievan throne. It was probably then that the dynasty gave up on the crown, which was blotted out of the collective memory as a dangerous innovation, showing dependence on the donor of the crown.

The crime was committed with the quiet assent of the other members of the dynasty, judging from the conspiracy of silence so effectively covering up the event and its circumstances. It indeed had a substantial impact on the country's subsequent political destiny, facilitating a takeover of the throne by Yaroslav, who then passed it to his own progeny. The dynastic murder also gave rise, in second half of the eleventh century, to a hagiographic tradition expressed in the *Lives* of the Saints Boris and Gleb, which acclaimed the deeply Christian attitude of the innocent victims, who renounced resistance and the struggle for earthly power for the sake of the Kingdom of Heaven. The cult of the martyred princes served first of all to maintain peace within the dynasty: it reinforced the obligation of subordination to seniority right, voiced by the saints, but in the case of a senior's abuse of power, it also granted the junior the right of resistance. Strengthening the ruling house's political religiosity for centuries to come, the veneration of saints Boris and Gleb soon became a nationwide cult.

The saints were venerated as martyrs in Christ, who, like the apostles, had signed the sacred act of the baptism of Rus' with the blood of their martyrdom and become, like a double-sided sword, the country's defenders against internal and external enemies. The dynastic drama, filled with Christian content, thus served to strengthen the new faith in Rus' and rendered the entire ruling family sacred in a very real way. Several other Rurikids joined the ranks of the saints in later centuries, but none of those cults, including that of St Vladimir, ever achieved the sincerity, scope and spread of the cult of the saintly martyred princes.

Yaroslav the Wise (born 978, died 1054) reaped the fruit of Vladimir's policies, once he had become sole ruler of Rus' (1036–1054). He maintained broad contacts with European courts and even had ambitions of influencing succession to the Byzantine throne (supporting the usurper George Maniakes in 1043). Strengthening the Church and conducting further, intensive Christianization of the country, he also invested bishops, and even, with the support of the synod of Rus'ian bishops succeeded in naming a metropolitan, ignoring the prerogative of the patriarch. He was given the nickname "Wise" many years later by those ecclesiastical and monastic circles which favoured him. The apotheosis of the princely house under his rule in the 1040s is recorded in the frescoes of the Cathedral of Divine Wisdom in Kiev, a church founded by him. A large composition, set in the western part of the nave, depicting the donor along with his family, is clearly arranged to correspond to the mosaic frieze with the Eucharist opposite it on the curved surface of the apse. Viewing the two compositions together, one cannot avoid the impression that the twelve-person princely procession, approaching Christ on the throne from two sides, parallels the procession of the Apostles in the Eucharistic scene. This striking juxtaposition, clearly readable in the context of the Christological theme of the other frescoes in the main nave and the transept, graphically symbolized the apostolic mission of the ruling dynasty to reign over its subjects and its realm — the Rus'ian land. With the passage of time, this depiction of the founder and its family became an ever stronger testimony to the fact that the Kievan throne was the rightful inheritance of Yaroslav's descendants.

To prevent struggles over the Kievan throne after his death, Yaroslav placed responsibility for Rus' in the hands of his three eldest sons: Iziaslav (husband of Gertrude, the daughter of Mieszko II of Poland and his wife

Richeza, and the niece of emperor Otto III), who inherited the Kievan seniorate; Vsevolod, the prince of Pereyaslav, and Sviatoslav, the prince of Chernihov. The triumvirate functioned well for nearly two decades, but failed at some critical junctures and ended (1078) in the sole rule of Vsevolod (d. 1093). In 1113 Vladimir Monomakh (b. 1053, d. 1125), the son of Vsevolod and the daughter of Byzantine emperor Constantine IX Monomakhos (from his earlier marriage to Maria Skleraina), assumed the Kievan seniorate, contrary to seniority right, but thanks to his political agility and personal charisma. In 1075, Vladimir, sent by his father, had accompanied the Polish prince Boleslaw the Bold in a campaign supporting the Saxon opposition to the German Emperor Henry IV, reaching as far west as the Bohemian Forest and Bamberg on that expedition. Around 1074 he married Guida, daughter of the English king Harald Godwinson. When, in the fifteenth century the Muscovite princes sought to legitimize their claim to the supreme imperial authority, it was said to lie also in their direct lineage from Vladimir Monomakh. A crown with a sable fur band preserved to this day and known, since the turn of sixteenth century, as the cap of Monomakh, was said to be part of the regalia Vladimir had received from his imperial Byzantine grandfather. (In reality, the cap was manufactured in Central Asia at the end of the fourteenth century.)

Of Vladimir Monomakh's eight sons, one of the youngest, Yury Dolgoruky, or the Long-Armed (b. around 1090, d. 1157), established a line known thereafter as the younger branch of the Monomakhs and is worthy of closer attention. Allotted a peripheral Rus'ian province, "beyond the woods" between the Oka and Volga rivers, he went down in history as the founder of the future might of Moscow. The meeting that he held with the prince of Chernihov in that city in 1146 has been seen by later historiographers as the beginning of this town's long development into the Russian capital. In the 1140s and 1150s, Dolgoruky was temporarily successful in grabbing the Kievan throne (hence his nickname), but the real arena of his success was in the Rostov–Suzdal land, intensively colonized by the Slavs.

Yury's sons, first Andrei Bogolubsky (d. 1174), whose nickname derived from his foundation of the residential complex of Bogoliubovo, near his new capital, Vladimir on the Kliazma, and then Vsevolod Big Nest (so named by historians because of his large progeny), resigned the attempt to attain the Kievan throne, instead striving to make the Vladimir–Suzdalian principality pre-eminent among the Rus'ian lands. In the 1160s, Prince Andrei tried, albeit unsuccessfully, to become ecclesiastically independent of Kiev by raising the diocese of Rostov–Suzdal to the rank of metropolitanate, a church province directly subject to the patriarch of Constantinople. Nor did he hesitate to seek the political degradation of Kiev: when he conquered the capital in 1169, in the midst of a dynastic struggle, he looted it savagely, carrying away countless cultural treasures, including many books and liturgical objects. He also exercised influence over the political life of Great Novgorod and other Rus'ian lands. Fifteen princes recognized him as their senior. Violent and power-hungry, he fell victim to an assassination plot, but his work toward creating a new political centre in Rus' was continued by his youngest brother, Vsevolod, who had spent six years in Byzantine exile (1162–1168). The Vladimir–Suzdalian realm expanded under Vsevolod's rule (1176–1212) to the regions of the Oka and Volga through the subjugation and assimilation of neighbouring Finno-Ugric tribes. Military successes in expeditions against the Polovtsians, Volga Bulgars and Mordvinians, subordination of the principality of Riazan and the republic of Great Novgorod, as well as continuing influence in Kiev, Chernihov and Halich all served to elevate Vsevolod to the position of a genuine senior — "father" to the other princes. The idea of divine legitimation of the dynasty and its representative, Vsevolod, found expression in the decorated facades of the churches he founded, which combined the Byzantine-Slavic architectural tradition with Romanesque bas-relief. Vsevolod was the first Rus'ian prince to consistently use the official title of "grand prince", expressing his aspiration to a position of superiority over Rus'. The appearance of such a title revealed how deeply the title of "prince" had depreciated through the growth of the dynasty in the number of its members and their claims to shared power. The title of "grand prince", translated externally as "great king" ("magnus rex" in Latin chronicles, "megas rex" in Byzantine documents addressed to Rus' from the second half of the twelfth century onward), was later adopted by many significant appanage princes, as well as by the Gedyminids.

Viewed from a historical perspective, Vsevolod's work can be seen to have been continued, despite the difficult conditions of the Mongol-Tatar conquest, by his grandson, Alexander (born c. 1220, d. 1263), son of Grand Prince of Yaroslav of Vladimir. Alexander first gained renown for his victorious battles against the Swedes on the Neva in 1240 (hence, his later nickname) and against the German Knights on ice-bound Lake Peipus in 1242. Deciding to recognize Mongol overlordship and to collaborate with the conquerors, he paid allegiance to Batu-Khan and the Grand khan in Karakorum, capital of Mongolia, in 1248, gaining a patent for the Grand Principality of Vladimir and later for Kiev as well. To consolidate his position, he did not hesitate to repress, with Mongol help, his own brothers and subjects.

Alexander Nevsky's Mongol policies met with a mixed reception among his contemporaries, and have continued to be controversial down to the present. These policies were supported by the upper social strata and the Church, who believed that resistance had no chance of success and could only lead to the liquidation of statehood. The life of Alexander, written as early as around 1282 — a kind of hagiographically coloured "gesta", praised his political wisdom. The local cult at his gravesite, dating back to 1380, led to his successful canonization in 1547. Thus Alexander Nevsky, grandson of Vsevolod Big Nest and great-grandfather of Ivan Kalita, who was the real founder of the Muscovite line, became the ideal of the far-sighted ruler, caring for the state as the highest good.

Despite the emergence of several lines of princes, ruling in the capitals of particular appanages (some of which shrank dramatically in size in the centuries that followed), the descendants of Monomakh managed successfully to assert their right to the Kievan throne in the first half of the twelfth century and, with the passage of time, to the Muscovite throne as well, though not without conflict with the princes of Chernihov. Although the younger line of Monomakh's descendants withdrew from the contest for direct control of Kiev after 1157, it continued, as we have seen, to exercise influence over the Kievan throne. At the same time, nation-building processes were taking place among the Slavs of the central Dnieper basin, heartland of the old Kievan Rus', long known to their neighbours and themselves as Rusiny (or, in the West, Ruthenians) and only in modern times as Ukrainians (from "Ukraina", the term for the broad borderland areas of the Polish Commonwealth). This southern group of the Eastern Slavs, inhabiting the lands on and between the Dnieper and Dniester, were ruled, from the outset, by their own branches of the Rurikid house. Apart from a number of smaller principalities, one should mention here the Chernihov-based descendants of Vsevolod, the older, Kiev-Volhynian line of Monomakh's offspring, and the line of Rostislav in Halich, ruling the Dniester basin since the 1070s. The last of these died out toward the end of twelfth century, while the Volhynian descendants of Roman (d. 1205) and Daniel (d. 1264) became extinct in the male line in around 1322, and in the female line with the death of Boleslav-Yurii of the Mazovian ducal family in 1340. Upon his death, the related dynasties of Piasts and Gedyminids staked claims to the Halich throne, resulting in 1352 and 1366 in the partition of the "kingdom of all little Rus'" between Poland and Lithuania. Rus'-Ukraine was doomed through the lack of a dynasty of its own.

The lands which lay, from the perspective of Kiev, on the far side of the massive Desna-Bryansk forest, between the Oka and Volga, and therefore known as Rus' "beyond the forests", were intensively colonized by the Slavs and provided the territory for a new state in the fourteenth century. That state, whose earlier centres had been Rostov, Suzdal and Vladimir on the Kliazma, now came to be known, from its new capital city, as Muscovy, or simply Moscow. Its inhabitants were likewise called Muscovites, Moskvins, Moskvitins, or Moskals in the Ruthenian-Lithuanian and Polish lands until, having evolved into the Great Russian nation, they assumed the name "Russians". Here, a process leading ever more clearly toward the formation of a great Russian empire was steered increasingly by the descendants of Daniel of Moscow, one of the younger lines of the junior Monomakh branch, which sought, with the support of the Orthodox Church, to provide an appearance of historical continuity to this undertaking, ultimately asserting its claims to all the lands that had ever been ruled by the "princes of Rus'", the descendants of the legendary Rurik and, most importantly, of the first Christian ruler of Rus', St Vladimir the Great. When, at the end of fifteenth century the Muscovite rulers were eager to adopt the title of tsar (emperor), the legend about Vladimir Monomakh's imperial-Byzantine regalia was born.

In pre-Mongol Rus', the imperial title of "caesar" was usually connected with the Byzantine emperor, or *basileus*, and it was applied to Rus'ian princes only in literary works that sought to praise the absolute character of a particular prince's power. On the other hand, the Mongol (Tatar) khan was at once recognized as an absolute ruler, whose authority was unlimited in all matters of internal and external policy. The khan, who confirmed the accession of the princes of Rus' to their individual thrones, who granted the patent for rule over the grand principality and "seniority among all the brothers", who served as judge in deciding conflicts between the princes, and who handed out sentences all the way down to capital punishment, was clearly befitting of the title of supreme sovereign. It was no accident, then, that possibly as early as the second half of the thirteenth century, and certainly by the fourteenth century, a new term "tsar", a corruption of the word "caesar", began to function in both popular parlance and written texts as the title of the ruler of the Golden Horde, ultimately replacing the imperial title altogether (even the Heavenly "Caesar" became the Heavenly "Tsar"). While any characterization of the prince of Rus' as a "tsar" in this era was out of step with realities of the age, it served nonetheless as an expression of the strivings and aspirations of the elites for a state liberated from the Tatar yoke, or at least sovereign in its internal affairs. In this manner, the monk Akindin writing in 1311 to the "grand prince and holy autocrat of the Rus'ian throne" Michael (the grand prince of Tver and, from 1304 to 1317, of Vladimir), reminded him that he (Michael) had the authority to serve as the judge over

I

ecclesiastical matters, and even over the metropolitan himself, since "you are, my Lord and Prince, the tsar in your own land".

Except in special cases, the Mongol-Tatar khans never sought to abolish local authority in their conquered territories. They avoided excessive interference in everyday matters in Rus', especially in its religious life, exhibiting tolerance and understanding for the Church's activities. The main objective of their rule was fiscal — the tribute, collected through local princely authorities for the conqueror. The Tatar protectorate over the Rus'ian lands consequently strengthened both the position of the Church through the privileged legal status that its institutions, clergy and dependent population enjoyed and a monarchical ideology envisaged in terms of absolute power by which the entire populace, whether native or foreign, was reduced to the status of servants or slaves. Such an understanding of sovereign power left its imprint on many institutions of the Muscovite state. Thus, in the fifteenth century one sees the emergence of the (actually untrue) notion that all social strata, including the highest ones, were equal members of a single estate of subjects, who, in addressing the Muscovite ruler in speech or in writing characterized themselves as his slaves (*kholopy*). They would additionally use the diminutive form of their names to underline their inferiority and humility in the face of the Majesty. Such degradation affected not only the numerous princely families of the Rurikids, who already, in the thirteenth century, had lost their monopoly to the princely title thanks to the Gedyminids, but also the Tatar princelings and *mirza*s who entered the Muscovite rulers' service. The lords of Moscow also proved most effective in winning over for their plans the Church, privileged by the Mongol-Tatars: both its hierarchy as well as the truly fundamental spiritual force of Orthodox Christianity, the monasteries, with the monastery of the Holy Trinity and St. Sergius of Radonezh in first place. Finally, the metropolitans of Kiev and of all Russia, who had already fled in 1299 from the Dnieper valley, where they had been harassed by the Tatars, to the more secure Vladimir-Suzdalian region, now made their permanent residence in Moscow.

The first prince of Moscow was Daniel, the youngest son of Alexander Nevsky, ruling between 1280 and 1303 over an appanage-principality with an area of around 12,000 sq. km. The Muscovite branch of the Rurikids, or Danilovichi, as they were also called, managed, in a relentless struggle for hegemony against the other lines of the house of Rurik as well as its own, to enlarge the territory of the realm nearly two hundred times over the course of two centuries and seven princely generations to control more than 2.5 million sq. km and 6 million inhabitants at the beginning of the sixteenth century. A considerable portion of those dazzling successes was due to Daniel's grandson, Ivan Kalita (i.e. the Purse, 1325–1341). Having gained the support of the metropolitans of Rus', who preferred to reside in Moscow rather than the more vulnerable city of Vladimir, he also won, in the course of a vicious rivalry against the other princes, the Tatar patent for the title of grand prince of all Rus'. Ruthlessly putting down an anti-Tatar uprising in Tver in 1327, he gained special favour with the Golden Horde, and along with that, the authority to collect the Tatar tribute from the other princes and Rus'ian lands. Aided by the Tatar troops, he did not hesitate to loot his neighbours' lands, extorting obedience and collecting the tribute. In the process, he benefited his own coffers, hence his nickname. The policy of closely collaborating with the Tatars, bringing substantial financial gains, and of allying with the Church, became the guiding principles of Kalita's successors, his sons Simeon the Haughty (d. 1353) and Ivan II (d. 1359). The latter was a rather dull character, but the Kalita policy was continued both during his reign and the regency during the minority of his son Dmitry "Donskoi" thanks to the efforts of the Muscovite nobility and the Church. Dmitry (b. 1350, d. 1389) aptly combined mobilization of Tartar support for actions against the grand principality of Tver' and Lithuania (particularly after the death of Lithuanian Grand Prince Olgerd in 1377) with successful manipulation of conflicts within the Golden Horde. At the battle of Kulikovo Pole near the Don River in 1380, he undertook to challenge Tartar sovereignty over Rus'.

The significance of Dmitry's victory at Kulikovo, commemorated in the nickname of the victorious prince but purchased at the price of heavy raids against his country and the destruction of Moscow, could only be appreciated from a longer-term perspective. Writing in the mid-fifteenth century, a biographer of Grand Prince Dmitry consistently refers to him as a *tsar*, in recognition of his efforts and role in liberating the country from the Tatar yoke. Nineteenth- and twentieth-century historiography clearly presents an idealized view of Donskoi, since the chronicles show the period of his reign to have been an unending series of feuds among princes, a time when Tartar, Lithuanian and home-based troops ravaged the country. Nevertheless, it is also true that the ruler was a skilful and cunning diplomat who, by defying the appanage princes, including those of his own family, forged a permanent union of the grand principality of Vladimir with Muscovy as a single realm with common titles, which he passed on as an inheritance, without seeking the permission of the Golden Horde, to his oldest son, Vasily I (d. 1425).

Vasily I married Sophia, daughter of Grand Prince Vitovt of Lithuania, which did not deter him from conducting an anti-Lithuanian policy of rivalry over the lands of Rus'. This policy continued, under his son Vasily II the Blind, despite the fact that, as an orphan, he had been brought up under the protection of Grand Prince Vitovt, his maternal grandfather. Throughout much of his reign, Vasily II fought ruthlessly with his paternal uncle and the latter's sons over Moscow and the throne of the grand principality. Although blinded in the course of this conflict, he was ultimately able to defend the principle of primogeniture, supported by internal forces, especially the nobility holding estates in return for service to the ruler. A completely new role in this dynastic war among the descendants of Dmitry Donskoi (1430–1450) was played by the Tatars. The Golden Horde, which had, since the times of Ivan Kalita, favoured the unifying policy of the Muscovite rulers in return for their recognition for its protectorate and the obligations that implied, was falling apart. Feuding Tatar clans found it advantageous to adapt themselves to the new circumstances. The opponents of Vasily the Blind blamed him for enlisting the services of Tatar princelings and *mirza*s alongside his own troops. Vasily and his successors followed the lead of Vitovt in actively settling Tatars on their lands. The Tatar dukes and their subjects were even granted contiguous areas with extensive internal autonomy. Such was the origin of the little realm of khan Kassim, which was established in 1445 around 110 kilometres away from Moscow. The allotment of appanages within the Muscovite state to Tatar clans revealed the habituation and assimilation of a once perilous enemy. A part of the Tatar elite joined the ranks of the service nobility, which was obliged to perform military service. The tables of history were thus turned under Vasily the Blind: now the Tatars began to serve Moscow, defending its interests against those of compatriots in the petty khanates that emerged as a result of the disintegration of the Golden Horde.

Vasily II took an ever firmer stand in defence of the Orthodox tradition against the Union of Florence (1439) than did the ecclesiastical hierarchy, in the process making the high clergy totally dependent on princely authority and paving the way for an autocephalic (jurisdictionally independent) Rus'ian Church, sealed by the fall of Constantinople in 1453. Under the banner of opposition to the union, he transformed the former Kievan and all-Rus'ian ecclesiastic province of the patriarchate of Constantinople into the metropolitanate of Moscow and all Rus', limited to the area of the territorially-expanding Muscovite state. With the abandonment of their jurisdiction over the Orthodox Church in the Grand Principality of Lithuania, the metropolitans resident in Moscow became ever more subordinated to the rulers of Muscovy. Domination of the Church strengthened the dynastic tradition, reflected in the rise to the cult of St. Vladimir the Great, founder of Christian statehood and apostle of Christianity in Rus'. This cult legitimized Muscovite rulers as his full successors and heirs to all the Rus'ian lands.

As a result of the successful expansionist policies of Gedymin, Olgerd and Vitovt, the Grand Principality of Lithuania absorbed a substantial part of the Rus' (roughly the area of present-day Belarus and Ukraine), becoming, in the course of the fourteenth century, an increasingly Rus'ian land, with a predominantly Orthodox population. Inheriting the central regions of Rurikid Kievan Rus', the Gedyminids emerged as dangerous rivals for Moscow in the gathering together of the Rus'ian lands. However, union with Poland and belated Christianization along with the growing influence of the Catholic Church, the related inability of Vilnius to inherit the spiritual traditions of Kiev, and schisms and quarrels within the Orthodox Church all combined to hinder the ability of the Grand Principality of Lithuania to complete with the Grand Principality of Moscow. The Gedyminids' chances were ultimately dashed by the defeat which Vitovt's troops suffered at the hands of the Tatars on the Vorskla river in 1399. The heavy losses suffered there by the Ruthenian boyars and nobility forced Vitovt to seek closer ties with the Polish Crown, while reducing his independent Eastern policy. Although, throughout the fifteenth century, and especially in the reign of Vitovt, Lithuania was still able to weaken and slow down Muscovy's unifying trends, it failed to capitalize on the internal strife among the claimants to the Moscow throne between 1430 and 1450, and the reign of Casimir IV of Lithuania and Poland witnessed a *de facto* withdrawal from involvement in Eastern politics.

The Rurikids resorted to diverse actions to undermine the claim of Vilnius to the Rus'ian lands, including a hereditary argument, contained in the "Genealogy of the grand princes of Lithuania", a pamphlet directed against the Gedyminid clan. The version in which it has come down to us, written by a Muscovite author, dates back to the turn of the sixteenth century, but it was already known in its basic form in Poland and Lithuania in the fifteenth century, where it may have appeared, not without inspiration from the hostile Teutonic Order, as early as the beginning of that century. The genealogy depicted "Gedyminek" as a serf and groom to the "princelet" of Smolensk, Witen. He was reported to have married the widow of his lord, producing seven sons, including "Olgerdik" and "Keistutik". Upon receiving the patent to the Vladimir Grand Principality, Yury, son of Muscovite prince Daniel, was said to have made the "Gedyminik" his governor of the Kievan and Minsk regions, and the latter to have taken advantage of strife between princes to rise as the grand prince of Lithuania. Olgerd, it was asserted, was a prince only by virtue of his marriage to princess Uliana from Tver', of the House of Rurik. The pamphlet served Moscow as an instrument in its rivalry against Lithuania especially during the first decades of the sixteenth century, although Muscovite diplomacy had resigned from indiscriminate genealogical assaults on the descendants of Gedymin by the time of the reign of Vasily III (after 1520), and certainly under Ivan IV.

Moscow's power was further constructed by Vasily II's son, Ivan III, who brought together the majority of the Rus'ian lands in a united Muscovite state between 1463 and 1505. The incorporation of Novgorod in 1478 on the pretext of countering a threat to the Novgorodians' confessional orthodoxy by the Latin heresy ushered in a series of repressions and mass resettlements, rapidly altering the pattern of land ownership. In general, a growing role came to be played in the state by the service nobility, living on lands granted in return for military and other state service (*pomest'ia*). This process in turn weakened the position of the hereditary *boiars*, who drew their strength from their patrimonial landholdings (known as *votchina*) and whose members included many descendants of Rurik.

Taking the advantage of disputes among the successors to the Golden Horde, Ivan III refused to continue to pay the Tatar tribute; historiography recognizes the year 1480 as the formal date when the Tartar yoke was thrown off. In 1487, Muscovy proceeded to impose its domination over the Tartar khanate in Kazan. Relations with Lithuania were disrupted by the continuing rivalry over border areas and by mutual efforts to lure the other's nobles into service across the border. Nor were relations improved at all by the marriage of Ivan's daughter, Helen, to Grand Prince Alexander of Lithuania in 1495. Ivan III's marriage to a Byzantine princess, Sophia (Zoe) Palaiologina, in 1472, preceded by several years of negotiations with the Papacy, opened up new European prospects for the growing state, as the West counted on Muscovy's adherence to the anti-Turkish coalition then being formed. Following the fall of Byzantium, the role of Moscow grew as the successor to Constantinople, known as the "new" or "second Rome". This notion was reinforced by historical reflections that superimposed Kiev's alleged links with the first Rome onto the relationship of that first Rome with "the third Rome". When, in the second half of the fifteenth century, under Ivan III and his successors, contacts with the Papacy were particularly frequent, and architects, doctors and various experts were all brought in from Italy, the activity of Vladimir the Great was readily held up as a model. Moscow's chroniclers at the turn of the sixteenth century asserted that that ruler, while engaging in the contacts with the "old" Rome and receiving Latin envoys, had remained true to Orthodoxy as it was understood by patriarch Photios. Byzantine tradition bequeathed adornments that could bolster the ruler's authority, such as the courtly diplomatic protocol, a coronation ceremonial, and imperial titles. It was in this period that the title of "tsar" came into official use, and that "the cap of Monomakh" appeared as a crown, at the coronation of Ivan III's grandson Dmitry as a co-ruler in 1498 (probably the first instance of this ceremony in Moscow). The double-headed eagle, which was introduced in this period as a symbol of the monarch's power in the official coat of arms, was related to the Byzantine and southern Slav emblems; at the same time, the grand state seal included borrowings from the Western imperial seal, with its double-headed Habsburg eagle.

The son of Ivan II and Sophia Palaiologina, Vasily III (1505–1533), crowned himself ruler of all Rus' in 1505. He incorporated Pskov in 1510 and the principality of Riazan in 1521, recovered Smolensk in a war against Lithuania in 1514, and continued to colonize the state's southern and eastern borderlands. Vasily's internal policies were characterized by a relentless drive toward the centralization of power: in 1509 he did away with his nephew, co-tsar Dmitry, a potential pretender to the throne, after throwing him into prison. His reprisals against stubborn noblemen and princes, accompanied by skilful manipulation of the feuds among the members of the elite, foreshadowed the bloody terror his successor would unleash. In an effort to enhance the internal and external stature of the state, new features were added to the official ideology. The dynastic legend now no longer drew upon St. Vladimir alone, but also retrieved Rurik from oblivion and provided him with a legendary ancestor, Prus, supposedly the brother of Emperor Augustus and ruler of a Prussian land stretching from the Vistula (Malbork and Gdansk) all the way to the towns on the Nieman. In the new version, Rurik was no longer invited to Novgorod from Scandinavia, but from the Prussian, or German, land. Moscow thus laid claim as well to the inheritance of declining Teutonic Prussia, with an eye to the lands of the Livonian Order as well. Seeking its roots in the Roman Empire and ancient history, a practice so popular in Renaissance historiography, the House of Rurik subscribed to European fashion and asserted the right of Moscow, the "third Rome", to the heritage of the "first Rome" as well as to the Othodoxy of the "second Rome" ("and a fourth there shall not be"). The tsar, ruler of Moscow and all Russia, had been transformed into a new Moses, new David, new Constantine the Great, and, lastly, a new Vladimir the Great in the role of defender and guardian of Christianity and Orthodoxy.

Ivan IV the Terrible (b. 1530, d. 1584) was the son of Vasily III and Helen Glinsky, who served as regent between 1533 and 1538. (The Glinskys, a princely family with Tatar roots, had once occupied high posts in the Grand Principality of Lithuania but entered Muscovite service in 1508.) Ivan IV's coronation as the tsar of all Russias in 1547 inaugurated a period of despotism and tyranny, shaped by the personal traits of this ruler, a sadistic psychopath. Suffering from paranoia, abnormally suspicious of his closest collaborators, cowardly in moments of crisis, lacking political insight or a sense of realism, he drove his country into ruin and decline, moral as well as physical. While currying the favour of the ruling European houses, he was completing the isolation of the Muscovite state, creating a model Asiatic despotism in which the authority was absolute and tyrannical, standing above all law. As Poland's King Stephen Bathory wrote to Ivan in 1580, "You are not the ruler, but the butcher of your people". The tsar tolerated no criticism, even when offered with humility. For example, when Metropolitan Philip asked him to consider the consequences of his acts, he had the prelate strangled. He killed his son and heir, Ivan (b. 1554, d. 1581), in a fit of anger. Contemporary Europe was aware of Ivan's crimes, but that did not prevent it from maintaining extensive contacts with the tyrant or according international recognition to his imperial title. The Habsburgs were keen to win Ivan IV for their anti-Turkish coalition, and he was a valued ally against the Polish Commonwealth. Rome was willing to gain his support for church union and Catholicism, unaware that a realization of these plans would have resulted in a confessional bloodbath. England saw nothing wrong with Ivan IV's advances toward Queen Elizabeth or her relatives. Lithuanian and Polish lords did not decline opportunities for service at the Muscovite court, nor was Ivan considered an unsuitable candidate for marriage with Catherine Jagiellonka, daughter of King Sigismund I of Poland, Ivan IV's exchange of letters with other rulers were full of dynastic arguments: the tsar emphasized his natural right to absolute power, resting his case on both the Byzantine heritage and his Roman "predecessor" Emperor Augustus. Demanding the return of Livonia from Bathory, Ivan called himself heir to the Jagiellons, and he justified his claim to the Grand Principality of Lithuania by the alleged kinship of both ruling houses with the princes of Polotsk, the descendants of Rogvolod.

An image of Ivan IV as great statesman and reformer was jointly created by his subjects, who one and all, from serf to prince, proclaimed themselves his slaves, by the ruling elites of the Europe of his day, and finally by scholarly historians. According to this view, his crimes (the institutionalized terror of the *oprichnina*, the public and secret killings, the expropriations, and extreme cruelty with which alleged conspiracies were crushed) were excused as an instrument, ruthless to be sure, yet necessary and effective, for bringing about change (redistribution of land and reforms of the judiciary, local and central administration, the military, and the Church). While twentieth-century historiography admitted that the costs of consolidating absolute power, centralizing the state, and conquering new territories (for example, the war over Livonia and access to the Baltic, 1577–1582) were disproportionately high in relation to the results, a persisting idealized evaluation of Ivan the

Terrible's actions was employed by some as an historical alibi for the crimes of Stalin's era.

Ivan IV was succeeded on the throne by Feodor (Theodore, b. 1557, d. 1598), the youngest son of his first wife, Anastasia Romanova, who was married to Irina, sister of a nobleman of Tatar descent, Boris Godunov. Boris wielded the real power on behalf of Feodor, becoming the unquestionable ruler of the Muscovite state in 1587 (or, as the English called him, lord protector). While performing the formal duties of a ruler, Feodor not only did not resist, but was clearly relieved to have his brother-in-law holding the reins of power. Instead, he busied himself with artistic handicrafts, supporting their development along with his wife, worked on the furnishing of his palatial residence, and above all else devoted himself to religion through unceasing prayer, alms-giving, and generosity to the monasteries. The question arises whether this last of the Rurikids was in fact, as he has been characterized by historians, a retarded mediocrity, a simple-minded fool, unfit to rule, smiling stupidly at the sight of visitors arriving at his court, or whether his personality had not simply developed in reaction to a childhood contaminated by a climate of crime, producing in him a revulsion toward a violent and murderous political power. Escaping into religion, he could consciously imitate the model of a "fool for the sake of Christ", a stance perceived in the society of his time as a special gift from God. Although Feodor was supposedly insane, he was proposed as a candidate to the Polish throne in 1573, 1574, and especially in 1587, and the Polish nobles were willing to see the feeble-minded Rurikid "to have Muscovy, Poland and Lithuania under one hand", provided Moscow was willing to open its coffers. It was even debated whether the state coat of arms should place the cap of Monomakh of the tsars above or below the Polish crown.

Feodor and Irina had no children, other than a daughter who died as a child, so the right to the throne passed to a son of Ivan IV by his seventh marriage, Dmitry (b. 1582, d. 1591). However, Dmitry died in his boyhood under circumstances which are still unexplained. Initially, a team of investigators concluded that the boy had suffered an attack of epilepsy while playing with his mates, and falling, stabbed himself with his own knife. On the other hand, after Boris Godunov's death, he was charged with the crime, supposedly plotting the assassination of Dmitry in order to pave his own way to the throne.

However, the dynasty of the Rurikids could not simply exit the historical stage with the last direct heir to the crown of the tsars: it was too strongly anchored in the consciousness and emotions of its subjects, who, whatever their place in the social hierarchy, could simply not imagine their lives and the state it embodied. The attitude was well illustrated in the words of the Muscovite envoys to the electoral convocation of the Polish Diet in Warsaw in 1587: "We have had natural rulers from the very beginning, and we are by nature their slaves". Boris Godunov understood this very well when he sought dynastic legitimation of his power after the death of Feodor and withdrawal of the widowed tsaritsa to a monastery. At this point, a truly theatrical performance took place: processions arrived to beg Godunov to accept the tsar's regalia, and witnesses appeared who claimed to have heard that Ivan IV had entrusted Feodor to Godunov's care, and how he stressed how much Irina was a daughter to him and her brother his natural son. Finally in the course of a lofty ceremony, the metropolitan proclaimed to the congregation, over Godunov's seeming protests, that "the Tsaritsa has given you her brother as your ruler and tsar".

Although Boris Godunov did everything to legitimize the continuity of the ruling house in his person, the burden of authority proved too heavy for a tsar lacking true dynastic charisma. Following the bad harvests of 1601–1603, which compounded the effects of the economically disastrous policies of Ivan IV, famine plunged the country into a whirlpool of uprising, rebellion, civil war, and foreign intervention. In the midst of this chaos, Polish-backed pretenders claiming to be the surviving Dmitry arose, the first of whom managed to take Moscow and remain on its throne for a year (June 1605–May 1606), and the second of whom, who arose after the violent death of the first, menaced Moscow for several years (1607–1610). Their appearance would not have been possible, even with the support of foreign forces, had it not been for the belief, widespread among many sections of society, that the Rurikids would survive, that the dynasty could not leave its people, that only it could save the country from the chaos.

On the other hand, the people were not willing to see a restoration of the dynasty in the accession of one genuine Rurikid, Vasily Shuisky of the Suzdal-Nizhny Novgorod line, descended from Alexander Nevsky's brother Andrei. Shuisky lacked credibility, since he had been involved for so many years in court and noble intrigues and had been suspected of plotting against the tsar, whose slave he once proclaimed himself to be. After agreeing to a limitation of his power, he was elected tsar at an assembly of the land in May 1606, but was overthrown four years later, on 17 July 1610. He was then taken away by a Polish army and died in Poland on 12 September 1612. By contrast, a Rurikid widely viewed by the public as having a legitimate right to the imperial crown was a distant relative of Tsar Vasily (they had a grandfather in common) Prince Michael Skopin-Shuisky, swordbearer to the first False Dmitry, a gifted commander who died at 24. Even Polish king Sigismund

Vasa alleged some genealogical connections to the house of Rurik, when he advanced his claim to the Muscovite throne in 1610 in an address to the people of Smolensk, allegedly in response to the appeals of "the people of the Muscovite state, prostrated before him", that he, "the Christian tsar and closest relative to the Moscovite rulers, remember his kinship and fraternal bonds with the earlier natural Muscovite sovereigns".

Relationship with the old dynasty was to be a major theme in the continuing rivalry for the throne in Moscow and ultimately in the ascension of the new ruling house of the Romanovs as well. The Romanovs were related to Feodor, the last Rurikid on the throne, through his mother Anastasia, who was also the aunt of Feodor Nikitich Romanov, who later became the patriarch of All Rus' under the name of Filaret, Feodor-Filaret was thus cousin-german, and his son Michael, who was to be the first tsar in the dynasty of the Romanovs, the nephew to the last tsar in the family of the Rurikids.*

* The Piasts and Jagiellons were related to the Rurikids through multiple marriages. The Rurikids have not died out today. Only the Muscovite line became extinct, and many Russian princely families correctly derive their origins from the Rurikids. A dozen or so Lithuanian-Ruthenian families, which later became Polonized, could also be added to the list.

Bibliography

1. S. Soloviev. *Istoriia otnoshenii mezhdu russkimi kniaziami Rurikova doma.* Moscow 1847.
2. N.I. Kostomarov. *Russkaia istoria v zhizneopisaniiakh ei glavneishykh deiatelei* I, 1–3, 1873–1888; reprint Moscow 1990.
3. A.V. Ekzempliarskii. *Velikie i udelnye kniazia Severnoi Rusi v tatarskii period s 1238 po 1505, Biograficheskie ocherki po pervoistochnikam i glavneishim posobiiam*, t. 1–3, St Petersburg 1889–1891; reprint 1966.
4. N. Baumgarten. *Généalogies et marriages occidentaux des Rurikides Russes du Xe au XIIIe siècle.* Rome 1927; idem *Généalogies des branches regnantes de Rurikides du XIIIe au XVIe siècle.* Rome 1934.
5. G. Olsr. "Gli ultimi Rurikidi e le basi ideologiche delle sovranita delle Stato russo", *Orientalia Christiana Periodica* 12, 1946: 322–373.
6. D.B. Miller. „The Coronation of Ivan IV of Moscow", *Jahrbücher f. Osteuropäische Geschichte* 15, 1967: 559–574.
7. J. Frossman. *Die Beziehungen altrussischer Fürstengeschlechter zu Westeuropa.* Bern 1970.
8. M. Cherniavsky (ed). *The Structure of Russian History. Interpretative Essays.* New York 1970.
9. M. Szeftel. "The Title of the Moscovite Monarch up to the End of the Seventeenth Century", *Canadian-American Slavic Studies* 13, 1979: 58–81.
10. A.V. Solov'ev. *Byzance et la formation de l'État russe. Recueil d'études.* London 1979.
11. G. Schramm. "Die erste Generation der Altrussichen Fürstendynastie", *Jahrbücher f. Geschichte Osteuropas* 28, 1980: 321–333.
12. A.P. Kazhdan. "Rus'-byzantine princely marriages in the eleventh and twelfth centuries", *Harvard Ukrainian Studies* 12/13, 1988–89: 414–429.
13. J. Pelensky. "The Contest for the 'Kievan Succession' (1155–1175)", *Harvard Ukrainian Studies* 12/13, 1988–89: 761–780.
14. A. Poppe. "Words that serve the authority. On the title of Grand Prince in Kievan Rus'", *Acta Poloniae Historica* 60, 1989: 159–184. [here ch. X]
15. L. Voytowich. *Genealohija dynastii Rjurykovychiv.* Kyiv 1990.
16. N. Kollmann Schields. "Collateral succession in Kievan Rus'", *Harvard Ukrainian Studies* 14, 1990: 377–387.
17. V. Vodoff. *Princes et principautés russes (X–XVII siècles).* Northampton: Variorum Reprints, 1989.
18. M. Dimnik. *The Dynasty of Chernihov 1054–1146* (Texts and Studies 116). Toronto 1994.

19. A. Poppe. "Der Kampf um die Kiever Thronfolge nach dem 15 Juli 1015", *Forschungen zur osteuropäischen Geschichte* 50, 1995: 275–295.
20. M. Bychkova. *Moskovskie samoderzhtsy. Istoriia vozvedenia na prestol.* Moscow 1995.
21. D.B. Rowland. "Moscow – the Third Rome or the New Israel?", *The Russian Review* 5, 1996: 591–614.
22. B.A. Uspenskii. *Tsar' i Patriarkh: kharisma vlasti v Rossii (Vizantiiskaia model i ee russkoe pereosmyslenie).* Moscow 1998.
23. N.V. Sinitsyna. *Tretii Rim. Istoki i evolutsiia russkoi srednevekovoi kontseptsii (XV–XVI vv.).* Moscow 1998.
24. A.F. Litwina, F.B. Uspenskij. *Wybor imion u Rjurikovicej X–XVI vv. Dinasticeskaja istorija skwoz prizmu antroponimiki.* Moscow (izd. Indrik) 2005.

I

Once Again Concerning the Baptism of Olga, Archontissa of Rus'

The Kievan princess Olga played a role of no small importance in the entry of Rus' into Christendom. To be sure, as the treaty of 944 between Byzantium and Rus' indicates, there was already a Christian community in Kiev during the reign of her husband Igor, and Christianity had already penetrated the upper strata of Rus' society. Nonetheless, Olga's conversion to Christianity ultimately paved the way for the Christianization of all Rus' in 988.

In recent years a number of papers have been written concerning the time, place, and circumstances of Olga's baptism.[1] Of these, G. G. Litavrin's proposed redating (from 957 to 946) of the visit to Constantinople of the archontissa and hegemon of Rus', Olga, described by Constantine VII Porphyrogenitus, has been particularly instrumental in encouraging a reexamination of the existing (and often contradictory) interpretations of these questions.[2] However, Litavrin's argument that 946 is the only possible date, for all its ingenuity, does not sufficiently consider the testimony of the other sources, and hence has met with well-founded objections.[3]

The present paper proposes a solution to the question of the conversion of Olga on the basis of all the known sources. It differs from earlier studies only in part of its interpretation of those sources. The arguments presented support the long-accepted date of Olga's conversion, closer to 955, and further develop an idea first advanced by G. Ostrogorsky, demonstrating that the baptism of Olga was associated with her elevation to the imperial rank of *zōstē patrikia*.[4]

After the death of the Kievan prince Igor (ca. 945), the regency of the widowed princess Olga (until ca. 960) supported the further Christianization of Rus'. The clearest expression of this policy was the baptism of Olga herself, although the precise time and place of that event has remained uncertain.[5] According to eleventh-century tradition, voiced by the *Primary Chronicle,* the baptism took place in Constantinople, with the participation of the patriarch and emperor.[6] The fact that Olga's baptismal name, Helen, was also the name of the wife of Constantine Porphyrogenitus suggests the involvement of the imperial couple as godparents.

I would like to thank Robert Scott and Simon Franklin for their help in translating this article into English.

[1] See, e.g., and for a consideration of earlier opinions, the important series of studies by D. Obolensky: "Russia and Byzantium in the Mid-Tenth Century: The Problem of the Baptism of Princess Olga," *GOTR* 28 (1983), 157–71; "The Baptism of Princess Olga of Kiev: The Problem of the Sources," *Byzantina Sorbonensia* (1984), 159–76; "Ol'ga's Conversion: The Evidence Reconsidered," *Harvard Ukrainian Studies* 12–13 (1988–89 [1990]), 145–58. Obolensky argues that Olga was baptized during a visit to Constantinople in 960.

[2] See G. G. Litavrin, "O datirovke posol'stva knjagini Ol'gi v Konstantinopol'," *Istorija SSSR* (1981), no. 5, 173–83; idem, "Russkovizantijskie svjazi v seredine X veka," *VoprIst* (1986), no. 6, 41–52.

[3] A. Poppe, "Christianisierung und Kirchenorganisation der Ostslawen in der Zeit vom 10. bis zum 13. Jahrhundert," *Österreichische Osthefte* 30 (1988), 460–65; A. V. Nazarenko, "Kogda že knjaginja Ol'ga ezdila v Konstantinopol'?," *VizVrem* 50 (1989), 66–83 (arguing for 957), and Litavrin's reply, ibid., 83–84.

[4] G. Ostrogorsky, "Vizantija i kievskaja knjaginja Ol'ga," in *To Honor Roman Jakobson* (The Hague-Paris, 1967), 1458–73. Ostrogorsky presumed that Olga visited Constantinople only once, in 957, when she was already a Christian, and he therefore follows the *Primary Chronicle* in dating her baptism to ca. 955, though he locates it in Kiev. A similar dating for the baptism—despite his proposal for an earlier visit by Olga to Constantinople in 946—is accepted by G. G. Litavrin, "K voprosu ob obstojatel'stvah, meste i vremeni kreščenija knjagini Ol'gi," in *Drevnijšie gosudarstva na territorii SSSR. 1985* (Moscow, 1986), 55–57.

[5] On the historiography of the question see Obolensky, "Russia and Byzantium," 157 ff; Nazarenko, "Kogda že knjaginja Ol'ga"; M. Labunka, "Religious Centers and Their Missions to Kievan Rus': From Ol'ga to Volodimer," *Harvard Ukrainian Studies* 12–13 (1988–89 [1990]), 165–70; also O. Pritsak, "When and Where was Ol'ga Baptised?" ibid., 9 (1985), 5–21.

[6] *PSRL,* I, cols. 60–62. For a commentary on the *Primary Chronicle*'s tale of Olga's conversion, see L. Müller, "Die Erzählung der 'Nestorchronik' über die Taufe Olgas im Jahre 954/55," *ZSl* 33 (1988), 785–96.

At the same time, however, the account in the chronicle has been embellished with folkloristic elements that attest to later traditions developed within an already Christian society.

The date assigned to the baptism in the *Primary Chronicle*, 6463 (September year 954/55), appears to find some confirmation in the eulogy to Olga included in the triptych *Memory and Eulogy of the Rus'ian Prince Vladimir.* That work, compiled at the end of the thirteenth century, contains annalistic entries dating from the eleventh century, some of which are clearly independent of the chronology of events outlined in the *Primary Chronicle.* The *Memory*'s indirect reference to the date of the baptism of Olga ("after holy baptism Olga lived 15 years . . . she died July 11 6477 [969]"[7]) may perhaps be considered an independent source, although this still does not constitute a decisive argument. It is rather the completely independent report found in the *Synopsis historiarum* of John Skylitzes that demonstrates that the chronicle's date of A.M. 6463 (= 954/55) is highly probable. Writing in the second half of the eleventh century, the chronicler made use of tenth-century sources. He notes that Olga came to Constantinople after the death of her husband and returned home a baptized Christian. All of the events before and after this entry relate to the reign of Constantine VII Porphyrogenitus and, more specifically, to the period between the dethronement of Romanos I Lekapenos in December 944 and the death of Patriarch Theophylaktos on 27 February 956. Skylitzes precedes his reference to the baptism of Olga with information about relations with the Hungarians in the years 948–955, and follows it with a report of the marriage of Constantine's son Romanos II to Theophano, an event that could not have taken place later than 956, and most likely occurred in 955.[8] Thus, the sequence of events permits us to conclude that Olga was baptized in Constantinople about 955. In light of the compilatory character of Skylitzes' work, we cannot of course rule out the possibility of a mistaken sequence, but its concurrence with the two reports from Rus' makes a 955 date for Olga's baptism most likely.

The description of the visit of the archontissa and hegemon of Rus' Olga as found in *De cerimoniis aulae byzantinae* does not state directly whether the princess was already a Christian at the time; the current argument over whether this autumn visit took place in 946 or 957 thus has no essential implications for the place and time of her baptism. It is possible, however, to draw certain indirect conclusions. The fact that Olga appears here under her princely pagan name (Elga) rather than her Christian one (Helena), proves nothing in and of itself—oft-repeated opinion to the contrary notwithstanding—for many Christian rulers of Rus', beginning with Vladimir, were known to Byzantine authors only by their princely names.[9] The presence of a priest in Olga's suite is likewise of no decisive significance: he could have been present to assist an already baptized princess (or catechumen), but he could also have been there simply because some of the individuals accompanying Olga were Christian (just as some of the emissaries concluding the treaty of 944 had been).

More significant, however, is the remark of *De cerimoniis* to the effect that, during the ceremonial banquet, Olga sat among the *zōstai,* in accordance with her rank, at the "separate" table. In other words, Olga was equated with a *zōstē* (literally, "girdled") *patrikia,* the highest female rank of the

[7]"Pamjat' i pohvala Jakova Mniha i žitie knjazja Vladimira po drevnejšemu spisku," ed. A. Zimin, in *KrSoobInstSlav* 37 (1963), 70. On Jakov's work see A. Poppe in *Słownik Starożytności Słowiańskich* 4 (1970), 16–18; also E. Fet in *Slovar' knižnikov i knižnosti Drevnej Rusi: XI–polovina XIV v.* (Moscow, 1987), 288–90.

[8]*Ioannis Scylitzae Synopsis Historiarum,* ed. I. Thurn (Berlin-New York, 1973), 237–40. The accepted view is that the reported baptism of the Hungarian prince Bulcsu took place in 948, and that of Gyula in 952/53: see, e.g., G. Moravcsik, *Byzantium and the Magyars* (Budapest, 1970), 104–6; G. Györffy, "Role de Byzance dans la conversion des Hongrois," in *Cultus et cognitio* (Warsaw, 1976), 174. If this was so, then in Skylitzes' sequence the baptism of Olga should be dated between 952 and 956. Skylitzes' sequence is called into question by G. G. Litavrin, "Putešestvie russkoj knjagini Ol'gi v Konstantinopol': Problema istočnikov," *VizVrem* 42 (1981), 40, who notes the reference to the death of Bertha-Eudokia, which occurred in 949. However, Skylitzes here does not break the sequence, but merely alludes to his own previous reference to Bertha's death (*Synopsis,* 231), just as in his account of Olga's baptism he alludes to the 941 campaign of Olga's deceased husband Igor.

[9]For the view that Constantine's use of Olga's pagan name indicates that she was not yet converted, see e.g., J.-P. Arrignon, "Les relations internationales de la Russie kiévienne au milieu du Xe siècle et le baptême de la Princesse Olga," in *Occident et Orient au Xe siècle* (Paris, 1975), 168, 171, 174; Obolensky, "Ol'ga's Conversion," 151; Litavrin, "K voprosu," 52–54. However, in the *De administrando imperio* Constantine on five occasions speaks of "Boris," ruler of the Bulgars, and only three times does he mention Boris' baptismal name of Michael. He refers to the princes of the baptized Croats only as Terpimir, Krasimir, and Miroslav, and to the prince of Moravia only as Swentopolk (five times). Skylitzes ignores Christian names in his notices on the baptism of the Magyar princes and of Olga. It appears that in public and diplomatic contexts the use of dynastic ("pagan") names was the norm, and the use of baptismal names was reserved for more private occasions. Cf. Theophanes, *Chronographia,* Bonn ed., I (1839), 687; II (1841), 214, who appears to assume that even the patriarch was unaware of the baptismal name of Leo III.

imperial court. The title of *zōstē* was used at that time by only two ladies-in-waiting of the wives of Emperor Constantine and his son, Emperor Romanos. However, one also finds in tenth-century sources that *zōstē* appears as an honorary title bestowed upon the females of neighboring dynasties, including the Bulgarians.[10] And only the *zōstē* had the right to sit at the table of the imperial family. Thus, the "fitting honor" that Skylitzes reports was shown to Olga after her baptism, if it is understood as the award of the title of *zōstē*, was not an exceptional event, particularly in light of the fact that the Hungarian princes were granted the title of *patrikios* after their baptism. The Byzantine custom of granting court titles to foreign rulers baptized with the participation of the emperor was continued in the tenth century, and an omission of this gesture in the case of Olga would be difficult to explain. It is also worth noting that there are no known instances of a non-Christian being granted the title of *zōstē*.

On the basis, then, of *De cerimoniis* and Skylitzes' *Synopsis*, it can be concluded that Olga received the title of *zōstē patrikia* after her baptism, an act also associated with the imperial pair's role as godparents of the archontissa of Rus'.[11] Likewise, the seating of the princess in the midst of the imperial family, enabling her at dessert to converse freely with the emperor, represented an exceptional degree of intimacy for the Byzantine court, with its cultivation of stiff ceremonial. Such honor to a pagan ruler would have been unheard of, but it would have been natural and appropriate for a *zōstē* and imperial goddaughter. Given the fact of Olga's spiritual kinship with the imperial family, we must date her visit as a Christian to the autumn of 957, and her baptism to an earlier trip to Constantinople, which could have taken place in 954 or 955.

Such a date would appear to be contradicted by the *Continuation of the Chronicle of Regino of Prüm*, probably written by Adalbert, a monk from Trier and later missionary bishop to Rus', who in 968 became the first archbishop of Magdeburg. In this work, under the year 959, we read that "ambassadors of Helena, queen of the Rus', who was baptized in Constantinople under Romanos, emperor of Constantinople, came to the king [Otto I], asking—insincerely, as it later turned out—for the appointment of a bishop and priests for that people."[12] A literal interpretation of this report would force us to move the date of Olga's baptism to the reign of Romanos II, between 9 November 959 and 15 March 963, but such a conclusion would merely serve to make this report even more confusing, for it would mean that in 959 it was the pagan Olga, not the Christian Helena, who sent the embassy to Otto I.[13] A more convincing argument would be that in light of the late date of the writing of this note (after 962 but no later than 967) we are dealing here with a typical lapse of memory, resulting in the mistaken substitution of Romanos' name for Constantine's.[14] Other in-

[10] Constantine Porphyrogenitus, *De cerimoniis aulae byzantinae*, I, CFHB (Bonn, 1829), 594–98 (bk. 2, 15). For the view that Olga at the reception had status equivalent to a *zōstē patrikia*, see Ostrogorsky, "Vizantija," 1458–73; cf. Obolensky, "Ol'ga's Conversion," 163; Arrignon, "Les relations," 173. On the title see R. Guilland, "Contribution à l'histoire administrative de l'Empire byzantin: La patricienne à ceinture," *BSl* 32 (1971), 269–75; also J. Deér, "Zur Praxis der Verleihung des auswärtigen Patriziats durch den byzantinischen Kaiser," in idem, *Byzanz und das abendländische Herrschertum*, Vorträge und Forschungen 21 (Sigmaringen, 1977), 424–37.

[11] Cf. Ostrogorsky, "Vizantija," 1469–71. Skylitzes mentions that both the Magyar princes were made patricians, so one can assume that his phrase ἀξίως τιμηθεῖσα implies an equivalent promotion for Olga: *Synopsis*, 239–41; cf. the similar terminology in Theophanes Continuatus, CFHB (Bonn, 1838), 469, 471. However, Olga could not be made a simple *patrikia*, since that title was granted only to the wives of patricians. Constantine's account of her reception provides strong support for the view that she was given the highest court dignity available to a woman, the title of *zōstē patrikia*. After baptism Olga would have been a spiritual daughter of the ruling couple, a member of the imperial family, so it could be appropriate—according to ceremonial rules—that at table she should take her place at the imperial table between the two *zōstai* (μετὰ τῶν ζωστῶν κατὰ τὸν τύπον: *De cer.*, 597, 1.4). Note also that her ceremonial garments as *zōstē*—especially the *loros* and the *propolema*—would have restricted her movements and prevented her from performing complete proskynesis. Olga limited herself to a slight inclination of the head: see Guilland, "Contribution," 271; on proskynesis see idem, *Recherches sur les institutions byzantines*, I (Berlin-Amsterdam, 1967), 144–48, esp. 145, 147.

[12] *Adalberti Continuatio Reginonis*, in *Quellen zur Geschichte der sächsischen Kaiserzeit*, ed. A. Bauer and R. Rau (Darmstadt, 1977), 214–15.

[13] Obolensky, "The Baptism," 163–73, and Arrignon, "Les relations," 177–78, accept as authentic the statement in Adalbert that Olga was baptized under Romanos, but fail to note this would put in question the other Kievan information in Adalbert: see Litavrin, "Putešestvie," 38–39. Libutius, a monk of the monastery of St. Alban, was consecrated bishop for the Rus' in Frankfurt in the presence of Otto I at Christmas 959. Otto must therefore have been informed of Olga's request by envoys at least two or three months earlier, i.e., *before* Romanos II came to the throne on 9 November 959. We must assume that the Kievan envoys set out not later than August or September 959.

[14] Adalbert heard about Olga's baptism from Olga herself, who may well have mentioned that the current emperor (Romanos) had attended, and thus there may have arisen the false information in the text. Adalbert was certainly well informed, but that does not mean that we are always well informed by him. Cf. Thietmar (bk. VII, 72) who manages to confuse Otto III with Otto II, and to refer to Anna Porphyrogenita as "Helen." See also below, note 15.

stances of imprecision and incorrect detail in the *Continuation* would tend to confirm this hypothesis.[15]

The visit of an embassy from Rus' in 959 is not itself in question, for already at Christmas of that year, at Frankfurt, in the presence of Otto I, the monk Libutius was consecrated as bishop "genti Rusorum." In light of this fact, the arrival of the embassy from Rus' should be dated to the fall of 959, while Constantine Porphyrogenitus was still alive. In any case, news of his death on 9 November and of the assumption of power by Emperor Romanos could hardly have reached the royal court by Christmas.

The reliability of the report would not be questioned if, instead of "sub Romano imperatore Constantinopolitano" one reads "sub Constantino et Romano imperatoribus Constantinopolitanis." The surviving manuscript tradition, it is true, does not exclude the possibility of such an earlier form, but neither does it provide grounds for such an emendation of the text. There are, however, other circumstances enabling us to explain such imprecision at the time of the writing of the *Continuation* entry. Romanos II became emperor and autocrator only after the death of his father Constantine Porphyrogenitus on 9 November 959, but he was nominally emperor from the moment of his coronation, at his father's wish, on 6 April 946. At the courts of Europe it was well known who the real ruler was, but that did not free one from the obligation of observing the established rules. "Regnal years" were numbered from the date of coronation (and hence, for Romanos, from 946), and in correspondence produced by the Byzantine chancellery, the titulature included the names of both emperors, Constantine and Romanos.[16] Moreover, the co-emperor was named along with the real emperor in the address of letters sent to the Byzantine court.[17]

The author of the *Continuation,* Adalbert, worked from 953 to 956 and, after his return from Kiev, 962 to 966 in the chancellery of Otto I, and thus was well acquainted with the formulary of Byzantine correspondence. From 946 Romanos had been named alongside Constantine in the addresses of letters sent to Constantinople from the Ottonian chancellery. When Adalbert returned to his duties in the chancellery after his visit to Kiev, Romanos, as emperor and autocrator, figured first in the address. Hence, it can be argued, Adalbert named him alone when he wrote the further installment of his chronicle in 966–967.[18]

We thus have the right to consider Adalbert's information reliable, if inexact by virtue of incompleteness, for in accordance with the "chancellery" view of the surrounding world, Olga-Helena had been baptized during the reign of emperors Constantine and Romanos.

This information about the princess of Rus' has come down to us from Adalbert solely because of the latter's need to comment on the Rus' episode of his biography and to justify his lack of success there. As fate had it, the departure of Bishop Libutius was delayed (his death on 15 February 961 suggesting that illness was the reason). The subsequent consecration of Adalbert to Rus' must have taken place fairly quickly, but not earlier than Easter, 7 April 961; in the summer Adalbert could have arrived in Kiev in order to return after spending less than a year there.

Emphasizing the difficulties and dangers of his journey, Adalbert grumbled against the agent of his advancement, Wilhelm Archbishop of Mainz, "from whom he had expected better treatment, since he had never done him any wrong."[19] From this comment it is already apparent that Adalbert belonged to that category of ecclesiastical dignitary

[15] Adalbert did indeed produce the "outstanding work of tenth-century German historiography," but one should not thereby assume that he is always an "accurate and valuable reporter" (see Obolensky, "Ol'ga's Conversion," 152, 154). On his errors and contradictions see M. Lintzel, *Ausgewählte Schriften,* II (Berlin, 1961), 399–406; also K. Hauck, "Erzbischof Adalbert von Magdeburg als Geschichtsschreiber," in *Festschrift für W. Schlesinger,* II (Cologne-Vienna, 1974), 276–353.

[16] See the intitulation formulae in *De cer.,* II, 28 (vol. I, 686–92). On this topic see F. Dölger, "Das byzantinische Mitkaisertum in der Urkunden," in *Das byzantinische Herrscherbild,* Wege der Forschungen, 341 (Darmstadt, 1975), 13–48; cf. Nazarenko, "Kogda že knjaginja Ol'ga," 76.

[17] These are not preserved, but cf. Hugo Capet, writing at the turn of 987 "to the Orthodox Emperors Basil and Constantine": *Die Briefsammlung Gerberts von Reims,* ed. F. Weigle, MGH, *Briefe,* II (Berlin, 1966), 139; trans. in H. P. Lattin, *The Letters of Gerbert* (New York, 1961), 151. Cf. also W. Ohnsorge, "Das Mitkaisertum in der abendländischen Geschichte des früheren Mittelalters," in idem, *Abendland und Byzanz* (Weimar, 1958), 261–87.

[18] Cf. S. Heider, "Zum Verhältnis von Kapellanat und Geschichtsschreibung im Mittelalter," in *Geschichtsschreibung und geistiges Leben im Mittelalter: Festschrift für Heinz Löwe zum 65. Geburtstag* (Cologne-Vienna, 1978), 107–8, 132. Adalbert's experience in the royal chancellery influenced his writing of the *Continuation,* but was no guarantee against inaccuracy or partiality. On the incongruity of the chronology if we accept that "sub Romano imperatore" must mean "during the sole reign of Romanos" (i.e., after 9 Nov. 959), see above, notes 13–15; also the comments by Müller, "Die Erzählung der 'Nestorchronik,'" 786.

[19] *Adalberti Continuatio Reginonis,* 214–19, under the years 961–62.

that had neither desire for nor understanding of the mission "ad maiorem gloriam christianitatis." Adalbert was the polar opposite to a zealous man of the Church like Bruno of Querfurt, who regarded the mission to the pagans, and even a martyr's crown in that cause, as the highest of distinctions.[20] The failure of the mission to Rus' thus had its "internal" reasons: the choice of Adalbert as its chief had not been a fortunate one. Even if he undertook his task without enthusiasm, the missionary bishop did not simply dream up all the difficulties he reported encountering on the Dnieper. Two full years had passed since Olga's invitation to the mission. Svjatoslav, who by this time had reached manhood and assumed power, was at the very least indifferent to the efforts of the mission, valuing more highly the opinions of his entourage, warriors who poked fun at Christianity.

Under these new conditions, the pro-Christian Olga was unable to offer effective support to these missionary efforts. The authorities were not quick "compellere intrare" (Luke 14:23), and the disappointed missionaries did not delay in returning to their homeland. The generally held view that the failure of the mission was a result of rivalries between Rome and Constantinople lacks any real foundation. Regardless of certain differences in rite, which could not have mattered to Olga in any case, there was still one Church at that time, and the activity of Greek or Latin missionaries therefore did not have to be mutually exclusive, even though a signal success of one or the other missions would have made the issue of ecclesiastical jurisdiction the order of the day. Olga clearly understood that the conversion of the country would be difficult to carry out without dynastic, political, and ecclesiastical contacts and sufficient aid from the outside; she could have felt justified in turning to any Christian ruler for this purpose.[21] Her appeal met, moreover, with a moderately favorable but short-lived response from the court of Otto I. Otto I ultimately viewed the missionary action from the perspective of his own political interests, and those did not extend too far east of the Elbe.[22]

Likewise, the practical recommendations on foreign policy toward northern neighbors laid out by Constantine Porphyrogenitus in *De administrando imperii* indicates that in the mid-tenth century the political horizon of the empire was dominated by the Khazars and Pechenegs. To be sure, political and commercial contacts with Rus' were valued, as were mercenaries from Rus', but in this conversion of its ruler the opportunity of opening Rus' to Christianity was not yet sensed. No doubt influenced by earlier failures, Byzantine politics in this period lacked a genuine missionary impulse. In both Rome and Constantinople in the tenth century there was a lack of the imagination that had earlier accompanied their mutual rivalry over Bulgaria. The limitless east European plain was only faintly sketched on the horizon of the Christian world of that time.

Why exactly would the princess of Rus' have appealed in 959 to the western ruler Otto I, given the established links between Kiev and the Eastern Empire?

We do not know for a fact that Olga linked her efforts to obtain personal baptism during her visit to Constantinople in 954/955 with the sending of a mission headed by a bishop to Rus', but it seems

[20] See R. Wenskus, *Studien zur historisch-politischen Gedankenwelt Bruns von Querfurt* (Münster-Cologne, 1956), 91 ff, 143–54, 198–201; J. Karwasińska, "Świadek czasów Chrobrego—Brunon z Kwerfurtu," in *Polska w świecie* (Warsaw, 1972), 91–105; also A. Poppe, "Vladimir as a Christian," in *The Legacy of St. Vladimir*, ed. J. Breck, J. Meyendorff, and E. Silk (Crestwood, N.Y., 1990), 44–46.

[21] See F. Dölger, "Die 'Familie der Könige' im Mittelalter," and "Die mittelalterliche 'Familie der Fürsten und Völker' und der Bulgarenherrscher," in idem, *Byzanz und die europäische Staatenwelt* (Darmstadt, 1976), 34–69, 183–96; A. Angenendt, *Kaiserherrschaft und Königstaufe* (Berlin-New York, 1984), 5–11, 292–93.

[22] There are various, mostly strained, interpretations of Otto I's letter of 968 in which he refers to Adalbert, archbishop of Magdeburg, as metropolitan "totius ultra Albam et Salam Sclavorum gentis": MGH, *DD*, I (1884), no. 366. A traditional opinion is that Otto's *Ostpolitik* aimed at building a Christian empire as far as Kiev. For a more sober assessment see E. Hlawitschka, *Vom Frankreich zur Formierung der europäischen Staaten- und Völkergemeinschaft 840–1046* (Darmstadt, 1986), 115, 125; also Angenendt, *Kaiserherrschaft*, 293–94. Otto could not ignore Olga's request, but neither did he attach great importance to the Kievan mission, to which he appointed first the sickly Libutius and then (after Libutius died) the unwilling Adalbert. Adalbert's own limited interest in this aspect of the life of the Church is reflected in his apparent indifference toward the newly founded Bavarian, Saxon, Slavic, and Danish bishoprics: see Linzel, *Ausgewählte Schriften*, II, 403–4. There is no evidence to support the hypothesis that the Ottonian Church was attempting to draw Kievan Rus' into the Latin sphere of influence: cf. T. Manteuffel, "Les tentatives d'entraînement de la Russie de Kiev dans la sphère d'influence latine," *Acta Poloniae historica* 22 (1970), 36–42; Labunka, "Religious Centers," 169. Note, in particular, that "Sclavorum gentes" meant only the western Slavs: in German sources of the 10th and 11th centuries Kievan Rus' is *Ruzzia, Ruszia, Ruzi, Russi*, after Adam of Bremen, who drew a clear distinction between *Sclavonia* and *Ruzzia;* cf. G. Labuda in *Słownik Starożytności Słowiańskich* 5 (1975), 225–27; A. V. Nazarenko, "Ob imeni 'Rus' v nemeckih istočnikah," *Voprosy jazykoznanija* (1980), no. 5, 47 ff.

probable.[23] It is also hard to imagine that it would have been possible for the Byzantines to refuse to honor such a wish expressed by the archontissa and hegemon of Rus'. However, the concrete implementation of this wish depended on the actions of the emperor and patriarch. Constantine VII Porphyrogenitus, a scholar and *literatus* with an engaging lifestyle, was no statesman, living more in the past than the present; generous in his promises, he was miserly in his deeds. The patriarch in that period, Theophylaktos, was a man found "more often in the stables than in the church."[24] When Emperor Romanos I Lekapenos forced the elevation of his sixteen-year-old son to the patriarchal throne, the opposition of the local bishops was so great that the consecration of the young man in 933 was performed by papal legates. This lamentable situation continued until the death of Theophylaktos on February 27, 956; moreover, as a result of a fall from his horse, he was in poor health during the last two years of his life, and was thus at the very least limited in his activities, which would have included the consecration of bishops. Finally, finding a willing and worthy candidate who would not consider this mission a sentence of exile, could well have compounded the difficulties.

If the view that Olga visited Constantinople as a Christian in 957 is well founded, then her presence here could be linked, perhaps, in addition to political and commercial affairs, with renewed efforts to obtain the dispatch of a bishop and mission to Kiev. The office of patriarch was now occupied by the more worthy Polyeuktos, who, standing up in defense of the principles and canons of the Church, quickly fell into conflict with some of the bishops and with the emperor himself. Constantine began to fear him, and hated him to his last breath.[25] No doubt both the emperor and the patriarch would have individually favored Olga's request, but when it came to agreeing to and advancing a candidate, intrigues and quarrels between the palace and Hagia Sophia would surely have led to a postponement of the decision. The failure of the expected pastor to appear in Kiev in 958 or in the summer of 959 could well have led Olga, in Skylitzes' words, authentically devoted to the true faith, to send her embassy to Otto I in early autumn 959. The fact that she appealed to the German ruler in particular attests to the regent's orientation in the prevailing ecclesiastical situation.[26] It was not rivalry between Constantinople and Rome over Rus', but local squabbles in both centers of the Christian world that had led to an ignoring of the great mission of the Church. The pontificate of John XII (955–964) marked the nadir of the papacy in a century characterized by the great historian Baronius as the "saeculum obscurum." John XII, much like Theophylaktos, had been elevated to his throne as an immature seventeen-year-old and led a life of scandal and even crime.[27] In both Churches there was no lack of striving toward renewal, but the very presence of unworthy individuals at the helm undermined the missionary efforts that had been undertaken. In such a situation, the regeneration of the Church in symbiosis with the state under Otto I could not have escaped the attention of the regent of Rus'.

Various factors contributed to the failure of the mission to Rus', Adalbert's own lack of spirit being the least among them. The attempts undertaken in Kiev to draw closer to the Christian world, strong in the power of a newly discovered faith, but weak in social support, exposed the lack of genuine interest in an evangelization of Rus' in Constantinople, where political skepticism and ecclesiastical inertia were reinforced by popular fears of the Rus', viewing them as a menace of apocalyptic proportions.

The conversion of Olga, whom the chronicler hails as the herald and dawning light of Christianity in Rus', had far-reaching consequences, even though it did not lead to an immediate breakthrough. The number of Christians continued to

[23] When the Hungarian archon Gyula was baptized in Constantinople ca. 952/53 the monk Hierotheos was consecrated bishop for Hungary and started his missionary work there: see Skylitzes, *Synopsis*, 239.

[24] Skylitzes, *Synopsis*, 242–44; cf. G. Ostrogorsky, *History of the Byzantine State* (New Brunswick, N.J., 1969), 272.

[25] Skylitzes, *Synopsis*, 244, 247.

[26] On the Ottonian Church see Hlawitschka, *Vom Frankreich zur Formierung*, 50–57, 212–215; J. Fleckenstein, "Problematik und Gestalt der ottonisch-salischen Reichskirche," in *Reich und Kirche vor Investiturstreit* (Sigmaringen, 1985), 83–98. For a different view of Otto I's "mission to Rus'" see A. V. Nazarenko, "Popytka kreščenija Rusi pri knjagine Ol'ga v kontekste meždunarodnyh otnošenij èpohi," in *Cerkov', obščestvo i gosudarstvo*, (Moscow, 1990), 24–40; idem, "Rus' i Germanija pri Svjatoslave Igoreviče," *IstSSSR* (1990), no. 2, 60–70. Nazarenko places the mission firmly in the context of Byzantino-German relations, and proposes that the appointment of Adalbert, the former bishop of Rus', to the newly created see of Magdeburg in 968 indicates a revival of the idea.

[27] See F. Gregorovius, *Geschichte der Stadt Rom im Mittelalter*, I.2 (Darmstadt, 1978), 614–26; H. Fichtenau, "Von Ansehen des Papsttums im 10. Jh.," in idem, *Beiträge zur Mediävistik*, III (Stuttgart, 1986), 98–107; H. Zimmermann, *Im Bann des Mittelalters* (Sigmaringen, 1986), 70–80.

grow, at the Kievan court, among the nobles, and among the townspeople. Olga's effort to win her son Svjatoslav over to the new faith was unsuccessful, although the overall impact of his Bulgarian policy would ultimately open Rus' more fully to the influence of Christianity. What remained to Olga was the possibility of influencing her grandchildren. One of these was Vladimir, raised at the court of his grandmother, where his mother Malusha, concubine of Svjatoslav, performed the duties of steward. Malusha, as a member of the closest retinue of Princess Olga, must have been baptized along with her mistress or not long thereafter, and even if Vladimir was raised according to pagan custom at the wish of his father, his grandmother and mother no doubt did much to ensure that he came to know the new faith. As a result, Christianity was not foreign to Vladimir from his earliest years.[28] More than two decades were to pass, however, before it became the official religion in Kiev.[29]

[28]See A. Poppe, "Vladimir, prince chrétien," *Studi storici* (forthcoming). Olga appears also to have had some influence on Vladimir's older brother Yaropolk: Yaropolk's relations with the Ottonian court, and his request for a marriage to Richtlint, a daughter of Graf Kuno of Ohningen, suggest that he was close to conversion before he died in 977/78. See Nazarenko, "Rus' i Germanija v 70-ie gody X veka," *Russia mediaevalis* 6.1 (1987), 38–89.

[29]After the completion of this study I was able to see a typescript of J. Featherstone's forthcoming article, "Olga's Visit to Constantinople," to be published in *Harvard Ukrainian Studies.* Featherstone has some sound observations on the difference between the reception ceremonies for Olga and those for Saracens, noting that Olga was entertained in the inner parts of the palace, which would probably not have been accessible to non-Christians (the Triclinium of Justinian, the Kainourgion, the Pentakouboukleion), and that this seems to confirm Olga's status as a goddaughter to the imperial family. Featherstone also takes the view that Olga was made a *zōstē patrikia,* whose ceremonial dress gave her dispensation from full proskynesis (see above). However, Featherstone's argument that Olga arrived and was baptized on 8 September 957 is vitiated by a weak grasp of the questions of chronology and of the scholarly literature thereon. He devotes much effort to showing that Basil (the future Basil II) was two years old and present at table with Olga. In fact the eldest child of Romanos and Theophano, present at table, could have been a girl (see my suggestion in "The Political Background to the Baptism of Rus'," *DOP* 30 [1976], 230 note 114); and, for Basil's age, Featherstone relies entirely on comments in Skylitzes (*Synopsis,* 369), apparently unaware that different chronicles give different information, and that the question has been a focus of discussion since G. Schlumberger, *L'épopée byzantine à la fin du dixième siècle* (Paris, 1896), 328. Featherstone's chronology also looks strained in the light of Constantine's statement that a reception was held on 9 September ἐπὶ τῇ ἐφόδῳ ("upon the arrival," *De cer.,* I, 594) of Olga.

ADDENDUM

The sensational discovery of palimpsest fragments of *De cerimoniis* describing Olga's visit to Constantinople, with additions made at the end of the 10th century noting, *inter alia*, that the *archontissa Rhosias* was baptized at beginning of the first indiction, which means sometime between 1 and 9 September 957, has opened up new possibilities for understanding the whole complex of events connected with the period of Olga's regency in Rus' (see P. Schreiner's note in *BZ* 97 [2004], no. 2637). The whole text will be published in *BZ* in the near future by its discoverers.

Michael Featherstone's visionary dating of Olga's baptism to 8 September 957 is to be congratulated,[1] though one wonders why he ignored the remark (see fn. 29 above) that a reception for Olga was held on 9 September "upon her arrival". We still need to take care to test all the "information" in those later additions to the palimpsest, since even after just a few years eye-witnesses can easily conflate two events occurring close to one another in time.

On the other hand, G. Litavrin's arguments over the past quarter of a century for a 946 date, supported by C. Zuckerman,[2] have also gained some strong support from O. Kresten's demonstration of the homogeneity of the whole relevant subchapter II,15 of *De Cerimoniis*, where the description of Olga's visit appears in close proximity to accounts of an Arab mission that, Kresten has shown, took place in 946.[3]

Even if it now turns out that preference must be given to 957, one must concede that these stimulating studies have nonetheless opened the way to a more well-grounded knowledge of Rus'ian history in the mid-10th century. One should also include here the very detailed, if debatable argument for 957 assembled by A. Nazarenko[4] and the open-ended review of the research "at the cross-roads" by Fr. Tinnefeld.[5]

The intention of my study was to establish the date of Olga's baptism through a critical examination of the Ottonian data. The question of why she should have

---

[1] M. Featherstone, "Olga's visit to Constantinople in *De cerimoniis*", *Harvard Ukrainian Studies* 14, 1990: 293–312, and a restatement of the question in *Revue des Etudes Byzantines* 61, 2003: 241–251.

[2] C. Zuckerman, "Le voyage d'Olga et la première ambassade espagnole à Constantinople en 946", *Travaux et mémoires* 13, 2000: 647–672; G. Litavrin, *Vizantija, Bolgaria i Rus' v X–XII vv.*, Moscow 2001: 174–190.

[3] O. Kresten, "Staatsempfange im Kaiserpalast von Konstantinopel um die Mitte des 10. Jahrhunderts", *Sitzungsberichte d. philos.-hist. Kl. d. Österr. Akad. d. Wiss.* 670, Vienna 2000: 3–61.

[4] A.V. Nazarenko, *Drevnjaja Rus' na mezdunarodnykh putjakh*, Moscow 2001: 219–310.

[5] F. Tinnefeld, "Zum Stand der Olga-Diskussion. Zwischen Polis, Provinz und Peripherie", *Beiträge zur byzantinischen Geschichte und Kultur*, Wiesbaden 2005: 532–567.

turned to the Ottonian Empire just two to four years after her baptism in Constantinople has yet to be answered. Since the late Rus'ian data on the baptism of Olga are evidently secondary, I based my answer on the chronological sequence of events given by Skylitzes' compilation. I am willing to concede that those calculations, which led me to propose 954/55 as the date of Olga's baptism may ultimately prove wrong, but the old (and recently revived) argument offered in opposition to it that Olga could not have visited Constantinople twice is unsound and rather reflects the perspective of our times. From the same emperor Constantine we know that in the 10th century a merchant fleet regularly travelled, on a yearly basis, between Kiev and Constantinople. Like all other rulers of Rus', the regent Olga would have had to overcome immense distances even to travel within her own country. A thirty-day journey to Constantinople would not have taken as long as some trips within Rus' and would have been less dangerous than many of those internal itineraries.

III

How the Conversion of Rus' Was Understood in the Eleventh Century

Scholars have long studied particular accounts of the baptism of Rus' for their veracity, and I too have investigated the relevant evidence.[1] A peculiarity of all the sources is that not one is contemporaneous with the event it describes; they were all recorded a dozen to several scores of years later, although in some cases one can detect passages from, or fragments of, records written closer to the crucial year of 988. Here I am not concerned with these records as a source to the baptism of Rus' per se, but as a repository of what different writers of the eleventh century knew about the conversion of Rus' and its ruler, Prince Volodimer of Kiev and how they perceived that event.

Decided ignorance is shown by the Byzantine writers. It was not a real ignorance, but one dictated by the internal situation of the Byzantine Empire, above all by the deep divisions evident during the civil war of 986–989, which did not disappear after Basil's victory. One can easily understand the efforts at concealment of Leo the Deacon, who was opposed to the policy of Basil II.[2] Leo portrayed the Rus' as a dangerous enemy threatening the very existence of the empire. His ignoring of the baptism of Rus' was at least justified in his own mind, because he believed it was announced for the sake of appearances and had no lasting significance. More surprising was the attitude of Michael Psellos, who wrote his *Chronographia* after 1059, that is, over seventy years after Christianity was promulgated in Rus' under the supervision of the metropolitan of Kiev, appointed in Constantinople. Psellos does not mention the baptism, but in his account of the participation of the Tauroscythians in the battle of

[1] A. Poppe, "The Political Background to the Baptism of Rus'. Byzantino-Russian Relations Between 986–989," *Dumbarton Oaks Papers* 30 (1976): 197–244; reprinted in idem, *The Rise of Christian Russia* (London, 1982).

[2] *Leonis Diaconi Caloensis Historiae libri decem*, ed. C. Hase (Bonn, 1828), pp. 149f., 175f.; especially book 10. Cf. J. Karayannopulos and G. Weiss, *Quellenkunde zur Geschichte von Byzanz* (Wiesbaden, 1982), pp. 368f.; Poppe, "Background," pp. 212f.; S. A. Ivanov, "Polemičeskaja napravlennost' 'Istorii' L'va Diakona," *Vizantijskij Vremennik* 43 (1982): 74–80; M. Ja. Sjuzjumov, "Lev Diakon i jego vremja," in *Lev Diakon*, ed. S. Ivanov and G. Litavrin (Moscow, 1988), pp. 143–46, 149–56.

Abydos (April 989), and particularly in his description of the Rus'-Byzantine war of 1043, he calls the Rus' "barbarians."[3] Thus, indirectly but pointedly, he contested their membership in the family of Christian nations. Highly educated and well-read, Psellos consciously made full use of the semantic possibilities of the Greek word *barbaros*. He delighted in using this word again and again in reference to Rus'. Because he knew the ancient tradition so well, by *barbaroi* Psellos could simply have meant foreigners: it was in this sense that the Greek writers of Constantinople used the term in referring to the inhabitants of Rome.[4] Psellos, reasoning in imperial categories of old and new Rome, included the Rus' among the *exterae gentes* from *oikumenē tōn rhōmaiōn*. As a courtier and a monk, an intellectual and an intriguer, an adviser and a friend of emperors and of patriarchs, Psellos must have met with the metropolitans of Kiev and the Greek bishops of Rus' who visited Constantinople. He contrasted the *orbis romanus*, as an expression of Christian civilization and humanity, with the barbarous Rus', to him an uncultured, unorthodox, brutal, and rude land. This attitude resulted from his conviction, inherited from Leo the Deacon, that the Rus' were an age-old enemy, with perpetual hatred for the empire. To Psellos, the East Slavs of the second half of the eleventh century were a pagan ethnos beyond the limits of the Christian community.

What forced Psellos to go so far in ignoring the Rus' as a Christian nation? Were the impressions he received from visiting Rus' and returning Greek clergy so negative? True, from Constantinople's vantage point Rus' was Christianizing very slowly. Yet the real obstacle to his understanding was unfamiliarity with the language of Rus' and, above all, the extreme contrast in culture, to say nothing about the noted persistence of pagan prac-

[3] M. Psellos, *Chronographie ou Histoire d'un siècle de Byzance (976–1077)*, ed. and trans. E. Renauld (Paris, 1926–28), vol. 1, p. 9, and vol. 2, p. 8f. (bk. 1, §13–15; bk. 6, §90–96); Eng. trans. E. R. A. Sewter, 1953 and 1966. Cf. Karayannopulos and Weiss, *Quellenkunde*, pp. 407f.

[4] Cf. F. Dölger, *Byzanz und die europäische Staatenwelt* (Darmstadt, 1976; reprinted from the 1953 edition), pp. 285, 292, 340; K. Lechner, *Hellenen und Barbaren im Weltbild der Byzantiner* (Munich, 1954); idem, "Byzanz und die Barbaren," *Saeculum* 6 (1955): 299ff.; D. Obolensky, "The Principles and Methods of Byzantine Diplomacy," in *Actes du XIIe Congrès International d'Études byzantines*, vol. 1 (Beograd, 1964), pp. 54–56 (reprinted in idem, *Byzantium and the Slavs: Collected Studies* [London, 1971]); H. Ahrweiler, *L'idéologie politique de l'Empire byzantin* (Paris, 1975), pp. 29ff., 46ff. Cf. also G. Vismara, "Barbaren," *Lexikon des Mittelalters*, vol. 1 (1980), pp. 1434f. On the question of why the Slavs did not call the Byzantines Romans, but simply Greeks, cf. an attempt by G. Litavrin, "Predstavlenija 'varvarov' o Vizantii i vizantijcax v VI–X vv.," *Vizantijskij vremennik* 46 (1986): 100–108, who likes to see here the renunciation of Byzantine rights to the Roman legacy. The actual case seems to be much simpler: in practice, the Slavs dealt with the Greeks and with the Greek language.

tices among the Rus'. Also, the human and spiritual qualities of the Greek clergy sent to Rus' must be considered: how many of them were real missionaries? One remark of a Kievan monk and chronicler at the turn of the eleventh century is hardly complimentary to most of the metropolitans of Kiev.[5] It can be assumed that opinions in Constantinople about the newly converted land were shaped in part by Byzantines returning from there. However, Psellos first and foremost was a Byzantine imperial historian, and one, moreover, uncommonly pliable and cunning. He knew how to select his materials. He must have considered it tactless and indiscrete to connect Volodimer's help for Basil during the civil war with the giving of a porphyrogenite princess in marriage to a barbarian prince, especially since he probably considered the conversion as unauthentic and insincere. He preferred to keep silent on the topic.

In any case, the inclination to insinuate and to pass over in silence was typical not only of Psellos. John Skylitzes, his contemporary, noted the Rus' military assistance and the marriage of Volodimer to the emperor's sister, but made no mention of the prince's baptism or the conversion of his country. Yet in treating the 860s Skylitzes repeated the testimony of Theophanes Continuatus on the conversion of Rus' and for the 950s he did record the baptism in Constantinople of the *archontissa* of Rus', Ol'ga.[6] Mention of these events might have suggested to his readers that when the emperor Basil later asked for Volodimer's help and gave him the hand of his sister Anna, he was dealing with a Christian ruler.

[5] See *Polnoe sobranie russkix letopisej* (hereafter *PSRL*), 1 (Leningrad, 1926), p. 208; Eng. trans. S. H. Cross and O. P. Sherbowitz-Wetzor, *The Russian Primary Chronicle* (Cambridge, Mass., 1953), pp. 169f.: "In this year, John the Metropolitan passed away. John was a man versed in books and study, generous to the poor and to the widows, affable to both rich and poor, calm-tempered and mild, reticent yet eloquent, and able to console the sorrowful with words of Holy Scripture. *There never was his like in Rus' before him, nor will there be in later days.*" Usually the metropolitans were much different. Cf. L. Müller, "Russen in Byzanz und Griechen im Rus'-Reich," *Bulletin d'information et de coordination*, no. 5 (Athens and Paris, 1971), pp. 96–118; G. Podskalsky, "Der Beitrag der griechischstämmigen Metropoliten (Kiev), Bischöfe und Mönche zur altrussischen Originalliteratur (Theologie), 988–1281," *Cahiers du monde russe et sovietique* 24 (1983): 498–515. For separate biographies of Kiev metropolitans, see G. Podskalsky, *Christentum und theologische Literatur in der Kiever Rus' (988–1237)* (Munich, 1982), pp. 282–301. For a more recent view on John II, see G. Podskalsky, "Metropolit Ioann II von Kiev (1076/77–1089) als Ökumeniker," *Ostkirchliche Studien* 2 (1988).

[6] *Ioannis Scylitzae synopsis historiarum*, ed. J. Thurn (Berlin and New York, 1973): 165, 240. See Karayannopulos and Weiss, *Quellenkunde*, pp. 407f.; Poppe, "Background," p. 201. On the "first conversion" of Rus', see Podskalsky, *Christentum*, pp. 14–17; L. Müller, *Die Taufe Russlands* (Munich, 1987), pp. 57–66; and A. P. Vlasto, *The Entry of the Slavs into Christendom* (Cambridge, Eng., 1970), pp. 244f., 391f.

Such was courtly historiography. In any case, in Byzantium during the years 987–988, when the Rus' church province was founded with the former metropolitan of Sebaste, Theophylaktos, a man loyal to Basil II, at its head, the event was thought of primarily as a dynastic alliance and a diplomatic mission to the Kievan court. That perception continued to some degree in the eleventh century.[7]

The Byzantine contribution to the Christianization and to the transformation of culture and public life in Rus' is indisputable. But this Byzantine impact was often passive in nature. Through Byzantine influences, a large Christian religious and cultural legacy was at the disposal of the Rus'. The needs, conditions, and possibilities of the Rus' limited the benefits they could derive. Reception was facilitated by the existence of the Cyrillo-Methodian and Bulgarian inheritance. Its adaptation created some problems, but in the main was conducive to acculturation.[8] There is some doubt about considering early East-Slavic receptivity to Byzantine Christianity and civilization as acculturation. The active party in the process was the recipient. The Byzantine merit could have lain in facilitating unhampered borrowing from this repository. Yet here too a civilization's attitude toward its lowly follower could have been in evidence. Acrimonious remarks made in Kiev about the Greeks simultaneously with expressions of deep respect to Greek Christianity seem to reflect this duality. The baptism and Christianization of the East Slavs and their acculturation into Byzantine civilization must be attributed to the initiative of the leading strata of Rus' society (including the clergy). In this case Spinoza's statement is especially apt: "the active one is not the one who influences but the one who receives the influence. . . . Receiving, in the language of scholastics, is always accomplished *modo recipientis*."[9]

[7] See Poppe, "Background," pp. 224–32; note, for instance, the creation in the 1060s of two titular metropolitanates in Černihiv and Perejaslav. Cf. A. Poppe, "Uwagi o najstarszych dziejach Kościoła na Rusi," pts. 2 and 3, in *Przegląd historyczny* 55 (1964): 557–72 and 56 (1965): 557–69; Podskalsky, *Christentum*, pp. 32f.

[8] Cf. D. Obolensky, "The Byzantine Impact on Eastern Europe," *Praktika tēs Akademias Athēnōn* 55 (1980): 148–68, reprinted in idem, *The Byzantine Inheritance of Eastern Europe* (London, 1982); also see other papers by this author there. For an attempt at recapitulation, see S. Franklin, "The Reception of Byzantine Culture by the Slavs," in *The 17th International Byzantine Congress. Major Papers* (Dumbarton Oaks, 1986), pp. 383–98, which omitted F. J. Thomson, "The Nature of the Reception of Christian Byzantine Culture in Russia in the Tenth to Thirteenth Centuries and its Implications for Russian Culture," *Slavica Gandensia* 5 (1978): 107–39 (with valuable data and controversial conclusions).

[9] See L. Kołakowski, *Jednostka i nieskończoność, Wolność i antynomia wolności w filozofii Spinozy* (Warsaw, 1958), p. 612. Cf. A. Gieysztor, "Kasztelanowie flandryjscy i polscy," in *Studia Historyczne (Festschrift S. Arnold)* (Warsaw, 1965), p. 107; cf. also I. Ševčenko, "Remarks on the Diffusion of Byzantine Scientific and Pseudo-Scientific Literature among the

Although in Constantinople itself, both in the imperial court and among the inhabitants, the view of Rus' as an apocalyptic force threatening the empire with extermination persisted and the baptism of Rus' was largely ignored, a somewhat different opinion prevailed in Byzantium's eastern provinces—for instance, in Antioch, which sided with the usurper Bardas Phokas during the civil war. The more informative view of Rus' was recorded by the Arab-Christian historian Yaḥyā of Antioch, who settled there in 1015. Writing his history a dozen or so years later, he made use of local sources. His description of the civil war of 986–989 sets out to explain how victory came to Basil.[10]

According to Yaḥyā, it was Emperor Basil who sent envoys seeking military assistance to Kiev. Volodimer's willingness to provide it led to a treaty and relationship by marriage. Volodimer "married the sister of the emperor after the latter had demanded his baptism along with all of the people of his land."[11] The emperor first sent clergy to baptize Volodimer and his subjects and then sent his sister. A simple deal is struck: the emperor, desperately in need of military aid, gets it at the price of kinsmanship. The porphyrogenite princess will be given in marriage after the baptism of Volodimer and his people. Volodimer's willingness to convert is what makes the realization of both men's intentions possible. The marriage of Anna Porphyrogenita to a barbarian and pagan would only have confirmed Basil's loss of the crown, whereas the baptism of Volodimer and the introduction of his country into the family of Christian nations helped to justify not only the dynastic alliance itself, but also the use of Rus' troops against the Byzantine ruler's kinsmen. This help was offered by a newly baptized Christian ruler who was, moreover, now also the emperor's brother-in-law. Thus, the political significance of the conversion of Rus' is preeminent in Yaḥyā's historical record.

The view of the Armenian historian Stephen of Taron (Asoghik) is based on the same facts, but differs from the one-sided Byzantine view of Yaḥyā. Asoghik wrote shortly before the year 1005 in connection with the participation of Rus' forces in the emperor's eastern campaign of the year 1000.

Orthodox Slavs," *Slavonic and East European Review* 59, no. 3 (1981): 322–25.

10 *Histoire de Yahyā-ibn-Sa'īd d'Atioche*, ed. and trans. I. Kratchkovsky and A. Vasiliev, fasc. 2 (=Patrologia Orientalis 23) (Paris, 1932), pp. 417–31; cf. also a very good literal translation and important commentary by V. R. Rozen, *Imperator Vasilij Bolgarobojca: Izvlečenija iz letopisi Jax'i antiohijskogo* (St. Petersburg, 1883; rpt. London, 1972), pp. 23–41, 194–216; Poppe, "Background," pp. 205f. For the Greek sources of Yaḥyā and the rebellion of Bardas Phokas, 987–89, see J. H. Forsyth, "The Byzantine-Arab Chronicle (938–1034) of Yaḥyā b. Sa'īd Al-Anṭākī," vol. 1 (Ph.D. diss., University of Michigan, 1977), pp. 186–92, 423–62.

11 *Histoire de Yahyā*, pp. 422–24; Rozen, *Imperator*, pp. 23–24.

Asoghik notes that "Basil got six thousand foot-soldiers from the king of Rus', when he gave his sister in marriage to the latter and at the time that this nation came to believe in Christ."[12] The timing and causality of the events are skillfully linked. The political action is prominent, but the military aid and matrimonial alliance are set against a "Christian background." Here the conversion of Rus' is depicted more autonomously as a primary occurrence, without the bald frankness of Antioch's version of events.

An Arabic view of the circumstances behind the conversion of Rus' was also written at the court of Baghdad. Abū Shujā', vizier of the Abbasid caliphs, who wrote after 1072, used the now lost Baghdad chronicle of Hilāl aṣ Ṣābī (for 970–1056) to describe the years 979–999. Byzantine affairs are related carefully, because regular military and diplomatic contacts required that attention be paid to Byzantium's internal situation. The conversion of Rus' was seen from that perspective. In this account Byzantium is said to have begun the action by asking the Rus' ruler for military help. Then the Rus' prince demanded from the emperor his sister's hand in marriage, but she refused to marry a non-Christian.[13] Significant is the emphasis on Anna's role because the condition of marriage she imposed won Volodimer for Christianity. Here, too, the baptism precedes the marriage. This order of events is unclear in the record of Yaḥyā. But also in Baghdad there arose the conviction that Rus' military strength was crucial in the defeat of Bardas Phokas.

We know next to nothing about the West European response to the baptism of Rus'. Bruno of Querfurt, in his letter to the German king Henry II written in 1008 after a visit to Kiev, evidently considered Rus' to be a fully Christian country. The Christian ruler of the Rus' supported Bruno's mission to convert the Pečenegs.[14] The missionary bishop, zealous to spread

[12] Asoghik, bk. 3, §43, French trans. by E. Dulaurier and F. Macler, *Histoire universelle par Etienne Asołik de Tarôn*, pt. 2, Publications de l'Ecole des Langues Orientales Vivantes, ser. 1, vol. 18 (Paris 1917–), pp. 161–65. An Armenian text was published twice (Paris, 1859, St. Petersburg, 1885); Russian trans. N. Èmin (Moscow, 1864), pp. 198–201; German trans. by H. Gelzer and A. Burckhardt (Leipzig, 1907), pp. 209–212. See Poppe, "Background," pp. 202f.

[13] *The Eclipse of the 'Abassid Caliphate*, vol. 6: *Continuation of the Experiences of the Nations by Abu Shuja' Rudhrawari...*, trans. D. S. Margoliouth (Oxford, 1921), pp. 118f.; Arabic text, *The Eclipse*, vol. 3, pp. 116f. Russian trans. by T. Kezma with Ukrainian introduction by A. Kryms'kyj, "Opovidannja arabs'koho istoryka XI viku Abu-Šodži Rudravers'koho pro te jak oxrestilasja Rus'," in *Jubilejnyj zbirnyk na pošanu D. I. Bahalija* (Kiev, 1927), pp. 383–87, trans. pp. 388–95. Cf. Poppe, "Background," pp. 206f.

[14] For Bruno's letter, see J. Karwasińska, ed., *Monumenta Poloniae Historica*, n.s., vol. 4, no. 3 (Warsaw, 1973), pp. 97–106, especially 98–100; on Bruno's stay in Rus', see M. Hellmann, "Vladimir der Heilige in der zeitgenössischen abendländischen Überlieferung," *Jahrbücher für Geschichte Osteuropas* 7 (1959): 397–412 (also on Thietmar); A. Poppe, "Vladimir as a Christian," forthcoming. For how Bruno understood the act of conversion, see D. H. Kahl,

Christianity among the pagans and traveling across the East Slavic land twenty years after the baptism of Rus', seemed unaware that Christianity was actually just beginning to take hold there. Apparently Bruno did believe it essential to win the ruling class over fully to the Christian faith.

That the baptism of Rus' was noted in Ottonian Europe we know from the chronicler and bishop of Merseburg, Thietmar (975–1018), a relative and schoolmate in Magdeburg of Bruno of Querfurt. Thietmar presented a very negative opinion of Volodimer's morality. Thietmar's text was written between 1015 and 1017; he corrected and supplemented that text in the fall of 1018. According to him, only after Volodimer married the Byzantine princess did he yield to his wife's persuasion and adopt the Christian faith (*christianitatis sanctae fidem eius ortatu suscepit, quam iustis operibus non ornavit*, bk. 7, chap. 72). Thietmar also maintained that the Polish prince Mieszko was won over to Christianity by his wife, the Czech princess Dobrava (bk. 4, chaps. 55–56). Did Thietmar stereotype these rulers? In any case, the passage about Volodimer's conversion stems from Thietmar's wish "to touch upon the wrongful deeds of the king of Rus' Volodimer" (*Amplius progrediar disputando regisque Ruscorum Wlodemiri accionem iniquam perstringendo*, bk. 7, chap. 72). These wrongful deeds were marriage with a Greek princess who was promised to the German king (*Hic a Grecia ducens uxorem Helenam nomine, tercio Ottoni desponsatam, sed ei fraudulenta calliditate subtractam*, bk. 7, chap. 72), and the seizure of Bishop Reinborn, who died in prison. The bishop had come to Rus' with a Polish princess who had married Volodimer's son Svjatopolk; about 1013 Volodimer came to suspect all three of conspiring against him and so had them imprisoned.[15]

Thietmar's indignation at Volodimer's marriage with *filia sancti imperii* is comprehensible in view of the writer's descent from the family of the Grafen (Earls) von Walbeck, which was closely related to other powerful Saxon families. His father Siegfried (d. 991) was a trusted person in the court of Otto II and Theophano. Already Thietmar's maternal grandfather, Henry, Graf von Stade, was an important person in the court of Otto I and was indeed related to him. Otto I's three-year effort to procure a porphyrogenite princess for his son Otto II was not forgotten. Partial success came only after the new emperor, John Tzimisces, decided to give in marriage his niece, Theophano, to Otto II, although the bride was not a porphyrogenite.

"Compellere intrare. Die Wendenpolitik Bruns von Querfurt im Lichte hochmittelalterlichen Missions- und Völkerrechts," *Zeitschrift für Ostforschung* 4 (1955): 161–93.

15 *Thietmari Merseburgensis episcopi Chronicon*, ed. R. Holtzmann, trans. W. Trillmich (Berlin, 1957; rpt. 1962) pp. 170–75, 432–37.

Thus, when in 988 news came of Anna's marriage to a barbarian ruler (hardly a true Christian), the Ottonian court nobility must have been cut to the quick. Bitterness revived and deepened during negotiations for a porphyrogenite princess for Otto III (995–1001). That lasted seven years and had a sad epilogue: Otto III died shortly after a porphyrogenite bride finally arrived.

The Greek arrogance toward the Ottonian dynasty lingered in Thietmar's memory. When writing about Volodimer's marriage nearly thirty years later, the chronicler mistook Helena for Anna and Otto III for Otto II. But Helena seems not to have been his invention: it is likely that the elder daughter of Romanos II was named for her paternal grandmother, the empress Helena Lecapena. So this porphyrogenite princess Helena could have been "the desired girl" requested in about 968 by Otto for his son Otto II (not Anna, who was born in 963).[16]

Thietmar connected Volodimer's baptism with the Rus' ruler's marriage to a porphyrogenite, a marriage recalling an affront to his own country. No wonder that Thietmar spoke about Volodimer as a "great and cruel fornicator" whose "Christianity was not adorned with acts of justice." Writing at the time of fratricidal rivalry for the Kiev throne following Volodimer's death in 1015, Thietmar pointed out that the sinful life and injustice of the late ruler were the source of the quarrels disintegrating his kingdom. Thietmar's animosity is so intense that his account should be read alongside the dispassionate one of Bruno of Querfurt. Yet Thietmar must have reflected the views prevailing among the secular and clerical German, particularly Saxon, nobility. The conversion of Rus' was seen primarily in terms of its political implications to the *renovatio imperii*, despite a divergence from the Ottonian manifestation of this *renovatio* during the reign of Henry II (1002–1024). The defeat of Bardas Phokas (a relative of the empress Theophano) and Byzantine military consolidation could not have pleased Germany, even if only regarding Italian matters. It was known that Rus' military strength had been a major factor in the reversal of Basil's military and political fortunes.[17] The estimation of the conversion of Rus' with

[16] See Poppe, "Background," pp. 202, 219, 230–34. For more detail, see A. and D. Poppe, "Dziewosłęby o porfirogenetkę Annę," *Cultus et Cognitio (Festschrift A. Gieysztor)* (Warsaw, 1976), pp. 451–68; Hellmann, "Vladimir der Heilige"; and A. Poppe, "Vladimir as a Christian."

[17] By saying that Volodimer "crudelis magnamque vim Danais mollibus ingessit" (*Chronicon*, VII, 72, p. 434), Thietmar shows the political orientation of the Ottonian court in 987–989. The "unmanly Greeks" vanquished by Volodimer, Thietmar implies, are Bardas Phokas and his partisans. Theophano was probably also related to Bardas Skleros. Unsuccessful historiographic attempts to make the wife of Otto II and mother of Otto III into a porphyrogenite ceased in the 1960s. See W. Ohnsorge, "Die Heirat Kaisers Ottos II mit der Byzan-

Byzantine participation did not result from confessional motives, but was connected with the rise of a new political situation in Eastern and Southeast Europe.

Outside Kievan Rus' itself, the Rus' conversion to Christianity was recorded by near and distant neighbors, mostly Christian, as a trivial event, a component of a political deal and the vehicle for a better position in the family of rulers. Even the intellectual and Christian philosopher Psellos was not imaginative enough to see the future significance of the event.

* * *

How was "the grace and truth brought to earth by Jesus Christ" understood, realized, and felt by the Rus' nation when it was baptized? The earliest native record of the baptism of Rus' known to us was written in Kiev in the year 1049 or 1050. This "Sermon on Law and Grace and the Eulogy of our prince Volodimer who baptized us" is more than a homiletic work: it is a philosophical and religious treatise composed by Ilarion, a native priest-monk who had a Byzantine cultural background.[18] Shortly after its deliverance, in 1051, Ilarion was elevated to the metropolitan see of Kiev. His work is widely known, so here we will deal only with its relevance to the topic at hand.[19] Ilarion's sermon was never considered a primary source on

tinerin Theophano," *Braunschweigisches Jahrbuch* 54 (1973): 24–60. For earlier literature, see J. Strzelczyk, "Teofano," *Słownik Starożytności Słowiańskich* (hereafter *SSS*) 6 (1977): 57f.

[18] Recently edited anew by A. M. Moldovan is *Slovo o zakone i blagodati Ilariona* (Kiev, 1984); still indispensable as an excellent commentary is the edition of L. Müller, *Des Metropoliten Ilarion Lobrede auf Vladimir den Heiligen und Glaugensbekenntnis*, nach der Erstausgabe von 1844 neu herausgegeben, eingeleitet und erläutert (Wiesbaden, 1962). Moldovan's dating of the *Slovo* between 1037–1050 (after A. Gorski, 1844) does not take into account the arguments brought up in the 1960s. The *terminus ante quem* is the mention of Jaroslav's wife Irene-Ingigerd, who died on 10 February 1051. The *terminus post quem* is the mention of the Churches of Sophia and of the Annunciation and a "wreath" of fortifications around Kiev built by Jaroslav; all of these were begun after 1036 and were completed near 1046. Present in church during Ilarion's speech were the grandchildren of Jaroslav (the eldest sons married in 1043/44). The sermon was probably recited in *capella palatina*—the Tithes Church—in front of Volodimer's tomb on the Sunday anniversary of his death, 15 July 1050. Cf. A. Soloviev, "Zur Lobrede des Metropoliten Hilarion," *Das heidnische und christliche Slaventum. Acta II congressus internationalis historiae Slavicae Salisburgo-Ratisbonensis 1967* (Wiesbaden, 1970), pp. 58–63; reprinted in idem, *Byzance et la formation de l'Etat russe* (London, 1979); A. Poppe, *Państwo i Kościół na Rusi w XI w.* (Warsaw, 1968), pp. 56–58; idem, "The Building of the Church of St. Sophia in Kiev," *Journal of Medieval History* 7 (1981): 15–66 (reprinted in idem, *The Rise of Christian Russia* [London, 1982]).

[19] For the literature, see Podskalsky, *Christentum*, pp. 84–86; N. Rozov, "Ilarion," in *Slovar' knižnikov i knižnosti Drevnej Rusi, XI–pervaja polovina XIV v.* (Leningrad, 1987), pp. 198–204. A clear treatment in English is J. Fennell and A. Stokes, *Early Russian Literature* (London, 1974), pp. 40–60, with many quotations from the sermon. As far as I know, only a short part of the sermon has been translated into English, in S. A. Zenkovsky, *Medieval*

the Rus' baptism, even though the conversion is its main subject. The theological treatise offers, in a sense, a historiosophical discussion on the introduction of the Rus' into the universal Christian history of salvation. It also constitutes a praise of Volodimer, as a ruler who converted his nation to the true faith and brought it into the family of Christian nations. The discourse is a proclamation of victorious Christianity and of the originator of the conversion who "raised us [the Rus'], prostrated by idolatry, from the deathbed."[20] In his historiosophical and theosophical vision of the salvation of mankind, Ilarion expressed the significance of the turn from paganism to Christianity in the history of Kievan Rus'.

Among medieval Christian writings Ilarion's sermon is a rare testimony to the self-consciousness of a newly converted nation. Several dozen years after its baptism, in a country where large regions did not yet know about or recognize its own Christianization, a record was produced reflecting Christian historiosophy and a sovereign kind of thinking. It presented the baptism of Rus' as an event glowing high above common terrestrial history. This view, as formulated in Rus', came through Byzantine mediation, giving Ilarion access to the wide range of Christian tradition.

For Ilarion, Rus' history begins with its baptism. Volodimer is not only the baptizer of Rus'—he is its apostle. Ilarion does not dramatically contrast pagan Rus' and Christian Rus', or pagan Volodimer and Christian Volodimer, as the hagiographical writings commonly do (a good example being the text in the Primary Chronicle). While Ilarion qualifies the period of idolatry as the time when darkness was dominant, he praises Volodimer as the son of glorious Svjatoslav and grandson of old Igor'. Volodimer is also praised for having ruled his land "justly, boldly, and wisely" even before the conversion; he "did not rule in a meager and unknown land, but in the land of Rus', known well and heard about to all corners of the earth."[21] So, according to Ilarion, Volodimer even as a pagan ruler showed he was predestined to his role by Divine Providence. And at that time "the Supreme Being came upon him. . . [to show him] how to understand the delusiveness of idolatry and to discover the one true God." And Volodimer, having thrown aside a panoply of false beliefs ". . . was christened in Christ. . . and announced to his whole land that it was to be baptized. . . and everyone was to be a Christian." Ilarion expressed public feeling in those days: "And no one dared to oppose his [Volodimer's] pious order. Even if someone was baptized not for love, he was baptized for fear of him who

Russia's Epics, Chronicles, and Tales (New York, 1974), pp. 85–90.

[20] Müller, *Ilarion Lobrede*, p. 126; Moldovan, *Slovo*, p. 98.

[21] Müller, *Ilarion Lobrede*, pp. 100, 101; Moldovan, *Slovo*, pp. 91–92.

gave the order, because his piety was linked with authority.''[22] Over thirty years later Nestor the hagiographer, in his Vita of Boris and Glěb, sketched a more idyllic picture: ''and all hastened to be baptized, and there was nobody opposed, but as if already educated a long time, they came joyfully for baptism.''[23]

Ilarion does not reduce the conversion to a single act. Noting that ''at the same time our land started to glorify Christ,'' he also points out that this was only the beginning: ''Then the obscurity of paganism started to recede from us, and the daybreak of the true faith dawned.''[24] By the end of the eleventh century, a chronicler praising Jaroslav would express the same thought more allegorically: ''His father Volodimer plowed and harrowed the soil, when he enlightened Rus' through baptism, while this prince [Jaroslav] sowed the hearts of the faithful with the written word; we in turn reap the harvest by receiving the teaching of the [sacred] books'' (the Primary Chronicle's entry under the year 1037).[25]

Ilarion attributes the conversion of Rus' exclusively to Volodimer's merits as a teacher of the true faith: ''Through you we came to know the Lord and got rid of pagan delusions.... The Savior himself assigned you.'' Unlike many other rulers who witnessed the power of Christ and of the saints but rejected the faith, Volodimer ''came to the true faith, came to Christ, without those witnesses...owing to an upright attitude of mind and sagacity in understanding that there is God, only one Creator,'' who ''sent to earth his one and only son for the salvation of the world.'' Volodimer's virtues are manifold because ''he converted not one person, not ten of them, not a city, but the whole of his land.''[26] Those virtues allowed Ilarion to equate the Rus' prince with Constantine the Great—the first Christian Roman emperor. According to Ilarion, the baptism of Rus' was a repetition of a previous historical situation, and Volodimer was a new Constantine. His interpretation gave the event in Rus' an autonomous character without direct reference to the ''terrestrial'' Byzantine connection. But for Ilarion it was inconceivable to equate Rus' with a Byzantium perceived as *orbis romanus*. He made parallels only between Volodimer and Rus' and the first Christian Roman emperor and first Christian empire. In any case, Ilarion's

[22] Müller, *Ilarion Lobrede*, pp. 102, 103–104, 105; Moldovan, *Slovo*, pp. 92–93.

[23] *Die altrussischen hagiographischen Erzählungen und liturgische Dichtungen über die heiligen Boris und Gleb*. Nach der Ausgabe von D. Abramovič in Auswahl neu herausgegeben und eingeleitet von L. Müller (Munich, 1967), 4.

[24] Müller, *Ilarion Lobrede*, p. 105; Moldovan, *Slovo*, p. 93.

[25] *PSRL*, 1: 152; Cross, *Primary Chronicle*, p. 137.

[26] Müller, *Ilarion Lobrede*, pp. 107, 108, 110, 116; Moldovan, *Slovo*, pp. 94, 95, 96.

treatise is by no means anti-Byzantine (today few authors maintain so).[27] True, he did not give Byzantium a major role in the Rus' recognition of the one true God, but he did convey essential elements that made the Byzantine impact clearly evident.

The Pantocrator guided the intentions and deeds of Volodimer. When the prince decided "to find the one true God," he, still pagan, showed very good acumen: "Then he heard of the Orthodox land of Greece, so Christ-loving and strong in faith." This recognition of Byzantine Christianity and, simultaneously, of the sources of the religious inheritance results directly from Ilarion's comparison of the acts and roles of Volodimer and Constantine: "He [Constantine] with his mother Helen brought the Cross from Jerusalem and, affirming the faith, spread it over all their land; so you with your grandmother Ol'ga carried the Cross from New Jerusalem, from the city of Constantine, and having placed it in your land, affirmed the faith."[28] The cross symbolizes not only the triumph of Christianity in Rus', but also shows its genealogy and institutional ties. The composition is an expression of utmost regard for Byzantine Christendom and at the same time a declaration of loyalty to one's own confessional affiliation, since for Kiev the city of Constantine is the New Jerusalem, a new terrestrial icon of God's City. Referring to the Byzantine capital as such, while emphasizing Volodimer's guidance directly by God, can only be interpreted as an expression of religious homage and of Kiev's desire to be a true icon of Constantinople as a New Jerusalem.[29] That in Kiev efforts were made to resemble Constantinople even in appearance is illustrated by the Constantinopolitan influence in early Kievan architecture,[30] and by travelers' impressions from about 1070 that the capital of Rus' imitates Constantinople, "the brightest ornament of Greece."[31]

[27] But M. Priselkov's thesis is still alive. See, for instance, M. Ju. Brajčevs'kyj, *Utverždenie xristjanstva na Rusi* (Kiev, 1988), pp. 171–73; *Vvedenie xristianstva na Rusi* (Moscow, 1987), pp. 149–208; *Kak byla kreščena Ruś* (Moscow, 1988), pp. 237f.

[28] Müller, *Ilarion Lobrede*, pp. 102, 118–19; Moldovan, *Slovo*, pp. 92, 97.

[29] Cf. N. Schneider, *Civitas Celestis: Studien zum Jerusalem Symbolismus* (Münster, 1969); Podskalsky, *Christentum*, pp. 119f.

[30] See C. Mango, *Byzantine Architecture* (New York, 1976), Reg.; Poppe, "Building of St. Sophia," pp. 30–56; A. I. Komeč, *Drevnerusskoe zodčestvo konca X–načala XII v.* (Moscow, 1987), pp. 133–232, 316–18. Cf. also P. A. Rappoport, "O roli vizantijskogo vlijanija v razvitii drevnerusskoj arxitektury," *Vizantijskij vremennik* 45 (1984): 185–91.

[31] "Magistri Adam Bremensis, Gesta Hammaburgensis ecclesiae Pontificum," in *Quellen des 9 und 11 Jahrhunderts zur Geschichte der Hamburgischen Kirche und des Reiches* (Berlin, 1961), p. 254. The information of the chronicler recorded between 1072–76 that "Ruzziae. . . metropolis civitas est Chive, aemula scerptri Constantinopolitani, clarissimum decus Greciae" (lib. II, §22) has been misinterpreted (also in English translation, by Tschan, 1959, p. 67) to mean that Kiev was a rival of Constantinople. But there are no grounds for such

Without diminishing the apostolic mission of Volodimer, Ilarion reached back to the prehistory of Christianity in Rus' when he called Ol'ga the grandmother of the Apostle-like ruler. Thus he showed that recognition of the true faith had begun in Rus' decades before the baptism, also with the participation of Constantinople. For Ol'ga, too, Constantinople was the New Jerusalem. In his homage to both heavenly and terrestrial powers, Ilarion knew how to strike the right chords and the right balance.

Although the vision of the Rus' conversion presented by Ilarion had above all a religious and theological shape, it also conveyed one political benefit for the newly converted country: Christian Rus' had become the equal associate of other Christian nations.

Subsequent authors did not add much to this conception of the conversion of Rus', but did borrow a good deal from it. The adopted ideas are readily found in Nestor's Life of Boris and Glĕb, in the anonymous "Memory and Eulogy of Volodimer," and finally in the Primary Chronicle.[32]

The Primary Chronicle's account did not stop with Ilarion's vision, formulated half a century earlier. That vision was strongly spiritual, but skipped over many historical realities and details associated with the conversion. With the passage of time, questions arose, many things were forgotten or remembered inexactly, and legends began to proliferate. The chronicle's entry for the year 988 cannot be considered "the principal source of our knowledge of the event" of the Rus' conversion.[33] Research shows that the chronicle's account of the conversion of Rus' was a legend "vested in historical garments," and that it was a compilation written over one hundred years after the conversion took place. Its core is the legend of Volodimer's conversion at Kherson. The compilation is comprised of "The speech of philosopher" and "The confession of faith." The Kherson

an interpretation. *Aemula* also means "imitation," and this sense no doubt corresponds to the reality in the eleventh century, when Kiev endeavored to resemble the Byzantine capital.

32 As it is, the compilation known as the "Memory and Eulogy of Volodimer" belongs to the thirteenth century, even though some components can be dated to the eleventh century. See Podskalsky, *Christentum*, pp. 116ff.; A. Poppe, in *SSS* 4 (1970): 16–18. Cf. also E. Fet, in *Slovar' knižnikov*, pp. 280–90, who repeats the improbable thesis that the Patriarchate of Constantinople opposed the canonization of Volodimer. The questions of the borrowings in "Memory and Eulogy" from Ilarion's sermon have yet to be investigated. On the Primary Chronicle, see L. Müller, "Ilarion und die Nestorchronik," *Harvard Ukrainian Studies* 12 (1988) (forthcoming).

33 Such treatment of the Chronicle, if with some limitations, prevails; it is clearly expressed by D. Obolensky in *The Byzantine Commonwealth: Eastern Europe 500–1453* (London, 1971), p. 193. Cf. also idem, *Byzantine Inheritance*, 2: 132. For remarkable revisions of this traditional opinion, see L. Müller, *Die Taufe Russlands* (Munich, 1987), pp. 107–116, and especially V. Wodoff, *Naisance de la chrétienté russe* (Paris, 1988), pp. 63–81.

legend may originally have been Greek in language but surely was Khersonian in spirit; it was formed in the second half of the eleventh century, under the influence of still lively contacts with the Crimea, promoted by the Kiev Monastery of the Caves.[34] These contacts originated during the time of the conversion, when some members of the Kherson clergy were forced to go north and take part in the conversion of Rus'. Also the spoils of war—holy relics, church items, and icons—were sent north, because they were urgently needed for new churches in Kiev and in other Rus' cities.[35]

The chronicler, following Ilarion, attempted to present the conversion as a significant religious occurrence. So his narration was composed without a logical sequence of events, but as an interpretation of the decrees of Providence. Although the chronicle cannot be read as a reliable source for the events of 986–989, it is remarkable primary evidence of the knowledge of Christian writings and of religious and historical consciousness in Rus' at the turn of the eleventh and the beginning of the twelfth century. The chronicle's providential account of the conversion provides sufficient terrestrial data while clearly focusing attention on and amplifying the Greek role. Now it is not the Pantocrator who visits and elucidates the faith to Volodimer, but a Greek philosopher who in a long speech persuades the Rus' ruler of the superiority of "the Greek faith." The choice of faith is left to Volodimer, but with the participation of the Rus' nobility and with emphasis on the magnificence of the Byzantine liturgical rite as a substantial argument. The nobles also influence Volodimer to adopt the "Greek religion" by pointing to the good example of his grandmother Ol'ga, "who was wiser than all other men." It seems that Volodimer is convinced, but he decides "to wait a bit."[36]

Now Providence begins to work: without any particular reason Volodimer undertakes a campaign against Kherson, captures the city, and claims from the emperors Basil and Constantine their sister Anna in marriage. The

[34] For the English text of the philosopher's speech, see Cross, *Primary Chronicle*, pp. 97–116; "Cherson Legende," ibidem, pp. 111–13, 116; "Credo," ibidem, pp. 113–15. On the literature, see Podskalsky, *Christentum*, pp. 18ff., 205ff.; A. Poppe, "Legende Korsuńska," *SSS* 3 (1967): 34f. The speech may have been translated much earlier, in Bulgaria, but its adaptation addressed to Volodimer could have appeared only sometime after 1054, because of its anti-Latin tendencies.

[35] The reliability of the Primary Chronicle in stating that the relics of St. Clement and St. Phebus were brought to Kiev (*PSRL*, 1: 116; Cross, *Primary Chronicle*, p. 116) and were there at the middle of the eleventh century is confirmed by a notice in the psalter "Odalrici praepositi Remensis ecclesiae." See B. de Gaiffier, "Odalric de Reims, ses manuscrits et les reliques de saint Clément à Cherson," in *Études de Civilisation Médiévale (IX–XIIe siècles). Mélanges offerts à E.-R. Labande* (Poitiers, 1974), pp. 315–20, esp. p. 318.

[36] *PSRL*, 1: 108, 106; Cross, *Primary Chronicle*, pp. 111, 110.

emperors, although equals to Volodimer, are reduced to acting as instruments of Providence, agreeing to the marriage on the condition of Volodimer's conversion. The prince informs them that he has already studied their religion and is ready to be baptized. Anna objects, but nonetheless the emperors send her to Kherson.

After Anna's arrival in Kherson, Volodimer mysteriously loses his eyesight. Upon his baptism, he is miraculously cured and says, "I have now perceived the one true God."[37] Volodimer returns Kherson to the emperors as a dowry for Anna, and together with his new bride and clergymen from Kherson returns to Kiev, where the baptism of its inhabitants soon takes place.

Eastern Orthodox tenets and the role of Kherson in the conversion of Rus' are visibly accentuated. The terrestrial reasons that made Basil II ask his prospective brother-in-law to capture the rebellious city that supported Bardas Phokas are passed over in silence.[38] Instead of a punished city, Kherson is depicted as a fortunate one, chosen by God to be the baptismal site of the ruler of Rus'. Volodimer's intent to marry a porphyrogenite becomes evident only after the city is captured. Kherson becomes the fitting site for the wedding of the Rus' prince with the Byzantine princess. So, several scores of years after Kherson was left defeated and humiliated, a pillaged and half-burned city, it was transfomed into a site chosen by Providence for glory. The Kherson legend implies that the city rendered good services both to the empire and to Rus'. For the small but influential groups (mostly clergy) from Kherson who followed Volodimer and Anna northward, Rus' became a new homeland. The legend, embellished by details of varying credibility, has held a durable place in the pragmatic exposition of the history of Rus' for nearly the last nine hundred years.

The chronicle's version of the conversion, when compared to Ilarion's, not only diminishes Volodimer's role, but also indirectly puts into question his apostolic mission. An insertion into the chronicle at the turn of the eleventh century relates the legend of the apostle Andrew wandering through Rus'.[39] The apostle's elevation of a cross on the hills that would become the site of Kiev has evident ecclesiastical and political overtones, because Andrew, according to tradition going back to the fourth century, was the first bishop of Byzantion, the city of Constantine. The cross raised

37 *PSRL*, 1: 111; Cross, *Primary Chronicle*, p. 113.

38 For more detail, see Poppe, "Background," pp. 221–24, 238–40, 242; and idem, "Cherson and the Baptism of Rus'," *Zapysky Naukovoho tovarystva im. Ševčenka* (forthcoming).

39 *PSRL*, 1: 7–9; Cross, *Primary Chronicle*, pp. 53–54. Cf. Podskalsky, *Christentum*, pp. 11ff.; Müller, *Die Taufe Russlands*, pp. 9–16.

at Kiev as an apostolic act reduced Volodimer to the role of executor of divine and apostolic predestination. Some Kievan writings contradict the legend: for instance, St. Paul is said to have been the first teacher of the Slavs.[40] Yet the departure from Ilarion's viewpoint must not be seen as a conscious attempt to discredit it. Rather, other accounts should be viewed as various answers to questions that began to emerge first among the clergy, especially in monasteries and at court. The frame of the Primary Chronicle's account is providential, but at the same time it gave the reader a colorful historical portrayal. The description well suited the perceptions of a generation whose grandfathers and great grandfathers had witnessed the conversion. A younger generation tried to reconstruct and to understand the conversion according to their own perceptions. In Kherson, tradition animated and shaped anew this Greek city's role in the event. The adoption in Rus' of Slavic writings of the ninth and tenth centuries, and the mostly ecclesiastical relations with the country of the "true faith," added some contradictory elements to the picture. Today, after the lapse of a millennium, scholars keep toiling over accumulated enigmas.

40 See *PSRL*, 1:28; Cross, *Primary Chronicle*, p. 63. On the whole problem, see my article, "Two Concepts of the Conversion of Rus' in the Kievan Writings," to appear in *Harvard Ukrainian Studies* 12 (1988).

IV

Two Concepts of the Conversion of Rus' in Kievan Writings*

On occasion a speaker has to begin his paper with statements so obvious as to be embarrassing to the listener. Here is one such statement. There is not a single *primary* source that refers to the baptism of Rus', an event of prime importance. This is why we are reduced to conducting a diligent, but not always critically pursued, search for the authentic tradition and its traces, both actual and merely presumed.

Be that as it may, we have acquired a better understanding of the knowledge—or at least the views—concerning the acceptance of Christianity by the Rus' held by those living in Kiev and some other centers of Europe and Asia Minor one or a few generations after Volodimer.[1] Moreover, we realize with some astonishment that European capitals did not, or did not wish to, acknowledge the appearance in Europe of a new and vast Christian state at the time of the baptism of the Kievan prince on 6 January 988. On the other hand, people in these same capitals followed closely the vicissitudes of civil war that was raging in the Eastern Empire; it was noted that the troops of the Rus' had become involved in that civil war. In Germany, memories of the affronts caused by the overweening Byzantines still lingered, both at the Ottonian court and the courts of nobles. Indignation mingled with satisfaction in gossip about the plight of the Byzantines and about the porphyrogenite princess, who was to be given in marriage to a pagan and a fornicator.[2]

* The translation of this article is a collective work: my friends and learned colleagues Henrik Birnbaum, Miroslav Labunka, and Ihor Ševčenko worked with me to make it readable in English. I owe them my thanks.

[1] For details on this topic, see A. Poppe, "How the Conversion of Rus' was Understood in the Eleventh Century," *Harvard Ukrainian Studies* 11, no. 3/4 (December 1987): 287–302.

[2] See *Thietmari Merseburgensis episcopi Chronicon*, ed. R. Holtzmann, trans. W. Trillmich (Berlin, 1957; rpt. 1962), p. 432, VII, 72: "Hic a Grecia decens uxorem,. . .christianitatis sanctae fidem eius ortatu suscepit,. . . Erat enim fornicator immensus." About the causes of this negative characteristic as well as suggestions to the effect that Volodimer became a Christian only after the contraction of a marriage union with the porphyrogenite, see A. Poppe, "Volodimer as a Christian," presented in Rome on 3 May 1988 at the international conference, "Le Origini e lo sviluppo della Cristianità slavo-bizantina: il baptesimo del 988 nella lunga

Rome, the city to which the empress Theophano was traveling at that time, was not spared from the decadent turn in mores.[3] Rome was the vantage point from which she could better observe the struggle between Emperor Basil II and the two usurpers, Bardas Phokas and Bardas Skleros. She was a relative of both Bardases, and a regent of the realm, but her goals were the same as those of her deceased husband Otto II.[4] In France, at the court of the usurper and founder of a new dynasty, Hugo Capet, news of the events in Kiev was received in confused silence. Indeed, this news put an end to the well-thought-out plan to marry the heir apparent, Robert, to the *filia sancti imperii* and thus extend Hugo's influence to Italy.[5] Finally, the inhabitants of Constantinople itself suffered from the presence in their midst of a contingent of Tauroscythians, several thousand strong and poised for military action. This presence must have been especially painful, given that many of these inhabitants of the city were lukewarm at best in their support of the legitimate power. Propaganda, skillfully handled by the usurper's forces, fed this doubtful loyalty by means of apocalyptic prophecies,

---

durata.'' The publication of a French version is foreseen in the *Studi Storici* of the Istituto Storico Italiano per il Medio Evo.

3 The pope, John XV (985–996), who was inclined toward nepotism, quarrelled with the Roman high clergy, and found himself, precisely during the years 988 and 989, in a situation of oppression and isolation. Threatened also by the formal loss of the throne, he sought support in the imperial Ottonian court. Cf. Gregorovius, *Geschichte der Stadt Rom im Mittelalter*, vol. 1, pt. 2 (Munich, 1978), pp. 647–60. Even Sylvester II (999–1003), a pope worthy of the title, an excellent scholar, seasoned diplomat, and experienced advisor to Otto III, was not able to, or perhaps was not capable of, rebuilding the authority and political significance of the throne of Peter's vicar. Cf. the recent work by P. Riché, *Le pape de l'an mil* (Paris, 1987), pp. 179–255. Those who uncritically repeat the theory of the alleged direct contacts of Volodimer with the Roman curia, referring to the Nikon Chronicle for the year 989 (*Polnoe sobranie russkix letopisej* [hereafter *PSRL*], 9, p. 57), must take into account that this and some other ''Roman'' entries were invented in Moscow at the turn of the fifteenth century. Cf. B. M. Kloss, *Nikonovskij svod i russkie letopisi XVI–XVII vekov* (Moscow, 1980), pp. 187–88. These opinions completely ignore the inability of the papacy at that time to conduct its own eastern politics. Cf., e.g., P. E. Schramm, *Kaiser, Könige und Päpste*, vol. 3 (Stuttgart, 1969), pp. 214–35.

4 Italian matters, which were linked to the situation in Rome as well as to the question of Byzantine possessions and the confrontation with the Arabs, already required the presence of the regent in 986. By the end of this year Theophano planned to go to Rome, but because of various circumstances this journey was postponed until the turn of the year 988–989. On Ottonian politics in Italy, see K. Uhlirz and M. Uhlirz, *Jahrbücher des Deutschen Reiches unter Otto II und Otto III*, vols. 1 and 2 (Berlin, 1902 and 1954); and E. Hlawitschka, *Vom Frankenreich zur Formierung der europäischen Völkergemeinschaft 840–1046* (Darmstadt, 1986), pp. 134–38.

5 See A. Poppe, ''The Political Background to the Baptism of Rus'. Byzantine-Russian Relations Between 986–989,'' *Dumbarton Oaks Papers* 30 (1976): 232–35, reprinted in A. Poppe, *The Rise of Christian Russia* (London, 1982). For more detailed information, see D. Poppe and A. Poppe, ''Dziewosłęby o porfirogenetkę Annę,'' in *Cultus et cognitio: In honorem A. Gieysztor* (Warsaw, 1976), pp. 451–68.

according to which the time was nearing "of the last days of the city that will be destroyed by the Rus'."[6] Even after Basil II's victory—a victory to which the Rus' had so significantly contributed—the fears and prejudices felt towards those in imperial service lingered for a long time among the Romans. Millennial beliefs no doubt contributed to this state of mind, for the oppressive prophecies of "the end of the city and the end of the world" pointed to the Rus' as the executors of these dreaded deeds. As for Emperor Basil II and his entourage, the Christianization of the Rus' was of interest primarily as the means to an effective military alliance. For Basil and his retinue were absorbed, above all, with the military and political concerns of the time. The court, calculating and sober as it was, saw a guarantee of a military alliance in the establishment of dynastic ties to the Rus' rather than the inclusion of the Rus' in the byzantine religious community.[7]

True, ecclesiastics were sent out and policies aimed at the Christianization of the Rus' were formulated upon imperial command. Yet the idea for that vast country's conversion was not initiated in the capital on the Bosphorus. While we fully grant that Byzantine theological contributions and Byzantine cultural heritage—both Christian and pre-Christian—were of prime importance in the Christianization of the East Slavs,[8] we are not inclined to ascribe the conversion of Rus' to Byzantium's initiative and activity alone. What we have tended to call the "Byzantine impact" was in fact the accomplishment of those in Rus' society interested in acquiring new spiritual values. Again and again we return to the most felicitous phrase based on Spinoza: "the active one is not the one who influences but the one who receives the influence." Receiving, to use the language of

6 *Patria Constantinopoleos* (compiled ca. 990), ed. Th. Preger, in *Scriptores originum Constantinopolitanorum*, vol. 2 (Leipzig, 1907), p. 176. Cf. A. Diehl, "De quelques croyances byzantines sur la fin de Constantinople," *Byzantinische Zeitschrift* 30 (1930): 192–95. In Western Europe, the approaching year 1000 did not have the same significance nor the same influence on the state of mind as it did in Byzantium, where the atmosphere of civil war and foreign threats fostered the feeling of menace and prophecies fell on fertile ground. Compare G. Duby, *L'an mil* (Paris, 1967) and P. Riché, "Le mythe des terreurs de l'an Mille," in *Les terreurs de l'an 2000* (Paris, 1976), pp. 21–30.

7 Cf. Poppe, "The Political Background," pp. 218–21, 228–32.

8 An elucidating picture of this influence and the state of research was given recently by G. Podskalsky, *Christentum und theologische Literatur in der Kiever Rus' (988–1237)* (Munich, 1982). A picture of the accomplished turning point was recently presented with befitting competence by L. Müller, *Die Taufe Russlands* (Munich, 1987), and V. Vodoff, *Naissance de la Chrétienté russe* (Paris, 1988). These two works complement each other wonderfully. While Müller emphasizes the period preceding and in preparation for the turn of the year 988, Vodoff examines the consequences of this act in the eleventh to thirteenth centuries as well, showing the process of the Christianization of Rus'.

scholastics, is always accomplished *modo recipientis*.[9] Still, it does remain true that the Byzantines could regard the conversion of Rus' as a considerable achievement,[10] even though they were not fully aware at the time of the significance of the accomplishment.

Whereas, in the century that followed, the outside world saw the conversion mainly as one element in a political game,[11] the elite of Rus' itself became heir to a number of multifaceted reflections upon the event of Christianization, and they felt deeply that a fundamental change had taken place, and that this change offered access to the world of Christian values. The educated people of Rus' then formulated a deliberate view of their own conversion. Two conceptions were submitted; they were complementary, but differed on some essential points.

One of these conceptions is represented by Ilarion's philosophical treatise, composed sixty-two years after the baptism, on the eve of his being called to assume the highest ecclesiastical office in the land—that of metropolitan of Kiev.[12] As Ilarion's work has been the subject of frequent discussions in secondary literature during recent years, here we shall deal only with those passages in Ilarion's text that are germane to the topic at hand.[13]

9 L. Kołakowski, *Jednostka i nieskończoność. Wolność i antynomia wolności w filozofii Spinozy* (Warsaw, 1958), pp. 610–12. Cf. A. Gieysztor, ''Kasztelanowie flandryjscy i polscy,'' in *Studia Historyczne. Księga jubileuszowa z okazji 70 rocznicy urodzin Stanisława Arnolda* (Warsaw, 1965), p. 107.

10 D. Obolensky, *The Byzantine Commonwealth. Eastern Europe 500–1453* (London, 1971), p. 201.

11 This was so in Christian Europe, as Thietmar attests, and in Byzantium itself, as reported by Yaḥyā of Antioch. For more details, see, Poppe, ''How the Conversion of Rus' was Understood in the Eleventh Century,'' pp. 287–95

12 The latest edition, taking into account more than fifty manuscripts in three wordings, was prepared by A. M. Moldovan, *Slovo o zakone i blagodati Ilariona* (Kiev, 1984); L. Müller's edition of *Des Metropoliten Ilarion Lobrede auf Vladimir den Heiligen und Glaubensbekenntnis*. . . (Wiesbaden, 1962) is also still important for its excellent commentary. The work, dated between the years 1037–1050, may be justifiably linked to the year 1049 or 1050, as the result of detailed inquiries. See A. Soloviev, ''Zur Lobrede des Metropoliten Hilarion,'' *Das heidnische und christliche Slaventum. Acta II congressus internationalis historiae Slavicae Salisburgo-Ratisbonensis 1967* (Wiesbaden, 1970), pp. 58–63, reprinted in idem, *Byzance et la formation de l'État russe* (London, 1979); N. Rozov, ''Sinodalnyj spisok sočinenij Ilariona—russkogo pisatelja XI wieku,'' *Slavia* 32 (1963): 147–48; A. Poppe, *Państwo i Kościół na Rusi w XI w.* (Warsaw, 1968), pp. 56–59. In English, see E. Hurwitz, ''Metropolitan Hilarion's Sermon on Law and Grace: Historical Consciousness in Kievan Rus','' *Russian History* 7, no. 3 (1980): 322–33.

13 For a comparison of the literature, see, Podskalsky, *Christentum*, pp. 84–86, as well as *Slovar' knižnikov i knižnosti drevnej Rusi XI–pervaja polovina XIV v.* (Leningrad, 1987), pp. 198–204; one must note that in this last edition, not only are there important gaps in the bibliography, but the entry ''Ilarion'' was written without taking into account the current state of research: even the dating of the ''Slovo'' was, in general, neglected. In the millennial literature—particularly in these congress reports—the work of Ilarion occupies a considerable

The second interpretation, which is preserved in the Primary Chronicle in the cycle of stories conditionally called the "Tales of the Spread of Christianity in Rus'," cannot be fixed concerning the authorship, chronology, or the exact order and inclusion of the stories. The main emphasis is on the entries for the years 986–989, which contain the story of the conversion of Volodimer and the Kievan people, and on the entry for 1015, which consists of praise for Volodimer.[14] To these tales also are ascribed the entries for 955 and 969 on Ol'ga; for 983 on the first Christian martyrs in Kiev; for 1015 on the assassination of Boris and Glěb; and for 1037, praise of the activities of Jaroslav the Wise.[15] The hypothesis which dates the composition of the whole cycle of the "Tales of the Spread of Christianity" to the 1040s is not defensible, because none of the tales included could have been created before the second half of the eleventh century.[16]

---

place. There is also no lack of extremely incompetent approaches. See, for example, A. Zamaliev and V. Zoc, *Mysliteli Kievskoj Rusi*, 2nd ed. (Kiev, 1987), pp. 41–45. The intentions of the popularizers justify neither the lack of acquaintance with the state of research nor the type of primitive formulation that ascribes to Ilarion the "rehabilitation" of paganism; according to these authors, Ilarion "proclaims the pagan peoples the true receivers of the belief of Christ," is himself "far from ecclesiastical orthodoxy," "conformed evangelical doctrine to secular politics," and is practically an Arian (idem, pp. 45, 47).

14 *PSRL*, 1 (1926–1928), cols. 84–122, 130–131. (I refer to volume 2 of *PSRL* only in those cases where the entry in the Laurentian Chronicle is not sufficiently clear and must be confirmed or verified by referring to the Hipatian Chronicle.) Cf. also the English translation: *The Russian Primary Chronicle. Laurentian Text*, trans. and ed. S. H. Cross and O. P. Sherbovitz-Wetzor (Cambridge, Mass., 1953). My translation sometimes differs a little from this one.

15 *PSRL*, 1, cols. 60–64, 68–69, 82–83, 132–34, 151–53. Cross, *Primary Chronicle*, pp. 82–84, 86–87, 95–119, 124–31, 137–38.

16 With this hypothesis on the "Tale of the Spread of Christianity in Rus'," D. S. Lixačev has attempted to surmount the deficiencies of the hypothesis of A. Saxmatov about the compilation of a chronicle in Kiev soon after 1039, and through this attempt to replace it. See D. S. Lixačev, *Russkie letopisi* (Moscow, 1947), pp. 62–75; cf. idem, *Izbrannyje raboty*, vol. 2 (Leningrad, 1987), pp. 81–93. Lixačev's hypothesis gained nearly universal recognition; see *Vvedenie xristianstva na Rusi* (Moscow, 1987), pp. 147, 149. It is surprising that O. V. Tvorogov, who is the author of one of the sections of this collective work, speaks of the secular nature of the chronicle. When it comes to the individual works from which this new tale was supposed to have been compiled in the 1040s, one can already see that the composition of the praise of Jaroslav could not have occurred earlier than during the generations of his sons or grandsons, since in it Volodimer is compared to a ploughman and Jaroslav to a sower, but the chronicler defines his own generation as that which reaped the harvest (*PSRL*, 1, cols. 151–52). The chronicler's story about the murder of Boris and Glěb is a recasting of the "Anonymous Tale"—a hagiographic work written ca. 1072. Cf. A. Poppe, "La naissance du culte de Boris et Gleb," *Cahiers de Civilisation médiévale* 24 (1981): 29–53. Even if the opposite position is taken, one has to agree that the chronicle's story could only have been written with the beginning of the cult of the holy prince martyrs, that is, after the year 1050. The very presence in the chronicle's relating of the choice of religion by Volodimer, of as many as two representatives of the Christian church, along with adherents of Islam and Judaism, with the intention of differentiating between them, would also have been unthinkable in the situation

The cycle could be made more complete with the inclusion of two other stories of the Christianization of Rus' belonging to the structure of the Primary Chronicle: one, in the introductory section of the chronicle, on the journey of the apostle Andrew through the "Slavic land," and the other, the entry for the year 898, based on the vitae of SS. Cyril and Methodius, called "The Tale on the Translation of the Books into Slavic," which names the Apostle Paul and his disciple Andronikos as the teachers of the Slavs and the Rus'.[17] Both tales were incorporated into the Primary Chronicle before its definitive arrangement in 1116: the presentation of the apostolic roots of Christianity in Rus' in both these tales contradicts the accounts not only by Ilarion in 1050 and Nestor the Hagiographer in 1085, but also that of the author of the entry for the year 983 in the Primary Chronicle itself: "the apostles were not by body here; they did not teach here; and also the prophets did not prophecy here."[18] Yet, in the introduction to the same Primary Chronicle we find the apostle Andrew arriving on the hills of the future Kiev, erecting the Cross, with the prophecy that "the favor of God shall shine upon them; that on this spot a great city shall arise and God shall erect many churches therein."[19]

In the entry for 898, the right to recognize Paul as the Apostle of the Slavs is augmented by his association with the common motherland (cradle) of all the Slavs on the Danube: "Apostle Paul reached Illiric where the Slavic people primarily lived. That is why Paul is the teacher of the Slavic people... and he ordained Andronikos as a bishop and vicar after himself for the Slavic people, and the Slavic people and the Rus' people are one and the same."[20]

The information in the Primary Chronicle on the roots and beginnings of Christianity in Rus', in spite of the heterogeneity and different dating of the tales, takes shape as a clear idea of the Christianization of Rus'. This concept of the conversion was formulated during the last three decades of the eleventh century and the first fifteen years of the twelfth. Later, as part of the Primary Chronicle structure, it circulated through the ages for the most

before the year 1054. The adaptation of the speech of the Greek philosopher, as if addressed to Volodimer, could also not have been made earlier. See fn. 30 below.

17 *PSRL*, 1, cols. 7–8, 26–28. Cross, *Primary Chronicle*, pp. 53–54, 62–63.

18 *PSRL*, 1, col. 83; cf. also Moldovan, *Slovo*, p. 95 (188[b]), and Müller, *Lobrede*, p. 109 (41[29]). See also L. Müller, *Die altrussischen hagiographischen Erzählungen und liturgischen Dichtungen über die Heiligen Boris und Gleb* (Munich, 1967), p. 3 (a partial reprint of D. I. Abramovyč, ed., *Žitija svjatyx Borisa i Gleba i služby im* [1916]).

19 *PSRL*, 1, col. 8; Cross, *Primary Chronicle*, p. 54.

20 *PSRL*, 1, col. 28; Cross, *Primary Chronicle*, p. 63.

part unchanged, although at times somewhat abbreviated.[21]

The concept of Ilarion differs from that of the Primary Chronicle not only in time and in detail, but also in substance. The vision of Ilarion was born of a conviction in the unity of the Church, its apostolicity and its orthodoxy, whereas the conception of the Primary Chronicle already recognized the division between the imperial city and Rome.[22]

Ilarion extolls Volodimer as a teacher and leader, worthy of the same veneration given other teachers of the Christian world: ''All countries, cities, and nations, each one of them honors and glorifies its teachers, who instructed each one in the Orthodox faith.'' And he mentions the first Rome, saying: ''The Roman land glorifies, with voices of praise, Peter and Paul.''[23] We can assume that ''the Roman land'' here means ''orbis romanus'' and that the use of the present tense means that in the eyes of Ilarion Rome is orthodox. His profession of faith has the same significance: ''I come to the Catholic and Apostolic Church.''[24] This confession, which in its original prototype was the Confession of Faith by Michael Synkellos (ca. 787), has been preserved, somewhat abbreviated, in the Primary Chronicle as an admonition to the newly baptized Volodimer. The above formula, quoted by Ilarion, has been omitted from the chronicle, perhaps accidentally. Instead, what Volodimer hears is: ''Do not accept the teachings of the Latins as their instruction is vicious.''[25]

21 Independent of the divergence in views on the beginnings of Rus' chronicling, there is no doubt that at the Caves Monastery historiographic work began in the 1090s and acquired its final form in the second decade of the twelfth century. The writing, on the other hand, of annalistic notes must have dated from the 1070s at the monastery and perhaps from the 1060s. A survey of the latest chronicle writing (compare Lixačev, *Russkie letopisi*, pp. 427–79, as well as the thirty-eight volumes of *PSRL*) indicates that the Primary Chronicle was incorporated into the greater part of the compilations of chronicles up to the sixteenth and seventeenth centuries.

22 This difference is clear evidence of the time which divides both concepts; hence, not only is the attempt at simultaneous dating surprising, but so also is the admittance of the possibility of the authorship of Ilarion in this cycle of tales in the Primary Chronicle about the spread of Christianity. Cf. *Vvedenie xristianstva*, p. 147; *Slovar' knižnikov*, p. 202.

23 Moldovan, *Slovo*, p. 91 (184^{b}); Müller, *Lobrede*, p. 99 (38^{3-8}).

24 For the Confession of Faith of Ilarion, see Müller, p. 54, as well as in the appendix the Greek text of the Confession of Faith of Michael Synkellos, pp. 189–92.

25 *PSRL*, 1, cols. 114–16; Cross, *Primary Chronicle*, p. 115. For the juxtaposition of the Confession of Faith of Michael Synkellos with the text of the Confession in the Codex of Svjatoslav of 1073 and in the chronicle, see M. Suxomlinov, *O drevnej russkoj letopisi kak pamjatnike literatury* (St. Petersburg, 1865), pp. 65–68. The likelihood of an unintended removal arises from the dissimilarity of the further text. The Confession of Faith in the chronicle replaces the data of Michael Synkellos about six councils with information about seven general councils. Taking into consideration that the Confession ascribed to Michael Synkellos mentions Trullo, therefore the synod completing (quinisextum) in the year 691, it seems necessary to assume that it was written around the time of the ecumenical council of 787 (II Nicae-

Ilarion's belief in the "Universal and Apostolic Church" is an expression of a still deeply rooted conviction—both in the East and in the West—of the unity of the Church. It is because of this conviction that it was possible to overcome the conflict with Rome of Photius's time and to achieve reconciliation after 877.[26] Differences exploded with new force only in the mid-eleventh century, and the year 1054 has been seen as the beginning of the deepening division.[27]

In the Primary Chronicle the realization of this division is clearly perceived. Attempts made by some scholars to explain the anti-Roman, anti-Latin commentaries found in the chronicle as later interpolations cannot be defended since they are an integral part of the concept of the "Choice of Faith" developed by the author. Hence, along with representatives of Islam and Judaism, there were in Kiev two Christian embassies: the "Germans from Rome" and a Greek philosopher.[28] When Volodimer learns from the papal envoys of "fasting according to the person's strength," he sends "them back home since our forefathers did not accept this."[29] His answer

---

num). The emphasis placed on the worship of icons and relics in this Confession places it with this last council and with the restoration of the veneration of icons. And in this case we can still consider the authorship of Michael Synkellos (born ca. 760) as possible. Cf. H. G. Beck, *Kirche und Theologische Literatur im byzantinischen Reich* (Munich, 1959), pp. 503–505. In any case, the dating of this Confession of Faith to the first half of the ninth century seems little justified.

[26] See Fr. Dvornik, *The Photian Schism. History and Legend* (Cambridge, Mass., 1948); French ed., *Le schisme de Photius. Histoire et Legende* (Paris, 1950), pp. 230–86.

[27] It seems that only the events of 1204 made this division irreversible. See P. Lemerle, "L'Orthodoxie byzantine et l'oecumenisme medièval: les origines du 'schisme' des Églises," *Bulletin de l'Association Guillaume Budé*, series 4, vol. 2 (Paris, 1965), pp. 228–46. Cf. D. M. Nicol, *Byzantium: Its Ecclesiastical History and Relations with the Western World* (London, 1972; Variorum rpt., pt. 2); M. Angold, *The Byzantine Empire 1025–1204* (London, 1984), pp. 28–31; J. Meyendorff, *The Byzantine Legacy in the Orthodox Church* (New York, 1982), pp. 79ff.

[28] *PSRL*, 2, col. 72; 1, col. 85. "Nemcy"—this word is used in Rus' writings in both the wide sense of the mainly Germanic peoples of northwestern Europe as well as in a more narrow sense. Considering the use in this same text of the term "Greeks" for representatives of Eastern Christianity, it appears that here "Germans" are the equivalent of Latin Christians.

[29] *PSRL*, 1, col. 85; the excessive mildness of the Latin fast was raised by Michael Caerularius in his letter to the Patriarch Peter of Antioch (*PG*, v. 120, p. 781^{B}), while in Rus' the theme was repeated by the Metropolitan Nicephorus in letters to two princes. A letter to Volodimer Monomax was published by K. Kalajdovič in *Pamnjatniki rossijskoj slovesnosti* (Moscow, 1821), pp. 157–63. About these letters, see *Słownik Starożytności Słowiańskich* (hereafter *SSS*) 3 (1967), 369–70 as well as *Slovar' knižnikov*, pp. 278–79. On the other hand, the anti-Latin treatise attributed to the Metropolitan George (ca. 1073) is only a rewriting of Nicephorus's letter. Compare *Slovar' knižnikov*, pp. 104–105. The very theme of the non-observance of the fast by the Latins stirred Metropolitan John II, around the year 1085, in § 4 of his Responses: *Pamjatniki drevne-russkogo kanoničeskogo prava*, pt. 1 (=*Russkaja istoričeskaja biblioteka*, vol. 6, p. 3) (St. Petersburg, 1880).

is one of an adherent of stricter fasting rules and of one turning to arguments ascribed to one's forebears. We can say, therefore, that the answer that was put in Volodimer's mouth rightly belongs to his grandsons or great-grandsons.

In the words of the Greek philosopher, "the Roman faith is only slightly different from ours since they celebrate the Holy Liturgy with unleavened bread, that is, wafers."[30] In these words we find in fact the main theme of the conflict which began in 1054 and was stubbornly repeated in polemical tracts for the remainder of this century and the following one.[31] This debate could have appeared in Kiev as early as the 1060s, but its wider spread seems to have occurred in the twelfth century.[32]

At about the same time, other minor Latin deviations against which Volodimer had been persuaded by the Greek philosopher began to circulate in Rus'. This Greek philosopher seems to give to Byzantium the exclusive rights to the pure, uncorrupted, Apostolic tradition when he says:

30 *PSRL*, 1, col. 86. The fact that the speech of the philosopher (*PSRL*, 1, cols. 86–106) in its basic shape is a text that arose earlier on Bulgarian ground (cf. A. L'vov, "Issledovanie Reči filosofa," in *Pamjatniki drevnerusskoj pis'mennosti* [Moscow, 1968], pp. 333–96) is not of any significance here. Rather, we are concerned with the chronicle adaptation of the speech that was done in Kiev and that was addressed to Volodimer. This adaptation was completed some time after 1054 and thus from a clearly anti-Latin stance. L'vov's attempt to interpret the presence of the term "oplatki" (wafers ["azymes," i.e., unleavened bread]) as a "late Czech interpolation from the X–XI centuries" (ibid., col. 394) indicates that neither the polemic about the azymes itself and its chronology, nor the anti-Latin treatises (both the original and the translated), which comfortably used the expression "oplatok," i.e., wafer, remained unknown to the author. The West Slavic origins of the expression "oplatki" (from the Latin *oblata*) is certain, as is the fact that its use in Rus' was not the result of literary borrowings but rather of everyday contact with the neighboring Poles. Anti-Latin polemicists stressed the dangers of such contact to the purity of the faith.

31 A work that is still valid is M. Čelcov *Polemika meždu grekami i latinjanami po voprosu o opresnokax v 11–12 vekax* (St. Petersburg, 1879); cf. also Beck, *Kirche*, pp. 318–20, 534.

32 A. Poppe, "Le traité des Azymes Leontos mētropolitou tēs en Rhosiai Presthlabas: quand, où et par qui a-t-il été écrit?" *Byzantion* 35 (1965): 504–527, where there is also earlier literature. See also Podskalsky, *Christentum*, pp. 171–84. It is necessary here to focus attention on the duration of two tracts against the Latins mistakenly attributed to Theodosius of the Caves († 1074), although the argued view dates the beginning of these monuments to the twelfth century and links them to a person associated with this monastery in the first half of the twelfth century—Theodosius the Greek. The basic arguments concerning this attribution were collected by K. Viskovatyj ("K voprosu ob avtore i vremeni napisanija 'Slova k Izjaslav o Latinex'," *Slavia* 16 [1939]: 535–67); see also further arguments completed by Podskalsky, *Christentum*, pp. 179–81, where there is also older literature. Articles about both Theodosiuses in *Slovar' Knižnikov*, pp. 457–61 appear not to know the cited literature and do not give a true picture of the state of research. For example, O. Tvorogov, writing about Theodosius of the Caves, gives in his bibliography the work of Viskovatyj, but appears not to know that this author came out against the attribution of this letter to Theodosius of the Caves. T. Bulanina also cites the works of Viskovatyj and Podskalsky, but ignores their arguments.

"...When the apostles taught [the people] throughout the world to believe in God, we Greeks inherited their teaching."[33] Otherwise, Ilarion praises Constantine the Great, "who among Greeks and Romans had subordinated his Empire to God...hence now both among them and among us it is Jesus Christ who is called the King."[34] Expressing the unity of the Universal church felt at that time, Ilarion entertains no doubts whatsoever about the extraordinary ties that linked Kiev with Constantinople. For Volodimer, the country that is the embodiment of piety, the country of "the true faith, which loves Christ and is strong by the faith" is "the Greek country." Constantinople is the new Jerusalem—the city of Salvation, an ideal model for all cities. Greece is for him the land "where the churches in the towns and villages are filled with the faithful who sing there their prayers."[35] The Holy Cross, which symbolizes the faith in Christ, but which also indicated the ecclesiastical ties, had been brought from this new Jerusalem by Ol'ga and Volodimer, and been erected in their own country to "strengthen the faith."[36]

In the Primary Chronicle, the initiative for the introduction of Christianity to Rus' is presented as a more complex process. Volodimer is presented as the most important actor, but the role of his boyars, of his retinue, is also duly recognized, as is the active role of the Byzantines. The Greek philosopher (or, more properly, missionary theologian) and bishops and priests from Constantinople and Cherson, as well as the imperial family, are also mentioned.[37]

Yet another important discordance between the treatise of Ilarion and the Primary Chronicle should be mentioned here. Ilarion stresses the direct vocation given Volodimer by God for apostolic mission. He also points out that Volodimer did not have a forerunner. Volodimer "did not see the

33 *PSRL*, 1, col. 105; 2, col. 92. Cross, *Primary Chronicle*, p. 109.

34 Moldovan, *Slovo*, p. 96 (191[a]); Müller, *Lobrede*, p. 118 (44[13–15]).

35 Moldovan, *Slovo*, p. 92 (185[b]); Müller, *Lobrede*, p. 103 (39[3–4, 7–8]).

36 Moldovan, *Slovo*, p. 97 (191[a]); Müller, *Lobrede*, pp. 118–19 (44[19–21]).

37 *PSRL*, 1, cols. 106, 107, 108, 110, 111, 116. The chronicle states that together with Anna came "sanovniki nekii i presvitery" (ibid., p. 110), which nullifies the justification for the assertion, generalized in the literature, that the arrival of the bishops received no mention in the chronicle. At that time, the expression "sanovnik" meant "dignitary" in both Greek and Slavonic—a holder of rank (*san, aksioma, dignitas*), also bishop. Cf. *Slovník jazyka staroslověnského*, 4 (1983), no. 36, p. 19; I. Sreznevskij, *Materialy*, 3, pp. 259–60. It is possible, therefore, in spite of the translators, to assume in principle that "some dignitaries" accompanying Anna are representatives of the high church hierarchy as well as secular officials. Besides, it is hard to imagine that it could be otherwise, since the chronicle speaks of this clearly (it appears that the later semantics of the Russian expression "sanovnik" obscured the correct interpretation). See, i.e., Cross, *Primary Chronicle*, p. 112: "some dignitaries and priests."

Apostle who would have come to his land.''[38] There was, then, no apostolic intercession. Nestor the Hagiographer (ca. 1085), and probably also the author of the story about the Varangian martyrs, also wrote that the apostles had not visited the lands of Rus'. The Primary Chronicle, however, contains the story of a journey through Rus' made by the apostle Andrew.

The tradition of the missionary journeys of the apostle Andrew, the origin of which, given the mention of Scythia, can be dated to the third or fourth century, was supplemented by certain articulars during the seventh to ninth centuries when the foundation of the bishopric in the city of Byzantion (later named Constantinople) began to be linked with the missionary activity of this apostle. In that later version the territory north of the Black Sea, as well as Sinope and Cherson, is mentioned. These two cities are referred to in the *Vita of St. Andrew* by the monk Epiphanius and in the *Laudatio* descended from this *Vita* (it should be noted that both these sources were written in the ninth century). It was these sources that provided a geographic reference point for the description of St. Andrew's journey through Rus'.[39]

We cannot discuss here details of the authorship and the circumstances surrounding the composition of the Rus' Andrew legend.[40] However, its late origin is definite: it could only have appeared after 1085, probably in the beginning of the twelfth century, shortly before the last arrangement of the Primary Chronicle in 1116. To Ilarion this legend was of course unknown, but it is difficult to accept that he did not know of those versions of the *Vita* from the ninth and tenth centuries, which linked St. Andrew with the apostolic tradition of the See of Constantinople.

It seems, therefore, that the apocryphal legend on the participation of the apostle Andrew in the foundation of the Byzantion See was not unknown to Ilarion, but that he did not accept its reliability, in accordance with the intellectual trend among the church hierarchy, expressed so clearly by Patriarch Photius. And neither Photius nor Patriarch Ignatius, during their controversies with Rome, referred to the apostolic succession in terms of the St. Andrew legend, since both were aware that this new idea had no authentic confirmation in ecclesiastical tradition.

38 Moldovan, *Slovo*, p. 95 (188^{b}); Müller, *Lobrede*, p. 109 (41^{30}).

39 Fr. Dvornik, *The Idea of Apostolicity in Byzantium and the Legend of the Apostle Andrew* (Cambridge, Mass., 1958), pp. 188ff., 223–63. Compare the note in *PSRL*, 1, cols. 7–8, that Andrew taught in Synop and came to Cherson, with Epiphanius's *Life of St. Andrew*, *PG*, vol. 120, 220^{B}, 244.

40 On the literature, cf. Podskalsky, *Christentum*, pp. 12–13; *SSS*, 7 (1984): 360–61; *Slovar' knižnikov*, pp. 49–54 (*Apokrify o Andree Pervozvannom*). For accurate observations about the later origin of this legend, see Müller, *Die Taufe Russlands*, pp. 9–16.

Pleading for the apostolicity of the Byzantion See, both Photius and Ignatius linked the See to the apostle John the Evangelist as founder of the bishopric of Ephesus. The apostolic prerogatives of Ephesus, together with its See and relics of the apostle, were transferred to Byzantion when this city became the capital of the Roman diocese of Pontus, that is, over Asia Minor.[41]

This is just the situation expressed by Ilarion. The ecclesiastic jurisdiction of the apostolic see of Ephesus over Asia Minor is registered with historical accuracy: "With panegyric voices Asia, Ephesus, and Patmos praise John the Theologian, their teacher, who brought them the Orthodox Faith."[42] Ilarion appears as a spokesman and a supporter of these historically grounded traditions, which served the Constantinopolitan See's bid for apostolicity.

Given all that we know about Ilarion and his work, it is difficult to assume that the entry on the geographic regions covered by the five apostles in their missionary activity was compiled by chance. This record is based on the Origenist tradition as reported in the account of Eusebius of Caesarea, passed down through later filters of church interpretation. Eusebius ascribed to Peter, besides Rome, a few provinces in Asia Minor. Ilarion refers only to the "Roman land"—a phrase more compact but less precise. Surprising is Ilarion's omission of the apostle Andrew's Scythian mission mentioned by Origen. This silence could be explained as evidence of suspicion of legendary motives surrounding the missionary activity of the apostle Andrew. Doubts as to the veracity of the Andrew legend were raised by Photius and were presumably carefully weighed by Ilarion, who was not merely a compiler, but was a learned bookman, well versed in the traditions of the Church and well acquainted with the question of the apostolicity of the imperial city.

The tendency to include the apostle Andrew as founder of the see of Constantinople in the official tradition of the Byzantine church, evident at the end of the tenth century (in the writings of Simeon Metaphrastes, in the *Menologion* of Basil II, and in the *Patria Constantinupoleos*), had still not been accepted in the patriarchate during the eleventh century since the question had never risen in contemporary polemics with Rome. Little was heard on this idea in the twelfth century. It became a burning issue only after 1204.[43]

41 Dvornik, "The Idea of Apostolicity," pp. 233f., 238–53.

42 Moldovan, *Slovo*, p. 91 (184^{b}); Müller, *Lobrede*, pp. 99–100 (38^{3-8}).

43 Dvornik, "The Idea of Apostolicity," pp. 244–46, 257–59, 280–90.

The Rus' connection to the travels of St. Andrew must have been added to the legend at the end of the eleventh or beginning of the twelfth century, clearly in response to the increased significance of that legend in Byzantine literature. The presence of Cherson in the Andrew legend is also suggestive.[44]

The Rus' version of the legend was inspired by the honest and naive desire to enrich one's own prehistory, one's own road to Salvation through association with the apostolic mission and its legacy. In reality, however, the concept, presented in the Primary Chronicle, of introducing the two apostolic motifs indirectly but clearly detracted from the apostolic role of Volodimer so markedly advanced by Ilarion. Could it have been this aspect which was one of the reasons that hampered the development of the Volodimer cult?[45]

St. Andrew's presence on Rus' soil and the raising of the Cross on the hills of the future Kiev constituted, as it were, the act of baptizing the land, the promise that one day it would be a Christian land. The introduction of the apostle Paul as teacher of the Rus', "since he taught the Slavic people. . . And the Slavs and the Rus' are one people,"[46] further complemented the mission of St. Andrew: the very presence of St. Paul blessed all Slavs in their Danubian ancestral home. Those Slavs who arrived on the banks of the Dnieper settled in territory blessed by St. Andrew. Thus, according to the chronicler's conception, Christ, through the mediation of his apostles, inscribed the Slavs and the Rus' land in the history of Salvation. Unlike the vision of Ilarion, for whom Volodimer was the disciple of Christ (for "it was the Savior himself who had appointed him"),[47] the chronicle version views Volodimer on a more human scale. This should not be seen as an attempt to cast doubt on Ilarion's testimony or to detract from Volodimer's achievement. The legend was merely an expression of the desire, typical of neophytes, to find their place in the genealogy and traditions of Christendom. The Rus' legend of St. Andrew's travels, integrated with the at first apocryphal and subsequently officially recognized Byzan-

44 The presence of and contacts with the Rus' in the Black Sea region (Cherson, Tmutorakan') were able to further the inception of this legend, which is, after all, similar to the legend that began in the eleventh century about the visit of the apostle Andrew to Georgia.

45 On the topic of the intricate circumstances surrounding the beginnings of this cult, see A. Poppe, "Vladimir," in *Histoire des Saints et de la Sainteté Chrétienne*, 5 (Paris, 1986), pp. 256–59; J. Fennell, "On the Canonisation of Prince Vladimir," in *Tausend Jahre Christentum in Rußland* (Göttingen, 1988), pp. 299–304; and V. Vodoff, "Pourquoi Volodimer n'a-t-il pas été canonisé?" in this volume of *Harvard Ukrainian Studies*, pp. 446–66.

46 *PSRL*, 1, col. 28; Cross, *Primary Chronicle*, p. 63.

47 Moldovan, *Slovo*, p. 94 (188^b); Müller, *Lobrede*, p. 108 (41^{17}).

tine tradition, added a note of apostolic predestination to the ties of Kiev with Constantinople.[48]

An important role in the chronicler's conception of the Christianization of Rus' must be attributed to the "Tale of the Assassination of Boris and Glěb." This entry under the year 1015 is an abridged version of a hagiographic text—the "Anonymous tale of the martyrdom of SS. Boris and Glěb," written shortly after 1072 and expanded by the chronicler with the encomium of the princely martyrs.[49] Added to the allegedly historical narrative of the events were some characteristics attesting to the conversion of Rus'. The chronicler clearly, though indirectly, conveys the idea that the act of conversion, begun with the baptism of Volodimer, was only completed when "the land of Rus' was blessed by the blood" of the princely martyrs.[50] By their act, Volodimer's two sons indicate that they belong among those who maintain the highest Christian values. Their voluntary sacrifice in a society recently turned Christian took on the meaning of martyrdom for the faith—a faith confessed not only in words, but in deeds. The martyrs' deaths of Boris and Glěb, accepted innocently and voluntarily (in the views of both the hagiographer and the chronicler), were interpreted as readiness to sacrifice their lives in the name of Christ's evangelical teachings. Their voluntary sacrifice became in the history of the conversion of Rus' the crowning act of its baptism. Volodimer led Rus' onto a new path, and his two sons, through their humility, nonresistance, and participation in Christ's martyrdom—by applying the teachings of the Gospel to life

48 The opinion suggesting that the legend arose with the aim of procuring sovereignty over Rus', with Andrew's vicar residing in Constantinople (A. Poppe, *Państwo i Kościół na Rusi w XI wieku* [Warsaw, 1968], pp. 234–35), appears to be a simplification since, during the forming of this legend, the idea linking the apostolicity of Constantinople with the apostle Andrew had not yet gained official sanction, although the tradition, consisting of legendary elements, could convey connections of some countries with the imperial city. At the same time, interest in the development of this tradition could have been stronger in the peripheries than in the center. For example, Nil Doxopatros in Sicily in 1143 already treated the connection between the apostolic mission of Constantinople with the person of the apostle Andrew as credible, and understood it as the official dogma.

49 The secondary relation of the tale in the chronicle in regard to the anonymous Tale is particularly clearly readable in the case of the comparison of both expositions of the events of the year 1072. Cf. *PSRL*, 1, col. 172 as well as *Die altrussischen hagiographischen Erzählungen*, pp. 55–56. See A. Poppe, "Uwagi o najstarszych dziejach Kościoła na Rusi, III," *Przegląd Historyczny* 56 (1965): 560–63; and idem, "La naissance du culte de Boris et Gleb," pp. 29–53.

50 *PSRL*, 1, cols. 138–39; 2, col. 126. This praise of Volodimer, given in conclusion to the report of the death of the ruler, seems to be a personal work by the chronicler who was also inspired by the well-known *Slovo* of Ilarion and the anonymous Tale.

itself—had demonstrated in what way the Gospel transforms man.[51]

In Ilarion's conception of the conversion of Rus', Volodimer's decision to be baptized is the turning point. By the same token, however, it was emphasized that the baptism merely opened the road to the country's true Christianization: "And then the darkness of heathendom began to recede from us and the dawn of the new faith appeared." By referring to Ol'ga's participation in the elevation of the cross on Rus' soil, Ilarion briefly yet unmistakably indicates that the conversion to the true faith covered the previous two generations of Rus' history. The Primary Chronicle praises Ol'ga as the "Herald of Christian Rus'," as the dawn before sunrise. But at the same time the chronicle's vision gives the intended impression that Volodimer begins everything anew. For again the pagan night had descended, and the darkness of the pagan deities had triumphed—dramatic contrast so necessary to the chronicler to highlight the turnabout accomplished by Volodimer.[52]

In Ilarion's *Slovo*, pagan Rus' and its rulers are not painted in black colors, though the description of the dramatic changes does use the literary device of imagery. Despite the darkness prevailing in this pagan land, both Igor' and Svjatoslav deserved recognition, and their grandson and son could be identified as a "wise, brave, and just" ruler. The Rus' land, though pagan, is a "land known and famous to all ends of the earth."[53] Ilarion's conclusion is characteristic of his way of thinking, so apparent in his view of the Old Testament phase of history (Law) in relationship to the New Testament phase (Grace).[54] The "Law" was necessary and useful to prepare for the knowledge of Christ. Just as the Old Testament prepares for and is

[51] In this opinion, we differ fundamentally with the existing literature, which, independent of orientation, does not consider Boris and Glěb martyrs for the faith, but victims of quarrels among princes. Cf. G. Fedotov, *Svjatyje drevnej Rusi* (Paris, 1985^3), p. 19; *Vvedenije xristianstva*, p. 147. Taking the matter historically, it really was so; somehow the reconstruction of the sequence of events after the death of Volodimer in 1015 is exceptionally difficult because of the already hagiographical character of the preserved records. But precisely this tradition—speaking of the voluntary character of their sacrifice—gave it a religious sense of following in the footsteps of Christ and by their atonement "removing the stigma [of paganism] from the sons of Rus'" (Nestor, "Life of Boris and Glěb," in *Die altrussischen hagiographischen Erzählungen*, p. 6). It is necessary to make note of this deep understanding of becoming a true Christian, when one passes from words to the actual application of the teachings of Christ in one's own life, so surprising in a society that just became Christian.

[52] Moldovan, *Slovo*, pp. 93 (186^b), 97 (191); Müller, *Lobrede*, pp. 105, 118–19 (40^{8-9}, 44^{18-21}); *PSRL*, 1, cols. 68 79–80, 82–83.

[53] Moldovan, *Slovo*, pp. 91–92 (184^b, 185^a); Müller, *Lobrede*, pp. 100–101 (38^{12-30}).

[54] Both of these expressions appear repeatedly in the *Slovo* of Ilarion, mainly on the principle of contrast (*zakon* = OT 29 times; *blagodat'* = NT 32 times). Compare Moldovan, *Slovo*, pp. 201–202, 211 (dictionary).

replaced by the New Testament, so the pagan Volodimer and his ancestors, who built a strong and populous state worthy of an honorable place in the world, though as yet submerged in darkness, are instruments in the path of the Rus' towards Grace.

Ilarion's *Slovo* is not a document of ecclesiastic policy as it is often taken to be; rather, it is a theological-philosophical treatise, an attempt at offering a philosophy of the history of Rus' with the aim of demonstrating its place in the general Christian history of Salvation. Ilarion conceives of the history of mankind as the process of spreading Salvation through Christ's teachings: "The faith of salvation spreads over all of the world and reaches also our Rus' people, drying out the lake of law while the wellspring of the Gospel is pouring richly, filling the earth and inundating us also."[55]

Many misunderstandings in the reading of Ilarion's message—including the search for anti-Byzantine overtones or the absence of loyality vis-à-vis the ecclesiastic authority of Constantinople—have resulted both from considering it a concealed ecclesiastic-political polemic and from comparing it with other Old Rus' texts, assuming contemporaneous (or even earlier) provenance to Ilarion's *Slovo*. This is true, for example, of the hypothetical chronicle of 1039, the equally hypothetical "Tales of the Spread of Christianity in Rus'," or of the Lives of Boris and Glěb, which have been given wrong, far too early dates. Mistaken assumptions concerning the dating of various texts by necessity lead to inaccurate conclusions.[56] However, it so happens that the most outstanding piece of Christian literature among the East Slavs originated at the dawn of Christianity in Rus', definitely predating the Primary Chronicle and the tales mentioned here that came to form this Chronicle's text. There can also be no doubt about the *Slovo*'s impact on that literature even though not all borrowings from it were aptly used.[57]

Only some aspects of both concepts of the conversion of Rus' were touched upon here. These concepts vary, not only in the element of time, but, more importantly, in the circumstances surrounding their formation

55 Moldovan, *Slovo*, p. 88 (180^{b}); Müller, *Lobrede*, p. 88 (34$^{6-10}$).

56 See fn. 22, above. Concerning the differences in the dating of the works dedicated to Boris and Glěb, see Poppe, "La naissance du culte de Boris et Gleb," pp. 30–37; *Slovar' knižnikov*, pp. 398–408.

57 On the influence of Ilarion's *Slovo* on the Primary Chronicle, see L. Müller, "Ilarion und die Nestorchronik," in this volume of *Harvard Ukrainian Studies*, pp. 324–45. We will add here that the author of the praise of Volodimer in the chronicle's entry for the year 1015 travestied Ilarion's definition of Volodimer as the imitator of the great Constantine ("podobniče velikago Konstantina"; Moldovan, *Slovo*, p. 96 [191^{a}]) in "he is the new Constantine of mighty Rome" ("se jest novyj Konstantin velikago Rima"; *PSRL*, 1, col. 130; Cross *Primary Chronicle*, p. 124).

with regard to the conversion of Rus', and—most importantly—in the differences in intent and the background of erudition and understanding of their authors.

V

The Christianization and Ecclesiastical Structure of Kyivan Rus′ to 1300

The Christianization of Rus′—the state of the East Slavs created with the participation of Scandinavian war bands in the course of the ninth century—was a pivotal event in the history of Eastern Europe. The reception of Eastern Christianity and the articulation of the faith in the Slavic language set the course for much of the religious, intellectual, and cultural development of the three East Slavic peoples—Belarusians, Ukrainians, and Russians—over the succeeding millennium.

Despite the obvious significance of the act of conversion itself, one should not confuse the conversion of Rus′ with its Christianization. Rather, the year 988, as the most important turning point in the process, marked but the opening of the Christian era for Rus′, providing new dimensions and a new quality to its contacts with the world of Christian culture. Christianization itself lasted for several centuries, with the most important portion, in terms of events and results, falling in the second half of the tenth and the first half of the eleventh centuries: that hundred-year period opened with the crucial, though individual act of baptism of the *hēgemōn* and *archontissa Rhōsias*, Princess Ol′ga, at Constantinople in the 950s. It closed with a major development: the first formulation of a theosophical vision of the converted land of Rus′, which placed its baptism into the context of a human history guided by the hand of Providence—the history of universal Salvation. That vision was pronounced by the monk-presbyter Hilarion (Ilarion), who was preparing in 1050 to assume the throne of the metropolitan of Kyiv.

Despite the visible progress of Christianity, it is clear from the events of the eleventh century that the common people were not as accommodating and quick in their reception of the new religion. Indeed, the tenth century merely demonstrated the possibility of, and the eleventh century created the conditions for, the extension of the Christian faith to the broader ranks of society, providing but a beginning to the Church's efforts to overcome the traditional mentality and ways of thinking of the common people. While the upper strata of society and the inhabitants of the chief urban centers can be considered completely Christianized in the eleventh century, the conversion of the majority of fortress-town centers in peripheral or recently colonized regions, particularly in the north and northeast, would continue throughout the twelfth century. The penetration of Christianity into rural areas, along with the rise of a parish network, comes only with the thirteenth century. Indeed, the disasters that befell Rus′ in that latter century expedited the conversion of its entire territory and deepened the religious allegiance of its inhabitants. Consequently, by the end of the thirteenth century, despite many survivals of the old beliefs and the existence of syncretistic tendencies, not only the state, with its elite and towns, but the whole populace of the lands of Rus′ had become a substantially Christian society.

Foredawn of Christianity on the Dnipro

The centuries-long influence of the Byzantine possessions of the northern Black Sea coast on the peoples of the southern tier of the East European plain began, in the ninth century, to extend as well to the East Slavic tribes, who now formed, together with bands of Scandinavian warriors and merchants, a new sociopolitical entity—Rus′. The cumulative effects of raids on the cities of the Black Sea coast and of the establishment of commercial contacts and diplomatic missions, had helped to acquaint the Rus′ people with Christianity. For its part, Byzantium was made quite aware of the danger posed by Rus′ in July 860, when the *Rhōs* (as they were recorded in Greek) laid siege to Constantinople. The empire reacted quickly, outlining two objectives to be achieved with the help of Christianization. In 861 a mission was sent to Khazaria, headed by Constantine, future apostle to the Slavs. His *Vita* allows us to conclude that the best means of preventing further Rus′ raids on Byzantine possessions was considered to be the winning over of the Khazar ruler to Christianity and, as a result, the baptism of the peoples under his rule, who included some of the Slavs on the Dnipro. A second Byzantine undertaking was aimed specifically at Rus′: negotiations were begun, the successful outcome of which, according to Byzantine accounts, was crowned by the arrival in Constantinople (ca. 865) of a Rus′ embassy requesting baptism. In connection with this event, Patriarch Photius reported in an 867 encyclical to the patriarchs of the East that "the wild people known as *Rhōs*, who not long ago dared to attack the empire of the Romans, have received the pure and uncorrupted Christian faith" and have "found a place among those obedient and friendly to us," and "been given a bishop and shepherd."[1] That bishopric, if in fact it was actually established, had an extremely short life, for it does not figure on any of the lists of dioceses from the period. This first attempt at Christianization, which was assumed on Byzantine initiative, was unsuccessful because Rus′ itself was not yet ready for conversion.

The absence of a bishop in Kyiv during Princess Ol′ga's period of rule is indicated by her efforts to obtain one from Otto I in 959. Nonetheless, Christianity continued to gain adherents on the Dnipro. We must consider credible, for example, the testimony of the Arab writer, Ibn Khurdādhbeh (d. 912), which dates to around 885 and concerns the *ar-Rūs* merchants of the *aṣ-Ṣaqāliba* people who represented themselves as Christians to the Byzantine customs authorities.[2] To be sure, they would have had good reason to do so, as Christians paid only half of the customs duty, but even if we assume, to be on the safe side, that these merchants merely wanted to be seen as Christians, this in itself indicates that Christianity was well known in Kyiv at the end of the ninth century. A few merchants no doubt really were Christians, for the international character of Kyiv, quite apparent in the tenth century, allowed for the existence of a Christian community. Still, there were no Christians in the Rus′ embassy that concluded the Rus′-Byzantine treaty of 911. The turning point must have come sometime after that year, for in 944 Christians do figure among the Rus′ envoys, who represented the social elite. There was already at least one church in Kyiv by 944, as indicated by the text of a treaty from that year and by an accompanying Primary Chronicle commentary, written at the beginning of the twelfth century. As the chronicler relates: "the Christian Rus′ took oath in the church of St. Elijah, which is by the stream . . . [and] since it was a parish church, for many of the Varangians were Christians."[3] Likewise, the fact that visitors from Kyiv to Constantinople prior to 944 regularly resided in the suburbs near the Monastery of St. Mammas suggests that part of the Rus′ were already Christianized. This is also indicated by the Christian names of a number of Dnipro islands (St. Gregory [Khortytsia] and St. Aitherios [Berezan]) on the road "from the Varangians to the Greeks" (attested by Constantine VII Porphyrogennētos in the mid-tenth century), as well as by the presence of "baptized Rus′" in the imperial guard.

The disappearance of the practice of cremation of the dead and its replacement by inhumation in the Kyiv region prior to the actual Christianization of Rus′ may possibly be linked with the influence of Christian traditions of burial. Archaeological data do not permit a definitive conclusion, since the chronology of cremation and burial practices among the Eastern Slavs is too heterogeneous. Nonetheless, it is indisputable that the transition along the middle Dnipro, from a prevalence of cremation in the sixth to tenth centuries to a predominance of skeletal burials in the second half of the tenth century, coincides chronologically with the opening up of Rus′ to Christianity.[4] Elsewhere among the Eastern Slavs, cremation continues to be in evidence throughout the eleventh century. The absence of cult objects (such as crosses or icons) of stone or metal among the items found in the graves of this period is as characteristic, with a few exceptions, as it was for the eleventh to thirteenth centuries as well. We do not know whether the wearing of crosses was widely practiced at that time. Nor is it clear whether those crosses, undoubtedly treated at first as phylacteries, would have accompanied the deceased to the grave. Still, such a syncretic treatment of this Christian symbol is suggested by bronze and silver crosses of the eleventh century used as female jewelry or amulets and found among cremated remains as well.[5]

Baptism of Ol'ga—Regent of Rus'

After the death of the Kyivan prince Igor′ (c. 945), the regency of his widow Princess Ol′ga (until ca. 960) supported the further Christianization of Rus′. The most salient expression of this policy was the baptism of Ol′ga herself. According to eleventh-century tradition, that ceremony took place in Constantinople. The fact that Ol′ga's baptismal name, Helena, matched that of the wife of Emperor Constantine VII Porphyrogennētos implies the participation of the imperial couple as godparents. The Primary Chronicle's account of these events has been embellished with many folkloristic elements clearly originating in an already Christian society. Nonetheless, the Primary Chronicle's date for the baptism—6463 (according to the Byzantine *anno mundi*; i.e., between 1 September 954 and 31 August 955 A.D.)—finds support in the eulogy of Princess Ol′ga included in the triptych *Memorial and Encomium for Prince Volodimer*. That work, compiled at the end of the thirteenth century, contains annalistic notes dating back to the eleventh century, and a few of them display an independence from the chronology of these events presented in the chronicle. The work's alternative, indirect way of indicating the date of Ol′ga's baptism, for example, suggests it is using a different source: "after holy baptism, Ol′ga lived fifteen years . . . she died on 11 July 6477 [969]."[6] However, it is the completely independent account in the *Synopsis historiarum* of John Skylitzes that really demonstrates the likely accuracy of the Primary Chronicle's date of 6463. Writing in the middle of the eleventh century, Skylitzes makes use of tenth-century sources. He notes that Ol′ga, after the death of her husband, came to Constantinople and returned home a baptized Christian. All the events preceding and following this note relate to the period of Constantine VII Porphyrogennētos' reign between the dethronement of Romanos I Lekapenos in December 944 and the death of Patriarch Theophylaktos on 27 February 956. Skylitzes precedes his reference to the baptism of Ol′ga with information about relations with Hungary between 948 and 955, and follows it with a discussion of the marriage of Constantine's son Romanos II to Theophanō, which probably took place in 955 and certainly no later than 956. The chronological order of these events permits us to conclude that Ol′ga was baptized in Constantinople in 954 or 955.[7] The agreement between the Skylitzes data and the two accounts from Rus′ makes this dating of Ol′ga's baptism most likely.

The description of the visit to the imperial palace of Ol′ga, *archontissa* and *hēgemōn* of Rus′, in *De Ceremoniis,* does not explicitly indicate whether the Rus′ princess was already a Christian. Thus, the current debate concerning the date of that autumn visit—whether it occurred in 946 or in 957—is not of essential significance for determining the place and time of her baptism.[8] Certain inferences are possible, however. The fact that Ol′ga appears here under her previous name (Elga) rather than her Christian one (Helena) proves nothing, for many Christian South Slavic rulers and rulers of Rus′ (including

Volodimer, for that matter) are likewise known to Byzantine authors only by their princely names. The presence of a priest in the suite of Princess Ol′ga is likewise not of special significance: he could have been present to assist a baptized or catechumen princess, but he could also have been there simply because some of those accompanying Ol′ga were Christians (just as some of the emissaries concluding the treaty of 944 had been).

More significant, on the other hand, is the indication of *De Ceremoniis* that, during the ceremonial banquet, Ol′ga sat, in accordance with her dignity, among the *zōstai* at the imperial table.[9] She was thus treated as the equal of a "girded" *patrikia*, the highest female rank at the imperial court. The title of *zōstē* was used in that period by the first ladies of the court, who would accompany both empresses, the wives of the two emperors and Constantine and his son, Romanos. In addition, the ninth and tenth centuries saw the use of the term as an honorary title bestowed upon wives of neighboring rulers, including those of Bulgaria.[10] Only the *zōstai* had the right to sit at the table of the imperial family. The "appropriate honor" that according to Skylitzes was shown to Ol′ga after her baptism would have been nothing unusual, if it is understood to have been an award of the title of *zōstē patrikia* ("Girdled Lady"), particularly since the Hungarian princes had received the title of *patrikios* following their baptism. The Byzantine custom of granting court titles to foreign rulers who were baptized with the participation of the emperor was continued in the tenth century, and the omission of this award in Ol′ga's case is unlikely and would be difficult to explain. It should also be noted that there are no known instances in which the title of *zōstē* was bestowed upon a non-Christian.

Thus, on the basis of *De Ceremoniis* and the *Synopsis* of Skylitzes, we can basically conclude that the *archontissa* of Rus′ received the title of *zōstē patrikia* after her baptism, as a result of the participation of the imperial pair as godparents. Likewise, the seating of the princess in the midst of the imperial family for dessert and informal conversation on various subjects with the emperor indicates an exceptional degree of intimacy for the imperial court, with its concern for strict ceremonial decorum. The bestowing of such honor to a *zōstē* and goddaughter of the emperor would have been natural enough, but it would have been completely unheard of for a pagan ruler to be accorded similar treatment. Since spiritual kinship with the imperial family can now be taken as a given here, the visit of the Christian Ol′ga must be dated to the autumn of 957, and her baptism to an earlier visit to Constantinople in 954 or 955.

The Ottonian Mission

This date appears to be contradicted by the *Continuation of the Chronicle of the Abbot Regino of Prüm* (*Reginonis abbatis Prumiensis chronicon, cum continuatione Treverensi*), probably written by Adalbert, monk of Trier and then missionary bishop to Rus′, who later, in 968, went on to become the first archbishop of Magdeburg. We read there, under the year 959, that "ambassadors of Helena, queen of the Rus′, who was baptized in Constantinople under Romanos, emperor of Constantinople, came to King Otto I asking—insincerely, it later turned out—for the appointment of a bishop and priests for that people."[11] A literal reading of this account would suggest that the baptism of Ol′ga must to be dated to the reign of Romanos II, that is, between 9 November 959 and 15 March 963, but such a conclusion merely serves to deepen the impression that the account itself is unreliable: were it true, then it would have been a pagan Ol′ga, and not a Christian Helena, who would have sent an embassy to Otto I in 959.[12] Given the later provenance of this note (written after 962, but no later than 967), we should probably see this as a typical error resulting from faulty memory (naming Romanos instead of Constantine). Other inaccuracies and inexactitudes in the *Continuation* would tend to support such a view.

The very fact of the appearance of a Rus′ embassy in 959 does not seem open to doubt, for already in Christmas 959 in Frankfurt, the monk Libutius was consecrated bishop *genti Rusorum* in the presence of Otto I. In light of this, the arrival of the Rus′ embassy should be dated to the autumn of 959, when Constantine VII Porphyrogennētos was still alive. The news of his death on 9 November and of the assumption of power by Romanos could barely have reached the royal court by Christmas.

There would be no question about the reliability of the account if, instead of *"sub Romano imperatore Constantinopolitano,"* we were to find *"sub Constantino et Romano imperatoribus Constantinopolitanis."* There are, however, circumstances permitting us to understand the appearance of such imprecision at the time of the writing of the work. Romanos II became *basileus autokrator* only after the death of his father Constantine VII Porphyrogennētos on 9 November 959, but he had been emperor in name from the moment of his coronation on 6 April 945. At the courts of Europe it was well known who the real ruler was, but this did not free one from the obligation to observe established procedure. It is well known that "years of rule" were numbered from the date of coronation (and hence, for Romanos, from 945) and that the titulature in correspondence issued by the Byzantine imperial chancellery included the names of both emperors, Constantine as well as Romanos. The co-emperor was likewise named on a par with the real emperor in the address of letters sent to them.[13]

The author of the *Continuation,* Adalbert, served in the chancellery of Otto I from 953 to 956 and again, after his return from Kyiv, from 962 to 966, and was thus perfectly acquainted with the formulae of Byzantine correspondence. Since 945, Romanos had been named alongside Constantine in the address of letters originating from the royal chancellery. When, after his stay in Kyiv, Adalbert returned to his duties in the Ottonian chancellery, Romanos then figured first in the address as the emperor *autokrator*. Hence, Adalbert could easily have named him alone when he wrote the further installment of his chronicle.[14]

We thus have the right to consider Adalbert's information reliable, though inexact (since it was incomplete), for, according to the chancellery's view of the surrounding world, Ol′ga-Helena did receive her baptism under the reign of Constantine as well as that of Romanos.

We owe the information about the Rus′ princess included in the *Continuation* solely to the need felt by Adalbert to comment on the Rus′ episode of his biography and to justify its unsuccessful outcome. Fate had it that the dispatch of bishop Libutius was delayed, and his death on 15 February 961 suggests that the delay must have been due to illness. The ordination of Adalbert in his place must have been carried out quickly, although not earlier than Easter (7 April) 961, so that in the summer of that year Adalbert could already have been in Kyiv, only to return home after less than twelve months.

Emphasizing the difficulties and dangers of his journey, Adalbert reproached the man responsible for his promotion, Archbishop Wilhelm of Mainz, "from whom better treatment should have been expected, since I had never done him any wrong."[15] From this comment alone it is clear that Adalbert belonged to that category of ecclesiastical dignitaries who had neither desire for nor understanding of the apostolicity *ad maiorem gloriam* of Christianity. He was the polar opposite of a zealous man, a pillar of the church like Bruno of Querfurt, who considered the mission to the pagans, even if it meant a martyr's crown, to be of the highest honor. The failure of the mission to Rus′ thus had its internal reasons: the appointment of Adalbert as helmsman was not the happiest of choices. Undertaking his task without enthusiasm, the missionary bishop did not, however, simply dream up all the difficulties he encountered along the Dnipro. Two full years had passed since Ol′ga's invitation. Her son Sviatoslav, who had reached adulthood and assumed power in the meantime, was, at best, indifferent to the goals of the mission. For him, the opinion of his soldiers, with their scorn for Christianity, mattered more.

Under these new conditions, the pro-Christian Ol′ga was unable to offer effective support to the missionary efforts. The authorities were not quick *compellere intrare* (Luke 14:23), and so the missionaries, disappointed by such double-dealing, did not delay in returning to their homelands. The generally held view that the failure of the mission was a result of rivalries between Rome and Constantinople lacks any real foundation. Regardless of certain differences in rite, which could not have mattered to Ol′ga in any case, there was still one Church at this time, and the activity of Greek or Latin missionaries, therefore, did not have to be mutually exclusive, even though a signal success by one or other mission would have placed the matter of ecclesiastical jurisdiction on the order of the day. Ol′ga clearly understood that the conversion of the realm would be difficult to carry out without dynastic, political and ecclesiastical contacts and sufficient aid from outside, and could have felt justified in turning to any Christian ruler for this purpose. Her appeal, moreover, did meet with a moderately favorable but short-lived response from the Ottonian court. Otto I ultimately viewed the missionary action from the perspective of his own political interests, and these did not extend much farther east than the river Elbe.[16]

Likewise, the practical recommendations on foreign policy toward northern neighbors offered by Constantine VII Porphyrogennētos in *De administrando imperio* indicate that, in the mid-tenth century, the political horizon of the empire in that region was dominated by the Khazars and Pechenegs. To be sure, political and commercial contacts with Rus′ were valued, as was the supply of mercenaries from that country, but the opportunity of opening Rus′ up to Christianity through the conversion of its ruler had not yet been recognized. No doubt, influenced by earlier failures, Byzantine politics lacked a genuine missionary impulse in this period. Indeed, in both Constantinople and Rome in the tenth century, there was an absence of the imagination that had earlier fuelled their competition over Bulgaria. The limitless East European plain was only faintly outlined on the horizon of the Christian world in that period.

* *
*

Why, though, would a princess-regent of Rus′ have appealed to the Western Emperor Otto I in 959, given the traditional ties between Kyiv and the Eastern Empire?

It is quite likely that Ol′ga, on her visit to Constantinople in 954–955, sought, in addition to her own baptism, the dispatch to Rus′ of a mission led by a bishop.[17] The fulfillment of this wish would have depended upon the emperor and the patriarch. Constantine VII Porphyrogennētos, a scholar and literatus with an engaging lifestyle, was no statesman, living more in the past than the present. Generous in his promises, he was parsimonious in his deeds. The patriarch in that period, Theophylaktos, for his part, was a man found "more often in the stables than in the church." When Emperor Romanos I Lekapenos had forced the elevation of his sixteen-year-old son to the patriarchal throne in 933, the opposition of the local bishops was so great that the consecration of the young man had to be performed by papal legates. This lamentable situation continued until the death of Theophylaktos on 27 February 956. Moreover, as a result of a fall from his horse, he was in poor health during the last two years of his life, and was thus at the very least limited in his activities, which would have included the consecration of bishops. Finally, finding a willing and worthy candidate who would not have considered this mission a sentence of exile could well have compounded the difficulties.

When Ol′ga visited Constantinople as a Christian in 957, her presence there was perhaps connected, in addition to political and commercial matters, with renewed efforts to obtain a bishop and mission for Kyiv. The patriarchate was from 3 April 956 occupied by the more worthy Polyeuktos, who, in standing up for the principles and canons of the church, quickly came into conflict with some of the bishops and with the emperor himself. Constantine began by fearing him and then went on to hate him with a passion that continued to his last breath.[18] No doubt, both the emperor and the patriarch, individually, would have favored Ol′ga's request, but when it came to agreeing on a candidate, intrigues and quarrels between the palace and Hagia Sophia would surely have led to a postponement of the decision. Thus, when the awaited pastor failed to appear in Kyiv in 958 or in the summer of 959, Ol′ga, sincere in her devotion to the faith, sent her embassy to Otto I in early autumn 959. The fact that she addressed her appeal directly to the German ruler attests to her good grasp of the prevailing ecclesiastical situation.

It was not rivalry between Constantinople and Rome over Rus′, but local squabbles in both centers of the Christian world that had led to an ignoring of the great mission of the church in this period. John XII, elevated to the papal throne as an immature youth of seventeen, much as Theophylaktos, led a life of scandal and even crime. In both churches there was no lack of striving toward renewal, but the presence of unworthy individuals at the helm undermined the missionary efforts that had been undertaken. Under the circumstances, Otto I's efforts to regenerate the church in symbiosis with the state could not have escaped the attention of the regent of Rus′.

* *
*

Various factors doomed the Rus′ mission to failure, Adalbert's faintheartedness being but the least among them. The attempts undertaken in Kyiv to draw closer to the Christian world, strong with the power of a newly discovered faith, but weak in social support, exposed the lack of any genuine interest in the Christianization of Rus′ in Constantinople. In the Byzantine capital, political skepticism and ecclesiastical inertia were reinforced by popular fears of the Rus′, who aroused a sense of apocalyptic doom.

Even though it did not lead to an immediate breakthrough, the conversion of Ol′ga, whom the chronicler hails as the herald and dawning light of Christianity in Rus′, had far-reaching consequences. The number of Christians continued to grow—at the Kyivan court, among the nobles, and among the townspeople. Ol′ga's efforts to win her son Sviatoslav over to the new faith were unsuccessful, however. Even though the need for a change in the ideology and structure of the young state of Rus′ was already strongly felt locally, there were still insufficient forces to break with the traditional worldview. Sviatoslav, the barbarous warrior and chieftain, taking the helm of rule from his mother after 960, became the guardian of this archaic order. In fact, however, his own activities ultimately served to destroy that system: his friendly contacts and military struggles with Byzantium, as well as his efforts to establish his rule in Bulgaria, opened Rus′ to a greater extent than ever before to the influence of Christianity. Ol′ga herself was left with the possibility of influencing her grandchildren. One of these was Volodimer, who was raised at his grandmother's court. Even if he was brought up as a pagan at the wish of his father, Ol′ga doubtless did much to ensure that he came to know the new faith.[19] More than two decades were to pass, though, before that faith became the official religion in Kyiv.

Civil War in Byzantium and the Conversion of Rus'

The year 988 opened the Christian era for all of Rus′. It unfolded against an exceptionally colorful political background, one that has tended to obscure some of the essential details of the events of 986–989. Let us thus examine the tangle of events of that period which determined the entry of Rus′ into the Christian fold.[20]

The significant role ascribed to the city of Kherson (*Gk.* Cherson; Korsun′ to the Rus′ chroniclers) in the baptism of Rus′ since the days of the Rus′ Primary Chronicle is in need of revision. The Primary Chronicle account of 988 should not be seen as the basic source of our knowledge about the events relating to the conversion of Rus′.[21] An investigation of all the sources enables us to see the Primary Chronicle's tale of the baptism as a myth clad in historical robes, a literary compilation patched together more than a hundred years after the events it purports to describe. Its author sought to portray the baptism of Rus′ as a great religious event, and so arranged his assembled materials in an order calculated to emphasize the ordinances of Providence, even if that order contradicted the logical flow of events.

A significant place in this compilation is occupied by a text known as the "Korsun′ Legend." That legend, originally Greek in language and, more importantly, Khersonian in spirit, came to Kyiv in the 1070s or 1080s as a result of the broad contacts of the Kyivan Caves Monastery and its branch in Tmutorokan. Passing in silence over the reasons for the campaign of the prince of Rus′ against Kherson, the legend has him capture the Greek city and demand the hand of the sister of Emperor Basil II on the threat of further war. In the finalization of the mutually successful negotiations, a significant role is played by Kherson itself as the site of Volodimer's baptism and of his marriage to the imperial princess Anna. The desire of the text to emphasize the role of this city in the Byzantine-Rus′ rapprochement is quite obvious.[22]

Historians assessing the marriage of Volodimer to the *porphyrogennēta* Anna, daughter of Romanos II and granddaughter of Constantine, in the light of an imperial doctrine categorically forbidding the marriage of members of the imperial family to foreigners, have viewed Volodimer's campaign against Kherson as an effort of that prince to win, by force of arms, the hand of an imperial princess earlier promised to him in exchange for military aid.[23] This interpretative approach grows out of the conviction, as unshakeable as if it could be demonstrated from the sources, that a barbarian—and a pagan at that—could not have achieved such a great honor without exerting considerable pressure. The capture of Kherson supposedly played just such a role. However, these historians have failed to recognize that the matrimonial practice of the imperial court was not as rigid as its declared principles, and they have forgotten that political decisions are influenced first of all by political realities, and only then by doctrinal considerations.[24]

In fact, there is no support in the sources for the universally held view that Volodimer captured a Byzantine city loyal to Emperor Basil II and the Macedonian dynasty. Indeed, the chronology of events as well as facts from the history of Kherson itself lead one to quite the opposite conclusion. From the mutually supplementary accounts of contemporary historians (Leo the Deacon, Yaḥyā of Antioch, and Stephen [Step‘anos] of Tarōn) about celestial phenomena it can be concluded that Kherson was captured probably by the end of 988 and surely before October 989.[25] During this same period, Basil II, with Rus′ aid, won an enormous victory over the usurper, and the armies of Rus′ continued to be involved until the late autumn in the crushing of still unextinguished centers of revolt in Asia Minor. It is inconceivable that at the same time as a Rus′ force of several thousand was fighting victoriously under the command of the emperor, other Rus′ troops sent by the same Volodimer would be capturing the city of Kherson, had it been loyal to the emperor. In fact, data from the tenth century permit us to conclude that in the civil war of 986–989, Kherson must have been in the camp of Basil II's opponents.

In the middle of the tenth century, Constantine VII Porphyrogennētos, referring to earlier attempts of Kherson to cast off imperial authority, had recommended measures to be taken in case of another revolt by this city. Among the most effective, in his view, would be an economic blockade, cutting off commercial contacts between Kherson and the Black Sea provinces of the empire: deprived of the possibility of selling hides and wax or importing grain and wine, the inhabitants of Kherson "will not be able to live."[26] The Byzantine emperor thus pointed to the circumstances that would dictate the choice of one political orientation or another by this city, so slow to surrender its traditional autonomy: it would have to submit to whoever controlled the southern coast of the Black Sea. Beginning in September 987, that coast was controlled by the pretender to the imperial crown, Bardas Phokas, who, as Leo the Deacon reports, "took all of the ports and coastal regions of Asia Minor with the exception of Abydos."[27] There must have been tensions in 970–971, when *patrikios* Kalokyros, one of the leading figures in Kherson and a trusted supporter of Emperor Nikēphoros Phokas, refused to recognize the new emperor, John Tzimiskes, after the palace coup of December 969, thereby tying his hopes for the future to the plans of the Phokas family and the bellicose

Sviatoslav.[28] At the beginning of the eleventh century, the revolt that broke out in Kherson was ultimately suppressed in 1016 by the joint actions of the imperial navy and a Rus′ force.

These facts suggest that in 988 and 989 Rus′ units were operating in the Crimea on the basis of the same understanding and to the same end as their comrades who had been sent to the Bosphorus by the Rus′ prince. The imperial possessions in the Crimea, with Kherson in the lead, had come out against the Macedonian dynasty, and so Rus′ troops besieged and captured the rebel city, returning it to the rule of Emperor Basil II—ally and brother-in-law of the ruler of Rus′.

This fundamentally different assessment of the place of Kherson in the developments of the years 986–989 thus leads us to a new interpretation of the sequence of events, showing how, on the one hand, they freed the Byzantine Empire from the confusion of civil war and, on the other, then placed Rus′ inside the orbit of Christian civilization.

* *
*

A painful military defeat, and an even more painful loss of face in a battle with the Bulgarians on 17 August 986, had forced Basil II to reassess the empire's Bulgarian policy laid down by John Tzimiskes. Fresh memories of Sviatoslav's conquest of Bulgaria encouraged thoughts about reviving those articles of the treaties of 944 and 971 that had provided for Rus′ military action against the enemies of Byzantium. It is quite probable that contacts were initiated with Kyiv for this reason soon after the retreat in Bulgaria. In any case, when the Byzantine aristocracy, emboldened by the misfortunes of the emperor, came out openly against the Macedonian dynasty a few months later, Basil, determined to break its political aspirations, no longer had any other way out. On news of the destruction of Basil's armies by the Bulgarians, Bardas Skleros mounted a new rebellion in December 986. Basil was forced to call back Bardas Phokas to his aid, a talented general and ambitious politician whose aspirations peaked in 970 and was suspected of participating in the conspiracy of 985. Phokas, though forced to swear an oath of loyalty to the emperor on everything holy, did not keep his word for long. Wasting no time, he already began negotiations with Bardas Skleros in May 987. Basil had already learned of Phokas' treason in June. After the pair of usurpers had agreed to a division of the empire, Phokas treacherously imprisoned Skleros at their second meeting in August, and on the day of the Exaltation of the Holy Cross, Wednesday, 14 September 987, proclaimed himself emperor.

Elite units of the Byzantine army were in the hands of Basil II's foes, with the Armenians casting their lot with Skleros and the Iberians backing Phokas. The emperor, faced with the hostility of the military and the landed aristocracy, with opposition in the bosom of the church, and an unfavorable attitude on the part of the populace of the empire in general, could have little doubt that the alliances against him spelled the beginning of the end of his reign. He did what he could to hinder the common action of these threatening forces, but in order to save his throne he had to be able to counter the armies of the enemy with an equally respectable force. The contacts already established with Kyiv following news of the agreement between the two usurpers in June now assumed a character of the highest priority: the embassy was instructed not only to ensure that military reinforcements were sent, but also to win Volodimer over entirely to the cause of the Macedonian dynasty. The embassy must have set off in June or the beginning of July 987—the period most favorable for navigation on the Black Sea—and then arrived in Kyiv in July or August of that year. If earlier attempts to obtain Rus′ military support had focused on action against Bulgaria, much more was hoped for and much more offered by the summer of 987. The rank of the embassy must have been appropriate to the gravity of the matters it was to discuss and the goals it was to achieve. It included, and was perhaps led by, Theophylaktos, the metropolitan of Sebastea. Entangled in violent conflicts with the Armenian clergy of that city, he had taken refuge in the capital in the spring of 987 after the outbreak of the revolt of the Armenians' supporter Skleros, thus linking his own fate with that of the Macedonian dynasty. The events of 986 and 987, the fact of the erection of the metropolitanate of Rus′ sometime between 976 and 997, and the transfer of Theophylaktos from Sebastea to the see of Rus′ during the reign of Basil II Porphyrogennētos, all show that the ecclesiastical dignitary, loyal to the emperor, was suited as no one else for a combined diplomatic and missionary undertaking of this kind. His success in this endeavor resulted in Theophylaktos becoming the first head of the church in Rus′.

* *
*

Three central issues were the subject of the discussions and mutually binding agreements in Kyiv: 1) the acceptance of Christianity by the ruler of Rus′ and his land, 2) his marriage to the *porphyrogennēta* Anna, and 3) his provision of effective military aid to the empire. Let us examine each issue individually.

1. Volodimer declared his readiness to accept baptism in his own name and in that of his subjects: "the boyars and all the people of the land of Rus′." It was decided, for the purposes of the propagation and strengthening of the Christian faith there, to found a separate Rus′ ecclesiastical province—a metropolitanate—jurisdictionally joined to the patriarchate of Constantinople, with the Byzantine side taking responsibility for its organization and the ruler of Rus′ providing his protection and the necessary means of support.

2. Through their emissaries, the Emperors Basil and (his brother) Constantine expressed their desire to become kinsmen of the prince of Rus′ and

their readiness to give their sister Anna to him in marriage as soon as he became a Christian.

3. Volodimer obligated himself to offer military aid against all the enemies of the empire by sending a contingent of several thousand to the Bosphorus to fight against the army of the usurpers as soon as possible. Probably then, or before long, an armed action against the Crimean city of Kherson, which had come out on the side of Bardas Phokas, was settled.[29]

Curiously, the most important stipulation of this now vanished treaty is nowhere reflected in Byzantine writings of the tenth and eleventh century.[30] The explanation should probably be sought in the fact that while Byzantine public opinion, alarmed by the threatening presence of the contingents from the north, doubted the sincerity of the conversion, court circles, for their part, sought just as resolutely to emphasize that the baptism of Rus′ was a long-accomplished fact. Justification of such a point of view could be found both in the 867 encyclical of Patriarch Photios and in the views expressed by Constantine VII Porphyrogennētos in his *Life of Basil I*, written around 950.[31] Doubtless, too, more than real weight was ascribed to the Christian community that already existed in Kyiv. Such an explanation was opportune, as it would not have been fitting to admit that at the battle of Abydos, "on the day that"—to quote the Byzantine philosopher and theologian, Michael Psellos— "decided the future of the Empire," the most Christian of rulers had been forced to rely on the aid of pagan Rus′ against his own subjects and fellow believers. For this reason, in order to maintain appearances in Constantinople, Rus′ was treated as if it were already a Christian country, and the terms of the agreement concluded were represented as simply involving the personal baptism of Volodimer and those of his subjects who were not yet baptized, as well as the establishment of jurisdictional and organizational bases for the church in Rus′.

For the Byzantine side, the most important issue was the arrival of a strong Rus′ force in Constantinople as soon as possible. If the alliance was concluded in August and September, there would still have been a possibility of sending a contingent of several hundred in the fall, before navigation became impossible, but months would have been needed to prepare and then dispatch an armada of several thousand warriors.[32] Volodimer must have provided additional troops, drawing them from various parts of his realm, as well as hired Varangians, perhaps from Scandinavia. Considerable time would have been needed to suitably equip an expeditionary corps of this kind and to prepare the 120 to 140 ships capable of carrying 40 to 60 warriors apiece down the river and across the sea. Volodimer must have ordered the assembled force to move southward no later than September of 987, as soon as circumstances were favorable for navigation, which would have meant April or May 988, when the high level of spring water would ease the passage of heavy war boats over the Dnipro cataracts. The route down the Dnipro was easier and faster at that time of year, taking about 20 to 23 days, and cabotage on the Black Sea—6 days. A fast-moving military fleet could thus complete the Kyiv-to-Constantinople journey in about 26 to 30 days. Even in the case of a slightly slower pace, it could have been expected on the Bosphorus sometime in June of 988.[33]

It was no problem to set a date for the baptism of Volodimer and his subjects (meaning, for all practical purposes, the lords and military servitors and the inhabitants of Kyiv). Part of the social elite and its clientele and part of the merchant class were already Christian. The fact that a portion of the Byzantine embassy remained in Kyiv for missionary work permitted the preparation of catechumens and the performance of the baptismal rite at a leisurely pace, just as long as it was completed before the agreed-upon date for the arrival of the *porphyrogennēta* Anna in Rus'.[34] The earliest possible date would have been sometime in the summer of 988.

The giving away of a *porphyrogennēta* in marriage within less than a year from the conclusion of the agreement seems quite startling, considering the earlier experience of the Ottonians. Otto I had negotiated for three years with Emperor Nikēphoros Phokas to obtain the hand of a *porphyrogennēta* for his son Otto II, and unsuccessfully at that. Moreover, his emissary, Bishop Liutprand of Cremona, was told, during an audience at the imperial palace in 968, that "It is an unheard-of thing for a *porphyrogenita* born of a *porphyrogenitus,* that is, a daughter of one born in the (imperial) purple, who was then herself born in the purple, to be given away in marriage to a foreigner."[35] Subsequent efforts to win a *porphyrogennēta* for Otto III lasted for more than six years (995–1001).

When the initiative was taken by the emperor himself, however, the matter could be settled much more quickly: in the course of one-and-a-half years, for example, a marriage was concluded between Otto II and Theophanō, who was, it is true, not a *porphyrogennēta,* but only a relative of Emperor John Tzimiskes. Even the temporary difficulties of Tzimiskes that had forced him to revise his predecessor's policy toward the Ottonians were hardly comparable to the plight of Basil II. The events of 986–987 had made Basil an emperor without an empire. The Asiatic provinces were dominated by the rebellious Bardas Phokas, while the Bulgarians held sway in a significant part of the European half of the empire. The Armenian and Iberian units had thrown their support to the usurpers. Nor could Basil count upon the Greeks. According to Psellos, an overwhelming part of the army had declared itself for Bardas Phokas, who had also won the support of the most influential aristocratic clans. Basil was aware of the disloyalty among the *Romaioi.*[36] In his efforts to save his throne he could not afford to pay heed to any tradition, nor be held back by the warnings of his grandfather, who had called down anathema upon anyone who, in violation of tradition and imperial law, might be receptive to a request from "the unbelieving and contemptible inhabitants of the North" to become kinsmen of the emperor of the *Romaioi.*[37] Aware of the danger to him and to the Macedonian dynasty itself, he decided to break with the hitherto binding principle of denying marriage of foreigners to daughters of the emperor born in the porphyrous chamber of the palace. Having concluded the agreement for the marriage of Anna to Volodimer, Basil was profoundly interested in carrying it to conclusion without delay. By having a sister in Kyiv, he could be certain of effective support from his brother-in-law and count on the arrival of Rus′ units to deploy against the rebellion. To be sure, the emperor and his entourage remembered well the lesson that Sviatoslav Igor′evich had taught the Byzantines almost twenty years before. And some close to Basil were aware that the Rus′ prince stayed true toward Nikēphoros Phokas and that Byzantine-Rus′ relations came to a volte-face and hostility only after this emperor's murder (11 December 969).[38] The thought of a new appeal for aid from Rus′ must have aroused some anxiety. Nonetheless, there was no alternative. All Basil could do was to take every possible step to avoid surprises from that quarter while assuring himself of continued military aid. The most reliable means of realizing this was the establishment of ties of kinship between the two dynasties. It was thus not the prince who forced this union, but it was the emperor himself, compelled by circumstances, who was the true initiator of the marriage of Volodimer and Anna. The "Korsun′ Legend" of the Primary Chronicle, which is oblivious to the civil war in Byzantium and the matter of Volodimer saving the throne for Basil II, betrays better knowledge of imperial matrimonial doctrine than of historical reality.

For Volodimer, an early wedding date was likewise most desirable. An honor that other Christian rulers had failed to attain had become the portion of the ambitious builder of a large and energetic state that was, after all, barbarian in the eyes of the heirs of the Roman Empire. The efforts of the Ottonians and their merely trifling success with the non-*porphyrogennēta* Theophanō, so poorly received, according to Thietmar, by many of the lords of the *Heiliges Römisches Reich*, was no secret to the court in Kyiv. Moreover, reports of the baptism of more and more Slavic and Scandinavian dynasts could well have encouraged a growing sense of isolation and a desire to open up Rus′ to the Christian world, an attitude no doubt encouraged by those members of the Kyivan ruler's entourage who had already converted to Christianity. The decision to accept baptism, already under consideration in Kyiv for some time and now coming to fruition, became particularly attractive in light of the opportunity to become a brother to the emperor of the *Romaioi.* The Kyivan ruler, making Rus′ part of the Christian *oikoumenē,* thus did not merely enter the European family of rulers, but, thanks to his marriage to a *porphyrogennēta,* immediately attained a leading position in that hierarchy.[39] The union between the two dynasties—Macedonian and Rurikid—significantly eased the difficult and historically important breakthrough that opened the road to the Christianization of Rus′. Hence the force of the political and ideological statement of the marriage of Volodimer I.

Since both sides were vitally interested in a hasty realization of their agreement, a Rus′ betrothal embassy must have arrived in Constantinople that same autumn of 987. In its presence the treaty was to be ratified by the emperor himself. The procedure must have been similar to that known from the agreement between John Tzimiskes and Otto I in 971.[40] Part of the Byzantine delegation, consisting chiefly of clerics, remained in Kyiv to prepare and carry out the baptism of the prince of Rus′ and his pagan entourage, but the rest, with the Rus′ embassy and perhaps, as noted above, a military contingent of several hundred, made its way by sea to Constantinople while that route was still open to navigation. The assumption that this matchmaking embassy must have reached Constantinople by October, or at the latest early November, is given greater credence by the news that Volodimer's betrothal reached the European courts by January 988. Light is shed on the timing of the agreement by the thwarted plans of King Hugh Capet of France to obtain a *porphyrogennēta* for his son Robert.[41] All of this endorses the dating of the Byzantine-Rus′ agreement to being concluded no later than September 987.

* *
*

An appeal to outside force in the course of a civil war could not have failed to have an impact on public opinion in the empire. Anxiety was fanned by circles opposed to the Macedonian dynasty, but even among neutral and loyal groups, the ruler's decision to bring in Rus′ troops aroused serious misgivings, even after the victory—no doubt out of fear about the long-range consequences of such an action. These misgivings are expressed in a clear though indirect manner by Leo the Deacon in his history, written at the beginning of the 990s. Leo belonged to court circles, but was not an apologist for Basil II. The historian's silence about the presence of the Rus′ at Chrysopolis and Abydos and about the marriage of the *porphyrogennēta* Anna should be understood as an expression of his disapproval of the means the emperor had employed to save his throne. Leo's treatment of the capture of Kherson by the "Tauroscythians" as yet another misfortune is witness to the fact that he was shocked by the turning over of what was, after all, a Greek city to pillaging by barbarians, whose excesses and cruelties in the wars with Sviatoslav were recalled and exaggerated, not by chance, just at the time of rapprochement. Leo, unsparing in his praise for Emperor Nikēphoros Phokas, and writing after the civil war had already ended in victory for Basil, paints a dark picture of the situation, so drastically different from the more fortunate reigns of Nikēphoros Phokas (963–969) and John Tzimiskes (969–976). He portrays the Rus′ as a sinister and dangerous foe and a genuine menace to their neighbors, supporting his warnings with the prophesies of Ezekiel (*Historiae* lib. IX, 6).[42]

Leo the Deacon was not alone in deriving a pessimistic vision of the empire's future from the years of civil war. In poetic works written between

986 and 990, John Geometres contrasts an idealized portrait of Nikēphoros Phokas and his times with an image of the empire of the present, one encompassed with ruin and oppressed by a fratricidal war in which "brother aims his ax at the breast of brother" and "noble cities are humiliatingly trampled by the feet of foreigners."[43]

Aversion to the Rus′ visitors is sharply expressed as well in a poetic epitaph for Nikēphoros Phokas. The poet appeals to the murdered emperor to rise up from his grave to defend his city against the Rus′. Particularly telling is the following five-line stanza:

> The armed forces of the Rus′ come out against us.
> The tribe of Scythians is thirsty for slaughter.
> The lowest of foreigners plunder our city,
> They, whom once your statue alone,
> Before the gates of Byzantion, struck full of terror.[44]

This verse refers to the presence of the Rus′ expeditionary corps in Constantinople in 988–989. The Rus′, despite their thirst for slaughter, limited themselves to pillage. The behavior of foreign troops, even allied ones, was always a heavy burden for the inhabitants of the host country, and the warriors from Rus′ were no exception, although the poet (whether under the influence of his own prejudices or of reports purposely spread by forces hostile to Basil or opposed to his policy) probably overstates the case. Evidence of misgivings and fears about Rus′ during the time of Basil II is offered by the *Patria Constantinopoleos*, which is a guide to the landmarks of the capital. Referring to a monument on the Forum of Taurus (Forum Tauri), it describes how one of the reliefs on its side portrayed "the last days of the city, when the Rus′ will destroy it."[45] The genesis of this legend about the future destruction of the city by the Rus′ dates back to their unexpected attack on Constantinople in 860. It is noteworthy that the prophesy was still alive a few years after Abydos, in the early 990s, when the guide was compiled. Despite the new state of relations with Kyiv since 988, in the years that immediately followed, while elite Rus′ units fought on the Bulgarian and Syrian fronts to restore the empire to its earlier strength and glory, a traveler guided across the Forum of Taurus was still treated to the same, unaltered commentary. The fact remains that the obsessive expectation of "the end of the city and the end of the world," a reflection of the growth of millennarian beliefs, singled out the Rus′ as the ones who would execute the sentence.[46] The divisions from the years of civil war had not yet been overcome, and the opposition of broad sections of society had not yet died down. The events that long since have enabled us to credit Basil II with rebuilding the empire's strength appeared in much more somber hues to his contemporaries. The new policy of Basil toward Kyiv aroused distrust and anxiety about the future of the empire among the Byzantines, and this was translated into the language of eschatological prophecy by the common people.

Alongside his chief diplomatic initiative to ensure Kyivan aid, the emperor negotiated an understanding with the Fāṭimid caliph of Egypt between September 987 and April 988. It was no coincidence that at a time when the eastern regions of the empire were under the domination of Phokas, Basil sent an embassy to Cairo and agreed, as Arab historians confirm, to heavy terms—inclusive of prayers for the Fāṭimid Caliph al-ʿAzīz recited in the mosque of Constantinople. At the cost of territorial concessions, he could count on Arab military action to tie down part of Phokas' forces on the Syrian border.[47] He did not hesitate to choose such means of assuring his victory, and likewise did not hesitate to sacrifice his own imperial sister to that goal. When his own existence was at stake, there was no time to follow the dictates of imperial doctrine.[48]

The Baptism of Rus' Viewed from Kyiv

At a time when the empire was wracked by civil war, three significant events were taking place: the baptism of Rus′, the marriage of Volodimer to Anna, and the siege and capture of Kherson by Rus′ armies. Our doubts about the reliability of the Primary Chronicle account also have to do with the sequence and location of events of which it writes. Not only the considerations outlined above, but an analysis of other Rus′ accounts as well, militate against the contention that the baptism of Volodimer and his marriage to the *porphyrogennēta* took place in captured Kherson. The Primary Chronicle's "Korsun′ legend" managed to forget the real reason for Rus′ action against Kherson and instead invested the city with splendor as the site of historical ceremonies. Nonetheless, in composing anew the history of those years, it conveyed details—still present in the eleventh century—connected with the siege and capture of the city, as well as with its real role in the Christianization of Rus′. Along with the trophies—relics of the saints, church vessels, and icons, urgently needed for the newly established churches of Kyiv—many clerics of Kherson also journeyed northward, though not of their own free will. Adapting themselves to life in Rus′, they came in time to be the propagators of this legend, one so flattering to their native city.

The date of Kherson's capture can be deduced from Leo the Deacon's reference to a comet that heralded the earthquake in Constantinople on 25–26 October 989. That comet appeared in July.[49] In accordance with the sequence of the Byzantine historian's account, the comet had appeared sometime after the battle at Abydos and the fall of Kherson, justifying the traditional view that Kherson was captured prior to July 989. In any case, the city fell before the earthquake of October 989. The breaking of the resistance of this Crimean fortress may have been linked with the arrival of news about the defeat and death of Bardas Phokas at Abydos on 13 April 989. The Rus′ action against Kherson grew out of the agreement of 987 and fits in well with the overall outlines of the imperial policy toward the rebellious city. This new act of treason brought the issue to life again. Basil II decided to break the political ambitions of Kherson, and in order to provide exemplary punishment for the city, he consciously handed the city over for plunder. As further retribution, Kherson was also deprived of the right to mint its own coins.[50] The extent of the destruction remains under discussion, but it seems certain that Kherson never regained its earlier political brilliance nor its economic significance.[51]

* *
*

In reconstructing the sequence of events associated with the baptism of Rus′, it is impossible not to notice the coincidence between certain of our conclusions and the account of the *Memorial and Encomium for Prince Volodimer* which notes that: "after holy baptism the blessed prince lived twenty-eight years. In the second [i.e., following] year after his baptism, he went to the cataracts, and in the third he captured Kherson."[52] The differences in the order and chronology of events here from those in the *Primary Chronicle* permit us to conclude that the concise annalistic notes used by the *Memorial and Encomium,* which itself was compiled in the thirteenth century, originate from a different tradition. That tradition was still alive in Kyiv in the second half of the eleventh century, as shown by the *vitae* of Boris and Glěb. If we subtract those twenty-eight years from the death of Volodimer in 6523 (1015), the date of his baptism falls in 6495 (March 987–February 988). The same conclusion is supported by the reference to the capture of Kherson in the third year after the baptism. Counting from 6495, that year turns out to be 6497 (March 989–February 990), corresponding closely to Byzantine information about the date of that city's fall.[53]

Thus, the dating of Volodimer's baptism to the year 6495 has all the earmarks of a reliable tradition. The mission, which remained in Kyiv after the conclusion of the understanding in September 6495 (987), would have had sufficient time to convert the Rus′ ruler before the end of the year (February 988). The sacraments of baptism and confirmation could only have been performed by a bishop, and so it must be concluded that at least one hierarch of episcopal rank headed the mission. Because there was no need for excessive haste, the missionaries no doubt sought to endow the ceremonies with the most spectacular character possible. Most likely, the feast of the Epiphany, one of the nearest canonically established days suitable for the baptism of a ruler, was chosen as the day of the ceremony.[54]

On the basis of the ritual requirements of the Constantinopolitan *euchologion,* the preparation for baptism would have taken about two months. The first stage of the catechumenate had probably already begun in October, and certainly no later than the first half of November 987: after receiving instruction in prayer and being conducted into the church, the prince became an "unbaptized Christian." Following forty days of prayer, fasting, catechism, and talks about the faith with his spiritual father, the bishop, Volodimer would have reached the second stage of the catechumenate, which had to last at least ten days, given the requirement of daily exorcistic prayers. The Christmas of 987 would have marked the beginning of the most significant period of this second stage: the renunciations required for the confession of faith. As one newly born into the faith, Volodimer received a new name at baptism: Basil (Vasilii). Since the rituals of baptism and confirmation contained formulae using the new baptismal name, the selection of the latter must have taken place beforehand. The name chosen was the same as that of the "Emperor of the Romaioi," thereby revealing Basil II as the patron of the Rus′ ruler's baptism and, as it were, *per procuram,* his godfather.[55] The feast day of the patron saint of both rulers, St. Basil the Great, was 1 January, coinciding with the feast of the Circumcision, and in 988 it fell on a Sunday. It could well have been the day for the catechumen Volodimer to decide on his new Christian name. Receiving the sacrament of baptism in the font and the sacrament of confirmation on 6 January 988, Volodimer thus became a Christian. The remaining heathen members of his court probably were baptized at the same time.

* *
*

The enigmatic reference in the *Memorial and Encomium* to Volodimer's trip to the Dnipro cataracts in the year 6496 (March 988–February 989) comes between two major events—his baptism in 6495 and the capture of Kherson in 6497. If the note was based on an original annalistic record, then its terseness would speak for it having been written at a time when the reason for the prince's trip to the cataracts would still have been obvious.

What could have led Volodimer to do this in the following year, shortly after his baptism—6496 or, to be more precise, during its first half (i.e., between the spring and the fall of 988)—the period favorable for navigation on the Dnipro? The prince of Rus′ undoubtedly went down to the cataracts to greet his betrothed and to ensure a safe journey for her entourage. The documented instances of later Rus′ princes' travel to the cataracts or even the mouth of the Dnipro to meet an entourage bringing a betrothed princess, support such an interpretation of this laconic "reference."[56] While Volodimer awaited the arrival of Anna at the cataracts, guarded by his warriors, a flotilla of Rus′ boats must have moved still further down the Dnipro nearer to the mouth to take the suite of the *porphyrogennēta* on board from their sea-going vessels. An understanding of these words of the *Memorial and Encomium* to be a reference to Anna's arrival in Rus′ in the calendar year (6496) after Volodimer's baptism, or, more precisely, in the summer of 988, is reinforced by the fact that both rulers had a genuine interest in carrying out their mutual obligations as soon as possible. A delay in cementing the alliance would not have been in the interests of the Macedonian dynasty.[57]

* *
*

If everything points to 988 as the year of Volodimer's baptism, then 6 January seems the most likely day for administering the sacrament, given its symbolism by twinning the baptism of the ruler with the feast of the Epiphany. Likewise, the day of the Descent of the Holy Spirit (Pentecost), which in 988 fell on 27 May, may well be linked with the mass baptism of the assembled Kyivans in the waters of the Dnipro as described in the Primary Chronicle: "Then Volodimer sent heralds throughout the city, proclaiming that if any inhabitant, rich or poor, did not betake himself to the river, he would risk the prince's displeasure. When the people heard these words, they wept for joy, and exclaimed in their enthusiasm: 'If this were not good, the prince and boyars would not have accepted it.'"[58] The equally zealous believer, Metropolitan Hilarion, provided a somewhat more sober assessment of the event: "No one dared to oppose Volodimer's pious command. And even if one did not come to baptism out of love, he did so out of fear of the one who had ordered it, for his piety was linked with authority."[59]

The "Korsun′ Legend" events surrounding the baptism of Rus′ are all related in the Primary Chronicle under the year 6496 (March 988–February 989). For the chronicler-compiler, the Kherson version seemed the most reliable, since it offered the most providential vision of the conversion of Rus′. But as he himself admitted, other versions were known to him, no doubt as laconic and mundane as the above mentioned notes from the *Memorial and Encomium*. He thus could have had the date of at least one of those events, and on that basis assigned a place to the "Korsun′ Legend" in the chronological structure of the chronicle. This could have been the date of Anna's arrival or of the departure of the expedition against Kherson, but most likely it was the year of the mass baptism of the Kyivans. In Kyiv, the memory of that Pentecostal day, that last Sunday in May of 988, when, along the Dnipro "a countless multitude assembled, [who] all went into the water [and] stood, some up to their necks, others up to their chests, the younger nearer the banks, the adults holding children in their arms waded while the priests stood by and offered prayers,"[60] must have lived on in the minds of several generations.

* *
*

This turning point in the religious, social, and political life of Rus′ is inseparably linked with the personality of its ruler, Volodimer. Already in the eleventh century a variety of commentators proclaimed the significance of his achievement, marking, as it did, the beginning of the spiritual transformation of the East Slavs, and the accuracy of their assessment was confirmed by the millennium that followed. Volodimer and his decision were soon compared to Constantine the Great and his achievement. The baptizer of Rus′ was styled "equal of the apostles," and "apostle among rulers." But his spiritual side, his personality, was treated in a purely stylized manner. Thus, the monastic chronicler sharply contrasts the dark figure of yesterday's pagan with the shining visage of the Christian prince. From the oral—knightly and folk—*bylina* tradition, written down centuries later, there emerges a more colorful but equally idealized figure of the Christian prince.[61] The historian of today, wrenching the account of Volodimer's "choice of a faith" out of its chronicle context and thereby overlooking the role assigned to Providence in that account, unintentionally endows the proceedings with a grotesque character: Volodimer is portrayed as an able and effective ruler, who, when his reform of paganism has failed, pragmatically considers various propositions and reaches out to Christian teaching as the best means of consolidating the structure of the state and elevating its position by joining it to the family of Christian countries.

There exists almost nothing about the actual personality and religious convictions of the ruler, who, after all, himself became a Christian. Hilarion, sketching his unambiguously positive portrait of a believer more than thirty years after Volodimer's death, placed his emphasis, above all, on the cultivation of those values on Rus′ soil of which he himself and his hero were zealous propagators.

The "baptism of Rus′" had been prepared by two preceding generations, and Volodimer's decision itself must have taken time to ripen. Hagiographic and bookish tradition notwithstanding, the transformation of Volodimer from pagan to Christian actually was not and could not have been a sudden one.

Volodimer, the third son of Sviatoslav, was born between 955 and 960 to Malusha, housekeeper of Princess Ol′ga and of an unfree court attendant's family. Her brother, Dobrynia, likewise made a career for himself at court. Malusha belonged to the inner circle of the regent's entourage, and as one of Ol′ga's closest servants must have been baptized along with her mistress. As a concubine of Sviatoslav and soon the mother of Volodimer, she continued to live at court, and thus Ol′ga, up until her death in 969, could easily have exercised an influence on the education of her grandson. Even if he was brought up as a pagan in accordance with the wishes of his father, his grandmother and mother would surely have imparted many of the ideas and values of the Christian faith to him. Shortly after Ol′ga's death, the young Volodimer, along with his tutor and uncle Dobrynia, was sent by Sviatoslav to Novgorod. The fact that it was Dobrynia whom Volodimer, after his own baptism in 988, entrusted with overseeing the introduction of Christianity in Novgorod, allows us to speculate that the brother of Malusha may already have been a Christian. One can thus confidently presume that Volodimer, from childhood, grew up in a Christian atmosphere and surely could not have been the convinced heathen as some insinuate. The baptism of the thirty-year-old Volodimer on 6 January 988, preceded by a period of catechumenate, had grown out of well-prepared soil. An emotional tie with Christianity, reaching back to childhood years, imbued with the religious zeal of his grandmother and mother, intertwined with another, rational path to a knowledge of God: "reason illuminated his heart as to how to find . . . the one God." Belief in the unseen, in that which the senses cannot comprehend, was viewed in the young Christian society as a higher stage of intellectual initiation, an attitude expressed well in Hilarion's characterization of Volodimer's decision to be baptized as an act of wisdom. An act of faith and an act of reason have at least one thing in common: both demand a conscious concentration, an internal tension, a new sense of responsibility toward oneself and one's surroundings. This was forcefully expressed by the chronicler's metaphor of Volodimer as the plowman "who plowed and harrowed the soil when he enlightened Rus′ with baptism," and Iaroslav the Wise as the sower, "who sowed the hearts of the faithful with the written word."[62]

Some sense of the natural, human dimension of the faith of the ruler and baptizer of Rus′ can be derived from a few laconic but substantive remarks by the missionary bishop, Bruno of Querfurt, in a letter to King Henry II at the very beginning of 1009. The zealous missionary, aiming to convert the Pechenegs, spent no less than two months in Kyiv in 1008. Out of their conversations, characterized by a common concern for the extension of the *terra christiana,* and out of joint participation in worship and prayer, a bond of spiritual friendship was forged between Bruno and Volodimer. The relationship culminated in a dramatic farewell at the edge of the steppe: the missionary and prince, and those accompanying them, joined together in the mystery of the liturgy, united in prayer by a common language of faith and doubt, fear and hope.[63]

* *
*

The *Senior Ruzorum* must have made a strong impression on Bruno, in light of how the latter undertook to present him to his own senior, King Henry, as a model Christian and a model Christian ruler. In Bruno's view, Volodimer belonged to that rare category of princes who, like Constantine the Great and Charlemagne, had earned from God the title of apostle by their work for the conversion of the heathen and the enlargement of the church. In the course of his visit to Kyiv, Bruno must have encouraged the baptizer of Rus′ and his lay and ecclesiastical entourage in their sense of the apostolic character of their mission. That conviction continued to live on in Kyiv after the death of Volodimer as well. Not only was it expressed by Hilarion and the chronicler, it was made part of the legacy of the ruling house by Iaroslav the Wise, who wrote it into the decorative program of the metropolitan cathedral of Kyiv in the 1040s. The foundation scene in the western portion of the chief nave of St. Sophia, a fresco of substantial dimensions (about 25 sq m) portraying Iaroslav the Wise and members of his family, clearly corresponds to the mosaic frieze depicting the Eucharist on the curving wall of the apse at the opposite end of the nave. Looking at the two compositions, one cannot help being struck by the way the twelve-figure princely procession approaching the enthroned Christ from either side echoes the procession of the apostles in the scene of the Eucharist opposite. This striking parallel, clearly comprehensible in the context of the overall Christological theme of the compositions in the main nave and transept (the central crossing of the church), is a visible symbol of the apostolic mission of the ruling dynasty toward its subjects and toward its domain—the land of Rus′.[64]

This charismatic apotheosis of the ruling house was reinforced—beginning in the mid-eleventh century—by the growing cult of saintly kinsmen: the princes Boris and Glěb, treacherously slain in the fratricidal struggle for the Kyivan throne that followed the death of Volodimer on 15 July 1015.[65]

By their very character, the two sons of Volodimer bore witness to their adherence to the highest Christian values. In this young Christian society, their voluntary sacrifice assumed the sense of martyrdom for the faith—a faith confessed in deed as well as word. The martyred deaths of Boris and Glěb, innocent and unresisting (as portrayed by both hagiographer and chronicler), began to be interpreted in due course as a readiness to lay down one's own life in sacrifice for the gospel of Christ. The chronicler, while drawing at the turn of the eleventh century on the hagiographic text, emphasized even more strongly the notion that the baptism of Rus′, undertaken by Volodimer, had been brought to fruition by the blessing of the land of Rus′ with the blood of the princely martyrs.[66] Such a voluntary sacrifice attested to a turning point of Rus′ on a new path: Volodimer's two sons, bringing the gospel to life by their example of humility, nonresistance, and participation in the sacrifice of Christ, demonstrated how that gospel could transform a human life.

Such reflections on the act of baptism in 988, combined with a deepening awareness of the history of the Christian community, also led to speculation about the original source and earliest beginnings of the conversion—speculation that was not content to stop with the deeds of Volodimer, "equal of the apostles," and those of his forerunner Ol′ga. The search was sparked by a sincere, albeit naïve, desire to embellish the searchers′ own prehistory, to trace their own path to salvation back to apostolic times. At the end of the eleventh century, the legend of the wanderings of the Apostle Andrew, who was also said to have established the episcopal see in Byzantion (the future Constantinople), had a Rus′ motif grafted onto it. The chronicle likewise adopted a South Slavic tradition that portrayed the Apostle Paul as teacher of all the Slavs.

The Apostle Andrew's setting foot on the land of Rus′, and his raising of the cross on the hills that would be become the site of future Kyiv, served, as it were, as a baptism of the land itself, a foreshadowing of the Christian realm that would one day arise there. The introduction of the Apostle Paul as a missionary among the Slavs in their prehistoric cradle, and the characterization of him as "the teacher of we Rus′, since he preached to the Slavic race," supplemented the mission of Andrew. From the very presence of the Apostle

Paul, blessing flowed down upon the Slavs in their ancient Danubian homeland. Those who migrated to the Dnipro, moreover, settled on a land already blessed by the Apostle Andrew. Thus, according to the chronicler's conception, Christ, by the agency of the apostles, had already written the Slavs and the land of Rus′ into the history of salvation. Both legends were an expression of a yearning, so typical of the newly converted, to find a place in the genealogy of the church and the traditions of ancient ties to Christianity. The Rus′ legend about the wanderings of Andrew, originally an apocryphal work and then in the thirteenth century an officially recognized Byzantine tradition, endowed the ties between Kyiv and Constantinople, moreover, with a character of apostolic predestination.[67]

* *
*

The integrative potential of the Slavic language was already recognized in Rus′ in the tenth century. The Slavicization of the social elite, led by the dynasty, had begun even earlier. Igor′'s son Sviatoslav, born in the 930s, already bore a Slavic name (Igor′ itself is the Slavic version of Norse Ingvarr). The process was also reflected in the contemporary Slavic translation of the treaties of 911 and 944. A role in the recognition of Slavic as the state language of Rus′, despite the Scandinavian origin (judging from their names) of the majority of the Rus′ emissaries concluding the treaties, was undoubtedly played by the linguistically related Bulgarian culture, which penetrated the Dnipro region in the course of the tenth century. The latter development also made it easier for Volodimer, when receiving Christianity directly from Byzantium, to don a linguistic garb of his own choosing. The choice bears witness to the self-consciousness of the ruling circles of Kyivan Rus′, who understood and valued the social and political benefit of offering praise to the "newly known Christian God" in the Slavic language. It also enjoyed the support of the church, conscious, thanks to the Cyrillo-Methodian experience, of the importance of the language of ecclesiastical books and liturgy for the Christianization of a large realm.[68] Only with Christianization did Rus′ become capable of full political and social self-consciousness, finding a place for itself in the universal history of humanity and its salvation. The right of the ruling elite to power was now based not only on birth, valor, and wealth, but also on membership in a particularly high religious and intellectual culture as well as on its distinctiveness from the unconverted and unenlightened. The Slavic *nevěglasъ* meant "a heathen," but, as is clear from translations from Greek and Latin, it also meant "an uneducated, ignorant man, one not belonging to the sphere of thought."

Christianity meant access to knowledge and became a source of intellectual experience. The spiritual union of faith and reason rather than the dichotomy between them, characterized a young Christian society. The newly converted elite must have been particularly susceptible to the charm of the well-conceived order linking church and written word with political authority and the fortress-town. In the era of the Merovingians and perhaps even more in the era of the Carolingians, Western Europe had lived through such a period, marked by the naïve absence of any distinction between religious ideals on the one hand and political and civilizational ones on the other—an era when Christianity was turned more toward rulers, their courts, their magnates and courtly and armed retinue, and appeared in harmony with earthly strivings toward legal order, building in stone, and education. Now it was the turn of the Eastern Slavs. For Emperor Basil and his entourage, preoccupied with immediate military and political goals, the conversion of the ruler of Kyiv and his subjects was of interest, above all else, from the point of view of an effective alliance. And so, for the moment, an assurance of its constancy was sought, with mercenary practicality, more in ties of kinship, though in the long run the imperial court was sensible to institute the foundations of a religious community.[69]

Although clerics and the means necessary to support the Christianization of Rus′ were dispatched from the imperial city on the order of the emperor, the conversion of that land was not decided on the Bosphorus. For all the importance of the theological, intellectual, and cultural achievement of the Byzantine and early Christian heritage in the transformation of the Eastern Slavs into a Christian society, there is no basis for ascribing the conversion of Rus′ to the initiative and activity of Byzantium. What we are accustomed to characterizing as "Byzantine influence" was in fact the work of the interested party itself, reaching out in search of new spiritual values. Nonetheless, the Byzantines who supported the measures and steps taken up by Anna and Basil II could consider the conversion of Rus′ a significant achievement on their part, even though many notables in fact failed to grasp the significance of the event in time.[70]

If, from the outside, it was the political aspect that was most clearly recognized, in Rus′ itself the newly converted elite had already managed in the course of the first century following the baptism to rise to a more complex appreciation of the event. The change itself and the new participation in the world of Christian values were understood, felt, and profoundly experienced. Moreover, this elite had succeeded in arriving at a considered understanding of its own conversion.[71]

The acceptance of Christianity was not dictated by chance. While the specific date and conditions of the baptism of the Rus′ ruler and his entourage grew out of a specific political situation, the entry of the Kyivan realm into the Christian community had been preceded by more than a century of infiltration of Christianity into the middle Dnipro region and of the growing stature of that faith among the Rus′ nobility and at the court in Kyiv (cf. the treaty of 944), particularly since the time of the baptism of Volodimer's grandmother, the regent of Rus′ Ol′ga-Helena, from 954, the imperial *zōstē patrikia*.

If the idea of the conversion of Rus′ had been born in Constantinople, a reversion to paganism would have been unavoidable—just as it had been shortly after the premature initiative of Photios in 867, or even after the attempt under Ol′ga and her son Sviatoslav (when the need for change was already felt, but the fear of breaking with traditional values was still strong).[72] This fear had weakened in the course of the succeeding decades, and the conditions proposed by Basil II, born in an international context that reflected the constellation of real political forces, greatly eased Volodimer's decision. The permanence of the reception was decided, however, by the political readiness of the Rus′ ruling strata to be baptized. The baptism of Rus′ was a great religious act, but, at the same time, it was a significant political event.

The Metropolitanate of Kyiv and All Rus': The Propagation of Christianity. The Building of an Ecclesiastical Framework

The most important stipulation of the treaty concluded in September 987 between Byzantine Emperor Basil and Volodimer was the latter's agreement to make Christianity the official religion of Rus′. The Byzantine side expressed its readiness to participate actively in the realization of this task.

In the *Notitia episcopatuum* of the patriarchate of Constantinople, prepared and promulgated around 1087 under Alexios I Komnenos, the metropolitanate of Rus′ is listed as number 60 among 80 metropolitanates. The metropolitanates are listed in the *Notitiae* in the order of their establishment. Immediately before the see of Rus′, in positions 58 among 59 are the metropolitanates of Serres (Sérrai) and Pompeiupolis, both of which were still only titular archbishoprics in the time of John Tzimiskes, but figure as metropolitanates in a synod document of 21 February 997. They thus had advanced in rank sometime between 969 and 996. The metropolitanate of Alania, following Rus′ in position 61, and thus established after it, was set up before 6506 (997–998), as indicated by a grant of privilege to its metropolitan in that year. The simple conclusion, then, is that the metropolitanate of Rus′ was created sometime after 969 and certainly before 997. From one of the versions of the treatise *"Peri metatheseon"* [*De translationibus*], it is known that Theophylaktos was transferred from the cathedra of Sebastea to the see of Rus′ during the reign of Basil II Porphyrogennētos (976–1025). It is likewise known that Theodore, the chronicler and metropolitan of Sebastea who was confirmed in his see in 997, must have become pastor of that city prior to that year. Moreover, the information about the translation was probably taken from Theodore's no longer extant chronicle of Sebastea. It would appear, then, that Theophylaktos was Theodore's predecessor in Sebastea and hence the very same metropolitan who had fallen into a violent conflict with the clergy and people of that Armenian city and region, and was forced, as a result, to leave Sebastea at the very beginning of 987.[73]

Thus, everything would seem to indicate that the metropolitanate of Rus′, sixtieth in rank in the ecclesiastical province of the patriarchate of Constantinople, had already been established in the princely capital of Kyiv by the time the *porphyrogennēta* Anna and her suite of lay and ecclesiastical dignitaries arrived there in 988. At the head of the clergy who had come to Rus′ was the former metropolitan of Sebastea, a trusted supporter of Basil II. The fact that he had already been consecrated a bishop made it easier for the emperor to nominate him to this new post, avoiding difficult and time-consuming ecclesiastical procedure.

The Byzantine genealogy of the Rus′ church was indicated ca. 1050 by Hilarion, himself soon to become metropolitan of Rus′, in his *Sermon on Divine Law and Grace*. There he praised the deed of Volodimer and described the ruler's path to a knowledge of the one God—"Most of all, moreover, he heard of the ever Orthodox Greek land, loving Christ and strong in faith"—and later compared the Rus′ prince to Constantine the Great—"That man, together with his mother Helena, brought the Cross from Jerusalem and established it, bringing glory to the faith throughout his world. You and your grandmother Ol′ga brought the Cross from the new Jerusalem, from the city of Constantine, and, establishing it on your land, affirmed the faith." The Cross serves here as a metaphor, expressing not only the triumph of Christianity in Rus′, but also its genealogy and institutional ties. Iaroslav continued the work of his father: "he does not alter your acts, but affirms them," while the whole princely family "guards Orthodoxy in accordance with your will."[74] Hilarion's express emphasis on the continuity between the ecclesiastical policy of Volodimer and that of Iaroslav the Wise confirms that the status of the Church of Rus′ had already been defined in the era of its baptizer.

The creation of an ecclesiastical province headed by a metropolitan (archbishop) meant the establishment of a number of bishoprics with suffragans subordinated to him within its structure. According to reliable data, several bishops came to Rus′ with the metropolitan. The Arab historian Yaḥyā of Antioch reports that Emperor Basil sent "metropolitans and bishops" to the leader of Rus′, and that they "baptized the king and all who inhabited his land."[75] This reference to "metropolitans" in the plural has led some to question the reliability of the account of Yaḥyā, who was a Christian historian. However, the circumstances under which Yaḥyā's report of the baptism came into being enable us to explain the remark. Yaḥyā wrote his history of events in Byzantium after moving in 1015 from Cairo to Antioch, where he was able to make use of local Greek sources. One of those sources, recounting the uprising of Bardas Phokas and the arrival of a Rus′ force in Byzantium, could well have used the Greek collective term for bishops of varying rank: *archiereis*. In translating this term into Arabic, Yaḥyā must then have sought to convey its meaning by using two words borrowed from the Greek and known to Arabic Christians: *maṭārinat wa asāqifat* (metropolitans and bishops). Because he knew nothing more about the ecclesiastical organization in Rus′ than his source provided, his translation could have been influenced by the situation in the patriarchate of Antioch, where many bishops used the title of metropolitan.

From a letter of the missionary bishop Bruno of Querfurt to the German King Henry II in 1008, we know that one of his missionary comrades was consecrated (*consecravimusque nos*) bishop to the Pechenegs during Bruno's visit to Kyiv in that year.[76] According to the decrees of the Council of Nicaea, a new bishop had to be consecrated by at least three bishops, and hence, other bishops must have participated alongside Bruno in the ceremony, which took place in Kyiv after the return of the mission from the steppe. This is likewise indicated by Bruno's use of the plural in his letter. There were at least two of them, probably the metropolitan of Kyiv and one of his suffragans. The Primary Chronicle, written a hundred years later, confirms the arrival of bishops in Kyiv along with the *porphyrogennēta* Anna and their presence in Rus′ during the time of Volodimer.[77] Also decisive here is the statement of Hilarion, who praised Volodimer, saying, "and you often gathered together with our new fathers—the bishops—and took counsel with them in humility, about how to establish law among the people, who had just come to know God."[78] Hilarion must have met some of those who had taken part in the mass baptism in the waters of the Dnipro in 988. In the 1060s, "another brother by the name of Jeremy, who remembered the conversion of Rus′," was still living in the Monastery of the Caves. Hilarion's own memory would have reached back at least to the final years of Volodimer's rule, for he was a contemporary of that prince's sons.

In 1018, Bishop Thietmar of Merseburg had no doubt that the cathedral complex of St. Sophia in Kyiv had been occupied for years by *"archiepiscopus civitatis illius,"* i.e., the head of an ecclesiastical province. In other words, the church in Rus′ already had its own ecclesiastical provincial structure. An archbishop with the title of metropolitan, administering his own diocese, stood at the head of a group of suffragans, each of them administering a diocese of his own.

Thus, from the outset, the church in Rus′ was a metropolitanate, an ecclesiastical province of the patriarchate of Constantinople. From this it follows that the patriarch enjoyed certain defined rights here in administrative, judicial, and legislative matters, as well as in the interpretation of canon law. The most important of these was the right of filling the metropolitanate. In the tenth through thirteenth centuries the exercise of that right lay within the competence of the *endemousa synodos,* i.e., the permanent, standing patriarchal synod of bishops residing or visiting in Constantinople, who presented to the patriarch three candidates satisfying the canonical requirements. The one selected then received his episcopal consecration from the hands of the patriarch. Even if there was a candidate in mind from the outset, and frequently the will of the emperor came into play here, an attempt was nonetheless made to preserve the appearance of proper procedure. This was also the path to the see of Kyiv, and the metropolitans of Rus′ also took part in the work of the *endemousa* when they were in the imperial capital. The difference from other metropolitanates of the empire lay in the fact that the act of enthronement in Kyiv was one not only of ecclesiastical, but of political accreditation as well. That enthronement would take place in Kyiv's cathedral of St. Sophia on a Sunday shortly after the arrival of the newly consecrated metropolitan. With the exception of three men of Rus′ (Hilarion, Clement [Klym], and Cyril [Kirill] II), all of them were Greeks. Reception of a new arrival, permission to proceed with the enthronement ceremony, and the participation of the princely court in that rite served as a *de facto* confirmation of the act that had been performed in Hagia Sophia in Constantinople.

This method of filling the metropolitanate meant that every vacancy in the see of Kyiv lasted at least a year or, not infrequently, longer. Likewise, the periodic visits to Constantinople, made less frequently than at the prescribed interval of every two years because of the difficulty of the journey, lasted several months and sometimes a whole year. In the nearly 300-year period under discussion here, the metropolitanate of Kyiv was vacant for at least 60 years, a fact that points, on the one hand, to the relative weakness of its incumbent, who came to what was for him a foreign land partly without a knowledge of the Slavic language or the realities of ecclesiastical life, and, on the other, bears witness to the internal strength of the Rus′ church.[79]

* *
*

With the establishment of a metropolitan see in Kyiv in 988 and, soon thereafter, episcopal sees in Bilhorod (Belgorod), Chernihiv (Chernigov), Novgorod, and Polatsk (Polotsk), the framework of an ecclesiastical organization for Rus′ came into being. In this way, the organizational preconditions for the Christianization of the Eastern Slavs were created. The seats of bishops were situated in politically distinctive centers, which already possessed, by the second half of the tenth century, an urban character. They lay on the north-south river route known as the "road from the Varangians to the Greeks," the axis of the political dominion of the Rurikids.[80]

From the beginning, a special place was held by the bishop in the town of Bilhorod, a powerful fortress some 23 kilometers from Kyiv, which served as Volodimer's second residence. As a kind of palatial bishop and above all else as *protōthronos* (i.e., the first bishop of the province after the metropolitan), he enjoyed precedence over the remaining suffragan bishops and took the place of an absent metropolitan in certain functions. The position of the Bilhorod see was emphasized by the choice of the Holy Apostles as its patrons, a choice clearly linked with the title of the metropolitan cathedral, named for the Wisdom of God, which was identified with Christ as the second person of the Holy Trinity. This symbolic expression was supplemented by the title of Transfiguration of the Lord bestowed on the third cathedral created on the lands of Rus′ proper—that of Chernihiv, the second most significant center on the middle Dnipro, about 150 kilometers from Kyiv.

The other centers chosen as the seats of bishops, the two most notable towns of the realm after Kyiv, lay far to the north: Polatsk, more than 700 kilometers from the capital of Rus′, and Novgorod, located more than 1,000 kilometers from Kyiv. In both, the cathedral churches were dedicated to the Wisdom of God—Sophia—and it was no coincidence. Traditionally, this has been seen as an expression of the rivalry of both cities with Kyiv, but the political conditions in the eleventh century, when Novgorod opposed itself to Kyiv on several occasions and the princes of Polatsk had to defend their rights against Iaroslav the Wise and his sons, cannot be projected back into the period of baptism and the building of the framework of ecclesiastical organization. In those days, Volodimer's oldest son, Iziaslav, was sitting in Polatsk, while in Novgorod paganism was being uprooted by Volodimer's governor, his uncle Dobrynia. The title of Sophia was consciously chosen by the bishops from Byzantium and approved by the newly baptized ruler. Since mostly metropolitan cathedral churches were dedicated to Sophia in the Byzantine domain, it cannot be excluded that the choice was made with intended long-range perspectives.

Three cathedrals in the three most important centers of Kyivan Rus′, each bearing the same name, were thus linked to Hagia Sophia on the Bosphorus and embodied the complex and rich theological content of such dedication. To the newly converted, they proclaimed: "God is in the land of Rus′, and with God's help it shall not be moved." This is the sense of the mosaic inscription of Psalm 45:6 in the conch of the Kyivan metropolitan cathedral, the thirteen copulas of which proclaimed the mission of Christ and his Apostles to the capital and all of Rus′. The Wisdom of God portrayed—and was, in and of itself—the victory of Christianity over paganism and the victory of Orthodoxy over heresy.[81] The latter victory had, since the reform of Byzantine Christianity in the eighth and ninth centuries, been understood above all as the triumph over the iconoclasts and found special expression in the iconographic programs of sacred edifices. It thus is no coincidence that, at the dawn of Christianity, the triumph of Orthodoxy among the Eastern Slavs manifested itself in the name of the three chief cathedrals of Rus′, and occupied a central place in the religious life of the newly converted, expressed externally in a profound cult of the holy icon. The introduction, adoration, and contemplation of the icon in Rus′ thus have their roots in the Christianization of that land, and we cannot accept those views that see the source of these practices in local and especially pagan and syncretistic traditions.[82] Only with the passage of time did a host of superstitions grow up around the cult of images. The Church in Rus′ opposed itself, ultimately unsuccessfully, to the influences of sculpted figures, not because of their supposedly pagan origin, but because of the rejection of sculpted figures in the sacred art of Byzantium, with its cult of the icon, that resulted from the victory of Orthodoxy.

The divergence between this most modest diocesan structure and the enormous task of Christianizing a realm measuring an area of more than one million square kilometers and inhabited by approximately five million people, forces us to conclude that the Byzantine Church was totally unprepared and not fully aware of the extraordinary significance of the changes taking place. So the

Christianization process and ecclesiastical structures could not spread over the whole land through decades. Undoubtedly, it was also a matter of routine: a Byzantine metropolitan ecclesiastical province usually consisted of three to six dioceses.

In Hilarion's conception of the conversion of Rus′, the crucial turning point was the decision of Volodimer. It is immediately emphasized, however, that the baptism merely opened the door to a genuine Christianization of the land: "Then the darkness of idolatry began to depart from us, and the dawn of a new faith appeared."[83] The Rus′ side was thus aware that Christianity would be accepted by the various strata of society primarily in those places where political authority had been firmly established. Hence, Christianization could not immediately embrace the whole expanse of territory under the rule of Rus′. For example, the populace of those broad sections of the country whose subordination to the state consisted primarily of an obligation to pay tribute at first remained outside the new faith for the simple reason that the tributaries met with the princely administration but once or, at most, twice a year. That is why Christianization was concentrated first of all in the region of the middle Dnipro.

Apart, however, from any question of the level of consciousness or limitations on or unevenness of activity, a basic obstacle limited the progress of Christianization. What was decisive was not the number of bishops but the number of clergy and, more importantly, the number of those who knew the Slavic language. The priests who carried out evangelization prior to 988 had been but a drop in an ocean of enormous need. Related to this was the problem of equipping the churches, particularly with ecclesiastical books, especially those necessary for the celebration of the divine service. To satisfy the suddenly pressing need, recourse was had to a standard practice of those times. The equipment of any churches of Kherson, the city punished by the Byzantine emperor and his Rus′ brother-in-law, went as booty to the north: undoubtedly, part of Kherson's clergy were also sent against their will to Rus′. However, the real, ongoing supply of church apparatus, and Slavic books in particular, flowed from Bulgaria, which was being conquered step by step during those years by Byzantine armies, half of which consisted of Rus′ units; in 1016, a third of the trophies fell to the Rus′.[84]

Rus′ troops participated in the Byzantine conquest with only short interruptions over the course of nearly twenty years, and the size of the spoils of war obtained must have been correspondingly large. It has long been known that many texts written in Bulgarian found their way to Rus′. The fate of the oldest manuscripts is an integral part of the history of Bulgarian-Rus′ linguistic and literary contacts.[85] The only thing remaining unclear has been the path by which those manuscripts made their way to the banks of the Dnipro and Volkhov. Such manuscripts as the Codex of Tsar Symeon—the prototype of the *Izbornik* of Sviatoslav of 1073 or the Macedonian Gospel of Tsar Samuel (d. 1014) from which the Ostromir Gospel was copied—were evidently from the palace church and library of the Bulgarian rulers. Their appearance in Rus′ can be explained convincingly only by *jus spolii*.[86] The ever growing number of churches constructed in the newly converted state had to be supplied with ecclesiastical books, and the choice of the Slavic language as the language of liturgy and evangelization encouraged recourse to this cheapest and fastest means of acquiring the needed materials. Plundering houses of worship in an enemy land with an eye to supplying one's own churches was quite customary in Christian Europe at the time, and, in this case, it provided the Byzantine ruler with a most convenient way of fulfilling the obligations he had assumed. It also helped to satisfy the wishes of his sister Anna and brother-in-law Volodimer, who were actively involved in the Christianization of Rus′. Probably, many literate Bulgarian clerics were also forced to journey to that region. The institution of an unfree clergy, known later in Rus′, undoubtedly had its origins in these early circumstances. Although it sounds paradoxical, the undeniable Bulgarian influence on Rus′ literature and more broadly, on its culture, was the result not of supposed ecclesiastical ties with Ochrid, but of the participation of Rus′ troops in the Byzantine conquest of Bulgaria. Ironically, the stripping of Bulgaria of Slavic books and clerics to meet the needs of the newly converted East Slavs had to facilitate the Hellenization of the church and religious life in Bulgaria itself after its conquest by the empire.

* *
*

The Christianization of Rus′, much as that of other regions, could not be carried out without the use of some coercion, both in the initial introduction of the new religion and in defense against various attempts at apostasy, especially on the part of the common people. The well-known uprisings of rural inhabitants under the leadership of soothsayers in the eleventh century and the apostasy of the people of Novgorod eighty years after the baptism of that city, forcibly suppressed by princely authority in collaboration with the clergy, were as much an expression of protest against the new order infusing the sociopolitical and economic fabric of the land as against the new religious order that supported it, imposed from above by the state.[87] The Church, in the words of its representatives, viewed compulsory baptism as a completely justifiable measure and pointed, with the sincerity characteristic of a proselyte, to fear of the ruler as the deciding reason for the recognition of the new religion by the majority.[88] A strong influence on the members of the simple urban mob was exercised by the example of the courts of the prince and the aristocracy, with whom they were linked by various ties. Religious instruction at the time of conversion to the new faith was something of an exception during the earliest period following the baptism of Rus′, a privilege reserved for the social elite. But the effectiveness of that instruction was also great. One hundred years after baptism, in the upper strata of society, the ecclesiastical sacrament of marriage had became a common practice, and the church could turn to the task of winning over "the simple people," who continued to avoid its blessing when contracting their marriages, although the threat to impose ecclesiastical penances on the latter suggests that they, too, were already within its reach.[89]

The Christian custom of commemoration of the deceased—including memorial services, about which there are written references in relation to the ruling dynasty as early as the eleventh century—found particularly fertile ground, and was facilitated by the existing tradition of an ancestral worship. It is in this sense that we should view the baptism of the exhumed remains of Volodimer's brothers, the pagan princes Oleg (d. 977) and Iaropolk (d. 980) and their burial in the princely church. Such acts, which were at variance with church canons, may be explained by a desire to include in Christian commemorations those members of the dynasty who perished in fratricidal struggles. Christian piety as expressed in commemorations of the dead was being quickly incorporated into family life.

A striking indication of the permanence of the ideological and religious transformation of the ruling circles of Rus′ is the fact that none of the competing parties in the interprincely struggles of the eleventh century sought to raise paganism as a banner to rally in support of its own political interests. The deep dynastic political crisis that exploded on the death of Volodimer in 1015, expressed in a fratricidal struggle for the throne of Kyiv and lasting with varying intensity until 1026, did not undermine the Christianization of the land. This is all the more remarkable in light of the fact that the Byzantine side supported the inheritance rights to the Kyivan throne of the children of Volodimer and the *porphyrogennēta* Anna.[90] The failure of this effort as a result of the assassination of Boris and Glěb did not slow the continued conversion of the country in the least, indicating that an authentic Christianization of the dynasty and the elites that supported it had taken place during the reign of Volodimer. An ability to distinguish between Christianity and its values, on the one hand, and the political undertakings of Byzantium, on the other, had likewise been fully attained.

What is more, once a curtain of total silence had fallen over the actual reasons for the political murder of Boris and Glěb, the official version of the violent deaths of these two sons of Volodimer found a sublimated interpretation in the cult of the two princes, who, by their example, offered a model of Christian attitudes and moral behavior worthy of imitation. The far-reaching effect of this dynastic political crisis was the entry of native martyr princes into the ranks of the saints and the creation of a tradition that gave young Rus′ Christianity a unique profile of its own.[91] The cult, originally directed at a princely milieu, spread with astounding speed. In May 1115, the celebration of the translation of the sarcophagi containing the relics of Saints Boris and Glěb to a new walled church in Vyshhorod drew countless people of varying rank from all over Rus′: princes, bishops, boyars—all with their retinues—clergy, monks, and common people, all come to pay homage, in continuous day and night processions, to their own martyrs in Christ and advocates for the land of Rus′.

Similarly, in the decades of conflict between Iaroslav and his sons, on the one hand, and the princes of Polatsk, on the other, the latter, though threatened with the loss of their principality, did not appeal to heathenism, even though soothsayers still enjoyed respect at the princely court in Polatsk. On the contrary, Vseslav of Polatsk, in his struggle with the sons of Iaroslav, opposed the stone church of St. Sophia in Polatsk to the walled church of St. Sophia in Kyiv. In 1067 he plundered St. Sophia of Novogrod to enrich his own church in Polatsk. Giving four of his seven sons the names of Boris-Roman and Glěb-David, Vseslav was among the first to contribute to the development of the cult of the martyr princes, in which he found a religious and moral justification for the right of opposition and the rights of his line to the throne of Polatsk. This political and ideological demonstration, incidentally, assured him the support of the Church, especially that of the Kyivan Caves Monastery.[92]

The support of the ruling strata for the new religion was so ostentatious as to create the appearance of a rapid Christianization of the whole land. The missionary archbishop Bruno of Querfurt, a zealous advocate of the conversion of all the remaining pagan peoples of Europe, when visiting Kyiv in 1008 considered Rus′ already to be a Christian land, able to support his intention to convert the Pechenegs—just twenty years after the baptism of Volodimer and the Kyivans. The forest of cupolas and crosses towering over Kyiv must have made a considerable impression on a visitor from Saxony, who in 1018 managed to report on his visit to that city to the chronicler and bishop, Thietmar of Merseburg. His reference to "more than 400 churches" has usually been questioned, despite the chronicle report of the destruction of 600 churches in Kyiv in the great fire of 1124. In both cases here, small wooden structures were mentioned. As is known from accounts from the thirteenth to fifteenth centuries, small churches of this type could be erected in a dozen days or so, or even, if prefabricated elements were used, in the course of a single day.

The capital city of Kyiv in 1018, with its 10-hectare princely fortress and eight marketplaces, was, from the perspective of observers west of the Elbe and the Salle, an exceptionally large and populous urban center.[93] Its houses of worship, however, with the exception of one stone palace church and about a dozen or so largish wooden communal churches (*publicae ecclesiae*), including the wooden metropolitan cathedral of St. Sophia (burned in 1017 and rebuilt in less than a year), consisted of hundreds of private oratories and chapels (*ecclesiae privatae*) belonging to the nobility of Kyiv. At the beginning of the eleventh century there must have been several hundred boyars' residences in Kyiv, considering that the city numbered no fewer than 15,000 inhabitants at that time (and a hundred years later—some 40,000). The example of the prince, and Byzantine (and probably even Western) custom as well, encouraged the establishment of such "houses of God" in individual residences, originally, at least, as an external expression of personal faith and loyalty to the ruler. Such churches bore witness at the same time to the position and prestige of boyar families in the new Christian reality. Linked to the ecclesiatical foundations of Volodimer himself, his nobles yearned to affirm in this way their role in the confession and propagation of the new faith.

Half a century later, when the city—now encompassing a considerably greater walled area, with a main city entrance called "the Golden Gate" (70 hectares)—had acquired a dozen stone churches along with the still impressive, in its mass and beauty, St. Sophia cathedral (built 1037–1046), Adam of Bremen saw Kyiv as an *aemula*, i.e., imitation, of Constantinople,[94] no doubt, in large part, because of its many churches. Despite the fact that the princely stone church of the Virgin (Church of the Tithe)—abutting the stone palace—built by Byzantine masters in the 990s, continued to be for half a century the exception, the broad scale of Kyiv's wooden ecclesiastical architecture ensured from the outset that the city impressed every visitor as an extremely Christian one. Only under Iaroslav and his sons did the new fashion of ecclesiastical building in stone and brick begin to effect changes in the landscape of the cities of Rus′, the impact of which gradually intensified in the twelfth and first decades of the thirteenth century. Today one can identify slightly under 300 relatively well-preserved remains of stone churches from the pre-Mongol era, just under a hundred of them in the middle Dnipro region, i.e., in Rus′ proper.[95] Throughout the Middle Ages, construction in wood would continue to dominate the sacral architecture of Rus′.

The baptism of Rus′ called into being a new group with a special social role, endowed with the exclusive right to represent the new religious ideology and possessing a significant unifying potential. Unlike the sacrificers, soothsayers, and other representatives of the old pagan religion, the whole Christian clergy was quite closely linked to the apparatus of political authority. That relationship resulted in a growing prestige for this social group, whose special status was underlined by distinctive dress and customs. outside as well as inside the church. The clergy in eleventh-century Rus′ consisted to a large extent of persons of local origin. The clerics from Bulgaria, no doubt originally more numerous, quickly integrated themselves into the local Slavic environment. A less numerous, but significant element was the Greek clergy, who, among other things, occupied the highest positions in the ecclesiatical hierarchy. The latter, coming to Rus′ with a strong sense of their own worth and a consciousness of their sociopolitical as well as ecclesiastical usefulness, brought with them ready-made models of relations between secular and ecclesiastical authority.

The formal ties linking the Rus′ and Byzantine churches grew closer in the decades following the baptism thanks to the ideological ties of Rus′ monasticism with the centers of monastic life in Byzantium.[96] It was these links that would ultimately decide the loyalty of the Rus′ church to the principles of Byzantine Orthodoxy. Rus′ monasticism, with its religious zeal and political sense, became, thanks to its intimate ties with the social elite of old Rus′ society, a crucial factor in the development of Christianity and the church in

Rus′. The aristocratic Monastery of the Caves in Kyiv achieved a high degree of religious and moral authority in the second half of the eleventh century, becoming a center of particular influence on ecclesiastical, cultural, and political life in Rus′. An exceptionally important contribution here was made by one ascetic holy man produced by this monastery, Hegumen Theodosius [Feodosii] (d. 1074), whose renown as a saint, local at first, acquired an all-Rus′ character in 1108.[97]

The primary activity of the clergy was concentrated in the religious field and in related social matters. Its constant, gradually growing influence on the mentality of society, and that of the upper strata in particular, led to a transformation of outlook that could not have been achieved at the moment of baptism itself in 988, but which it would be wrong to assume took centuries to accomplish. The adoption by old Rus′ culture of the Christian value system progressed with varying degrees of success on various fronts, but much had already been accomplished in the course of the first century.[98]

The clergy as a whole, distinguished by its literacy, by its extensive reading, and sometimes by its knowledge of languages, production of books, and literary activity, served as an intermediary in transmitting the values of Christian culture to the Eastern Slavs. The beginnings of intellectual activity inspired by Christianity must be dated to the tenth century, for the personality and activity of Hilarion—such an outstanding example of a Byzantine education and the Christian worldview—who was capable of independent historiosophic speculation, could not have sprung out of a culturally virgin soil.[99] The clergy, a kind of medieval intelligentsia, likewise assisted in the diffusion of reading and writing and other elements of education among the laity—not only the princes, the boyars, and their retinues, but townspeople as well. In the generation after baptism, an ability to read and write was shared by all the members of the dynasty, women included, and traces of four princely libraries of the eleventh century had been preserved.[100]

The clergy, and particularly erudite monks drawn from aristocratic families, enriched the store of historical thought, which had hitherto developed as an oral tradition, by giving it a written form, adapting various genres of historical writing—the annalistic note, the relation, the narrative, and the tale—for this purpose. This development of a historical method and combination of varied forms into a single chronicle genre, produced, at the beginning of the second century after baptism, the Primary Chronicle, which was the result of historical thought spun out in monastic cells but driven by the ideas and political passions of this world. The central theme of this work was the state and Christianity in Rus′, in which the creation and maintenance of princely authority were linked directly to the propagation of the Christian faith.[101]

These new cultural values became an important ally in the transformation of the local order and local ways of thinking. The very appearance of the churches, in their upward rising profiles contrasting with the surrounding wooden, earthen, and semi-earthen huts, had already begun to exercise an influence on the psyche of the still really half-pagan Rus′ Christian. The church, moreover, as an artistic composite, adorned with frescoes and icons, costly vessels and objects, and serving as a place of divine service, of liturgical activity and song, offered an unequalled setting for emotional, esthetic, and, ultimately, religious experiences.

From the very beginning, the church ascribed sacral traits to princely authority. Preachers and scholars propagated the conviction that the prince, like the biblical David and the Byzantine emperor, was the Lord's anointed; that princely authority was established by God; and that the prince, ruler of the land, was an icon of Christ, an earthly reflection of the ruler of the heavens.[102] To the prince, the church ascribed the roles of guardian of the flock of Christ, defender of Orthodoxy, and teacher and guide; it endowed him with the character of shepherd and archpriest, and taught all of his subjects that "disrespect for authority is disrespect for God himself." In the rich array of epithets added to the princely title in Rus′ ("beloved of God, Christ-loving and beloved of Christ, Orthodox, most pious," etc.), expression was given to the charismatic character of authority and of the person of the prince. The same character was assumed by the ceremony of enthronement of the prince, which already in the eleventh century had become an ecclesiastical rite.

Princely authority certainly contributed to the Christianization of the country, but the contribution of the church and Christianization to the transformation of princely authority into a genuine state organization was likewise crucial. Christianization and the formation of the state were closely linked in the case of every people emerging onto the historical stage, and the East Slavs were no exception.

* *
*

We cannot exclude the possibility that the fifth diocese, with its cathedral of the Archangel Michael at Pereiaslav, 85 kilometers southeast of Kyiv, was founded under Volodimer, but there is more in favor of its having been erected together with the bishopric of "St. George on the River Ros′" in Iuriev, and thus during the reign of Iaroslav the Wise, after his victory over the Pechenegs in 1036. It is notable that both of these cathedrals were entrusted to the patronage of holy warriors—the leader of the heavenly forces and the destroyer of the dragon, patrons of Christian soldiers in their struggles against unbelievers.

Both dioceses were created, not in the interior of the land, but on its steppe frontier. To be sure, after the disaster suffered by the Pechenegs before Kyiv in 1036, settlement in these regions intensified, as did the building of forts to guard the settlers, but this was chiefly colonization of a military type, aiming to create an effective barrier against the raids of the nomadic Pechenegs who roamed the steppes. The creation of the two border bishoprics, however, was not aimed merely at moral and religious reinforcement of the barrier shielding the country from the steppe. Both patron saints were revered as humblers of the dragon—the symbol of the devil, of evil, of unbelief, of paganism—and the creation of the two bishoprics likewise had as one of its goals missionary work among the pagans, a program that was also in the interest of Byzantium, pressed as it was by the Pechenegs in the Danubian territories of the empire.[103] An attempt to Christianize these mobile and dangerous nomads was also the aim of the mission of Bruno of Querfurt and his successor, the anonymous bishop *in partibus Pezenegorum*. The subordination of the Pechenegs was an exceptionally vital matter for Kyiv as well as Constantinople. The results achieved by these missionary efforts were modest, but only with the appearance of new nomads—the Polovtsians, who visited disaster upon the Rus′ princes at Pereiaslav in 1068—and with the crushing of the Byzantine army at Manzikert in 1071, did the situation change so drastically as to make Byzantine-Rus′ efforts to draw closer together and establish secure communications lines through newly Christianized regions of the Pontic and Danubian steppe appear unrealistic.

Before Byzantium and Rus′ were made aware of the insurmountability of the steppe barriers that hindered contacts on either side, significant developments on another front had threatened to divide the ecclesiastical province of Rus′. In the 1060s and 1070s the bishops of Chernihiv and Pereiaslav were also granted the title of metropolitan. They received the title for life, and the dioceses they administered likewise achieved the status of titular metropolitanates for that period.[104] They differed from ordinary metropolitanates in that they did not represent ecclesiastical provinces with suffragan subordinate bishoprics, but in accordance with their new standing were directly subordinate to the patriarch. In Byzantium one can clearly observe the efforts of titular metropolitans to transform their sees into ecclesiastical provinces by setting up suffragan bishoprics on their territory. The strength of this tendency is suggested by the compromise imperial novella of 1084, which stipulated that only those titular metropolitanates that had enjoyed this status for more than thirty years could be recognized as regular metropolitanates.

In practical terms, the erection of titular metropolitanates in Rus′ resulted in the temporary removal of two dioceses that together represented nearly half of the territory of the state (almost all of the region east of the Dnipro) from the jurisdiction of the metropolitan of Kyiv. The elevation of the bishoprics of Chernihiv and Pereiaslav to the rank of titular metropolitanates was purely political in character, undoubtedly connected with the events of 1060, when the Rus′ princes Iziaslav, Sviatoslav, and Vsevolod inflicted a crushing defeat on the Uzes, who were threatening Byzantium. Since the Byzantine holdings in the Crimea as well as on the Danube frontier were vulnerable to pressure from the steppe dwellers, the Byzantine court was quick to recognize the value of Rus′ armies in the struggle against the nomads. The transformation of the two bishoprics into titular metropolitanates should be ascribed to the initiative of the imperial court, which was well informed about the political situation in

Rus′. After the death of Iaroslav the Wise, rule over Rus′ was assumed not only by his eldest son Iziaslav, the senior in Kyiv, but by two other sons as well: Sviatoslav, prince of Chernihiv, and Vsevolod, prince of Pereiaslav. Their joint decisions on matters of war, law, and the assignment of other princely thrones permit us to speak of a triarchy in this period.[105] This balance of forces found its counterpart in the realm of ecclesiastical organization as well, as the Byzantine court needed to maintain direct, friendly contacts with all three rulers of Rus′.

Through the intermediary of these titular metropolitans, acting as Byzantine ambassadors *sui generis* in direct ecclesiastical contact with Constantinople, the imperial court sought to strengthen the alliance and make it more effective. It was encouraged in this approach by internal upheaval within the empire, which limited its own ability to oppose the Pechenegs and Uzes. Although the Byzantine side emphasized the ecclesiastical primacy of Kyiv by granting its metropolitan, George (Iurii), the high court rank of *synkellos* (member of the imperial senate), Kyiv was well aware of the danger threatened by the division, as clearly indicated by points 31 and 32 of the canonical answers of Metropolitan John (Ioann) II, dating from ca. 1083.[106] And even though subsequent political developments in Rus′ removed the underlying causes, this temporary ecclesiastical-political arrangement had a braking effect on the further development of a diocesan structure.

The first and probably only titular metropolitan in Chernihiv was Neofit, who already held his title before 1072. He no doubt died not long after 1080, for in 1088 Bishop John had already been the incumbent in Chernihiv for some time. One may thus infer that the metropolitanate of *Maurokastron* (i.e., Chernihiv), that is, *Nea Rhōsia*, mentioned in one of the manuscripts of the *Notitiae*, compiled around 1072, was created in the 1060s.[107]

The situation was different in the case of the diocese of Pereiaslav. Its first titular metropolitan was the Greek Leo (Leontii), known for his polemical anti-Latin treatise against azymes (unleavened Eucharistic host). His successor, sometime before 1072, was Bishop Peter (Petr), who probably did not possess the honorary metropolitan title. In any case, he appears as an ordinary bishop in the account of the translation of the relics of Saints Boris and Glěb on 20 May 1072, in which Metropolitans George of Kyiv and Neofit of Chernihiv also took part. The vacancy in the see of Pereiaslav must be dated somewhere from 1068 to 1071, when the unstable political situation in Rus′ (as a result of princely quarrels) and Byzantium (as a result of the defeat at Manzikert) would have supported a reassertion of the Kyivan metropolitan's rights over the diocese of Pereiaslav through the ordination of Peter as a regular suffragan bishop. However, after the death of Peter and, shortly thereafter, Metropolitan George, the situation changed, and probably in 1076–1077, or in any case prior to October 1078, Ephrem (Efrem), a former monk of the Kyivan Caves Monastery, returned from Byzantium with the title of titular metropolitan of Pereiaslav. The appearance of this metropolitanate before 1080 is registered by three versions of the *Notitiae episcopatuum.*[108] Despite the change in the situation, when Vsevolod, the youngest member of the triarchy, became sole ruler of Rus′ after the death of his brothers, Ephrem retained his title until his own death in the 1090s.

In the midst of these changing political and ecclesiastical circumstances, a new diocese came into being in Rostov. Rostov at that time was the center of a region in the northeast of Rus′ that later was to be known as the Vladimir-Suzdal land. In the eleventh century it belonged to the principality and diocese of Pereiaslav. When Iziaslav was driven out of Kyiv on 22 March 1073, and his two brothers divided Rus′ between them, in the process establishing new spheres of influence and authority, the Rostov region passed under the rule of Sviatoslav—the new prince of Kyiv. Sometime later, this political decision was followed by an ecclesiastical one: the Rostov land became an independent diocese subordinate to the metropolitanate of Kyiv. The metropolitan at the time, George, was conscious that by this measure he would not only immediately broaden the range of his jurisdiction, but would also circumvent, or at least lessen, the threat that the titular metropolitanate of Pereiaslav might be transformed into a regular ecclesiastical province. The decision was undoubtedly facilitated by the fact that the current bishop of Pereiaslav, Peter, did not have the title of honorary metropolitan or, even more likely, that the see had already been vacated by Peter's death. The first bishop of Rostov was Leo (Leontii), a monk of the Kyivan Caves Monastery. Shortly after his arrival, perhaps as early as 1074, the new bishop died a martyr's death during disorders probably growing out of the crop failure of 1073 and the ensuing famine.[109] In Rostov, pagans still represented the majority. A similar uprising took place at this time in Novgorod: here the cause was the apostasy of significant numbers of the townspeople. The death of Bishop Leo bore witness to the fact that Christianity had not yet been accepted in peripheral areas such as Rostov, and indicated the degree of importance the continuing development of its diocesan structure was for the Christianization of the domain.

Despite the violent death of Rostov's first bishop, the diocese was able to maintain itself, being filled again by the new metropolitan of Kyiv, John II, in 1077–1078. The new bishop was Isaiah (Isaiia), hegumen of the Kyivan monastery of St. Demetrius. After his death in 1095, however, Rostov did not receive another pastor. As a result of changes on the Kyivan throne, the Rostov land had again passed, in 1094, to the rule of the prince of Pereiaslav, and the titular Metropolitan Ephrem succeeded in returning it to his jurisdiction. From the point of view of the metropolitan of Kyiv, this represented an ongoing vacancy in the see. Only around 1137 did Rostov regain its own bishop, when Iurii Dolgorukii, the first independent prince of Rostov and Suzdal, abandoned efforts to win the throne of Pereiaslav for himself. The restitution of the Rostov bishopric is also supported by the list of its bishops: the next after Isaiah (d. 1095) was Nestor, mentioned in the 1140s. The history of efforts to establish the diocese of Rostov shows how difficult the initiation and maintenance of a bishopric could be. The difficult inception of the bishopric of Rostov must have provoked resentments, echoed in the later attempt of Prince Andrei Bogoliubskii of Vladimir-Suzdal to break away from the Kyivan ecclesiastical province and create a metropolitanate of his own in the 1160s.[110] This initiative, along with the plunder in 1169 of the churches and shrines of Kyiv—which this prince took as a model for the construction of his own capital—was an initially unsuccessful attempt at *translatio regni*, but with time acquired significance as a harbinger of things to come.

* *
*

The Christianization and ecclesiastical administration of a broad territory, often separated from the seat of the bishop by hundreds or even a thousand kilometers, was nearly impossible. Where the creation of new dioceses was too difficult, local units of episcopal administration, which could be characterized as territorial vicariates, were set up to satisfy a constantly growing demand. The bishop's representative, known as a *naměstnik* (vicar), exercised certain defined rights over a given part of the diocesan territory. The Byzantine church, with its dense network of dioceses, had no need of such subunits, and so could not serve as an example here. The institution was created locally, and the name given to these vicars was taken from terminology customarily applied to princely officials.[111] Some inspiration may also have been drawn from various early Christian officers created to assist the bishop in his work, such as the *chorepiscopos, periodeutēs,* or *archidiakonos.* And while the likelihood of actual borrowing is small, a comparison of the *naměstnik* in Rus′ with the archdeacon in Western Europe seems justified, given that both offices grew out of a rationalization of episcopal administration in an effort to avoid division of dioceses. The progressive Christianization of the country dictated the creation of smaller units within the broader framework of the bishopric—the vicariates—which were naturally suited to the administrative structure of the state. For this reason, the bishop's vicars first appeared in the seats of the prince's sons or of his governors (*posadniki* or *naměstniki*). The bishop's *naměstnik,* an ecclesiastical personage charged with administration of a fixed portion of the diocese, exercised his office with the aid of a collective organ similar in certain respects to the bishop's *kliros,* a collegial administrative-judicial body corresponding to the Greek *presbyterion* or Latin *capitulum*—chapter. Such vicariates must have already begun to appear in certain centers in the eleventh century. Under favorable circumstances, where a city was the center of a principality, there was a possibility of the transformation of one of these subunits into an independent diocese. This was encouraged by the functioning of a *kliros* alongside the *naměstnik,* just as one did alongside a bishop. In such a case, it would simply be transformed into an episcopal *kliros.* The legal and property status of the *kliros*, it would appear from the foundation document of the bishopric of Smolensk (ca. 1136), was independent of that of the bishop.[112] When and how an episcopal vicarship became an independent diocese depended on many circumstances, and undoubtedly involved more than just ecclesiastical circles in Rus'. A special need to create more dioceses emerged in the second half of the eleventh century, despite, and, in a certain sense, because of the appearance of the two titular metropolitanates. Kyivan Metropolitan John II even had to address this matter in his canonical responses: a diocese could be created, he explained, "particularly where there is a large population, many people and towns," and where it was a question of "Christian protection and pastoral care over them." This was to be done, however, "in a God-fearing manner," and was only permissible "when the incumbent of the first see of Rus' [i.e., the metropolitan] and the synod of the whole country give their permission."[113]

The metropolitan's reiteration of the general rules of the Church was obviously connected with specific events. At the beginning, he indicated that the question at hand involved a division planned by the princely authority and noted that while the prince naturally might propose the establishment of a new diocese, the decision lay ultimately in the hands of the bishops of the Rus' ecclesiastical province (i.e., the metropolitan and his suffragans). This commentary may well be connected with the establishment of new bishoprics in Volodymyr-in-Volhynia in 1078–1086 and Turaŭ (Turov) in 1088.[114] Despite the absence of any direct evidence in the sources, we can basically assume that both these centers were located within the boundaries of the metropolitan diocese proper, so that the new bishoprics had to be carved out of its territory.

When Vsevolod became the sole ruler of Rus' in October 1078, he assumed certain obligations vis-à-vis the sons of his older brother, Prince Iziaslav of Kyiv, who had just fallen on the field of battle. According to the law of seniority, the throne of Kyiv was to pass to the oldest son of Iziaslav, Iaropolk, on the death of his uncle Vsevolod. Among Vsevolod's first decisions was to grant Volhynia, with its seat at Volodymyr, and Polisia, with its center at Turaŭ on the Prypiat River, to Iaropolk. Iaropolk-Peter is the Rus' prince whose visage is known to us from the miniatures of the Cividale Codex (the "Trier Psalter").[115] Thanks to his sojourns at the courts of European rulers as well as at the papal court in Rome, he was one of the members of the Rurikid dynasty more conversant with the world, who understood well the need for and the value of ties between princely authority and the church. Moreover, in Rus' and at the Caves Monastery in particular, Iaropolk was viewed as a model Christian and a just Christian ruler. Suggestions about the supposed "Roman Catholic orientation" of Iaropolk and his parents Iziaslav and Gertrude are the result of an exaggerated, anachronistic view of the year 1054 as a sharp dividing line in ecclesiastical history. In Rome and Kyiv alike, Princes Iziaslav and Iaropolk were considered proper Christians. Also, Iziaslav's Polish wife was already active in Kyivan religious life in the 1050s and 1060s. She helped to admit the mother of Theodosius to the convent of St. Nicholas, which she founded, and was held in high respect at the Kyivan Caves Monastery.[116] Thus, what we know of Iaropolk permits us to see him as the initiator of the founding of the bishopric of Volodymyr-in-Volhynia. Vsevolod and John II responded favorably to this wish, since it was a question of a country "with a great population" requiring pastoral care. It is significant that the first bishop of Volodimer was Stephen (Stefan), a former hegumen of the Caves Monastery. Volhynia at that time was considerably more Christianized than the Rostov land. In the 1060s there was and had been for some time past a "Holy Mountain" monastery near Volodymyr-in-Volhynia, which, as its very name indicates, owed its establishment to close contacts with the center of Byzantine monasticism, the Holy Mount of Athos.[117] Hence, while political considerations were decisive in the establishment of this bishopric, circumstances of an ecclesiastical nature were clearly at work here as well.

Political considerations are most obvious in the case of the founding of the bishopric of Turaŭ on the Prypiat. After the death of Prince Iaropolk of Volodymyr-in-Volhynia (22 November 1086), the anticipated successor to the throne of Kyiv became the second son of Iziaslav, Sviatopolk, who at that time held Novgorod. Sviatopolk's uncle, Prince Vsevolod of Kyiv, clearly understood the danger that would threaten his own heirs, should Sviatopolk follow him on the Kyivan throne while still retaining Novgorod. In order to avoid this, he persuaded his nephew, on the pretext of his impending succession, to move to a nearer center, Turaŭ, just about 200 kilometers from Kyiv. At the same time, a bishopric was established there. Here, for the first time, it can be seen clearly—although it was already detectable in the case of Volodymyr-in-Volhynia—how important, for reasons of prestige, was the presence of a bishop in a princely residence. Sviatopolk realized this fact, although he must have viewed Turaŭ as merely a temporary residence (in fact, he ended up ruling as prince there from 1088 to 1093). Accustomed to the presence of a bishop in Novgorod, he wanted one in Turaŭ as well. This indicates not only that the social elite had been Christianized, but that collaboration with the church had become characteristic of princely authority. And even though the erection of the bishopric of Turaŭ was the result of a temporary situation, it became a permanent feature of the country's diocesan organization.

* *
*

The names of the cathedral churches in the newly erected bishoprics in Rostov, Volodymyr-in-Volhynia, and Turaŭ on the Prypiat were identical: all were dedicated to the Holy Assumption of the Mother of God (*Uspenie, Koimēsis*—i.e., "Dormition"). In the twelfth and thirteenth centuries, still other cathedrals were dedicated to the Dormition of the Mother of God. It is, in fact, no accident that all seven cathedral churches established between 1073 and 1213 bear this name. Indirect data permit us to trace the source of this custom to the Kyivan

Caves Monastery, the main church of which was dedicated to the Dormition. This pattern highlights the significant role that this monastery played in the Christianization of the Eastern Slavs and in the Slavicization of the ecclesiastical hierarchy. Its significance in the history of the church in Rus′ can be read not only in the widespread occurrence of churches of the Dormition, but also in the consecration of about 50 bishops from that single monastery during the period prior to 1220.[118] In both the twelfth and the first half of the thirteenth centuries, half of the dioceses were occupied by bishops who had formerly been monks at the Kyivan Caves Monastery. And this is only one aspect of the activity of the Caves Monastery in transforming Rus′ into a Christian land. Its contacts were not limited to the princely court in Kyiv: through its branches and episcopal curiae, it reached the courts of the appanage princes as well.

The clergy of the Dnipro region and the monks from the Caves Monastery in particular also played an important role in the religious life and ecclesiastical structures of the rest of the East Slavic lands in the second half of the thirteenth century—for example, in the intensive colonization and Christianization of the Oka-Volga mesopotamia, a process underway since the twelfth century.

It is a telling circumstance that, from the second half of the eleventh century, bishoprics were established on foundations prepared by *naměstnik*s in vicariates, where a main church dedicated to the Dormition of the Mother of God already existed. With the erection of a bishopric, this church was elevated to the rank of a cathedral. It is possible to infer from this that the organization of diocesan vicariates was likewise closely connected with the Caves Monastery. Undoubtedly, the questions posed to John II about the preconditions for creating a diocese were often discussed in this community, deepening the conviction that further Christianization and the development of a diocesan structure were inseparably linked with one another.

Indirect but eloquent testimony from Hegumen Daniel's (Daniil's) account of his pilgrimage to the Holy Land suggests that the question of the establishment of new bishoprics was very much alive at the beginning of the twelfth century. On his road to the holy places in Palestine in 1106, Daniel visited Cyprus, where he paid special attention to the diocesan structure, noting that there were "fourteen bishoprics but only one metropolitanate" on that island. It is interesting that it was precisely the church in Cyprus, and not the ecclesiastical organization in Palestine or any of the other lands or localities along the route of his pilgrimage, that attracted Daniel's attention. Obviously, there must have been something similar in the situation of the church in Cyprus to that in Rus′. Daniel underlined such an analogy by referring to the Cypriot church as a metropolitanate, rather than, in accordance with the Greek custom, as an archbishopric.[119]

Daniel had set off on his pilgrimage a dozen or so years after the special status of the two titular metropolitanates had died out. However, fears about a possible division of the heretofore unified Rus′ ecclesiastical province had not yet disappeared. At the same time, the question of creating new dioceses had come to a head as a result of the successes in Christianizing the realm and the need to continue the process, as well as a result of changes in the political structure of Rus'. In various circles, including the court of the metropolitan of Kyiv, the future must have seemed unsettling. The experience of the Greek metropolitanates suggested that an increase in the number of suffragan bishoprics encouraged the more dynamic among them to seek the status of independent metropolitanates. In Cyprus, Daniel observed something that made him think about his own church. By this time there were nine bishoprics subordinate to the metropolitan of Kyiv. By pointing to the fourteen bishoprics in Cyprus, Daniel wanted to calm the doubts of those who feared an increase in the number of dioceses in Rus', and by emphasizing the presence of "just one metropolitanate" (*mitropolia zhe edina*), he expressed himself clearly in favor of preserving the unity of the Rus' ecclesiastical province. Such was the position of the majority of the Rus' clergy during the eleventh to thirteenth centuries. Addressing himself to his readers—princes and bishops, boyars and hugemens—for whom he had prayed in the Holy Land, Daniel sought to dispel any fears about an increase in the number of bishoprics in Rus', by pointing out that an even greater number of dioceses had not prevented the church in Cyprus from continuing to be a single ecclesiastical province. He represented here a position shared by the Kyivan Caves Monastery, which was, on the one hand, a proponent of the unity of the ecclesiastical province and, on the other, an active supporter of the further development of its diocesan structure.

There were, however, forces in the church in Rus' that, while they did not basically question this view, nonetheless opposed the establishment of new bishoprics in concrete instances. The history of the bishopric of Smolensk provides a good example of these tendencies. As long as the Smolensk land was part of the principality of Pereiaslav, it was under the jurisdiction of the bishops of that latter town. Sometime in the second half of the eleventh century, an episcopal vicariate was established in Smolensk to facilitate the ecclesiastical administration of this region, located some 600 kilometers away from Pereiaslav. After 1094, when the suzerainty of the princes and bishops of Pereiaslav over the Smolensk and Rostov-Suzdal lands was restored after a temporary hiatus, some thought was also given to the creation of a local ecclesiastical organization. At about the same time, immediately after 1096, the new prince of Pereiaslav, Volodimer Monomakh, and his bishop, the titular Metropolitan Ephrem, built a stone church in Suzdal in honor of the Dormition of the Mother of God. The building of the first stone church in the Rostov land just after the lapse of the bishopric in Rostov was designed to emphasize that decisions affecting the region were made in Pereiaslav, for with this action the episcopal vicariate was transferred to Suzdal. In Suzdal, moreover, a branch of the Kyivan Caves Monastery had already been in operation for some time. In 1101, probably after the completion of the edifice in Suzdal, Volodimer Monomakh and Ephrem's successor, Bishop Simon (Symeon) of Pereiaslav, began the construction of a stone church of the Dormition of the Mother of God in Smolensk. The case of Suzdal makes it clear that no far-reaching plans for change in the structure of the metropolitanate were connected with the building of these churches. It was only a matter of ensuring, from the point of view of Pereiaslav, effective administration in the north. Only after 1113, when Volodimer Monomakh was seated upon the Kyivan throne, and particularly after 1117, when his political intentions and those of his heir Mstislav became clearer, did the two princes want to establish a bishopric in Smolensk. When Bishop Sylvester (Sil'vestr) of Pereiaslav died on 12 April 1123, the vacancy in the see provided a suitable opportunity for a division of the diocese. But here Volodimer ran up against the opposition of Metropolitan Nicetas (Nikētas). In revenge, the prince denied investure to the new candidate to the Pereiaslav see. Only after the death of Monomakh (19 May 1125) did his son Iaropolk, the new prince of Pereiaslav, accept Abbot Mark as bishop-elect, and finally on 4 November 1125, Metropolitan Nicetas consecrated him as bishop of Pereiaslav. The Kyivan Prince Mstislav continued, however, to strive for the establishment of a bishopric in Smolensk, the seat of his son Prince Rostislav. The sudden death of Metropolitan Nicetas on 3 March 1126, and the ensuing vacancy of several years in Kyiv contributed to further delay. The new metropolitan, Michael (Mikhail), who came to Kyiv in 1130, was clearly prepared to carry out the wish of the Kyivan ruler, as can deduced by the fact that he brought with him, in his entourage, the candidate designated to serve as bishop of that see, Manuel (Manuil). Nonetheless, Metropolitan Michael encountered opposition from Pereiaslav to the erection of a bishopric in Smolensk. Only after the death of Bishop Mark of Pereiaslav on 6 January 1135 was it possible to return to the project, and Manuel, the as yet unconsecrated bishop-elect, began administering his future diocese. The political situation—specifically, quarrels among the princes and continual changes on the princely throne of Pereiaslav—delayed a final decision, so that only in 1136–1137, was Manuel consecrated by Metropolitan Michael as the first bishop of Smolensk.[120] At the same time, the bishopric of Rostov was restored. The opposition of the Pereiaslav hierarchy and of the cathedral *kliros* in particular must have been quite stubborn, as the vacancy in the see of Pereiaslav lasted until 1141. With the creation of the Smolensk bishopric and the restitution of the Rostov bishopric, the jurisdictional area of the diocese of Pereiaslav had been reduced by three-quarters, being limited now only to the Pereiaslav land proper in the south.

The development of a diocesan structure was essential for further Christianization. This did not, however, prevent political motives from playing a part in the establishment of the new bishoprics. This was certainly true in the case of the bishopric in Halych. That region, roughly encompassing the upper and middle course of the Dnister and San rivers, took shape at the end of the eleventh and the first decades of the twelfth centuries as the domain of the heirs of Rostislav, grandson of Iaroslav the Wise. In characteristic fashion, the idea of an indigenous bishopric was born, but encountered misgivings in Kyiv and stiff opposition from the princes and bishops of Volodymyr-in-Volhynia. Only the interprincely struggles that broke out in 1146, particularly the clash over an appointment to the metropolitan see connected with the elevation of Clement Smoliatich in 1147, made it possible to establish a bishopric in Halych, which only shortly earlier had become the capital of this principality. The efforts of Prince Volodimer of Halych were eased by the fact that Metropolitan Clement and the bishop of Volodymyr were supporters of Iziaslav Mstislavich, who was both the Kyivan senior prince and the prince of Volodymyr-in-Volhynia. In the struggle for the Kyivan throne between Iziaslav Mstislavich and Iurii Dolgorukii, Volodimer of Halych supported the latter. In addition, his alliance with Byzantium against the Hungarians, who were Iziaslav's allies, assured him the support of the empire in this ecclesiastical matter. Since Clement's elevation to the metropolitanate was viewed as an illegal act in Constantinople, the Halych church had the right not to recognize its earlier obedience. Only after the return to a legal situation acceptable to the patriarch, with the arrival of Metropolitan Constantine (Konstantin) in Kyiv in 1156, did it become possible to consecrate bishop-elect Kosmas as bishop of Halych.[121] In this way, the *de facto* existing bishopric of Halych was carved *de iure* out of the diocese of Volodymyr-in-Volhynia, to which it had heretofore belonged, territorially partly as the vicariate of Peremyshl (*Pol.* Przemyśl) as well.

Considerably less troubled was the birth of the bishopric of Riazan on the Oka. The Riazan-Murom principality had already split off from the principality of Chernihiv at the beginning of the twelfth century, but continued to be part of the diocese of Chernihiv. The princes of Riazan had no great interest in ecclesiastical independence. In order to counter the pressures of the princes of Vladimir-Suzdal, they were forced to seek the support of Chernihiv, and could count on the intervention of its bishop on their behalf. The ecclesiastical alienation of Riazan arose only when the princes of Riazan, as a result of their defeat of 1186, fell into dependence on Prince Vsevolod of Vladimir-Suzdal. Vsevolod was interested in breaking the ecclesiastical ties between Riazan and Chernihiv. The creation of the bishopric should be ascribed to the diplomatic skill of Metropolitan Nikēphoros II, who managed to take advantage of the favorable conditions and bring the princes of Chernihiv and Vladimir-Suzdal into agreement in the 1190s, and was able to obtain their consent to the creation of a Riazan bishopric' out of the diocese of Chernihiv. Despite the changing fate of its principality and the destruction of the city in 1237, Riazan was to remain permanently as a diocese of the Rus' ecclesiastical province.[122]

The division of the Rostov-Suzdal diocese and the creation of a second bishopric alongside Rostov in Vladimir-on-the-Kliazma took place as a result of the division of the domain of Vsevolod "Big Nest" among his eldest sons. The bishops of Rostov had already resided for some time in Vladimir-on-the-Kliazma, so the separation in fact returned its function of episcopal see to Rostov while recognizing the ecclesiastical role that Vladimir-on-the-Kliazma had played for nearly 50 years. The division of the diocese was also a result of the progress in the Christianization of northeast Rus′. In November 1213 and at the beginning of 1214 bishops descended from the Caves community were consecrated for the two sees.[123]

King Danylo and Metropolitan Cyril: The Church in the Face of the Mongol Invasion

Shortly thereafter, a bishopric was established in the western borderlands of Rus′ at Peremyshl, where—one can presume—there had already been a vicariate of the diocese of Volodymyr-in-Volhynia at the turn of the eleventh and twelfth centuries. During that period a princely stone church dedicated to St. John the Baptist, which later became a cathedral, was also built here. After 1130, Peremyshl lost its primacy in the western lands of the Dnister basin to Halych.[124] Peremyshl, as the center of a land already advanced in its Christianization, was well suited to be the seat of a bishop, but in fact the city owed this status to an accident. Political events in Novgorod, the bishop of which had borne the honorary title of archbishop since 1165, resulted at the end of 1219 in the return of Archbishop Mitrofan to his throne, from which he had been removed on 23 January 1211. Because Mitrofan's successor since 1211, Archbishop Anthony (Antonii), was not inclined to withdraw, however, it was decided to send both bishops to Kyiv to submit to the mediation of the metropolitan. Metropolitan Matthew (Matfii) settled the problem by rehabilitating Mitrofan, who had originally been consecrated in 1201, and sending him back to Novgorod. The metropolitan also "honored" Anthony, giving him the bishopric of Peremyshl.[125] This was possible on the strength of an understanding between the metropolitan and Mstislav the Bold, who had become the ruler of the Halych principality in 1219. The latter, as prince of Novgorod (1210–1218), had become friends with Archbishop Anthony. Probably a vacancy in the see of Halych permitted the separation of the diocese of Peremyshl from the diocese of Halych without any great difficulties. And even though Bishop Anthony returned to Novgorod in 1225, this change could not threaten the existence of the newly created bishopric. Despite the passing circumstances behind the erection of an episcopal see and the political complications into which the town had fallen, there were also real justifications for such a step, and so the bishopric of Peremyshl became a permanent component of the ecclesiastical geography of *mikra Rhōsia* or "little Rus′."

Not long after the division of the diocese of Halych, there was a further partition of the diocese of Volodymyr-in-Volhynia. Before joining Halych and Volhynia together under his rule (1238), Prince Danylo had already established a bishopric in his residence at Uhrusk on the Buh, about 80 kilometers northwest of Volodymyr, conceived, no doubt, as a bishop's see at the ruler's court. Only when the princely court moved between 1240 and 1250 to Kholm (*Pol.* Chełm), which now emerged as the new capital of a unified Halych-Volhynian principality, was the office of court bishop transformed into a regular bishopric.[126] At about the same time, probably before 1240 and in any case before 1250, a bishopric was established in Lutsk, one of the most important cities in eastern Volhynia.[127] That foundation mirrored the further development of ecclesiastical-religious life; it must be viewed, however, like that of Kholm, in the overall context of Danylo's political plans. As a ruler, he yearned to be a "prince of princes," a crowned king surrounded by bishops. The coronation of Danylo must be seen against the background of his political ambitions. As a ruler connected with European courts, he understood quite well that he could become a true king (*rex coronatus*) by receiving a crown from the pope.[128] The earlier foundation of a bishopric in Peremyshl furnished him with a good example, and, furthermore, a comparison with his neighbors—Hungary, Bohemia, and Poland—inclined him to further foundations. There are thus good grounds to suggest that Danylo consciously set out to increase the number of dioceses on the territory of his realm. There is no evidence, however, from which to infer that he sought to join his five dioceses into a new ecclesiastical province or to break up the metropolitanate of Kyiv. Nonetheless, his ecclesiastical administrative activity laid the basis for the future metropolitanate of *mikra Rhōsia*.

In the difficult years of the Mongol invasion, Danylo was a spokesman for the unity of the Kyivan ecclesiastical province: in the years 1239–1243 and 1246–1249 it was he who bore the title of Grand Prince of Kyiv. He held Kyiv the first time until 1243, when Khan Batu named Grand Prince Iaroslav Vsevolodovich of Vladimir-Suzdal the "eldest among all the princes of Rus'." After the death of Iaroslav, Danylo probably became grand prince of Kyiv again, being the only one to return to Rus' of all the princes who had traveled to the court of the Great Khan to pay homage in 1246.[129] Metropolitan Joseph (Iosif), who had come to Kyiv from Nicaea in 1236, quickly disappeared from the scene, either returning to his homeland or losing his life in Kyiv when it fell to the Mongols on 6 December 1240. In 1241 or at the latest in 1242, in this exceptional situation—further complicated by a vacancy on the patriarchal throne in Nicaea (1240–1244)—Danylo, as the nominal Grand Prince of Kyiv, entrusted the administration of the metropolitanate to metropolitan-elect Cyril.[130] The latter, however, could not have gone to Nicaea until after Danylo's journey to pay homage to Khan Batu in the spring of 1246, which resulted in the return of the title of Grand Prince of Kyiv to him. Only in 1247 was Cyril finally consecrated in Nicaea. Not long after his return to Kyiv in 1249, it was decided at the court of the Great Khan to entrust the title of Grand Prince of Kyiv to Alexander Nevsky, who also became Grand Prince of Vladimir-Suzdal in 1252. The new Grand Prince of Kyiv and the metropolitan of Kyiv developed a close working relationship with one another. Nonetheless, speculation about a supposed loosening of Cyril's ecclesiastical ties to Halych-Volhynian Rus' is groundless. A change in the bearer of the grand princely title was simply accompanied with the normal retention of Cyril as metropolitan of Kyiv. From the very fact that the edition of the *Nomokanon* produced under the direction of Metropolitan Cyril was accepted in Volhynia in its earliest form and copied there in 1286, it follows that *mikra Rhōsia* continued to be as much under the jurisdiction of the metropolitan of Kyiv as were the other lands of Rus'.[131] Equally baseless is the assertion that Cyril transferred the seat of the metropolitanate to the Vladimir in the Suzdal land. Kyiv and its metropolitan see continued to function: synods took place there (e.g., in 1273 and 1284), and bishops were consecrated there as late as the 1290s (e.g., Clement of Novgorod and Theodore of Vladimir-on-the-Kliazma in 1276). The Kyivan St. Sophia likewise continued to be the final resting place of Kyivan metropolitans: the remains of Cyril, who died on 27 November 1281 in Pereiaslav Zaleskii during a pastoral visit to the Suzdal land, were transported back to Kyiv and buried on 6 December in the St. Sophia Cathedral there.[132]

Under Cyril's administration, two more bishoprics were established. Despite the fact that the principality of Tver was established in the 1240s, the advance of Tver to the rank of a bishopric can be confirmed only in connection with the treaty (1255–1258) between Grand Prince Alexander Nevsky and his brother Prince Iaroslav of Tver.[133]

The year 1261 witnessed the consecration of Mitrofan, first bishop of Sarai, which was the capital of the Golden Horde on the Volga. His successor, Theognostos, was made bishop both of Pereiaslav (near Kyiv) and Sarai in 1269. Theognostos journeyed three times to meet with the emperor and the patriarch in Constantinople at the behest of Metropolitan Cyril and Khan Möngke Temür. He was there on 12 August 1276, as indicated by an act of the patriarchal synod.[134] In literature on the subject, the bishop of Sarai has tended to be viewed more as a diplomatic representative than a pastor, but these synodal documents portray the involvement of Theognostos in matters of a strictly pastoral nature, related to the special circumstances of his post. It is known that the bishopric of Sarai had a precisely delineated area of jurisdiction. This is demonstrated by a quarrel with the bishop of Riazan about the boundary of the diocese. From the end of the thirteenth century, these two episcopal sees, located 750 kilometers one from the other, argued over the course of the boundary line running midway between them. One would have expected in that period to find open steppe and an absence of settlement between the rivers Don, Khopor, and Vorona. But even in the stormy thirteenth century, not only settlements, but Christian communities and a functioning ecclesiastical organization existed there. The settlers recognized the jurisdiction of the bishop of Sarai, counting on his effective defense of the Christian communities against abuses on the part of the Tatar-Mongol administration.[135]

* *
*

These events in political and ecclesiastical life lead us up to the hiatus associated with the Mongol invasion. While one certainly should not underestimate the significance of the invasion itself, which began in 1223 and reached its peak of destruction and slaughter in the years 1237–1240, it is also true that the catastrophe, no matter how vast its immediate proportions may have been, proved truly fatal only in the long run, when it turned out to be irreversible. The deep dividing line thus comes not so much with those few years of armed conquest as with the continuing rule of the Mongols in the decades that followed. It was not defeat on the field of battle, but the ensuing half century that turned the course of history toward a permanent division of Europe.[136] Economic, political, and ecclesiastical life went on after 1240, despite the destruction of the many fortresses and towns that had put up resistance to the invaders. There were, after all, many remaining centers and settlements that had surrendered without a fight. The destruction of Kyiv meant the decline of a European city, but not the end of its existence.[137] Resistance was not entirely quelled, moreover, and continued to smolder in the decades that followed. Even the trips of the Rus' princes to pay homage at the court of the khan, the recognition of Mongol suzerainty, and the readiness to collaborate with the foreign conquerors do not lend themselves to a one-sided interpretation, but rather need to be evaluated within the context of the overall situation of the time. The tactic of collaboration with the victors enjoyed increasingly strong support from the upper strata and the church, as the conviction grew that resistance was hopeless and could only lead to a demolition of what remained of the state and to the total destruction of Christian society.[138]

From the political and religious points of view, the thirteenth century was a very difficult but fruitful one for the Church. It was a period in which the common experience of disaster, of the defeats and humiliations suffered, awakened a common confessional consciousness and served to enrich spiritual life. Despite the heavy human losses and the material destruction—the ruin of many churches and the loss of countless monuments of artistic and spiritual value—it became forcefully apparent just how deeply Christianity had penetrated the various strata of society. Christian consciousness, pitted against a godless, or, rather, religiously indifferent, invader, came to life in a defense of indigenous values expressed in a growing religious intolerance.

Ecclesiastical institutions were not only spared by the characteristically tolerant conquerors but were even encouraged in their activity by a variety of privileges (the oldest such charter/*iarlyk* dating from 1267). The Church and ecclesiastical hierarchy achieved a greater independence from their own princes in this period, but at the same time had to take greater responsibility upon themselves. It is worth noting that Metropolitan Cyril in the course of his long tenure (1242–1281), did not once appear at the khan's court. However, there is no evidence to support the contention that, because of his ties with King Danylo, Cyril did not enjoy the trust of the Horde.[139] Cyril managed to obtain privileges and benefits for the Church without involving himself in the excursions to pay homage at the court of the khans, and from this stance, a certain model of behavior for the bishops of the Rus' church took shape. Bishop Ignatius (Ignatii) of Rostov was even required to justify his journey to the

Golden Horde before a metropolitan tribunal in 1281.[140] For the metropolitan, who wanted to avoid such visits to the court of the khan, the maintenance of a permanent representative in the person of the bishop of Sarai became a necessary and valuable expedient. The permanent presence of a Rus′ bishop at Sarai was also valued by the Golden Horde, in view of its need for closer diplomatic ties with the Byzantine Empire.

One cannot help noting that, as a result of the Mongol invasion, the young Rus′ church was confronted with tasks of exceptional difficulty well before reaching maturity. But after more than thirty years of Mongol lordship over Rus′, a synod held in Kyiv in 1273 was able to come to a conclusion that, while containing nothing new, did offer a decisive pastoral program of ecclesiastical reform for coping with this difficult era of foreign rule.[141] The need to collaborate with the conqueror in the ecclesiastical-political sphere was not translated into the language of pastoral care, and sermons were not embellished with praise for the invaders. On the contrary, the pastoral letter of Metropolitan Cyril from Kyiv in 1273 reminded the faithful of the dark and humiliating realities: "Has not God scattered us throughout the whole land? Have not our cities been captured? Have not our powerful princes been cut down by the sword? Has not our youth been led away into captivity? Have not our houses of divine worship been violated? Do not the godless and criminal pagans torment us day after day?" Metropolitan Cyril's suffragan, Bishop Serapion of Vladimir-on-the-Kliazma, who had been until recently (1249–1273) archimandrite of the still functioning Caves Monastery in Kyiv, struck a similar chord in his admonition of 1274. Warning of extermination, he called for a purification of souls and a moral renewal, and did not fear to say of the Mongol yoke: "Has not our country fallen into slavery? Have not our strongholds been captured? Was it so long ago that our fathers and brothers lay down in battle? Have not our women and children been led away into captivity? Have not those who survived been trapped in a bitter yoke by the foreigners? And it has lasted nearly forty years, this torment and suffering, and heavy dues bear down upon us without ceasing . . . ." Likewise, in another sermon, Serapion complains that "our riches have been taken by the pagans, our country has become the possession of foreigners, our neighbors look upon us with scorn—we have become the laughingstock of our enemies."[142]

Such was the Church of Rus′ and such were its pastors in the first decades of the Mongol yoke. They succeeded in obtaining privileges from the conquerors and in strengthening their own position. They also stood guard, however, over national and spiritual traditions. Recounting the defeat and suffering, urging the preservation of values inherited from the past, they awakened a spirit of resistance, an internal rejection of the imposed reality. It is true that the young church as an institution and its pastors as individuals did not always act with appropriate dignity, but the Church was not broken: it found the inner strength and social support necessary to continue its mission.

The devastated and depopulated cities and settlements, and the burned and profaned churches, evoked horror in the accounts of those who survived. The armed invasion of the Mongols in 1237–1240 was a heavy defeat and was perceived by contemporaries as utter annhihilation, but in fact it did not result in a total destruction. Despite everything, life continued; finding support in the Church, the conquered remained unreconciled to their fate.

The Mongol invasion inaugurated a major break in the continuity of the history of Rus', but the further course of events was not immediately apparent. The fatal turning point was the result not of the invasion of the Mongols itself, not of the plundering and mass slaughter of the population, not of the fall of Kyiv or Vladimir-on-the-Kliazma, but above all of the profound changes in the internal life of the country that took place under the influence of these events and the continuing presence of the Mongols in the life of Rus'. The increasingly coercive course, so disastrous for the land, was influenced more by the Tatar register of 1257–1259 than by the destruction of the years 1237–1240.[143]

These changes meant, among other things, an end of the Kyivan era in the history of the Church in Rus', an era of a single Church common to all the East Slavs. Metropolitan Cyril, probably of Halych-Volhynian origin, was the last pastor to preside over such a unity. His successor, the Greek Maxim (Maksim) who arrived in 1283, sought to uphold tradition, but, in 1299, in the face of a difficult reality, he decided to transfer his court and the Sophia *kliros* to the Vladimir in the Suzdal land.[144]

Four years later, in 1303, a decision was made by Constantinople to carve a second ecclesiastical province—with the seat of the new metropolitan at Halych and his five suffragans initially in Volodymyr-in-Volhynia, Peremyshl, Lutsk, Turaŭ, and Kholm—out of the metropolitanate of Kyiv with its twelve bishoprics.[145] In the official note of the Patriarchate of Constantinople concerning the erection of the metropolitanate of Halych we find for the first time the phrase "*mikra Rhōsia*," paralleling the name "*Megale Rhōsia*," which had been used for the first time in the twelfth century in reference to the metropolitanate of Kyiv. Both of these names, despite their subsequent roles as ethnopolitical and geographical terms,[146] function here exclusively as Byzantine conceptions of ecclesiastical geography, serving, on the basis of the number of suffragans in each, to distinguish the smaller Rus' ecclesiastical province from the larger.

In tenth- to twelfth-century Byzantium, it was known that the geographical term "Rus'" (*Rhōsia*) was employed in Rus' first and foremost in referring to the territory on the middle Dnipro with its center in Kyiv, while the domain of the Kyivan princes extended to a significantly broader territory. At the same time, this geographical term was also used, for practical purposes, in referring to the whole area of Kyivan rule just as it is, for that matter, in contemporary historiography. However, sometimes the need for greater precision was felt. Hence, Constantine VII Porphyrogennētos localizes Novgorod in "outer Rhōsia," having in mind the extent of Kyivan rule beyond Rus' proper. Similarly, in the chancellery of the patriarch, use of the term "great Rhōsia," served to emphasize the congruency between the jurisdictional range of the metropolitanate of Kyiv and the territorial domain of Rus′ as a state.

Moreover, the identification of the metropolitanate of Kyiv as the metropolitanate of "great Rus′," in the sense of all, or the whole, of Rus′, may already have begun in Byzantium at the end of the eleventh century in the face of political and ecclesiastical centrifugal forces that challenged the unity of the patriarchate's Rus′ province. The counterpart of this "great" Rus′ is the phrase "*pasēs Rhōsias,*" or "*vseia Rusi,*" employed by metropolitans and princes of Kyiv alike. From the moment of the division into two metropolitanates, the adjective "great" regained its basic semantic sense, serving, in a pairing with "little" or "minor," to distinguish a larger structure.

As later history would show, it was no easy matter to translate this division, deepening in the fourteenth and fifteenth centuries, into the language of definitive ecclesiastical administrative decisions, but the course had been set. The processes leading to these transformations had begun earlier, but the events of the thirteenth century had accelerated them dramatically.

The metropolitanate of Halych was not a stable structure. Among the factors responsible for this was the crucial one: the extinction of local branches of Rurikids. When, toward the end of the twelfth century, the line of Rostislaviches of Halych died out, it seemed that they would be successfully replaced by the Volhynian line of the scions of Volodimir Monomakh: Prince Roman (d. 1205) and his son King Danylo (d. 1264; he even competed successfully for Kyiv). Their successors, in the face of the persistent Mongol-Tatar pressure, increasingly limited themselves to local matters and rivalries, and then by the year 1322 came the extinction of the male line of the Halych-Volhynian Rurikids. Claims to the throne and power in Halych on the part of related neighbors—members of the dynatsies of the Piasts, Gediminids and Arpads—had a negative impact on the history of these lands, though they initially brought political order and economic prosperity. There is no doubt, however, that in the longer perspective the loss of its own dynasty, whose roots reached back to the Kyivan era, weighed heavily on the fate of Rus′-Ukraine and found reflection in its religious life as well.

NOTES

This essay was originally conceived as an introduction to a collection of essays on the history of religious life in Ukraine, which was not published because of the landmarks of 1991. It was based largely on my analytical studies, which I reference below, as well as on my critical discussion of previous studies on this subject. Here I consider mainly studies related to the Millennium of Christianity in Rus'/Ukraine.

1. "Photii epistolae," no. XIII, chap. 35, in Jacques-Paul Migne, ed., *Patrologiae cursus completus. Series graeca*, 161 vols. (Paris, 1857–1866), vol. 102, pp. 735–38. Cf. Ihor Ševčenko, "Religious Missions Seen from Byzantium," *Harvard Ukrainian Studies* 12/13 (1988/1989): 7–27 (reprinted as "Religious Missions Seen from Byzantium: The Imperial Pattern and its local Variants," in his *Ukraine Between East and West: Essays on Cultural History to the Early Eighteenth Century* (Edmonton, 1996), pp. 27–45). The interchangeability of [ō] and [ū] (graphemically, ω/Ω) in the Greek of the Byzantine era (until the thirteenth century?) permits us to hypothesize confidently that the name "*Rhōs, Rhōsia*" was pronounced in Byzantium in a manner similar to the Slavic "*Rus*′" and the Latin "*Rusia*." Compare Liudprand, Bishop of Cremona's (ca. 960): "*gens . . . quam Graeci vocant . . . Rusios*" (*Antapodosis* b. V, c. 15). Ω was pronounced as a long ū, as shown by the Latin spelling of the Greek sound of the name, Theophanu (Theophanō in Greek spelling). For literature on the Christianization before 988, see the second Russian edition, with corrections and bibliographic additions, of Gerhard Podskalsky [Podskal′skii], *Khristianstvo i bogoslovskaia literatura v Kievskoi Rusi 988–1237 gg.* (St. Petersburg, 1996), pp. 17–29.

2. Tadeusz Lewicki, *Źródła arabskie do dziejów Słowiańszczyzny,* vol. 1 (Wrocław, 1956), pp. 76ff, and the commentary on pp. 126–38. See Omeljan Pritsak, "An Arabic Text on the Trade Route of the Corporation of Ar-Rūs in the Second Half of the Ninth Century, " *Folia Orientalia* 12 (1970): 242–59; cf. M. Hrushevsky [Hrushevs′kyi], *History of Ukraine-Rus′,* vol. 1 (Edmonton, 1997), pp. 217, 218, 316, and 388. On some implications in reconstructing the original text and in enlarging the dating for the whole ninth century, see Thomas S. Noonan, "When Did Rūs/Rus′ Merchants First Visit Khazaria and Baghdad?" *Archivum Eurasiae Medii Aevi* 7 (1987–1991): 213–19.

3. Samuel Hazzard Cross and Olgerd P. Sherbowitz-Wetzor, eds. and trans., *Russian Primary Chronicle: Laurentian Text* (Cambridge, MA, 1953), p. 77. Since the term *sobornaia tserkvi* has often been translated as "cathedral church," which would assume the presence of a bishop in Kyiv even prior to 944, it should be remembered that *sobornaia* represents an exact translation of the Greek *katholiki*, in this context, meaning a common, public church; in other words, a church serving the congregation of believers [*publica ecclesia*] in contrast to an oratory or private church [*privata ecclesia*].

4. A. P. Motsia, *Naselennia pivdenno-Rus'kykh zemel' IX–XIII st. za materialamy nekropoliv* (Kyiv, 1993), pp. 6–46 and 74–102; A. Chernetsov, "Nachalo khristianstva na Rusi v svete arkheologicheskikh dannykh. Sostoianie izuchennosti voprosa," *Slavia antiqua* 38 (1997): 81–93. It seems that it is too early to evaluate the degree of Christianization on the basis of findings of 2 to 9 percent of the graves with Christian signs on them from the eleventh-thirteenth centuries, if one considers that in the thirteenth century there was a decline in the number of such graves, as compared with the twelfth century. There is no clear proof to state that "by the end of the 12th century almost all urban graves were Christian" (Simon Franklin and Jonathan Shepard, *The Emergence of Rus' 750–1200* [London, 1996], p. 352); cf. also pp. 174–76; the white stone rotunda in Peremyshl (*Pol.* Przemyśl) cannot be dated to the tenth century (p. 159) but only to first half of the eleventh, and it is most likely a fragment of a palatium not of a church.

5. Cf. also N. A. Makarov, "K otsenke khristianizatsii drevnerusskoi derevni v XI–XIII vv.," *Kratkie soobshcheniia Instituta arkheologii* 205 (1991): 11–21; V. V. Sedov, "Rasprostranenie khristianstva v drevnei Rusi," *Kratkie soobshcheniia Instituta arkheologii* 208 (1993): 5–11, takes into account earlier writings (controversial). See also Tat'iana Panova, "Khristianskaia simvolika v gorodskom pogrebal'nom obriade Rusi (XI–XVvv.)," *Russia mediaevalis* 9(1) 1997: 54–77.

6. Aleksandr Zimin, ed., "Pamiat' i pokhvala Iakova Mnikha i Zhitie kniazia Vladimira po drevneishemu spisku," *Kratkie soobshcheniia Instituta slavianovedeniia* 37 (1963): 72; *The Hagiography of Kievan Rus'*, trans. and with an introduction by Paul Hollingsworth (Cambridge, MA, 1992), p. 171.

7. Joannes Scylitzes [John Skylitzes], *Ioannis Scylitzae synopsis historiarum,* ed. Johannes Thurn (Berlin–New York, 1973), p. 282. If we accept Gyula Moravcsik's *(Byzantium and the Magyars* [Budapest, 1970], pp. 104 and 106) dating of the baptism of both Hungarian princes (Bulcsu 948 and Gyula 952) then the baptism of Ol'ga should have followed shortly after 952.

8. Gennadii G. Litavrin ("Russko-vizantiiskie sviazi v seredine X veka," *Voprosy istorii* 1986 [6]: 41–52) dates Ol'ga's baptism in a similar way, although he dates the princess' visit, described in *De ceremoniis*, as having taken place in the year 946. See A. Poppe, "Once Again Concerning the Baptism of Olga, archontissa of Rus'" *Dumbarton Oaks Papers* 46 (1992): 271–77.

9. Constantine VII Porphyrogenitus [Porphyrogennētos] *De ceremoniis aulae byzantinae*, vol. 1 (Bonn, 1829), pp. 594–98 (hereafter, *De ceremoniis*); G. Ostrogorsky has already noticed that Ol'ga had been equated with *zōstē patrikia.* I have only developed that idea (see above n. 8). Here it can only be added that in the fall 957 Ol'ga was evidently Christian. As a *zōstē* she had the right to wear imperial *loros* for a palace reception, a very heavy garment which reduced her act of *proskynēsis* to

the bending of her head (*De ceremoniis*, p. 597). Since the *loros* symbolized the cross as the implement of Christ's victory, as stated by Constantine himself on another occasion (*De ceremoniis,* p. 638), Ol′ga's baptism prior to that visit cannot be questioned.

10. R. Guilland, "La patricienne à ceinture," *Byzantinoslavica* 32(2) 1971: 269–75; A. J. Deér, "Zur Praxis der Verleihung des auswärtigen Patriziats durch den byzantinischen Kaiser," in *Byzanz und das abendländische Herrschertum* (Sigmaringen, 1977), pp. 424–37.

11. "*Continuatio Reginonis Chronicon*" in *Ausgewählte Quellen zur deutschen Geschichte des Mittelalters*, vol. 8 (Darmstadt, 1977), pp. 214–15.

12. So oversimplified by J.-P. Arrignon ("Mezhdunarodnye otnosheniia Kievskoi Rusi v seredine X veka i kreshchenie kniagini Ol′gi," *Vizantiiskii vremennik* 41 [1980]: 121–23), who met with the right reply by G. G. Litavrin ("Puteshestvie russkoi kniagini Ol′gi v Konstantinopol′. Problema istochnikov," *Vizantiiskii vremennik* 42 [1981]: 38–39).

13. See the intitulation formulae in *De ceremoniis*, pp. 686–92, especially p. 691; cf. E. Dölger, "Das Byzantinische Mitkaisertum in den Urkunden," in *Das Byzantinische Herrscherbild* (Darmstadt, 1975), pp. 13–48. The office of *conregni more Graecorum* was known very well to Adalbert, the supposed author of the *Continuatio Reginonis Chronicon*, since Otto I had crowned his son Otto II in this way in 961.

14. While Adalbert should be appreciated as an historian, we have to keep in mind that his works contain many mistakes and inaccuracies. See M. Lintzel, *Ausgewählte Schriften II* (Berlin, 1961), pp. 399–406 (especially pp. 400–401).

15. *Continuatio Reginonis Chronicon,* pp. 214–19.

16. See Otto I's letter of 968 in *Monumenta Germaniae Historica* I (1884), no. 366. For the limits of Magdeburg archbishops' early jurisdiction, see J. Fried, *Otto III und Bolesław Chrobry* (Stuttgart, 1989), pp.144–47. The myth about the continuity of the German "Drang nach Osten" was often politically modernized first of all in German historiography, but also in Polish and Russian approaches. The hypothesis that the Ottonian dynasty attempted to involve Rus′ in the sphere of the Latin church has no basis, but has been repeated to this day. For a preliminary revision of this hypothesis, see A. Poppe, "Polityka Ottonów wobec Rusi Kijowskiej," in *Katolicyzm w Rosji i Prawosławie w Polsce, XI–XX w.* (Warsaw, 1997), pp. 24–28.

17. The Hungarian Prince Gyula, baptized ca. 952, received at the same time a missionary bishop. The monk Hierotheos, to whom Hungary was known earlier, obtained consecration from the patriarch (Scylitzes, *Synopsis historiarum,* p. 239). Cf. P. T. Antonopoulos, "Byzantium, the Magyar Raids and Their Consequences," *Byzantinoslavica* 54(2) 1993: 263, 265–66.

18. Scylitzes, *Synopsis historiarum*, pp. 242–44, 247. The view presented in patriotically oriented historiography, which maintains that in Constantinople Rus′ was the focus of political and diplomatic attention, has no basis. As has been rightly stressed, "for Constantine VII alliance with the Pechenegs was the key to Byzantine diplomacy in the north." See D. Obolensky, "Byzantium, Kiev and Cherson in the Tenth Century," *Byzantinoslavica* 54(1) 1993: 109. It was not until the year 987 that a sudden shift in politics occurred— Rus′ came into prominence.

19. See A. Poppe, "Vladimir als Christ. Versuch eines psychologischen Porträts des Kiever Herrschers," *Österreichische Osthefte* 35 (1993): 553–75.

20. This section is based on my study "The Political Background to the Baptism of Rus′," *Dumbarton Oaks Papers* 30 (1976): 197–244; reprinted with eight other papers in my *The Rise of Christian Russia* (London, 1982). For a historiography, see Hrushevsky, *History of Ukraine-Rus'*, vol. I, pp. 444–49; Podskalsky, *Khristianstvo i bogoslovskaia literatura*, pp. 28–41. Ihor Ševčenko, in his brilliant essay, "The Christianization of Kievan Rus'" (in *The Polish Review* V (1960), reprinted in his *Ideology, Letters and Culture in the Byzantine World* [London, 1982], pp. 29–35), noticed that researchers and organizers of the future *Russiae sacrum millenium* had enough time to agree on the exact date and place of Volodimer's baptism. The organizers of meetings have more than fulfilled expectations, while researchers lagged behind, despite help offered by a multitude of amateurs. We continue to argue about the date, place, and circumstances of Volodimer's baptism.

21. This traditional opinion still has many followers, but is most clearly articulated (and for years) by D. Obolensky. See his "Byzantium, Kiev and Cherson in the Tenth Century," pp. 108–13; in compatibility with Obolensky's view and in polemic with me is J. Shepard —"Some Remarks on the Sources for the Conversion of Rus′," in *Le Origini e lo sviluppo della cristianità slavo-bizantina* (Rome, 1992), pp. 59–95.

22. Cf. A. A. Shakhmatov, *Razyskaniia o drevneishikh russkikh letopisnykh svodakh* (St. Petersburg, 1908), pp. 133–61; D. S. Likhachev, *Izbrannye raboty v trekh tomakh*, vol. 2 (Leningrad, 1987), pp. 99–104.

23. This traditional interpretation predominates in writings on the Millennium, most cogently by D. Obolensky, "Cherson and the Conversion of Rus′: An Anti-Revisionist View," *Byzantine and Modern Greek Studies* 13 (1989): 244–56; perplexedly (in all religious and church matters), in Franklin and Shepard, *The Emergence of Rus′ 750–1200*, pp. 158–69; already hesitantly and inconsistently (and with many inaccuracies), by S. Senyk, *A History of the Church in Ukraine*, vol. 1 (Rome, 1993), pp. 61–71; and, unskillfully, in the jubilee publication of W. Seibt, "Der historische Hintergrund und die Chronologie der Taufe der Ruś (989)" in A.-E. N. Tachiaos, ed., *The Legacy of Saints Cyril and Methodius to Kiev and Moscow: Proceedings of the International Congress on the Millen-*

nium of the Conversion of Rus' to Christianity (Thessaloniki, 1992), pp. 289–303.

24. See Franz Tinnefeld, "Byzantinische auswärtige Heiratspolitik vom 9. zum 12. Jh. Kontinuität und Wandel der Prinzipien und der praktischen Ziele," *Byzantinoslavica* 54(1) 1993: 21–28; J. Fennel, *A History of the Russian Church to 1448* (London, 1995), pp. 37–38.

25. There is nothing surprising in the fact that the focus of the discussion is the time of events. Thus, Obolensky, ("Byzantium, Kiev and Cherson in the Tenth Century," especially p. 248) stresses that the events took place later than 989, and so moves the conquest of Kherson to the year 990. Although I basically maintain my arguments in agreement with the way of dating astronomical phenomena by V. G. Vasil′evskii (1876) and V. R. Rozen [*Imperator Vasilii Bolgaroboitsa. Izvlecheniia iz letopisi Iakh"i Antiokhiiskogo* (St. Petersburg, 1883)], I have decided to disregard the phenomenon of pillars of fire because of its uncertain character, linked, perhaps, to biblical reminiscences. Unprofessional attempts to compile chronological data based on previously made assumptions (O. M. Rapov, *Russkaia tserkov' v IX–pervoi treti XII v.: priniatie khristianstva* [Moscow, 1988]) have been criticized, and rightfully so, by N. M. Bogdanova, "O vremenii vziatiia Chersona kniazem Vladimirom," *Vizantiiskii vremennik* 47 (1986): 39–46 and A. L. Ponomar′ev, N. I. Serikov, "989 (6496) god—god kreshcheniia Rusi (Filologicheskii analiz tekstov, astrologiia i astronomiia)," in *Prichernomor'e v srednie veka*, vol. 2 (Moscow, 1995), pp. 157–85. In the latter article, the authors propose an original solution: after Basil II's defeat in Bulgaria in August 986, Volodimer decided to take advantage of the weakness of the empire in order to conquer Kherson in 987 and 988, and later demand the hand of the *porphyrogennēta* and agree to be baptized (989). While the remarks on the dating of astronomical phenomena are noteworthy, the authors of this paper ignore the fact that the famous earthquake that caused the western cupola of Hagia Sophia to collapse has been confirmed by a few independent testimonies, which point to 25–26 October 989. See Poppe, "The Political Background to the Baptism of Rus′," pp. 211–12; G. Downey, "Earthquakes at Constantinople and Vicinity, A. D. 342–1454," *Speculum* 30 (1955): 599–600; A. P. Kazhdan, ed., *The Oxford Dictionary of Byzantium*, vol. 1 (New York and Oxford, 1991), pp. 669–70; C. Mango, "The Collapse of St. Sophia, Psellus and the Etymologicum Genuinum," in *Gonimos: Neoplatonic and Byzantine Studies Presented to L. G. Westerink* (New York, 1988), p.168. Ponomar′ev's and Serikov's suggestion (ibid., pp. 178–80) to date this earthquake as having taken place two years earlier (987) cannot be accepted. The authors ignore or dismiss records that contradict their thesis. Thus, they claim that Asoghik [Asołik] (Stephen of Tarōn) made a mistake when he wrote several dozens of years later about the event; however, the earthquake took place in the lifetime of this Armenian historian, who finished writing his history around the year 1003.

26. Constantine Porphyrogenitus [Porphyrogennētos], *De administrando imperio,* Greek text ed. by Gy. Moravcsik; English trans. by R. J. H. Jenkins, revised ed., vol. 1 (Washington, DC, 1967), p. 53.

27. *Leonis diaconi Caloensis Historia libri decem,* ed. C. B. Hase (Bonn, 1828), p. 173.

28. A. Poppe, "Nie mieczem a piórem: Swiętosław Igorewicz i Leon Diakon," in *Człowiek w społeczeństwie średniowiecznym* (Warsaw, 1997), pp. 341–46.

29. Kalokyros, a member of Kherson's nobility, was evidently a trusted person of Emperor Nikēphoros Phokas, and in 970–971, of his brother Leo and nephew Bardas, while they kept struggling for power against Tzimiskes. What wonder, then, that Kherson's magnates sided with the same Bardas Phokas seventeen years later? Obolensky,"Byzantium, Kiev and Cherson in the Tenth Century," p. 255, is right in understanding that it is "hard to believe that the Byzantine government, which attached the highest importance to its Crimean possessions, and had struggled for centuries to prevent neighboring peoples from interfering in the affairs of Kherson, should have conceded by treaty this right of interference to the ruler of a people that had shown itself four times in the past seventy-five years a determined enemy of the empire." Such reservations could have their place in the context of traditional interpretations of the Khersonian campaign; it bears remembering that "for centuries" the emperors had problems with the rebelliously inclined Kherson and that in the past seventy-five years, Constantinople, without any pressure to protect the Byzantine Crimean possession in terms of the treaties of 944 and 971, entitled this "determined enemy" to interventions (to stop the Black Bulgars from raiding Kherson) in order to provide direct military assistance, and practically made the Rus′ occasional allies (*symmachoi*) of the empire. I refer here to F. Wozniak's opinion which is very close to Obolensky's view and who did not know my 1976 published interpretation of those treaties (Poppe, "The Political Background to the Baptism of Rus′," p. 239 and nn. 144 and 145). I am already taking into account Obolensky's reservations—pertaining to the withdrawing of linguistic amendments to the 944 treaty and to remain explicit— (see "Cherson and Conversion of Rus′: An Anti-Revisionist view," pp. 247 and 254): "By the terms of the treaty of 944 the Greeks sought to utilize this naval and military potential of the Russians not only in recruiting them into their army, but also in the protection of Kherson even though the Rus′ themselves potentially threatened this city." See Frank E. Wozniak, "The Crimean Question, the Black Bulgarians and the Russo-Byzantine Treaty of 944," *Journal of Medieval History* 5(2) 1979: 115–26, especially p. 122. So a 987 allied treaty between Constantinople and Rus′ referring to Kherson was of a traditional nature only under totally different circumstances. Not the Byzantine government, but personally Basil and the Macedonian dynasty were in grave danger, and Anna, as the wife of the Rus′ ruler, could help her brother and assure the constancy of the close alliance.

30. A. Poppe, "How the Conversion of Rus' Was Understood in the Eleventh Century," *Harvard Ukrainian Studies* 11(3/4) 1987: 287–302.

31. Constantine Porphyrogenitus, "De Basilio Macedone," in *Theophanes continuatus, Ioannes Cameniat, Symeon Magister, Georgius monachus*, ed. Immanuel Bekker (Bonn, 1838), pp. 342–43. Cf. L. Havlikova, "À propos de la Christianisation de la Russie en IX siècle," *Byzantinoslavica* 54(1) 1993: 102–107. H. Birnbaum, "Christianity before Christianization: Christians and Christian Activity in Pre-988 Rus'," *California Slavic Studies* 16 (1993): 42–62.

32. On the mobilization potential of Rus' and the figures of operational units see Poppe, "The Political Background to the Baptism of Rus'," pp. 228–9. The campaign against Kherson (2,000–3,000 warriors) could be easily simultaneous to the main expedition of about 6,000 soldiers. Obolensky's suggestion ("Cherson and Conversion of Rus': An Anti-Revisionist view," pp. 248–49) that the main military aid was sent by Volodimer to the Bosphorus already in the fall of 987, can be accepted. But we must remember that the first battle (Chrysopolis) they engaged in happened by the turn of January 989, and indirectly their presence on the Bosphorus comes to light in the summer of 988. For detailed arguments on the dating of the Chrysopolis battle, see my "The Political Background to the Baptism of Rus'," pp. 235–38. M. Kotliar (*Zaprovadzhennia khrystianstva na Rusi* [Kyiv, 1988], p. 68) questions my way of dating events, deferring to the authority of V. Vasil'evskii. But it was precisely Vasil'evskii's suggestion (his *Trudy*, vol. 1 [St. Petersburg, 1908], p. 197n. 2) that prompted me to collect evidence for the correctness of such dating.

33. For travel conditions and time, see D. Obolensky's commentary on the *De administrando imperio* reprinted in his *Byzantium and the Slavs: Collected Studies* (London, 1971), pp. 31–32, 37–40, 48, 54–55, and A. Poppe, "La dernière expédition russe contre Constantinopole," *Byzantioslavica* 32(2) 1971: 239–45, 249.

34 Matchmaking and various procedures, as well as the preparation of wedding ceremony documents for *filiae sancti imperii*, must have been similar to the ones we know from the agreement between Tzimiskes with Otto I regarding the marriage of Otto II and Theophanō. But the Byzantine side must have been more active due to its experience and requirements. See W. Ohnsorge, "Die Heirat Kaiser Ottos II mit der Byzantinerin Theophano (972)," *Braunschweigisches Jahrbuch* 54 (1973): 35–37; W. Georgi, "Ottonianum und Heiratsurkunde 962/972," in *Kaiserin Theophanu. Begegnung des Ostens und Westens um die Wende des ersten Jahrtausends*, vol. 2 (Cologne, 1991), pp. 148–54.

35. *Liutprandi Legatio*, chap. 15 in E. Dümmler, ed., *Liutprandi episcopi Cremonensis opera omnia* (Hannover, 1987), p. 133.

36. Michael Psellus [Psellos], *Chronographie; ou, Histoire d'un siècle de Byzance (976–1077)*, ed. and trans. E. Renauld, vol. 1 (Paris, 1926), pp. 18–19 (libs. 1, 10, 13).

37. Constantine Porphyrogenitus, *De administrando imperio*: 73, chap. 13.
38. See n. 28.
39. See G. Ostrogorsky, "The Byzantine Emperor and the Hierarchical World Order," *The Slavonic and East European Review* 35(84) December 1956: 5–14; T. Wasilewski, "La place de l'État russe dans le monde Byzantine pendant le haut Moyen-Age," *Acta Poloniae Historica* 22 (1970): 43–51.
40. See n. 34.
41. For a more detailed discussion, see Poppe, "The Political Background to the Baptism of Rus'," pp. 232–35.
42. *Leonis Diaconi Caloensis,* p. 149; cf. M. Ia. Siuziumov, "Lev Diakon i iego vremia," in G. Litavrin, ed., *Lev Diakon. Istoriia* (Moscow, 1988), pp. 137–65.
43. See J. A. Cramer, comp., *Anecdota graeca e codd. manuscriptis Bibliothecae regiae parisienses*, vol. 4 (Oxford, 1841), pp. 271, cf. 282–83, 322–25, 341–42; Vasil'evskii, *Trudy*, vol. 2, pp. 112–23; F. Scheideweiler, "Studien zu Johannes Geometres," *Byzantinische Zeitschrift* (1952): 300–19.
44. Scylitzes, *Synopsis historiarum*, p. 282; cf. Vasil'evskii, *Trudy*, vol. 2, pp. 114–15; Scheidweiler, "Studien zu Johannes Geometres," pp. 307–309. This poem is preserved in Skylitzes' chronicle where he says that the poem's author is John, the metropolitan of Melitene. The latter has usually been identified as John Geometres. On dating and attribution, see A. Poppe, "The Political Background to the Baptism of Rus'," pp. 215–17. For different opinions of contemporaries on Nikēphoros Phokas, see A. Markopoulos, "Zu den Biographien des Nicephorus Phocas," *Jahrbuch der Österreichischen Byzantinistik* 38 (1988): 225–33, R. Morris, "The Two Faces of Nikephoros Phokas," *Byzantine and Modern Greek Studies* 12 (1988): 83–115.
45. In T. Preger, ed., *Scriptores originum Constantinopolitanarum*, vol. 2 (Leipzig, 1907), p. 176; A. Berger, *Untersuchungen zu der Patria Konstantinopoleos* (Bonn, 1988), pp.187–93, 323–24.
46. C. Diehl, "De quelques croyances byzantines sur la fin de Constantinople," *Byzantinische Zeitschrift* 30 (1930): 194–95. For a new look at state of mind, religiosity, and human activities while expecting Judgment Day, see J. Fried, "Endzeiterwartung um die Jahrtausendwende," *Deutsches Archiv für Erforschung des Mittelalters* 45 (1989): 381–473.
47. But in 995 Basil II, with the participation of Rus' troops, expelled the Fatimid army from Syria. See A. Hamdani, "Byzantine-Fatimid Relations Before the Battle of Mantzikert," *Byzantine Studies* 1(1) 1974: 200–209.

48. And the unheard-of thing happened: a *porphyrogennēta* became the wife of a barbarian ruler. Was she forced to go to Kyiv, as the traditional historiography tells us, in order to save the imperial city from an attack by Rus′? It could have been that way, but it was not. A twenty-six-year-old young woman went to Kyiv; she was raised in a palace and well-educated. She went there because she was flexible, knew methods of ruling, and also because she felt responsible for her new domain and the success of its conversion. It suffices to take a look at her mother Theophanō, her nieces who later became empresses—Theodora and Zoe—as well as the German empress, the Greek Theophanō, to realize that Anna was an intellectually mature woman, and well aware of the role she had to play: *filia sancti imperii,* married to the newly converted Volodimer. As a Christian, she must have liked the idea of spreading the new religion, which she did through building new churches, as we know thanks to Yaḥyā. She may have been afraid of the severe climate and heathen customs, but at least she knew the language: as a girl, she was frequently in the company of Bulgarian princes and princesses of her age, who were related to her and who lived for a few years in the imperial palace. Thus, the Slavic vernacular was not alien to her. It may have been for this reason that she was called a Bulgarian in Kyiv. Political and religious roles were also known to her. The emperor could rely upon his sister and help her spread the new faith. For details on Anna and her political role, see A. Poppe, "Der Kampf um die Kiever Thronfolge nach dem 15. Juli 1015," *Forschungen zur osteuropäischen Geschichte* 50 (1995): 275–95. Anna's recognized activities in Rus′ have also been examined by F. Kämpfer, "Eine Residenz für Anne Porphyrogenneta,"*Jahrbücher für Geschichte Osteuropas* 41 (1993): 101–10.

49. According to Ponomarev and Serikov ("989 [6496] god—god kreshcheniia Rusi," pp. 171, 181) it was not Halley's comet but an ordinary one that was seen on 17 July 987, so there are grounds to consider that the comet which was seen in Asia Minor on 27 July 989 was another one.

50. It was not until the end of the eleventh century that native Khersonian coins were produced again, but on a smaller scale. See I. V. Sokolova, *Monety i pechati vizantiiskogo Khersona* (Leningrad, 1983), pp. 52–63, 116–17.

51. The interpretation on dating of archaeological excavations leaves much to be desired. In the 1980s (A. Romanchuk) a trend began toward the revision of earlier results (A. L. Jakobson and his school) about the decline of Kherson after 989. The traces of ruin and fire are no longer adduced in connection with Volodimer's action. But it is out of the question that "some parts of the city were destroyed and burned, but the causes are unknown." The new proposition that "it happened sometime in the eleventh century" lacks clear arguments. See N. M. Bogdanova, "Kherson v X–XV vv. Problemy istorii vizantiiskogo goroda," in

Prichernomor'e v srednie veka, vol. 1 (Moscow, 1991), pp. 92–94, 134n89, 145–46. The style of revision arouses suspicions that the archaeological dating has no stable, fixed criterion and demonstrates too extensive an adaptability. Some could think that it is improper to portray Kherson—a place of the baptism of Volodimer and his wedding with the *basilissa* Anna—as a destroyed city.

52. Aleksandr Zimin, ed., "Pamiat' i pokhvala Iakova Mnikha i Zhitie kniazia Vladimira po drevneishemu spisku," p. 72; *The Hagiography of Kievan Rus'*, p. 175, but here there is an error in translation: reference is made to "eight years" and "ten years," where instead it should be "in the eighth year" and "in the tenth year."

53. It is usually supposed that the dates as given in the *Memorial's* annalistic records are in the March style (the standard used in eleventh century Rus'), but dating with the Byzantine (September) year cannot be excluded. Ponomarev and Serikov ("989 [6496] god–god kreshcheniia Rusi," pp. 163–65) made the right critical remarks about the interpretation on *Memorial's* dates by O. M. Rapov, but that cannot be the reason to dismiss this tradition itself, since it has other sequences not supporting their suggestion that Kherson was taken by Volodimer before his baptism (ibid., p. 182).

54. See M. Arranz, "Catecumenado y bautismo en tiempos de Volodymyr," *Orientalia Christiana Periodica* 54 (2) 1988: 277–308; and the Russian version, "Chin oglasheniia i khreshcheniia v drenei Rusi," *Simvol* 19 (1988): 69–100. The ritual of catechumenate and the sacrament of baptism, based mainly on the Byzantine *Euchologion*, has been thoroughly presented by M. Arranz in *Orientalia Christiana Periodica* 49 (1983): 42–90, 284–302; 50 (1984): 43–64, 372–97; 51 (1985): 60–85; 52 (1986): 145–78; 53 (1987): 59–106. S. Senyk's doubts (*A History of the Church in Ukraine*, p. 67) concerning M. Arranz's and my own attempt for reconstruction of Volodimer's baptism have remained unfounded. I did not claim that Volodimer's baptism had two parts to it because the selection of the name on 1 January belonged to the final part of the catechumenate. The choice of the name must have been made before its conferment during the the baptism itself, which Senyk should have known. Her claim that any other day would have been equally good for Volodimer's baptism shows that she does not know the history of the baptism and the close connection between Theophania and the theological meaning of this sacrament, so important in the case of a ruler's baptism.

55. On the imperial patronage, see A. Angenendt, *Kaiserherrschaft und Königstaufe: Kaiser, Könige und Päpste als geistliche Patrone in der abendländischen Missionsgeschichte* (Berlin, 1984), pp. 5–11, 91–105, 295–96. E. Patlagean, "Christianisation et parentés rituelles: Le Domaine de Byzance," *Annales* 3 (1978): 625–36; R. Macrides, "The Byzantine Godfather," *Byzantine and Modern Greek Studies* 11 (1987): 139–62.

56. Cf. *Polnoe sobranie russkikh letopisei* (hereafter, *PSRL*), 2nd ed. vol. 1 (*Lavrent'evskaia letopis′*) (Leningrad, 1926–1928), pp. 340–41.

57. The author of the jubilee "debut" was so impressed by the rebuff Otto I experienced when he tried to secure a "*porphorogenita*" for his son's wife that he excluded the possibility of Basil II's breaking of the matrimonial doctrine. The same author also deemed the idea that Volodimer conquered rebellious Kherson at the emperor's wish as impossible (W. Seibt, "Der historische Hintergrund und die Chronologie der Taufe der Ruś (989)," pp. 297–99). Therefore, he did not notice that the "unheard-of thing" became a fact after twenty years. Also, if it is assumed that Basil was forced to give his sister away in order to regain Kherson, why would it have been absurd for the emperor to arrange his sister's marriage in order to save much more, that is, his throne and life?

58. *Russian Primary Chronicle,* p. 116.

59. A. M. Moldovan, ed., *Slovo o zakone i blagodati Ilariona* (Kyiv, 1984), p. 93; cf. Simon Franklin, trans., *Sermons and Rhetoric of Kievan Rus'* (Cambridge, MA, 1991), p. 19. Hilarion expressed here, shortly before Bruno of Querfurt, the acceptability to conduct the conversion of people under pressure, according to the evangelical principle *compellere intrare* 'compel them to enter in' (Luke 13:23).

60. *PSRL*, vol. 1, p. 117.

61. On Volodimer as he is portrayed in literary and oral tradition, see Hrushevsky, *History of Ukraine-Rus′,* vol. 1, pp. 407–409, 447–49.

62. Moldovan, ed., *Slovo o zakone i blagodati Ilariona*, pp. 92, 95; *Sermons and Rhetoric of Kievan Rus'*, pp. 18, 20; *Russian Primary Chronicle*, p. 137.

63. See Bruno of Querfurt's letter to King Henry II (as edited by J. Karwasińska), in *Monumenta Poloniae Historica* n.s., vol. 4 fasc. 3 (Warsaw, 1973), pp. 101–102.

64. A. Poppe, "Kompozycja fundacyjna Sofii Kijowskiej," *Biuletyn Historii Sztuki* 30(1) 1968: 1–29; F. Kämpfer, *Das Russische Herrscherbild von den Anfängen bis zu Peter dem Grossen* (Recklinghausen, 1978), pp. 78ff.

65. See Poppe, "Der Kampf um die Kiever Thronfolge nach dem 15. Juli 1015," pp. 275–96.

66. *Russian Primary Chronicle*, pp. 129–30. See A. Poppe, "O zarozhdenii kul′ta svv. Borisa i Gleba i o posviashchennykh im proizvedeniiakh," *Russia mediaevalis* 8(1) 1995: 21–68.

67. A. Poppe, "Two Concepts of the Conversion of the Rus′ in Kievan Writings," *Harvard Ukrainian Studies* 12/13 (1988/89): 488–504. On the Rus′ legend of the Apostle Andrew, see Podskalsky, *Khristianstvo i bogoslovskaia literatura*, pp. 17–20.

68. Podskalsky, *Khristianstvo i bogoslovskaia literatura*, pp. 94–107; V. Vavřínek, "The Introduction of the Slavonic Liturgy and the Byzantine Missionary Policy," in *Beiträge zur byzantinischen Geschichte im 9.-11. Jh.* (Prague, 1978), pp. 255–81; G. A. Khaburgaev, *Pervye stoletiia slavianskoi pis'mennoi kul'tury. Istoki drevnerusskoi knizhnosti* (Moscow, 1994), pp. 12–18, 80–113, 155–65.

69. According to a widespread opinion, Basil II had an aversion toward culture and intellectuals and focused only on military affairs. Based on that, I stated in my earlier works that the emperor had been interested mainly in a lasting military alliance with Rus′, while he treated other relations as more or less necessary accessories. However, in light of Barbara Crostini's studies, I have to change my view. Not only does she show Basil's broad interests and deep religiosity, but also his role in inspiring cultural and spiritual life which was rapidly developing in the eleventh century. See B. Crostini, "The Emperor Basil II's Cultural Life," *Byzantion* 66(1) 1996: 55–80. In light of Crostini's well-documented arguments, it could be concluded that the emperor had great understanding for his sister's project of Christianization of Rus′ and that he actively helped her and his brother-in-law in their endeavors. Such a view becomes more plausible if we take into account that the lifestyle of the emperor-warrior was steeped in asceticism and religiosity. He felt personally responsible for the empire and the church also after his life. Therefore, Basil willingly directed northward church accouterments, books taken from the Bulgarian churches, and, last of all, the clergy themselves.

70. Cf. A. Poppe, "How the Conversion of Rus′ Was Understood in the Eleventh Century," pp. 287–95; for a discussion of the shortsightedness of political and cultural activity in the tenth century, see H. G. Beck, *Das Byzantinische Jahrtausend* (Munich, 1978), pp. 297–303. It seems relevant to quote, in the context of Byzantine external activities, the sentence by C. Mango, *Byzantium: The Empire of New Rome* (London, 1988), p. 55: "The Byzantines were content to sit at home and wait for foreign traders to come to them."

71. See Poppe, "Two Concepts of the Conversion of the Rus′ in Kievan Writings," pp. 488–504.

72. Cf. A. Poppe, "Christianity and Ideological Change in Kievan Rus′. The First Hundred Years," *Canadian-American Slavic Studies* 25(1–4) 1991: 3–26; cf. D. Obolensky, "The Byzantine Impact on Eastern Europe," in his *The Byzantine Inheritance of Eastern Europe*, vol. 3 (London, 1982), pp. 148–68; on the prejudices towards the "bloodthirsty barbarians," see H. Ahrweiler, *L'idéologie politique de l'Empire Byzantin* (Paris, 1975), pp. 49–59.

73. For a more detailed discussion, see Poppe, "The Political Background to the Baptism of Rus′," pp. 203–205, and my "The Original Status of the Old Russian Church," *Acta Polonica Historica* 39 (1979): 5–10, both

reprinted as chapters in my book *The Rise of Christian Russia* (London, 1982).

74. Moldovan, ed., *Slovo o zakone i blagodati Ilariona*, pp. 92, 96–98; *Sermons and Rhetoric of Kievan Rus'*, pp. 18, 22–24.

75. I. Kratchkovsky and A. Vasiliev, eds. and trans., "Histoire de Yahya-ibn-Saïd d'Antioche," *Patrologia Orientalis* 23(2) 1932: 423. See the Russian translation in Rozen, *Imperator Vasilii Bolgaroboitsa. Izvlecheniia iz letopisi Iakh"i Antiokhiiskogo*, pp. 23–24.

76. Bruno of Querfert to King Henry II, p. 100. As a missionary archbishop (honored by the pallium), Bruno was able to consecrate the bishop to the Pechenegs himself, but he did not do it during his stay in the steppe. The consecration took place in Kyiv after his return. Also, the fact that Bruno uses the plural form makes it more plausible that a few bishops participated in the consecration; when the author of the letter speaks only about himself, he uses the singular form.

77. *PSRL*, vol. 1, pp. 110, 126. A sentence in *The Primary Chronicle* s.a. 988, "*sanovniki někii i presvitery*," has been misunderstood and mistranslated. As a result, it has been thought that there were no bishops present in Anna's entourage. However, *sanovniki* means one in a position of dignity (*san* = Greek *aksiōma*, Latin *dignitas*) in their midst, a clergyman of the highest order; that is, a bishop regarded equally with lay dignitaries.

78. Moldovan, ed., *Slovo o zakone i blagodati Ilariona*, p. 96; *Sermons and Rhetoric of Kievan Rus'*, p. 23. *PSRL*, vol. 1, p. 189. On Thietmar's 1018 record and the wooden cathedral in Kyiv see A. Poppe, "The Building of the Church of St. Sophia in Kiev," *Journal of Medieval History* 7 (1981): 15–66 (reprinted in *The Rise of Christian Russia*).

79. A recent attempt at evaluation of Greek metropolitans who supervised the church in Rus′ is not very flattering; it basically reiterates the view that has been current over the last hundred years. See Ia. N. Shchapov, *State and Church in Early Russia: Tenth to Thirteenth Centuries* (New Rochelle, NY, 1993), pp. 169–79. Gradually, we have more and more access to data that allow us to form more just opinions. There is complete lack of data about candidates' lives prior to their appearance in Rus′. Nevertheless, the presence of such distinguished Greek personalities as John II Prodromos (1076–1089)—about whom the chronicler says with admiration: "there was no such one in Rus′ before him and there will be none after him" (*PSRL*, vol. 1, p. 208)—among the Kyivan metropolitans did not have to be an exception. Constantine I (1155–1159) was a distinguished theologian and he was sent to Rus′. On the metropolitans, see Podskalsky, *Khristianstvo i bogoslovskaia literatura*, pp. 446–71. The candidacy for Rus′ of Leontios from Strumitsa, the hegumen (abbot) of Patmos monastery, (shortly afterwards appointed Patriarch of Jerusalem in 1176), who was recommended by Emperor Manuel I Komnenos, proves that Constantinople saw a need for sending exceptionally quali-

fied church dignitaries to Rus′ (a study is in preparation); see also G. Podskalsky, "Der Beitrag der griechischstämmigen Metropoliten (Kiev) Bischöfe und Mönche zur altrussichen Originalliteratur (Theologie)," *Cahiers du monde russe et soviétique* 24 (1983): 498–513. S. Franklin, "Greek in Kievan Rus′," *Dumbarton Oaks Papers* 46 (1992): 69–81.

80. The order in which the dioceses are positioned determines their rank. The oldest list of dioceses in Rus′, recorded around 1162, has been preserved as part of *Notitia episcopatuum* (*Codex Athen.* no. 1371), which was compiled around 1170. Hence the bishop of Belgorod is listed as the first *protōthronos* of the Kyivan metropolitan, although this dignity was taken over by Novgorod in 1165. See J. Darrouzès, *Notitiae Episcopatuum Ecclesiae Constantinopolitanae* (Paris, 1981), p. 367; Podskalsky, *Khristianstvo i bogoslovskaia literatura,* p. 458; for information and bibliography concerning dioceses, see ibid., pp. 52–60. For a detailed study of the diocesan structure of Rus′ in the eleventh-thirteenth centuries, see. A. Poppe, "L'organisation diocésaine de la Russie aux Xe–XIIe siècles," *Byzantion* 40(1) 1970: 165–217 (reprinted in *The Rise of Christian Russia*); and my "Werdegang der Diözesanstruktur der Kiever Metropolitankirche in den ersten drei Jahrhunderten der Christianisierung der Ostslaven" in *Tausend Jahre Christentum in Russland* (Göttingen, 1988), pp. 251–90.

81. For the theological sense of a Greek inscription on a mosaic in a conch of the Kyivan cathedral and its connection with the idea of the Holy Wisdom, see. S. S. Averintsev, "K vyiasneniiu smysla nadpisi nad konkhoi tsentral′noi apsidy Sofii Kievskoi," in *Drevnerusskoe iskusstvo. Khudozhestvennaia kul'tura domongol'skoi Rusi* (Moscow, 1972), pp. 25–49; K. K. Akent′ev, "K proiasneniiu smysla nadpisi nad konchoi sv. Sofii Kievskoi," in *Vizantiiskoe iskusstvo i liturgiia: novye otkrytiia: kratkie tezisy dokladov nauchnoi konferentsii, posviashchennoi pamiati A.V. Bank (11–12 aprelia 1990 g.)* (Leningrad, 1991), pp. 16–19; K. K. Akent′ev, "Mozaiki Kievskoi sv. Sofii i 'Slovo' mitropolita Ilariona v vizantiiskom liturgicheskom kontekste,"*Vizantinorossica*, vol. 1 (St. Petersburg, 1995), pp. 75–94.

82. Those tendences, widely known in every religion, were and are, in a very exaggerated way, imputed to the East Slavs under the magically untranslated definition of *dvoeverie* and discussed as a specifically Slavic occurrence. Cf. the apt remarks of V. M. Zhivov, "Dvoeverie i osobyi kharakter russkoi kul′turnoi istorii," in *Philologia Slavica* [a collection of essays to honor N. I. Tolstoi] (Moscow, 1993), pp. 50–59; it should also be remembered that some discoveries of "pagan relics" in pieces of Christian art must be connected with a noble desire to save them at a time when they were in danger of being eliminated or destroyed. Some Western Slavists took these vestiges very seriously.

83. Moldovan, ed., *Slovo o zakone i blagodati Ilariona*, p. 93; *Sermons and Rhetoric of Kievan Rus'*, p. 19.

84. Scylitzes, *Synopsis historiarum,* p. 355; cf. A. Dain, "Le partage du butin de guerre d'après les traités juridiques et militaires," in *Actes du VIe Congrès International d'Études Byzantines* (Paris, 1950), pp. 347–54. While the numerical force of the Byzantine army operating in Bulgaria was ca. 14,000, the number of Rus′ warriors can be estimated at approximately half this number, since a third of the booty belonged to the emperor's fisk and a third was given to the domestic troops.

85. See D. Freydank, "Byzantinische und bulgarische Tradition in der altrussischen Literatur," in *Byzanz in der europäischen Staatenwelt* (Berlin, 1983), pp. 127–33. Francis J. Thomson, "The Bulgarian Contribution to the Reception of Byzantine Culture in Kievan Rus′: The Myths and the Enigma," *Harvard Ukrainian Studies* 12/13 (1988–1989): 214–61. For a survey of writings in translation, mainly of Bulgarian origin, see Podskalsky, *Khristianstvo i bogoslovskaia literatura,* pp. 95–127. Khaburgaev, (*Pervye stoletiia slavianskoi pis'mennoi kul'tury*, p. 163). explains the appearance of old Bulgarian texts in Rus′ in an original but puzzling way. According to him, many Slavic books written in Cyrillic appeared in Byzantine monasteries during lively Byzantine-Bulgarian relations in the second quarter of the tenth century during Tsar Peter's reign. Beginning with the end of the tenth century, they were gradually sent to Rus′. Such splendid manuscripts of the Preslav school as Tsar Symeon's codex, copied in Kyiv as Prince Sviatoslav's miscellany in 1073, or Ostromir's *Gospel* of 1057, copied (in Novgorod) from the *Macedonian Book of Gospels* that belonged to Tsar Samuel, could have appeared in Rus′, only as trophies. But the codex was not booty from Sviatoslav's 971 expedition, as its editors claim, repeating an outdated opinion. Cf. P. Dinekov, ed., *Simeonov Sbornik (po Svetoslavoviia prepis ot 1073 g.*), vol. 1 (Sofia, 1991), p. 97.

86. This phenomenon was widespread; cf. A. T. Lucas, "The Plundering and Burning of Churches in Ireland. Seventh to sixteenth century" in E. Rynne, ed., *North Munster Studies* (Limerick, 1967), pp. 172–229. As early as 1063, Prince Vseslav of Polatsk took advantage of this rule when he pillaged St. Sophia Cathedral in Novgorod in order to benefit his own cathedral in Polatsk, for which he was competing at the time. Under the year 1202 the Kyivan chronicler recorded that much evil was done in Rus′ of the kind—plundering, burning of churches, and conquest—Kyiv had not experienced since its baptism. (*PSRL*, vol. 1, p. 418). So it seems that in 1169 the plundering of Kyiv and the taking of icons, church books, and other articles from its churches by the troops of Prince Andrei Bogoliubsky of Suzdal-Vladimir (*PSRL*, vol. 1, p. 354) was not all that harmful, although in the historical perspective it turned out to be a political turning away of Rus′ "beyond the forests" from Kyiv. Cf. J. Pelenski, "The Sack of Kiev of 1169: Its Significance for the Succession to Kievan Rus′," *Harvard Ukrainian Studies* 11(3/4) 1989: 303–16.

87. Cf. A. Gieysztor, "Mouvements para-heretiques en Europe centrale et orientale du IXe au XIe siècle: Apostasies," in *Heresies et sociétés dans l'Europe pre-industrielle, XIe–XVIIIe siècles* (Paris, 1968), pp.159–67.

I. Ia. Froianov, *Drevniaia Rus'. Opyt issledovaniia istorii sotsial'noi i politicheskoi bor'by* (Moscow, 1995), pp. 160ff. See also the additional commentary by M. B. Sverdlov in *Povest' Vremennykh Let* (St. Petersburg, 1996), 2nd edition, pp. 623, 629–30.

88. Moldovan, ed., *Slovo o zakone i blagodati Ilariona*, p. 100.

89. *Pamiatniki drevnerusskogo kanonicheskogo prava* (St. Petersburg, 1880), part 1 (no.1), p. 30. Cf. Shchapov, *State and Church in Early Russia*, pp. 121–27. But we have to remember that John II wrote on the basis of Byzantine experiences, while in Western Europe in the eleventh century the church wedding was still not practiced by the majority of the population, which was, after all, Christian.

90. Poppe, "Der Kampf um die Kiever Thronfolge," pp. 275–95.

91. Poppe, "O zarozhdenii kul'ta svv. Borisa i Gleba," pp. 45–56, 66–68. See also a suggestion on the dating of the origins of the cult to the 1030s in L. Müller, "O vremeni kanonizatsii sviatykh Borisa i Gleba," *Russia Medievalis* 8(1) 1995: 5–20.

92. *PSRL*, vol. 1, pp. 155, 167, 172, 193, 274, 281, 283;

93. Thietmar, Bishop of Merseburg, *Chronik,* trans. with commentary by Werner Trillmich (Darmstadt, 1957), pp. 530–31, VIII, 32; *PSRL*, vol. 1, 293.

94. Adam of Bremen, "Magistri Adami Bremensis Gesta Hammaburgensis ecclesiae pontificium," in *Quellen des 9. und 11. Jahrhunderts zur Geschichte der hamburgischen Kirche und des Reiches* (Berlin, 1961), p. 226, II, 22 [=*Ausgewählte Quellen zur Deutschen Geschichte des Mittelalters*, vol. 11]; In the English translation by Francis J. Tschan (*History of the Archbishops of Hamburg-Bremen* [New York, 1959]), it is also wrongly translated as *rival.*

95. See P. A. Rappoport, *Building the Churches of Kievan Russia* (Brookfield, VT, 1995), pp. 313–41.

96. In the eleventh century, especially with the Mount Athos and Stoudios monasteries. An attempt to question the connections between the Kyivan Caves Monastery and Mount Athos, especially the statement that the Holy Mountain (*Hagion Oros*) is absent in the accounts of the origin of the Caves Monastery around the middle of the eleventh century, is flawed because of the monosemantic evidence of *The Primary Chronicle* and the *Life of Theodosii of the Caves*. On the other hand, the role of St. Anthony of the Caves and of the Rus' monastery at Athos, especially in the eleventh–thirteenth centuries, must be seriously discussed with Francis J. Thomson; see his "Saint Anthony of Kiev—the Fact and the Fiction: the Legend of the Blessing of Athos Upon Early Russian Monasticism," *Byzantinoslavica* 56 (1995): 637–68; cf. the helplessness of S. Franklin in dealing with Thomson's overskepticism in *The Emergence of Rus' 750–1200*, pp. 303–305, 308. My own polemics on the subject are being prepared for publication.

97. For pertinent literature, see Podskalsky, *Khristianstvo i bogoslovskaia literatura*, pp. 84–93, 207–14. The best monograph on the monastery is still L. Goetz, *Das Kiever Höhlenkloster als Kulturzentrum des vormongolischen Russlands* (Passau, 1904). See also the English translation of the Caves Paterikon by M. Heppell, *The* Paterik *of the Kievan Caves Monastery* (Cambridge, MA, 1989) and the English translation by P. Hollingsworth of "The Life of Our Venerable Father Feodosij, Superior of the Caves Monastery," in *The Hagiography of Kievan Rus'*, pp. 33–95. Cf. also F. von Lilenfeld, "The Spirituality of the Early Kievan Caves Monastery," in *Christianity and the Eastern Slavs* (Berkeley, 1993), pp. 63–76.

98. Cf. A. Poppe, "Christianity and Ideological Change in Kievan Rus′: The First Hundred Years."

99. Podskalsky, *Khristianstvo i bogoslovskaia literatura,* pp. 49–50, 148–55, 449–50; cf. N. N. Rozov, "Ilarion," in D. S. Likhachev, ed., *Slovar' knizhnikov i knizhnosti Drevnei Rusi,* vol. 1: *XI–pervaia polovina XIV v.* (Leningrad, 1987), pp. 198–204.

100. On Iaroslav, his sons Volodimer in Novogorod, Sviatoslav in Chernihiv/Kyiv and Volodimer Monomakh, see A. Poppe, "Książki, skryptoria i biblioteki na Rusi," in *Słownik Starożytności Słowiańskich*, vol. 2 (Wrocław, 1965), pp. 544–48; idem, "Dans la Russie médiévale X–XIIIe siècles. Écriture et culture," *Annales* 1 (1961): 12–35. This instant education could be connected rather with the palatial manners brought by Anna. Her granddaughter Anna, queen-widow of France, wanted surely to impress her courtly circle by personally signing in Cyrillic letters one of the documents in 1063, thereby going against the custom. Cf. G. Shevelov, *In and Around Kiev* (Heidelberg, 1991), pp. 44–51. *

101. The formation of Rus′ historiography (which was obviously Christian in approach as well as in the choice of themes) in the eleventh century and the compilation of the framework, the *Primary Chronicle* itself at the beginning of the twelfth century, are still disputed and many questions are still as open now as they were at the beginning of the twentieth century. Cf. the English translation, M. Hrushevsky, *History of Ukraine-Rus′*, vol. 1, pp. 450–71; Podskalsky, *Khristianstvo i bogoslovskaia literatura*, pp. 330–75; for a useful characterization of the *Primary Chronicle* in English, see Franklin and Shepard, *The Emergence of Rus′ 750–1200*, pp. 317–19. A setback in the studies on the oldest chronicle-writing was the necessity to defend research work from the pre-Soviet era, especially those by A. A. Shakhmatov. A good example of countering the growth of ignorance is Ia. A. Lur′e's astute critique of A. G. Kuz′min's guesswork, addressed to a wider audience. The "canonization" of Tatishchev's history from the eighteenth century as a treasury of lost information from the Middle Ages created a serious confusion. Also, attempts at "revealing" ever older chronicles, supposedly existing as early as the eleventh or even tenth century, played a negative role.

* See the Postscript on p. 392

102. See A. Poppe, "Le prince et l'Église en Russie de Kiev depuis la fin du Xe s. jusqu'au debut du XIIe s.," *Acta Poloniae Historica* 20 (1969): 95–119 (reprinted in *The Rise of Christian Russia*). Podskalsky, *Khristianstvo i bogoslovskaia literatura,* pp. 61–71, 244–47, 508–509, 511; I. S. Chichurov, *Politicheskaia ideologiia srednevekoviia: Vizantiia i Rus′* (Moscow, 1990), pp. 127–53. It is a misconception to say that Rus′ princes were not God-anointed. Certainly, they were not anointed with oil mixed with balsam in the presence of the church, but they were anointed by God in the same sense that Byzantine emperors were. The act of anointing was not a material one, which was so important for rulers from Latin culture, but it was a spiritual, invisible, and imperceptible act taking place directly between the celestial emperor and the terrestial one. Therefore, in the Byzantine refined and subtle understanding of these matters, there was no place for and no necessity of mediation by the church's hierarchy. Byzantine writers often call emperors "the anointed ones" but it is obvious that they give this expression a higher, figurative sense. It was only in the thirteenth century that this act came into being and evolved into a "real anointment," following the Western example. See G. Ostrogorsky, *Zur byzantinischen Geschichte* (Darmstadt, 1973), pp. 142–52; cf. J. L. Nelson, "Symbols in Context: Rulers' Inauguration Rituals in Byzantium and the West in the Early Middle Ages," in her *Politics and Ritual in Early Medieval Europe* (London, 1986), pp. 259–81. When inheriting the throne was at stake in Byzantium, the successor (usually the emperor's son) was considered as anointed "in his mother's womb." That is why in the Rus′ dynasty all of the Rurikids were jointly considered as anointed by God. The metropolitan wrote to Volodimer Monomakh "by God . . . in womb consecrated and anointed." See N. V. Ponyrko, *Epistoliarnoe nasledie Drevnei Rusi XI–XIII v. Issledovaniia, teksty, perevody* (St. Petersburg, 1992), p. 67; cf. also 56 (another letter). But what is even more important, the princes themselves were aware that they were the Lord's anointed. When the same Monomakh writes a letter to his German cousin Oleg in 1096 and summons him to make peace, he quotes "by God anointed David" as an example to follow (ibid., p. 45). Finally, we have to point out the ceremony of enthronement of Prince Konstantin, son of Vsevolod, in the St. Sophia Cathedral in Novgorod, which took place on 20 March 1205. During the ceremony, the newly enthroned prince was lauded with the words of the Bible: "God anointed thee, thine God" (*PSRL*, vol. 1, p. 423). Therefore, if a researcher states that it is unfounded to refer to the Rurikids as anointed by God, it obliges a medievalist to work on this topic. A study of the ceremony of enthronement of princes in Rus′, as well as their anointment by God, is in preparation.

103. See E. Malamut, "L'image byzantine des Petchenegues," *Byzantinische Zeitschrift* 88 (1995): 105–47, especially pp. 115–32. A. P. Kazhdan, "Once More About the 'Alleged' Russo-Byzantine Treaty (ca. 1047) and the Pecheneg Crossing of the Danube," *Jahrbuch der Österreichischen Byzantinistik* 26 (1976): 65–77; cf. L. S. Chekin, "The Godless

Ishmaelites: The Image of the Steppe in Eleventh–Thirteenth-Century Rus′," *Russian History* 19(1–4) 1992: 9–28.

104. A. Poppe, "Uwagi o najstarszych dziejach Kościoła na Rusi, cz. 2 i 3," *Przegląd Historyczny* 55 (1964): 557–72; 56 (1965): 557–59; Poppe, "Titularmetropolien im 11. Jh. Ruś," in *Das heidnische und christliche Slaventum* (Wiesbaden, 1970), pp. 64–75. Cf. Shchapov, *State and Church in Early Russia*, pp. 56–62. Since then, the thesis about the existence of two ephemeral metropolitan sees has gained a more solid foundation. Among the newly published lists of metropolitan seats, there is Pereiaslav (*hē Rhōsia Presthlába*), known to us in this role up to now only from Rus′ sources. It makes it more plausible to identify the metropolitanate of Maurokastron as Chernihiv (*Nea Rhōsia*), known to us from a similar list. See *Notitiae episcopatuum Ecclesiae Constantinopolitanae,* pp. 124–25, 344, 350, 382.

105. Cf. M. Hrushevs′kyi, *Istoriia Ukraïny-Rusi*, vol. 2 (Lviv, 1905; reprint, New York, 1954), pp. 51–60; A. Presniakov, *Kniazhoe pravo v Drevnei Rusi* (St. Petersburg, 1909; reprint, Moscow 1993), pp. 42–47; A. V. Nazarenko, "Rodovoi siuzerenitet Riurikovichei nad Rus′iu," in *Drevneishie gosudarstva na territorii SSSR* (Moscow, 1986), pp. 146–57.

106. *Pamiatniki drevnerusskogo kanonicheskogo prava*, pp. 31 and 32. On the seal belonging to John, the metropolitan of *pasēs Rhōsias* which has been ascribed to John II (1077–1089), the addendum "all" could have been caused by these concerns. See A. Soloviev, *Byzance et la formation de l'État russe* (London, 1979) IXa and IXb, pp. 294, 317–19. But according to V. L. Ianin this attribution is not certain; it could be dated almost a hundred years later to John IV.

107. Maurokastron is mentioned in only one notitia (the manuscript *Coislinianus*, 211), where this metropolitanate is listed after Basileion (founded in 1059–1071) and before Nazianzos (founded in 1068–1071). That means that the advance of Neofit to the rank of titular metropolitan of Chernihiv must have happened in the 1060s. See n. 105 above. During the ceremonies at Vyshhorod on 20 May 1072, the metropolitan of Chernihiv, Neofit, is listed second, according to the hierarchy of ranks, just after the metropolitan of Kyiv, George. Cf. *The Hagiography of Kievan Rus'*, pp. 122–23. This text from the *Tale of the Miracles* (about the events of 20 May 1072) is original in relation to the Primary Chronicle for the year 1072 (*PSRL*, vol. 1, pp. 181–82); cf. *The Hagiography of Kievan Rus'*, pp. 200–201.

108. *Notitiae episcopatuum Ecclesiae Constantinopolitanae* (Paris, 1981), pp. 344, 350, 382 (*Notitiae*: 11; 12; 15 in the sequence of 78, 80 or 81 positions). Pereiaslav was mentioned as a metropolitanate in six manuscripts. See *Notitiae episcopatuum Ecclesiae Constantinopolitanae*, p. 382. It is always listed between Rhusion and Lakedaimon—metropolitan sees that had been founded closer to 1080. However, we know that the titular metropolitanate of Pereiaslav had already existed in the 1060s.

An ephemeral titular metropolitan see did not occupy a constant position in the *ordo thronorum,* but was put on the list when a given bishop was given this honorary title and was crossed out after his death. The notitia which preserved the metropolitanate of Pereiaslav reflects the conferment of this title on Ephrem, which took place between 1073 and 1078. Because Attalea is mentioned last (founded 1084), the notitia must have been edited around 1085, which would explain why Maurokastron-Chernihiv is absent from the list. It was recorded after the titular metropolitan. Neofit had died, and his successor was an ordinary bishop. That is the reason why we know more precisely the time of the editing of the list from the manuscript *Coislinianus,* 211: it was compiled after the death of the metropolitan of Pereiaslav, Leo, but before the nomination of Ephrem—that is, at a time when Peter was the bishop of Pereiaslav (without the honorary title), around 1072.

109. The founding of this diocese took place in the early 1070s, according to M. D. Priselkov, *Ocherki po tserkovno-politicheskoi istorii Kievskoi Rusi X–XII vv.* (St. Petersburg, 1913), pp. 135–40. Shchapov (*State and Church in Early Russia*, pp. 46–48) proposes to ascribe the establishment of the Rostov see to Metropolitan Ephrem of Pereislav, but he has not taken into account that titular metropolitans had no right to found bishoprics and divide their dioceses. For the dating of disorders, see A. Kuchkin, *Formirovanie gosudarstvennoi territorii Severo-Vostochnoi Rusi v X–XIV vv.* (Moscow, 1984), p. 64. According to the Kyivan Caves Paterikon, written in the 1220s, Leo "was the first to occupy the Rostov see, and suffered many torments at the hands of unbelievers; he was the third citizen of the land of Rus′, together with the two Varangians, to be crowned by Christ, for whose sake he suffered" (*The* Paterik *of the Kievan Caves Monastery*, p. 118). But we must remember that since the twelfth century to the begining of the twentieth, the foundation of the Rostov see was generally connected with the baptism of Rus′ at the turn of the tenth century. For this reason Leo is named the "third martyr" (after the two Varangians murdered in 986). Hence Saints Boris and Glěb are not passed over in silence, as some thought, because they were not recognized as martyrs "in Christo."

110. See P. Sokolov, *Ruskii arkhierei iz Vizantii i pravo ego naznacheniia do nachala XV veka* (Kyiv, 1913), pp. 93–158 (still the basic text); Podskalsky, *Khristianstvo i bogoslovskaia literatura,* pp. 77–78; cf. also Pelenski, "The Sack of Kiev of 1169: Its Significance for the Succession to Kievan Rus′," and W. Vodoff, "Remarques sur la politique ecclésiastique d'André de Bogoljubovo," *Cahiers de civilisation médiévale* 17 (1974): 193–215.

111. In the colophon of a Greek psalter from the fourteenth century, a Greek priest, the hieromonk Malakhias, who was the vicar of the Moscow metropolitan in Vladimir-on-Kliazma calls himself *"namestnikos tou Volodimirou."* Cf. E. E. Granstrem, "Chernets Malakhiia filosof," in *Arkheograficheskii ezhegodnik za 1962 g.* (Moscow, 1963), pp. 69–70.

112. The document pertaining to the founding of the bishopric in Smolensk shows the legal and financial status of the *kliros* as independent from the bishop. In this case we are not dealing with the constitution of a new bishop's *kliros*, but with the transformation of a vicariate's *kliros,* under the Pereiaslav bishop, into the *kliros* of the Smolensk diocese. See the document edited by Ia. Shchapov in *Drevnerusskie kniazheskie ustavy, XI–XV vv.* (Moscow, 1976), pp. 141–46. It is noteworthy that the Greek *kleros*, serving to define clergy in its entirety, when it became part of colloquial speech in Rus′, was exclusively associated with "chapter" clergy; the meaning of this word became much more narrow and institutional. For information on the institution of the *kliros* and the bishop's *namĕstnik*, see E. E. Golubinskii, *Istoriia russkoi tserkvi*, vol. 2, part 1 (Moscow, 1901; reprint, 1969), pp. 376–88; A. Poppe, "Fundacja biskupstwa smoleńskiego," *Przegląd Historyczny* 57 (1966): 552–55; Shchapov, *State and Church in Early Russia,* pp. 124–31.

113. *Pamiatniki drevnerusskogo kanonicheskogo prava*, p. 32.

114. For a more detailed discussion, see Poppe, "Werdegang der Diözesanstruktur," pp. 275, 277–78.

115. The prince is presented in them with his wife, Irene, and his mother, Gertrude; see Kämpfer, *Das Russische Herrscherbild von den Anfängen bis zu Peter dem Grosse*, ill. 64 and 67.

116. See the life of St. Theodosius in S. I. Kotkov et al., eds., *Uspenskii sbornik XII–XIII vv.* (Moscow, 1971), pp. 84–85.

117. Ibid., p. 95. It was a monastery, on the land route to Constantinople and Mount Athos, that was founded surely before 1066—probably, but not necessarily, as a branch of the Kyivan Caves Monastery.

118. See *The* Paterik *of the Kievan Caves Monastery*, pp. 118–19; Podskalsky, *Khristianstvo i bogoslovskaia literatura,* pp. 84–92.

119. See Abbot Daniel's *Khozhdenie. Wallfahrtsbericht. Mit einer Einleitung und bibliographischen Hinweisen von Klaus Dieter Seemann* (Munich, 1970), p. 10. W. F. Ryan's English translation, "Journey to the Promised Land" in John Wilkinson, ed., *Jerusalem Pilgrimage, 1099–1185* (London, 1988); A. Poppe, "Soobshchenie russkogo palomnika o tserkovnoi organizatsii Kipra v nachale XII veka," in *Epetēris tou Kentrou Epistēmonikōn Ereunōn Kyprou 8* (Leukosia, 1978), pp. 53–72; cf. *Notitiae episcopatuum Ecclesiae Constantinopolitanae*, pp. 157, 338; Podskalsky, *Khristianstvo i bogoslovskaia literatura,* pp. 321–26.

120. *PSRL*, vol. 1, pp. 238, 293, 296; The reference by the founder to "the prayers of the father and the grandfather" allows one to assume that Volodimer Monomakh contemplated the foundation of the bishopric of Smolensk; cf. Shchapov, *Drevnerusskie kniazheskie ustavy, XI–XV vv.*, pp. 141, 144. It is well worth analyzing in depth the remarks made by V. L. Ianin, "Zametki o komplekse dokumentov Smolenskoi eparkhii XII veka," *Otechestvennaia istoriia* 6 (1994): 104–20. I accept his criticism that the date of the consecration of Bishop Manuel as 26 April 1136 is

based on the not very credible Nikonian chronicle and must be verified. As for the date of the writing of the act of foundation, I lean toward the view that the draft of this document preceded the ordination and hence there are additions made at the moment of its formal issuing. However, V. Ianin is of the opinion that the foundation document was written a few years later (between 1138 and 1142). The fontologic problems are exceptionally complicated and even if not all of the proposed solutions seem correct, they are important enough to make us reevaluate our own solution and encourage us to study the issue further.

121. M. Hrushevs'kyi, *Istoriia Ukraïny-Rusi*, vol. 2, pp. 150–54, 417–20. Poppe, "Werdegang der Diözesanstruktur."

122. After 1237, the residence of the bishops of Riazan was Murom, and in the second half of the fourteenth century the bishop moved to the new political center of Pereislavl Riazanskii (called Riazan from the sixteenth century, but officially only since the eighteenth).

123. See Golubinskii, *Istoriia russkoi tserkvi*, vol. 1, part 1, pp. 697–98; Podskalsky, *Khristianstvo i bogoslovskaia literatura*, p. 296; Kuchkin, *Formirovanie gosudarstvennoi territorii*, pp. 98–103; J. Fennell, *The Crisis of Medieval Russia, 1200–1304* (London, 1983), pp. 46–51.

124. Golubinskii, *Istoriia russkoi tserkvi*, vol. 1, part 1, pp. 698–99; M. Hrushevs'kyi, *Istoriia Ukraïny-Rusi*, vol. 2, p. 418 ff. and index; I. P. Kryp'iakevych, *Halyts'ko-Volyns'ke kniazivstvo* (Kyiv, 1984), pp. 30–32, 90–91; Podskalsky, *Khristianstvo i bogoslovskaia literatura*, pp. 457, 464, 467–68; Shchapov (*State and Church in Early Russia*, p. 50) suggests moving the date of the founding of the bishopric in Halych back to 1139–1145, but he thinks that until that time the Dnister region was directly a part of the metropolitan diocese and did not belong to the bishopric of Volodymyr-in-Volhynia.

125. *PSRL*, vol. 1, p. 502; A. N. Nasonov, ed., *Novgorodskaia pervaia letopis' starshego i mladshego izvodov* (Moscow, 1950), pp. 52, 60; Podskalsky, *Khristianstvo i bogoslovskaia literatura*, p. 464; Shchapov (*State and Church in Early Russia*, pp. 40–42) is ready, with reference to Tatishchev, to date the Peremyshl episcopal see to 1119–1128, because Prince Volodar "founded there the church dedicated to John the Baptist which later was a cathedral"; this is uncritically repeated by Senyk, *A History of the Church in Ukraine*, pp. 141–42.

126. Golubinskii, *Istoriia russkoi tserkvi*, vol. 1, part 1, p. 699; M. Hrushevs'kyi, *Istoriia Ukraïny-Rusi*, vol. 2, pp. 381–84; Podskalsky, *Khristianstvo i bogoslovskaia literatura*, p. 465; cf. Shchapov, *State and Church in Early Russia*, pp. 52–54.

127. Golubinskii, *Istoriia russkoi tserkvi*, vol. 1, part 1, p. 700; M. Hrushevs'kyi, *Istoriia Ukraïny-Rusi*, vol. 2, pp. 384–85 (but his view that the bishopric of Lutsk was founded already in the twelfth century is not plausible); Shchapov, *State and Church in Early Russia*, p. 54. In any case, Lutsk became the capital of the diocese before 1237 but after

Peremyshl (1220), which follows from the chronicle and notitia of dioceses. (*PSRL*, vol. 2, p. 926; *Notitiae episcopatuum Ecclesiae Constantinopolitanae*, p. 403). Unfortunately, the order of the bishoprics was compiled in this notitia after 1303.

128. Cf. the basic collection of data on Danylo (still to this day) by M. Hrushevs′kyi, *Istoriia Ukraïny-Rusi*, vol. 3, pp. 17–91. A convincing characterization of Danylo's policies is presented by G. Stökl in *Handbuch der Geschichte Russlands,* vol. 1 (Stuttgart, 1980), pp. 508–26.

129. See *PSRL*, vol. 1, pp. 470, 472; vol. 2, pp. 782, 785–86, 806, 808–809.

130. Podskalsky, *Khristianstvo i bogoslovskaia literatura,* pp. 427–29, 468–71; concerning Cyril II's first years, see also G. Stökl, "Kanzler und Metropolit," in his *Der Russische Staat im Mittelalter und früher Neuzeit* (Wiesbaden, 1981), pp. 98–123. Various assumptions about the role that a hegumen from Kyiv, Petro Akerovych, who had escaped the Tatars, was supposed to have played in contacts with the Roman church, were properly disproved by O. Tolochko ("Petro Akerovych—hadanyi mytropolyt vseia Rusi," *Ukraïns'kyi istorychnyi zhurnal* 1990 (6): 45–54). One might say that a puzzling "quidam archiepiscopus de Russia nomine Petrus . . . a Tartaris exterminatus" (Matthaeus of Paris, *Chronica maiora*), who participated in the 1244 Council of Lyons, was a usurper but perhaps he could have been an archimandrite (abbot) of a monastery in Rus′ because archbishops were also given that title in the West, and so it could have been simply a mistake in reversible translation (cf. Charles Du Cange, *Glossarium mediae et infimae Latinitatis* 1: 891; *Mittellateinisches Wörterbuch,* vol. 1 [Berlin, 1967], p. 891). The surprising and ephemeral title of *protōthronos* for Rus′ metropolitans, which the Bulgarian despot Iakov-Svietoslav gives to Cyril II around 1261 (cf. Podskalsky, *Khristianstvo i bogoslovskaia literatura*, p. 470n15), would most easily be explained by recalling the confusion in the Byzantine church, which caused a temporary transfer of the patriarch's residence to Nicaea in Bithynia (until 1261). At that time, Caesarea in Cappadocia, where the metropolitan was the patriarch's *protōthronos*, was destroyed to such an extent, especially after being conquered by the Mongols in 1243, that it ceased to be the seat of the metropolitanate. In this situation the patriarch could have come to the conclusion that rapid changes in church geography and the need for improving contacts with the Mongols justified such a promotion of the metropolitan of Rus′. If this patriarch was Arsenios Autoreianos, then it becomes understandable that after 1265 the new solution was forgotten.

131. See Ia. Shchapov, *Vizantiiskoe i iuzhnoslavianskoe pravovoe nasledie na Rusi v XI–XIII vv.* (Moscow, 1978), pp. 146–57, 209–12, 240–46, 270–72.

132. Podskalsky, *Khristianstvo i bogoslovskaia literatura*, p. 469n14. The first mentioned synod took place in Kyiv in 1273 (and not 1274), as Shchapov rightly proved (ibid., pp. 181–85).

133. V. Borzakovskii, *Istoriia Tver'skogo kniazhestva* (St. Petersburg, 1876; reprint, 1993), pp. 68–83, 205–206. Kuchkin, *Formirovanie gosudarstvennoi territorii*, pp. 111–21; J. Fennell, *The Crisis of Medieval Russia, 1200–1304*, pp. 107–18, 127.

134. For the Greek and Rus′ texts, see *Pamiatniki drevnerusskogo kanonicheskogo prava*, part 1, pp. 129–40 (no. 12), supplement 1–12 (no. 1). Cf. *PSRL*, vol. 1, p. 476, and Golubinskii, *Istoria russkoi tserkvi*, vol. 2, part 1, pp. 41, 60–61.

135. *Pamiatniki drevnerusskogo kanonicheskogo prava*, part 1 pp. 159–66 (nos. 18 and 19), supplement 1, paragraph 15. Cf. A. Nasonov, *Mongoly i Rus'* (Moscow, 1940; reprint, 1969), pp. 45–47.

136. Cf. Nasonov *Mongoly i Rus';* B. Spuler, *Die Goldene Horde. Die Mongolen in Russland 1223-1502,* 2nd edition (Wiesbaden, 1965); Charles J. Halperin, *Russia and the Golden Horde. The Mongol Impact on Medieval Russian History* (Bloomington, 1985). In the discussion about the Mongolian influence on the history of Rus′, an important place belongs to J. Fennell. *The Crisis of Medieval Russia, 1200–1304.* After this and other studies on the Mongols in Rus′ (see, for example, Podskalsky, *Khristianstvo i bogoslovskaia literatura*, pp. 142–45), Leo de Hartog's clear yet simplistic book, *Russia and the Mongol Yoke* (London, 1996), is disappointing. Eurasian studies are useful if we wish to gain some distance from issues at hand. As far as new publications are concerned, the books of the historiosophically oriented, talented writer Lev N. Gumilev dominate the field. Gumilev, who prefers to cross boundaries and refuses to be a professional historian or a medievalist, easily exaggerates and, although he has a critical mind, at times falls into the trap of becoming a visionary or, as he would say himself, of falling prey to excessive *passionarium.* Gumilev's constructs are built on a grand scale, but not without a nationalistic narrowing of the mind. Huge colorful canvasses and panoramic pictures can either be accepted wholesale or rejected, but one can also enrich one's knowledge through a view that goes beyond Eurocentric borders, in this case exceptionally so, without differentiating between Western and Eastern Europe. See, for example, L. N. Gumilev, *Drevniaia Rus' i velikaia step'* (Moscow, 1989). Gumilev, who was persecuted earlier but has become very popular today, is to be commended for always being true to himself and refusing to guard himself with an academic shield.

137. See M. Hrushevs'kyi, *Istoriia Ukraïny-Rusi*, vol. 3, pp. 147–53. And his *Ocherk istorii kievskoi zemli* (Kyiv, 1891; reprint, 1991), pp. 427–43, 506–509. This excellent historian's thesis about the survival of Kyiv is also substantiated by new studies of G. Ivakin; see, for example, his *Kiev v 13–15 vekakh* (Kyiv, 1982), pp. 12–23, 57–65, 82–102.

138. An exaggerated idealization and perpetuation of a hagiographical-like image of Alexander Nevsky in historiography had to trigger a reaction, which, however, was usually ignored or relabelled (for example, the earlier contrast between "Soviet historiography" and "bourgeois histori-

ography" is now replaced by a new opposition: *zarubezhnaia* (foreign)–*otechestvennaia* (native). But the crux of the matter is the scaling down of Prince Alexander's image to the proportions that it had in the thirteenth century, although a certain amount of exaggeration in historicizing his image cannot be avoided. See Fennell, *The Crisis of Medieval Russia, 1200–1304*, pp. 97–124; cf. W. Leitsch, "Einige Beobachtungen zum politischen Weltbild Aleksander Nevskijs," in *Forschungen zur osteuropäischen Geschichte* 25 (1978): 202–16; cf. also my attempt in *Lexikon des Mittelalters* 1 (1980): 370–71.

139. See Nasonov, *Mongoly i Rus′,* pp. 40–49, 329n95. This interpretation gave rise to the thesis about the founding of the bishopric in Sarai as a result of Mongolian mistrust toward the metropolitan of Rus′ and of a need for closer diplomatic ties with Byzantium.

140. Cf. *PSRL*, vol. 1, pp. 525–26; a later report focuses on accusing the bishop of removing the grave of Rostov's Prince Glěb, who died in 1278, from the cathedral.

141. *Pamiatniki drevnerusskogo kanonicheskogo prava,* part 1, pp. 83–100 (no. 6), especially p. 86. Cyril's pastoral letter played a preparatory role for resolutions made at the Kyivan Synod in 1273; cf. Podskalsky, *Khristianstvo i bogoslovskaia literatura,* pp. 427–32. Extreme judgments and accusations against the Rus′ church of servility during the Mongol Yoke have been replaced by more moderate assessments. See N. A. Okhotina, "Ruskaia tserkov′ i mongol′skoe zavoevanie," in *Tserkov', obshchestvo i gosudarstvo v feodal'noi Rossii* (Moscow, 1990), pp. 67–83; A. L. Khoroshkevich and A. I. Pliguzov, "Russkaia tserkov′ i antiordinskaia bor′ba v XIII–XIV vv. Po materialam kratkogo sobraniia khanskikh iarlykov russkim mitropolitom," *Tserkov', obshchestvo i gosudarstvo v feodal'noi Rossii,* pp. 84–102. See also the original panoramic view of the thirteenth century Rus′ church and Christianity by V. N. Toporov, *Sviatost' i sviatye v russkoi dukhovnoi kul'ture,* vol. 2 (Moscow, 1998), pp. 203–94.

142. The Five Sermons of Serapion are published in *Pamiatniki literatury drevnei Rusi: XIII vek* (Moscow, 1981), pp. 440–55, especially pp. 444, 448; See also the English translation partly edited by S. A. Zenkovsky, *Medieval Russia's Epics, Chronicles and Tales*, 2nd edition (New York, 1974), pp. 243–48; cf. Podskalsky, *Khristianstvo i bogoslovskaia literatura*, pp. 179–83. On Serapion's conciousness, see W. Philipp, *Ansätze zum geschichtlichen und politischen Denken in Kiever Russland* (Darmstadt, 1967), pp. 60–64.

143. Cf. T. T. Allsen, "Mongol Census Taking in Rus′, 1245–1275," *Harvard Ukrainian Studies* 5(1) 1981: 32–53; D. Ostrowski, "The Mongol Origins of Muscovite Political Institutions," *Slavic Review* 49(4) Winter 1990: 525–42.

144. *PSRL*, vol. 1, pp. 485, 528; cf. D. Ostrowski, "Why Did the Metropolitan Move from Kiev to Vladimir in the Thirteenth Century?" *California Slavic Studies* 16 (1993): 83–101.

145. *Notitiae episcopatuum Ecclesiae Constantinopolitanae*, pp. 399, 403; M. Hrushevs'kyi, *Istoriia Ukraïny-Rusi*, vol. 3, pp. 269–74, 543–44. The attempt to date the foundation of the Lithuanian metropolitanate before 1303 (instead of around 1316) in light of the notitia is unfounded. Cf. M. Giedroyć, "The Arrival of Christianity in Lithuania: Between Rome and Byzantium (1281–1341)," *Oxford Slavonic Papers* 20 (1987): 15–19.

146. Cf. the article by M. Hrushevs'kyi, "Velyka, Mala i Bila Rus'," reprinted in *Ukraïns'kyi istorychnyi zhurnal* 1991(2): 77–85.

Postscript

Continuation of fn. 100 (on p. 383): Tangible evidence of the education and emotional life of Anne, dowager queen of France (the daughter of Jaroslav the Wise) is her signature in Cyrillic on a document of the juvenile king, Philip I. Thus Anna demonstrated her position as a member of the regency council, which had been questioned in courtly circles after her second marriage, ca. 1062. See D. & A. Poppe, "Anna-Regina Francorum", *O rzeczach minionych* [Festschrift for Anna-Płachcińska] (Warsaw, 2006), pp. 239–246.

VI

Leontios, Abbot of Patmos, Candidate for the Metropolitan See of Rus'

Nineteenth- and twentieth-century church historians have largely expressed the view, successively repeated with little additional reflection, that the ecclesiastics sent to the Kievan see during the period of its dependence on the Patriarchate of Constantinople were mostly bishops appointed to be metropolitans there purely by chance; they also were ill-prepared to pilot that major church province encompassing the vast land of the Eastern Slavs, and still being in the early process of christianization.[1] Moreover, when we look at the circumstances in which a candidate was nominated in Constantinople, we can observe that often, and above all as a result of political considerations, the opinion of the emperor on the matter held more sway than that of the Synod and the Patriarch. Though in practice the selection process could, and did, vary, the historians' view of it has generally been negative; this may have been due to lack of data that would help these historians to produce balanced assessments and characteristics of the candidates being sent to Rus'.

After the Synod had proposed three nominees to the Kievan See, one of them was selected by the patriarch, with the emperor taking part in the procedure; thereupon, the candidate was appointed. He became the helmsman of the Rus' metropolitanate in the fullest sense, however, only after the enthronement that took place in his own cathedral, i.e. the Kievan cathedral of the Wisdom of God. The enthronement usually occurred on the first Sunday after the candidate's arrival and during the concomitant festive service, which would take place in the presence of the prince of Kiev, the local princes, the nobility and the clergy, including the local bishops, abbots and the clergy of the Kievan cathedral. The newly arrived bishop was thus invested with full metropolitan authority, first and foremost with authority relating to the ordination of bishops and clergy and the consecration of churches in his own diocese.

---

[1] For this assessment, current since the nineteenth century, see: Ia. N. Shchapov, *Gosudarstvo i Tserkov' Drevnei Rusi X–XIII vv.* (Moscow, 1989), 169–178, repeated in the translation of the same: Ia. N. Shchapov, *State and Church in Early Russia: Tenth to Thirteenth Centuries* (New Rochelle, N.Y., 1993), 200–209.

It is important to remember all this, for the prevalent and somewhat simplistic view is that the election to the metropolitanate of Rus' was decided entirely on the Bosphorus. This is true as far as it goes, provided that we also add that elections were decided with full consideration of Kievan sentiments and wishes as to the candidate, and taking into account all related local political circumstances, none of which the Byzantine Empire could ignore.

As a rule, nothing is known of the past of the Greek bishops arriving in Rus' as future metropolitans, and drawing plausible conclusions *ex silentio* is justified only in exceptional cases.[2] Even the assertion that bishops sent to Rus' did not speak the vernacular must be considered an unsubstantiated conjecture. Even if that should have been the case upon arrival, the bishop, as usually happens, would master the vernacular for practical purposes in the course of time, if he wished to be a true shepherd of the local church, that is, of local religious community, and to communicate with them in their own language. Moreover, the church service itself made it indispensable for him to know the local language in order to be able to perform the liturgy in Slavic.

The above considerations lead us to one exceptional case when we do have enough information on a candidate for the Rus'ian See and thus are able to form an idea of demands placed upon other candidates. The case in question is the nomination of Leontios, abbot of the Monastery of Patmos, to the Kievan metropolitan see by emperor Manuel I Komnenos (1143–1180). Manuel was fully informed on Russian political and church affairs; his selection is, therefore, of vital importance to our topic.[3]

*

* *

What is known of Leontios, whose ecclesiastical career culminated in the title of patriarch of Jerusalem, is based, first and foremost, on his *Vita*, composed in the early years of the thirteenth century by a younger contemporary of his, Theodosios Gudelis. Like Leontios, Gudelis was a monk of Patmos and was his companion during his patriarchate; later, Theodosios became abbot of the

---

[2] Eleventh–thirteenth century biographies of metropolitans effectively demonstrate the scarcity of available evidence; cf. G. Podskalsky, *Khristianstvo i bogoslovskaia literatura v Kievskoi Rusi (988–1237)*, 2nd enlarged ed. (Saint-Petersburg, 1996) 446–471 (= *Subsidia Byzantinorossica* 1).

[3] Generally speaking, Manuel I Komnenos exercised a crucial influence in church affairs and decided the Empire's church policy in accordance with his reconciliatory and "ecumenical" tendencies. On his church policy, see chs. 1, 5 and 6 of P. Magdalino, *The Empire of Manuel I Komnenos, 1143–1180* (Cambridge, 1993), especially ch. 5: "The Guardians of Orthodoxy", 316–412.

monastery. A recent edition of this *Vita*, with an English translation and a detailed commentary[4] that confirms the *Vita*'s main verifiable facts, will be our main source; it will allow us to gather pertinent information, and to focus on the considerations that emperor Manuel had in mind when he suggested to Leontios that he become metropolitan of Rus'.

Leontios's place of birth, Strumitsa, gains significance in this respect. Strumitsa was a region populated by Slavs, but, after the fall of the First Bulgarian Empire in 1018, it was successfully hellenized by the newly-arrived Greek settlers. There is no evidence (the *Vita* is silent on the names of Leontios's parents) for ascribing Slavic origins to Leontios.[5] Undoubtedly,

---

[4] *The Life of Leontios, Patriarch of Jerusalem.* Text, Translation, Commentary by Dimitris Tsougarakis. (Leiden–New York–Köln, 1993 = *The Medieval Mediterranean Peoples, Economies and Cultures 400–1453*, vol. 2). An earlier edition of *The Life of Leontios* was published by Makarios Chrysokephalos (Vienna, 1793), 381–433, also containing, on pp. 443–440, selections from both of Leontios' works mentioned below (cf. pp. 5–6). Iv. Troitskii also published an extract from the *Life,* with some lacunae regarding the patriarchal period of the Saint's life, both in the original and in a Russian translation; it appeared in the introduction to his edition of *Skazaniia Ioanna Foki o ... sviatykh mestakh Palestiny* (John Phokas being a contemporary of Leontios), *Pravoslavnyi Palestinskii Sbornik*, vol. 8, issue 23 (Saint-Petersburg, 1889), xv–xxxvii. The Russian and Cypriot episodes are missing from this edition. For the most thorough encyclopedic article on St. Leontios, see: D. Stiernon, "Léonce de Jérusalem", *Dictionnaire de spiritualité ascétique et mystique*, vol. 9 (Paris, 1975–1976), 664–666.

[5] The sentence concerning the nobility and wealth of the Saint's parents is a typical cliché to emphasize that the ascetic's choice had not been motivated by misfortunes in his previous life. The editor (*The Life of Leontios*; comm., p. 163) finds it strange that the author of the *Vita* of Leontios should pass over his parents' names in silence and sees here a desire to conceal something (their barbarian origin?). Any purpose here, however, was more likely linked to the author's wish to stress his hero's complete renunciation of worldly vanity and desire to be a man of God. The author of the *Life* does, however, undoubtedly feel the need to justify the city's barbarian name, claiming that Strum[n]itsa's population was "half-barbarian"; see *The Life of Leontios,* 34: Οὗτος τοίνυν ὁ μεγαλώνυμος, πατρίδα μὲν εὐτύχησε τὴν μέσον Μυσῶν καὶ Παιόνων κειμένην, ἄσημόν τινα πόλιν καὶ ἀνώνυμον, ἢ βαρβαρικήν τινα τὴν κλῆσιν κεκτημένην ὡς μιξοβάρβαρον. Στρούμβιτζα γὰρ ἡ κλῆσις τῆς πόλεως ("Thus, this glorious <man> was fortunate to have been born in a city situated between Mysia [Bulgaria] and Paeonia [Hungary], insignificant and nameless, or rather having received some barbarian name, <its dwellers> being half-barbarian. For the name of that city is Strubitsa [ms M: Strumitsa]"). — In the eleventh and twelfth centuries the Strumnitsa region in northern Macedonia was still populated by Slavs despite encroaching hellenization. The toponymy of the city itself and of its outskirts illustrates this fact. Cf., for example, the names of the settlements granted to the Greek Monastery of Our Lady of Pity (*Eleousa*) in Strumnitsa, according to the typikon of the years 1085–1106; see L. Petit, "Le Monastère de Notre Dame de Pitié en Macédoine", *Izvestiia russkogo Arkheologicheskogo Instituta v Konstantinopole* 6/1, (1900), 10–12; W. Swoboda, "Strumica", *Słownik Starożytności Słowiańskich* 5 (1975), 440–441; G. G. Litavrin, *Vizantiia i slaviane* (Saint-Petersburg, 1999), 410–420; cf. also I. Bozhilov, *B"lgarite v"v Vizantiiskata Imperiia*

however, having been raised in a bilingual environment (he was born ca. 1113), the Greek Leontios must have known Slavic, at least on a level that would have allowed the emperor to count on his ability to converse with the members of his flock upon his arrival in Kiev; Leontios thus would be able to concentrate right away on his tasks as helmsman of an important church province of the Constantinopolitan patriarchate.

Leontios exhibited piety from his very childhood, pursuing such extravagant ascetic practices as fasting and mortification of the flesh,[6] acting as a Fool-in-Christ,[7] self-flagellation,[8] and dwelling among the dead.[9] At the same time, he enjoyed travelling; he managed to visit Constantinople in his youth and, around 1130, decided to accompany the bishop of Tiberias in Galilee to

---

(Sofia, 1995), 14–22, 77–78; the author points to the Bulgarian origins of the Gudelis family, of which the author of *The Life of Leontios* was a member, but a survey of the numerous representatives of that family confirms (ibid., 294–303) that they were all Byzantine Greeks.

[6] See *The Life of Leontios*, § 5, p. 38: Καὶ μέχρις ἑσπέρας ἄσιτος ἵστατο ... φορυτὸν ἀκανθῶν συμφορήσας ... ἐπ᾽ αὐτῶν γυμνὸς ἀνεκλίνετο ("And he would stand without food until nightfall … Making a rubbish heap out of thorns … he would remove his clothing and lie upon them"; see also § 6 [further description of fasting and self-torture]; § 7–9 [his carrying incense and coal in his bare hands; plunging into a burning stove]; § 25 [his desire to reject food intake entirely]).

[7] See *The Life of Leontios*, § 7, p. 40: Καὶ τὸν ἔκφρονα πλασάμενος, νέον τέρας ἐδόκει τοῖς Βυζαντίοις ἐπιδεδημηκέναι, μῖμος ἑκούσιος αὐτοῖς ἐμποιεῖν δυνάμενος γέλωτα ("And, feigning madness, he appeared <to the inhabitants of the city> of Byzantium; a strange monster come unto them, a voluntary mime, capable of making them laugh").

[8] See *The Life of Leontios*, § 22, p. 58: Καὶ τοιοῦτος ὢν καὶ οὕτως ἐσχάτως ταπεινούμενος καὶ τῶν κυνῶν ἑαυτὸν ἡγούμενος χείρονα, ὅμως οὐ παρῆκε τὴν προρρηθεῖσαν μάστιγα, ἀλλ᾽ ἀδιαλείπτως ἑαυτὸν ἐμάστιζε ("Being as he was, abasing himself to the utmost and considering himself worse than a dog, he nevertheless did not leave off the aforementioned scourge but scourged himself incessantly"; see also § 19 [self-flagellation with a detailed description of the lash]). — Perceptions within Rus' of the self-abasing practices in contemporary Byzantine asceticism varied. When Leontios' contemporary, Constantine I, metropolitan of Rus' († 1159), disposed that his body be thrown to the dogs as unworthy of burial, this caused general embarrassment (see *Polnoe Sobranie Russkikh Letopisei*, vol. 1, *Lavrent'evskaia Letopis'*, 2nd ed. [Leningrad, 1926; repr. Moscow, 1997), 349).

[9] See *The Life of Leontios*, § 20, p. 54: Ἵνα δὲ καὶ διηνεκὴς αὐτῷ ἡ τοῦ θανάτου μνήμη παραμένῃ καὶ σύντροφος, πολλάκις ἡμέρας διαφαυούσης λανθανόντως ἐξῄει τῆς κέλλης αὐτοῦ καὶ ἀπερχόμενος ἐν τῷ κοινῷ κοιμητηρίῳ τῶν ἀδελφῶν ἀπεδύετο μὲν αὐτοῦ ἱμάτια, συναπεδύετο δὲ καὶ πᾶσαν δειλίαν τὴν τῆς ψυχῆς, καὶ θάρσος ἀναλαμβάνων πνευματικὸν ἐν μιᾷ τῶν σορῶν τῶν τὰ τῶν ἀπελθόντων φυλαττουσῶν λείψανα ἑαυτὸν ἐτίθει νεκρὸν ἑκούσιον ("In order that remembering death remain his constant companion, often he would stealthily leave his cell at dawn, go to the communal cemetery of the brethren, take off his clothing, and with it all timidity of the soul, and, his soul having gained in spiritual daring, he would lie down as a voluntary corpse in one of the coffins containing the remains of the departed").

the Holy Land as his disciple. However, possibly due to the crusaders' refusal to admit an orthodox clergyman, Leontios' journey took him to Patmos. There he entered the Monastery of St John the Theologian (before 1132), and the monastery's abbot, Theoktistos, became his spiritual advisor.[10] In the monastery, where he continued to mortify his flesh, Leontios perfected his spiritual and intellectual life by studying theology,[11] was appointed to serve under a *kanonarches* and, from 1145, became the steward (*oikonomos*) of the monastery, that is, the man in charge of its housekeeping and property.[12] Years of monastic life, albeit quite a busy one due to his responsibilities as a steward, confirmed Leontios' aspirations to become a stylite in the capital, i.e. to pursue his asceticism in full view of everybody, and thus to become a visible reproach to the inhabitants of the reigning city, ridden by vice, and an example of asceticism in Christ's name.[13] However, the death of abbot Theoktistos in 1157, who saw his successor in Leontios, ruined Leontios' plans.

Leontios' position as abbot strengthened his ties with the capital, which he had visited before on various kinds of monastery business, showing, according to his biographer and disciple, efficiency in the pursuit of affairs. It was on account of his efforts that patriarch Luke Chrysoberges bestowed its stauropegial status upon the monastery in October of 1168. [14]

During the sessions of the Constantinopolitan Council of 1166, the main subject of which was the exegesis of the words of the Gospel: "For my Father is greater than I" (John 14:28), Leontios may have demonstrated his ability to discuss and analyze abstract theological arguments concerning teachings about Holy Trinity. Indeed, the views of the Council of 1166 coincide with those of Leontios outlined in his "Chapters on Holy Trinity" (κεφάλαια

---

[10] D. Tsougarakis has convincingly established the dates for Leontios' birth (between 1110 and 1115) and of his acceptance of monastic vows on Patmos (no later than 1132; see *The Life of Leontios*, commentary, 172–173). The previously suggested date for Leontios' birth (ca. 1100) is not supported by facts.

[11] See *The Life of Leontios*, § 24, p. 60, where the author emphasizes Leontios' familiarity with not only the *Vitae* of saint by monks and ascetics (βίβλους .... οὐ μόνον ὅσαι βίους πατέρων ἢ μαρτύρων ἀπαγγέλλουσι) but also with those that discuss... deep dogmas, inaccessible to many (ἀλλὰ καὶ ὅσαι περὶ δογμάτων ὑψηλῶν καὶ τῶν ὀλίγοις βατῶν διὰ τὸ τῆς ἀνόδου πρόσαντες).

[12] See *The Life of Leontios*, § 21, p. 56 (Ὑπηρετούμενον αὐτὸν τῷ τῶν ἱερῶν ὕμνων κατάρχοντι ἐν τῇ τοῦ ναοῦ ὑπηρεσίᾳ ὁ προεστὼς κατεστήσατο; ...); § 27, p. 62–63 (Οἰκονόμος ... γεγονώς).

[13] See *The Life of Leontios*, § 37, p. 74 (on his desire to live in the retreat of Daniel the Stylite near Constantinople). — See also P. Magdalino, "The Byzantine Holy Man in the 12th Century", *The Byzantine Saint* (London, 1981), 51–66.

[14] See *The Life of Leontios*, commentary, pp. 176–177.

περὶ ʽΑγίας Τριάδος). We cannot exclude the possibility of his influence on the Council's decision, even though this question still awaits a detailed investigation. The treatise Περὶ διαφορᾶς ἔρωτος (*On various [kinds] of Love*) is also attributed to Leontios.[15]

During one of his visits to the capital on monastery business, fate brought Leontios together with the *megas droungarios* (at that time, a high member of the judiciary) Andronikos Kamateros. The spiritual connection established between the two must have been close, for the biographer of the Saint noted that one of the emperor's closest advisers "loved [Leontios] as a friend, respected him as a father, venerated him as a man of God". Everyone marvelled at the refined simplicity of Leontios' speech, and at the astonishing ease with which he was able to interpret difficult passages of the Scriptures.[16]

The meeting between Andronikos Kamateros and the abbot of Patmos perhaps occurred about the time of the Council of 1166. Their relationship grew stronger over the course of Leontios' visits to Constantinople. Leontios' theological learnings prompted Andronikos to introduce Leontios to the emperor himself. The three offers that followed one upon another, first to be installed in the See of Rus', then, soon after, in that of Cyprus, and, in the spring of 1176, to ascend the patriarchal throne of Jerusalem, all testify to the great importance that emperor Manuel Komnenos and his entourage attached to Leontios as a prominent man of the Church.[17]

---

[15] V. Grumel, *Les Regestes des Actes du Patriarcat de Constantinople*, vol. 1, fasc. 3 (Paris, 1974), nos. 1049, 1059–1062, 1065, 1067, 1075: H.-G. Beck, *Kirche und theologische Literatur im byzantinischen Reich* (München, 1959), 342–343, 628 (Beck calls Leontios' work on the Trinity "The 14 Theological Chapters" [14 Κεφάλαια θεολογικά]; *The Life of Leontios*, 9–11. — For commentaries on the Councils of 1166 and 1170, see J. Gouillard, "Le synodikon de l'Orthodoxie", *Travaux et Mémoires* 2 (Paris, 1967), 216–222; cf. F. Uspensky, *Ocherki po istorii vizantiiskoi obrazovannosti* (Saint-Petersburg, 1891; repr. Moscow, 2001), 185–195.

[16] See *The Life of Leontios*, § 63, pp. 104–107; commentary, pp. 191–192. We cannot determine from *The Life* when exactly the two first met. Circumstantial evidence points to the winter of 1172/1173. Kamateros and Leontios met (for the first time?) after the latter's arrival in Constantinople. Considering that for the author of the *Life* the calendar year began in September and that he says that Leontios came to Constantinople the year following upon his illness (he was ill in the year of the Creation of 6680), his arrival in the capital should be dated to 6681, that is between September 1, 1172 and August 31, 1173. Since we know, however, that in September of 1172 Leontios visited Crete, returned to Patmos and only then set off for the Capital, the most probable date for his arrival there must have been the winter of 1172/1173.

[17] See *The Life of Leontios*, § 64, p. 106: ʼΕν τούτοις ὄντων τῶν πραγμάτων καὶ οὕτω τὰ κατ᾽ αὐτὸν οἰκονομοῦντος τοῦ κρείττονος, θνήσκει μὲν ὁ τοῦ ἔθνους τῶν Ρῶς κατάρχων ποιμαντικῶς, καὶ ὁ βασιλεύων ἀντὶ τοῦ τεθνηκότος εἰς ἀρχιερέα τοῦτον τῶν Ρῶς προβάλλεται καὶ διὰ τοῦ δρουγγαρίου αὐτῷ τὰ τοῦ πράγματος διαμηνύεται· ὁ δ᾽

Leontios' refusal of the emperor's first two offers was considered extraordinary by his contemporaries. His hagiographer felt compelled to explain both rejections by the fact that the Saint had had a revelation in a dream to the effect that he was to become a patriarch (with no specification as to where the See in question would be located).[18] The ambiguity of this revelation allows us to speculate that Leontios was quite ambitious and could have envisaged himself as the patriarch of Constantinople, i.e. as the successor to Michael of Anchialos (1170–1178). Refusing the dignity of patriarch of Jerusalem, however, could have appeared as a sign of arrogance even to Leontios.

At this point it is appropriate to say a word on Leontios' patron. Andronikos Kamateros, the emperor's closest advisor, also possessed a wide knowledge of theology and took part in the conciliar sessions of 1157, 1166 and 1170. We know a treatise, compiled and edited by him in the form of a disputation on the errors of the Latins and the Armenians and entitled Ἱερὰ ὁπλοθήκη *(The Sacred Arsenal)*.[19]

ἀπαναίνεται καὶ τὴν ἀρχὴν τῶν Ρῶς ἀποβάλλεται ("Such being the state of affairs and such the disposition that Divinity was making concerning him [the saint], the shepherd governing the nation of Rus' died and the emperor promoted the Saint to be archbishop of these Rusians in the place of the deceased. The emperor announced the details of this affair to the Saint through the *droungarios*, but the Saint refused and rejected the rule over the Rusians"); § 65, p. 106: Χήρα προσεχῶς καὶ ἡ τῶν Κυπρίων νῆσος τοῦ ἐφισταμένου ταύτης ποιμαντικῶς καθίστατο, καὶ ὁ βασιλεύων αὖθις τὸν μάκαρα διὰ τοῦ προλεχθέντος ἀνδρὸς ὑπεμίμνησκε καὶ ἀρχιερέα θήσειν τῶν Κυπρίων ἐδοκίμαζεν. Ὁ δὲ τὰ ἴσα ἐποίει καὶ παρῃτεῖτο τὸν θρόνον ("Soon afterwards, the island of the Cyprians also became widowed, <having lost> its shepherd. Again, the emperor notified the blessed one <of this> through the aforementioned man [i.e., the *droungarios*] and was considering appointing him metropolitan of the Cyprians. But the Saint did the same and refused the see"); § 66, p. 108: Ὀλίγου γὰρ καιροῦ παραρρεύσαντος, ἐτεθνήκει μὲν ὁ τὴν Ἱερουσαλὴμ οἰακίζων ("For, after a short time, the helmsman of Jerusalem died"). — The imperial nomination took place soon after April, 1176, the last time Leontios was mentioned as the abbot of Patmos (cf. F. Dölger–P. Wirth, *Regesten der Kaiserurkunden des oströmischen Reiches*, 2. Teil [München, 1995], no. 1521a). Already in the fall of 1176, Leontios set out for the Holy Land; see *The Life of Leontios*, pp. 108–109; commentary, pp. 195–196. Leontios' predecessor, patriarch Nikephoros II of Jerusalem, is recorded as present at the July session of the Council of 1173 (see Grumel, *Les Regestes* ..., no. 1126).

[18] The hagiographer reports that after his two refusals Leontios was showered with questions by his disciple Antonios, then a monk, later the abbot of Patmos Monastery, who expected benefits to accrue to the monastery from Leontios' promotion; Leontios finally disclosed his reasons: "If the Heavenly Ruler decreed that I be patriarch, then the earthly ruler cannot make me bishop." To an additional question, he replied: "To *which* see, that has not been revealed unto me" (*The Life of Leontios*, § 65–66, p. 108).

[19] Beck, *Kirche* ..., 618, 626–627, 662, 682; G. Stadtmüller, "Zur Geschichte der Familie Kamateros", *Byzantinische Zeitschrift* 34 (1934), 352–358; A. P. Kazhdan, *Sotsial'nyi*

Considering that the emperor's first offer made to Leontios concerned Rus', we may suppose that Leontios was originally presented to Manuel for this very reason and that this nomination was suggested to the emperor by the *megas droungarios* who, it seems, took into account not only Leontios' excellent grounding in theology, but also his ability fully to apply his learning in Rus', owing to his knowledge of the Slavic language.[20]

*
* *

Problems of church and state related to Rus' emerged almost from the very start of Manuel's reign. Drawn into conflicts between various princes, metropolitan Michael of Kiev had to abdicate in 1146 during a crisis which he himself helped to create. In 1147, Hieromonk Kliment Smoliatich was elected metropolitan, in disregard of the views of Constantinople.[21]

Unrest in the patriarchate itself was the reason why Constantine I could be ordained in Constantinople as metropolitan of Kiev only in 1155, with the support of the coalition of Rus'ian princes led by Iurii Dolgorukii. An expert theologian as witnessed by his speech on the presentation (*podnoshenie*) of the Eucharistic sacrifice to the indivisible Trinity, he was, in his own words, quite familiar with the situation in Rus'. True, the severity of the measures he undertook in his struggle with the "insubordinates" prolonged the period of the schism and contributed to his own defeat; however, he was later capable of passing severe judgment upon his failure as a shepherd, for, as we already

---

sostav gospodstvuiushchego klassa Vizantii XI–XIII vv. (Moscow, 1974), 107–114; Magdalino, *The Empire*, 259–260, 290.

[20] Andronikos Kamateros himself entertained quite close ties with Rus' for decades. Sometime before 1199, his niece, Maria Kamateros, was married to prince Roman Mstislavich of Halyč and Volyn'. Upon Leontios' refusal, the new candidate to the metropolitan see of Rus', Nikephoros II, was apparently put forward by the same Kamateros; cf. H. Grala, "Drugie małżeństwo Romana Mścisławowicza", *Slavia Orientalis* 31 (1982), 122–126.

[21] On events of church and state in the middle of the twelfth century, see: P. Sokolov, *Russkii arkhierei iz Vizantii i pravo ego naznacheniia do nachala XV v.* (Kiev, 1913), 55–156; W. Vodoff, "Remarques sur la politique ecclésiastique d'André de Bogoljubovo", *Cahiers de civilisation médiévale* 17 (1974), 193–215; Grumel, *Les Regestes*, no. 1052; Podskalsky, *Khristianstvo*, 77–81, 163–164, and in Appendix 1, pp. 454–462 (biographical information on Kievan metropolitans during the reign of Manuel I: Michael I, Kliment Smoliatich, Constantine I, Theodore, John IV, Constantine II, Michael II and Nikephoros II). For an overview of Byzantine primary sources, see M. V. Bibikov, *Drevniaia Rus' v svete zarubezhnykh istochnikov* (Moscow, 1999), 143–150.

saw (note 8 above), in his will he acknowledged himself unworthy of a Christian burial.

Discord in the Church led the princes to decide to side with neither of the opposing metropolitans, Kliment or Constantine, but to petition Constantinople for a new one instead, in March 1159. Theodore, the new choice, pursued his reconciliatory efforts, on the whole successfully, from the time of his arrival in August, 1160, right up to his death in June, 1163.

Meanwhile, two new developments began to threaten the reconciliation within the Church of Rus': the controversy concerning fasting and Andrei Bogoliubskii's manifest goal to found a second, that is, new, metropolitanate in northeastern Rus'. Emperor Manuel demonstrated his interest in the situation when, in the summer of 1163, he took part in person in the public debates that resulted in extending support to the Kievan metropolitan Theodore in the matter of the so-called Leontian heresy, i.e. in providing a solution to the dispute over fasting during the Feasts of Our Lord.[22]

The successful resolution of the discord in the Church found its expression in the title of Theodore's successor John IV (1164–1166), for this title, 'Shepherd of all Rusians' (τῶν πάντων Ῥῶς), confirmed that a single Church jurisdiction in Rus' had been restored.[23] Even if the prince Rostislav Mstislavich was hardly burning with the desire to accept John, the emperor's envoys were able to convince him to do so. The fragile understanding between Constantinople and Kiev, established through the work of metropolitans Theodore and John IV, was shattered by metropolitan Constantine II, who ascended the Kievan see in 1167. This was due to his conflict with the Cave Monastery, caused by his overly rigid interpretation of the rule prescribing Wednesday and Friday fasting, even during the Feasts of Our Lord. On Christmas Day, 1168, he imposed penance on abbot Polikarp of the Cave Monastery; moreover, he applied Byzantine civil law (mutilation) to the appointed but not yet ordained bishop Feodorets of Rostov and

---

[22] Grumel, *Les Regestes*, no. 1053. On Andrei Bogoliubskii's attempt to institute a second metropolitanate, see the observations of I. Ševčenko, *Byzantium and the Slavs* (Cambridge, Mass., 1991, but reprinting an article of 1966), 269–272; G. Prinzing, "Wer war der bulgarische Bischof Adrian der Laurentius-Chronik sub anno 1164?", *Jahrbücher für Geschichte Osteuropas* 36 (1988), 552–557.

[23] A. Soloviev, *Byzance et la formation de l'État russe* (London, 1979), no. IXa, p. 294; no. IXb, p. 318; cf. also V. L. Ianin, *Aktovye pechati drevnei Rusi*, vol. 1 (Moscow, 1970), 49, 52. Despite difficulties in reading the inscription, we cannot exclude the possibility that Constantine II was the first to use the formula "all of Rus'" on his seal. In 1966, I. Ševčenko (as in the previous note) aptly drew our attention to the possible emergence of this formula under Constantine II. In any case, Michael II employed the formula "of all Rusians" (see above, n. 17, text in *The Life of Leontios*).

Suzdal', who had supported Andrei Bogoliubskii in his plans to create a new metropolitanate. The cruelty and severity of Constantine II's administration led to new conflicts that began to threaten the unity of the Church; in 1170, Constantine II was forced to return to Constantinople, and Michael II was sent in his place. He conveyed upon the abbot of the Cave Monastery the rank of archimandrite, bestowed by the patriarch, and to the monastery itself, the status of a laura — granted either at the time of Michael II's arrival or soon thereafter. The new patriarch Michael III of Anchialos, ordained in January 1170, was a patron of monasticism and enjoyed the support of the monks; he appreciated the Kievan Cave monastery for its steadfast allegiance to Constantinople and its importance to Rus'. So did the emperor himself.

We do not know for how long Michael II occupied the Kievan See. Under the year 1183, chronicles refer to the activity of metropolitan Nikephoros II, who evidently must have come to occupy the see at an earlier date. Considering that Leontios had been nominated to the metropolitanate of Kiev no earlier than 1173 and no later than 1175, we may suggest that the "Shepherd of all Rusians" Michael II died within this period. Nikephoros II's appointment to the see of Rus' must have followed upon Leontios' refusal.

Information on the succession of archbishops in Cyprus does little to help us determine when exactly the emperor offered the Kievan see to Leontios. From 1152 on, one John had been archbishop of Cyprus; he was still alive and well on 21 February 1170, taking part in conciliar deliberations in the Constantinople which concluded with the deposition of the archbishop of Corfu. It is evident from the *Vita of Leontios* that Cyprus "was widowed" soon after Rus' had been. John's successor, archbishop Barnabas, was carrying out his duties already in the fall of 1176 and, as D. Tsougarakis correctly surmised, had been ordained one or two years earlier.[24]

Having overcome a serious illness in the fall of 1172 and succeeded in visiting Crete on monastery business soon afterwards, Leontios arrived in the capital no sooner than early 1173. Only "when the time came", i.e. not immediately upon his arrival, was he received by the *megas droungarios* Andronikos Kamateros. This was, most likely, a renewal of contacts that had begun during the abbot's visits to Constantinople in the 1160s. Quite some time may have passed before Kamateros presented Leontios at the court and to the emperor himself. Thus we should date the emperor's offer of the metropolitan see of Rus' to Leontios to 1174 or, perhaps, to 1175; for it is more probable that the governing metropolitan of all Rus', Michael II, passed

[24] Grumel, *Les Regestes*, nos. 1109, 1112; *The Life of Leontios*, 106–107, 124–125; commentary, 194–195, 200.

away in 1174 and that news of his death reached Constantinople in the same year, in any case no later than early 1175. When Leontios declined the offer, a new candidate had to be found. Metropolitan Nikephoros II could have arrived in Kiev already in 1175, and certainly by 1176. He remained on the Kievan metropolitan throne for over a quarter of a century, a period second only to Cyril II (40 years); next longest was that of Nikephoros I (17 years).

Leontios stood out not only by his pronounced religiosity, theological acumen and exceptional intellect, but also by his spiritual independence, which he exhibited even in his declining years. Despite the fact that, as patriarch of Jerusalem "in exile", he was staying in the Capital solely at the emperor's discretion, in 1183, after Manuel's death (September 24, 1180), Leontios opposed the incestuous marriage of the new emperor Andronikos I Komnenos, repudiating all compromise. It is notable that the patriarch of Constantinople, Theodosios I Boradiotes, who, too, had attempted to oppose this marriage, was forced out in August 1183. It likewise testifies to the respect paid to and authority enjoyed by Leontios that, when he passed away on 14 May 1185, Andronikos I ordered him to be buried with all due honours and reverence.[25]

*

* *

A more detailed knowledge of the biography of one of the candidates to the metropolitanate of Rus' helps us supplement the scant data concerning other Kievan metropolitans of Manuel I's reign. The offer made to Leontios of Patmos allows us to understand better the motives that guided the Byzantine ecclesiastical and imperial policies towards Rus'. Here, the religious factor came to the fore: once resolved, the theological questions troubling the Byzantine Orthodox universe had to be made part of Rus' patrimony as well. Candidates, we may surmise, were selected with due attention paid to their theological learning, their strict adherence to ecclesiastical principles and their

---

[25] Grumel, *Les Regestes*, no. 1161; *The Life of Leontios*, 142–143, 134–137; W. Heckt, "Der Bios des Patriarchen Leontios von Jerusalem als Quelle zur Geschichte Andronikos' I. Komnenos", *Byzantinische Zeitschrift* 61 (1968), 40–43. The suggestion, accepted in earlier scholarly works, that Leontios' rank was that of the "titular" Patriarch of Jerusalem (so Beck, *Kirche*, 629) is erroneous. After his ordination, Leontios set off for the Holy Land (in late fall of 1176); he stayed there for a year, but was forced to return to Constantinople in the summer of 1178, for he was unable to establish a firm base in Jerusalem due to obstacles set up by Crusaders. The Latin patriarchate even prevented Leontios from celebrating mass in the Cathedral of the Holy Sepulchre. Leontios remained a patriarch "in exile" (ὑπερόριος).

ability to communicate with their flock on various levels. This meant that their knowledge of Slavic was also a consideration.[26] Some nominations were unfortunate, such as those of candidates overly severe both towards themselves and towards their milieu, i.e. candidates lacking the gift of "oikonomia," or compromise (such was the case of both Constantines), but no nominations were made at random. Quite possibly, the selection of fully deserving candidates was characteristic not just of the Comnenian era, but of earlier times as well. Overawed by metropolitan John II Prodromos (1077–1089), a chronicler, who was also a monk of the Cave Monastery, exclaimed, "such a man was never seen before in Rus', nor will there be one hereafter." This should in no way be seen as a negative evaluation of that metropolitan's predecessors or his immediate successors. It is rather an expression of the exceptional recognition given to John II by the Kievan monastic milieu that had always placed high demands on the metropolitans of all Rus'.[27]

The story of Leontios was not the only case when the metropolitanate of Rus' appeared in contemporary sources in conjunction with the archdiocese of Cyprus. The Emperor's offers to him, accidental in the sense that both were dictated by the almost simultaneous "widowhood" of both sees, were *not* accidental in the sense of their having been regarded as the two positions most worthy of the abbot of Patmos. On the one hand, Rus', from the point of view of the Byzantine Church's hierarchy of sees, was just a province of the Constantinopolitan Patriarchate occupying the sixtieth place in that hierarchy, whereas Cyprus, while also a metropolitanate, had been long ago made autonomous by the Church, which is why its helmsmen, to avoid misunderstandings, also enjoyed the rank of full autocephalous archbishop.

On the other hand, however, the singularity of the Churches of Rus' and Cyprus, as well as of that of Ochrid, was clearly outlined by Neilos Doxapatres in his ecclesiastico-geographical overview of the Byzantine world

[26] The assertion that the Greek metropolitans first wrote their epistles and pastoral admonitions in Greek and then had them translated into Slavic is unfounded. S. Franklin has brought to our attention the erroneous interpretation of the words of metropolitan Nikephoros to this effect in his "Greek in Kievan Rus'", *Dumbarton Oaks Papers* 42 (1992), 71–72; cf. also G. Podskalsky, "Der Beitrag der griechischstämmigen Metropoliten (Kiev), Bischöfe und Mönche zur altrussischen Originalliteratur (Theologie)", *Cahiers du monde russe et soviétique* 24 (1983), 498–515.

[27] On John II and his authorship of the most ancient *Sluzhba svv. Borisu i Glebu*, see G. Podskalsky, "Mitropolit Ioann II. von Kiev (1076/77–1089) als Ökumeniker", *Ostkirchliche Studien* 37/2–3 (1988), 178–183; A. Poppe, "O zarozhdenii kul'ta Borisa i Gleba i o posviashchennykh im proizvedeniiakh", *Russia Mediaevalis* 8/1 (1995), 31–44; see also F. v. Lilienfeld, "The Spirituality of the Early Kievan Caves Monastery", *Christianity and the Eastern Slavs* (Berkeley, Cal., 1993), 63–76.

(1142).[28] Prior to finding himself at the royal court of Sicily, Neilos served as notary to the patriarch of Constantinople and belonged to the clergy of Hagia Sophia, which meant that he was exceptionally well versed in church affairs. The exceptional character of the Churches of Rus' and Cyprus was also noted, apparently not by accident, by Abbot Daniil of Chernigov during his stay in Cyprus in 1106.[29]

This exceptional character was recognized in the 1170s when Manuel I offered Leontios the two newly vacant prestigious sees one after another. The emperor, having been refused twice and perhaps made aware that the reason for the refusal had not been arrogance but the gift of prophecy (at any rate, that is the explanation that the *Vita of Leontios* offered its readers), used the opportunity of a vacancy on the patriarchal see of Jerusalem to express, symbolically at least, his recognition of the merits and talents of an exceptional man of the Church.

---

[28] G. Parthey, *Nili Doxopatrii notitia patriarchatum* ... (Lipsiae, 1866), 296; Beck, *Kirche*, 619–620.

[29] A. Poppe, "Soobshchenie russkogo palomnika o tserkovnoi organizatsii Kipra v nachale XII veka", *Epetēris tou Kentrou Epistēmonikōn Ereunōn Kyprou* 8 (1978), 53–72.

VII

Losers on Earth, Winners from Heaven. The Assassinations of Boris and Gleb in the Making of Eleventh–Century Rus'[*]

On July 15, 1015 Prince Vladimir of Rus', who had led his people to join the family of Christian peoples, breathed his last. In a reign spanning over three decades, he had achieved much. By forging a political and military alliance with Byzantium in 987, he secured the Macedonian dynasty on the throne, and princely authority in Rus' gained a new level of statehood thanks to the marriage tie and the Church organization that the alliance brought[1]. Vladimir's will power drove on the Christianization of the main centres of Rus', but a vital stimulus came from Constantinople in the form of Vladimir's wife, Anna, who had been born in the Purple Chamber of the Great Palace. Her building of churches in Rus' soon after the conversion earned her fame even in far–away Antioch[2]. Vladimir in his own lifetime won high praise for his apostolic achievements from Bruno of Querfurt, who met him in 1008. Bruno, a missionary bishop renowned for his zeal "to subject to the true God" all the peoples of Europe, compared Vladimir's feats with those of Constantine the Great and Charlemagne[3]. Decades later, on the thirty–fifth anniversary

---

[*] This reconstruction of what are inevitably obscure events sums up the findings of research begun more than forty years ago. The results of the first stage of my investigations together with a review of the historiography may be found in: A. Poppe, *La naissance du culte de Boris et Gleb* // Cahiers de civilisation médiévale 24, 1981: 29–53. The second stage is registered in A. Poppe, *O zaroždenii kulta svv. Borisa i Gleba i o posviaščennykh im proizvedenijakh* // Russia Mediaevalis 8/1, 1995: 21–68. These studies together with my other works cited below provide basic bibliographical guidance. Primary sources that are cited verbatim in our text will be given full annotation. For the translation, more precisely, for a native English rendering of my paper I am indebted to my friend Jonathan Shepard from Cambridge/Oxford.

[1] Cf. A. Poppe, *The Political Background to the Baptism of Rus'. Byzantine–Russian Relations between 986–989* // Dumbarton Oaks Papers 30, 1976: 197–244.

[2] *Histoire de Yahya–Ibn–Sa'id d'Antioche*, ed. et trad. en français par. I. Kratchkovsky et A. Vasiliev, vol. 2 // Patrologia Orientalis 33/3, Paris 1932: 423. Cf. F. Kämpfer, *Eine Residenz für Anna Porphyrogenneta* // Jahrbücher für Geschichte Osteuropas 41, 1993: 101–110.

[3] A. Poppe, *Vladimir als Christ. Versuch eines psychologischen Porträts des Kiever Herrschers* // Österreichische Osthefte 35, 1993: 553–575.

of Vladimir's death, probably on Sunday, July 15, 1050, the priest Hilarion spoke in memory of him, standing beside the marble sarcophagus where he lay. Extolling Vladimir and likening him to Constantine the Great, Hilarion presented reasons for regarding him as equal to the Apostles and tried to give the anniversary of the *Great Kagan*'s death the character of a saint's festal commemoration, a saint to be revered for his conversion of the Rus'[4]. However, the entry of Vladimir into the company of saints, in the sense of passing through the canonical procedures, failed to come about. It was only imperceptibly that the cult of Vladimir as enlightener of the land of Rus' developed and, towards the end of the thirteenth century at a time of Mongol domination, he came to be regarded as a saint since time immemorial[5]. But judging by the utter, seemingly incomprehensible, silence of Hilarion's *Sermon on Law and Grace*, Vladimir's wife, the basilissa Anna, who had spread the faith together with the Apostle–like prince, had vanished into utter oblivion by the middle of the eleventh century.

Extraordinary as it was on any scale of achievement, Vladimir's reign concluded with the open rebellion of his two elder sons and the violent deaths of the two youngest ones. The infighting between his children shook the young political structure to its foundations over the ensuing decade. It is striking that in the lengthy struggle for the throne of Kiev not a single prince raised the banner of apostasy, even though paganism was anything but extinct among the broad masses of the population. Vladimir's sovereign act did not mark the very beginning of Christianity in Rus', but it did set the new religion on a firm base and the twenty–eight years he spent instilling it ensured that the changes were irreversible.

Christianity arrived in Rus' before Vladimir's formal conversion in 988, but his personal example was followed by leading members of Rus' society and their various retainers, arms–bearers and servants, as well as by a substantial proportion of the inhabitants of the urban centres. The extent of the transformation was clear even at the court of Polotsk's prince. Wizards and sorcery had not yet left the scene at Polotsk in the 1030s, but its princes relied on Christian teachings and standards to defend them from Iaroslav and his offspring. It is no accident that Vseslav of Polotsk was one of the first to venerate his late kinsmen, Boris and Gleb, and it is no coincidence that the Caves Monastery of Kiev was well–disposed towards the princes of Polotsk[6].

---

[4] Hilarion, *Sermon on Law and Grace // Sermons and Rhetoric of Kievan Rus'*, transl. by S. Franklin, Cambridge, Mass. 1991: 3–31, encomium to Vladimir: 17–26.

[5] Cf. A. Poppe, *Vladimir Sviatoj. U istokov cerkovnogo proslavlenija* // Byzantinorossica 3, Sankt Petersburg [hereafter: SPb.] 2003: 9–55. Cf. B. Uspenskij, *Kogda był kanonizirovan kniaz' Vladimir Sviatoslavič? // For Ihor Ševčenko on his 80th birthday*, Paleoslavica X/2, Cambridge, Mass. 2002: 271–281; V. Vodoff, *Autour du mythe de la Sainte Russie. Christianisme, pouvoir et société chez les Slaves Orientaux*, Paris 2003: 119–133.

[6] Cf. Poppe, *O zaroždenii kulta*: 63–65. *The Russian Primary Chronicle Laurentian Text transl. and ed.* by S. H. Cross and O. P. Sherbowitz–Wetzor, Cambridge, Mass. 1953: 139, 149, 162, 199, 204 (hereafter: *Primary Chronicle*). Our bias will be in favour of citing from published English translations of the Old

Why, though, had Boris and Gleb come to grief, or, more precisely, why had they been put to death in secret? It is striking that, with the exception of these two boys born to Vladimir by a Bulgarian woman according to their hagiographer, none of the other participants in the bitter struggle for Kiev, not even the "accursed" exile, Sviatopolk, lost his life[7].

One can find a neat, even convincing, answer in the works dedicated to them: that the author of their secret murder, their brother Sviatopolk, wanted complete power in Rus' for himself, liquidating all his brothers in the process. But this raises a key question: why should Sviatopolk, already entitled to the Kievan throne as Vladimir's eldest son, have ordered the murder of Boris and Gleb as soon as he mounted it? Seeing that Boris and Gleb were among the youngest of all Vladimir's sons, they posed no threat to Sviatopolk's right to Kiev — unless, perhaps, there were changes in the line of succession that the *Primary Chronicle* and the *Lives* of Boris and Gleb pass over in silence.

The murder of Boris and Gleb was a quintessentially political crime. Yet the very fact that they perished unawares and secretly at the hands of assassins, not battling for power and their lives, gave the death sentence passed on them and their lack of resistance the air of sacrificial death and martyrdom. It is no accident that in a newly Christianized society princes who forswore resistance and the power struggle in favour of the heavenly kingdom and paid for this with their lives, gradually came to be seen as witnesses to the true faith. The deaths of Boris and Gleb were taken to be the sacrifice of martyrs imbued with Christian teachings: through their conduct they had borne witness and shown that they were true followers of Christ in word and deed. Thus it was that a politically inspired death sentence came — from the way it was executed and the way it was accepted by the victims — to be viewed as an example of suffering for Christ's sake. Boris and Gleb were believed to have sealed the birth of Christian Rus' with their own blood.

The appearance of this tradition about Boris and Gleb in written form together with their cult all took place in the course of the eleventh century. The mystery of their deaths and the date and the way in which they found sainthood will be addressed below, but on one point there is now general agreement: these holy blissful martyrs, who paid the supreme price for putting their Christian ideals into practice, were already the inalienable property of all Christian Rus' by the time the century ended.

Rus' primary sources, but sometimes there is reason to give a fresh translation (made by J. Shepard). On those occasions, a direct reference is given to the original edition, the existence of a published translation is noted with "cf".

[7] The claim of *Primary Chronicle*: 130 that a third son of Vladimir, Sviatoslav, was killed, dates from not earlier than the end of the eleventh century. It should be regarded as untrustworthy in the light of the emphasis of Nestor the hagiographer around 1080 that Sviatopolk was predestined to fail in his scheme to do away with all his other brothers after murdering Boris and Gleb. See *The Hagiography of Kievan Rus'*, transl. with introduction by P. Hollingsworth, Cambridge, Mass. 1992: 16–17, cf. 191 [hereafter: *Hagiography of Kievan Rus'*]. On Sudislav see below pp. 29–30 and fn. 35.

***

The tradition about Boris (whose baptismal name was Roman) and Gleb (baptismal name: David) is crystallized in the hagiographical works devoted to them[8]. These are as follows:

1 (a) The anonymous *Tale of the Passion and Encomium of the Holy Martyrs Boris and Gleb*, composed around 1072 and supplemented by,

1 (b) *The Tale of the Miracles of the Holy Passion Sufferers of Christ Roman and David*, composed in the years 1072–1073 and continued around 1116,

2 *The Lesson on the Life and Murder of the Holy Passion Sufferers Boris and Gleb and on their Miracles*, written by Nestor the hagiographer around 1080,

3 The oldest *Office for the Holy Martyrs Roman and David*, composed around 1084[9],

4 The entries for the years 1015, 1072 and 1115 in the *Primary Chronicle*[10].

Whatever one may think about the origin of the *Primary Chronicle*'s account *On the Killing of Boris and Gleb* or about its interrelationship with their *Lives*, the *Chronicle* entry for 1015 is patently dealing with princes already deemed martyrs. Both its style and its content have a markedly hagiographical character[11].

Our evidence for the events in the lives of Boris and Gleb, their assassination and the beginnings of their cult is obviously bound up with writings in praise of their self–sacrifice and their sanctity. Even so, we must not forget that hagiography forms part of history. For all its lack of chronological, topographical and, to some extent, factual bearings and its attempts to create a picture which could be regarded as unhistorical, hagiography is a form of historical writing with its own ideological agenda, in this case of a politico–religious type. In plain words, belonging to the genre of hagiography does not disqualify texts from being first–class historical

---

[8] For an English translation of these works see: Hagiography of Kievan Rus': 3–32 (The *Lesson* by Nestor); 97–134 (The *Tale of the Passion* and The *Tale of the Miracles*); 183–206 (from the *Chronicle*). F. Thomson's critical remarks (Byzantinoslavica 55, 1994: 364–375), important as they are for textual analysis, do not detract from the value of this translation in providing an overall picture of the contents of the works. For the circumstances of composition and the dating of these writings, see A. Poppe, *Opowieść o męczeństwie i cudach Borysa i Gleba. Okoliczności i czas powstania utworu* // Slavia Orientalis 18, 1969: 267–292, 359–382; idem., *Chronologia utworów Nestora–hagiografa* // Slavia Orientalis 14, 1965: 287–305.

[9] The oldest *Office*, which defies precise rendering, was discussed and supplied with an English translation of some of its hymnal verses by G. Lenhoff, *The Martyred Princes Boris and Gleb*: A Socio–Cultural Study of the Cult and the Texts, Columbus, Ohio 1989: 56–71, 132–134. For the dating, see A. Poppe, *O zaroždenii kulta*: 31–45.

[10] *Primary Chronicle*: 124–131, 154–155; *Hagiography of Kievan Rus'*: 183–206. For the secondary status of the 1072 entry, see A. Poppe, *Uwagi o najstarszych dziejach Kościoła na Rusi*, cz. 3 // Przegląd Historyczny 56, 1965: 560–563.

[11] For the essentials of the dispute over the interrelationship between these texts, see L. Müller, *O vremeni kanonizacii sviatykh Borisa i Gleba* // Russia Mediaevalis 8/1, 1995: 5–20; A. Poppe, *O zaroždenii kulta*: 21–68.

sources and they are fair game for analysis by the rules of source criticism, like any other material drawn on by the historian. Not that one should draw a hard and fast line between medieval historical writing and the writing of saints' *Lives*: each in its way is highly literary moralizing and rhetorical.

Having set out the approach, methods and direction that our arguments will take, we can dispense with polemic or exhaustive examination of the sources. We shall make do with references to our earlier publications and draw on their conclusions. Thus equipped, we shall follow up the surviving clues bit by bit and hazard a reconstruction of the chain of events. These involved the failure of Vladimir's plans to alter the order of succession to the throne, the downfall on earth and consignment to oblivion of Boris and Gleb — and their eventual heavenly triumph and emergence as spiritual protectors of the land of Rus'.

***

In accordance with the agreement reached with Byzantium in early autumn, 987, Vladimir, the ruler of Rus', completed his catechumenate towards the end of that year and was baptized on January 6, 988. Then, in the summer of 988, he met his Porphyrogenitan bride at the Dnieper Rapids and married her in a Christian ceremony in Kiev. Anna, who became the sole lawful wife of Vladimir, was the sister of the Byzantine emperors Basil II and Constantine VIII. The *Primary Chronicle* describes her as *tsesaritsa* (i.e. *basilissa*), and she was, in the words of the future pope Silvester II, "daughter of the holy empire". Born on March 13, 963, Anna was in her twenty–sixth year at the time of her marriage. She was several years younger than Vladimir and there are no grounds for supposing that the marriage was childless, even if direct evidence of children is lacking. Moreover, there is a strange silence about Anna in the *Chronicle*, which mentions her only in the context of its story of Vladimir's baptism in Cherson and in connexion with her death in 1011. The silence is particularly strange in the case of the *Sermon on Law and Grace*, where Hilarion lauds Vladimir on the eve of his own installation as metropolitan of Kiev. Hilarion takes care to mention Vladimir's father, Sviatoslav, his grandfather and grandmother, Igor and Olga, and also his son, Iaroslav, together with his wife, Irene, and their children[12]. Yet no mention is made of Anna, the imperial consort of Vladimir, despite Hilarion's attempt to rank this prince among the saints. And this encomium was delivered by Hilarion while he stood over Vladimir's marble sarcophagus in the princely — Tithe church. As we know from Thietmar of Merseburg's chronicle, as late as August 1018, Anna's remains also rested in the middle of that same church[13]. It was probably towards the middle of

---

[12] Hilarion // *Sermons and Rhetoric*: 17, 23, 24.

[13] *Thietmari Merseburgensis episcopi Chronicon*, lib. VII, 74; ed. by R. Holtzmann, W. Trillmich // Ausgewählte Quellen zur deutschen Geschichte des Mittelalters, Bd. IX, Berlin 1957: 436 transl. 437 [hereafter: *Thietmari Chronicon*]. Cf. A. Poppe, *Politik und Heiligenverehrung in der Kiever Rus' // Politik und Heiligenverehrung im Hochmittelalter* (Vorträge und Forschungen 42), Sigmaringen 1994: 405–409.

the eleventh century that Anna's sarcophagus was moved from its central position under the cupola to beneath the tiled floor. One has the impression of attempts being made to turn Anna into an unperson and to nullify the works of enlightenment which she carried out with Vladimir in the newly converted land. These attempts seem to have been highly effective.

Circumstantial evidence tends to suggest that Vladimir and Anna were not in fact childless. There are serious grounds for believing that Theophana, wife of Ostromir — the governor of Novgorod — was their daughter, named after Anna's mother. If Theophana was the half–sister of prince Iaroslav and the aunt of Iaroslav's son, Iziaslav, then her husband Ostromir would have been Iziaslav's relative by marriage. And a colophon of the *Ostromir Gospel–Book* directly indicates that they were related in this way[14]. There have long been suspicions and surmises of an imperial lineage for Boris and Gleb. Already in the late fifteenth century the Tver chronicler averred, "and from the *tsarevna* Anna, Boris and Gleb". S. M. Soloviev made full allowance for this possibility, noting that it would explain much about the events of that period[15].

The only really clear hint of an imperial origin for Boris is, admittedly, a remark made by the author of the earliest *Saints' Office* (liturgical Service): "Thou, Romanus, the most richly endowed, adorned with the imperial crown from thy youth onwards, great was thy authority over all creation in thy fatherland"[16]. Boris could have received this baptismal name in honour of Anna's father, Emperor Romanus II, while his princely name of Boris could have been given out of respect for Boris–Michael, the baptizer of Bulgaria, or perhaps even as an echo of Sviatoslav's links with Tsar Boris II. Sviatoslav had, after all, been his overlord and intended to shift the centre of his realm down to the Danube[17]. Boris–Romanus was born around 990 AD, when Basil II was beginning the conquest of Bulgaria with the assistance of a Rus' contingent, and when the outcome was far from certain. This was a matter for speculation in Kiev as well as Byzantium. There are grounds for supposing that Anna and Vladimir were planning to secure the Bulgarian throne for their first–born.

---

[14] A. Poppe, *Theophana von Novgorod* // Byzantinoslavica 58, 1997: 131–158. Anna, born in 963, could still have been child–bearing up to the age of forty–two to forty–four. Cf. J. B. Post, *Ages at Menarche and Menopause: Some Mediaeval Authorities* // Population Studies. A Journal of Demography 25, 1971, no. 1: 83–87.

[15] *Polnoje sobranije russkikh letopisiej* [hereafter: PSRL] 15, SPb. 1863: 73; S. M. Soloviev, *Istoria Rossii* I–1, Moscow re–ed. 1962: 204, fn. 290. An imperial ancestry for Boris and Gleb may also have some connotations for the history of the Ottonian empire in general. See J. Shepard, *Otto III, Boleslaw Chrobry and the "happening" at Gniezno AD 1000: some possible implications of Professor Poppe's thesis concerning the offspring of Anna Porphyrogenita* // Byzantium and East Central Europe, Cracow 2001: 27–49.

[16] *Žitija sviatykh mučenikov Borisa i Gleba i služby im*, ed. D. Abramovič, Petrograd 1916: 136–137 [hereafter: *Žitija*].

[17] G. Ostrogorsky, *History of the Byzantine State*, New Brunswick N.J. 1969: 292–296. Cf. S. Franklin, J. Shepard, *The Emergence of Rus' 750–1200*, London 1996: 139–150.

In this period, the Old Testament king David was held up as a model of Christian rulership and each successive Byzantine emperor was extolled as a "new" or "second" David. The bestowal of the name on Gleb, who was born around 1000 AD, sheds light on the designs of his mother. Having lived in Kiev for years, Anna realized perfectly well that, with the arrival of male offspring from her Church–sanctioned union with Vladimir, the question of the succession was squarely on the agenda. To a Byzantine *basilissa* it was self–evident that Vladimir's throne was the rightful inheritance of her sons of imperial blood, and she well understood that without a struggle their rights would never become a reality. The Biblical David, the embodiment of kingly authority, had in fact reached the throne as God's Elect and Anointed One after single combat with Goliath, not as legitimate heir. To Anna as a mother, the name probably appeared to have prophylactic powers, protecting her son from harm. A queen mother's ambition to secure the throne for her sons was so habitual (as, for example, in the cases of Charles the Bald's mother Judith or Constance, the wife of Robert the Pious)[18] that it should really be viewed more as a political and moral imperative. The Byzantine institution of co–emperorship provided a way of reconciling the interests of the two sons of Vladimir and Anna easily enough[19]. And the fact that the role of co–ruler, i.e. direct heir, had been secured for the under–age Gleb helps explain why he was "slaughtered like a lamb" by those sent to carry out the sentence, once they had dealt with Boris.

***

The inclination of, above all, Anna to Byzantinize the form of succession to the Kievan throne is suggested by one other important detail, which has not received much attention hitherto.

In Christian Rus', a prince's accession to the throne took the form of a solemn religious ceremony in church. The enthronement ritual was staged in the core part of the church, where the prince's throne stood. One can reasonably maintain that

---

[18] E. Temp, *Die Überlieferung der Vita Hludovici imperatoris des Astronomus* (MGH Studien und Texte, Bd. 1) Hannover 1991: 141–142, fn. 306. See also *Rodulfi Glabri Historiarum Libri Quinque*, ed. and transl. J. France, Oxford 1989: 150–159 (book 3, ch. 32–35). It is no accident that the theme of David's rise to kingly power was also celebrated by the court scholars of Charles the Bald, who himself greatly venerated David: J. L. Nelson, *Charles the Bald*, London 1992: 15, 92, 158–159. At about the same time, Basil the Macedonian's (and Patriarch Photius') interest in the anointing of David is shown by a number of artworks and literary texts: L. Brubaker, *Vision and Meaning in Ninth–Century Byzantium*, Cambridge 1999: 185–191, 208–210.

[19] See Gerbert of Aurillac's letter to Archbishop Egbert of Trier of 984: *more grecorum conregnantem instituere vultis*: Gerbert d'Aurillac, *Correspondance*, ed. P. Riché and J. P. Callu, Paris 1993: 52 (text), 53 (French tr.). Byzantine court culture is very likely to have informed Anna's keen sense of imperial dynastic legitimacy. See H. Hunger, *Zum Dynastieproblem in Byzanz* // Anzeiger der phil.–hist. Klasse der Österreichischen Akademie der Wissenschaften 131, 1994: 273–277; O. Kresten, A. E. Müller, *Samtherrschaft, Legitimationsprinzip und Kaiserlicher Urkundentitel in Byzanz in der ersten Hälfte des 10 Jahrhunderts* // Sitzungsberichte der Österreichischen Akademie der Wissenschaften 630, Wien 1995: 1–43.

the Church ceremonial for installing a ruler on the throne was, in its basic features, brought to Rus' ready–made, by Anna Porphyrogenita[20].

But if the Christian ritual for enthroning a ruler was introduced to Rus' so successfully, this raises the question why coronation did not catch on, too. It is all the more curious, seeing that already in the tenth century pagan barbarians, Rus' among them, were susceptible enough to marks of imperial rank to be asking for the emperor's vestments and crowns in Constantinople, albeit to no avail. But times had moved on. The *basilissa* who had arrived in a Rus' fast becoming Christian had no wish to be demoted to the rank of mere princess (*archontissa)*. She preferred to raise her husband to her own status, crowning him with a stemma. This would not put him on a completely equal footing with the emperor of the Romans, but it meant a place next to the emperor in the family of Christian rulers. If the Bulgarian rulers Simeon and Peter could be accepted in Constantinople as duly crowned *basileis*, such an honour was all the more becoming for the master of Kiev, husband of "the daughter of the holy empire". Kiev did not renounce this honour, as witness the gold and silver coins that show Vladimir resplendent in Byzantine imperial regalia. His stemma has a cross in the middle of the hoop with pendants hanging down on either side, and he is sitting on a throne with a nimbus round his head and holds a sceptre in his hands. Scholars differ in their interpretations of Vladimir's coin designs, but the prevailing view is that the imitations of the Byzantine *nomismata* of Basil II and Constantine VIII do not reflect the actual symbols of "monarchical" authority then in use in Rus'. This point of view rests on the assumption that if a coronation ceremony involving imperial regalia had been introduced, it could not simply have been abandoned to vanish without trace.

But in fact there are faint traces of these regalia. They may be detected on the coins of Vladimir's sons, Sviatopolk–Peter and Iaroslav–George, as well as on a couple of seals discovered recently[21]. Leaving aside the differences between their various coin types, there is a particular point of interest to us here. In one group of Sviatopolk's coins, he is shown wearing a crown, sitting on the throne and holding a sceptre (approx. 25 examples), but another group (approx. 45 examples), while still maintaining the dies of Vladimir's coins, shows the Apostle Peter, Sviatopolk's patron saint, instead of the prince with his monarchical regalia. And on all the coins of Iaroslav save for two imitations of Vladimir's coins, the prince's portrait is replaced by a bust of St George, from whom Iaroslav took his Christian name. So it emerges that Sviatopolk in due course and Iaroslav from the very start of his reign, around

---

[20] A. Poppe, The *Enthronement of the Prince in Kievan Rus' // The 17th International Byzantine Congress. Abstracts of Papers*, Washington DC 1986: 272–274.

[21] M. P. Sotnikova, I. G. Spasskij, *Tysiačeletie drevnejsikh monet Rossii. Svodnyj katalog X–XI vekov*, Leningrad 1983: 115–179 (the coins of Vladimir); 180–195 (the coins of Sviatopolk); 196–203 (the coins of Iaroslav). Altogether 340 coins (75% of them belonging to Vladimir) with 220 die–stamps are known: V. L. Janin, *Dve drevnierusskie vislyje pečati nacala XI v. // Gennadios (Festschrift for G. G. Litavrin)*, Moscow 1999: 292–303. On one seal Sviatopolk is represented as wearing a crown; on the other seal Iaroslav wears a helmet.

1017, passed up the honour of being depicted on their coins in imperial regalia and, one might add, from actually using such regalia. In other words, each of these rulers forbore from styling himself as a *rex coronatus*. It seems that Sviatopolk kept to Vladimir's dies during his first spell as lord of Kiev from July 1015 to December 1016, merely introducing his own name onto the coins. Then, when he returned to Kiev in August 1018, he began striking a new type that portrayed his patron, St Peter. Without entering into the other reasons why princes stopped issuing their own coins soon after Vladimir's death, one may detect in the changes in Sviatopolk's and Iaroslav's coins the abandonment of the *actual use* of Byzantine imperial regalia. The regalia would have been seen as part and parcel of the "Byzantinization" of the succession to the Kievan throne.

One may surmise that the testament resulting from Anna's efforts enabled Vladimir and Anna to follow through their decision and settle the succession in their own lifetimes. They did this by solemnly installing Boris and Gleb as co–rulers, Byzantine–style, accompanying the enthronement with a coronation rite. But the other Rurikids nipped this attempt at Byzantinization in the bud, in their determination to maintain the dynastic tradition of the eldest son's right to the throne. They eliminated all traces of it even from their own symbols of sovereign authority. To them a crown probably signified dependence upon the emperor conferring it, even if it also carried some "royal" connotations[22]. The imperial crown, in particular, was consigned to oblivion so that when, centuries later in Moscow, it was decided to introduce an imperial coronation ceremonial, bookmen trying to invent an ancestral tradition pinned their conjectures on the great–grandson of Vladimir the Great and grandson of Emperor Constantine IX, Vladimir Monomakh.

***

Although the hagiographer of Boris and Gleb was not particularly interested in the origins of the sons of Vladimir whom he listed by their mothers (with the exception of Rogneda of Polotsk), he did refer, fleetingly but deliberately, to the mother of Boris and Gleb, calling her "a Bulgarian". In reality, Anna was Greek, but the hagiographer either did not know this or, not wanting to break the taboo, used the everyday nickname for her, which he had picked up and which did not necessarily serve as an indicator of ethnic identity. Those ill–disposed towards Emperor Basil I, the founder of the Macedonian dynasty, called him "the Slav", albeit cautiously. The Byzantine empress Maria, a Georgian by origin, was known to her Byzantine contemporaries in the 1070s as "the Alanian"[23]. Anna could have been commonly known by the epithet "the Bulgarian" in the streets of Constantinople,

---

[22] See the important observations, supported by ample comparative evidence, of T. Wasilewski, *La couronne royale — symbole de dépendance à l'époque du haut Moyen Âge. Les deux couronnements de Boleslas la Vaillant prince de Pologne // La Pologne au XV Congres historique*, Wrocław 1980: 25–50.
[23] *The Oxford Dictionary of Byzantium*, vol. 2, 1991: 1298; N. Tobias, *Basil I (867–886). The Founder of the Macedonian Dynasty*, New Brunswick 1969: 2–18. A. M. H. Shboul, *Al-Mas'udi and His World*, London 1979: 251, 277.

while in Kiev there were grounds for doing so. As is well-known, Emperor Nicephorus' Phocas, in a bid for the Bulgarians' good-will in 968/69, declared himself ready to betroth both the young *porphyrogeniti*, Basil II and Constantine VIII, to Bulgarian princesses. So it is all the more plausible that he or his successor John Tzimisces (969–976) may have betrothed the boys' sister to the Bulgarian heir to the throne[24].

These passing diplomatic manoeuvres came to nothing, but the nickname of "the Bulgarian" could have stuck to Anna. In fact, for several years she had the chance to mingle with the aforesaid Bulgarian princesses in the palace of Blachernai, as well as with the eminent hostages Boris and Romanus, Tsar Peter's sons. They were, like Anna herself, descended from the emperor Romanus Lecapenus and thus were her distant relatives. No doubt, the children chattered among themselves — the girls were no more than seven to ten years of age — and Anna, then about seven years old, could have picked up Bulgarian Slavonic, especially as this language was not unfamiliar in the court. Arriving in Kiev, Anna may still have have spoken Slavonic with a Bulgarian accent and therefore to the Kievans she would have been "the Bulgarian". It is also worth recalling that the half-brother of Anna's grandmother, Basil the chamberlain, the most educated man of his time, the *éminence grise* of emperors up to 985 and an outstandingly influential court dignitary, had a Bulgarian mother. Bishop Liudprand, the envoy of Otto I in 968, was outraged at the special attention and prominence given to the Bulgarians in court receptions.

The hagiographer's purpose in listing the mothers of Vladimir's sons must have been to impress upon his readers the fact that the mother of the martyrs whom he was glorifying had been a Christian. Their killer, Sviatopolk, was of sinful stock: his mother was a defrocked nun, the serial concubine of the pagan brothers Iaropolk and Vladimir. Finally, through listing the four sons of Vladimir by Rogneda, he clearly reminds the reader that the elder brothers of Boris and Gleb were born from a union contracted before Vladimir's baptism.

***

As the years passed, with Vladimir under the influence of his porphyrogenita and her Byzantine courtiers, and with some input from the clergy at court, the idea that his sons by "the daughter of the holy empire" were the sole legitimate heirs to the throne began to gain ground. Their blood tie with the Macedonian dynasty together with the fact that Emperor Basil himself was their uncle — all this must have left its mark on Vladimir's political testament. It secured the Kievan throne

---

[24] Traces of this episode, albeit in a highly legendary form, may be found in Stephen of Taron (Asolik)'s *Universal History* III, 22, French tr. E. Dulaurier and F. Macler // Publications de l'Ecole des Langues Orientales Vivantes, ser. I, vol. 18 bis. Paris 1917: 74, 124; see Poppe, *Political Background*: 203–304. This marriage agreement might seem to have been demeaning to the empire, but it was not unprecedented: J. Shepard, *A Marriage too Far? Maria Lekapena and Peter of Bulgaria // The Empress Theophano. Byzantium and the West at the Turn of the First Millennium*, ed. A. Davids, Cambridge 1995: 121–149.

and supreme rights over all Rus' for Boris and Gleb while requiring Vladimir's other sons to make do with peripheral seats, giving up all prospects of inheriting Kiev. This order of succession was, seemingly, in place soon after the autumn of 1008, when Vladimir sent to the Pechenegs as a hostage Sviatopolk, his eldest, or possibly — if Vysheslav was still alive — his second oldest son. Vladimir's decision, taken in Anna's lifetime (i.e. before 1011), was accompanied by Byzantine–style ceremonial, the enthronement and coronation of Boris–Romanus as prince of Kiev, in direct succession to Vladimir, together with Gleb–David as his co–ruler. At any rate Boris, "adorned with the imperial crown from his youth onwards", was with Vladimir in Kiev at the time of his death and his father gave him the task of repelling the Pecheneg marauders. This is an important indication that Vladimir had designated Boris as his heir[25].

***

After marrying the daughter of Boleslaw the Brave around 1011, Sviatopolk ensconced himself in the region of Pinsk and Turov, which his father had assigned to him. Evidently, the "Byzantine" party lost ground after the death of Anna and discontent simmered among those of Vladimir's sons not born of a Church–sanctioned marriage. A wedding ceremony held actually in church was *de rigueur* in the upper and, to a considerable extent, the middling echelons of Byzantine society in this period, but it was still far from the norm in other parts of Christian Europe. In fact, it was still quite usual for people to get married without a priest or a church being involved (albeit sometimes with the priest's benediction in a private house). One must remember that in this traditional order of things membership of the ruling dynasty was determined by who one's father was, not by one's mother, with only very rare exceptions. Thus Vladimir himself, born of Sviatoslav's liaison with Malusha, the unfree court key holder of Sviatoslav's mother, Olga, did not forfeit his inheritance rights on this account — even though a full century and a half later in Polotsk and elsewhere people could still taunt the descendants of a "slaveling", that is, a slave woman's son[26].

---

[25] Already (1913) suggested by M. Hrushevsky, *History of Ukraine–Rus'*, vol. 1, Edmonton–Toronto 1997: 404; see A. Poppe, *Der Kampf um die Kiever Thronfolge nach dem 15 Juli 1015* // Forschungen zur osteuropäischen Geschichte 50, 1995: 277–282. In his Essays on the international relations of Rus' in the ninth to twelfth centuries, a work summing up the results of twenty years of research on the topic, A. V. Nazarenko eschews discussing in depth the thesis that Anna Porphyrogenita was Boris' and Gleb's mother. He thus remains within the mainstream of the historiographical tradition that excludes these princes' earthly fate from the purview of students of historical events of the early eleventh century. Nazarenko focuses instead on their role as Holy Martyrs, already assured by hagiography. See Chapter X, "Volodimer's Sons' Struggle for Kiev in the Years 1015–1019", in A. V. Nazarenko, *Drevnjaja Rus' na meždunarodnykh putjakh*, Moscow 2001: 449; 451–504.

[26] See PSRL 1, 1927: 299–300. The Nikonian Chronicle (PSRL 9, 1862: 155–156) contains the text s.a. 1128 in almost the same words as those of the original, and is available in an English translation: *The Nikonian Chronicle from the Beginning to the Year 1132 (Volume One)*, tr. S. A. and B. J. Zenkovsky, Princeton 1984: 252–253. Almost all the volumes of the PSRL have been reprinted more than once. The year of the reprint is not given here.

The protest against their father's decision by the sons excluded from the succession developed into an understanding that had the hallmarks of a conspiracy. Sviatopolk and Iaroslav were involved and so, probably, was the ruler of distant Tmutorokan', Mstislav. Nothing is known about the demeanour of the other sons who had been passed over. The compact came to Vladimir's knowledge in the first half of 1013 and he took effective counteraction, putting Sviatopolk in prison. Since he also detained Sviatopolk's wife and Bishop Reinbern, one may conclude that Vladimir, like Thietmar of Merseburg, suspected Boleslaw the Brave of being behind the conspiracy. In any case, that summer the Polish ruler made an incursion into Kievan territory, but an armed clash with Sviatopolk's allies, the Pechenegs, led to its failure. In this expedition, as also in the expedition to Kiev of 1018, Saxons were involved and thanks to them Thietmar, writing his chronicle in Merseburg, is fairly well–informed[27]. This was probably the detachment sent by Sviatopolk's brother–in–law, Margrave Hermann of Meissen. Hermann was married to Regelindis, the sister of Sviatopolk's wife.

In 1014 Vladimir prepared an expedition to send against Novgorod. His aim was to bring to heel Iaroslav who, in S. M. Soloviev's words, "was disinclined to become Boris' governor in Novgorod and so made haste to declare himself independent"[28]. But the expedition never took place. The prince of Kiev, who was now nearing sixty years of age, fell ill. As the expedition was prompted by Iaroslav's refusal to pay the annual tribute due from Novgorod to Kiev, one may conclude that Iaroslav had refused to send the two thousand grivnas (ca 400 kg of silver) — due as tribute for, probably, the previous year (1013). Iaroslav had reason to show displeasure, for although at that time the eldest of the sons — Sviatopolk — was first in line of succession to the Kievan throne, Vladimir's decision also dashed any chance of Iaroslav ever gaining Kiev. In the light of the steps taken by Vladimir against Sviatopolk and Iaroslav, another of Thietmar's statements is highly suggestive: that Vladimir "left all his inheritance in its entirety to two sons, while a third one was in prison"[29]. Taking this statement in isolation, one might interpret it in a variety of ways, especially as the Saxon chronicler's information is rather scrappy. But it carries particular weight here, seeing that these chronicle entries register Thietmar's anguish concerning his fellow alumnus from the school of Magdeburg, Bishop Reinbern: Reinbern had been landed in this dubious enterprise and did not survive his imprisonment. The statement in itself suggests that Thietmar gained his information about this

---

[27] *Thietmari Chronicon*, lib. IV, 58; VI, 91; VII, 65, 72, 73, 74; VIII, 31, 32, 33; cf. Poppe, *Der Kampf*: 282—290.

[28] S. M. Soloviev, *Istoria Rossii* 1–(1): 205.

[29] *Thietmari Chronicon*, lib. VII, 73: *rex* [Vladimir]... *obiit, integritatem hereditatis suae duobus relinquens filiis, tercio* [Sviatopolk] *adhuc in carcere posito. Relinquens* corresponds exactly with the English "relinquishing", i.e. "leaving" but also "transferring" (*relinquo aliquem heredem*). In any case, taking into account all the circumstances, the translation "abandoning" is unacceptable here. The problem is to identify Thietmar's "two sons": I propose Boris and Gleb.

episode during Vladimir's lifetime or, at any rate, that he did not hear of Sviatopolk's release at the same time as learning of Vladimir's death. In the light of what we now know, Thietmar's statement offers clear confirmation that Vladimir's testament was essentially in favour of the two sons borne to him by Anna.

Boris was in effect already co–ruler with Vladimir in Kiev by the time of Vladimir's death. News of the death reached Boris while he was on a campaign against the Pechenegs, who had been harassing Kiev with their raids. Their incursions were linked with — and in any case gained a *casus belli* from — the detention of Sviatopolk, who was their blood brother. The numerous warriors amassed under Boris' command were, in the words of the written tradition, ready to secure "his father's throne" for him[30].

In the palace, attempts were made to conceal Vladimir's death until Boris could get back with his retinue. The circumstances are unclear, as firstly Vladimir's courtiers and then Sviatopolk himself had an interest in temporarily suppressing the news. But as soon as Sviatopolk's supporters had sprung him from jail, he mounted the throne in Kiev. He immediately sent a message to Boris, declaring his readiness to form an alliance of friendship, and he summoned Gleb to his sick father's bedside in Kiev, without revealing that he was in fact already dead. It is not in doubt that Sviatopolk managed to suborn Boris' retinue and warriors, and that they abandoned their commander, the rightful heir to the throne by the terms of Vladimir's will. The question is merely whether this happened (as the aforementioned hagiographical tradition makes out) because of Boris' renunciation of the Kievan throne in an attempt to avert a succession struggle; or whether Sviatopolk managed to win over the retainers accompanying Boris on his expedition, and then Boris, realizing his utter isolation, decided to renounce the Kievan throne and recognize his eldest brother's right to it. This right is axiomatic in the hagiographer's scale of values. His emphasis on Boris' recognition of the seniority principle and thus of Sviatopolk's right to the Kievan throne is very insistent and one may reasonably suspect that his audience was not, in fact, fully in sympathy with this point of view, though he himself was a fervent advocate of succession in order of chronological seniority.

From the events of 1015 it emerges that Boris and Gleb's fate was sealed regardless of anything they had actually done. If the hagiographical tradition has preserved the authentic dates, they were done away with on, respectively, July 24 and September 5, 1015. This drastic solution was favoured as the one sure way of ruling out further attempts at "Byzantinizing" the succession to the throne. Although the various *Lives* name and shame the instigator of this crime, one should note that the perpetrators were despatched to do their work furtively. The effect was to conceal the identity of the true ringleaders in the first years after the murders; at any rate, the brothers' disappearance was shrouded in silence. One measure of

[30] Cf. *Hagiography of Kievan Rus'*: 13 (*Nestor*); 102 (the *Tale*); 185 (*Primary Chronicle* s.a. 1015).

the cover–up is the fact that the Saxons then in Kiev heard nothing about the bloodletting in the Rus' ruling family. Had Thietmar received word about it from the Saxons, he would not have passed up the opportunity of vilifying Boleslaw, whom he loathed, for protecting a son–in–law who had butchered his own brothers. Moreover, in August 1018 the metropolitan of Kiev laid on a solemn reception for Sviatopolk, involving the Kievan nobility and part of the princely family, including nine daughters of Vladimir. The metropolitan greeted and blessed the participants, accompanied by his clergy in full ecclesiastical vestments, bearing relics of the saints with crosses and icons. This ceremonial, together with the enthronement of the eldest brother in the Tithe church on the feast of the Assumption, strongly implies that Sviatopolk was not viewed at that time as a fratricide. The Christian character of a prince's office and exercise of authority required solemn confirmation in the house of God, and the metropolitan and his clergy did not deny Sviatopolk the rites appropriate for his enthronement. There is no reason to lift the imputation of fratricide that hagiography levelled against Sviatopolk from 1072 onwards, branding him "the Wretched". But one must emphasize that Boris and Gleb were assassinated by means of a *covert* operation. The rumours circulating about the affair do not seem to have heaped the blame on Sviatopolk unequivocally, insofar as the question was raised at all in the immediate aftermath of the murders. So in 1018 the Church authorities had no grounds for denying Sviatopolk the right to cross a church's threshold, banning him from participation in Church life until he did public penance, something that happened to more than one emperor in Byzantium.

While the semi–official indictment of Sviatopolk for eliminating Boris and Gleb must be viewed in a highly critical light, it gains support from the fact that Vladimir's testament debarred Sviatopolk first and foremost from his due position as prince of Kiev. At the same time, it must be remembered that *every* member of the dynasty wishing to maintain the traditional order of succession, and resenting the attempt to "Byzantinize" it, had an interest in the disappearance of the sons of their stepmother, Anna. Thus without dropping all charges against Sviatopolk, one must bear in mind that the accounts of the assassination of Boris and Gleb — written as they were within the culprits' penumbra — harp on the theme that the murderers were on a clandestine mission, sworn to secrecy. For a long time members of the dynasty were loath to let any light be shone on the affair. Years passed before rumours began to surface about the mysterious deaths. And in the *Lives*, aside from a number of understatements, the "Establishment" point of view prevails.

For a long time nothing was known about the circumstances of Gleb's death, and he could be posted as missing without trace. It is also significant that the hagiographer chose to regard the perpetrators as non–Christians or as "crooked", "false" Christians. Gleb was stabbed by the cook, Torchin (i.e. a Turkic man), while the names of the four Vyshgorod characters in the story have diminutive suffixes implying that they were aliens. They were called Talets' — a captive; Liashko — diminutive from Liakh (a Pole?), Elovets (?), Put'sha — a princely agent in charge of the roads, but also perhaps a newcomer, if not simply a vagrant, roaming around the highways. In the *Primary Chronicle* entry, this disdainful attitude towards the men of Vyshgorod is accentuated by giving them the diminutive "boiarlings" (instead of boiars)[31]. It is significant that Boris was the target of two Varangians' swords, and this has prompted speculation that Iaroslav was involved, or at least complicit, given that he relied on a Varangian retinue. This theory should not be ruled out altogether, in that the introduction of Varangians into the plot can scarcely be accidental. But bearing in mind the period when the works about Boris and Gleb were composed, one may detect a strong hint that Sviatopolk's executioners were not orthodox Christians so much as "false believers". Varangians professing the "Varangian", i.e. Latin, creed were beginning to be classified as such at that time[32].

A key point is that Boris and Gleb did not die in battle or fighting to inherit the Kievan throne from their father: they were killed in secret, covertly. This, regardless of their spiritual condition at that particular moment, accounted for their failure to put up a fight. Their non–resistance, as enshrined in tradition, may also have given a fillip to the idea that they died in a spirit of Christian humility and teaching. In princes' dealings with one another during this period, religious and ethical axioms dovetailed with a particular political maxim. The maxim is encapsulated in Boris' apostrophe to Sviatopolk after he had mounted the Kievan throne upon Vladimir's death: "Thou will be as a father to me, Thou will be my brother and senior"[33]. These words should not be dismissed as a hagiographer's fantasy: they were drawn from everyday princely life. Abandoned by his retainers and servants, Boris realized the futility of a power struggle and, perhaps more importantly, he did not want to take such a course. The hagiographer merely presented his explanation for Boris' decision, seeing in it conscious imitation of Christ. It was, in fact, the interaction of all these events, the hagiographer's conjectures and a Christian's bid for redemption that produced a code of ethical behaviour for — mainly — princes to observe in their daily lives. This did not mean tailoring the Christian faith to the facts of political life; on the contrary, it demanded of princes a truly Christian approach to public affairs, above all, in their treatment of one another. The effect was to introduce a religious dimension into princely power play. However, before being fully articulated, these values developed gradually in the court and Church circles of Rus'. They crystallized as the cult of princes who had laid down their lives "for the love of Christ", upholding Christian spirituality, faith and morality in deeds as well as words.

---

[31] PSRL 1: 132. Cf. *Hagiography of Kievan Rus'*: 102–185.

[32] See *Žitija*, ed. Abramovič: 16, 53 and 143; *The Hagiography of Kievan Rus'*: 19, 106, 118. A stark contrast between "Latins" and "Christians" is drawn in one of the twelfth–century tales incorporated into the Cave Monastery *Paterikon* during the 1220s: "Simon... who had once been a Varangian became by Christ's grace a Christian, having... abandoned the folly of the Latins...". *The Paterik of the Kievan Caves Monastery*, transl. by M. Heppell, Cambridge Mass. 1989: 5.

[33] The *Tale of the Passion* // *Žitija*: 30. Cf. *Hagiography of Kievan Rus'*: 100.

But for some time the very fact that they had been murdered was shrouded in uncertainty. The struggle for the Kievan throne continued, but it was now a ding–dong contest between Sviatopolk and Iaroslav. Decades later, the hagiographer would justify Iaroslav's bid to topple Sviatopolk from the throne as God's punishment for shedding his brothers' blood. Towards the end of 1019 Iaroslav succeeded in defeating Sviatopolk and driving him from Kiev, where the incessant raids of his sworn allies, the Pechenegs, cost him the support of most of the citizens. However, in 1022 Iaroslav made for Brest, on the edge of Sviatopolk's appanage of Turov–Pinsk, where he was holding out with the help of the Poles. It was probably while in league with Sviatopolk and taking advantage of Iaroslav's preoccupation with Kievan affairs that Prince Briacheslav of Polotsk sacked Novgorod. Iaroslav did not manage to gain a firm hold on the Kievan throne and his rights there were disputed by Mstislav of Tmutorokan', who — despite what the *Primary Chronicle* maintains — was in fact older than Iaroslav. In 1023 Mstislav launched an expedition against Iaroslav with the aid of the Kasogians and Khazars and, after being recognized by the Severians as lord of Chernigov, he defeated Iaroslav at the Battle of Listven' in 1024. Two years later, in 1026, Mstislav and Iaroslav came to an agreement: the lands east of the line along the Dnieper went to Mstislav, while the western lands, including Kiev, were to be Iaroslav's. However, Kiev did not become Iaroslav's permanent residence until 1036, and he preferred to make his base at Novgorod[34]. Only after the death of Mstislav that year and the rout of the Pechenegs outside Kiev did the town see rapid development, involving the construction of new quarters and churches.

At this point it is worth noting "the Sudislav affair", which is mysterious yet quite revealing about the struggle between Vladimir's sons for the throne of Kiev. On becoming sole ruler in 1036, Iaroslav secured full power over all Rus' except for the principality of Polotsk, consigning the only one of his brothers still alive, Sudislav, to a prison in Pskov. Where Sudislav had been ruling as prince before that time remains unknown, although one can discount the ludicrous notion that it is identical with the place where he was imprisoned! What is clear is that Sudislav had laid a claim to the south, most probably to Chernigov, after Mstislav died without issue. Iaroslav's extreme nervousness is shown by the fact that he kept his unexpected rival in prison until the end of his own life; and even then a further five years and a bit elapsed before Iaroslav's sons and successors, still very cautious, agreed to release their uncle, who had spent a grand total of twenty–four years behind bars. In order to extinguish any lingering notions of "going for the throne", they ordered

[34] The data in the *Tale* (*Hagiography of Kievan Rus'*: 98) and *Primary Chronicle*: 94, 119, 135 concerning the relative ages of Iaroslav and Mstislav is contradictory, but circumstantial evidence — the rivalry over Kiev, Mstislav's baptismal name being that of Emperor Constantine VIII (his uncle by marriage) and the fate of Sudislav — points to Mstislav being the elder. Cf. also N. F. Kotlar, *Mstislav Tmutarakanskij i Iaroslav Mudryj // Drevneišie gosudarstva vostočnoj Evropy*, Moscow 2000: 134–142.

him to take an oath on the cross, tonsured him and thus made him a monk. Only Sudislav's death in 1063 fully relieved the sons of Iaroslav of their fears[35]. The twenty–eight–year seclusion of Sudislav from "this world" demonstrates how very exceptional the killing of Boris and Gleb had been. There can be no doubt that Iaroslav and his sons were extremely apprehensive that Sudislav might pursue his very strong claims. Yet none of them presumed to put him to death. Had behaviour changed so very drastically since the time of Boris and Gleb? Or perhaps the power game for the throne was normally played out in a different way? The Byzantinization of the order of succession debarred all descendants of Vladimir save Boris and Gleb from the Kievan throne, whereas rivalries between princes usually involved wrangling over rights to particular seats, not the rights of the entire dynasty. After physically eliminating Boris and Gleb, the ringleader together with those other members of the dynasty conniving in the operation kept the crime *sub rosa* for a very long time indeed. In 1063 Sudislav, the last remaining son of Vladimir to know all the details, passed on, taking his secrets with him to the grave.

***

Only one thing is certain in all this: Iaroslav was trying hard to reserve sway over Rus' exclusively for his own descendants. This is obvious from the special case of Sudislav and also from the way that founder's portraits of Iaroslav and his family were inserted in the programme of frescoes in St Sophia in Kiev. Facing the mosaic of the Apostles in procession towards Christ, the painting of Iaroslav together with his wife and children presenting to Christ the cathedral of Holy Wisdom (begun in 1037 and completed in 1046) conveyed the idea of heavenly favour for the land of Rus' under the care of Iaroslav and his offspring[36].

The year 1036 marked a turning point in Iaroslav's reign. Only then did he feel fully in charge as lord of Kiev, inheriting and continuing Vladimir's achievements. Construction works on a vast scale were carried out, with new fortifications enclosing some 70 hectares, so that Iaroslav's town covered seven times the area of Vladimir's, and grandiose churches were built, most strikingly St Sophia itself. The aim was blatantly to make Kiev comparable with Constantinople, something that attracted notice even in Western Europe. Admittedly, when Iaroslav intervened in the empire's internal affairs and in 1043 despatched an expeditionary force to help George

---

[35] On Sudislav's fate, see *Primary Chronicle*: 119, 137, 143–144. That Sudislav, who was incarcerated in Pskov for 24 years, "can be regarded as prince of Pskov" has been claimed without substantiating evidence by G. Pickhan, *Gospodin Pskov. Entstehung und Entwicklung eines städtischen Herrschaftszentrums in Altrußland*, Berlin 1992: 65–71.

[36] A. Poppe, *The Building of the Church of St Sophia in Kiev* // Journal of Medieval History 7, 1981: 38–42; idem, *Christianity and ideological change in Kievan Rus'. The first hundred years* // Canadian–American Slavic Studies 25, 1991: 21–22. Cf. F. Kämpfer, *Das Russische Herrscherbild von den Anfängen bis zu Peter dem Großen*, Recklinghausen 1978: 110–116.

Maniaces try and seize the *basileus'* throne, he failed dismally[37]. In Constantinople it was noted that Iaroslav hankered after the role that his father had momentarily assumed in the history of the "Empire of the Romans". But after sidelining him for a few years, the Byzantines concluded a peace treaty in 1046. Relations were restored and the alliance reinforced with the betrothal of Emperor Constantine IX Monomachus' daughter to Vsevolod, one of Iaroslav's sons. The actual marriage took place around 1050 and Vladimir Monomakh was born in 1053[38].

During this period Iaroslav forged links with the ruling houses of Europe through a series of marriages involving his sons and daughters, bolstering his family's international standing. At the same time, he could hardly have failed to mull over the succession to the throne. Trying to provide for all of his sons, Iaroslav pondered over how he could strike a balance and avert another round of fratricidal conflict. Scenes from the struggle for Kiev after July 15, 1015 lived on in the minds of Iaroslav and his sons, while faint memories lingered of the internal strife after the death of Igor's son, Sviatoslav, in 972. Sviatoslav's own sons, Iaropolk, Oleg and Vladimir had been at daggers drawn, and the conflict had claimed the lives of the former two. Finally, a worm in the conscience and a standing reproach, Sudislav was festering away in captivity. For Iaroslav, political expediency was all, the interests of his children being the overriding consideration. It is no coincidence that, at Iaroslav's initiative, an ancient cult long harboured amongst his dynasty revived — the solemn honouring of forebears. The Christian practice of remembrance of the departed made it easier to Christianize this cult, through instituting an annual commemoration service in churches where one prince or another was buried. Suggestive nomenclature also had a part to play in the commemoration: a prince might choose the names of close or distant kinsmen in the interests of the dynasty or of a specific branch of it. Choosing a name emblazoned the prince's ties with that particular ancestor. This was a form of good will that staked a claim to inherit not only the ancestor's name and general rights to rule over the land of Rus', but also his personal share of the land.

One clear instance of this cult of ancestors is the transfer in 1044 of Vladimir's brothers, Iaropolk — whom Vladimir had killed — and Iaropolk's own victim, Oleg, from their burial mounds, the baptism of their remains and their interment inside the Tithe church, the *capella regia*. Baptizing the bones of those who had died as pagans was not in the spirit of Church law, but it could happen even in Byzantium itself, judging by the mention as late as the ninth century of the ancient

---

[37] A. Poppe, *La dernière expedition russe contre Constantinople* // Byzantinoslavica 32, 1971: 1–29, 233–268; polemically: J. Shepard, *Why did the Russians Attack Byzantium in 1043?* // Byzantinisch–Neugriechische Jahrbücher 22, 1979: 147–212. Attempts at reconciliation in G. G. Litavrin, *Vizantija, Bolgarija, Drevnjaja Rus'*, Moscow 2000: 228–276.

[38] The princess could have been a daughter of Constantine Monomachos either by the *sebaste* Maria Skleraina or by an earlier concubine also belonging to the Skleros family. See A.V. Soloviev, *Marie, fille de Constantin IX Monomaque* // Byzantion 33, 1963: 241–246; A. Poppe, *Theophana*: 142.

prohibition on the practice. In a newly converted country this sort of induction into the Church could be treated with a measure of latitude[39]. It amounted to honouring one's forebears in a manner sanctioned by the Church without, however, any sense of starting a religious cult. The fact that the remains of Iaropolk and Oleg were buried beneath the church floor shows that the respect they received as members of the dynasty in no way implied veneration on a formal devotional basis. Soon afterwards, probably around 1047, a first child was born to Iziaslav Iaroslavich and his wife Gertrude–Elisabeth, the great–granddaughter of Otto II and Theophano. They gave him Iaropolk for a princely name, and christened him Peter. A son of Sviatoslav was born in 1052 or 1053, and was called Oleg, with the Christian name of Michael. Very soon afterwards Vsevolod Iaroslavich gave his son, borne to him around the same time by the *basilissa* (*tsesaritsa*), the name of Vladimir, the brother of Iaropolk and Oleg. Things are, however, slightly more complicated in this last instance, for the grandson of the mighty Vladimir, Vladimir Iaroslavich, had died in Novgorod only the year before, and it may be that Monomakh received the name with his own uncle in mind[40].

Naming an infant after an ancestor or long dead relative highlighted the child's ties with him, gaining posthumous good will even to the extent of acquiring the deceased's dynastic rights. Sometimes the choice of names served to by–pass the deceased's direct descendants. It then acted as a kind of programmatic declaration of one's own claims to his inheritance, resting on the collective kin rights of the dynasty. For example, Iaroslav's pretensions to Polotsk as being part of his realm were signalled very clearly in 1024, when he gave his second son the name of his late brother, Iziaslav (died 1001), founder of the Polotsk branch of the dynasty, thus contriving a notional sort of "hereditary" bond with both man and place[41]. May not this have been a riposte to the expedition that Briacheslav, the son of this Iziaslav, had launched from Polotsk against Novgorod in 1021?

---

[39] *Primary Chronicle*: 139; J. Korpela (Jahrbücher für Geschichte Osteuropas 46, 1988: 161–176) took this outburst of convert zeal to signify that holy water was sprinkled over the remains of princes who were *already* Christian. But all such attempts to ignore the true meaning of *krestiti* (=baptize) and to make Christians of Oleg (died 977) and Jaropolk (died 980) are ill–founded. One may note that King Harald (died 985) of Denmark, who baptized his subjects c. 966, reburied his parents in a church at Jelling. His father Gorm was not just a heathen but an active persecutor of Christians. Cf. H. Ehrhardt, *Gorm der Alte* // Lexikon des Mittelalters IV, 1983: 1561. It is worth noting the hypothesis, based on comparative Scandinavian data, that the ban on baptism of the dead was disregarded in the case of those believed to have received the *prima signatio*, i.e. to have died as catechumens. See F. B. Uspensky, *Skandinavy, Variagi, Rus'*, Moscow 2002: 141–168. However, this would virtually amount to supporting that Olga exercised her authority as Christian *archontissa* of Rus' to make all her grandsons — Oleg, Iaropolk and Vladimir — catechumens.

[40] On the significance of the names chosen by the Rurikid dynasty for their children, see A. Poppe, O zaroždenii kulta: 56–67.

[41] This is reminiscent of Clovis, who gave his sons the names of members of the defeated dynasty (Theodoric, Theodebert) in the early sixth century: K. F. Werner, *Les Origines (avant l'an mil)*, Paris 1984: 319.

Almost half a century later, Iaroslav's son, Iziaslav, proceeded to lodge a claim to Polotsk, assigning his son Mstislav to the throne there. He also gave the name of Sviatopolk (with the Christian name Michael) to his and Gertrude's second son, born in 1050. This shows that the name of Sviatopolk "the Wretched" was not yet charged with the odium incurred once Boris and Gleb were numbered among the saints. It may seem odd that Iziaslav should have chosen for his son the name of one of his father's old enemies. However, the practice of honouring deceased members of the dynasty left no room for nursing old grudges. It was before 1050 that Iaroslav installed Iziaslav in the principality of Turov–Pinsk, and they were both well aware that Iziaslav was following in the footsteps of his uncle Sviatopolk, who had been assigned it as an appanage by his father, Vladimir the Great. It was precisely to reaffirm his blood–right to this principality, both for himself and his successors, that Iziaslav "resurrected" the name of Sviatopolk. This was a way of enrolling his late uncle among the protectors of his own children, whose claims to Turov would become long and firmly entrenched. With an eye to the future, Iziaslav had given his first–born (before 1044, the child of a concubine) the name of Mstislav, an apparent allusion to the throne of Chernigov, vacant since 1036.

The idea that one might have a higher call on an uncle's inheritance, over and above that of any of his direct progeny — who were to be treated as "premature orphans" (*izgoi*)[42] — also features clearly in Vsevolod's treatment of the sons of his nephew Rostislav while Vsevolod was lord of Kiev from 1078 to 1093. In fact, it was already in evidence in 1070, when Vsevolod gave his new–born son the name of Rostislav, three years after the death of Rostislav of Tmutorokan' (Tamatarcha) in February 1067. Rostislav, having been disinherited as a "premature orphan" by his uncles (the sons of Iaroslav), tried to set himself up at Tmutorokan'. But it is striking that earlier, while still secretly coveting Novgorod's throne and before his move south in 1064, he had invoked the ancestor cult and brazenly given his own first–born the name of the first recorded prince of Novgorod, Riurik. In enlisting the founder of the dynasty as patron of his son, Rostislav was aiming high — and far from randomly.

In fact, Iaroslav and his kindred made several other attempts to secure top places for their children in the ranking order of princes through invocation of the names of ancestors. As early as 1027 Iaroslav named his third son in honour of his grandfather, Sviatoslav Igorevich, and in 1038 he gave his youngest son the name of his great–grandfather, Igor. By parading these names Iaroslav highlighted the direct links between himself and "the glorious Sviatoslav" and "Igor of old", and Hilarion was not slow to draw attention to the continuity of the line. Commemorative

---

[42] The term *izgoi* denotes the son of a prince who had predeceased his own father; the "orphans" succession rights were severely limited, if not annulled altogether, to the benefit of the other members of the dynasty. Thus Rostislav and his sons became *izgoi* because Rostislav's father Vladimir had died (†1052) earlier than his grandfather Iaroslav (†1054).

lists of one's ancestors and the prayers said for them made the blood bonds between the living and the dead all the more indissoluble[43].

Thus one can make out a policy pursued both by Iaroslav and by his sons, notably Iziaslav, Sviatoslav and Vsevolod. These, the three eldest sons of Iaroslav to survive him, held princely seats in a triangle spanning the Middle Dnieper region, respectively at Kiev, Chernigov and Pereiaslavl', and the term "triad" is apt enough to describe their style of mutual collaboration in the first fifteen years after Iaroslav's death in 1054[44]. Like their father before them, Iaroslav's sons wanted to secure for themselves ancestral rights to "the land of Rus'" in the broad sense of all the territory that had been subject to the clan of Rus' princes. This would have been to the exclusion of the other branches of the dynasty. Before and after 1050, the offspring of Iaroslav "resurrected" the names of those princes whose rights to authority had apparently not expired with them. They stood out as grand symbols of the dynasty, more specifically of dynastic rights of dominion, influencing both political programmes and the way in which they were carried out.

***

It goes without saying that the names of Boris and Gleb could not have been left out of this roll of honour of departed relatives. Due care was shown over their interment, seemingly around the time of the transfer of the remains of Iaropolk and Oleg in 1044 and at any rate after 1036, when Iaroslav took over all power in Rus'[45]. Boris had been buried secretly in Vyshgorod "in the earth by the church of St Basil", immediately after his murder. Until May 20, 1072 Boris' relics lay in a wooden coffin and only then were they translated to "a casket of stone". It was harder to find out exactly where Gleb had first been buried near the banks of the Smjadin', not far from Smolensk. It was probably at the time when Gleb's burial site was located, around 1045, that his remains were conveyed to Vyshgorod and placed in the stone casket in which they were found in 1072. Gleb was then laid in the earth beside Boris —

---

[43] The Christian connotations of these bonds are illustrated by the funeral of Gleb, son of Sviatoslav, on July 23, 1078 in the church of the Redeemer in Chernigov. Gleb had been killed on May 30 in a clash with Finns several hundred kilometers to the north–east of Novgorod, his seat at the time. He was, according to the *Primary Chronicle*, "zealous toward the church and warm in the faith" (tr. Cross: 165). The body was transported almost 1,500 kilometers, not to ensure a church burial — which could have been carried out perfectly well in Novgorod — but primarily so that it could be laid to rest next to Gleb's father and kinsmen. There was good reason to expect that the surviving relatives would maintain prayers for these princes' salvation, together with an annual commemoration in the church in Chernigov. More information is available from the West European tradition; see the pioneering study of K. Schmid and J. Wollasch (*Die Gemeinschaft der Lebenden und Verstorbenen in Zeugnissen des Mittelalters* // Frümittelalterliche Studien 1, 1967: 365–405) and the observations of P. Geary, *Echanges et relations entre les vivants et les morts dans la société du haut Moyen Âge* // Droit et Cultures 12, 1986: 3–17.

[44] The "triad"'s rule did not go unremarked in Byzantium, and this led to the promotion of the sees of Chernigov and Pereiaslavl' to titular metropolitan status. See A. Poppe, *L'organisation diocésaine de la Russie aux XIe–XIIe-siècles* // Byzantion 40, 1970: 177–184.

[45] According to the *Tale*: *Žitija*: 48. Cf. *Hagiography of Kievan Rus'*: 113 (*preja* means "took over", not "received").

and not beneath the floor of the church of St Basil. So it seems that Boris' and Gleb's remains were not at that time revered to the same degree as those of Iaropolk and Oleg. Their graves stayed *sub rosa* until the day that St Basil's burnt down.

Both the secular and the Christian names of the two princes began to be used by the dynasty during the second half of the 1040s. The first–born of Sviatoslav's sons was called Gleb. The precise year of Gleb's birth is uncertain, but he was born not before 1047 and not later than 1050. At that time, Sviatoslav was ensconced in Vyshgorod, and he was thus to some extent involved in the transfer of his uncle's remains, seeing to their deposition in the stone casket. He marked this event by giving Gleb's name to his first–born. This serves as further confirmation that the date of the transfer of Gleb's remains from the banks of the Smjadin' was close in time to the burial of Iaropolk and Oleg in the Tithe church. It seems quite clear that in Iaroslav's project for uniting dead ancestors with Iaroslav's own living descendants, the brothers of Vladimir the Great were initially more privileged, as being direct heirs of the glorious Sviatoslav Igorevich, than were Boris and Gleb. In other words, when Gleb's remains were transported from the Smjadin' to be buried beside Boris — probably around 1045 — there was no sense of *religious* devotion for them. The anonymous *Tale of the Passion* offers a hint of this with its remark that many people were unaware of the brothers' burial in Vyshgorod. But that Sviatoslav, at least, was mindful of his late uncles is attested by the names Roman and David given to his sons born after Gleb at the very end of the 1040s and before 1052/53, when Oleg was born[46]. Thus two of his boys received the same baptismal names that Boris and Gleb had, and this could perhaps be taken to mark a shift from ancestor reverence to a full–blown cult of them as Passion Sufferers who had shown marks of sanctity. But it is more straightforward to suppose — and the dynasty's naming habits support this — that the baptismal names came to enjoy the status of "princely" names simply because earlier princes had borne them: for this reason Sviatoslav conferred them on his sons. It is worth recalling that Iuri Dolgorukii received as his *princely* name the baptismal name — George (Iuri) — of his great–grandfather, Iaroslav, while Iuri's brother Andrei received the baptismal name of his grandfather, Vsevolod, in the same capacity. Reverence for Boris–Roman and Gleb–David as deceased kinsmen is in play here, even if one cannot wholly rule out the possibility that the first shoots of a religious cult were beginning to appear.

Sviatoslav's conspicuous regard for his slaughtered uncles contained a political subtext. By parading his reverence for them and claiming to be the heir to their rights and their willingness to submit to their elder brother, Sviatoslav, highlighted

---

[46] See N. Baumgarten, *Généalogies et mariages occidentaux des Rurikides russes du Xe au XIIIe siècle*, Roma 1927: 18–21, tabl. IV. See also the 1073 miniature showing the family of Sviatoslav // Kämpfer, *Das Russische Herrscherbild*: 118, 119, ill. 65. On the devotion of Sviatoslav and his sons, especially Oleg, to the cult of Boris and Gleb, see M. Dimnik, *Oleg Svyatoslavich and his Patronage of the Cult of SS. Boris and Gleb* // Mediaeval Studies 50, 1988: 349–370.

the right to take vengeance for injuries and death inflicted upon one's relatives. After all, Vladimir wrought vengeance on Iaropolk, who had killed Oleg — hence Oleg became one of the names used by the Sviatoslavichi — while Iaroslav had taken up arms against Sviatopolk, the killer of Boris and Gleb.

It is striking that Prince Vseslav of Polotsk began to compete with Sviatoslav in adopting the names of his grandfather's half–brothers. The Polotsk branch of the family stemmed from Vladimir's eldest son, Iziaslav, who had died prematurely in 1001. By the very act of choosing both the princely and the Christian names of Boris and Gleb, Roman and David, for his sons, Vseslav gave these forebears the role of protectors of the Polotskian offspring of Vladimir by Rogneda, the daughter of the Scandinavian newcomer and first prince of Polotsk, Rogovolod[47]. But was he not also tacitly posting an inheritance claim to their rights to the Kievan throne? In giving his four sons these names, Vseslav was setting out a programme for the Polotsk house, overcoming the handicap of being "premature orphans". Two of his sons fought in the battle on the Nemiga on March 3, 1067, were taken prisoner and ended up in a Kievan jail together with Vseslav himself. So they must have been born around the year 1050. In the extraordinary circumstances of the flight of Iaroslav's three elder sons and their feeble performance against the Polovtsians, Vseslav was in 1068 proclaimed prince of Kiev. His rights within the dynasty to occupy the Kievan throne undoubtedly counted for something here, in the sense that he had inherited his dead ancestors' rights to a general stake in the land of Rus'. The ruling "triad" may well have been unnerved by Vseslav's predilection for the names of their slain uncles; for shortly after resolving their differences with one another, they convened in Vyshgorod on May 20, 1072 and venerated their uncles in a solemn act of worship.

***

It is remarkable that not a single one of the sons of Iaroslav born in the 1020s and 1030s received the name of their uncles so untimely snatched in 1015, and this even though Iaroslav had avenged their deaths with conspicuous zeal. Of the fifteen grandsons of Iaroslav known to us, five bore one or other of Boris' and Gleb's names. The younger sons of Iaroslav made use of these names, as well as Sviatoslav. Viacheslav (–Mercurius?), who was born in 1036 and died at the age of twenty, gave what seems to have been his only son the name of Boris; this child's baptismal name is unknown to us. The youngest of Iaroslav's sons, Igor, born after 1036 and dying in 1060, gave his son the name, both Christian and princely, of David. The designs on five of David Igorevich's seals dating from his politically active years (from 1080 to 1112) attest that his heavenly protector was the Prophet King David of the Scriptures[48]. Consequently, towards the end of the 1050s Gleb–

---

[47] N. Baumgarten, *Généalogies*: 32, table VIII. On Vseslav cf. *Primary Chronicle*: 144–150.
[48] V. L. Janin, *Aktovyje pečati Drevnej Rusi X–XV vekov*, vol. I. M. 1970: 171, 251 (table 3).

–David was still not accepted by the Church, at least, as a full saint in whose name a baby prince could be christened. Thus one and the same name could imply two protectors: prince David (Gleb) at the level of princely affairs and, in heaven, the Prophet King David. Bearing in mind that David Igorevich was born in the last years of his father's life and that Igor died in 1060, one may fairly interpret this choice of names as Igor's response to having his seat switched from Vladimir–in––Volynia to Smolensk by the dominant "triad" of Iaroslav's elder sons. It had a double meaning, linked to the fate of both Davids, his own uncle and the biblical king. David Igorevich was keenly aware that his uncles had slighted his father and he stubbornly insisted upon his rights to Vladimir–in–Volynia. In contrast to Sviatoslav, to Vseslav and to the younger sons of Iaroslav, neither Iziaslav nor Vsevolod showed signs of special reverence for Boris and Gleb in choosing names for their sons. But they joined whole–heartedly in the solemn veneration of them on the eve of the ceremonies in Vyshgorod in May 1072.

***

The idea of reviving ancestor worship in the dynasty at the same time as Christianizing the country and channelling it into Christian forms of commemoration is datable to the time when Iaroslav ruled alone over all Rus' from 1036 onwards. Iaroslav was blatantly trying to invoke the dead princes of the Riurikid dynasty's various branches in order to inherit their rights, whether or not they were close relatives, for the benefit of his own offspring. That is why the sons of Iaroslav immediately took up and developed their father's initiative. This commemoration of dead princes was tinged with piety, but the underlying agenda was understood all too clearly by the prince of Polotsk and, with the aim of furthering the interests of "Rogovolod's grandsons", Polotsk even overtook Kiev. The Polotsk prince's intentions are plain enough in his choice of the names Boris–Roman and Gleb––David. However, the rivalry between these two branches of the dynasty in honouring their ancestors was apparent earlier still. As has been noted above, in 1024 Iaroslav "borrowed" for his son the name of his late brother, Iziaslav of Polotsk. And in 1030 the latter's son, Briacheslav, named his own first–born after Vseslav, his brother, who had died in infancy in 1003. This was clearly a way of staking a claim to the entire inheritance of Polotsk for Briacheslav himself and for his descendants.

The three sons of Rostislav were no more reconciled to their "orphan" status than were the princes of Polotsk. The names of two of them, Riurik and Vasil'ko (a diminutive of Vladimir's Christian name Basil–Vasily, connected with the fact that he was born after his father's death) boldly proclaimed their inheritance rights within the Riurikid dynasty's dominions. But unlike the princes of Polotsk, the offspring of Rostislav, from their hard–won perch on the Dniester, did not join in the cult and start venerating their relatives Boris and Gleb as saints from 1072 onwards. Very likely, in fact — and in stark contrast with the other branches of the dynasty — they deliberately refrained from giving their children these names, whether as princely or baptismal ones. The stance of faithful, compliant princes loath to stand up to their elder brother and suffering uncomplainingly was alien in the extreme to these princes, as they struggled to carve out their own hereditary principality. This is in fact what the principality of Galich (pronounced "Halich") became, and the line of Rostislav's descendants ruled there as princes until the close of the twelfth century[49].

***

The cult of deceased ancestors must have done something to keep the dynastic peace between the various members of the house of Iaroslav. The cult of kinsmen who were recognized as Christian saints fostered unity even more effectively. But when did veneration of Boris and Gleb merely as dead relatives, their "cult" as members of the princely dynasty, turn into their cult as Christian martyrs?

The change unfolded over two or three decades. As late as the 1040s Boris' and Gleb's remains still lay beneath a mound outside the church of St Basil. Considering that it was customary in the eleventh century to bury princes inside churches, usually underneath the floor, burying the two princes outside St Basil's might seem strange. But the hagiographer insists upon this location so forcibly and repeatedly[50] that one can hardly deny it — still less so in the light of excavations that have uncovered the grave of a prince directly adjoining the outer side of the Tithe church's wall. It may be that the two brothers' graves at Vyshgorod lay in the earth beneath the gallery that curved around the wooden church.

In 1049 or, most likely, 1050 Hilarion commemorated and extolled Vladimir, the equal of the Apostles, but said not a word about Boris and Gleb. Yet he found time for a eulogy and salutations for Iaroslav, his wife, children and grandchildren[51]. How is the lack of any mention of Boris and Gleb to be explained? The silence is so total that it may be taken as evidence that Boris and Gleb were not yet recognized as saints at that time. But in 1051 or 1052, twenty years before Iziaslav raised a one–cupola church in Vyshgorod dedicated to Sts Roman and David (the patron saints of Boris and Gleb), his father Iaroslav had built a five–cupola church (left unnamed by the author of the *Tale of the Miracles*). The coffins of Boris and Gleb were transferred to it from their temporary resting–place in a small makeshift chapel on the site of the burnt–out church of St Basil. It was then that an annual service was instituted for joint commemoration of the murdered relatives – on July 24, the day of Boris' death[52]. As time went by, the memorial service took on the character of a full–blown feast day for saints. Thus payment of respects to dead members of

---

49 See N. Baumgarten, *Généalogies*: 15 (table III). Strange as it may seem, in the Dniester region — in the principality of Halich — no churches were dedicated to Boris and Gleb in the eleventh or twelfth centuries, or even as late as the sixteenth century.

50 *Hagiography of Kievan Rus'*: 18, 19, 20 (*Nestor*); 113, 118, 119 (*Tale*).

51 Cf. *Sermons and Rhetoric of Kievan Rus'*: 23–24.

52 *Hagiography of Kievan Rus'*: 120–121.

the dynasty turned into veneration of them as saints and it was described in these terms once their journey to sainthood reached its goal, on May 20, 1072[53].

The meeting of Church hierarchs and the "triad" of Iaroslav's sons at Vyshgorod in May 1072 confirmed that Boris and Gleb were saints in the eyes of the Church. Between 1072 and 1115 what had begun as a ruling dynasty's cult of its murdered innocents became common property, and the princes were venerated as Passion Sufferers at every level of society in Christian Rus'.

***

The path leading from initial reverence for Boris and Gleb to their official recognition as saints is obscured by inconsistent and misleading signposts in the sources. One might surmise that the starting–point lay in Iaroslav's last years (1051–53) and that Metropolitan Hilarion was also involved in instituting the new dynastic cult. But this would be sheer conjecture.

There was no particular need or reason for the prince and the metropolitan to perform a "U–turn" and initiate a cult of Boris and Gleb. The cult's roots lay deep in the practice of ancestor veneration, but it also owed something to prayers and commemoration for the dead, rites that were engrained in Christianity, in its priesthood and its believers[54]. The merits of Boris and Gleb, embroidered with tales of how they had coped with violent death, could not fail to invite interpretations in terms of Christian ideals. Their assassination without having had any chance to defend themselves, and their obvious readiness to renounce the throne and refrain from fighting their eldest brother, in themselves raised them to a higher level of Christian confession — the level requiring witness in deed as well as word. In a newly converted land, such behaviour, idealized over time and in a variety of circumstances, inevitably invited comparison with figures from the Christian past. It evoked the ideals of following in Christ's footsteps, martyrdom for His sake and standing on behalf of others before the Almighty. Obviously this association owed something to bookmen and clergy, and it also tapped into the zeal of princely relatives, eager to hallow the entire dynasty with saints coming from their ranks. For younger princes aware that they had to submit to their elders but afraid of skulduggery, there was great attraction in the model of princely innocents who obeyed their elder brother as if he were their father, refused to resist and paid for this with their lives. As Christians, Boris and Gleb showed an outstanding grasp of common humanity, while setting an example of sanctity as members of the ruling house. There was no need to go in for special pleading in their case. Lingering traditions about the brothers restored details that had faded and gave them a Christian

---

[53] For further details of these celebrations, see Poppe, *O zaroždenii kulta*: 45–56.

[54] On the commemoration of the dead in Old Rus', see the pioneering study of L. Steindorff, *Memoria in Altrußland. Untersuchungen zu den Formen christlicher Totensorge*, Stuttgart 1994. 294 pp. See also J. Lind's review // Russia Mediaevalis 9–1, 1997: 193–196.

touch, turning the veneration of departed kinsmen into a new cult of saints. To a Christian of the time, it seemed obvious that the moment they were killed, Boris and Gleb gained a sanctity, which had only gradually become apparent to those on earth. The progression was natural enough, in that Boris and Gleb had not laid down their lives for political ideals: they were martyred simply for putting their profession of Christianity into daily practice — in their case, in political life. Their model of behaviour became a criterion by which to judge human failings.

And so the wheel turned full circle. The vicious struggle for the Kievan throne following Vladimir's death was metamorphosed into a tradition which hailed two of his sons as sufferers for Christ's sake and as bulwarks of the land of Rus'. Together with their father Vladimir, they were given roles as "instigators of the holy conversion, like unto the Apostles"[55].

***

We have traced the murkiest and poorly documented phase of the fortunes of Boris and Gleb and their cult from the failure of the plan to "Byzantinize" the succession to the Rus' throne through to 1072, when their veneration as saints was formalized and received the Church's blessing.

On Sunday May 20, the caskets containing the holy princes' relics were translated to the new church that Iziaslav had constructed. The three reigning sons of Iaroslav took part — Iziaslav himself, Sviatoslav and Vsevolod. So did five prelates headed by Metropolitan George of Kiev, together with a large number of abbots of Kievan and other monasteries, with Abbot Feodosii (Theodosius) of the Caves Monastery at the head of the list. The act of translation was not the only momentous event that day: those present at the ceremony also witnessed the incorrupt state of the bodies and their odour of fragrance. When Boris' remains were transferred from a wooden coffin to a stone sarcophagus, participants in the ceremony kissed the head of Boris. Then the metropolitan blessed the princes with the hand of Gleb. Sviatoslav took this opportunity to halt the metropolitan's gesture. He applied the holy relic to an ulcer on his neck as well as to his eyes and the top of his head in hopes of a cure for the illness afflicting him. When one of the saint's fingernails stuck in his hair, this was taken to be a sign of special favour. After Sviatoslav's own death on December 27, 1076 the incident lost its significance and it was omitted from the *Primary Chronicle* altogether. We may infer that the ceremonies at Vyshgorod were written up very soon afterwards. There is no mention of the start of work on Sviatoslav's stone church dedicated to Boris and Gleb in 1074 in the first part of the *Tale of the Miracles*. These omissions and also the reference to Feodosii of

---

[55] *Letopisiec Perejaslavlja Suzdalskogo* // PSRL 41, Moscow 1995: 52 (this version of the *Primary Chronicle*'s text dates from the end of the thirteenth century).

the Caves Monastery as alive and well — when in fact he died on May 3, 1074 — also point to 1072–73 as being the composition date of this part of the *Tale*[56].

The *Tale of the Miracles*' author remarked upon the doubts expressed by Metropolitan George as to the status of Boris and Gleb as saints. These doubts reflect upon the metropolitan's dual role in the rites confirming their sanctity. The fleeting nature of George's scepticism is borne out by the very fact that, at the time of the relics' translation, he consecrated the newly built church dedicated to them as the martyrs Roman and David. It also emerges from the clear–cut decision, registered in the *Tale*, to glorify the princes under their Christian names. In no sense was this a "Greeks versus Rus'" dispute. It merely registered the viewpoint of the Church authorities, which had every reason to expect that princes newly recognized as saints should be known by their Christian names. However, under the influence of everyday usage, this preference was not followed through consistently. The inclination of local Christians to call native saints by their everyday names made itself felt, and this usage soon won the day. This is already apparent in the *Lesson* written by Nestor, who usually observes Byzantine hagiographical conventions so conscientiously. In the case of Boris and Gleb, he widens Christian horizons by calling them by their everyday princely names.

It is, then, with the proceedings around May 1072 that the documented period of the cult of Boris and Gleb as saints begins. In the *Tale of the Miracles* dedicated to them, they feature as the new saints Roman and David. The *Tale of the Passion of the Holy Martyrs Boris and Gleb* was composed about this time, on the eve of the ceremony at Vyshgorod on May 20, 1072. The *Tale of the Passion* gives no clear–cut indication as to when it was written, but it does specify that Gleb's remains were translated to Vyshgorod from the Smjadin' after Iaroslav had "taken over all authority in Rus'", i.e. after Mstislav of Chernigov's death in 1036. Judging by the *Tale of the Miracles*' introduction, some time elapsed from the burial of Gleb next to his brother in Vyshgorod until "God glorified them with abundant grace and with miracles"[57] and people began to realize that holy martyrs were buried in Vyshgorod. So that part of the *Tale of the Miracles* which places the glorifying of Boris and Gleb in the period of Metropolitan John's tenure of office, a tenure ending several years before 1036, is obviously incompatible with the chronology of the *Tale of the Passion*. The "glorifying" began, most probably, only in the 1060s. It would thus be difficult to date the start of the cult of Boris and Gleb as outright saints to the closing years of Iaroslav's reign[58]. This raises the question whether by

---

[56] *Hagiography of Kievan Rus'*: 122–124; see also the *Primary Chronicle*'s entry for 1072, ibidem: 200–201.

[57] *Hagiography of Kievan Rus'*: 118.

[58] Further details about the composition date and context of the *Tale of the Passion* and the *Tale of the Miracles* are given in A. Poppe, *Opowieść o męczeństwie i cudach Borysa i Gleba. Okoliczności powstania utworu* // Slavia Orientalis 18, 1969: 267–292, 359–382.

the time the *Tale of the Passion* was composed, just before their admission into the ranks of the saints, veneration of Boris and Gleb as forebears had not gradually led to full recognition of their extraordinary Christian virtues. Solemnly commemorating them every year, people would come to view them as worthy of sainthood. Instituting a memorial day for the brothers as departed relatives — adapting traditional notions to Christian ritual — may well have been the joint action of Iaroslav and Sviatoslav, carried out while Sviatoslav was ensconced in Vyshgorod. By the time they were solemnly recognized as saints in 1072, all these episodes had fused together in the popular consciousness. Looking back from this later perspective, people took to be acts of full veneration what had really only been routine respects paid by princes to their deceased relatives. Thus features of a limited dynastic cult — burial of Gleb beside his brother in Vyshgorod; the building of a temporary structure on the site of the burnt–out church; Iaroslav's construction of a five–cupola church as a fitting burial chapel for princes, and making July 24 the day for annual prayers of commemoration for them — all came to be viewed in hindsight, after the "official" sanctification in May 1072, as a premeditated process, leading to their recognition as saints.

Literary models made it possible to project the beginnings of the cult of Boris and Gleb back into the mists of time. After the fire at the church of St Basil's, where their coffins were buried, Iaroslav's replacement building with five cupolas was, most probably, dedicated not to Boris and Gleb but to their patron saints, Romanus the Melodist and David, prophet and king, and their remains were transferred to the new church. This would explain why it was only in 1072 that Boris' remains were transferred from a wooden coffin to a stone sarcophagus like Gleb's. Clearly, after the fire at St Basil's around 1052 and the opening up of the two brothers' graves (i.e. the time when the five–cupola church was built, some twenty years before Iziaslav's construction of a one–cupola wooden church in 1072), the coffin of Boris was either too well–preserved to need replacing or was in fact replaced with a new one, but also of wood. At that time, the brothers received decent reburial as kinsmen, and arrangements were made for annual prayers to be said for them, but without any notion of glorifying Boris and Gleb as saints. Yet it was in this very five–cupola church, the scene of the annual commemoration every July 24, that their cult as saints took hold.

***

While the literary scenes in the *Tale of the Miracles* point towards an early date for the development of the cult of Boris and Gleb as saints, the encomium concluding the *Tale of the Passion* creates confusion, not so much through general praise for their gift of miracles as with its mention of the churches being built in their name on the site of their murders, on the rivers Lta and the Smjadin'. For churches could only be built and dedicated to those formally recognized by the Church as saints. In Boris' and Gleb's case this sort of church could only have been built from May 20, 1072 onwards.

Several details in the *Tale of the Miracles* point clearly enough to a composition date of around 1072, and one particular episode holds the key to dating the entire text to that time. We learn that the peace of the princes buried outside the church was disturbed by Varangians: when one of them trod on the grave, a flame shot up and scorched his legs. These Varangians — who had not believed in the miraculous phenomena occurring above the princes' grave — were written out of the script by the author of the *Saints' Office* when he came to compose *Hymn 9*, the *heirmos*. He simply replaced the name "Varangians" with terms that were easier to understand, "the impure, the impious", in other words, those who were not sound in the orthodox faith. From 1054 onwards, monks and clergy in Rus' as well as Byzantium were beginning to apply such terms to those professing the Latin faith, and in late eleventh–-and twelfth–century Rus' Roman Catholicism was also called "the Varangian faith". The case of the flame shooting up from the grave invites comparison with the *Tale of the Passion*, where St Boris is finished off by Varangians. Both incidents reflect a desire to place on record the fact that Boris' and Gleb's killers were not orthodox Christians but "ungodly" Varangians. These details, seemingly marginal and arising from a sense that the Varangian, i.e. "Latin" faith, had become somewhat perverted, will have appeared in Kiev some time after the "Schism" of 1054[59]. Consequently, in the light of what has been said above, the *Tale of the Passion* cannot have been composed before the 1060s: it is most likely to have been written while planning for the Church ceremonies at Vyshgorod in 1072 was underway. The preparations had been agreed by the "triad" of Iaroslav's elder sons after Iziaslav's return to Kiev in 1069 and his attempts to wrest Polotsk from Vseslav in 1069–70. This dating might seem incompatible with what the *encomium* says at the end of the *Tale of the Passion*: that "on the sites where martyrs' crowns were bestowed upon them, churches were built in their names", i.e. referring to the churches on the Smjadin' and the Lta, the respective death sites of Gleb and Boris. But work on these churches is most likely to have started just after May 20, 1072, when it became fully permissible to build churches dedicated to them as saints[60]. The possibility that these churches date from the first onrush of zeal for the cult in the summer of that same year, 1072, takes the force out of objections to dating the *encomium*, too, to 1072–73.

What prevents a definitive answer, however, is the fact that the manuscript tradition of our anonymous *Tale* goes back to a full text containing both the *Tale of*

---

[59] Cf. *Primary Chronicle*: 115. What may be the earliest indication of the "Schism" is to be found in an anti–Latin tract ascribed to Metropolitan Ephrem of Kiev (Vatic. graec. 828, datable to the 13th or 14th cent.). Ephrem was in post from the end of 1054/beginning of 1055 until the mid–1060s. There is no reason why a senior churchman arriving from Constantinople soon after his appointment, only a few months after the events of July 1054, should not have written such a tract and brought it with him to Rus as a work of reference. No Slavic translation was made and this tract probably remained unknown outside the Church hierarchy's upper reaches, in contrast to later anti–Latin writings. See I. Čičurov, *Ein antilateinischer Traktat des Kiever Metropoliten Ephraim* // Fontes minores X, 1998: 319–356.

[60] The little wooden chapels were built in a day, while larger wooden churches were assembled from "prefabricated" logs over a period of several days.

the Passion (written in or just after 1072) and the *Tale of the Miracles* which was augmented with a *Continuation* soon after the translation of the saints' relics to the new stone church in Vyshgorod on May 2, 1115. Analysis of the extensive manuscript witnesses of the *Tale* confirms that all surviving texts — irrespective of whether they comprise solely the actual *Tale of the Passion* (the Chudov redaction), or whether they only contain, in one shortened form or another — the *Tale of the Miracles* — ultimately derive from the full (Uspensky Ms.) version, drafted after 1115, probably in 1117[61]. This has encouraged some scholars to conclude that the entire text comprising the anonymous *Tale of the Passion* and the *Tale of the Miracles* was composed at a stroke after 1115, drawing on the *Chronicle* entry for 1015 and on Nestor's *Lesson*. Since this interpretation fails to answer all the questions that arise upon collation of these texts, scholars have supposed that other primary sources existed and are now preserved most fully in the *Tale*. But if one accepts that the *Tale of the Passion* and the *Tale of the Miracles* were both composed around 1072–73, and that the latter's *Continuation* covered the whole period from the start of work on the stone mausoleum church dedicated to Sts Boris and Gleb in 1074, right down to the church's completion and the translation to it of their sarcophagi on May 2, 1115, there is no need to invoke hypothetical lost sources. Nestor the hagiographer, toiling over his *Lesson* on the life, death and miracles around the year 1080, took what he needed from the *Tale of the Passion* and the *Tale of the Miracles*. The only material he added was the miracle of the imprisoned men, a tale later reworked and used by the second author of the *Tale of the Miracles* when he wrote the *Continuation* soon after 1115. A marked feature of Nestor's *Lesson* is its use of the martyrs' princely names as if these were already well–established Christian names. In contrast, the author of the *Office* for the saints, perhaps Metropolitan John II Prodromos, writing after 1080, kept to the usage of his main source, the *Tale of the Miracles*, and referred to the princes by their Christian names, even though he was familiar with Nestor's *Lesson* and its usage.

The *Primary Chronicle* entry of 1015 relating the murder of Boris and Gleb abridges the *Tale of the Passion* without sacrificing its hagiographical flavour. What

---

[61] The basic study on the manuscript tradition (over one hundred and seventy manuscripts) was carried out by S. A. Buhoslavsky. He completed his work in 1939/40, but it is still unpublished. Some of Buhoslavsky's findings feature in his introduction to the texts published in Kiev in 1928. Pertinent criticisms of some of Buhoslavsky's views on the origins of the *Tale* and his attempts to reconstruct it are made by, for example, H. Goldblatt, *Authorship and* [textual] *identity in the Tale of the Holy Martyrs Boris and Gleb* // Annali dell'Istituto Universitario Orientale di Napoli, Slavistica 1, 1993: 102–106. Even if these reservations are valid, they do not detract from the overall scholarly worth of Buhoslavsky's textual study. Thanks to his scrupulous handling of the source material, I have been able to build on his findings to arrive at rather different conclusions. A fresh attempt has been made by G. Revelli to analyze the manuscript tradition and publish the texts: *Monumenti litterari su Boris e Gleb*, Genova 1993, 706 pp. This is described as a "quirky edition" by F. Thomson in his review of the work: // Ricerche Slavistiche 41, 1994: 329–336.

is really interesting is that the chronicler, while signalling awareness of the *Tale*'s concluding *encomium*, composes his own eulogy in praise of the saints and deliberately highlights the political aspects of the cult. The *Primary Chronicle* entry for 1072 is wholly dependent on the corresponding text in the *Tale of the Miracles*, apart from making some abridgements in the light of current circumstances, at the end of the eleventh/beginning of the twelfth century, and at any rate before the relics were translated to the new stone church in Vyshgorod (if not before 1111, when the church was completed). The earliest *Office*, composed in the 1080s and containing forty–four hymns, was supplemented by twenty–one additional hymns around the time of the translation to the stone church on May 2, 1115 or somewhat later, and in any case before 1160. The *Office* has been preserved in this state, with a number of abbreviations and minor additions, in scores of manuscripts and it was in regular use by the Church in the centuries that followed[62].

The ceremonies of 1115 gave a final boost to the composition of works dedicated to Sts Boris and Gleb. The texts looming largest in their cult from then onwards were those composed between 1072 and 1115/1117, i.e. the anonymous *Tale* (one part or another of which is preserved in over one hundred and eighty manuscripts), the *Lesson* (around thirty manuscripts) and the *Chronicle*'s entries for the years 1015, 1072 and 1115; these entries feature in all the later compilations of chronicles incorporating the full text of the *Primary Chronicle*, with modifications of greater or lesser import. The *Office for Sts Boris and Gleb*, composed for use in the liturgy, was transmitted mainly by means of the monthly *Service–Books* (*menaia*). From the beginning of the twelfth century onwards, various abbreviated and truncated versions were also utilized for *Synaxaries* (short accounts of saints or feasts arranged in calendar form for morning service) and for the readings on Boris and Gleb made at vespers[63].

***

The distinctive features in the development of the cult of Boris and Gleb have been presented above. They are also reflected in the iconography, which will be receiving special consideration elsewhere[64].

From its inception, the cult of the holy martyrs held up peace–making as an intrinsic virtue. This was true at the personal level of compromise and forgiveness of insults and injuries, but it also applied on the political plane to princes' relations with one another across the lands of Rus' and to their protection of Rus' from the assaults of the ungodly. Turning to the two *Lives* penned by Nestor, who was

---

[62] The earliest and the later versions of the *Office* were published by D. Abramovič // *Žitija*: 136–150.
[63] A strong–minded interpretation of the historical content of these readings, compiled after 1115 but still mostly before the end of the twelfth century, is proposed by B. A. Uspenskij, *Boris i Gleb*: *Vosprijatie istorii v drevnej Rusi*, Moscow 2000, 124 pp.
[64] The iconography of the cult of Sts Boris and Gleb is being investigated by the eminent art historian, E. S. Smirnova (Moscow).

a monk at the Caves Monastery, one is struck by the importance which Abbot Feodosii himself attached to peace–making and by how far this idea pervaded the monastery. Rebuking Sviatoslav in 1073 for seizing the throne from his eldest brother, Feodosii demanded that Iziaslav's rights be restored to him unconditionally, in accordance with their father's testament[65]. Even if Nestor, writing the *Life of Feodosii* some twelve years later, pictured him as more unyielding than was really the case, bearing in mind the needs of the Caves Monastery in Nestor's own day, his essentially reliable evidence conveys to perfection the general climate in which the cult of Boris and Gleb developed during the 1060s and 1070s. Combing through the anonymous *Tale* and the *Lesson*, one can see how the accent shifted markedly in favour of obedience to one's eldest brother between 1072 and about 1080, when Nestor wrote the *Lesson*. Nestor holds up Boris' and Gleb's readiness to obey Sviatopolk as an example to be followed: "Do you see, brethren, how profound was the obeisance the two holy ones offered to their eldest brother? For had they resisted him they would scarcely have been deemed worthy of this gift of miracles from God. In the present day there are many cadet princes who do not obey their eldest brothers, who oppose them and are killed: they are not vouchsafed such grace as these holy ones received"[66]. Equally in the *Tale*, the brothers are praised for giving up authority for the sake of the Gospel's teachings: this is set "before the eyes" of all Riurikids as a model of behaviour, direct allusion being made to the first Epistle of St John the Evangelist: "He who says, «I love God», but hates his brother, he is a liar"[67]. However, the cult of Boris and Gleb did uphold the right to resist, especially in defence of the weak, if the elder prince misused his authority. The chronicler sets out the right of resistance more clearly than Nestor does, when he invokes the Lord God Himself with words put into the mouth of Iaroslav: "It was not I who began the slaughter of the brethren... but him... may God be the avenger of the innocent blood of my righteous brethren"[68]. It is no accident that some time in the twelfth or thirteenth century this fragment of the *Primary Chronicle* was inserted into the text of the anonymous *Tale*[69].

Obeying one's elders, in other words, accepting hierarchical principles for society in general as well as in the princely family, together with the right to resist force used unjustly, are interlaced with basic Christian values in the cult of Boris and Gleb. The message is directed at princes in the first instance, seeing that they have the power. The two martyr princes rise above the squalor of this passing world but do not abandon it: they stand by their fellow countrymen as holy wonder–workers, interceding on behalf of each and every one of them before God. They are peace–

---

[65] Nestor, *Life of Feodosiy // Hagiography of Kievan Rus'*: 82–86.
[66] Nestor, *Lesson // Žitija* 25. Cf. *Hagiography of Kievan Rus'*: 30.
[67] *Žitija* 30. Cf. *Hagiography of Kievan Rus'*: 100.
[68] PSRL 1: 141. Cf. *Primary Chronicle*: 130–131 and *Hagiography of Kievan Rus'*: 111–112, 193, 196.
[69] *Žitija*: 44–46.

–makers, but with their two–edged swords at the ready they can overcome "internecine strife", repel "the assaults of the heathen" and, like a "bulwark", protect the "land of Rus'" from the attacks of unbelievers[70].

This interweaving of piety with polity created a religious sensibility that was Rus' in its external features and yet thoroughly medieval at heart. It allowed for many different forms of veneration of Sts Boris and Gleb and resonated at every level of society.

***

A sense that the sacrifice of the princes symbolized Rus' transformation into a Christian country with clear ethical and religious goals pervaded public discourse. A preacher addressing his congregation around 1170 in the church of Sts Boris and Gleb in Chernigov could thunder: "You princes, come to your senses! Those of you at odds with your elder brothers, raising up enmity and calling in the pagans against them, [take heed] for fear that God will unmask you at his terrible Last Judgement. [You know] that Sts Boris and Gleb suffered at the hands of their eldest brother, losing not just power but their lives... Imitate and follow the great wonder–workers Boris and Gleb, and learn from their example! If Satan sows hatred amongst you brothers, remember these saints — how they chose death rather than fight with one another. Whoever among you suffers injury and is the first to seek after peace, God will grant him recompense equal to theirs"[71]. It is no accident that feuding princes met with one another in the church at Vyshgorod, by the actual shrines of their sainted relatives, and were reconciled there.

When in 1139 Vsevolod, the son of Oleg, abused his position of seniority as lord of Kiev and relieved Andrey, the son of Vladimir Monomakh, of his principality in Pereiaslavl', transferring him to Kursk, Andrey with the backing of his retinue declared: "... My father was not installed in Kursk but in Pereiaslavl'. I wish to end my days in my own patrimony, whereas you, my brother, are not satisfied with holding all the land of Rus' but want to take this dominion, too. If you kill me, then this country will be yours, but I shall not give up my dominion so long as there is breath in my body. Yet do not suppose that this is unheard of among our kin, for it has been so before. Didn't Sviatopolk put Boris and Gleb to death for their dominions — but did he live very much longer himself?"[72]

These and other eleventh– to thirteenth–century texts address issues arising from princely politics, but they had far–reaching implications for Rus' society as a whole. The quotations should not be interpreted merely in terms of religious intrigue and politicking so familiar to us today. Trimming principles to suit political expediency was essentially alien to the medieval Christian. Believing that the Invisible

---

[70] Cf. the *Tale // Hagiography of Kievan Rus'*: 114–115.

[71] *The Discourse on Princes // Pamiatniki literatury drevnej Rusi, XII v.*, Moskva 1980: 338. Cf. *Hagiography of Kievan Rus'*: 222.

[72] PSRL t. 1: 307, t. 2, SPb. 1908: 305.

God was present in every corner of the universe and all too aware of their personal failings, Rus' newly enlightened citizens had real religious needs. A longing for the Good raised fundamental questions as to what were the principles underpinning their political structure. The stand taken by Prince Andrey of Pereiaslavl', articulated in the words cited above, shows quite clearly how central religion was to politics for the Christian in Rus'[73].

The sense of man enmeshed in his own vice and vileness made it all the more urgent to find saints of proven Goodness, who might serve as intermediaries, protectors and defenders before God. And who, in the thinking of medieval Christians, could do this better than local saints already familiar with their native land? Religious thought in the upper echelons of Rus' society was governed mainly by an assortment of Byzantine models, axioms of State and Church being pre–eminent among them. It is quite understandable that these considerations predominated so far as the princes' promotion of "home–grown saints" was concerned. Driven by this sort of dynastic imperative, the cult of Vladimir the Great doggedly reached saintly status, but it took three centuries to do so. The cult of Boris and Gleb likewise originated in, essentially, dynastic *esprit de corps.* But it soon gained momentum and intensity from a real sense of God bestowing Grace on the brothers. Before long, the cult had become the property of prince and pauper alike in the land of Rus'. This is shown clearly by the ceremonies at Vyshgorod in May 1115: for no less than three days and nights in an uninterrupted stream "the rich and the humble, the healthy and the sick", very probably more than ten thousand pilgrims overall, "thronged past so as to be allowed to touch the two holy shrines"[74].

***

In the cult of Sts Boris and Gleb, political considerations were so closely intertwined with selfless faith that early Rus' writers remarked on the phenomenon more than once. The chronicler sums up the consequences of their translation to the new stone church in Vyshgorod on May 2, 1115, when he apostrophizes: "you who are the pride of our princes and protectors of the land of Rus', who put aside the glory of this world and loved Christ, desiring to follow in his steps... neither resisting nor shunning violent death! For this you have come to reign with Christ!"[75].

In twentieth–century historiography it was often said that the two princes should not be regarded simply as martyrs for Christ: they had been made saints for political reasons which had nothing to do with their confession of the faith[76]. To say this is to take an anachronistic approach to the Christians in Rus' and the way they saw

---

[73] See Poppe, *Politik und Heiligenverehrung in der Kiever Rus'*: 403–422.

[74] The *Tale // Žitija*: 65. Cf. *Hagiography of Kievan Rus'*: 133.

[75] PSRL, t. 2: 281–282. Cf. also transl. *Hagiography of Kievan Rus'*: 205.

[76] This was the view of such outstanding students of Rus'ian piety and Church life as E. E. Golubinsky and G. P. Fedotov, and it has been repeated countless times since. See, for example, G. P. Fedotov, *The Russian Religious Mind*, vol. 1, Cambridge Mass. 1946: 104–105. In the Soviet era the idea of

the world around them. Things may well have been very different from twentieth–century suppositions. Boris and Gleb were the victims of a crime calibrated to the interests of the Riurikid dynasty, falling foul of *raisons d'état.* The circumstances triggering it were forgotten, but the brothers' clandestine killing inspired a religious reading of their conduct. This gave credit to their obedience to Christian precepts and their following of Christ to the point of sacrifice. Boris and Gleb were revered simply for upholding Christian virtues, suffering martyrdom for Christ and making the Word flesh in the land of Rus'. They had taken literally the demand that St John the Evangelist makes of every Christian: heed God not only in word but also in truth and deed. Boris' and Gleb's high–mindedness became an axiom of early Rus' piety, shaping ideas about the place of religion in political life. It had a particularly strong impact on the upper strata of Kievan society.

The question that absorbs modern researchers — what actually happened in 1015? — is apt enough if one is trying to reconstruct the lead–up to the murders. But viewed from a historical perspective, it is not the crime itself that moulded Rus' so much as the religious "construction" placed upon whatever may have happened. One can safely say that the cult of the martyr princes in all its manifold forms went far beyond the original expectations of the princes trying to enrol their murdered relatives among the saints. Nestor the hagiographer captured this when he represented the brothers as rounding off their father's work: Vladimir may have led the Rus' people out of the murk of paganism and showed the way ahead, but Boris and Gleb obeyed Christ to the last and shared in His Passion. They demonstrated in blood that the Gospel's message transforms the life of man. And this belief in their freewill sacrifice took firm hold at a variety of social levels in early Christian Rus'.

"political sainthood" facilitated research and publication without undue attention having to be paid to politically incorrect subjects such as spirituality. B. A. Rybakov claimed from the 1960s onwards that the cult of Boris and Gleb was essentially pagan, with roots deep in native tradition. This belief system has left traces in English–language publications, too (e.g. E. Reisman in Russian Review 37, 1978: 141–157). For a more critical appraisal, see P. Hollingsworth's introduction // *Hagiography of Kievan Rus'*: p. LI, and W. Goldblatt, *Authorship*: 112.

To sustain the view that Boris and Gleb were not recognized as martyrs for the faith in Rus', some scholars refer to the *Paterikon*'s citation of bishops who had formerly been monks of the Caves Monastery. Bishop Leontii of Rostov figures among them: "And behold, he was the third citizen of the Rus' world: he was crowned by Christ with that pair of Varangians for whose sake they were slain" (*Paterik of the Kievan Caves Monastery*, transl. M. Heppell, Cambridge Mass.1989: 118). One must remember that in the 1220s (when Simon and Policarp corresponded about the history of the Caves Monastery) and even in the twentieth century, many supposed the bishopric of Rostov to have been founded at the time of the conversion of Rus', at the end of the tenth century. It is therefore understandable that Leontii, the first bishop of Rostov, should have been taken for the third martyr for the faith after the Varangian father and son, who had perished according to *Primary Chronicle* s.a. 983 on the eve of the conversion. This false conclusion is the result of divergent views as to the date of the foundation of the Rostov see. As has been established, this in fact occurred long after the conversion, at the beginning of the 1070s. (A. Poppe, *L'organisation diocésaine*: 193–197).

VIII

The Sainthood of Vladimir the Great: Veneration in-the-Making*

1. Some observations regarding the Christianity of Vladimir. 2. When and how Vladimir was recognized as a saint. 3. The emergence of the veneration of Vladimir the Great.

The deeds of King Vladimir, "the equal of Constantine the Great", who "enlightened the land of Rus' with holy baptism", were not long in achieving recognition. As early as the mid-eleventh century, Hilarion's *Sermon on Law and Grace* and then, at the beginning of the twelfth century, *The Primary Chronicle* offered eloquent tribute.[1] More recently, the homage paid

---

* In memory of John Meyendorff, priest and historian, who inspired me to undertake this study. The research which has resulted in this triptych was begun in 1986–87. By the time of the jubilee in 1988, enough had been completed to publish a conceptualization of Vladimir's Christianity, found in the first section of this work. Subsequent unanticipated hold-ups in the completion of both the English and Russian versions of this work considerably delayed the time and place of its publication, but have allowed further additions and corrections to be made. This current English version was completed with the assistance of Robert Scott, for which the author expresses his thanks.

ABBREVIATIONS:

BZ	*Byzantinische Zeitschrift*
DOP	*Dumbarton Oaks Papers*
HUS	*Harvard Ukrainian Studies*
MPH	*Monumenta Poloniae Historica*
LMA	*Lexikon des Mittelalters*
RM	*Russia Mediaevalis*
ВВ	*Византийский Временик*
ДДГ	*Духовные и Договорные грамоты великих и удельных князей*
ИзвОРЯС	*Известия отделения русского языка и словесности*
НПЛ	*Новгородская Первая летопись старшего и младшего изводов*
ПСРЛ	*Полное Собрание Русских Летописей*
РИБ	*Русская Историческая Библиотека*
ТОДРЛ	*Труды Отдела Древнерусской Литературы*

[1] On the treatment of this topic in Hilarion's *Sermon on Law and Grace* (from which both quotations are taken) and *The (Russian) Primary Chronicle*, see A. Poppe "Two Concepts of the Conversion of Rus' in Kievan Writings", *HUS* 12/13 (1988/1989): 488–504.

throughout the world to this "apostle among kings"[2] during the celebrations marking 1000 years of Russian Christianity, reflected a widely-held understanding of the importance of the spiritual transformation of the Eastern Slavs that begun under his patronage.

Paradoxically, the millennial observance owed much of its universal resonance to the importance of a state that had struggled hard to make the Christian period of East Slavic history a thing of the past. Today, however, it is clear that faith can continue to look toward the future with hope.[3]

Taking a long perspective, it is clear that the events of the tenth and eleventh centuries had a decisive impact on Old Rus'ian society, bringing about radical changes in its individual and collective consciousness. The development of the spiritual side of human life, manifesting itself in ideology and in the psychology of the individual and society can and must be the subject of historical research, even if the sparseness of sources from the period of interest appears to present an insuperable obstacle. Even if we lack new sources, it is possible to examine the old ones anew and try to read well-known texts in new ways, without prejudice or predisposition.

The earliest image of Vladimir to emerge in the historiography was that of an idealized Christian ruler. That image was, in turn, supplanted by the slightly more complex, but ultimately no less reductionist, characterization of Vladimir as a crafty and able statesman prepared, for the sake of the internal progress and international interests of his country, first to renew the religion of his ancestors and then to repudiate it entirely for a new creed, choosing from among the various options as if they were the wares of a street vendor.

Many questions associated with the veneration and sainthood of Vladimir the Great have yet to be satisfactorily answered. This study seeks to elucidate various moments in the long process of their emergence. The roots of that process extend back into the life of the venerated one himself, to the contemporary recognition of his genuine achievement in bringing Rus' into the Christian world. Far from everything that can be said about Vladimir as a Christian has been said, and the first part of this triptych therefore attempts to understand his Christianity in a rather new and different way. The second section of the paper seeks to define more precisely the time when Vladimir came to be recognized as a saint. It also takes note of several peculiarities of

---

2 Since, in early medieval Europe, the Slavic title *kniaz'* was equivalent to the Latin title *rex*, and since the Rus'ian rulers are consistently referred to in medieval sources as *reges*, I break here with the historiographic tradition of the nineteenth and twentieth centuries and return to the medieval usage and meaning of this title.

3 In the years 1987–1992 more than twenty conferences were held and over forty volumes of collected studies were published on the Millennium of Rus'ian Christianity.

the initial period of that cult – the fourteenth and first part of the fifteenth centuries. Finally, the third section pulls together a variety of observations about the emergence, during the eleventh to thirteenth centuries, of a religious veneration of Vladimir that led ultimately to his inclusion in the ranks of Rus'ian saints as a sovereign equal-of-the-apostles (*isoapostolos*).

1. Some observations regarding the Christianity of Vladimir

When we seek to turn our attention to Vladimir himself as a Christian rather than to his deeds, we are confronted with a tradition heavily coloured by the conventions of hagiography. The monastic chronicler, while drawing on legends entwined around the baptism of Rus', constructs his life of Vladimir around the evangelical theme: "where sin has grown great, there grace abounds as well" (Romans 5:20). He therefore seeks to draw a sharp contrast between the dark image of the former pagan and the shining visage of the new Christian prince. Through comparison with Solomon, his blackened portrait of a polygamist and sensualist assumes virtually Old Testament proportions.[4]

The chronicle account of Vladimir's selection of a faith, however brilliant as a piece of literature, must be read as an attempt to look back symbolically on the events preceding the conversion and is of little use for reconstructing the actual facts. As the chronicler presents it, everything takes place in the course of eight years. King Vladimir, as soon as he is enthroned in Kiev, is shown undertaking a reform of paganism, creating a pantheon of divinities headed by the god Perun, only to abandon this attempt "to create a state-wide polytheistic cult"[5] shortly afterwards. News of the king's religious strivings seemingly spread throughout the world, for soon, in rapid succession, adherents of Islam, Judaism, Latin and Greek Christianity are shown hastening to Kiev. All are quickly sent on their way again, greater attention being accorded only to the more-than-5000-word speech of the Greek philosopher. Intrigued by the opportunities open to him, Vladimir now dispatches his own embassy, which visits, in turn, Bulgar on the Kama, Rome, and Constantinople in order "to examine closely the worship of each of them

---

4 *The Russian Primary Chronicle*, tr. S.H. Cross (Cambridge 1953), 94.

5 H. Łowmiański, *Religia Słowian i jej upadek* (Warsaw, 1979): 113–119. An intriguing, but utterly fanciful characterization of the "pagan reform" of Vladimir is presented by B.A. Rybakov, *Язычество древней Руси* (Moscow, 1987): 38–49. Cf. Ia.N. Shchapov, "'Священство' и 'царство' в древней Руси в теории и на практике", *BB* 50 (1989): 131–133.

to learn how they serve God". The result of the embassy is an unambiguous victory for the Greek variant. Its rightness is underscored by reference to the earlier choice of that same faith by Regent Olga. Vladimir then undertakes a military campaign against Byzantine Cherson as the place of his forthcoming baptism.[6] The providential course of events recounted by the chronicler, when taken as a straightforward accounting of the facts by contemporary historiography, cutting out the role he ascribes to Providence, takes on a grotesque character. The question whether the account of Vladimir's selection of a faith is fact or fiction likewise oversimplifies a complex question and is methodologically inappropriate,[7] as are attempts to confirm the accuracy of the *Primary Chronicle*'s literary portrait of the pagan Vladimir on the basis of testimony from the contemporary German chronicler Bishop Thietmar of Merseburg.[8]

Thietmar does reproach Vladimir for wrongdoing (*accionem iniquam*) and brand him an "unheard-of lecher" (*fornicator immensus*), but he makes these charges against a Christian, asserting that while Vladimir had "received the holy Christian faith, he did not adorn it with righteous deeds" (VII, 72). Research has in fact demonstrated the bias in Thietmar's account, with its colouration of fact by personal prejudice. Nonetheless, it is not our intention here to dismiss his testimony for its tendentiousness, but to attempt to explain how he came to hold these views and by doing so, begin to shed some light on their reliability. At the outset, however, attention should be drawn to Thietmar's peculiar penchant for moralizing on the theme of "our times, when the decay of morals is spreading everywhere at an immeasurable and unprecedented rate" (VIII, 3).

Just which act of Vladimir's Thietmar considered unjust emerges clearly from his account (VII, 72, 73), three-fourths of which is devoted to the chronicler's countryman, Bishop Reinbern of Kolberg. Reinbern had accompanied the daughter of the Polish king, Bolesław the Brave, to Rus',

---

6 *The Primary Chronicle*: 96–119; *ПСРЛ* I: 84–124.

7 Cf. P. Toločko, "Volodimir Svjatoslavič's Choice of Religion, Fact or Fiction?", *HUS* 12/13 (1988/1989): 816–829. The correct conclusion is that various conflicting traditions with little historical value were combined into one authoritative account of Vladimir's baptism, see D. Ostrowski, "The Account of Volodimer's Conversion in the *Povest' vremennykh let:* A Chiasmus of Stories", *HUS* 28 (forthcoming 2007). This account could have been composed only some time after 1054, since the Latins are characterized in it by their taking the Holy Communion in *azymo* (i.e. in unleavened bread).

8 These and subsequent pages of the Chronicle are quoted according to the edition *Thietmari Merseburgensis episcopi Chronicon*, ed. R. Holtzmann and W. Trillmich (Berlin, 1957): 404, 432, 434, 436, 442. References are also provided to the specific books of this Chronicle, in order to facilitate the use of any edition or translation.

where she was married to Vladimir's son Sviatopolk. In 1013 the bishop, princess, and Sviatopolk were all imprisoned on the order of Vladimir "when the latter learned that his son, at the urging of Bolesław, was secretly conspiring against him" (VII, 72). Although Thietmar does not question the existence of the conspiracy, he condemns the imprisonment of the innocent, "honourable pastor", who died in captivity. The chronicler indirectly lays the blame for the death of the bishop on Vladimir, expressing his indignation with the words of the apostle Paul (Hebrews XIII: 4), "*adulteros iudicat Deus*" and adding, in a manner hardly Christian but very much in the spirit of his times, that, "sitting safely in heaven, the bishop laughs at the threats of that unrighteous man and... awaits the burning retribution the lecher will receive" (VII, 73).[9]

Thietmar himself was apparently bothered by the bareness and irrelevance of his charge of adultery in this context, for the chronicle bears a later note in the bishop's his own hand explaining that "the aforementioned king wore a girdle on his loins to heighten his innate lustfulness" (*rex predictus habuit lumbare venereum, innatae fragilitati maius augmentum*, VII, 74). Thietmar did not simply dream up this detail, but was repeating a coarse anecdote circulating in Kiev probably even during the lifetime of the ruler and brought back to Germany in October of 1018 by a Saxon who had just taken part in the military campaign against that city. Thietmar eagerly seized upon the story, since he had been unable to bolster his earlier accusation of adultery with any concrete examples, despite his fondness, as a writer, for lively detail.

For that matter, Thietmar probably had not invented the charge of dissoluteness itself, but had heard it much earlier, under completely different circumstances. Significantly, at the very beginning of his account of Vladimir, Thietmar mentions the marriage of that ruler of Rus' to the daughter of the Byzantine emperor, who had been "earlier promised to Otto III but then denied to him as a result of deceitful intrigue" (VII, 72). Leaving aside for a moment the factual inaccuracies of Thietmar's statement, it seems clear that the bishop is expressing the indignation that his family, the Walbecks, closely linked with the court of all three Ottonians, must have felt over the Byzantine affront to their masters. The insult experienced by the Ottonian court as a

---

[9] *Thietmari Chronicon*, 934/5: 436/7. On the rebellion following Vladimir's death and the struggle for the throne of Kiev, see A. Poppe, "Losers on Earth, Winners from Heaven. The Assassinations of Boris and Gleb in the Making of Eleventh-Century Rus'", *Quaestiones medii aevi novae* 8 (Warsaw, 2003): 133–151 [=this volume no. VII].

result of the unsuccessful suit of 968 was, moreover, repeated by the equally abortive marriage project of 995–1001.[10]

Thietmar, stirred by news of the death of his imprisoned countryman, who may have been a close friend, probably returned in his memory to the troubling atmosphere of those earlier episodes, except that now, at the distance of so many years, he got the details mixed up. In 988 he had been 13 years old. The protracted efforts to obtain a *porphyrogenita* for Otto III (which Thietmar's chronicle confused with the earlier project) must have been the subject of much discussion and irritation, both in the family of the Walbecks (Thietmar maintained lively contacts with his many kinsmen) and in Magdeburg, where Thietmar received his education. In this context, the name of the fortunate rival suitor, who, though a pagan, had been able to achieve fairly easily something that had been denied for years to the arch-Christian Ottonians, must have come up again and again in conversation, accompanied by a far from flattering commentary in which charges of adultery must have been a constant theme.[11]

While seeking the sources of Thietmar's condemnation in the events of 988, we are not trying to suggest that Vladimir completely changed his way of life after his baptism and marriage to Anna the *porphyrogenita*, although there were, no doubt, some significant changes at the Kievan court. The private and public life of Christian rulers everywhere in the Europe of that day was far from the postulated Christian ideal. For that matter, the institution of legal marriage only gradually came to be held as sacrosanct, and the Church was long forced to tolerate marital ties of a lower rank, most notably concubinage. The vulnerability of Vladimir's private life to censure was not the result of a departure from the accepted behavioural norms of his time. Nonetheless, the ascetic Thietmar, scornful of worldly matters and the needs of the flesh, could stigmatize Vladimir without the fear of troubling comparisons with local conditions because of the exceptional piety and morality of the German emperor Henry – presumed by many of his contemporaries to be ruling over

[10] For more on this question, see A. Poppe, "The Political Background to the Baptism of Rus'. Byzantine-Russian Relations between 986–989", *DOP* 30 (1976): 230–231; A. Poppe, "How the Conversion of Rus' was Understood in the Eleventh Century", *HUS* 11, 1987: 293–294.

[11] Cf. K. Ritzer, *Formen, Riten und religiöses Brauchtum der Eheschließung in den christlichen Kirchen des ersten Jahrtausends* (Münster, 1981): 102–128, 256–297, 326–333. On marriage in Rus', see Ia.N. Shchapov, *State and Church in Early Russia 10th–13th Centuries* (New Rochelle, N.Y., 1993): 121–127; N.L. Pushkareva, *Женщины древней Руси* (Moscow, 1989): 70–79. In spite of Byzantine law, concubinage continued to exist in the 13th century – A. Laiou, "L'institution familiale en l'Epire", *Forschungen zur byzantinischen Rechtsgeschichte. Fontes Minores*, VI (Frankfurt a/Main, 1988): 284 ff.

the last days of this world.[12] Moreover, the conviction voiced in clerical and monastic circles that the disorder of the world was the result of debauchery struck a resonant chord in the eschatological and millennarian anxieties of societies long ago Christianized. Nonetheless, the bias of Thietmar's indignation toward the ruler of Rus' is revealed by a comparison with his attitude toward King Robert of France, whom the bishop described as "*pacificus et per omnia venerabilis rex*" (VII, 46). Thietmar could not have been ignorant of the fact that this monarch, "honourable in all things", had in fact been accused of two acts of incest and bigamy. The scandals of Robert's private life were known all over Europe and were debated even in the Roman curia (a fact which did not, however, prevent the king from earning the posthumous epithet of "the Pious").[13]

A kinsman and schoolmate of Thietmar, the missionary bishop Bruno of Querfurt, who met Vladimir in 1008 and spent no less than two months at his court, was of a completely different opinion: he saw Vladimir very much as a Christian and as a Christian ruler.[14] When the king warned Bruno of the all but certain death that awaited if he continued on his missionary journey to the Pechenegs, the bishop responded: "May God open heaven to you as you have opened the road to the pagans to me."[15]

Thietmar, despite his hostility to Vladimir, includes a report by Bruno describing the prince's great generosity in the distribution of alms. To be sure, the bishop provides a negative commentary, ascribing this to the ruler's desire

---

[12] Cf. *Thietmari Chronicon*, Books VI: 11; VIII: 6. On beliefs in the coming of the apocalypse in connection with the millennium of the Crucifixion, see J. Fried "Endzeiterwartung um die Jahrtausendwende", *Deutsches Archiv für Erforschung des Mittelalters* 45 (1989): 381–473; W. Brandes "Liudprand von Cremona (Legatio, cap. 39–41) und eine bisher unbeachtete west–östliche Korrespondenz über die Bedeutung des Jahres 1000 A.D.", *BZ* 93 (2000): 435–463.

[13] G. Duby, *Le Chevalier, la Femme et le Prêtre. Le mariage dans la France féodale.* (Paris, 1981[2]): 83–93.

[14] As is emphasized by M. Hellmann in "Vladimir der Heilige in der zeitgenössischen abendländischen Überlieferung", *Jahrbücher für Geschichte Osteuropas* 7 (1959): 397–412.

[15] See Bruno's letter to king Henry II, written in Poland at the end of 1008, after his return to Kiev – *MPH* s.n. IV, fasc. 3, ed. J. Karwasińska (Warsaw, 1973): 97–106, here: 99. Still essential for an understanding of Bruno's personality and work are: H.G. Vogt, *Brun von Querfurt, Mönch, Eremit, Erzbischof der Heiden und Märtyrer* (Stuttgart, 1907); R. Wenskus, *Studien zur historisch-politischen Gedankenwelt Bruns von Querfurt* (Munster–Cologne, 1956). For a detailed commentary on the Pecheneg episode see W. Meysztowicz, "Szkice o świętym Brunie-Bonifacym", *Sacrum Poloniae Millennium* 5 (Rome, 1958): 488–494, but his attempt to date the beginning of the Pecheneg mission precisely to 22 February 1008, the day commemorating the accession of the Apostle Peter to the cathedral of Rome, is hard to justify on the basis of the sources. Bruno's five-month stay in steppe can be dated to the spring and summer of 1008, so his visit to Kiev must have fallen in the same year.

to "wipe away the stains of committed sin" in accordance with the Gospel injunction (Luke XI: 41): "*Facite elemosinam, ac omnis sunt vobis munda*" (VII, 74). By making such a claim, he thereby contradicts his own statement of a year or two earlier, when he wrote that Vladimir had "received the holy Christian faith, but did not adorn it with righteous deeds" (VII, 72).

The renown of Vladimir's aid to the weak, sick, and poor of this world lived on for some time after him in Kiev. Thirty-five years after the king's death, Metropolitan Hilarion, standing above Vladimir's tomb in the Church of the Tithe, proclaimed: "Your generosity and almsgiving have remained in the memory of the people." Hilarion, describing Vladimir's Christian character, placed special emphasis on the theme of mercy and charity. The guiding thrust of his panegyric is that Vladimir had taken to heart and put into practice the advice of the prophet Daniel to King Nebuchadnezzar: "cleanse your sins with almsgiving, and your unrighteousness with liberality toward the poor." Thanks to his generosity, Hilarion asserted, Vladimir was worthy of the name of true servant of Christ, but, as if disputing those who might find this insufficient, he cited the epistle of James to bolster his claim: "Let him know that he who turns a sinner from the error of his way will save a soul from death and cover a multitude of sins."[16] Addressing the king, Hilarion adds: "If such a great reward is due from gracious God to him who has converted a single sinner, then what a salvation, Vasilii, have you obtained, you who have converted not one man, or ten, or a whole city, but your entire dominion." While praising the ruler-apostle, Hilarion is not silent about his sins, even if he does not devote any special discussion to them. Without reproach, but also without any attempt at justification, he lays them on the scales. Vladimir did not have his Einhard, so one can only speculate that his private life must have been comparable in more than one respect to the colourful life of Charlemagne. The Christianization of the marital customs of rulers and nobles in the tenth and eleventh centuries was marked by the ongoing conflict of two moralities: that of the priests and that of the warriors.[17]

* * *

[16] Hilarion, "Sermon on Law and Grace", *Sermons and Rhetoric of Kievan Rus'*, transl. by S. Franklin (Cambridge, Mass., 1991): 17, 20–23 (Encomium to Vladimir), 20–23 (below: Hilarion, *Sermons*).

[17] Cf. Duby, *Le Chevalier*: 27–59. A. Angenendt, *Das Frühmittelalter* (Stuttgart, 1990): 371–372.

This overwhelmingly positive image of Vladimir the Christian, so diametrically opposed to the picture that emerges from Thietmar's condemnation of the prince, could simply be ascribed to the greater distance in time and the subsequent acceptance by broader circles in Rus' of these values – values zealously promoted by, among others, Hilarion himself – were it not for a significant detail learned by Thietmar, along with the aforementioned ribald Kievan anecdote, from that same Saxon participant in the Kievan campaign. In August 1018, the latter reported, he had seen, in the palace church (the Church of the Tithe) the sarcophagi of Vladimir and his wife – i.e., the *porphyrogenita* Anna – standing "in full view, in the centre of the church" (VII, 74).

The expression "in full view, in the centre of the church" could be variously understood, depending on the architectural layout of the building, but in any case, it is clear that the reference is being made to the central nave. Since the Church of the Tithe was cruciform domed building, with a clearly delineated crossing, it is natural to assume that the Saxon visitor had in mind the space beneath the central dome. Possibly the sarcophagi of the royal pair were positioned slightly back, beneath the western arch, but they could not have been placed forward, beneath the eastern arch, as the altar screen, standing in front of the eastern pillars, would have made this impossible.[18]

The burial of a ruler before the main altar was nothing exceptional in Western Europe during this period.[19] In Byzantium, on the other hand, neither the presbytery nor the main nave under the central dome were used for interments, not even those of imperial personages.[20] The sole exception was the reliquary tomb, containing the remains of sanctified or beatified individuals. On the whole, moreover, such a grave was not the original place of interment. Translation of remains to the centre of the church was

---

[18] *Thietmari Chronicon*: 436. On the royal church "of the Tithe", cf. A. Poppe, "The Building of the Church of St Sophia in Kiev", *Journal of Medieval History* 7 (Amsterdam, 1981): 16, 24–26; A.I. Komech, *Древнерусское зодчество конца X – начала XI века* (Moscow, 1997): 168–178.

[19] F. Oswald, "In medio Ecclesiae. Die Deutung der literarischen Zeugnisse im Lichte der archäologischen Funde", *Frühmittelalterliche Studien* 3 (1970): 313–326. On the practice of burying near the altar, cf. K.H. Krüger, *Königsgrabkirchen der Franken, Angelsachsen und Longobarden bis zur Mitte des 8. Jhs. Ein historischer Katalog* (München, 1971): 422–423, 427–436, 430–431, 497, 500.

[20] Cf. Ph. Grierson, "The Tombs and Obits of the Byzantine Emperors (337–1042)", with Appendix by C. Mango and I. Ševčenko, *DOP* 16 (1962): 1–63. For new observations on the complicated primary history of those burials, see C. Mango, "Constantine's Mausoleum and the Translation of Relics", *BZ* 83 (1990): 57–62, 434.

associated with canonization or preparation for it.[21] The report of the Saxon newcomer seems all the more trustworthy in light of the fact that neither he nor Thietmar, as Westerners, would have associated it with a preparation for sainthood.

In light of the confusion and disorder of the struggle for the Kievan throne that broke out shortly after the death of Vladimir on July 15, 1015, it seems most likely that the prince's body had been laid in the aforementioned place immediately after his demise. For that matter, the decision to place the graves of the royal pair before the altar could already have been made at the time of the burial of Anna, who died in 1011, perhaps with the idea of eventually inducting the royal pair into the company of the saints. The placement of the tombs under the crossing of the church, before the altar, in full view of the praying parishioners, put the remains of Vladimir and Anna at almost the very centre of the liturgical space, according fully with their remembrance in the liturgy as well as with an annual celebration of their memory.

Given the absence of any local tradition of this sort, we can only conclude that the initiative must have come from the Byzantine elements of the Kievan court as well as from the Greek ecclesiastical hierarchy. In other words, already at the end of Vladimir and Anna's lives, their role in the conversion of Rus' and the implantation of Christianity must have been recognized within those circles as worthy of exceptional and indeed – for Christians – the highest honour. The decision to place the sarcophagi in the palace church, the only stone church in Kiev at that time, was not the same thing as beatification, but it foreshadowed such an act in the very near future. The confusion born of the fratricidal struggles between Vladimir's sons for the throne of Kiev would have imposed a delay on any such plans. However, three decades later the matter of glorifying the baptizer of Rus' could be taken up again, this time by the victorious Iaroslav and the Presbyter Hilarion.[22]

---

[21] See S. Ćurčić, "Medieval Royal Tombs in the Balkans: An Aspect of the 'East or West' Question", *The Greek Orthodox Theological Review* 29 (1984): 175–186. From this point of view, the argument between Vladimir Monomakh and David and Oleg of Chernigov, sons of Sviatoslav, on the eve of the translation of the coffins containing the relics of Saints Boris and Gleb into the new church at Vishgorod on 2 May 1115 (II: 281) is worthy of attention. Vladimir sought to place the coffin beneath a silver ciborium in the centre of the church, while the Chernigov princes, in accordance with the will of their father and the traditions of princely burial, wanted to place the coffins in a niche beneath the arch (*komara*) to the right of the altar. By casting of lots, the matter was settled in favour of the Sviatoslavichi.

[22] It was precisely here, over the grave of Vladimir, on an anniversary of his death, that Hilarion delivered his *Sermon.*

And so, thanks to Thietmar, so eager to avenge himself against the king of Rus', authentic images of the life of Kiev in the second decade of the eleventh century have been preserved for us: on one hand, in a coarse anecdote expressing admiration for the vital forces of the already aged ruler, repeated on the streets of Kiev along with other jokes about the king and, on the other, in indications of a ripening intention within court and ecclesiastical circles to pay supreme homage to "our teacher and guide" in the matter of conversion.

* * *

The hagiographer Nestor, writing nearly one hundred years after the baptism of Rus', conceived the conversion of the country's ruler – much as did the somewhat later the compiler of *The Primary Chronicle* – as a sudden turn of events, an act of divine Providence: "yesterday he did not know who Jesus Christ was, today he has become his proclaimer, yesterday he was known as the pagan Vladimir, today, as the Christian Vasilii."[23] This literary rendering produces its intended effect, but in reality the transformation of Vladimir from pagan into Christian could not have been so sudden.

Vladimir was the third son of Sviatoslav, born sometime between 955 and 960 to Malusha, housekeeper of Queen Olga and daughter of a ministerial family of unfree origin. Her brother Dobrynia had likewise made a career for himself at court. As a member of the closest entourage of the regent of Rus', Malusha could well have accompanied Olga along with other "notable female servants" on the journey to Constantinople, taking part in one of the receptions at the imperial palace there.[24] Whether then, in 954 or 955, or at some other time, Malusha, as one of Olga's intimates, must have been baptized just as her mistress had been. As a concubine of Sviatoslav and later the mother of Vladimir, she naturally would have remained at the court while her son was growing up. Olga, until her death in 969, could also have exercised an influence on the education of her grandson. Even if he was

---

[23] D. Abramovich, *Жития святых мучеников Бориса и Глеба и службы им* (Petrograd, 1916): 4; *The Hagiography of Kievan Rus'*, transl. by P. Hollingsworth (Cambridge, Mass., 1992): 4–7 (below: *The Hagiography*).

[24] For a summary of the debate over the dates of the visit of Olga noted by Constantine Porphyrogenitus, see the addendum to essay no. II in this collection of reprints. For a return to the traditional dating of Olga's baptism in Constantinople (954/955), see A. Poppe, "Once Again Concerning the Baptism of Olga, Archontissa of Rus'", *DOP* 46 (1992): 271–277. For an attempt to fix the time of Olga's inclusion in the ranks of the saints, see J. Fennell, "When was Olga canonized?", *California Slavic Studies* 16 (1993): 77–82.

raised as a pagan in accordance with the wishes of his father, his grandmother and mother no doubt sought to imbue him with a "secret" – i.e., not publicly proclaimed – Christian faith. Shortly after the death of Olga, the young Vladimir was sent by Sviatoslav, along with his *nutritor* (tutor) and uncle Dobrynia, to Novgorod. The fact that Vladimir, after his baptism in 988, would entrust Dobrynia with overseeing the introduction of Christianity in Novgorod permits us to speculate that the brother of Malusha may also have been a "secret" Christian.[25]

There are thus good grounds for presuming that Vladimir had grown up in a Christian atmosphere from childhood. He likewise favoured the already quite numerous Christians found in court circles. Hence the words of Hilarion: "In addition, he heard constantly of the Orthodox Greek land, loving Christ and growing stronger in faith... and knowing this, he yearned in his heart and burned in his soul to become a Christian...."[26] The baptism of the thirty-year-old Vladimir on January 6, 988, preceded by a three-month catechumenate, had thus been well prepared.[27]

This emotional tie with Christianity, reaching back to his childhood years and informed by the typically feminine religious zeal of his grandmother and mother, was now entwined with another, more rational road to the knowledge of God: "reason enlightened his heart [as to] how to find... the one God". Hilarion continues: "How did you come to believe, how did there come to dwell in you a reason surpassing the reason of the wise of this earth, such that you came to love the Unseen and dared to strive for the Heavenly? A wondrous miracle! Other emperors and rulers, seeing all these things taking place through the agency of holy men, did not believe. But you, o blessed one, without any of this, strove toward Christ. By the maturity of your thought and the quickness of your reason alone you came to understand that there is one God the Creator... and reflecting upon this, you drew near to the sacred font."[28]

Hilarion, born around the time of the baptism of Rus', belonged to the second generation of the converted. For him, belief in one God was not only

---

[25] The idea of "secret Christianity" was proposed by E. Golubinskii in his *История русской церкви*, vol. 1, part 1 (Moscow, 1901): 85ff, 151–154.

[26] A.M. Moldovan, "*Слово о законе и благодати" Илариона* (Kiev, 1984): 92; Hilarion, *Sermons* (Encomium to Vladimir): 18.

[27] See Poppe, "The Background": 240–242. On catechumanate and baptism itself cf. M. Arranz, "Чин оглашения и крещения в древней Руси", Символ 19 (1988): 69–100; cf. A. Angenendt, "Der Taufritus im frühen Mittelalter", *Settimane di Studi del Centro italiano di studi sull'alto Medioevo* XXXIII (Spoleto, 1987): 275–336.

[28] Moldovan, *Слово*: 95; Hilarion, *Sermons* (Encomium to Vladimir): 20.

an act of spiritual righteousness but a sign of wisdom as well, since belief in the Christian God was more rational than honouring the primitive pagan deities. Belief in things unseen, which could not merely be comprehended by the senses, required, in his view, a higher degree of initiation, as his words to Vladimir above suggest. In at least one respect the act of faith and the act of reason have a common characteristic – both demand a conscious concentration, an internal tension, and a new sense of responsibility toward oneself and one's fellows. The chronicler expressed this emphatically under the year 1037 in his metaphorical characterization of Vladimir as the plowman and Iaroslav the Wise as the sower, "who sowed the hearts of the believers with the written word".[29] Faith expressed itself first of all in a special relationship to the Holy Writ, but also to writing in general, and to reading, arousing one to a love of wisdom, including its highest form, originating from the Wisdom of God (St Sophia). It was namely to her, who embodied the Word of God, that, beginning in the late tenth century, the wooden cathedral churches of Kiev, Polotsk, and Novgorod were dedicated, a symbol of Wisdom's triumph over the "false error of idolatry".[30]

---

[29] *The Primary Chronicle*: 137–138. *ПСРЛ* I: 151–152. Speaking here of "books", "book learning", and "the words of books", the chronicler has in mind the Holy Writ. The Slavonic language must have been in use by Kievan Christians prior to 988. Otherwise it would be difficult to explain such a rapid resolution of the issue of a liturgical language for the Rus'ian church, already in the reign of Vladimir. Vladimir and Anna (who probably knew Bulgarian and quickly learned Old Russian) were faced with the complex task of Christianizing an enormous land with a mass of local centres scattered far away from one another. An urgent need emerged for a vast number of ecclesiastical books and liturgical apparatus, as well as for clergy able to speak a language understood by the people. The resolution of this problem was helped by the conquest of Bulgaria, taking place in the same period, by the Emperor Basil, assisted by Rus'ian troops. It ensured several years' flow to Rus', as trophies of war, of the greatest literary heritage of the South Slavs, including many liturgical books (the seizure of ecclesiastical property in the Middle Ages was a perfectly normal phenomenon for all of Christian Europe), and the Bulgarian clerics forcibly resettled in Rus' became, by force of circumstance, full-fledged missionaries to the East Slavs.

[30] Concerning St Sophia, the Wisdom of God see: F. von Lilienfeld, "Das Patrozinium der Heiligen Sophia in Europa und besonders in Rußland", *Tausend Jahre Taufe Rußland. Symposium in Halle, April 1988* (Leipzig, 1993): 467–476. Cf. the interesting ideas of S.S. Averintsev in "К уяснению смысла надписи над конхой центральной апсиды Софии Киевской", *Древнерусское искусство: Художественная культура домонгольской Руси* (Moscow, 1972): 25–49, and J. Meyendorff, "Тема 'Премудрости' в восточноевропейской средневековой культуре и ее наследие", *Литература и искусство в системе культуры* (Moscow, 1988): 244–252; K.K. Akent'ev, "Мозаики киевской Св. Софии и 'Слово' митрополита Илариона в византийском литургическом контексте", *Византинороссика* 1 (St Petersburg, 1995): 75–94. Interesting reflections on the intellectual reception of the "lexical structure" of Wisdom in the Greek and Cyrillo-Methodian

Christianity implied access to knowledge and served as a source of intellectual experience. It was not a divergence between faith and reason but their spiritual harmony that characterized young Christian society. The newly converted elites must have been particularly drawn to its ideas of a reasoned order and a beneficial organization of human life, gracefully joining Church and political authority, ecclesiastical book-learning and the fortress town into a unified whole. It had been like this in Western Europe, too, in the epoch of the Merovingians and (perhaps even more) the Carolingians, when Europe, with a child-like sincerity, still perceived a clear interrelationship between its religious and political and social ideals, when Christianity, addressing itself first and foremost to rulers and their courts and entourages, coexisted harmoniously with a very earthly striving for legal order, the building of towns, and the education of society. Now it was the turn of the Slavs.

Only with Christianization could Rus' become fully conscious of itself as a state and society, find its place in the universal history of humanity and its salvation. The claim of the ruling elite to authority was no longer based solely on birth, valour, and wealth, but also on its participation in a high-level religious and intellectual culture, distinguishing it from the mass of unbaptized and unenlightened pagans (the Slavic word for "pagan" was *neveglas*, literally "uneducated" or "ignoramus", a word serving in translations as an equivalent of the Greek *anoetos* – "not belonging the sphere of thought", *homo nullius experientiae*).[31]

In the perception of the ruler and his associates, the reception of Christianity was closely related to the construction of political authority, whose concrete expression, defining its range and viability, was the fortress and town. It is for this reason that such an important place in the work of the Kievan prince was devoted to the intensive building of fortress-settlements and fortified towns. The enclosed urban space, centred around its main church and protected by a powerful wall from the wild natural world of the limitless steppe and its wandering nomads, serving as residence of the prince and his great men, seat of ecclesiastical life and book-learning, and centre of gravity for priests and bookmen, manifested itself in a fresh and unstudied perception as the visible image of the House of the Wisdom of God, walled off from the "outer darkness". Even if we assume that Vladimir never managed to see Constantinople, even a Byzantine city like Cherson could have exercised a sufficiently powerful impression upon him. There is nothing

---

tradition can be found in V.N. Toporov, *Святость и святые в русской духовной культуре*, vol.1 (Moscow, 1995): 17–90.

[31] Cf. *Словарь древнерусского языка (XI–XIV вв.)*, vol. 5 (Moscow, 2002): 239.

surprising in the identification of the city with the church in the perception of the newly converted Christian, for the city was like a spacious church, and the church was the very heart of the city, and both were incarnations of the ideal city – the heavenly Jerusalem.[32]

Vladimir met frequently with the bishops to consult on matters of faith and on strengthening of the law of God among the newly converted, as well as to discuss the exercise of political authority and the justification of earthly law. The trustworthiness of the later testimony to this effect in Hilarion and *Primary Chronicle* is confirmed by Bruno of Querfurt in his letter to King Henry from the end of 1008.

Upon his arrival in Kiev, Bruno saw the "senior Ruzorum" in a dual capacity as Christian ruler and simple Christian. Vladimir, stirred by the words of the zealous missionary, but knowing the savage obstinacy of the Pechenegs, sought to restrain him, to warn and dissuade him against his mission to them.[33] Vladimir was unable, however, to divert the missionary, so eager for the crown of a martyr of Christ, from his intended quest. Some indication of the emotions of the Kievan ruler toward Bruno's intention "to take the Gospel of Christ... to such an unreasonable people" is provided by "the menacing vision concerning my unworthy self [that came] in sleep [to Vladimir]." This passing remark in the midst of Bruno's admittedly self-

---

32 On the reception and interpretation of the idea of the Heavenly City, see N. Schneider, *Civitas. Studien zur Stadtoptik und zu den Prinzipien der Architekturdarstellung im frühen Mittelalter* (Munster, 1973), esp. 9–15, 20–21, 35–39, 74–82, 111–113, 139, 147–149, 186–187. Cf. W. Phillipp, "Die religiöse Bergründung der altrussischen Hauptstadt", *Festschrift für Max Vasmer* (Wiesbaden, 1956): 375–381; Averintsev, "К уяснению": 42–49; K.K. Akent'ev, "К прояснению смысла надписи над конхой Св. Софии Киевской", *Византийское искусство и литургия (Тезисы конференции памяти А.В. Банк)* (Leningrad, 1991). 16–19; idem, "Мозаики": 75–80, 83–88; I.N. Nikitenko, "София Киевская как образ новообращенной Руси (Концепция "Нового Иерусалима" в монументальном комплексе собора)", *BB* 55 (1994): 169–174.

33 Letter of Bruno of Querfurt to King Henry II in *MPH* s.n. IV/3 (see above note 15): 99: "de me indigno visio quaedam eum terruit"; further references: 98–100. Ludolf Müller drew my attention to the "dream of Vladimir". In combination with the reference that "on Friday they led us three times to execution" the "prophetic dream" of Vladimir permits Bruno to emphasize the fact that he consciously set out on a way of the cross, following the example of Christ, and that he managed to remain alive only by the providence of God (see below, note 46). The dream of Vladimir here is not a literary device but an important component link in the development of events. Belief in visionary dreams, one of the characteristic features of religious consciousness in this period, ought not to be characterized as a survival of paganism, as it sometimes is, by reference to the prophetic dream of Sviatoslav in the *Lay of the Host of Igor*. On the interpretation of prophetic dreams in Christian writing of the Middle Ages, see H.H. Lauer, "Traum", *LMA* VIII (1997): 962–963.

serving account, unintentionally sheds light on the already Christian mentality of the king of Rus'. Daytime discussions about missionary work and godly matters with this zealous, even fanatic man of faith pressed themselves deeply into the king's subconscious, continuing to work on his psyche at night in sleep. This seemingly petty detail bears eloquent testimony to the fact that Vladimir was clearly more than a Christian in name only.

Finally, after a month of meetings and conversations with Bruno, who echoed the sentiments of the Apostle Paul that "...[I do not] count my life dear to myself, so that I may finish my race with joy, and the ministry which I received from the Lord Jesus, to testify to the gospel of the grace of God" (Acts 20: 24), Vladimir, spellbound by the exceptional personality and spirit of the missionary, paid him the highest homage, accompanying Bruno along the road to the border of his dominions as he set off on his journey to the Pechenegs.

The spiritual kinship that had grown up between Vladimir, now entering his sixth decade, and Bruno, a man perhaps 20 years his junior, permits us to postulate a direct interaction between the two, one not requiring a translator. The Kievan prince, married to a Greek princess, in regular contact with Greek clerics and the Byzantine dignitaries in the court of his Porphyrogenita spouse, undoubtedly knew the Greek language. In all likelihood, Bruno could also speak Greek, thanks to his contacts with Greek monasteries in Italy. Moreover, as a missionary and a native of Saxony, where local Slavs were the chief target of Christianization, Bruno was probably acquainted with the Slavic tongue as well. And among his companions there were undoubtedly Saxons who could speak the Western Slavic dialects and could fully claim to be *natione Saxones, gente Slavi* (of the Saxon land and the Slavic race).

Five months later, having met with success, Bruno returned from the steppe. "Christianity was more or less accepted by thirty souls", and all expressed readiness to accept the faith "if the peace which he concluded will be lasting."[34]

---

[34] The conversion would, of course, have involved only the Pecheneg elite, in accordance with the commonly-held view of that era (shared by Bruno) that the decisive role in the spread of Christianity was played by evangelization of the social elite. Reports of the heroic labours of Bruno of Querfurt in spreading the faith, even to the point of a martyr's death, in imitation of Christ, recounted by the returning members of the Pecheneg and Prussian missions, found their reflection in Latin writing, though unfortunately in such a distorted form that even in the works of Peter Damiani, composed so close to the time of Bruno, they amount to little more than a confused, unbelievable legend. An effort to decode them, an undertaking of enormous complexity was begun by A.V. Nazarenko, but ultimately met with insuperable obstacles. Nonetheless, he did succeed in fishing out a comparison of Vladimir as enlightener of the pagans with the

The favourable outcome of Bruno's mission must have had a powerful impact on Vladimir: faith had triumphed over experience and reason. In order to enforce the concluded peace, so that Christian law might rule among the "cruellest of all the pagan peoples living on earth", the leader of the Rus', "for the sake of God, met the demands [of the Pechenegs] and gave them his son as a hostage",[35] sending him to their country in the company of a bishop consecrated for them. That bishop had been ordained by Bruno with the assistance of at least two local bishops, and Vladimir, his family, and his court had undoubtedly taken part in the ceremony.[36]

It is worth noting that, in travelling to the Pechenegs from Hungary, Bruno had taken a roundabout route, probably counting on receiving help in Kiev. As a fighter for Christian enlightenment and the conversion of the whole world to the Church of Christ, he was undoubtedly attracted by the figure of this ruler, actively engaged in spreading the Church to the far reaches of his vast Rus'ian realm. If so, his calculation proved correct. As a missionary bishop (*episcopus gentium*) on whom the pope had bestowed the *pallium* (leading him to be described after his death as an archbishop even though he was not) Bruno had the power, under exceptional circumstances, to consecrate bishops by himself. Nonetheless, up until the end of his stay among the Pechenegs, he chose not to exercise this right, even though he had a satisfactory candidate for bishop with him. He understood perfectly well that a "Pecheneg bishop" could carry out his work of enlightenment only with the cooperation of the sovereign of Kiev and the ecclesiastical hierarchy of Rus'. Therefore, he consciously preferred to consecrate a bishop for the Pechenegs in Kiev, in full accord with the statutes of the Council of Nicaea – i.e., in a church, with the participation of no fewer than three bishops, in this case Rus'ian prelates (probably the metropolitan of Kiev and the nearby bishop of Belgorod).

Apostle Paul, a motif that can, with a high degree of probability, be ascribed to Bruno. See A.V. Nazarenko, *Древняя Русь на международных путях* (Moscow, 2001): 435–450.

[35] Since the time of N. M. Karamzin, it has been customary to identify this son with Sviatopolk, whose alleged status as the offspring of Iaropolk was nothing more than a hagiographic motif, clearly contradicted by the events of 1013–1019. That the story about Sviatopolk's birth has a legendary nature see L. Müller, "Studien 5/III. Die Quellen der Chronikerzählung: 1. Die Erzählung über die Geburt Svjatopolks von einer griechischen Nonne", *Zeitschrift für Slavische Philologie* 63 (2004): 23–49

[36] The use of the plural in Bruno's letter (*MPH*, s.n. IV/3:100 – *consecravimusque nos episcopum de nostris*) confirms our conclusion, all the more so since Bruno speaks of himself at the beginning of this sentence in the singular (*Hoc rationi perveni ad seniorem Ruzorum...*). Speaking of himself, Bruno uses the singular in his letter. "We" appears only when he has his fellow missionaries in view as well (*ivimus, exivimus, pervenimus*).

The consecration of a pastor *ad partes infidelium* with the active participation of bishops of two different rites – a bishop under the jurisdiction of Rome and others belonging to the Rus'ian province of the patriarchate of Constantinople – testifies eloquently to the fact that the unity of the Christian world was still very much alive in this period in the consciousness of the "people of God" and of the ecclesiastical hierarchy of the two different regions. At the turn of the millennium there was still one universal (Catholic) and Orthodox Church in Europe.

In response to the not infrequent but completely ahistorical debates about the proper adjective with which to qualify the Christianity of Vladimir, it would suffice to call him a member and guardian of a Christian community subject in its obedience to the bishop of the city of Constantine. Both Olga and Vladimir, while they had accepted baptism from the latter city as the New Jerusalem, were free of the prejudices of a later era. Olga, christened in the "New Rome", could still ask Otto I to send a bishop and priests for her people,[37] and Vladimir, playing host to Bruno, saw him, as much as he did the Greek bishops, as a charismatic spiritual father, a pastor of the people of God, and a teacher and guide in matters of faith. Bruno himself, in close contact with the Greek monastic clergy in Italy, where, at the end of the tenth century, the unity of both halves of the Church, particularly in the monastic sphere, was a daily affair,[38] certainly emphasized his obedience to the see of the Apostle Peter, but the ancient thirst for Christian labour that drove him onward accorded his mission a truly universal flavour. The exceptional personality of Bruno merely underlined the ecumenical character of his mission.

The meeting in Kiev of this bishop "to the pagans" with the ruler-enlightened of Rus', marked by an undoubted mutual understanding between the two participants and a special spiritual character, soon found passing expression in a letter sent by Bruno from Poland to German King Henry II at the end of 1008, in which Bruno held up Vladimir to his own sovereign as an example of a true Christian ruler. In an indirect but clear fashion, Bruno

[37] Concerning the embassy of Olga to Otto in 959 and its immediate motivation, see. A. Poppe, "Once Again Concerning the Baptism of Olga, Archontissa of Rus'", *DOP* 46 (1992): 271–274 [chapter II in this volume].

[38] See B. Hamilton, *Monastic Reform, Catharism and the Crusades* (London, 1979), № I: 5–26 (The City of Rome and the Eastern Churches in the Tenth Century); № III: 265–310 (The Monastery of S. Alessio and the Religious and Intellectual Renaissance in Tenth-century Rome); M. Dunn, "Eastern Influence on Western Monasticism in the Eleventh and Twelth Centuries", *Byzantium and the West c. 850–1200*, ed. J.D. Howard-Johnston (Amsterdam, 1988): 245–257; J.M. Sansterre, "Le monachisme byzantin à Rome", *Settimane di Studi del Centro Italiano di Studi sull'Alto. Medioevo* XXXIV (Spoleto, 1988): 701–746.

numbered the Rus'ian king among that small body of leaders, warriors of Christ (including, by implication, Poland's Bolesław the Brave as well), who, following the example of St Constantine and the "pious zeal" of Charlemagne, spared no effort in converting the pagans and spreading the Church of Christ throughout the earth and were, for this reason, "worthy of the name of apostle before God"[39]. The idea of comparing Vladimir to the apostolic emperor was probably not new to Bruno. Most likely he had already expressed it in Kiev, both at court and in his communications with the clergy. Hence, it can be asserted that the notion of the "apostolic" accomplishment of Vladimir as a ruler in all things "like the Great Constantine, both in wisdom and in love for Christ" – a notion attaining such vivid expression in Hilarion's encomion to Vladimir around 1050 – had already emerged during the lifetime of the baptizer of Rus' and was current in Kiev at the time of Bruno's visit there in 1008.

* * *

Bruno's account includes a dramatic scene of his leave-taking from Vladimir as the missionary set off on his journey to the Pechenegs. Enchanting in its early Christian simplicity and grandeur, it also sheds interesting light on the personality of the Kievan ruler.

Upon reaching the boundary of the Kievan state, which was marked by a fortified wall, the entire party dismounted from its horses.[40] A celebration of

---

[39] The letter of Bruno (*MPH* s.n. IV/3:104). Just how straightforward Bruno was in his sense of principle is revealed by the fact that while, describing Henry as "named by God", "blessed by God", "most Christian", and "most religious", he did not hesitate to condemn the latter's alliance with the pagan Liutichi against the Polish prince Bolesław, whom he valued highly for his services to the Church. While imbued with a profound sense of loyalty to his sovereign, to whom he ascribed a leading role in the Church, Bruno knew how to maintain a sober, pragmatic approach. Cf. Wenskus, *Studien*: 157–158, 186–197. This characteristic of Bruno's accords a special value to his reports about the ruler of Rus', combining, as they do, an economy of expression with an attentive fixation on essential detail.

[40] Noting the "exceptionally strong and unusually lengthy fortifications" (*MPH* s.n. IV/1: 99 – *firmissima et longissima sepe*), Bruno had in mind the so-called "serpentine walls", located to the south of Kiev. See E. Koval'chik, "Еще раз о Змиевых валах", *RM* VII (1992): 151–160, where the author disputes the conclusions of M. Kuchera (1987). According to Thietmar (bk. VI, 96), soon after returning from the Pechenegs, Bruno set off for Prussia, where he perished on 9 March 1009 along with 18 of his fellow missionaries (survived by only one, or perhaps just a few of his party). Since it is highly probable that a group of no fewer than 4 or 5 missionaries would have been sent along with the bishop to the Pechenegs consecrated in Kiev, one can presume that the mission

the liturgy began: concentrated in meditation on the final road of Christ, those departing and those who had come to see them off marched in silent procession across the border, the symbolic edge of the Christian world at that time. Bruno, bearing on his shoulders the cross of Christ, symbol of the Lord's passion, led the way with his company. Behind them trod Vladimir in the company of his great men. All came to a halt on the low hills nearby, looking out over the limitless steppe beyond.

By hoisting a large cross onto his shoulders, in a clear reference to Golgotha, Bruno not only emphasized that he was following the example of Christ, but that, before these witnesses, he was explicitly answering the call of Christ to "take up your cross and follow Me" (Mk 10:21; cf. Mt 10:38, 16:24, Lk 9:23; Mk 8:34). At that same time, he was expressing his readiness to suffer and die for Christ.[41]

A responsorial chant began.[42] Bruno intoned a verse from the Gospel of John (21:15–17) – "*Petre, amas me? Pasce oves meas*" – and the words echoed back antiphonally from the choirs on the two hills – "*Petro, amas me? Pasce oves*

---

which came to Kiev under Bruno's leadership must have numbered no fewer than twenty-five.

41 Describing the harsh treatment to which the Pechenegs subjected him and his comrades, Bruno did not forget to note even the days of the week, clearly having an eye to the Gospel model, to the Passion and the Way of the Cross (*MPH* s.n. IV/3: 99). In this way, too, Bruno gave his royal correspondent to understand (just as he probably had the Kievans before) that by grace of God he was already in communion with those suffering for Christ. In the time of Bruno, the cult of the Holy Cross was experiencing a new rise, accompanied by a deepening of its eschatological content. It is precisely in this context that one should understand Bruno's account, with all of its detail.

42 In the interests of ease of exposition, we have translated the word *responsorium* in Bruno's letter (meaning the "answer" of a choir, repeating the verse sung by a soloist) by the closely related Greek term *antiphon*. In contrast to the responsorium, the antiphon was sung not by a single choir, following the lead of a soloist, but by two choirs in turn. In our case, Bruno's song was answered by choirs on two hills, one occupied by his comrades, and the other by Vladimir and his retinue. It is quite possible that this second choir sang in Greek, for in this early period Greek was still broadly used in the liturgy of the Kievan church – cf. W. Vodoff, "Quelques questions sur la langue liturgique à Kiev au début du XIe siècle", *The Legacy of Saints Cyril and Methodius to Kiev and Moscow*, ed. A.E. Tachiaos (Thessaloniki, 1992): 435–448. For a discussion of the date of the beginning of the Slavonic liturgy, see V. Vavřinek, "Культурные и церковно-политические предпосылки возникновения славянской литургии", *Кирило-Методиевские студии*, bk 4 (Sofia, 1987): 130–137 and A. Dostal, "The Origins of the Slavic Liturgy", *DOP* 19 (1965): 69–87. The connection between responsorium and antiphon was sufficiently close and always preserved in the tradition. Cf. H. Hucke "Das Responsorium", *Gattungen der Musik in Einzeldarstellungen: Gedenkschrift L. Schrade* (Bern–München, 1973): 144–171, 190–191, J. Haurlier, "Notes sur l'Antiphon", *ibid*: 138–143, and C. Kucharek, *The Byzantine-Slav Liturgy of St John Chrysostom: Its Origin and Evolution* (Combermere, Ontario, 1971): 366–380.

meas" and "*Petre, liubieši li mja? Pasi agncy moja.*" Verse after verse, cantor and choirs continued the solemn chant. The Latin, Slavic, and possibly Greek words of the two groups, intertwining in sublime song, were ideally suited to the atmosphere of a mission *ad partes infidelium*, drawing together those praying there in a common language of faith and uncertainty, hope and fear.[43]

The choice of these lines from the Gospel was carefully conceived. After all, on the shore of the Sea of Galilee, the Lord not only asked Peter three times if he loved Him, and entrusted His flock to him, but also foretold Peter's martyrdom. Thus it was made clear that, in setting off to the Pechenegs, Bruno was directly following the example of "his lord" Saint Peter. Bruno's readiness to humble himself even for the death of the cross could not have failed to leave a deep impression on the participants in this common service, could not have failed to leave a trace in their spiritual lives and their Christian consciousness. Vladimir, his boyars, and his retinue, knew the Pechenegs well and realized that Bruno was heading for almost certain death. But the cross he bore was for them, as Christians, not only an instrument of suffering and death but also a symbol of life and resurrection. And from this was born the hope, however faint, for a successful outcome, strengthened by reliance on the mercy of God.

In the choir of the respondents we can pick out a dissonant strain, born of deep anxiety for this holy man, setting off on his way to seemingly certain death, but we can sense a strain of humility as well: the majesty of earthly authority submitted before the Christian "Thy will be done." It is this voice in the choir of the faithful that reveals to us the natural human dimension of King Vladimir's belief.

2. When and how Vladimir was recognized as a saint

The precise time of Vladimir's induction into the ranks of the saints, a procedure frequently but inaccurately referred to as canonization (a term

[43] It has been suggested elsewhere that Bruno's choice of Gospel text served once again to emphasize his subordination to Rome. One thinks that our explanation is more likely. On the special veneration of the coryphaeus of the apostles in the Byzantine East, see J. Meyendorff, "St Peter in Byzantine Theology", *The Primacy of St Peter in the Orthodox Church* (London, 1963): 7–29 and V. von Falkenhausen, "San Pietro nella religiosità bizantina", *Settimane di Studi sull'Alto Medioevo* XXXIV (Spoleto, 1988): 627–658. It is true that churches in Rus' were, as a rule, dedicated jointly to both leaders of the apostles, Peter and Paul, but there were exceptions. Among them was the 11th-century church of St Peter in the Kievan monastery of St Demetrius, founded by Iziaslav Iaroslavich (*ПСРЛ* I: 206, cf. p. 209). Churches dedicated to St Peter alone were also known in Byzantium.

borrowed from the West and specifically denoting the process by which saints were recognized in the Roman Catholic Church), has interested scholars for many years. G.P. Fedotov, writing on the 950th anniversary of the Baptism of Rus', produced a good summary of the research on this question. This well-known historian confirmed the opinion expressed earlier by E.E. Golubinskii in 1880, namely, that the feast of St Vladimir was established sometime soon after Alexander Nevskii's defeat of the Swedes on 15 July 1240, an event which occurred on the anniversary of the death of the baptizer of Rus'.[44]

As source and textological studies of old-Rus'ian writings have improved, this first reference to St Vladimir in connection with the battle on July 15, set forth in the *Life of Alexander Nevskii*, has been examined more closely, and more precise conclusions drawn about it. It turns out that the original redaction of the *Life*, composed about the year 1283, makes no mention whatsoever of St Vladimir. The victory over the Swedes is attributed to the intercession of Boris and Gleb, and Sunday, 15 July is noted as being the day of commemoration of "the 630 holy fathers assembled at the Council of Chalcedon and of the holy martyrs Cyriacus and his mother, Julitta". However, the addition of the words "and the holy Prince Vladimir, who baptized the Russian land" was probably made not too long after 1283, since it appears in the majority of the copies of the first variant of the original redaction, and in any event must have been added before 1305, the year in which the compiler of the protograph of the Laurentian Chronicle completed his work, since that work cites this amended version.[45]

* * *

---

[44] E. Golubinskii, *История канонизации святых в русской церкви* (Moscow, 1903): 63–64; G.P. Fedotov, "Канонизация святого Владимира", *Владимирский сборник в память 950–летия крещения Руси, 988–1938* (Belgrade, 1938): 188–196. For a review of the historiography, see G. Podskalsky, *Christentum und theologische Literatur in der Kiever Rus' (988–1237)* (hereafter, *Christentum*) (Munich, 1982): 17–24, 116–121, 211–212. For an attempt to find an explanation of the timing, see W. Vodoff, "Pourquoi le prince Volodimer Svjatoslavič n'a-t-il pas été canonisé?", *HUS* 12 (1988/90): 446–466. The canonization of St Vladimir was attributed to Metropolitan Maximos (1283–1305) by J. Fennell in "The Canonisation of Saint Vladimir", *Tausend Jahre Christentum in Rußland. Zum Millennium der Taufe* (Göttingen, 1988): 299–304.

[45] N.I. Serebrianskii, *Древнерусские княжеские жития: Обзор редакций и тексты* (Moscow, 1915): 56–57, 153, 176–177, texts: 113. *ПСРЛ* I (1962): 479; I.K. Begunov, *Памятники русской литературы XIII века: Слово о погибели русской земли* (Moscow–Leningrad, 1965): 48–49, 55–61, 164, 188. Cf. V.I. Okhotnikova, "Повесть о житии Александра Невского", *Словарь книжников и книжности древней Руси, XI–первая половина XIV в.*, vol. 1, gen. ed. D.S. Likhachev (Leningrad, 1987): 354–363.

The naming practices the Rurikid dynasty over time are of crucial importance for determining the time of the recognition and veneration of Vladimir as a saint. In accordance with the accepted custom, members of the ruling dynasty were given two names: a princely one and a baptismal one. With time, it became possible for a princely name to be the same as the baptismal name, provided that it had been the name of the patron saint of an ancestor – e.g., Iurii (George) Dolgorukii, named after his great-grandfather Iaroslav-George, had only one name. Indeed, during the second half of the thirteenth century, undoubtedly as a result of deepening Christianization and probably in connection with the Mongol invasion, we observe a complete adoption of Christian names in daily life by the branches of Rurikid dynasty.[46]

The fact that at least until the middle of the thirteenth century all princes with the princely name of Vladimir also had another baptismal name indicates that he had not yet been recognized as a saint. One such bearer of two names, born in 1214, was a grandson of Vsevolod "Big Nest". His father Constantine, prince of Rostov, also named him Dmitrii "in holy baptism".[47] Dmitrii had also been the baptismal name of the child's grandfather Vsevolod and of his uncle, Prince Vladimir of Pereiaslav, who was born on the eve of St Demetrios' day, 25 October 1194. Describing the birth of that earlier Vladimir, the chronicles note that, while celebrating his own name-day, Great Prince Vsevolod had "decided to give his son the name Dmitrii in holy baptism, but to assign to him the princely name of Vladimir, the name of his grandfather, Vladimir Monomakh." The brother of this latter Vladimir-Dmitrii, the aforementioned Prince Constantine of Rostov, undoubtedly called his third son by this princely name in honour of his own brother. Their older brother Iurii also named his third son, born in 1218, Vladimir, but we do not know his baptismal name.[48]

About the year 1249 Vladimir Vasil'kovich, nephew of Daniel of Halich, was born. His baptismal name was John.[49] The coincidence of the two names, Vladimir and John, probably reflected an attempt of his powerful uncle to

---

[46] Cf. N.P. Likhachev, *Материалы для истории византийской и русской сфрагистики*, vol. 1 (Leningrad, 1928): 86–89; A. Poppe, "О времени зарождения культа Бориса и Глеба", *RM* 1 (1973): 10, 11–14; Podskalsky, *Christentum*: 304–305.

[47] *ПСРЛ* I: 438

[48] *ПСРЛ* I: 411–412, 438; II: 674–675. See N. de Baumgarten, *Généalogies et mariages occidentaux des Rurikides russes du Xe au XIII siècle* (Orientalia Christiana vol. 9/1, nr. 35; Rome, 1927) table X 45, 46.

[49] Vladimir-John was born about 1248 and no later than 1249, since in 1263 he married Princess Olga-Helena of Brian'sk. See *ПСРЛ* II: 861–862; Baumgarten, *Généalogies et mariages*, table XI: 47, 48, 50; cf. D. Dąbrowski, *Rodowód Romanowiczów – książąt halicko-wołyńskich* (Poznań, 2002): 77–98, 187–196.

underscore the rights of his nephew to the throne of Halich, which had passed to him from the extinct Rostislavich line of Galician princes. The Hypatian Chronicle's panegyric to this Vladimir-John, prince of Vladimir in Volhynia, who died on 10 December 1288, reveals that Vladimir, baptizer of the Rus'ian land, was still, long after 1249, not recognized as a saint.[50] The author of this extensive panegyric utilized Hilarion's *Sermon on Law and Grace and Praise of Kagan Vladimir* as a literary source,[51] but while borrowing a number of Hilarion's expressions and applying them to Vladimir Vasil'kovich, he does not even once mention the original addressee of Hilarion's encomion: Vladimir, the baptizer of Rus'. (In his references to Mstislav Danilovich, Vladimir Vasil'kovich's cousin and successor to the throne of Vladimir in Volhynia, the chronicler uses the same terms of praise that Hilarion had applied in his *Sermon* to Iaroslav the Wise.)

Such utilization of excerpts from literary works and their reapplication to new people and circumstances was no rarity in the writing of the Middle Ages,[52] but such an *anonymous* usage of Hilarion's *Sermon* makes clear that "old

---

[50] *ПСРЛ* II: 914–927. This is seemingly contradicted by the Hypatian chronicle's naming Vladimir "с[вя]тыи" ("holy" or "saint") in an entry under the year 1254. But the content of that notice about the campaign of Daniil Romanovich "against the Czechs" (in which the chronicler notes that "never before had the Rus'ian land made war on the Czech land, not [even] brave Sviatoslav or holy ["стыи", i.e., saint] Vladimir"), and the closeness of the lettering allows one to hypothesize that an original "старыи" (i.e., "old") was transformed by the hand of a fourteenth-century copyist into "стыи" (an abbreviated form of "с[вя]тыи"). In the same Hypatian Chronicle under 1229, recounting the campaign of prince Daniil against the Polish city of Kalisz, the writer, who was also the author of the entry under 1254, adds "for no other prince except great Vladimir had gone so far into the Polish land" (*ПСРЛ* II: 758). Here "великыи" [great] is used in the same sense as "старыи" [old], i.e., "of long ago", living before any other princes by that name. In the same way, Hilarion in the middle of the eleventh century refers to Vladimir the grandson of "old [старыи] Igor'." On the use of "стар" cf. V.L. Vinogradova, *Словарь-справочник «Слово о полку Игореве»*, vol. 5 (Leningrad, 1978): 210–212; on the use of "великыи" [great] in the sense of "старыи" [old], "давнии" [bygone], see A. Poppe, "Words that serve the Authority. On the Title of 'Grand Prince' in Kievan Rus'", *Acta Poloniae Historica* 60 (1989): 172–173 (essay no. IX in this collection of reprints).

[51] For the text taken from the *Sermon,* see *ПСРЛ* II: 915–916, 922–924, in English translation G. Perfecky, *The Galician-Volynian Chronicle* (Munich, 1973):106–107,108–110; L. Müller, *Des Metropoliten Ilarion Lobrede auf Vladimir den Heiligen und Glaubensbekenntnis* (Wiesbaden, 1962): 144–145. Cf. A.V. Nikol'skaia, "«Слово» митрополита Киевского Илариона в позднейшей литературной традиции", *Slavia* 7 (1928): 549–563; Moldovan, *Слово*: 30.

[52] A closer example that can serve us here is the afterword on folios 216 and 216v of the Gospel of Ivan Kalita (1339/1340), where clear traces of the influence of Hilarion's *Sermon* are apparent, but not a hint about the great ancestor, who was by this time already recognized as a saint. The textual dependency is limited to the section praising the teacher-

Vladimir" was still not recognized as a saint. A careful reading of the manuscript praising Vladimir-John Vasil'kovich reveals that its author, praising the deeds and moral qualities of the deceased prince, unambiguously sought to place him in the ranks of the saints, emphasizing the incorruptibility of his body after the opening of his tomb on 6 April 1289 – about four months after the prince's death on 10 December. Had Vladimir the Great already been recognized as a saint, the author, drawing on Hilarion's work, could easily have offered a list of comparisons, beginning with the fact that the princes bore the same name. Instead, the chronicler made use here of the baptismal name of the prince, attributing the following words to the widowed princess weeping at his grave: "O my Caesar, good, meek, humble, and just: rightly were you named in baptism John, for in every virtue you are like unto him."[53] The Volhynian chronicler wrote his panegyric shortly after April of 1289, and in any case no later than 1292.[54]

The fact that Vladimir was still not recognized as a saint in the 1270s and 1280s is also reflected in the Rus'ian version of the *Nomocanon* (*Kormchaia Kniga*), literally, "Helmsman's Book", a collection of Byzantine church law (with local Rus'ian additions) compiled in this period, which included Prince Vladimir's "Ecclesiastical Statute" along with other local texts. Neither the

---

apostles of various lands, with the addition – "the Rus'ian land...praises...Andrew, first-called of the Apostles, and the Greek land, emperor Constantine." See *Пергаменные рукописи библиотеки АН СССР* (Leningrad 1976): 76–80, and *Сводный каталог славяно-русских рукописных книг XIV в.*, vol. 1. (Moscow, 2002): 237–240 (№ 119). The probability of the use in 1340 of an already edited borrowing is confirmed by the fact that the writer of the encomion is comparing the deeds of Kalita not to those of Vladimir, but to those of Constantine. An intentional ignoring of St Vladimir would hardly be possible. Neither the cult of St Vladimir, nor Hilarion's point about Vladimir's equality with the apostles were as yet part of the broad common property of Christian Rus', not even in the setting of a princely court, although the situation would change dramatically by the end of the century. The Gospel (*Сийское евангелие*) was copied from a Southern or South-western prototype of the twelfth-thirteenth century; St Vladimir is also not indicated in the monthly calendar, nor are any other Rus'ian saints save Boris and Gleb – O. Loseva, *Русские месяцесловы XI–XIV вв.* (Moscow, 2001): 384. On the history of this work, see E.M. Smorgunova, "Древнейший московский рукописный памятник", *Источниковедение и история русского языка* (Moscow, 1964): 119–141.

53 *ПСРЛ* II: 919–920, 927. Borrowings from the *Sermon* are abundant and clearly direct. In other words, the author of the panegyric to Vladimir Vasil'kovich was familiar with the full redaction of Hilarion's work. The fact that the author chose not to take advantage of the shared name has to be strong support for an argument that, at least in Halich-Volhyn Rus', Vladimir the Great was not yet venerated as a saint around 1290, when this panegyric was written.

54 See A.I. Gens'ors'kii, *Галицько-волинський літопис, процес складання редакції і редактори* (Kiev, 1958): 5–7, 25–54. Cf. O.P. Likhacheva, *Словарь книжников*: 240.

Rostov-Vladimir (Varsonof'ev) redaction from the end of the thirteenth century nor the Volhynian redaction of 1286 (recopied by order of Vladimir Vasil'kovich), although they are preserved in later manuscripts, offer any hint of Vladimir's sainthood. They simply entitle him prince (*kniaz'*), not even "Grand Prince" as he is usually called in the fourteenth and fifteenth centuries. Only with *The Statute of the holy Prince Vladimir, Baptizer of the land of Rus', concerning Ecclesiastical Courts*, added as supplement in the mid-fourteenth century to the Novgorod *Nomocanon* of 1282, are we presented with a new situation, and the manuscript tradition of this work also permits us to conclude that, in its original form, going back to the twelfth-thirteenth centuries, down to its insertion into the *Nomocanon* somewhere around 1280, it, too, was simply attributed to King Vladimir, with no reference to any sainthood.[55]

* * *

And so, at least until about the year 1290, Vladimir clearly was not honoured as a saint. But by 1311 he was recognized as one, for a stone church bearing his name was erected in that year.[56] We cannot be certain, however, that this was the first church to have been dedicated to the newly-glorified saint.[57] Most churches built in Rus' were constructed of wood, and these were only rarely mentioned in the chronicles. In the fourteenth and fifteenth centuries a number of churches were dedicated to St Vladimir, but from the surviving evidence it would appear that only two of them were made of stone: one in

[55] *Древнерусские княжеские уставы XI–XIV вв.*, ed. Ia.N. Shchapov (Moscow, 1976): 22, 62, 68–69; cf. Ia.N. Shchapov, *Княжеские уставы и Церковь в древней Руси* (Moscow, 1972): 38–47, 63–72.

[56] *НПЛ*, ed. A.N. Nasonov (Moscow–Leningrad. 1950): 93: "In this year Archbishop David built a stone church to Saint Vladimir on the gates to the Nereva quarter." (So reads the Synodal manuscript of the first half of the 14th century. The Commission manuscript of the mid-15th century already represents a secondary remaking of the text – cf. *ibidem*: 334.)

[57] The fire of 28 July 1311 in the Nereva quarter, in which 40 churches were burned, allows us to hypothesize that among them could have been a wooden church named in honour of the isoapostolic saintly prince. The building of new stone gates with churches on them was part of a general program of construction, beginning at the end of the thirteenth century, of stone fortifications around Novgorod. (*НПЛ*: 328). In 1305, a stone church of Boris and Gleb was built "on the gates from Prus'skaia Street", *НПЛ*: 91, 92. Cf. A.L. Mongait, "Оборонительные сооружения Новгорода Великого", *Материалы и исследования по археологии СССР*, vol. 31 (1952): 87–89.

Novgorod in 1311 and another in Moscow sometime before 1417 (in "the gardens" at the princely residence outside the city).[58]

The fact that the founder of the church in Novgorod was none other than the archbishop himself signifies beyond a doubt that Vladimir now belonged to the company of the saints. As noted above, an insertion made into the *Life of Alexander Nevskii* sometime before 1305 reflected a retrospective recognition of the coincidence of the dates of the victory on the Neva and the day of the death of the baptizer of Rus'. The link between Alexander Nevskii's battle and Novgorod, which continued to battle the Swedes for control of the Karelian isthmus and Neva waterway before and after the year 1300, permits us to posit that it was precisely here, on the Volkhov, that this coincidence of dates provided a basis for honouring the memory of St Vladimir. That the celebration of the memory of St Vladimir did in fact originate in Novgorod through association with the victory on the Neva in 1240, with the successful campaign against the Swedes in 1311 possibly providing an additional impulse, is suggested by the church itself. Built of stone and placed over one of the gates of the city, it served as a part of system fortifications defending Novgorod, clearly demonstrating that St Vladimir was perceived as a guardian and protector of the city. [59]

* * *

In connection with these questions, it is worth paying closer attention to the somewhat mysterious figure of Vladimir, son of Andrei and grandson of Alexander Nevskii, who has been hitherto overlooked in most genealogical research. He is mentioned only once, but quite reliably, in a surviving original charter of Prince Andrei Aleksandrovich and the city of Novgorod to the King of Denmark: "we have sent to you our son, and your nephew, Vladimir." On the basis of the chronicle account of conclusion of peace with the Danes, this letter of ambassadorial credentials can be dated to 1302. If Vladimir Andreevich was the head of the Novgorodian delegation for the negotiation of peace in Revel, he must have been an adult capable of

---

[58] *ДДГ*, ed. L.V. Cherepnin, (Moscow 1950), № 21: 58. Most likely, the latter church was originally built in connection with the birth of Vladimir Andreevich in 1353. Both he and his father, the prince of Serpukhov, had a share of Moscow.

[59] The sea campaign against the Swedes across the Neva and the Gulf of Finland took place early in the summer of 1311. Satisfaction with the victorious outcome (*НПЛ*: 334) resulted in the foundation, on 15 July, of a church dedicated to St Vladimir as protector of the city. Cf. I.P. Shaskol'skii, *Борьба Руси за сохранение выхода к Балтийскому морю в XIV в.* (Moscow, 1987): 69–70, 70–78.

responsible work by this date, meaning that he could not have been born any later than the 1280s. If we assume that he was the last prince to bear Vladimir's name as a princely name only, we might want to inquire about his baptismal name, and the question arises whether he might not be one and the same person as Prince Boris Andreevich, likewise known to us only from a single mention, describing his participation in the ceremony of installation of Archbishop-elect Theoktist in the archiepiscopal residence in 1299. Active participation in the investiture suggests that, in order to act as the representative of the grand prince his father, Boris must have been relatively mature and hence could not have been a son of Andrei Aleksandrovich's 1294 marriage to Vasilissa of Rostov. This had not been the only marriage for Andrei Aleksandrovich, who was nearly forty years old at the time. An indirect indication that before Vasilissa, Andrei had been married to a Dane, is the diplomatic document of 1302, indicating Vladimir's relation to the Danes ("your nephew"). That marriage must have taken place in the 1270s or early 1280s, and Vladimir-Boris can be considered its offspring. In such a case, his appearance as the representative of Grand Prince Andrei Aleksandrovich at the end of the thirteenth century would have been completely natural. Support for the identity between Vladimir and Boris could be the fact that his princely name is used only once in the sources, explicable not only as reflection of an old, nearly extinct dynastic tradition, but also as a reflection of Prince Andrei's decision to use this name, with its ties to the Scandinavian "Valdemar", as a way of emphasizing his ties to the Danish aristocratic clans.

However, the identity of Vladimir and Boris cannot be accepted without qualification. It cannot be ruled out that Prince Andrei had two sons from his first marriage – Vladimir and Boris. In such a case, the name Vladimir could be considered not only a princely name but – for the first time – a baptismal name, bestowed on one of his sons by Andrei Aleksandrovich. That prince, in his political activity, continued the policies of his father, not only on the grand princely throne, but with respect to Novgorod as well, striving to defend it from attacks by its neighbours. This could mean that the connection between the victory on the Neva and Vladimir's memorial day made in Novgorod originated precisely at the court of Prince Andrei Aleksandrovich, who ruled the city from 1281/82 to 1284. That development would then quickly have been reflected in an addition to the *Vita of Alexander Nevskii* that had just been composed around 1282. If all of this is true, it would not then be surprising for one result of such attention to the coincidence of those two important dates to have been the baptism of a son of Andrei in the name of his great ancestor, recognized at long last as a saint. Considering this possibility, we can also speculate that the first church – wooden, of course – dedicated to St Vladimir might have in fact been built on the occasion of the birth and baptism of that son of Prince Andrei.

However attractive this hypothesis may be, it nonetheless must be emphasized that we do not have the facts to prove it. We are, however, probably safe in assuming that this Vladimir Andreevich was either the last Rurikid to bear the name "Vladimir" as a purely dynastic one, or the first to be baptized in the name of his great forebear.[60]

* * *

If, sometime between 1282 and 1305, they began honouring Vladimir as a saint in Novgorod, it follows that it must have been precisely in this period that the Church officially added Vladimir to the company of the saints. It was along these very lines that John Fennell attributed the sanctification of the king to Metropolitan Maximos (1283–1305).[61] Indeed, only Maximos, as the bishop of Kiev, would have had the right to perform this act during that period. The mere absence of any mention of such a major event in the sources for these years does not, in and of itself, discredit this hypothesis, but a number of other considerations do serve to raise some doubts. Inclusion into the ranks of the saints, as a rule, was associated with the presence and discovery of the relics of the saint. In this instance, this means that sanctification could have taken place only in Kiev. But as we know, the sarcophagus containing the remains of King Vladimir was buried beneath the collapsed vaults and walls of the Church of the Tithe in December 1240. It remained there, covered by those ruins, until about 1635, when Peter Mogila restored the church and recovered the relics of St Vladimir.[62] Ascribing such an act to Metropolitan Maximos, one would have to assume that at the time of his move from Kiev to Vladimir on the Kliazma, he brought with him part of the relics of St Vladimir, an event that would surely have evoked some echo in the ecclesiastical and political life of Muscovite Rus'.

---

[60] *Грамоты Великого Новгорода и Пскова* (Moscow–Leningrad, 1949), № 35: 64; V.L. Ianin, *Новгородские акты XII–XV вв.* (Moscow, 1990), № 10.

[61] J. Fennell, "The Canonization of Saint Vladimir": 299–304.

[62] See *Акты юго-западной России*, vol. 3 (St Petersburg, 1861), № 18: 28–29; № 39: 44; S.T. Golubev, *Киевский митрополит Петр Могила и его сподвижники*, vol. 1 (Kiev, 1883): 530–539, 550–552; vol. 2 (Kiev, 1898): 411–434, 460–463. Cf. M.K. Karger, "К вопросу о саркофагах кн. Владимира и Анны", *Краткие Сообщения Института Истории Материальной Культуры*, 7 (1941): 79–80.

A more plausible approach is to consider the reception at the turn of the thirteenth-fourteenth centuries of the celebration of St Vladimir in Novgorod to have been the result of a conviction, formed on the basis of the already existing documents dedicated to Vladimir (especially Hilarion's *Sermon on Law and Grace*), that King Vladimir had been numbered in the ranks of the saints even in the Kievan period, but was not glorified in a manner worthy of his accomplishments. All that would have been necessary, according to such a view, would have been to restore his veneration as a saint.[63]

Whatever the case, the veneration of St Vladimir, so clearly attested in Novgorod at the beginning of the fourteenth century, gradually spread to other Rus'ian lands as well, initially at a rather modest pace. This pattern indirectly confirms the notion that there was no formal act of sanctification of Vladimir at the turn of the thirteenth–fourteenth century. Had such an initiative been undertaken by the Church, in all likelihood with the close cooperation of the dynasty, there would surely been an immediate and energetic spread of veneration for the isoapostolic sovereign. In reality, commemoration of St Vladimir was reflected in the ecclesiastical calendar only gradually over the course of the fourteenth and fifteenth centuries, with texts dedicated to St Vladimir appearing first in the *prologi* (synaxaria), and only later, in the fifteenth century, in the *service Menaion*. A full Office (service) to the saint was composed only at the turn of the fifteenth–sixteenth century.[64]

---

[63] The point of view we ascribe to the Novgorodians of the thirteenth century is shared by a contemporary author: "In the second half of the thirteenth century, the church revived the cult of Vladimir, "baptizer of Rus"', whose commemoration in the form of ecclesiastical veneration has been dated by us to the eleventh century" – A.S. Khoroshev, *Политическая история русской канонизации (XI–XVI вв.)* (Moscow, 1986): 85. However, combining various points of view found in the literature, Khoroshev falls into clear contradiction, associating the legend about the foundation of the town of Vladimir' on the Kliazma by "the holy and blessed and great king Vladimir" with the ecclesiastical-political measures of Andrei Bogoliubskii and confusedly asserting that "evidence for early veneration is the consecration to St Vladimir of a church altar on the Golden Gates of Vladimir' on the Kliazma, in 1174, long before the official establishment of a day of commemoration for the prince" (*Ibid.*: 48, 61, 85). The author uncritically cites the Nikon Chronicle (*ПСРЛ* IX:222), forgetting that the description there of the efforts of Andrei Bogoliubskii to obtain a metropolitan for his capital at Vladimir' reflect later Muscovite strivings, which gave a new meaning to the veneration of St Vladimir.

[64] Cf. N. Nikol'skii, *Материалы для повременного списка русских писателей и их сочинений* (*X–XI в.*), (Saint Petersburg, 1906): 444–451. Here are noted manuscripts with services and canons to St Vladimir, and it is suggested that the first redaction of that service is preserved in a manuscript of the thirteenth century (Saint Petersburg, Дух. Акад. Новг. Соф. перг., № 332, pp. 67–71). This *Mineia Prazdnichnaia*, belonging to the Novgorod cathedral and containing a service of "the dormition of Prince Vladimir, 15 July" dates

* * *

Side by side with developments in Novgorod, a cult of St Vladimir began taking root in princely courts, where we begin to see sons baptized in the name of the their saintly ancestor. One of the first of these was a child born to Prince Alexander Mikhailovich of Tver' at the end of the 1320s or beginning of the 1330s.[65] Another Vladimir baptized in the 1330s was the son of Prince Constantine of Rostov and his wife Maria, daughter of Ivan Kalita, who were married in 1328.[66] At least two others were so christened in the 1330s or 1340s: one, who later died at the battle of Kulikovo, was the son of Prince Fyodor of Viaz'ma (of the princely line of Smolensk), and the other, later Prince of Pronsk, was the son of the Prince Iaroslav-Dmitrii of Riazan

---

from the end of the thirteenth or beginning of the fourteenth century (*Сводный каталог славяно-русских рукописных книг, хранящихся в СССР, XI–XIII вв.* (Moscow, 1984), № 454: 354), i.e., to the time when the veneration of Vladimir as a saint was established in Novgorod. Careful dating fixes the time of this *Mineia* generally to the thirteenth or fourteenth century (see *Словарь древнерусского языка XI–XIV вв.*, vol. 1, (Moscow, 1988): 50). Confirmation of dating is required for a fragment of a collection of homilies, vitae, and sermons in Middle Bulgarian (with Russicisms) ГПБ Q п. 1. 61, dated to the thirteenth century, in which are noted remembrance of Princess Olga on 11 July, the Varangian martyr and his son Ioann on 12 July, and the dormition of Prince Vladimir on 15 July (see *Сводный каталог*, № 304: 276). Worthy of closer study is the "Studion monastery church statute" in a Novgorodian manuscript of the end of the twelfth (?) century, with a fragment containing the remembrance of saints with indication of chant and readings from 11 June to 18 August (See *Сводный Каталог*, № 107: 135 and № 139: 161), where, on f 4–4v. under the date 24 July is the service for Boris and Gleb, in which, on f 4v, it is noted that, as part of the commemoration of these saints, "the vita of prince Vladimir is read, in which is the martyrdom of Saints Boris and Gleb" (see *Сводный Каталог*: 161). Here, perhaps, is a trace of the informal commemoration, without the naming Vladimir as a saint. In the monthly calendar of the Service Book, compiled prior to Easter of 1332, on folio 6, under 15 July, immediately after the saintly martyrs Cyricus and Julitta is added, in the hand of the same scribe "on the same day Vladimir" (under 2 May and 24 July are noted the saintly martyrs Boris and Gleb), but curiously, not preceding the name with the usual abbreviation of "saint." See A.H. Van den Baar *A Russian Church Slavonic Kanonnik (1331–1332): A comparative textual and structural study including an analysis of the Russian computus (Scaliger 38B, Leyden University Library)* (The Hague, 1968): 30–31, 192, 269, 272 (folio 6r).

[65] Vladimir was one of the younger sons of the prince of Tver' from a marriage concluded in 1320, and he was probably born after the departure of the grand prince and his family to Pskov in 1327. It is not to be ruled out that Vladimir was younger than his brother Mikhail, who was born in Pskov in 1333 (*НПЛ*: 345). Cf. Eksempliarskii, *Великие и удельные князья*, vol. 2: 476, 539, 641; N. Baumgarten *Généalogies des branches regnantes de Rurikides du XIIIe au XIVe siècle*, (Orientalia Christiana 35:1; Rome 1934), table VIII: 47,49.

[66] Eksempliarskii, *Великие и удельные князья*, vol.1: 50, 52, 54; Baumgarten, *Généalogies des branches*, table XI, 31: 61.

(d. 1344).[67] Finally, one of the sons of Olgerd, grand prince of Lithuania, born at the beginning of the 1340s, most likely from Olgerd's marriage to a princess of Polotsk, was also named Vladimir.[68] Although in all of these instances the princely name of the child was also his baptismal name, we do not know precisely why the parents selected that of the baptizer of Rus'. However, given that in none these cases does the name Vladimir occur among near ancestors, so that the bestowal of the name did not represent an "inheritance", it seems permissible to posit that the baptisms of these princely sons were inspired by the existence, however modest, of an emerging ecclesiastical veneration of the isoapostolic king. It should also be noted that recognition of Vladimir as a saint made it possible to christen children of families unrelated to the dynasty with this originally princely name. The name Vladimir thus begins to appear in baptisms of the sons of boyar, merchant, and even peasant families in the fourteenth and fifteenth centuries, accompanied by the appearance of a diminutive form, Volodia, applied to adults as well as children. The earliest known use of the name in these non-dynastic circles is associated with Vladimir Vsevolodovich, the Muscovite military commander in 1380 (who must have been born around the year 1340).[69]

---

[67] Eksempliarskii, *Великие и удельные князья*, vol.2: 584–585, 628–630. The biography and even the very existence of Vladimir, son of Vsevolod, mentioned as commander of the forward regiment at the battle of Kulikovo in one manuscript of the *Skazanie o Mamaevom Poboishche* are not entirely clear. His association with the family of princes of Smolensk is probably not trustworthy. Cf. *Повести о Куликовской битве* (Moscow, 1959): 56; *«Слово о полку Игореве» и памятники Куликовского цикла* (Moscow–Leningrad., 1966): 492. It is possible that a Muscovite commander has been mistakenly elevated here to the rank of prince.

[68] In the lists of the sons of Olgerd in the chronicles, Vladimir is named as the fifth child of his first marriage, which would exclude him from inclusion among the seven sons of Iuliana Aleksandrovna, princess of Tver', who was married to Olgerd in 1350. Iuliana was preceded by Anna, who probably was his second, childless wife, who managed to insist on the baptism of the sons of Olgerd by his first wife. Cf. *ПСРЛ* VII: 215; 13: 109; XXV: 193, 211; XXXV: 223, T. Wasilewski "Trzy małżeństwa Wielkiego Księcia Olgierda", *Kultura średniowieczna i staropolska. Studia ofiarowane Aleksandrowi Gieysztorowi w pięćdziesięciolecie pracy naukowej* (Warsaw, 1991): 673–682. This would place the baptism of Vladimir sometime in the 1340s, but his birth some time in the 1330s, which is indirectly supported by the participation of his son Yurii as an envoy of his grandfather, grand prince Olgerd, at the conclusion of peace in 1371. See *ДДГ* 6: 21.

[69] *ПСРЛ* XI: 54, 59, cf. Index of *ПСРЛ* XIV: 32; M. Wojtowicz, *Древнерусская антропонимия XIV–XV вв. Северо-восточная Русь* (Poznan, 1986): 191–192. All mentions relate to the fifteenth century, although the birth of a few of the baptized individuals could be dated either to the fourteenth or very beginning of the fifteenth century. The name also penetrates into the peasant stratum, and in monasteries comes to be used as a tonsure name (for example, there is mention in 1507 of a Vladimir, abbot of the Trinity Monastery

But the most convincing proof of the actual veneration of King Vladimir as a saint is contained in the chronicle record of the birth and baptism in 1353 of Prince Vladimir Andreevich of Serpukhov, future comrade in arms of his cousin Dmitri Donskoi and known to later generations as "the Brave" on account of his military exploits.[70]

Vladimir, the third son of Andrew, prince of Serpukhov and grandson of Ivan Kalita, was born on the fortieth day after the death of his father, on 15 July 1353. It was a terrible period, when the "Black Death" which had raged across throughout Western Europe, now galloped into Rus', plunging its voracious teeth into the land, sparing no one, not even those of princely rank. Andrei Ivanovich died one month or so after his older brother, the Great Prince Simeon the Haughty, who had been preceded in death by his four sons, ranging from one to five years in age. The oldest son of Prince Andrei, born about 1350, was named Ivan after his grandfather; we do not know the name of the second son, who died in infancy. Through five generations of Muscovite princes, beginning with Alexander Nevskii and his father Iaroslav, the son of Vsevolod the "Great Nest", i.e., through the entire thirteenth and the first half of the fourteenth century, the name Vladimir does not appear.[71] It is easy to imagine the despair of the princess over the death of her husband and her fear for her newborn child. It seems natural to suggest that, under

---

in Kashira district. Cf. *ДДГ* 7: 251 (Volodia 1477 г.); 18: 221 (1472 г.); *Акты Московского Симонова монастыря 1506–1613*, comp. L.I. Ivina. (Moscow, 1983), № 66: 78 (1541 г.); № 91: 103 (1548 г.), № 95: 106 (1549 г.); *Акты русского государства 1505–1526* (Moscow, 1975), № 223: 225 (1523 г.: Олексей, внук Володимиров), № 207: 35 (1507 г.: игумен В.).

[70] *ПСРЛ* VII: 217; VIII: 10,15; X: 226; XV: 62–63, (see here under 6862, i.e., 1354); XXV: 179; Eksempliarskii, *Великие и удельные князья*, vol. 2: 293–305. In a substantial article devoted to the actions and holdings of Prince Vladimir Andreevich of Serpukhov, V.A. Kuchkin ("Сподвижник Дмитрия Донского", *Вопросы истории* (1979), № 8: 104–106) proposed a revision of the date of his birth to 1354 instead of the heretofore accepted 1353. However, the clever reasoning of the author is undermined by the other accompanying events – the death of Metropolitan Theognostos and Grand Prince Simeon – which, in light of the evidence of other chronicles and Byzantine ecclesiastical sources, can in no way be moved from 1353 to 1354. Therefore the death of prince Andrei (who, like the rest, died as result of the plague raging in Europe) and the birth of his son Vladimir must be associated with the same year, 1353. N.S. Borisov, *Русская Церковь в политической борьбе XIV–XV веков.* (Moscow, 1986): 129, note 114, while correctly drawing attention to the special circumstances of the birth of this son of Prince Andrei, errs in asserting that Vladimir was named in honour of the "the great autocrat Vladimir of Kiev" (*Ibid.*: 78). He was simply baptized in the name of *Saint* Vladimir.

[71] Baumgarten, *Généalogies des branches*, table I, II, for the one exception among the descendants of Nevskii, mentioned above, his grandson, the newly discovered Vladimir Andreevich.

such circumstances, the birth of a son on the day of the remembrance of St Vladimir could have been eagerly grasped at as a sign from God, pointing to the heavenly protector of her child. The selection of this name also demonstrates that by the year 1353, the memory of Vladimir as a saint was widely celebrated on 15 July throughout Rus'. The predominantly religious motive behind the choice is further suggested by the fact that, in the four following generations of the line of princes of Serpukhov and Borovsk descended from Vladimir the Brave, the name Vladimir does not appear again.[72]

* * *

The continuing vitality of the cult of St Vladimir in the Muscovite ruling family is attested not only by the above-mentioned church of St Vladimir at the princely court outside the city walls, but also by an *aer* (embroidered cloth) portraying "the Saviour not-made-by-human-hands", sewn in the year 1389 for Princess Maria, widow of Simeon the Haughty. On it, in the midst of eight figures, we see Saints Demetrios of Thessalonica and Vladimir, the patron saints of the Great Prince of Moscow, Dmitri Donskoi, and his companion-in-arms, Vladimir the Brave. It is the earliest known depiction of St Vladimir.[73]

The mere fact of the portrayal of St Vladimir on this *aer* presupposes the existence of an iconographic model, for which a need would have emerged along with the rise of his cult. The stone church dedicated to him in 1311, for example, would have had to include his image in the local row of its iconostasis. The first icon painters did not, of course, have portraits of Prince Vladimir at hand. His earlier portrayals on coins and seals were merely stereoptypical renderings of the image of the *basileus* appearing on Byzantine coins and seals. However, the icon painters were able to draw the basic idea for their glorification of Vladimir from the figures of the apostles and other ruler-teachers. Thus, on icons there appeared the figure of a gray-haired,

---

[72] See the branch of Serpukhov-Borovsk princes in Baumgarten, *Généalogies des branches*, table VI: 33. That the prince of Serpukhov was conscious of himself as bearer of the name of his holy ancestor is suggested by his own unusual (for that time) choice of a name for the son born to him on 18 January 1388, Iaroslav, a name chosen, no doubt, in honour of the son of Vladimir, Iaroslav the Wise. In baptism this prince received the name Afanasii, for the day of his birth.

[73] See N.A. Maiasova, *Древнерусское шитие* (Moscow, 1971), tables 5 and 6. Substantial results in the study of the iconography of St Vladimir have been achieved by E.S. Smirnova, whose fundamental study on this topic is close to completion.

elderly man, his face reminiscent of Basil the Great, in whose name Vladimir had been baptized. A late sixteenth-century icon-painter's guide of Novgorodian redaction describes the rules for portraying the holy prince in this way: "... Prince Vladimir, gray and curly-haired, with the beard of St John the Theologian, dressed in purple garb and underneath, blue garb, with a cross in his right hand and a sword in its scabbard in his left, and on his head an imperial crown...."[74]

In the known depictions of St Vladimir, he is portrayed either with a princely cap or an imperial crown (as was the case on the aforementioned *aer* from 1389). Portrayals in a princely cap are encountered more frequently in the early iconography from the fourteenth and fifteenth centuries. For example, in all of the icons of Saints Boris and Gleb with scenes from their lives, beginning with the earliest examples from the fourteenth centuries, in the miniatures of the pictorial *Tale of Saints Boris and Gleb,* in the collection of Sylvester from the mid-fourteenth century, and in the miniatures of the Radziwiłł chronicle manuscript from the end of the fifteenth century, Vladimir appears in a princely cap, his head surrounded by a nimbus.[75]

---

[74] See I. Okunev, "Изображение святого Владимира", *Владимирский сборник* Belgrade (1938): 197–200. For a series of general questions concerning the iconography of St Vladimir, see also: E.S. Smirnova, V.K. Laurina, E.A. Gordienko *Живопись Великого Новгорода XV в.* (Moscow, 1982): 40–50, 192–198. The suggestion that we can see a depiction of St Vladimir in A. Vesterfeld's 1651 drawing of the still extant patron's fresco of St Sophia in Kiev, done when the church was painted in the first half of the 11th century and only touched up in the 17th, cannot be considered well founded (see S.A. Vysotskii, *Светские фрески Софийского собора в Киеве* (Kiev, 1989): 69, 74–76, 79, 91–98). Even if we were to concede that a figure of St; Vladimir was originally included in the patron's composition, one must agree with the widespread view (V.N. Lazarev, M. Karger, and others) that the image of St Vladimir noted by Vesterfeld was painted by the restorers working for Peter Mohila after 1633, and corresponds completely to the iconography of the saintly prince taking shape in that period (cf. V.N. Lazarev "Групповой портрет семейства Ярослава", *Русская средневековая живопись* (Moscow, 1970): 36–37; A. Poppe "Kompozycja fundacyjna Sofii Kijowskiej. W poszukiwaniu układu pierwotnego", *Biuletyn Historii Sztuki* 30/1 (1968): 10–11).

[75] Cf. *Сказание о Борисе и Глебе. Факсимильное воспроизведение из Сильве-стровского сборника* (Moscow, 1985): pp 117, 128; V.N. Lazarev, *Русская иконопись от истоков до начала XVI века.* (Moscow, 1983), table 85: an icon with scenes from the life of Saints Boris and Gleb, with the first image depicting Vladimir in a nimbus; it is dated here to the first quarter of the fourteenth century. This famous icon from Kolomna, in the collection of the Tret'iakov Gallery, is considered a monument of early Muscovite art: E.S Smirnova, *Московская икона XIV–XVII вв.* (Moscow, 1988), table. 46: 267; with dating to end of the fourteenth century; see also: *Радзивиловская или Кенигсбергская летопись: Факсимильное воспро-изведение рукописи конца XV в. Текст исследования. Описание миниатюр* (Saint Petersburg., 1994), where, on f. 62v and subsequent pages, beginning with the baptism in Cherson and in succeeding miniatures, depicting the construction of churches and campaigns against the

Although these works stem from illustrated prototypes of the twelfth and thirteenth centuries, the portrait of Vladimir began to be adorned with a gold nimbus only in the fourteenth century. Arguments for the existence of an illustrated *Vita* of St Vladimir, supposedly used for the illustrated chronicle, appear to be without substance. The portrayal of Vladimir in an imperial crown should viewed not so much as an association with the image of David as with that of Emperor Constantine, to whom he was compared.

With rare exceptions, St Vladimir is not represented in small sculpted works of metal, stone, and bone. The earliest known work of this kind, a slate icon (24 x 15 cm) dating from 1544 and belonging to Vladimir Golokhvastov is, as the written evidence indicates, of a family character. In the top tier is portrayed the Nativity of Christ, to which the church in the family estate of the Golokhvastovs not far from Dmitrov was dedicated, and in the lower tier are presented three saints, St Vladimir in the middle and the holy Metropolitans Peter and Aleksei at his side, easily identifiable as the heavenly patrons of the Golokhvastovs – Vladimir and his sons Peter and Aleksei.[76] This well-documented stone icon enables us better to understand another work, a wooden two-tiered icon, dating from the century before, from Pskov (128 x 70 cm) with a portrayal of the Dormition of the Virgin in the top tier and Saints Vladimir, Boris, and Gleb in the lower.[77] This, too, is probably a family icon. Finally, special attention should be paid to a Novgorodian portrayal of St Vladimir in an imperial crown from a *deesis* composition along with Saints Peter and Paul, dating from the first half of the fifteenth century. Here the apostolic and imperial dignity of the saint are consciously and fully presented. This *deesis* icon appears to have been part of the iconostasis of a church of St Vladimir, perhaps the very one erected in 1311 and restored after the fire of 1414.[78]

* * *

Pechenegs, Prince Vladimir is portrayed with a nimbus. (pp. 67 image, 68, 69 image, 73, 74), added by the third painter (V), who corrected and supplemented the miniatures painted by master A. These supplements, as well as the miniatures themselves, are dated to the end of the fifteenth century

[76] I. Окunev, "Шиферная икона XVI в.", *Seminarium Kondakovianum* 8 (1936): 187–192.

[77] Псковскoе муз. собр. NN 14–16; see *Псков. Сокровища искусства и памятники зодчества XII–XVII вв.* (Leningrad. 1978).

[78] *НПЛ*: 405; E.S. Smirnova et al., *Живопись*: 393.

Over the course of a hundred years, during which the veneration of the saint was increasingly accompanied by the use of his name as a baptismal one, first in various princely lines and then by other social groups, a qualitative leap in the reception of the cult, especially in Moscow, was gradually being prepared. To no small degree, this leap was linked with resistance to the union of the Eastern and Western Churches at the Council of Florence and with the establishment of Muscovite autocephaly.[79]

However, the first serious step toward the utilization of a cult of St Vladimir in political affairs was taken by the grand prince of Lithuania, Olgerd, who placed his son Vladimir on the throne of Kiev in 1363. The selection from six grown sons of the one named Vladimir cannot be considered accidental, especially when one takes into account Olgerd's plans regarding the Kievan metropolitanate.[80]

The veneration of St Vladimir in the Muscovite realm acquired the features of a fully developed state-church cult as early as the middle of the fifteenth century, when the Muscovite sovereign Vasilii the Blind (1441) and Metropolitan Ionah (1451) began to stress that, for its membership in the

---

[79] In his polemic with the supporters of the Union of Florence, written about 1440, Simeon of Suzdal, praising Grand Prince Vasilii Vasil'evich, emphasized that he, in uprooting the Latin heresy "was like the isoapostolic Grand Emperor Constantine, who created Orthodoxy, and the pious Grand Prince Vladimir, who baptized the Rus'ian land and established the Orthodox faith of the Greek rule." See A. Popov, *Историко-литературный обзор древнерусских полемических сочинений против латинян.* (Moscow, 1875): 357, cf. 377; W. Vodoff, *Princes et principautés russes, Xe–XVIIe siècles* (Northampton, 1989), IV: 58; VII: 97–98. A new signification of the apostolate of St Vladimir, not yet fully apparent in the time of Ivan Kalita, was expressed by Epiphanius the Wise at the end of the fourteenth century in the Vita of St Stefan of Perm (see below, note 122).

[80] On the Rus'ian and ecclesiastical policy of Olgerd, see his letter to the patriarch from 1370 (*РИБ* 6, appendix: 135–145) and P. Sokolov, *Русский архиерей из Византии и право его назначения до начала XV века* (Kiev, 1913): 345–482; G.M. Prokhorov, *Повесть о Митяе. Русь и Византия в эпоху Куликовской битвы* (Leningrad., 1978): 175–176; J. Meyendorff, *Byzantium and the Rise of Russia* (Cambridge, 1981): 145–146, 159–172, 188–199, 288–289; M. Giedroyč, "The Arrival of Christianity in Lithuania: Baptism and Survival (1341–1387)", *Oxford Slavonic Papers*, n.s., v. 22, (1989): 34–57. The political pretensions of Vladimir Olgerdovich himself as the heir to the authority of the Kievan sovereigns were sharply revealed by his arresting in 1384 the newly consecrated Metropolitan of Rus', Archbishop Dionisii of Suzdal', on the charge that he had been consecrated without the approval of the ruler of Kiev: "you went to obtain the metropolitanate in Constantinople without our permission" – *ПСРЛ* XV-1: 149. Cf. also N.P Likhachev, *Материалы для истории византийской и русской сфрагистики*, [fasc. 2, Leningrad. 1930]: 257–264 and N.A. Soboleva, "К вопросу о монетах Владимира Ольгердовича", *Нумизматика и Эпиграфика*, vol. 8 (Moscow, 1970): 81–87.

Orthodox Christian world, Rus' was indebted to "our forefather, the holy equal-of-the-apostles and great king of Kiev and all Rus', Vladimir".[81]

3. The emergence of the veneration of St Vladimir

It is customarily argued that the initiator of the ecclesiastical veneration of the baptizer of Rus' was the monk-priest Hilarion, who gave substance to the notion in his famous *Sermon on Law and Grace*. Without lessening the importance of Hilarion's contribution, we should also take note of the early attempt to prepare the way for ecclesiastical veneration of Vladimir, described earlier, that has come down to us in the chronicle of Thietmar. We have already had an opportunity, in the first section of this article, to examine in detail the reasons behind the sharply negative view of Vladimir and his Christian life held by the bishop of Merseberg.[82] It is this very ill-will of the bishop toward the Rus'ian king that accords objectivity and trustworthiness to the important information he noted, in his own hand, in October or the first part of November 1018, not long before his death (on December 1), based on a report from a Saxon knight who had taken part in the Kievan campaign of Bolesław the Brave.[83]

That Saxon knight had come to Kiev in August of 1018 as part of an auxiliary detachment sent by Herman, the margrave of Meissen, in support of his brother-in-law, the Kievan prince, Sviatopolk (who was also the son-in-law of the Poland's ruler Bolesław the Brave). He described his visit to the Church of the Tithe, where Vladimir and his wife were buried next to each

---

[81] This or a parallel formula becomes, from this time onward, an inseparable part of grand princely charters dealing with ecclesiastical political questions. See *Памятники древнерусского канонического права*, part. 1 (*РИБ*. vol. 6) (Saint Petersburg, 1880), № 62 (1441 г.): 526; № 66 (1451 г.): 560; № 71 (1451/52 г.): 581; № 85 (1459 г.): 635; № 86: 640, а также с. 708, 648, 723. Cf. *Русский феодальный архив XIV–XVI вв.*, part. 1 (Moscow, 1986), № 5: 71; № 34: 147; № 64: 217. In the Muscovite state the development of the cult of St Vladimir as an ideal ruler was perhaps delayed by the focus on his isoapostolic similarity to Constantine the Great, while the supreme power of both was ignored or left unaccentuated. For this interpretation, see M. Plyukhanova, who uses this to explain the late addition of the king to the ranks of the saints: *Сюжеты и символы Московского царства* (Saint Petersburg, 1995): 120–124, 153–156, 256.

[82] Cf. the first part of the triptych above.

[83] On the Kievan expedition of the Polish sovereign Bolesław the Brave to restore Sviatopolk to his seniority rights, see A. Poppe, "Der Kampf um die Kievan Thronfolge nach dem 15. Jule 1015", *Forschungen zur Osteuropäischen Geschichte* 50 (1995): 275–295.

other, noting that "Their sarcophagi stand in full view in the centre of the church" (*sarcofagis eorundem in medio templi palam*).[84]

In sources of the period, the expression "*in medio ecclesiae* (*templi*)" did not, as noted above, always refer to the very centre of the church, i.e., the crossing, but was always associated with the longitudinal axis of the church and its central nave. Sometimes, it was used to refer to the eastern, or altar section, and sometimes to the western, though generally a spot close to the crossing.[85] In this case, the Saxon's description of the burial is clearly not of something hidden but, rather, set out where all could see it. Furthermore, considering the cruciform, domed layout of the church of the Tithe and the highly segmented character of its interior,[86] it seems clear that the sarcophagi of Vladimir and Anna must have been at the crossing, though conceivably set back slightly under the supporting western arch of the dome (but not under the eastern one, where the altar screen stood).

This burial of a pair of rulers precisely in a court church (*capella palatina*)[87] such as the church of the Tithe (built in the 990s and still, in 1018, the only stone church in Kiev) was not in itself atypical for the period, when the burial of rulers and other prominent individuals within church buildings was a common practice, and when, in Western Europe, since the ninth, and particularly the tenth centuries, the central portion of the church was used for this purpose. However, such burials were usually placed beneath the church floor, although the tombs were occasionally placed in open view, so that Thietmar recounts this particular instance, drawn from an eyewitness report, as a perfectly natural one.

However, for the Byzantine tradition, the fact that the sarcophagi of Vladimir and his *porphyrogenita* spouse were not placed beneath the floor of the church, but stood in full view and, moreover, in the centre of the church building, has to be considered most exceptional. During that period in Byzantium, neither the altar area nor the crossing served as a place even for imperial burials.[88] The only exceptions were reliquary tombs containing the

---

[84] *Thietmari Merseburgensis episcopi Chronicon*, lib. VII, 74, ed. R. Holtzmann and W. Trillmich, Berlin 1957; (repr. 1962): 436.

[85] Oswald, "In medio Ecclesiae" (see n. 19 above).

[86] Komech (see n. 18 above). Cf. also the article of N. Gribanova, Iu. Assev, and A. Reutov on the various issues about the reconstruction of the Church of the Tithe, in a collection devoted to its 1000th anniversary, *Церква Богородиці Десятинна в Києві* (Kiev, 1996): 24–34.

[87] On the status Church of the Tithe as a princely, palace church from its establishment, see A. Poppe, "Русские митрополии Константинопольской патриархии в XI в.", *BB* 28 (1967):85–109.

[88] See nn. 20 and 21 above.

remains of saints, whether broadly or locally recognized, which had usually been moved to that spot from their original location in connection with the induction of those individuals into the ranks of the saints.

The fact that the interment of the deceased ruler in the centre of the church in a marble sarcophagus alongside that of his *porphyrogenita* spouse took place under conditions of political upheaval, which had broken out quickly after his death on 15 July 1015, shows this decision must have been made while Vladimir was still alive, and most likely at the time of the entombment of Anna, who died in 1011.[89] Already at that time, it seems, the possibility of adding the royal pair to the congregation of the saints was already under consideration. Since it is not possible to speak of any kind of local tradition, the idea must have been born in the Byzantine retinue of the princely court and among the ecclesiastical hierarchy of Kiev, who were capable of correctly assessing the great service rendered by Vladimir and Anna in bringing Christianity to Rus'.[90]

The decision to place the sarcophagi of the pair in the nave of the palace church accorded to the latter the character of a mausoleum and immediately created favourable conditions for honouring them and, later, for venerating them as saints. However in the upheaval of the fratricidal struggle for the Kievan throne, all these plans fell into obscurity.

Only three decades later was the question of the saintliness of "our teacher and instructor in the faith" raised again, by the monk-priest Hilarion, soon to become metropolitan of Kiev. This initiative, from all indications, enjoyed the full support of the Kievan king, Iaroslav, once a rebellious son, but now the faithful heir to the programme of his father, coming to the conclusion of his stormy reign and preparing to "present himself, unashamed", before the throne of the Most High.[91]

---

[89] *ПСРЛ* I: 129. The formulation of Thietmar's note (Bk. VII, 74) that Vladimir after his death, "was buried next to his aforementioned wife" (*sepultus iuxta predicatam coniugem suam*) clearly indicates the order of the burials.

[90] An indirect, but clear evaluation of Vladimir's activity of this kind emerges from the aforementioned letter of Bruno of Querfurt after his stay in Kiev in 1008. Undoubtedly, his understanding with the Kiev ecclesiastical hierarchy was complete at this point. It should also be noted that strivings toward sainthood were common in Byzantine imperial circles, and clearly, neither Anna nor, as recent research indicates, her brother, the warrior Emperor Basil II were free of them. See B. Crostini, "The Emperor Basil II's Cultural Life", *Byzantion* 66 (1996) 55–80.

[91] This and subsequent quotations from the work of Hilarion are presented in accordance with the edition of A.M. Moldovan, *Слово о законе и благодати Илариона* (Kiev, 1984): 95–96, 102–103. Engl. transl. by S. Franklin, *Sermons*: 17–26 (Encomium to Volodimir). Cf. A. Poppe "La tentative de réforme ecclésiastique en Russie au milieu du

* * *

The Sermon on Law and Grace and the Praise of our Kagan, Volodimir is a well and widely known literary classic. It presents no substantial divergences from the perspective we have been developing concerning the question at hand. It clearly conveys the idea that Vladimir, by baptizing Rus' and leading her into the family of Christian peoples, had earned a place for himself in the assembly of the saints. Clearly, it would be wrong to reduce the *Sermon* to a mere argument for sanctification. Its philosophical, religious, theological and historiosophical aims and content are far richer than that. However, it does present, more eloquently and effectively than any subsequent text, a brilliant exposition of the right of the baptizer of Rus' to the halo of sainthood.[92]

Hilarion's oration was delivered in the presence of Iaroslav, his large family, and the Kievan nobility and clergy at the tomb of Vladimir in the Church of the Tithe in 1049 or 1050 AD,[93] probably on the anniversary of the death of the king on Sunday 15 July 1050. When we compare this panegyrical oration with what we know from Thietmar, however, we are very much struck by its omission of any mention of Anna. Her sarcophagus ought still to have been standing, as it was in 1018 AD, next to the sarcophagus of Vladimir. But did it, in fact, continue to remain in that location?

Anna's contributions to the work of Christianizing Rus' can scarcely be doubted. Her zeal in the building of churches was known even in distant Antioch, as can be seen from the chronicle of Yahya al-Antaki, compiled in the third decade of the eleventh century from sources contemporary with

---

XIe siècle", *Acta Poloniae Historica* 25 (1972): 5–31, reprinted in idem, *The Rise of Christian Russia* (London 1982): V.

[92] Engl. introduction to Hilarion's work by S. Franklin, *Sermons*: xvi-xlv; J. Fennel and A.D. Stokes, *Early Russian Literature* (London, 1974): 57–60. Cf. the interesting observations of V.N. Toporov in his *Святость и святые в русской духовной культуре*, vol. 1, (Moscow, 1995): 257–340.

[93] The dating of the *Sermon* to 1049 or 1050 has been substantively established by A.V. Solovyev "Zur Lobrede des Metropoliten Ilarion", *Das heidnische und christliche Slaventum* vol. 2 (Wiesbaden, 1970): 58–63 and A. Poppe, *Państwo i Kościół na Rusi w XI w.* (Warszawa, 1968): 54–58, 63–66. The attempt of K.K. Akent'ev (*Byzantinorossica* I, 1995: 75–94) to date the sermon of Hilarion to the time of the consecration of St Sophia on 11 May 1046, does not take into consideration the fact that, as clearly follows from the text, the *Sermon* was delivered over the tomb of Vladimir, and therefore, in the Church of the Tithe, or the fact that by 1046 Sophia had just been finished, while the Golden Gate, and in particular, the Church of the Annunciation raised upon it, given the order of the building projects, could yet have been, and yet Hilarion refers to the latter as completed at the time of his sermon.

Anna.[94] Hilarion's consistent silence on the subject of Vladimir's *porphyrogenita* spouse therefore speaks in favour of a deliberate rather than accidental omission of her name. Was it perhaps because Anna was seen as the perpetrator of the decision regarding succession to the Kievan throne that had sparked conspiracy and rebellion on the part of Sviatopolk and Iaroslav even during their father's lifetime and led to fratricidal war after his death? Whatever the reason, the "absence" of Anna from the oration of Hilarion is an enigma which scholars need to address.[95]

It was not only by influencing all subsequent works dedicated to Vladimir that the *Sermon* had an impact on the further development of his cult. A special role in the emerging veneration of the king was also played by the so-called second redaction of the *Sermon*. While the first full edition of *The Sermon on Law and Grace* has come down to us in just a single manuscript (Sinod. 591), the second redaction is represented by thirty-eight. (A third, of which 13 copies survive, was derived from the second.) The fundamental feature of the second version is the absence of a concluding panegyric to King Iaroslav. The appearance of such a redaction may be explained by a desire to adapt the *Sermon* to liturgical use.[96] Certainly Hilarion's panegyric to Iaroslav and his family would have been superfluous at a reading of the *Sermon* in church on 15 July in commemoration of Vladimir. The presence of this "truncated" version of the *Sermon* in various collections of homilies, hagiographies and teachings, in manuscripts dating from the fifteenth and even fourteenth centuries, tends to confirm the view that it was designed for liturgical use, and provides a link to ecclesiastical celebration of the memory of St Vladimir, which began at the turn of the thirteenth to fourteenth centuries. Two items, however, testify to the existence of this "truncated" edition even earlier, in the first half of the thirteenth century: one is a parchment fragment containing the *Sermon* in an anthology of homilies and teachings (BAN 4.9.37) dated, on the basis of paleography, to the second half of the thirteenth century.[97] The other is the *Life of Monk Simeon* (Stefan Nemanja) composed in 1264. Its author, the Serbian monk Domentian, clearly had a copy of the second

94 *Histoire de Yahya-ibn Sa'id d'Antioche*, ed. and transl. by I. Kratchkovsky and A. Vasiliev (Patrologia Orientalis 23, 1932): 423, 442–443.

95 On the questions of the succession of the Kievan throne and the part played by Anna see Poppe, "The Losers": 133–168 [essay no.VII in this collection of reprints].

96 N.K. Nikol'skii, *Материалы для повременного списка русских писателей и их сочинений (X–XI вв.)* (Saint Petersburg, 1906): 75–90, 509–510.

97 F.I. Pokrovskii, "Отрывок Слова митрополита Илариона о законе и благодати в списке XII–XIII вв.", *ИзвОРЯС* 11, bk 3 (1906): 412–417; *Описание рукописного отдела БАН СССР*, vol. 3, extract 1 (Moscow–Leningrad, 1959).

version at his disposal. Even if one accepts the argument of some that the first of these texts dates from the turn of the thirteenth to fourteenth centuries, the testimony of the Serbian hagiography is less open to question.[98] It is therefore difficult to connect the appearance of the "truncated" version of the *Sermon* to liturgical needs arising in Novgorod around the year 1300. Its presence in the didactic ecclesiastical literature of the first half of the thirteenth century is undoubted, and its origins may date back as early as the twelfth.

A truncation of the panegyric to Iaroslav occurred not because "in the eyes of posterity the authority of King Vladimir was incomparably higher than that of his eldest son",[99] but simply because Vladimir, despite not being officially recognized as a saint, was nevertheless venerated in practice, possibly on a local basis. The inclusion of the truncated version into the corpus of didactic writings on the one hand reflected this veneration, and on the other helped gradually to spread the practice more widely. Those in Novgorod at the end of the thirteenth or beginning of the fourteenth centuries who discovered the *Sermon* in an anthology of religious orations and teachings would have been able to conclude that they were dealing with a panegyric to a King Vladimir whose sainthood dated from "time immemorial" (*ab immemorabili tempore*) and had simply fallen into oblivion in the disastrous years of Mongol devastation. As noted above, in doing so, the Novgorodian Church would have been travelling along a path well-worn in Byzantine ecclesiastical practice: the existence of a cult from "time immemorial" had been sufficient basis to legitimate the official veneration of many saints.[100]

In seeking to determine when this "truncated" version of the *Sermon of Law and Grace* first made its appearance, one probably need consider only a single setting: well before 1240 there was a stone church in Kiev, whose founder was Vladimir, where his remains reposed in a marble sarcophagus, and where his memory as patron would have had to have been observed every 15th of July. Such an annual reading of the "truncated" version of the *Sermon*, along with a requiem mass, in commemoration of the death of the founder of the palace church, would surely have helped promote the growth of his veneration as a saint. Crossing the boundary between regular

98 M. Petrovskii, "Иларион митрополит Киевский и Доментиан, иеромонах Хилендарский", *ИзвОРЯС* 13 (1908), bk. 4: 81–133.

99 Rozov, *Словарь книжников*, vol. 1: 201.

100 See H.-G. Beck, *Kirche und theologische Literatur im byzantischen Reich* (Munich, 1959); H. Delehaye, *Sanctus. Essai sur le culte des saints dans l'antiquité* (Paris, 1927); A. Angenendt, Das *Frühmittelalter* (Munich, 1990): 59, 190, 334, 339–341.

commemoration of a deceased individual on the anniversary of his death to his veneration would have been all the easier here since it was a question of the baptizing sovereign of Rus'. Praise of his deeds would thus naturally have evolved into the prayerful glorification of a saint.

* * *

It is frequently assumed that the phrase to "observe the memory" [*pamiat' tvoriti* (*ustaviti*)] of someone referred only to a commemoration on the day established "in memory of a saint", when in fact the establishment and annual observance of such a memorial might also have in view a simple remembrance, a service commemorating the departed. Such an ordinary remembrance, the so-called *godina,* conducted with the participation of clergy and the family and friends of the deceased, was established by the ecclesiastical authorities (the bishop) and took on an ecclesiastico-social character. It seems appropriate to distinguish between a *celebration* of the memory, referring to the saints, and an *observance* of the memory, applied by the Church in relation to those who had not yet achieved sainthood, but who were distinguished by the Church for their works or way of life. In this context the 1439 decision of Archbishop Euthemius of Novgorod, establishing an annual remembrance of Vladimir, son of Iaroslav the Wise and of his mother, both of whom were buried under the portico of St Sophia in Novgorod is instructive. The prelate directed that the church was to "keep their memory and remember them each year on the fourth day of October, the day of the memory of the sainted priestly martyr, Hierotheus", [101] a good example, in a single phrase, of both meanings ascribed to the word "memory" by the Church.

[101] The Novgorod Second (Archival Ms.) Chronicle (*ПСРЛ* XXX, 1965): 199. How deeply accepted was the religious obligation to honour the memory of the departed already in the third generation after baptism is shown by the words of Vladimir Monomakh, addressed to his cousin Oleg, concerning advice on soul-saving: "But what are we, sinful men? Today alive, tomorrow dead, today in glory and honour, tomorrow in the grave and unremembered (*и без памяти*) while others divide our treasures" – *The Primary Chronicle*: 217; *ПСРЛ* I: 253. In its religious didactic context, Monomakh's expression "*bez pamiati*" cannot be understood to mean "forgotten by all", but precisely in the sense of the lack of religious, ecclesiastical commemoration of the departed. Not coincidentally, they willed in their testaments for their heirs to take care for the remembrance of their souls ("and after me to do remembrance as much as possible" – testament of abbot Vasilii c. 1350. see Sreznevskii, *Материалы для словаря*, vol. 2: 872). The foundation for research on the remembrance of the dead in old Rus' was laid by L. Steindorff, *Memoria in Altrussland. Untersuchungen zu den Formen christlicher Totensorge.* (Stuttgart 1994); rev. J. Lind, *RM* 9/1 (1997): 193–196.

There are, therefore, good reasons here to speculate that the observance each year of the memory of the founder of the church of the Tithe on the 15th of July, an event established immediately after death for an individual who had been slated from the outset for inclusion into the ranks of the saints, acquired an exclusively solemn character in the year 1050, thanks to Hilarion and the hearers of his *Sermon*.

A continuing observance of the memory of the one who "by holy baptism enlightened the whole Rus'ian land" is indicated by *The Primary Chronicle* somewhere near the end of the eleventh or beginning of the twelfth century. A panegyric to Vladimir is placed just after the chronicle's tidings about his death in 1015.[102] The panegyric was composed not earlier than the very end of the eleventh century, but not later than 1110, when the *Primary Chronicle* itself was completed. The influence of Hilarion's *Sermon* on this text is obvious. It has frequently been adduced as proof that, at the time of compilation of the aforementioned chronicle record, Vladimir was not yet recognized as a saint.[103] While this fact is indisputable, the remarks of the chronicler must be understood to indicate, not a total absence of veneration in his day, but rather, insufficient veneration: "But we, though Christians, do not render him honour in proportion to this benefaction... If we had been zealous for him, and had offered our prayers to God in his behalf upon the day of his death, then God, beholding our zeal, would have glorified him."[104] The chronicler indicates that Vladimir was not venerated to a degree proportionate to his accomplishments (more precisely: to what "he gave to us"), and that prayers for Vladimir on the day of his falling asleep were not sufficiently fervent (in translation, the original words of the *Primary Chronicle,* "потщанье и мольбы" must not be treated separately, as "zeal *and* prayer." Their relationship is not merely conjunctive. "Zealous" (the word used in the Cross translation above) is an intensifier here, to be taken together with prayer as "zealously praying", or "petitioning God with fervent zeal".

The fact that the chronicler took a critical view of the degree of Vladimir's veneration and saw it as insufficient for his "glorification", i.e., his inclusion

---

102 Laurentian Chronicle, *ПСРЛ* I, 1926): 130–131; *The Primary Chronicle*: 125.

103 Cf. the commentary of D.S. Likhachev, *Повесть временных лет*, ed. 2, Saint Petersburg 1996: 471.

104 *The Primary Chronicle*: 125; *ПСРЛ* I: 130–131. The accepted interpretation of "would have glorified him" in the sense of "by miracles" is not necessary here, all the more since it was obvious to people of the Church that miracles did not create sainthood, but only confirmed it. Of course, it was understood otherwise by the broad masses of believers, for whom sainthood and the performance of miracles were one and the same. This was realized by Vladimir's contemporary Bruno of Querfurt, and in his *Vita* of St Wojciech-Adalbert he strongly emphasized that "miracula sanctitatem non faciunt".

into the ranks of the saints, is obvious from one of the sentences that follows: "The people of Rus', mindful of their holy baptism, hold this king [Vladimir] in pious memory..."[105] This statement does not represent a contradiction. It is not the result of an unsuccessful combination of two different texts, as has been proposed.[106] Here the chronicler has in mind the observance of Vladimir's memory ("hold this king in pious memory", i.e., perpetuate his memory), whereas earlier he pointed out that such veneration was disproportionate to the accomplishments of a "righteous man" worthy of sainthood. It is precisely the chronicler's reference to the Rus'ian people's remembrance of Vladimir in connection with their baptism that allows us to suggest that the perpetration of his memory had already spread beyond the limits of the "mausoleum" Church of the Tithe. In addition, the chronicler's appeal for zealous prayer on the day of the death of Vladimir and the words of a prayer concerning his glorification which he cited, suggest the existence of an ecclesiastical framework for such a mode of prayerful address to God, i.e., liturgical services in observance of the memory of "the one who baptized us". The very existence of an annual observance of the memory of Vladimir in connection with the baptism of the Rus'ian land, even if limited to selected churches (initially probably some cathedrals and monastic churches), already contained within itself the potential for transition into a feast in memory of St Vladimir.

The growing readiness for such a change is evident in the written accounts of the life and deeds of one worthy of sainthood. Much had already done here, beginning with the *Sermon* of Hilarion and excerpts from the Chronicle containing a description of Vladimir's great accomplishment: the baptism of Rus'. Such an excerpt found its way into the Synaxarion in the form of a short "Life of Prince Vladimir" most likely even before Vladimir was recognized as a saint, as the oldest manuscript, dating from the thirteenth century, suggests.[107] In this regard, a thorough investigation is required of the well-known *Memory and Encomium to the Rus'ian King Vladimir*.[108] The influence of Hilarion's *Sermon* and *The Primary Chronicle* on this work are beyond question, although its attribution to Iakov, a monk of the Kievan Monastery of the

[105] *ПСРЛ* I: 131; *The Primary Chronicle*: 125.

[106] Serebrianskii, Жития: 47.

[107] ГПБ, fond 147, see catalogue # 294; cf. # 304, *Сводный каталог славяно-русских рукописных книг, хранящихся в СССР. XI–XIII вв.* (Moscow, 1984): 271 (№ 294), cf. 276 (№ 304).

[108] Serebrianskii, *Жития* (survey of manuscripts, 32–36, 49–51), texts: 12–13. *Память и похвала Иакова мниха и житие князя Владимира по древнейшему списку*, ed. A. Zimin (Краткие Сообщения Института Славяноведения, fasc. 37, 1963): 67–72.

Caves in the second half of the eleventh century, is without foundation.[109] In the form in which it has been preserved, this compilation appears to be a work of the second half of the thirteenth or first half of the fourteenth century,[110] although there is some doubt about the possibility of fully analyzing and dating those strata and components. Nevertheless, the inclusion in this document of annalistic entries relating to events confirms their trustworthiness precisely in reference to the events connected with the baptism of Rus'.[111] Without a detailed investigation of the entire manuscript tradition devoted to Vladimir, the issue of the chronology of the material presented in this document cannot be resolved. Tentatively, however, it may be said that the composition of the first part, the *Memory and Encomium* itself, dates from somewhere in the twelfth or thirteenth centuries, especially since nowhere in this section is Vladimir called a saint, and since its language is typical for that period of time. In this part of the text, Vladimir is four times called *блаженыи* (*μακάριος* in Greek, *beatus* in Latin) in the sense of "blessed", "worthy of veneration". Here the author follows Hilarion, who addressed Vladimir as "O blessed one". It is worth noting that while mentioning Vladimir eighteen times, only in the panegyric itself does the author call him blessed, which seems more an effort to glorify the prince than to offer praise to one already glorified.[112] As the very title of the work indicates, it could only have been composed for the purposes of commemoration the kind of observance about which the chronicler speaks.

* * *

The well known scholar B.A. Uspenskii has identified a whole series of references to the glorification of Vladimir in the writings of the pre-Mongol

---

[109] Bibliography of editions and literature on the question can be found in O.V. Tvorogov, E.A. Fet, *Словарь книжников* 1: 191–192 (Iakov); 288–290 (Память). However, Podskalsky (*Christentum*: 198–202) is inclined to see Iakov as an author of the end of the eleventh century. "Memory" Engl. translation and introduction by P. Hillingsworth, *The Hagiography of Kievan Rus'*: LXXXI–XCVI, 165–181.

[110] S.A. Bugoslavskii, "К литературной истории «Памяти и Похвалы» князю Владимиру", *ИзвОРЯС* 29, 1924/1925: 105–141; cf. A. Poppe, *Słownik Starożytności Słowiańskich* 4 (1970): 16–18.

[111] Cf. A. Poppe, "The Political Background to the Baptism of Rus'." *DOP* 30, 1976: 240–242.

[112] The author of the *Memory...* like Hilarion perhaps, senses the subtle difference between the terms "saint" (holy), i.e., ecclesiastically glorified, and "blessed", meaning likewise holy but, one might say, not always with a defined ecclesiastical status. The term "blessed" (*blazhenyi*) provided broader semantic possibilities See *Словарь древнерусского языка XI–XIV вв.*, vol. 1, (Moscow, 1988): 22–226.

period, filling out our picture of the gradual construction of a cult of an isoapostolic prince, which began with Hilarion's encomion to the teacher of Rus'. The fact that the dating of a few of these references is debatable is unimportant in this case, since the evidence of veneration, "creation of memory", is clearly present from eleventh and twelfth century in the Old Russian manuscript tradition. The only question is whether they should be seen as traces of a veneration of Vladimir as a saint, growing in the twelfth and thirteenth centuries, and leading by the end of the thirteenth to official ecclesiastical inclusion of the baptizer of Rus' in the company of the saints as one honoured since time immemorial, as proposed by the author of this article, or whether they should be seen as traces of a much earlier ecclesiastical recognition, perhaps accorded almost immediately following the official recognition of Boris and Gleb as martyr saints (1072), as Uspenskii has proposed.[113]

Gratefully accepting the materials assembled by his "competitor" as a supplement to his own observations, this author is nonetheless inclined to take a second look at the inscription on birchbark to which such great significance is accorded in Uspenskii's account. This surviving fragment of a larger text has been reconstructed as follows:

> х҃а: б҃цѣ: петра и п[ав]ла[:] коꙁмадьмьана: о[ть]ча василья: и бориса и глеба: и свѣхъ стхъ.[114]

Uspenskii proposes that "father Vasilii" is a reference to St Vladimir. Such an argument concerning this fragment of an unknown larger text, discovered in excavations in Novgorod, can even be bolstered by reference to the procedure by which Boris and Gleb were added to the ranks of the saints, in which a clear effort was made to declare the sons of Vladimir saints under their baptismal names.[115] The hypothesis is spoiled, however, by too strict of a dating of this note to the third quarter of the eleventh century, for in the works of the 1070s and 1080s devoted to Saints Boris and Gleb, there is not the slightest indication that the father had followed his sons into the ranks of the saints. The final stumbling block is the *Pokhvalnoe Slovo* in the *Povest' Vremennykh Let*, clear proof that at the very beginning of the twelfth century,

---

113 B.A. Uspenskii, "Когда был канонизирован князь Владимир Святославич?", *For Ihor Ševčenko on his 80th birthday* (*Paleoslavica* 10/2; Cambridge, Mass., 2002): 271–281.

114 Uspenskii, "Когда был канонизирован": 274–275.

115 A. Poppe, "О зарождении культа свв. Бориса и Глеба и о посвященных им произведениях", *RM* 8/1, (1995): 31–45, 50–51.

there had not yet been any ecclesiastical recognition of Vladimir's sainthood,[116] as noted above.

That we are dealing here with an ordering according to the calendar has not been fully demonstrated. Another weak point in the argument is the unusual combination of "father Vasilii" with "Boris and Gleb", requiring too subtle a dual interpretation of the fatherhood of "Vasilii" in the literal sense of being actual father of the holy martyrs and in the figurative sense of "father of all Rus'" as teacher of the land.[117] One must concede, however, that the text remains as much of a mystery if we posit a reference to the Church father Basil the Great, archbishop of Caesarea.

Likewise, Uspenskii's arguments about the genesis of princely names derived from Vladimir-Vasilii (Volodar', Vasil'ko, etc.), while interesting in itself, does nothing to bolster the reliability of the birchbark fragment (no. 906) and continues to arouse uncertainties.

This attempt to decipher the mysterious note, one must admit, represents an extremely promising investigative approach, but in the final analysis it must result in a decision not to draw upon it as a fully-fledged historical source.

* * *

The boundary between the observance and the celebration of the memory of Vladimir must have been gradually erased, and it seems that the ecclesiastico-didactic texts devoted to the blessed Vladimir sometimes permitted him to be accepted as a saint. Thus, for example, in a manuscript of a South Slavic synaxarion dating from the end of the thirteenth or beginning of the fourteenth century, in a segment about the transfer of the relics of Boris and Gleb, the following clarification is added: "The sons of Saint Vladimir the Great, Rus'ian King, a second Constantine, who baptized the whole Rus'ian land."[118] The Serbian synaxarion did utilize an old redaction of the Rus'ian one, which had made its way south probably as early as the first half of the thirteenth century. In all likelihood, however, calling Vladimir a saint here is the work of a Serbian scribe acquainted with some other text (probably Hilarion's) comparing Vladimir to Constantine the Great.

---

[116] *The Primary Chronicle*: 125–126; *ПСРЛ* 1: 130–131.

[117] Uspenskii, "Когда был канонизирован": 275. If forced to guess, one might also hypothesize that the fragment of text before us here is part of an order given to an icon painter.

[118] Serebrianskii, *Жития, тексты*: 168. ГИМ, Увар., 70. See *Сводный Каталог*: 361–362 (№ 469).

In the development of the veneration of Vladimir, an ever fuller and more widespread recognition of his isoapostolic accomplishment as the most important event in the history of Rus'ian Christianity accompanied his imperceptible entrance into the ranks of the saints. This bold notion was expressed with utmost clarity by Hilarion in the middle of the eleventh century, but the three more centuries were needed for it to become the property of all Christian Rus'.

Hilarion not only called Vladimir an "apostle among rulers" and likened him to Constantine the Great. He also ranked him among the apostolic teachers of the true faith. In subsequent periods, efforts to identify the roots of Rus'ian Christianity saw the reception and development of traditions about the role of the apostles Andrew, Paul and Andronicus in the preparation of the Slavs and the Rus'ian land for Christian enlightenment.[119] Introduced into the *Primary Chronicle* at the beginning of the twelfth century, these traditions preordaining the course of historical events unintentionally but undoubtedly weakened the appreciation of the apostolic accomplishment of King Vladimir and his significance as "our teacher, our guide in devotion."[120] A brief *Life of Vladimir* from a synaxarion going back to the first half of the fourteenth century (and the oldest manuscript, the Tipografski ms. 169/364, may even date from the turn of the thirteenth to fourteenth centuries),[121] in essence coinciding with the account in the chronicle about the baptism of Rus', adopts, in its treatment of the apostleship of Vladimir, the text of Hilarion, expands it and adds to it a point of view that found its confirmation in the *Life of Stephan of Perm* by Epiphanius the Wise, written at the turn of the fourteenth to fifteenth century,[122] and perpetuated in the ecclesiastical and political life of the fifteenth and sixteenth centuries (cf., for example, *The*

[119] Cf. A. Poppe, "Two Concepts of the Conversion of Rus in Kievan writings", *HUS* 12/13, (1988/89): 488–504 [=this volume, no. IV]; Podskalsky, *Christentum*: 17–23. I.S. Chichurov, "Хождение апостола Андрея» в византийской и древнерусской церковно-идеологической традиции", *Церковь, общество и государство в феодальной России. Сборник статей* (Moscow, 1990): 7–23.

[120] Moldovan, *Слово*: 96; Hilarion, *Sermons*: 25.

[121] Serebrianskii, *Жития,* texts: 14–16. Such an early dating of the parchment manuscript raises doubts and requires careful examination. In the Orsha gospel of the second half of the thirteenth century, (now in Kiev), on f. 139v the note "pamiat' kniazia Vladimira" is written in the margin in a later *ustav* hand. See *Сводный Каталог*: 295 (№ 342).

[122] *Житие св. Стефана, епископа Пермского, написанное Епифанием премудрым*, ed. V.G. Druzhinin (Saint Petersburg, 1897; reprinted 1959 with an introduction by D. Chizhevskii): 89–90. On the possibility that not only Bruno and Hilarion but Vladimir could see himself as an apostle to the heathen, a new apostle Paul, see the thought-provoking observations of S. Senderovich, "К мифопоэзису св. Владимира", *ТОДРЛ* 49 (1996): 300–313.

Sermon about the Life and Death of Dmitri of the Don). The author of the *Life* in the synaxarion addresses Vladimir thus: "How can we worthily praise you, who have accomplished a work equal to that of the apostles. The Roman land praises Peter and Paul, Asia – John the Theologian, Egypt – Mark, Antioch – Luke, and the land of Greece – Andrew, but the whole land of Rus' praises you in prayerful songs, O Vladimir, and celebrates your memory as an apostle of the Lord."[123]

The observations presented above concerning the emergence of the veneration of King Vladimir, performer "of a work equal to that of the apostles", is but an attempt to mark out a fresh direction approach to the study of his cult. It begins with the affirmation that the addition of Vladimir into the company of saints never took place as a formal ecclesiastical procedure. Attempts to fix the time of the canonization of Vladimir must therefore lead to a dead end. The very term "canonization" unwittingly refers to a mode of thinking and a calculated, centralized mechanism for canonization developed in the Roman Catholic Church since the eleventh century. As a result of the acceptance of such a point of view, Constantinople, the patriarch and Greeks in general have been accused of preventing the raising up of the local righteous and ascetics into the ranks of recognized saints. In like manner, the delay in the glorification of Vladimir has been attributed to the intrigue of the Greeks.

The gradual, imperceptible growth of the veneration of Vladimir led to a moment at the end of the thirteenth century when, in extreme circumstances, existing written works and an already established tradition of an annual observance of the memory of Vladimir were perceived as evidence of a veneration from time immemorial of "the one who ploughed the whole land with baptism". Such a process only seems accidental. In view of the decades of Tatar rule and the threat of a collapse into the indifferent Mongol world, the Christian faith and self-awareness of the old-Rus'ian society, and the religious-national and state instinct of its leaders were manifested in a deepening of the inner spiritual world of man. This involved a greater emphasis on religious life and spiritual awakening through "our head, our leader and teacher, thanks to whom we are saved from darkness saw the light."

This was without doubt not a mass movement. Vladimir's accomplishment lends to his cult a more intellectual-religious character and, more than

---

[123] Serebrianskii, *Жития*, texts: 16. The citations below are from the version of the synaxarion vita of St Vladimir composed no earlier than the beginning of the 14th century (see n. 121 above regarding the ms.)

anything else, in the face of a new darkness, Rus'ian Christians began to understand all the importance and significance of Vladimir's deed. This perception became the cornerstone of the sainthood of the "worker for the Christian faith".[124]

124 "*Delatel'*" used here in its Old Rus'ian sense of "labourer".

IX

WORDS THAT SERVE THE AUTHORITY
On the Title of "Grand Prince" in Kievan Rus' *

The origins of the title of "Grand Prince" in Old Rus' are still unclear. Divergent opinions have been expressed on this topic despite the fact that for decades V. O. Ključevskij's assertion that "from the middle of the 11th century the highest dignitary—the prince of Kiev—was called Grand Prince" was a point of reference for most experts.[1] During the 1960s and 1970s the view that this title was applied to the rulers of Kiev as early as the 9th century

---

* Since the modern meaning of the word Russia (Russian) concerns only one (Greatrussian) but not two other Eastern Slavic nations (Ukrainians and Byelorussians) the medieval term Rus' (and adj. Rusian) which embraces all Eastern Slavs in Middle Ages is used here for the sake of greater accuracy. Kievan Rus' (or Kievan Russia) is a learned term used for dominated by the Eastern Slavdom, multination statehood under the hegemony of Kiev between the 9th and the 13th centuries. The communication on the title of Kievan ruler was presented in 1974 in Münich (Kommission für die Geistesgeschichte der östlichen Europa) and 1976 in Moscow (Institut Istorii Akademii Nauk). The Polish version of the present paper was published in: "Przegląd Historyczny", vol. LXXV, 1984, No. 3, p. 423—439.

For contribution on the English wording of this text I am obligated to my learned friends and collegues Henrik Birnbaum from Los Angeles, Richard Bosley from Düsseldorf and Simon Franklin from Cambridge.

[1] V. O. Ključevskij, *Sočinenija*, vol. VI, Moskva 1959, p. 136. J. P. Arrignon took this point of view as the basis for his own reflections: *Usage et valeur du titre de Grand Prince (Velikij Knjaz') dans la Russie du nordest aux XIIIe et XIVe siècles*, in: *Les Principautés au Moyen Age* Bordeaux 1979, pp. 176, 178. W. Vodoff has recently presented two articles of rulers' titles in medieval Rus'. His views, which are in keeping with mine, form an appropriate background for the thoughts presented here; see: W. Vodoff, *La titulature des princes russes du Xe au debut de XIIe siècle et les relations extérieures de la Russie Kiévienne*, "Revue des Etudes Slaves", vol. LV, 1983, pp. 139—150; idem, *La titulature princière en Russie du XIe au début du XVIe siècle. Questions de critique des sources*, "Jahrbücher für Geschichte Osteuropas", vol. XXXV, 1987, pp. 1—35.

found increasing acceptance.[2] Nearly eighty years ago L. K. Goetz attempted to trace the origin of this title to the second half of the 12th century; although his work still offers the most lucid overview of the sources, the limitation of his inquiry to the text of three chronicles prevented him from providing a satisfactory answer to the question.[3]

Certain historians, aware of the chronological and semantic difficulties, accepted that the grand princely title was used to elevate Kievan ruler, but denied that it had any fundamental importance, and emphasized instead the institution of the eldest among the princes of Rus'.[4] Some even categorically denied that the grand princely title had any official status in the 11th and 12th centuries.[5] To a certain extent the difference of opinion is attributable to the different views of the political organisation and supremacy in the Kievan state. Yet it also results from an underestimation of the need to verify the textual transmission: thus

---

[2] This opinion, which has remained unchanged in the face of criticism for years, is held by B. A. Rybakov; see most recently his *Kievskaja Rus' i russkije knjažestva XII—XIII vv.* Moskva 1982, pp. 328, 416, 476; see also, for example: V. P. Šušarin, *Sovremennaja buržuaznaja istoriografija drevnej Rusi*, Moskva 1964, p. 158; J. Frojanov, *Kievskaja Rus'*, Leningrad 1980, p. 24f; M. B. Sverdlov, *Genezis i struktura feodalnogo obščestva v drevnej Rusi*, Leningrad 1983, p. 32ff; P. Toločko, *Drevnjaja Rus'*, Kiev 1987, pp. 37, 42—43, 49, 76, 216—218; Ju. Limonov, *Vladimiro-Suzdalskaja Rus'*, Leningrad 1987, pp. 27, 32, 35—36, 73. Also for both last authors (who ignore my own and Vodoff's studies mentioned here) the grand princely title of Kievan ruler seems to be self-evident; cf. further the academic text books such as: *Istorija SSSR s drevnejših vremën do konca XVIII v.*, ed. B. A. Rybakov, Moskva 1983, pp. 56, 93ff. *Istorija gosudarstva i prava SSSR*, vol. I. ed. O. Čistjakov and I. Martysevič, Moskva 1985, pp. 28—30.

[3] L. K. Goetz, *Der Titel "Grossfürst" in den ältesten russischen Chroniken*,—"Zeitschrift für Osteuropäische Geschichte", vol. I, 1911, pp. 23—66, 177—213. See also K. R. Schmidt, *Soziale Terminologie in russischen Texten des Frühen Mittelalters bis zum Jahre 1240*, Copenhagen 1964, pp. 293 f., 524.

[4] B. D. Grekov and subsequently V. T. Pašuto and L. V. Čerepnin referred, albeit inconsistently, to the senior of Kiev as Grand Prince. G. Stoekl also appears to share this view, although he is aware that this title was accepted quite late; see *Die Begriffe Reich, Herrschaft und Staat bei den orthodoxen Slaven*, "Saeculum", vol. V, 1954, p. 108; idem, *Der russische Staat in Mittelalter und früher Neuzeit*, Wiesbaden 1981, p. 78. For comments on the right of the eldest, see L. V. Čerepnin *K voprosu o haraktere i forme drevnerusskogo gosudarstva X—načala XIII v.*, "Istoričeskie Zapiski", vol. LXXXIX, 1972, p. 369 ff.

[5] V. L. Janin, *Aktovye pečati drevnej Rusi X—XV vv.*, vol. I, Moskva 1970, p. 22.

adjective *velikyi*, which accompanies the word *knjaz'*, is interpreted exclusively as one of the standard epithets of the Kievan prince, as his official title. No one has reflected on the semantic subtleties of the attribute *velikyi*, which, in the Middle Ages, was equivalent to the Greek *megas* and Latin *magnus*.[6]

The earliest references to "Grand Prince" are found in the Byzantine-Rusian treaties of the 10th century, which are preserved in manuscripts from the 14th—15th centuries. For this reason L. K. Goetz was prepared "to consider these treaties spurious in the form in which they are preserved, solely because of the use the term *velikyi knjaz'*, of which we find no other examples from such an early period".[7] The textual form of this passage as it has been transmitted to us is admittedly not perfect, and one can identify small omissions or interpolations made at the beginning of the 12th century, that is, at the time when these treaties were first added to the *Primary Chronicle*. Yet the sceptical opinion of this accomplished historian of the Rusian Middle Ages does not seem well-founded.[8] By the same token, however, one must add that the view is unfounded according to which the treaties prove that already in the 10th century a "Grand Prince" was at the head of the old Rusian state.[9] Neither point of view takes into account

---

[6] See P. Schreiner, *Zur Bezeichnung "Megas" und "Megas Basileus" in der byzantinischen Kaisertitulatur*, "Byzantina", vol. III, 1971, pp. 175—192; W. Kienast, *Magnus, der Ältere*, "Historische Zeitschrift", vol. CCV, 1967, pp. 1—14; R. Macrides, *What's in the Name "Megas Komnenos"?*, "Archeon Pontou", vol. XXXV, 1979, pp. 328—345; P. Bührer, *Studien zu den Beinamen mittelalterlicher Herrscher*, "Schweizerische Zeitschrift für Geschichte", vol. XXI, 1972, pp. 205—236.

[7] L. K. Goetz, *Der Titel...*, p. 26. See the objections raised by G. Stoekl (*Die Begriffe...*, p. 108, note 21), who views *velikyi knjaz'* in the treaties as a laudatory expression "great prince". A. Kuźmin, *Načal'nye etapy drevnerusskogo letopisanija*, Moskva, 1977, p. 83, considers the adjective "great" appended to the princely title in the treaties an interpolation of the 12th century.

[8] For the current state of research see J. Bardach, *Traktaty* [*Treaties*] in: *Słownik Starożytności Słowiańskich*, vol. VI, 1977, pp. 130—133; S. M. Kaštanov, *Russkije knjažeskije akty X—XIV vv.*, "Archeografičeskij Ežegodnik za 1974", Moskva 1975, pp. 94—99.

[9] In addition to those works mentioned in footnote 2 see A. N. Saharov, *Diplomatija drevnej Rusi*, Moskva 1980, p. 239, where the author concludes that "the treaty of 944 makes use of the title officialy recognized in Rus', "Grand Prince". G. Vernadsky,—see his *Kievan Russia*, New Haven 1948, (7th ed., 1973), pp. 31, 36,—expressed a similar opinion.

the irrefutable fact that the Slavic text of the treaties is a translation from Greek;[10] but this fact must form the point of departure of all further studies.

In Byzantine practice it was common to call the ruler of Rus' *archōn*. The custom of translating *knjaz'* as *archōn* had taken root during the centuries of constant contacts between Byzantium and the Southern Slavs. From the forms of address listed in the book *De caerimoniis* authorized by Constantine Porphyrogenitus, we learn that in the 10th century (that is, in the very period in which the Byzantine-Rusian treaties were concluded) imperial letters were addressed to Rusian princes with the simple phrase *pros ton archonta Rhōsias* without the addition of any established *epitheta ornantia*. The author of the book is clearly unaware of the term "Grand Prince" when he speaks about particular rulers of Kiev: Igor is called *archōn Rhōsias*, Olga *archontissa Rhōsias* and once *hēgemōn kai archontissa tōn Rhōs*.[11] The Rusian princely seals with Greek inscriptions from the 11th and the beginning of the 12th centuries testify to the fact that the members of the Rurikid dynasty were satisfied with the title *archōn Rhōsias*.[12]

The Byzantines, on the other hand, who were aware of the multitude of semantic possibilities of this contemporary term, which was also used by the officials of the Empire's provincial administration, complemented the title *archōn* directed at the

---

[10] The fundamental study of the linguistic dependence of the treaties on the Greek original remains N. Lavrovskij, *O vizantijskom elemente v jazyke dogovorov russkich s grekami*, St. Petersburg 1853, reprinted Warszawa 1904.

[11] *De caerimoniis aulae byzantinae*, vol. II, ed. Bonn 1830, pp. 511, 596, 691; see also G. Ostrogorsky, *Die byzantinische Staattenhierarchie*, "Seminarium Kondakovianum", vol. VIII, 1936, p. 49 ff.; J. Ferluga, *Die Adressenliste für auswärtige Herrscher aus dem Zeremonienbuch Konstantin Porphyrogennetos* in: idem, *Byzantium and the Balkans*, Amsterdam 1976, p. 261 ff.

[12] See A. Soloviev, *Archōn Rhōsias*, "Byzantion", vol. XXXI, 1961, pp. 237—248; vol. XL, 1970, p. 435 f. Reprinted in idem, *Byzance et la formation de l'Etat russe*, Variorum, London, 1979; V. L. Janin, *Aktovye pečati...*, vol. I, p. 14 ff. The titles of the extant diplomas are equally modest: the ruler's name is placed first, sometimes without any title at all. Only in the 13th century did the mention of the title before the name of the prince take precedence. Cf. S. M. Kaštanov, *Intitulacija russkih knjažeskih aktov X—XIV vv.*, "Vspomogatel'nye istoričeskie discipliny", vol. VIII, Leningrad 1978, pp. 69—83.

princes of Rus' with various epithets. It is known that in the practice of the imperial chancery the epithets were more significant then the title itself. Indirect evidence permits us to conclude that one of the epithets used by Byzantine emperors and patriarchs in their correspondence with princes of Rus' was *eugenestatos* and possibly *paneugenestatos*. Given the monodynastic nature of the princely dignity this tautological addition to the princely title did not take immediate root in Rus'. Proof of this is seen in the fact that works written in old Rusian avoided its use even in titles with many epithets, favouring instead terms which accentuated the Christian nature of the prince's power. One example of this is found in the canonical responses of the Kievan metropolitan Johannes II: the expression *tou eugenestatou archontos* was translated as *blagovernago knjazja* in which the Christian epithet was considered more suitable.[13]

In the treaty of 911 the Kievan ruler Oleg is called *velikyi knjaz' russkyi*, *svetlyi knjaz' russkyi* and *naša svetlost'*.[14] The last, a typical Byzantine title, is a calque of *hē periphaneia* (or *lamprotēs*) *hēmōn* and corresponds to the familiar *cesarstvo naše* (*hē basileia hēmon*) of the treaties.[15] Oleg's successor, Igor, was called six times *velikyi knjaz' russkyi* in the treaty of 944 and *knjaz' russkyi* equally often. In the treaty of 971 (or rather in the declaration intended for Johannes Tzimiskes) Igor's son Svjatoslav is called *velikyi knjaz' russkyi* in the third person in the preliminary protocol but *Az Svjatoslav knjaz' russkyi* in the disposition in the first person. In the report on the preliminary negotia-

---

[13] *Kirchenrechtliche und kulturgeschichtliche Denkmäler Altrusslands*, ed. L. K. Goetz, Stuttgart 1905, p. 138 f. See also A. Poppe, *The Rise of Christian Russia*, Variorum, London 1982, IX, p. 111 f.; A. Soloviev, *Byzance...*, No. VI, pp. 241—248.

[14] Among the many editions of the treaties, the editions in the *Polnoe sobranie russkih letopisej* [hereafter PSRL] must be considered the basic one: vol. I, Leningrad 1926 (reprinted 1962), cols. 32—38 (Treaty of 911), cols. 46—54 (Treaty of 944), cols. 71—73 (Declaration of 971); and vol. II, St. Petersburg 1908 (reprinted 1962) corresponding cols. 23—28, 35—42, 60—61. For a translation into English which primarily follows the text of the Laurentian MS see *The Russian Primary Chronicle, Laurentian Text*, transl. and ed. by S. H. Cross and O. P. Sherbowitz-Wetzor, Cambridge, Mass. 1953, pp. 64—65, 73—77, 89—90: A. Zimin offers an emended text based on that in the PSRL with variants from several MSS in: *Pamjatniki russkogo prava* [PRP], vol. I, Moskva 1952, pp. 3—63.

[15] See Lavrovskij, *O vizantijskom elemente...*, pp. 104—107.

tions and in the document itself Tzimiskes is called *cěsar'* ; only once is he called *velikyi cěsar'* when he is mentioned together with "Basil and Constantine, the emperors enlightened by God". This turn of phrase reflects precisely the situation at that time : as was customary, Tzimiskes, being the eldest and the true holder of power, was called the *megas basileus.* The plural *velicyi cěsari* occurs in the treaties of 911 and 944 when, according to the common practice of the imperial chancery, the names of the joint emperors were mentioned together with the name of the true emperor-autocrat.[16]

From the text of all three documents we can clearly infer that *velikyi/megas* was not part of an official title for the Kievan ruler, but was rather an adjectival epithet which was used by the Byzantines not only for the princes of Kiev but also for their own emperors. On the contrary, the full title of the Kievan ruler in these texts is *knjaz' rus'kyi/archōn Rhōsias,* whereas other princes are mentioned without reference to the country.

It appears that the meaning of the epithet *megas* added to *archōn Rhōsias* does not differ from that found in Byzantine documents in the phrase *megas basileus.* This is supported by the very clear use of *megas* by Constantine Porphyrogenitus in the sense of "elder", "principal", "chief" in the report about the ruler of Moravia (*ho Morabias archōn*) Svetopluk who divided his country among his three sons, with the eldest to be the chief prince *ton prōton kataleipsas archonta megan.*[17] The term *megas archōn/velikyi knjaz'* should, therefore be translated as "chief prince", since it is less likely that the Byzantine dictating the document intended *megas archōn* to mean "famous" or "important prince". The information contained in the treaties themselves appears to support the interpretation "chief prince" (keeping in mind many Grecisms left by translator, the complex MS tradition

---

[16] See Fr. Dölger, *Byzanz und die europäische Staatenwelt*, Ettal, 1953 (reprinted 1976) pp. 286 f., 312 ; G. Ostrogorski, *Vizantija i Slovienie*, Beograd 1970, pp. 285—288, 290—292, 302 ; P. Schreiner, *Zur Bezeichnung...*, pp. 179 f.

[17] *De administrando imperio*, ed. Gy. Moravcsik, Washington 1967, p. 181 (cap. 41, see also cap. 37, 38 and 40). *Ibidem*, pp. 166 f., 172 f., 178 f., where the leader of the Pečenegs and the Magyar ruler Arpad are consistently called *archōn* and only once *ho megas Tourkias archōn.*

of the texts, and the clear traces of corrections made by a Rusian bookman).[18]

In the treaty of 911 the Rusian envoys appear in the name of Oleg as well as *ot vseh iže sut' pod rukoju jego svetlyh i velikyh knjaz' i jego velikyh bojar*. According to the treaty of 944 the envoys are sent by Igor as well as "by all the princes" (*ot vsjakaja knjažija*); later on, however, the text mentions the ruling prince and "his princes and boyars" or only "his boyars". The document of 971 mentions, in addition to Svjatoslav, only his boyars. From this we see that the terms "princes and boyars", "princes" or simply "boyars" were used indiscriminately in the treaties to designate one and the same social group close to the Kievan prince. This observation led H. Łowmiański to conclude that the terminological confusion in the Byzantine-Rusian treaties of the 10th century reflects the "transformation of the clan chieftains into an early feudal aristocracy. The former, deprived of the title prince, which was reserved for members of the ruling dynasty, was fused into the group of boyars".[19] It is difficult to agree with this ingenious interpretation of the inconsistent use of social terminology in the treaties, in view of the fact that the form of the documents is a product of the Byzantine side. An examination of the MS tradition of the treaties reveals the tendency (undoubtedly of the old Rusian bookman-chronicler) to replace the "princes" subordinated to the Kievan prince by boyars. One can see the clear traces and at the same time results of these corrections in the two edited versions of the treaty of 911:

Laurentian MS (PSRL I, p. 33)	Hypatian MS (PSRL II, p. 24)
poslani ot Olega velikogo knjazja rus'kago i ot vseh iže sut' pod rukoju jego svetlyh i velikih knjaz' i jego velikih bojar	*poslani ot Olega velikago knjazja ruskago i ot vseh iže sut' pod rukoju jego svetlyh bojar*

[18] See A. A. Šahmatov, *Povest' vremennych let i eë istočniki*, *Trudy otdela drevnerusskoj literatury*, vol. IV, 1940, pp. 111—122; B. A. Larin, *Lekcii po istorii russkogo literaturnogo jazyka X—seredina XVII v.*, Moskva 1975, pp. 24—52.

[19] H. Łowmiański, *Początki Polski* [*The Beginnings of Poland*], vol. III, Warszawa 1967, p. 481. The influence of this thesis is clearly seen in the studies mentioned in footnote 2.

In view of the MS tradition, in particular the wording of the treaty of 944, it is impossible to accept the simplest explanation, namely that *i velikih knjaz' i jego velikih* is a later interpolation intended to complement the original wording *svetlyh bojar.*[20] On the contrary, it appears that marginal notes were present in the common protograph of both versions, which attempted to lend precision to the terminology by substituting "boyars" for the enigmatic "princes" who were subordinated to the prince of Kiev. The scribe of the version transmitted in the *Laurentian Chronicle* mistakenly treated these marginal notes as a completion and thus interpolated the word "boyars". In contrast the scribe of the version in the *Hypatian Chronicle* correctly understood the intention of the writer of the MS, which he copied, and eliminated the word "princes". In the original version of the translation they figured as Oleg's subordinates : *pod rukoju* is a literal translation of *hypocheirioi* or *hoi hypo cheira.*[21]

It must seem surprising that these subordinate princes were furnished with two epithets *svetlye i velikye* whereas the chief prince Oleg had to be content with one. It cannot be excluded that the Greek original read *lamproi kai megaloi archontes* and that the second epithet had to be interpreted in another manner than when referring to Oleg ; perhaps it was translated as "recognized", "respected" or simply as "many".[22] Another poss-

---

[20] A. A. Zimin proposed such an emendation in PRP I, pp. 6, 25. Compare also with Cross's translation, p. 66 : "...sent by Oleg, Great Prince of Rus', and by all the serene and great princes and the great boyars under his sway". It is perplexing to encounter the view that the *svetlye knjazi* of the treaty of 911 are closely analogous to *Svet* (*-malik*), the ruler of the Slavs mentioned in an Arabic source from the 9th century. This exercise in popular etymology serves to support the thesis that Kievan Rus' possessed a feudal structure roughly a century before Oleg ; see B. Rybakov, *Kievskaja Rus'...*, pp. 274—276. In fact it is not clear whether the Arabic source contains the name or the title of the Slavic ruler. The original account cannot be older than the last third of the 9th century. Unfortunately B. Rybakov has not familiarized himself with the present state of research ; see Fr. Kmietowicz, *Die Titel der Slavenherrscher in der sog. "Anonymen Mitteilung"—einer orientalischen Quelle (Ende des IX. Jahrhunderts)*, in : "Folia Orientalia", vol. XIX, 1978, pp. 13—34.

[21] Cf. N. Lavrovskij, *O vizantijskom elemente...*, pp. 93—96.

[22] Constantinos Porphyrogenitos (De adm. imp. 32, p. 154) relates the imprisonment by the Serbians of the son of the Bulgarian ruler together with twelve distinguished boyars : *meta kai boiladōn dōdeka megalōn.* For *bojare velicii* in the sense of distinguished, noble boyars, see PSRL II, cols : 724, 730, 910. Cf. also *velikie i menšie bojare* in the church Statute of

ibility is that the two Slavic adjectives were equivalent to a composite Greek superlative of one of the epithets with which Byzantine dignitaries were honoured; the text might have read *archontes periphanestatoi (splendissimi, illustrissimi), lamprotatoi (clarissimi, illustrissimi), peribleptotatoi (spectabilissimi), megaloprepestatoi (magnificentissimi).*[23]

We can gain an insight into the sense of the passage in question in the treaty of 911 by comparing the Greek text of the decisions of the council of Chalcedon of 451 with its Slavic version found in the *Nomocanon* translated in Bulgaria in the first half of the 10th century. The oldest extant MS *Efrem's kormčaja*, was copied in Rus' at the beginning of the 12th century. The members of the council, *oi megaloprepestatoi kai endoxotatoi archontes kai hē hyperhyēs synklētos* were translated as *velelepotnii i slavnii knjazi i velicii boljari.*[24] The Slavic translator rendered the second *kai* as a connective "i/and" whereas it is actually the equivalent of "namely", "indeed". The church fathers attending the council were first called "magnificant and glorious archontes" and thereafter their gathering was termed an "extraordinary senate".[25] In

the 13th century attributed to Yaroslav the Wise (*Drevnerusskie knjažeskie ustavy XI—XV vv.*, ed. Ja. Ščapov, Moskva 1976, p. 86). See also the frequent phrase ot *mala i do velika*, that it to say, from all walks of life: the lower and the noble upper classes (PSRL II, pp. 192, 348, 369, 639, 710). Georgios Hamartolos reports that Mohammed's wife came from a "famous" family: *velika* [*periphanēs*] *bo rodu i bogata*; see *Hronika Georgia Amartola v drevnem slavjanorusskom perevode*, ed. V. M. Istrin, vol. I, Petrograd 1920, p. 449. For the use of the adjective *velik, velii* for the Greek *polys* [*numerous*] and *mnog* [*many*] for *megas*, see *ibidem*, vol. III: *Lexicon*, Leningrad 1930 (reprint 1972), pp. 120, 152; *Slovnik Jazyka Staroslověského*, vol. I, Praha 1966, (henceforth SJS), p. 171 f.

[23] For the translation of Greek compound adjectives into simple words in Slavic see A. Budilovič, *Issledovanije jazyka drevneslavjanskogo perevoda 13 slov Grigorija Bogoslova po rukopisi XI v.* St. Petersburg 1871, p. 101 ff., and the Greek-Slavic dictionary in *Hronika Georgia Amartola...*, ed. V. M. Istrin, vol. III, Petersburg 1920. *Megaloprepēs* (magnificent) is translated as *velmi lep* or *velmi česten*. *Lampros* is translated as *svetl* or *slaven* and *periphanēs* as *slaven, svetl, velik*.

[24] *Drevneslavjanskaja Kormčaja XIV titulov bez tolkovanij*, vol. I ed. V. N. Beneševič, St. Petersburg 1906, p. 129. It is not unusual to call the bishops *archontes*; (cf. Apostolic Constitutions 2, 28).

[25] *Synkletos* means frequently the senate which assisted the emperor in Constantinople and was usually translated as *boljare*, sometimes as *boljarskij čin, boljarskij sbor*. *Hronika Georgia Amartola...*, vol. III, p. 172, 210, S—S I, p. 136 f. Cf. further S. Zavadskaja, *"Boljarin"—"Bojarin" v drevnerusskih piśmiennyh istočnikah*, in: *Drevnejšie gosudarstva na territorii SSSR (za 1985 god)*, Moskva 1986, pp. 89—94.

two other places in the same resolutions, when the members of the council are called *archontes*, the Slavic translator used alternatively as *knjazi* and *boljari*.[26]

Consequently the assumption appears justified that the preliminary protocol of the treaty of 911 employed similar alternating terms for the entourage of the ruler of Kiev. The translator who preferred verbatim rendition, had difficulties with the text. This was noted by the editor of the *Primary Chronicle*, who attempted to make corrections, when included the texts of the treaties in his work.

The preceding discussion suggests a number of possible solutions in order to emphasize more strongly the groundlessness of mechanically applying foreign socio-political terminology to the East Slavic society.

The oldest translations demonstrate that *archōn* was translated as *knjaz'* to designate not only the ruler but also various subordinate dignitaries.[27] Byzantine sources also use the term *archontes*, together with *dynastoi* and *megistanes* to designate representatives of the Slavic ruling class; the magnates who appear in South Slavic sources are usually referred to by the generic term *boljary*, whereas Latin sources refer to them as *principes*, *primates*, *maiores*, *optimates*, or *meliores*. The indentification of *archōn* with *knjaz'* must have been deeply rooted in the language of those Slavs who were within the Greek sphere of influence, since the Hellenized author of the *vita* of Constantine-Cyril, the apostle of the Slavs, designated those belonging to the entourage of Moravian prince Rostislav as *knjazi* (cap. XIV: "*Rostislav bo, Morav'skij knjaz'... svet stvori s knjazi svoimi i s Moravlany*"[28]).

---

[26] *Drevneslavjanskaja Kormčaja...*, p. 126, 127. The phrase *hoi megaloprepestatoi kai endoxotatoi archontes* was first translated as *velelepotnii i slavnii boljari* and later as *vellepii slavnii knjazi*.

[27] See SJS, vol. I, p. 136 f., vol. II, p. 94; J. Ferluga, *Byzantium on the Balkans...*, p. 311—319 and index; idem, "*Archōn*" in *Lexikon des Mittelalters*, vol. I, 1970, p. 911; H. Łowmiański, *Początki Polski*, vol. III, pp. 474—476. On p. 480 the author does not share A. Presnjakov's skepticism of the value of the treaties as a source of social terminology. However, this terminology cannot be considered in the abstract but is a translation of a well-known and commonly used Greek terminology. See the semantic diversity of the word *archōn* in Constantine Porphyrogenitos, *De administrando imperii*, ed. 1967, in the Index.

[28] *Vita Constantini*, ch. 14, ed. P. Lavrov in *Materialy po istorii*

By contrast the Latin sources use terms such as *primates*, *primores*, *comites*, *seniores* when refering to the mighty of Moravia. The semantic freedom in the use of the term *knjaz'/knęź* is without doubt derived from an older period, when the title was not reserved exclusively for members of a single hereditary ruling dynasty. As is shown by history of Rogvold, prince of Polock, and by that of Mal, prince of the Drevljane, the clan chieftains of ancient Rus' disappeared together with the independence of their territories, over which the dynasty of Ryurik extended its rule.

The conviction that the princely title was of the highest order and applicable to the sovereign ruler is clearly confirmed in the second "Miscellany" of Svjatoslav, a collection of various texts translated from the Greek and compiled in 1076. The term *ho basileus* is translated here as *cesar'* when it refers to a specified Roman or Byzantine emperor, but as *knjaz'* when referring to a ruler as such. The term *archōn* which appears in the original in the sense of ruler is translated by the more general term *vlastel'*.[29] It is characteristic that the Rusian translator of Georgios Monachos rendered *archōn as knjaz'* when the subject was the Bulgarian ruler, but in other cases, depending on the context, as *boljarin*, *vlastel'* or *starejšina*.[30]

Summing up, we have established that the text of the treaties provides no grounds for the supposition that the official title "Grand Prince" existed in Rus' in the 10th century, or that a group of nobles close to the Rusian ruler—barring his relatives—used the princely title. Clear testimony to the fact that

---

vozniknovenija drevnejšej slavjanskoj pis'mennosti, Leningrad 1930, p. 26, H. Łowmiański, *Początki Polski... [Poland's Beginnings...]*, vol. III, p. 470, views this account as the complete confirmation of his thesis of "the dynastic origin of the magnates". However, he underestimates the literary nature of the work which is closely related to Byzantine hagiography. The absence of ties between the noble families and the Mojmir dynasty, which would give them the right to ascend the throne, has been pertinently underlined in the relevant literature; see T. Wasilewski, *Morawskie państwo [Moravian State]*, in: SSS III, p. 292.

[29] See *Izbornik 1076*, Moskva 1965, p. 296/715, 367/776, 335/777, 515, 517, 518/741, 674, 675/816 and Index. The notes refer to both Slavic and Greek text.

[30] *Hronika Georgia Amartola*, vol. III, p. 33. Similarly, in an 11th century MS of the homilies of Gregory of Nazianzus *archōn* corresponds to *knjaz'*, *vlastel*, *boljarin*; see A. Budilovič, *Issledovanie jazyka...*, p. 71. See also SJS, vol. I, p. 136, 199; vol. II, p. 94 ff.

the title "Grand Prince" did not even exist in Byzantium in the middle of the 10th century is given by the Emperor himself who concluded the treaty of 944 with the "great", that is the chief, prince of Rus' Igor' and who received later Igor's widow Olga in his palace on the Bosporus. When he wanted to emphasize the sovereignty of Olga's power he added *hēgemōn* to her title *archontissa Rhōsias.* Nor can one find any confirmation for the suggestion that the princely titles of the Byzantine-Rusian treaties of 911 and 944 is due to the influence of Scandinavian terminology : *yfirkonungr/velikyi knjaz'* and *smalkonungar/knjazi* —subordinate princes.[31]

Recourse to the first "Miscellany" of Svjatoslav of 1073, as proof that the ruler of Kiev used the grand princely title in the 11th century is also misguided. In the colophon Svjatoslav is indeed given the title *velikyi knjaz'* and *velikyi v knjaz'eh knjaz'* ; however no one has noted in this connection that the miscellany was translated from the Greek for the Bulgarian ruler (*velikyi v cesar'eh*) Symeon (893—927), and that the Rusian scribe copied the rhetorically inflated colophon substituting the name of his patron for the name of Bulgarian tsar. Similarly, therefore, the colophon of the Kievan bookman who wrote "this miscelanny for the great prince Svjatoslav", should be seen as another specimen of such adaptation, influenced by the panegyric for Symeon."[32] The influence of the epithet *megas* in Byzantine encomia to praise the ruler also plays a role here. The term had the same semantic import not only in the Bulgarian but also in

---

[31] A. Soloviev, *Byzance...*, No. I, p. 252 ; No. VIII, p. 148, advanced this hypothesis. In view of the Scandinavian origins of the Rusian envoys, he endeavored to show that *rex Russiae* in the Latin sources was inspired by the title *yfirkonungr/velikyi knjaz'*. However, in the texts which Soloviev himself produces in his article *"Reges" et "Regnum Russiae"* (reprinted in his *Byzance...*, No. VIII, pp. 143—173) the title *knjaz'* was the exact equivalent of the Latin *rex*. Perhaps the clearest proof of this is found in Abbot Daniel who addressed Balduin I, King of Jerusalem, as *knjaže moi* (*my king* !) ; see A. Poppe, review of K. Seemann, *Abt Daniil, Wallhahrtsbericht*, in : *Russia Mediaevalis*, vol. II, 1975, p. 172.

[32] *Izbornik Svjatoslava 1073 goda. Faksimil'noe izdanie*, Moskva 1983, folium 2v., 263v. ; E. F. Karskij, *Slavjanskaja kirillovskaja paleografija*, Moskva 1979 (reprint of the edition of 1928), p. 282. See also B. St. Angelov, *Pohvala carju Simeonu*, in : *Izbornik Svjatoslava 1073 g. Sbornik statej*, Moskva 1977, p. 247 ff.

the old Rusian translated literature. The colophon of 1076 miscellany, proves that the epithet was not part of the princely title: the Kievan ruler Svjatoslav is given the simple title *knjaz' rus'sky zemlja.*[33]

Not even the text of the Chronicles from the 11th and beginning of the 12th century, contrary to some assertions, furnishes proof that the lord of Kiev used an expanded title: in all three chronicle entries the adjective *velikyi* added to the princely title carries a distinctly panegyric characterisation. The entries for 1054, 1093 and 1125 are drawn from the necrologies of the Kievan princes Yaroslav, his son Vsevolod and his grandson Vladimir Monomach. We know of Byzantine examples from the time of the Comneni of the use of *megas* for a recently deceased ruler.[34] To assume however on the basis of the necrology of Yaroslav for the year 1054 that this usage was known on the Bosporus even earlier would be too risky, since the entire entry for 1054 shows signs of subsequent editing, dating to the end of the 11th century. One must note that this epithet is not used in the necrologies of other Kievan rulers of the 11th and the beginning of the 12th century. From this we may conclude therefore that the Byzantine model was adopted only in the milieu of Vladimir Monomach, no doubt with the intention of emphasizing the special rights of the descendants of Vsevolod to the throne of Kiev. That the title "Grand Prince" was unknown to the ruler of Kiev in the last quarter of the 11th century is proven clearly by the period in which Prince Vsevolod reigned alone (1078—1093). After the death of his brother Izjaslav, Vsevolod ascended the throne of Kiev "having assumed sovereignty over all Rus' " (*priim vlast' rus'skuju vsju*). At that time, resisting the centrifugal tendencies in the land, Vsevolod added the title "Prince of all Rus"/*archōn pasēs Rhōsias* to the legend of his seal to emphasize his sovereign rights.[35]

33 *Izbornik 1076*, Moskva 1965, p. 701.

34 See: PSRL I, cols. 161, 215, 293; II, cols. 149, 207, 289. See also S. A. Vysockij, *Drevnerusskie nadpisi Sofii Kievskoj*, Kiev 1966, p. 18 (graffitto No. 4); P. Schreiner, *Zur Bezeichnung "Megas"*, p. 179.

35 See: A. Soloviev, *Byzance...*, No. V, p. 435 f., V. L. Janin, *Aktovye pečati*, pp. 168—170. See also A. Poppe, *Pieczęć ruska z Kruszwicy* [A Rusian Seal from Kruszwica], "Slavia Antiqua", vol. XXVI, 1979, pp. 121—126.

Even when Vladimir Monomach "took over the rule over all the Russian land" (*preja knjaženie vseja russky zemlja*),[36] (1113-1125) there is no evidence for the title of "Grand Prince" in Kiev. The best demonstration of this is epistle of the Greek metropolitan of Kiev Nikephoros, in which he addresses the Kievan ruler more than twenty times, comparing his power with that of the emperor, yet calling him simply "my prince" (*knjaže moi*). Not once do we find the word *velikyi* among the *epitheta ornantia* which accompany the title.[37]

The adjective *velikyi* also appears before the names of deceased princes in expressions equivalent to those containing *megas* characteristic of a deceased Byzantine emperor. The epithet "the Great" is used to embellish the name of the Baptiser of Rus', Vladimir, very late and then inconsistently. In the entries in the *Hypatian Chronicle* under the years 1149 and 1229 we read: "Vladimir the Great, who baptised the land of Rus'." However, in the entries for 1169 and 1173 in the Hypatian as well as in the *Laurentian Chronicle* we read: "Vladimir, who baptised the land of Rus',".[38] This panegyrical epithet was certainly added to Vladimir's name as a result of comparing him with Constantine the Great.[39] One can not, however, positively determine whether the accompanying epithet *velikyi*, when added to the names of other deceased princes, signifies praise and recognition, or is used in the sense of "former", "old", "elder". In the 12th century this epithet is applied particularly to the descendants of Vladimir Monomach and doubtless served in many cases to

---

[36] *Die altrussischen hagiographischen Erzählungen und liturgischen Dichtungen über die heiligen Boris und Gleb*, (after 1916 edition of D. Abramovič, chosen by L. Müller), Münich 1967, p. 64.

[37] Published in *Russkie dostopamjatnosti*, vol. I, Moskva 1815, pp. 61—75 and by A. Dölker, *Der Fastenbrief des Metropoliten Nikifor an den Fürsten Vladimir Monomach*, Tübingen 1985, pp. 16—73 (with German translation). The Lenten epistle is preserved in three MSS, the oldest being from the end of the 15th century or beginning of the 16th. However, Vladimir is called "Grand Prince" only in the heading, which from the 15th century on was typical of the additions to the titles of rulers of the Kievan era.

[38] PSRL I, col. 357; II, cols. 383, 554, 758; cf. col. 821 under the year 1254, where Vladimir is already called *svjatyi*. See also PSRL I, col. 479 under the year 1263.

[39] See *Des Metropoliten Ilarion Lobrede auf Vladimir den Heiligen*, ed. L. Müller, Wiesbaden 1962, p. 117: *podobniče velikago Konstantina.*

distinguish them from their namesakes who were the chroniclers' contemporaries.[40] The oldest use of *velikyi* occurs in the *Primary Chronicle* in the entry for 1030 concerning the death of the Polish prince (*umre Boleslav velikyi v Lasěh*), and is generally understood to mean "the Great". However this event was recorded in the Kievan Caves Monastery only in the 1070s, when Boleslav's namasake reigned in Poland, and it was a matter of distinguishing the well-know Boleslavs. Consequently the Kievan scribe called the first of them "Boleslav the elder".[41]

Princes were also given the epithet *velikyi* during their lives. When the *Novgorod Chronicle* reports that *Svjatoslav velikyi Vsevolodič* entered Novgorod in 1180—1181 he uses the epithet to distinguish the eldest prince from other contemporary princes with the same name. Svjatoslav was indeed prince of Kiev from 1176 until 1184 but precisely in the time between September 1180 and the summer of 1181 he was driven from throne by his rival Ryurik.[42] On the other hand the author of the *Lay of the Host of Igor* uses epithet *Velikyi Svjatoslav* to designate the position of this Kievan senior.[43] However, Svjatoslav did not use the title "Grand Prince" as a senior of Kiev. Two isolated exceptions are the traces of a later redaction of the text of the *Kievan Chronicle* by Moisej, abbot of Vydubiči, in 1200. This panegyrist of Ryurik, Svjatoslav's successor in Kiev (1194 until 1202 and with interruptions until 1210) very frequently bestowed the grand princely

---

[40] This is how one should interpret the references to Mstislav and Yurij Dolgorukij although gradually the term was linked with their role as the founders of two princely lines, the senior and junior lines of the Monomachoviči. See PSRL II, col. 303 under the year 1140, col. 525 (year 1164) cols. 609, 619, 702 (under the years 1179, 1180, 1197); PSRL I, cols. 379, 406 (under the years 1177, 1188); *Novgorodskaja pervaja letopis' staršego i mladšego izvodov*, ed. A. Nasonov, Moskva—Leningrad 1950; (hereafter LN I), p. 37 (year 1182).

[41] PSRL I, col. 149; II, col. 137.

[42] "Vnide Svjatoslav velikyi Vsevolodič Novugorodu", L. N. I, p. 36. Several lines above the chronicler distinguishes him as "the grandson of Oleg". It is clear that the compiler of the chronicle copilation, who worked at the beginning of the 13th century, took pains to distinguish between this Svjatoslav and the other Svjatoslav, who was also Vsevolodovič, but the grandson of Yurij Dolgorukij and who became prince of Novgorod in 1200 (LN, I, p. 44).

[43] Cf. A. Poppe, *On the Title of Grand Prince in the Tale of Ihors' Campaign*, in: *Eucharisterion: Essays to Omeljan Pritsak*, "Harvard Ukrainian Studies", vol. III—IV, 1979—1980, pp. 684—689.

title upon his protector, even when he wrote about the time when Svjatoslav reigned in Kiev.[44]

The first Rusian prince who regularly made use of the grand princely title was Vsevolod, prince of Vladimir-Suzdal', son of Yurij Dolgorukij, later given the sobriquet "The Big Nest". L. K. Goetz' observation remains to the point, that Vsevolod is the first prince to whom "Grand Prince" is systematically applied during his life as an official title.[45] To this one must add that the systematic use of the grand princely title is not found from the first years of his rule in Vladimir (1176—1212) but only from the end of the 12th century. Apart from the isolated references from the 1180s, which could be the result of a later reworking of the chronicle, the consistent application of the grand princely title to Vsevolod begins in 1190 and becomes predominant after 1195.[46] The references to *velikyi Vsevolod*, on the contrary, under the years 1179, 1181, 1186 and 1187 could be interpreted as hints of Vsevolod's preeminence over other princes; but at least in a few cases the chronicler simply wanted to emphasize Vsevolod's age

---

[44] See PSRL I, col. 397, under the year 1186; II, col. 651 under the year 1185. A good example of the editorial zeal of the panegyrist of Ryurik Rostislavič are the entries under the year 1183 and 1185 in which Ryurik is mentioned after the current senior of Kiev but given the title of "Grand Prince": "The Lord God gave victory to the princes of Rus', to Svjatoslav Vsevolodovič and to Grand Prince Ryurik Rostislavič". PSRL II, col. 630; see also col. 636.

[45] L. K. Götz, *Der Titel Grossfürst...*, p. 59, A similar view was advanced by M. Hrushevsky in 1905, as well as by A. Shahmatov and M. Prislkov in 1940. For the author of the monograph devoted to Vladimir-Suzdal' principality the grand princely title of Vsevolod is obvious (cf. Ju. Limonov, *Vladimiro-Suzdalskaja Rus'*, p. 106), but the whole issue of adoption of this title by the ruler of Suzdalia does not exist. That this title was still not instituted before 1176 is evident from the Chronicle-records about prince Mihalko (PSRL I, col. 373—379), elder brother and predecessor of Vsevolod. Mihalko is named without title or simply as *knjaz'* and only once it is mentioned that the townspeople at Vladimir were happy to see *velikogo knjazja vseja Rostovskija zemla* (PSRL I, col. 377). Since the second prince after Mihalko in "the whole land of Rostov" (older description of Vladimir-Suzdal principality) was Vsevolod, it is clear that Mihalko is called here *velikyi knjaz'* in the sense "chief prince".

[46] See the almost consistent use of the grand princely title in the chronicle of Vladimir-Suzdal' after the year 1196 (PSRL I: col. 412 ff.). This title is also found in the Kievan chronicle but one notes the tendency to call Vsevolod simply "Prince of Suzdal'". In many other references worded in the customary manner the prince is named but not given a title; see PSRL II: 694 ff. Cf. also W. Vodoff, *La titulature...*, p. 23.

vis-à-vis other princes with the same name.[47] We should consider the appearance of the "Grand Princess" in the chronicles as an important indication of the permanence of the grand princely title among Vsevolod's titles.[48]

The recognition of Vsevolod's grand princely title in other Rusian lands must have been met with certain reservations. We can observe in the Kievan Chronicle writing that Vsevolod was inconsistently called "Grand Prince" in the south ; the chronicler's reservation reflects the inconstancy of the political influence of the ruler of Suzdal'. Novgorod took an unusual position : local chroniclers clearly avoided calling Vsevolod "Grand Prince", undoubtedly because they rightly assumed that they would not only be recognizing a fact but also Vsevolod's right to suzerainty over the city. The reality of their mutual relations, however, compelled them to be flexible : the Novgorod envoys who arrived in Vladimir in the autumn of 1199 knew full well that they could not permit themselves a breach of protocol and therefore addressed Vsevolod *Ty gospodine knjaže velikyi Vsevolod Gjurgevič*.[49]

The use of the grand princely title by the sovereigns of Kiev has a markedly secondary character and is much more a response to the ambitions of Vladimir on the Kljazma River and an emphasis of the traditional position of Kiev. The title of "Grand Prince" was not the official title of the Kievan ruler Svjatoslav (d. 1194). However the situation changed during the reign of his

---

[47] See PSRL II, cols. 658, 659, 613, 624, 653. Only once does the chronicler clearly state that he is referring to Vsevolod as to the elder of the Prince of Pronsk Vsevolod, son of Gleb : *Vsevolod že ide s nimi na svet ko Vsevolodu velikomu Jurgeviču*, PSRL I, col. 402 (under the year 1186).

[48] See the entries for 1202, 1205, 1206 (PSRL I, cols. 417, 421, 424). The last reference is the necrology. It is not clear whether the title *knjagini velikaja*, applied to Roman's widow, reflects his grand princely title or to her role as regent. See the entries in the chronicle of Halič-Volhynia under the years 1208, 1209, 1213, 1215, (PSRL II, cols. 726, 727, 733—735). Cf. W. Vodoff, *La titulature...*, p. 20, n. 117. It is obvious at any rate that *velikaja* did not denote the "elder princess" or "princes mother" since none of her sons, all of whom were minors, could have been married. An example of *velikaja* used in this sense appears to be the reference under the year 1258 to the widow of Prince Constantine, who died in 1230, as "Grand Princess" See PSRL I : col. 475.

[49] PSRL I, col. 415 ; see also LN I, p. 49. Vsevolod is given the title of "Grand Prince" once under the year 1205, but the political change in Novgorod in 1210 was such, that even the death of this influential ruler was not noted. Cf. also W. Vodoff. *La titulature...*, pp. 21, 23.

successor, Ryurik Rostislavič, the nominal sovereign of Kiev, who clearly adapted himself—albeit inconsistently—to the situation created by Vsevolod. Even Roman, the Prince of Halič-Volhynia, who took possession of Kiev shortly before his death in 1205 appears to have acquired the new title.[50] In the 13th century the rulers of other Rusian principalities, but above all the sons and successors of Vsevolod, followed his footsteps.[51]

Yet another view is erroneous, namely that, which maintains that the grand princely title was originally used by the ruler of Kiev, and that the rulers of other principalities already assumed the title in the first half of the 12th century. Evidence for this is found in the inscription on a drinking bowl which belonged to Prince Volodimir of Černihov, who was killed in battle in May of 1151 : *a se čara knjazja, Volodimirova Davidoviča, a kto iz neě p'et', tomu na zdorov'e a hvalja Boga svoego ospodarja velikogo knazja* ("this is the drinking bowl of Prince Vladimir Davidovič, and this is to the health of him who drinks from it, praising God

---

[50] See PSRL II : col. 715 under year 1201 where the grand princely title is linked with the dominion over all of the land of Rus'. However, this entry was made after Roman's death in June of 1205, PSRL II, col. 716 f., 721 (*velikago Romana*), 726. Once again in the Chronicle of Vladimir-Suzdal' we see the clear tendency to ascribe to Roman the recognition of Vsevolod's supremacy, even though the chronicler admits that both of these princes acted in unison to occupy the throne of Kiev in 1202 (PSRL I : col. 418 ff.).

[51] Although the title is not used consistently hereafter, this can be explained by the nature of the chronicle account which has been abridged. On the other hand, the facts of the chronicle should be carefully analyzed, since the author of the study on the grand princely title in Vladimir-Suzdal' in the 13th—14th century devoted most of his attention to the 14th century : see J. P. Arrignon, *Usage et valeur du titre de Grand Prince*, pp. 173—184. One must also take account of the information in western sources. In his chronicle covering the years 1186—1227, written in 1227, Heinrich of Lettland titled the prince of Rus' as *rex* and *rex magnus*. This adjective appears to be less a part of the title than to mean "the elder" or "the late" when applied to the deceased. The terminology used by John de Plano Carpini, *Ystoria Mongalorum*, Florence, 1929 is clearer : once he calls Yaroslav Vsevolodovič, Grand Prince of Vladimir-Suzdal' and Kiev, *magnum ducem Ruscie* (p. 46) but later simply *ducem Ruscie* (pp. 112, 128). He also appears to hint at the grand princely title when he refers to Michael of Černihov as *qui fuit unus de magnis ducibus Ruscie* (p. 38). He calls the ruler of Halič-Volhynia *rex Daniel Ruscie* (p. 128). One must also consider the custom of the Halič-Volhynian chronicle to refer to several of the Polish princes of the 13th century as *velikyi knjaz'*, undoubtedly in the sense of "main prince" or "senior" ; see PSRL II, cols. 754, 756, 809, 880, 897.

and the lord of the house, the great prince").[52] The wording of this panegyric inscription is somewhat contradictory : The prince appears at the beginning without an epithet, and at the end with the term *velikyi*, which can refer to *ospodar* (here in the sense of host, lord of the house) as well as to *knjaz'* and which evidently is used in the sense of "famous, glorious".[53]

It is tempting to answer the question of what role Byzantine customs played in the origin of the grand princely title in Rus'. The first bearer of the title, who was born in 1154, spent his formative years in Byzantium (1162—1168), where he and his mother, who was probably Greek, had been banished by his older brother Andrej Bogoljubskij. Vsevolod's stay in the empire must have influenced his views on imperial ideology even though the actual idea of expanding the titles of the mightiest prince, must have matured earlier.

It is unfortunate that Byzantine-Rusian correspondence of the 11th—12th centuries is no longer extant, since it would permit us to determine whether the imperial chancery continued the 10th century custom of applying the title *megas archōn* to the princes of Rus'. The seals with reading *archōn Rhōsias*, from the 11th and the beginning of the 12th century, including those of the monarchs of Kiev from Yaroslav the Wise to Vladimir Monomach permit us to conclude that the princes of Rus', even when they were confronted with the epithet *megas*, did not take it as a part of their

---

[52] V. F. Ržiga, *Očerki iz istorii byta domongolskoj Rusi*, Moskva 1929, pp. 51—53 and 4 photographs of the inscription. B. A. Rybakov, *Russkie datirovannye nadpisi XI—XIV vekov*, Moskva 1964, No. 24, S. 28 f., plate XXIX. Rybakov treats the abbreviation *knja* which appears twice, as a suspension, which permits him to read the first one as (*čaša*) *knja[ža]* and the second as *knja[zja]*. It is to assume, however, that both are a common contraction from genitive of substantive *kn[jaz]ja*.

[53] For *ospodar'—gospodar*, in the sense of "lord of the house", see *Pravda Russkaja*, vol. II, Moskva—Leningrad 1947, pp. 477 f., 486, 609, I. Sreznevskij, *Materialy dlja slovarja drevnerusskogo jazyka*, vol. I, col. 563 ; vol. II, col. 735. In view of the subject of the inscription on the drinking bowl, it appears likelier in this case that *velikyi* belongs with *ospodar'* in the sense of "great host". For the title of ruler *gospodar/gosudar'*, see G. Stoekl, *Die Begriffe*, pp. 114 ff. ; W. Vodoff, *La titulature...*, pp. 5—19, 31 ; to Vodoff's observation we add that this title originated on the beginning of the 14th century in the bilingual chancery of the last prince of Halič (*gospodar' zemli russkoj* as translation of *Dominus terrae Russiae*) and was adopted in turn by rulers of Poland, Lithuania, Moscovy and other Rusian lands.

stock of titles but considered it to be only an occasional epithet. Otherwise they would have included it in the Greek inscriptions on their seals. Had *megas* belonged to their stock of titles they would have used it in the opening formulae as the issuers of diplomas.[54]

There is one well-known exception to this : the seal with the likeness of the Apostle Andrew and the clearly legible inscription : *Mestisthlabos megas archōn Rhōsias.*[55] This seal very likely belonged to Mstislav-Andrej, grandson of Igor and great-grandson of Yaroslav the Wise, who is mentioned several times in the *Primary Chronicle* at the turn of the 11th—12th century and who died in 1116. He was probably a prince—*izgoi* (his father is unnamed) : that is to say, a prince without land, who was constantly on some campaign. In the year 1100 fate brought him to the coast of the Black Sea, to the Byzantine possessions on the northern coast, or to Tmutorakan'. Other attempts to attribute this seal, which assume that the *megas archōn* could only refer to the ruler of Kiev and which therefore consider other Kievan princes named Mstislav, are difficult to accept for two reasons. Firstly, none of these other princes named Mstislav bore the Christian name Andrew ; and secondly, the seal exhibits no features which could permit us to date it later than the second half of the 11th century or the first quarter of the 12th century. In view of these considerations one may suppose that Prince Mstislav-Andrej, a nomadic

---

[54] The diploma of "Grand Prince" Izjaslav Mstislavovič recording a gift to the Monastery of St. Panteleimon in Novgorod (PRP, vol. II, Moskva 1953, p. 104) is no exception. The diploma is conventionelly dated 1146—1154, precisely because of this title : that is, to the period in which Izjaslav was senior in Kiev. This date was convincingly rejected by V. L. Janin, *Iz istorii zemlevladenija v Novgorode v 12 v.*, in : *Kultura drevnej Rusi, Festschrift for N. N. Voronin*, Moskva 1966, pp. 313—324. Janin proposes that the diploma was written in 1134 and suggests the possibility that the title was modernized by a later copyist (p. 321). Although the date of this otherwise trustworthy diploma remains a moot point, its presence in a copy from end of the 16th century permits us to suppose that we are confronting the tendency, apparent already in the 15th century, to supplement the title of old princes. Confirmation of this is found in the diplomas of Izjaslav's brother Vsevolod, prince of Novgorod from 1125 to 1137. In contrast to the original diploma for the Monastery of St. George from 1130 the two others diplomas in late 16th century copies call Vsevolod "Grand Prince" even though he never ruled in Kiev ; see PRP, vol. II, pp. 102 f. Cf. further K. R. Schmidt, *Soziale Terminologie*, p. 442.

[55] V. Janin, *Aktovye pečati...*, vol. I. No. 31, pp. 20—23, 172.

prince who stood on the lowest rung of the princely dynasty, recommended that the epithet *megas* with which he had probably been honored in correspondence, be repeated in the inscription of his seal. Vladimir Monomach acted similarly, causing the inscription *sphragis Basileion tou paneigenestatou archontos Rhōsias tou Monomachou* to be engraved on one of his seals.[56] Regardless of the accuracy of the attribution to the landless Mstislav (once can consider two other princes with the same name : Mstislav Izjaslavič, who died in 1061, and Mstislav Svjatopolkovič who died in 1097, neither of whom ruled in Kiev), it is difficult to have any doubts as to the dating of the seal. This would seem to indicate that the Byzantines tended to add the epithet *megas* to the Rusian princely title, regardless of the political position of the bearer. The Rusian princes could have interpreted this epithet in particular as "famous", "glorious", "powerful", since the adjective *velikyi* is used in this sense in contemporary Old Rusian literature.[57]

Perhaps the entire matter is much simpler. Possibly *megas* on the seal should not be linked with the title *archōn* but with the name Mstislav. *Megas* after the name would be odd in Greek if the inscription were not a translation from the Old Rusian : *Mstislav velikyi*. For among the living princes of the same name, Mstislav, the grandson of Igor and the great grandson of Yaroslav the Wise was the elder. Perhaps Mstislav, who was something of an outcast, used this epithet to compensate for his position. The *Novgorod Chronicle* furnishes a good example of the occasional

---

[56] *Ibidem*, No. 25, pp. 16, 170.

[57] See, for example, PSRL I, col. 124 : *Volodimir že velikim mužem stvori togo* ; *velikyi* frequently occurs in the sense of "famous", "powerful", "noble" in the *Kievan Caves Patericon*, several times alone in the tale about Moisej. Cf. *Das Paterikon des Kiever Höhlenklosters nach der Ausgabe von D. Abramovič*, ed. D. Tschižewskij, *Slavische Propyläen*, vol. II, Munich, 1964, pp. 142—147. See also footnote 22 supra ; see PSRL II, col. 807 ff. under the year 1250, which reads : "*o zleje zla čest' tatarskaja : Danilu Romanoviču knjazju byvšu veliku, obladavšu Rus'skoju zemleju... nyne sedit' na kolenu i holopom nazyvajetsja*". This is not an allusion to the grand princely title ; *velik* is used here in the sense of "powerful" or "famous". About different meanings of *velikyi* see also : V. Peretz, *K izučenju Slova o polku Igoreve, IV : Epitety v "Slove" i v ustnoj tradicii*, in : *Izvestija otdelenija russkogo jazyka i slovesnosti*, vol. XXX, Moskva 1926, pp. 155—158.

emphasis of age-seniority: in the account of the construction of the Church of the Savior at Neredica the donor, who is mentioned frequently, is called *velikyi knjaz' Jaroslav, syn Vladimirov, vnuk Mstislavov* only once. The chronicler clearly intended to distinguish between this Yaroslav, the brother-in-law of Vsevolod, Prince of Suzdal', and Vsevolod's son Yaroslav who was younger and well-known in Novgorod.[58]

In the 14th century the imperial chancery always used the title *rex* or *megas rex* for the ruler of Rus' in its correspondence; this was equivalent to the title *knjaz'* or *velikyi knjaz'* which was common in Rus'. These latinized titles, applied to the princes of Rus', cannot be traced beyond the second half of the 13th century, and must, therefore, be associated with the experience of the Latin (i.e. Western) domination of Byzantium.

Henceforth the Byzantines took into consideration the previously institutionalized nature of the grand princely office in Rus' and, without sparing other decorative epithets, reserved the epithet *megas* exclusively for the grand princely title.[59]

This information from the 14th century cannot, therefore, be applied retrospectively to the period before the Tatar invasion of Eastern Europe and the Latin conquest of Constantinople. The situation in the second half of the 12th century is nevertheless, somewhat illuminated by the 17th century copy, which contains signs of authenticity, of the old Rusian translation of an epistle of the Patriarch Lukas Chrysoberges to the Prince of Vladimir and Suzdal' Andrej Bogoljubsky, from about 1168. The patriarch, restraining the ambitious prince from the idea of founding a new metropolitan bishopric in Vladimir, calls him *preblagorodivyi knjaže (paneugenestate archōn)*, as opposed to the prince of Kiev whom he calls *velikyi knjaz' vseja Rusi (megas archōn pasēs*

---

[58] LN I, p. 44; see also pp. 35, 37, 51, 53 ff.

[59] See the extant Greek diplomas from the 14th century in *Pamjatniki drevnegò russkogo kanoničeskogo prava*, vol. I, St. Petersburg 1880, Appendix Nos. 3, 20, 21, 28, 29, 40, 41, 46. The Byzantine-Rusian term *megas rex/velikyi knjaz'* influenced the *intitulatio* and *inscriptio* in the chancery of the Polish kings; see, for example, Casimir's diploma from the year 1351 ...*velikogo korola krakovskogo i gospodarja ruskoje zemle* and Jagiello's from the year 1388 *velikyi korol polskoi*, see: A. Sobolevskij, S. Ptašycki, *Paleografičeskie snimki s russkih gramot preimuščestvenno XIV v.*, St. Petersburg 1903, Nos. 6, 7, 9, 10, 23.

Rhōsias). The jurisdictional rights of the metropolitan of all Rus' were also emphasized.[60] The substitution of *pasēs Rhōsias* for the brief *Rhōsias* in the title of the prince and the metropolitan had a specific political implication and expressed not only the position of the patriarch but also the policy of the Empire towards Rus'. It was precisely in the second half of the 12th century that the titles of the metropolitans of Kiev—documented in particular by their seals—accentuated their ecclesiastical sovereignty over all of Rus'. The princely feuds of the 1140s and 1150s, the political and ecclesiastic chaos, clearly underlined the danger that the archdiocese of Rus' would distintegrate, and that the jurisdictional dependence on Constantinople be broken. The Byzantines naturally understood the necessity of repeatedly recognizing and supporting sovereignty of the metropolitan and the prince of Kiev over all of Rus'. This policy did not fully succeed owing to overpowerful centrifugal tendencies. However, its partial success meant the maintenance of the ecclesiastical unity of Rus'—thanks to the support of her clergy—until the end of the 13th century.

The epistle of the Patriarch to the Prince of Vladimir and Suzdal' contains a trace of the Empire's diplomatic initiative at that time. In this context the epithet *megas/velikyi*, combined with an emphatic emphasis of the extent of the Prince of Kiev's dominion, acquired a clearly, political content and was intended to mean that the *megas archōn pasēs Rhōsias* was the chief prince, the foremost ruler of Rus'. This title, whose use was dictated by concern for the centrifugal tendencies in Rus', undoubtedly was constantly used in Byzantine correspondence with Rus' during that period. From here it was only one step to transforming the adjective *velikyi* into a permanent element of the Rusian ruler's title. As it turned out it was not the Kievan senior who first adopted this title, but the ruler of the dynamically developing northeastern region of Rus'.[61] The fact that Andrej Bogoljubsky's

[60] *Pamjatniki* No. 3, cols. 63, 66, 68; cf. with P. Sokolov, *Russkij arhierej iz Vizantii*, Kiev 1913, (repr. 1971), pp. 98 ff., 136 ff. N. N. Voronin, *Andrej Bogolubski i Luka Hrizoverg*, "Vizantijskij Vremennik", vol. XXI, 1962, pp. 29—50. A thorough study of this epistle is found in L. K. Götz, *Staat und Kirche in Altrussland*, Berlin 1908, pp. 175—195.

[61] See V. A. Kučkin, *Rostovo-suzdal'skaja zemlja v pervoj tret'i XIII v.*, "Istorija SSSR", 1969, No. 3, pp. 76—94. M. Hellmann,

troops conquered and sacked Kiev in March of 1169 and that Andrej placed a man loyal to himself on the throne of Kiev is characteristic of this change. Andrej, who was the brother and predecessor of Vsevolod, had ambitious political plans to "acquire the right of the eldest in Rus' ". However, contrary to the view based on isolated chronicle accounts edited shortly after the prince's death, these plans did not include assuming the grand princely title.[62] The attempts to reestablish the unity of the lands of Rus' with Kiev at the center failed despite the fact that during the entire second half of the 12th century attempts were made to preserve at least the appearance of unity.

The origin of the grand princely title is not, therefore—contrary to a widely held opinion—to be found in the period in which the Kievan dominion grew, its internal structure strengthened and in which the international position of its ruler was enhanced. From the time that the Kievan state was founded, expanded and grew powerful, to the era when the Kievan monarchy was at its height, that is, from the reign of Vladimir the Great at the end of the 10th century until the era of Vladimir Monomach and his son Mstislav, that is, until 1132, the rulers of Kiev were satisfied with an inalienable hereditary title to which only the members of the ruling dynasty were entitled. It included the concrete and exhaustive notion, established by custom, of sovereign power and therefore did not require any semantic elaboration. The addition of various *epitheta ornantia* could not occur without foreign influence, and when necessary one relied upon precise terms by making use of already developed Byzantine terminology. Con-

---

Wandlungen in staatlichen Leben Altrussland und Polens während des 12. Jahrhunderts, in: *Vorträge und Forschungen*, vol. XIII, 1968, 279—282. D. Wörn, *Studien zur Herrschaftsideologie des Grossfürsten Vsevolod III Bolšoe Gnezdo von Vladimir (1176—1212)*, "Jahrbücher für Geschichte Osteuropas", vol. XXVII, 1979, pp. 1—40, with extensive bibliography.

[62] The term *velikyi knjaz'* in the necrology of Andrej Bogoljubskij (see PSRL I col. 367) has another meaning, known at least from the turn of the 11th—12th centuries. That the Byzantine custom was commonly used in Rus' is evident from the Rusian chronicles' treatment of the German King Philipp of Swabia, who never formally became emperor. While Philipp was alive the chronicler refers to him as *nemečskim cesarem*, LN I, pp. 46—47. However, after Philipp had died, the chronicler wrote: *Ubien byst' cesar' velikyi Filip Rimskyi* (PSRL II col. 723).

temporary sources call those princes of Kiev who exercised power over all of Rus' "autocrat" and "sole ruler" (*samoderžec, edinoderžec, edinovlastec*). The Rusian princes did not aspire to the imperial title even though the thesis that imperial and princely power were equal is found in old Rusian literature of the 11th—12th centuries. The view that certain princes assumed the imperial title is the result of an excessively literal interpretation of the sources in which a prince is in fact given the title *cesar'*. These isolated references from the 11th—12th centuries provide, on the contrary, interesting information regarding the literary influence on, and views of the nature of princely power common to court and ecclesiastical circles. By contrast the verb *cesarstvovati*, a translation of *basileyō* was employed to accentuate the sovereign nature of princely power.[63]

The necessity of expanding the ideological content of the title of the ruler of all Rus', which perhaps first became apparent beyond the borders of Rus'—on the Bosporus—appeared in the era of the declining authority of the princes of Kiev, of the diffusion of the dynasty, of the growth of centrifugal forces and of the devaluation of the title itself. The title "Grand Prince" could not take on the function of a connecting link for the disintegrating Kievan Rus'. On the contrary, it served those princes who, while solidifying their own principalities, strove to acquire influence on matters of common concern. However, they were not backed by the throne of Kiev but by the "right of the eldest in the land of Rus' ". The new title was intended to ensure the lasting nature of their success ; even though it was not originally intended for them, it accurately expressed their own aspirations and the position which they had in fact assumed. Therefore, it was not by

[63] W. Vodoff proved that this view of the imperial title of the princes of Rus' is untenable. See his *Remarques sur la valeur du terme tsar appliqué aux princes russes avant le milieu du XVe siècle*, "Oxford Slavonic Papers", N. S., vol. XI, 1978, pp. 1—41 ; idem, *La titulature...*, pp. 28—30. One should note that the term *car'* derived from *cesar'* is not evident in Rus' before the 13th century. The paleographic reception—a contraction with a superscript letter c(s) and then its omission—certainly contributed to the phonetic transformation. However, for a long time thereafter, translations from Greek rendered *basileus* for *cesar'*. See also G. Stoekl, *Die Begriffe*, pp. 109—111.

chance that it was the ruler of the vigorous state between the Oka and Volga who was first to usurp the title of "Grand Prince". In a period in which the various lands and principalities of Rus' were rapidly growing apart, the spread of the title of "Grand Prince" was only a question of time.[64]

[64] See in detail W. Vodoff, *La titulature...*, pp. 5—12, 17—19, 21—27, where also the "inflation" of this title specially during the 15 c. is good shown.

ADDENDUM I

On M. Dimnik's study of 2004

All results of research should be subject to criticism and revision. It is therefore not inappropriate that the author of another article with the same title as ours has challenged its thesis "that the title of 'grand prince' in Rus' came into systematic use towards the end of the twelfth century, not in Kiev, but in Suzdalia." As a result of his own work, he suggests, (and in accordance with some earlier views), "the prince of Kiev styled himself *velikyj knyaz'* from the time of Yaroslav the Wise" onward, i.e., from the mid-eleventh century.[1]

To assert that a ruler's title is an "official" one implies that it is used fairly consistently by the ruler himself, his subjects, and by others abroad, at least in diplomatic relations. Only such a title can be characterized as an institutionalized one. An accurate translation of the East Slavic "*knjaz'*" in the Latin Europe of the period was "*rex*", i.e. "king", while for West Slavic rulers in the orbit of the Papacy and Reich it diminished to "*dux*" *(princeps, duke, Fürst)*, an exception being made for a *rex coronatus*.[2] The Byzantine Empire, for its part, avoided the use the titles *basileus* or *caesar* for foreign rulers, preferring instead the vague term "*archon*". MD appears to have overlooked the possibility that the adjective "*velikyj*" alongside the title of a given ruler (*knjaz', rex*, or *basileus*, etc.) could also be used in a variety of descriptive senses ("famous" or "glorious", "old", "elder", "chief", "former", "late", etc. – cf. p. 161ff., fn. 31 *above*)

MD's frequent reference to Rurikid "dynasties" ruling over Rus' is a misnomer: from the 9th until the end of 16th century, Rus' had but one Rurikid dynasty, embodied, over time, in an increasing number of branches.[3] Only the members of that Rurikid dynasty were perceived (and perceived themselves) to be the Lord's anointed; a *knjaz' ruskij* (*archon Rhosias*) had the right to rule in the territory of Rus' (i.e., receive an appanage) as part of the general jurisdiction of the dynasty. However, the actual transmission of power was a liturgical act – enthronement – and had its own terminology (*nastolovanie*).[4]

---

[1] Martin Dimnik, "The Title *Grand Prince* in Kievan Rus'", *Mediaeval Studies* 66 (2004): 253–312; the references directly to him use the initials MD, with references in brackets to pages of his paper, while those to my essay include the note "*above*".

[2] Modern English-language historiography, taking into account the later depreciation of the title *knjaz'*, has adopted the incorrect translation "prince" rather than "king" in reference to the early medieval setting, an approach that leads in turn to additional misunderstandings.

[3] See the essay "The Rurikid Dynasty or Seven Hundred Years of Shaping Eastern Europe", at the beginning of the present volume.

[4] The existence of this ceremony seems not to be fully known (cf. Dimnik: 275–276). See: Fr. Dvornik, "Byzantine Political Ideas in Kievan Russia", *DOP* 9/10, 1956: 116–121;

MD broadens the source base for addressing this question in his article, having recourse to the venerable field of sphragistics, in this case, princely seals. Nearly one hundred such seals of the 11th and 12th centuries have come down to us, about 40 of them with a portrait on the obverse of the saintly patron whose name had been bestowed on the ruler in baptism, and on the reverse, an inscription calling for divine protection. Up to the beginning of the 12th century, the inscription is in Greek, but in the reign of Vsevolod (1078–1093), texts in Cyrillic begin to appear. The only exception to the above-described pattern known to date is a seal with the Greek inscription "*Mstislav, megas archon of Rusia*". All attempts thus far to attribute this seal (including my own – see pp. 178–179 *above*) have produced dubious results, but the additional weakness of MD's proposal (267–268) arises from a one-sided interpretation of the conclusion, pushed too far, about the use of the title of "grand prince" by Jaroslav's brother Mstislav (d. 1036). For the moment, at least, the lack of any other discoveries of princely seals bearing the terms "*megas*" or "*velikyj*" means that the only correct conclusion one can draw from the sigillographic evidence of the 11th and 12th centuries is that the title of "grand prince" had not yet been established in Rus'.

MD also points to an inscribed silver drinking vessel belonging to prince Vladimir Davidovich that has been the subject of varying interpretations (176–177 *above*), and concludes, with a view supported by only one compilation chronicle of the 16th century (PSRL IX: 173, 176) that "there can be little doubt that the inscription refers to Vladimir as *grand prince*" (281–282). However, we should bear in mind that such a feast-cup was designed to be drained of its contents by a chosen guest, who thus also had an occasion to honour and praise the master of the house. It was laudatory cup and its inscription would, consequently, have been a flattering one. It is also quite possible that the cup could have been a gift, rather than something produced by the owner himself. Furthermore, it should be noted that the inscription refers once to the host as "*velikyj knjaz'*", but a second time simply as "*knjaz'*." Under these circumstances, simply to choose the desired reading out of varied choices seems very risky.

A doubtful contribution is MD's effort (255–259) to broaden the source base with the text of some 20 to 22 chronicles compiled in the 15th and 16th centuries, surviving mostly in later manuscripts containing earlier syntheses beginning with *The Primary Chronicle* (PVL), also known as *The Tale of Bygone Years*.[5] Such later

---

A. Poppe, "The Christianisation" [=Study V above], 349, 384, fn.102 and addendum 2 below.

[5] MD (255–256) asserts that the "*Novgorod First Chronicle* has the earliest version of *PVL*, known as the *Nachalnyy Svod*, which contains information up to the early 1090s, when it was compiled." But the hypothesis about the existence of such an "elementary" compilation, once firmly accepted as a "*fait accompli*" has, since the 1990s, been drawn increasingly into question (cf. S. Senderovic, T. Vilkul). It still has its defenders (e.g., A. Gippius) but it cannot serve MD's purposes.

texts, especially those produced by circles close to the rulers of Muscovy, taking into account the spreading of the title of *velikyj knjaz'*, tended to apply the title retrospectively to all direct ancestors of the Muscovite ruling line. Drawing upon such late references as evidence of earlier use of the title needs to be backed up by some observance of the established rules of investigation.

* * *

MD also declares his intention "to determine if the evidence of late copies of non-chronicle documents is truly untrustworthy or if it reflects conventions from the Kievan Rus' period" (259). In conclusion he writes: "...the evidence of independent documents seemingly corroborates the chronicle data" (306). Let us take a closer look at those documents .

He argues that the text of the "*Paterikon of the Cave Monastery* suggests that, by the beginning of the thirteenth century, the monks of the monastery acknowledged Izjaslav as *velikyj knjaz'*" (270–271). Such a conclusion is clearly incorrect. The collection of lives of the fathers of the Caves Monastery was indeed composed in the 1220s, on the basis of written and oral monastic tradition, but the *Paterikon* survives only in three redactions of the 15th century and later, with obvious linguistic additions and corrections. Despite that fact, the core text was basically not deformed in the process, and of the more than 20 references to Izjaslav contained in the work, only two refer to him as "grand prince". The first of those exceptions is found in Kasian's 1462 redaction of the *Paterikon*, which has come down to us in a manuscript from 1554, and its clear source is an entry of the *Primary Chronicle* under the year 6576 in which no such title is used. In the so-called "Basic" redaction, preserved in a manuscript of the 16th century, and in that of Theodosius from the beginning of the 15th (MSS. *O* and *T*), the wording of the entry is simpler: "*v knjaženje Izjaslavlě*". The second use of "grand prince" is in the text of a letter to Izjaslav listing the errors of the Latins, which was appended to the text only in the 1462 redaction of the *Paterikon.*[6] Unfortunately, the author has misled both himself and his readers at this point.

* * *

[6] See *Das Paterikon des Kiever Hohlenklosters* (reprint of D. Abramovič edition, Kiev 1931). Munich 1963: 17, 82, 190; it is regrettable that MD did not make use of D. Tschizewsky's introduction to that edition. MD refers to a passage in the Paterikon whereby "blessed *grand prince* Yaroslav appointed Ilarion in 1051" (264) without taking into account that this is only a repetition of a sentence (lacking the term "*velikyi*", however) from the *Primary Chronicle* s.a. 1051. Jaroslav's sons Svjatoslav and Vsevolod, as well as his grandson Vladimir Monomakh, are never referred to in *Paterikon* as "grand prince", and Svjatopolk II, who appears in eight passages, is only once given that title, which is, again, only a repetition of a sentence (once again, without any "*velikyj*") from the *Primary Chronicle* s.a. 6616 (1108).

An important role in MD's thinking is played by the ecclesiastical statutes of Vladimir and Jaroslav. MD regrets that both "privileges are problematic because the original has not come down to us". The Statute of Prince Jaroslav "seemingly proves that Yaroslav was using the title [of *grand prince*] by the middle of the eleventh century" (262–265). The Novgorod Church privilege he cites, dated to the 1130s, was actually composed in the 14th century. MD does note, with some delicacy, that "the credibility of the texts is suspect". Indeed, all of these documents were composed in the 13th to 15th centuries and, on the basis of internal and external evidence, must be characterized as falsifications, at least in their formal aspects – i.e., their use of titles and the alleged circumstances of their issue, the very elements at issue here.[7]

* * *

MD refers to the colophon of Svjatoslav's *Miscellany* from the year 1073 as further evidence for the grand princely title, overlooking the fact that this panegyrical colophon was originally composed in Greek and addressed to Symeon, ruler of Bulgaria (271–273; 170–171 *above*). Moreover, he completely disregards the other *Miscellany* from 1076, where Svjatoslav is titled simply "*knjaz'*" (see 171, fn. 33 *above*). MD also attributes the title of *grand prince* to Svjatoslav since both he and his father Jaroslav were entitled *kagans* (272). Such argumentation is hard to follow.[8] MD refers also to graffiti with a notice about the death of Jaroslav in which he is called *c[es]ar'* [9] as an argument for his having been entitled "*grand prince*". Surprisingly MD, who dedicated so much attention of the grand princely title of Vladimir Monomach (274–277), totally ignores the well-known Lenten epistle of metropolitan Nikephoros addressed to that prince, referring to him

[7] This has been known for over hundred years (E. Golubinskij, M. Hrushevsky, etc.). The rights and privileges provided to the Church in Rus' at its beginnings are another matter. Hence, there are varying assessments of the contents of these documents, as to whether they reflect the establishment of a new status or the confirmation of a pre-existing one. The confusion results, perhaps, from a misunderstanding of some of the conclusions of Ja. Ščapov, *Knjazeskie ustavy i cerkov v drevniej Rusi* (Moscow 1972), which MD cites. It is unfortunate that MD is not familiar with the excellent encyclopedia article of J. Bardach ("Statuty kościelne na Rusi", *Słownick Starożytności Słowiańskich* V, 1975: 403–408), which notes the unsatisfactory progress of source studies in this area.

[8] Instead of informing us that the inscription (graffiti) in Sophia Cathedral was written under a fresco with an icon of St Nicholas, the patron saint of Svjatoslav-Nicholas, which provides basic grounds for hypothesizing that the writer must have been referring here to Svjatoslav, MD describes this conclusion as the outcome of a "meticulous investigation".

[9] MD (266, 270) does not take into account the fact that the word and title "*tsar*" (a contraction of "*caesar*") did not yet exist in the 11th century (cf. p. 183, fn. 63 *above*)

over twenty times as "my prince" and containing the title of "grand prince" only in the heading (see p. 172, fn. 37 *above*).

*   *   *

MD hoped to show that his observations are in accord with the testimony of the available sources. To be sure, such "sources" are available, but many of them are uncertain, dubious, or simply falsifications.

In situations where there is a basic difference in understanding of the sources, questions of broader interpretation are of secondary importance. The *instrumenta studiorum* must be applied in accordance with the rules of the medievalist's tool kit. This fruit of university seminars, assimilated by adepts of the craft, has continued to develop successfully in our day despite various challenges by those who would attempt to ignore or even break its basic principles, often the result of an ignorance of those principles.

Although MD's article directs us largely to later references, it is here that he has actually performed his greatest service. Indeed, I would have little problem with his article, were its title qualified by the addition of the words "...in the View of the Bookmen of the 14th to 16th Centuries".[10] On the basis of certain details, one can speculate that the core of his work must have been done in the 1970s or early 1980s. This would seem to be suggested, among other things, by the observation, made independently by both us, that an important proof of the institutionalization of the grand princely title was its application to consorts or widows of the ruler in the early 13th century (p. 279, fn. 48 *above*).

In light of these considerations, I would ask the reader for indulgence of both authors and to consider this reissue of my text as a response to the arguments raised by MD in *Medieval Studies* of the year 2004.

[10] One should note here the recent article of S.N. Kisterev, "Великий князъ всея Руси в XI–XV веках", *Очерки феодальной России*, вып. 6, Moscow 2002: 47–85, which concentrates on the addition of the phrase "of all Rus" to grand princely titulature in the 14th and 15th centuries. The author hastily attempts to find the origins of this formula in the 11th- and 12th-century inscriptions referring to the *князь русьскии (archōn Rhōsias)*. However, that title was used primarily to refer to members of the ruling dynasty (their characterization as "Rurikids" came considerably later). The use of the phrase "*всея Руси*" *(pasēs Rhōsias)* could simply express the claim of those metropolitans or princes who aspired to jurisdiction over "all of Rus'".

ADDENDUM II

The Enthronement of the Prince in Kievan Rus'*

The installation in power of a prince in Kievan Rus' was formally expressed by an act of enthronement. But despite what some think, there was no coronation[1] nor was anointing as a sacrament conferring a title to rule known in Rus'. Each prince of the ruling dynasty was seen by birth as Lord's anointed.[2]

According to Francis Dvornik this enthronement was primarily a secular act without a fixed ceremony; the involvement of the clergy was at first largely a matter of chance and it first gained importance in the principality of Vladimir-Suzdal about the year 1200.[3] But the analysis of chronicle data permits the conclusion that during the 12th century enthronement was regularly a religious and ecclesiastical ceremony, which can be reconstructed.

As a rule the enthronement took place on a Sunday and consisted of the following ceremonial acts: the festive entrance of the prince into his city; the populace (commoners, nobles, and clergy in mass vestments) acclaimed the prince with "honour and glory"; the bishop blessed the prince; probably immediately thereafter the prince swore to rule righteously and according to tradition; the oath culminated in kissing the cross – a visible symbol of Christian nature of the ruler's power.[4] Afterwards the prince, accompanied by his suite and the clergy, entered the cathedral where the liturgy was celebrated. The prince prostrated himself and prayed to Christ and the Virgin while the clergy chanted invocations (Biblical passages about God as the source of every earthly power; the ruler as God's elect, and as one called by God). The actual elevation to the princely throne, which was regularly located in the cathedral, followed. Probably at this moment the prince was handed the sword. Finally the enthroned prince

---

* A previous version of this notice was published in *The 17th International Byzantine Congress 1986. Abstracts of short papers*, Washington, D.C. 1986: 272–274.

[1] A coronation ceremony introduced in Rus' to byzantinize the form of succession to the Kievan throne after the death of Vladimir the Great was abandoned by Yaroslav supported by other Rurikids in their determination to maintain the dynastic tradition and vanished without trace. See the present volume, Studies I: 8–9; VII: 139–141.

[2] See A. Poppe, "Christianisation" = the present volume, Study V: 349, 384 fn.102

[3] Fr. Dvornik, "Byzantine Political Ideas in Kievan Russia", *Dumbarton Oaks Papers* 9/10,1956: 116–121

[4] For the previous literature see H.W. Dewey, A.M. Kleimola, "Promise and Perfidy in Old Russian Cross-Kissing", *Canadian Slavic Studies* 2, 1968 #3: 327–341. For more on this topic see П. С. Стефанович, "Крестоцелование и отношение к нему в древней Руси", *Средневековая Русь* 5, Moscow 2004: 86–113. Research on this topic should be continued.

accepted the allegiance of those present who "prostrated themselves before him and kissed him with awe".[5]

We may assume that this ecclesiastical ceremony also existed in the 11th century. Svjatopolk II was enthroned on a Sunday, 24 April 1093 and the chronicler records the prince's festive advent into the city, as well as the acclamation and homage of the populace. If we examine the statements that Vladimir Monomakh assumed the throne "of his father and grandfather", that is of Vsevolod and Jaroslav, and that Vsevolod assumed the throne of his father (Jaroslav, † 1054) and brother (Izjaslav † 1078) in the light of the information from the 12th and 13th centuries, then it appears that the throne mentioned is the real throne of Jaroslav in Sophia Cathedral which he built. It is to be noted that Jaroslav too sat on the throne "of his father" in the year 1016.[6] This, however, must be the throne of Vladimir the Great (d. 1015) in the Church of the Tithe, the *capella regia*, which was only stone church in Kiev at that time.

It is to be assumed that the custom of enthronement in church and the idea that the Church conferred divine approval at the beginning of the reign were brought to Kiev by Anna Porphyrogenita. The rulers of Kiev and those around them were aware that the Christian nature of the princely (royal) office required legitimation in this manner. Therefore the most important elements of the religious ceremony of enthronement were taken over in their finished form. When then Rus'ian chronicler began to speak of the ceremony at the end of the 11th century, it was already an established tradition the details of which did not seem any longer to deserve mention.

---

[5] See the Laurentian Chronicle, s.a. 6714, PSRL 1 (1928 or reprint): 423. With these *laudes* we are near to those presented in detail by E. Kantorowicz, *Laudes regiae. A Study in Liturgical Acclamations and Mediaeval Ruler Worship*, Los Angeles 1958. Rus'ian chronicles have many references to enthronement but all are very short and very stereotyped. The earliest and more detailed information was given by Thietmar of Merseburg, *Chronicon*, ed. K. Holzman (Berlin 1935) books VII,65; VIII,32.

[6] PSRL 1:129; 2:142, The phrase "and of his grandfather", found only in the Laurentian Ms., is apparently a later interpolation and strong evidence that the archetype was free of this addition (cf. also Novgorod First Chronicle s.a. 1016).

X

On the Title of Grand Prince in the *Tale of Ihor's Campaign*

Whether the princely titles used by the anonymous author of the *Tale of Ihor's Campaign* reflect the actual usage prevailing at the time of the battle against the Cumans (Polovcians) in 1185 — and if so, how accurately — is a question that hitherto has not been raised, although otherwise this famous epic has been subjected to the most intense scrutiny. The omission is not surprising, however, for no thorough studies of princely titles in pre-Mongol Rus' have been undertaken. It has simply been assumed that the title "grand prince" dated from the tenth or eleventh century. In any case, the question could be dismissed entirely on the grounds that accuracy in every historical detail cannot be expected from a literary work, especially in matters of such marginal importance as the titles borne by the princely host who figure in it.

A recent investigation of the appearance of the title of grand prince in Rus' encourages us, however, to take another look at the *Tale of Ihor's Campaign* from that perspective. That study[1] concluded that the adjective "grand" (*velikyi*) accompanying the word "prince" (*knjaz'*) was not consistently used as a component of the official title to indicate the hierarchical superiority of some Rus' princes over others before the end of the twelfth century. Although it is often attested in the sources before that time, they do not use it as an official title for the rulers of Rus'; it occurs simply as an attribute having different meanings.

In Old Rus'ian the semantics of this adjective were differentiated, as

[1] The present article was published in advance of the larger work to honor Omeljan Pritsak, whose work includes contributions to research on the *Tale of Ihor's Campaign,* especially its Turkological tradition ("The Igor' Tale and the Eurasian Steppe," unpublished work), and an attempt to establish the *post quem non* for its creation as August 1201 ("The Igor' Tale as a Historical Document," *Annals of the Ukrainian Academy of Arts and Sciences in the United States* 12 [1972]:33–61).

were those of its medieval Greek and Latin equivalents — μέγας and *magnus*. In the oldest records — the Byzantine-Rus' treaties of the tenth century — "grand prince" is simply a translation of μέγας ἄρχων, that is, chief prince. Under Byzantine influence the attribute μέγας/*velikyi* was used in Rus' to praise the ruler or to refer to a deceased ruler, especially in eulogies. It was also used in the sense of "old-time, old, elder, senior," but in such cases the term *velikyi* was associated with the name of the ruler, rather than with his title. It was not used as a constituent part of the official princely designation even by Kievan senior princes.

The first ruler to adopt the appellation "grand prince" as a title was the senior prince of Vladimir-Suzdal', Vsevolod the Big Nest (1176–1212).[2] Its systematic use dates not from the beginning of Vsevolod's rule in Vladimir, but only from the 1190s.[3] Then the title began to be used derivatively, if inconsistently, by the Kievan senior princes, but they obviously regarded it as having only secondary importance. It was a way of stressing the traditional preeminence of Kiev in response to the ambitions of Vladimir on the Kljaz'ma. It was not yet part of the official title of the Kievan senior prince Svjatoslav (1180–1194). The situation changed under his successor, Rjuryk Rostyslavyč (1195–1201), the nominal Kievan senior prince; he adopted the title already used by Vsevolod.[4] In the thirteenth century senior princes of other Rus' lands also followed Vsevolod's example.

The need to expand the semantic context of the title of the Rus' ruler arose during the period when the Kievan prince's authority was in decline, the dynasty was growing in numbers, centrifugal processes were intensifying, and the title itself was losing value. The necessity of strengthening the Kievan prince's title and of emphasizing the scope of his rule may have

[2] L. K. Goetz ("Der Titel 'Grossfürst' in den ältesten-russischen Chroniken," *Zeitschrift für osteuropäische Geschichte* 1 [1911]:59) aptly observed that Vsevolod "ist derjenige Fürst, für dem 'velikyi kniaz" systematisch als Amstitel während seines Lebens gebraucht wird." A similar view was expressed by Hruševs'kyj, *Istorija Ukrajiny-Rusy*, vol. 3 (Lviv, 1905), p. 205.

[3] A. Šaxmatov (*Obozrenie russkix letopisnyx svodov XIV–XVI vv.*[Moscow and Leningrad, 1938] , p. 12), and M. Priselkov (*Istorija russkogo letopisanija XI–XV vv.* [Leningrad, 1940], p. 81), thought that Vsevolod had styled himself grand prince beginning in 1186, but the title is used consistently for Vsevolod in chronicles only after 1195. One can assume, therefore, that earlier references to it are later interpolations into the text.

[4] The reference to Rjuryk Rostyslavyč as grand prince should be attributed to the author of the Kievan redaction of around 1200. An example of an obvious later interpolation is in the Hypatian Chronicle under the year 1183, where Svjatoslav is called simply "Kievan prince," but Rjuryk is called "grand prince." *Polnoe sobranie russkix letopisej* (hereafter *PSRL*), vol. 2, 2nd ed. (St. Petersburg, 1908), col. 630.

first been realized beyond the borders of Rus'. When the political and ecclesiastical turmoil of the 1140s and 1150s threatened to disintegrate the Rus' church, Byzantium recognized that it must support the Kievan prince and the supremacy of his authority in order to guarantee the church's unity. Hence, a designation with clearly political intent appeared in Byzantium's correspondence with Rus'. The Kievan prince was referred to as the supreme prince—ruler of all Rus' (μέγας ἄρχων πάσης 'Ρωσίας). Similarly, the metropolitan of Rus' emphasized the scope of his jurisdictional rights by designating himself, and being designated, "Metropolitan of all Rus' (πάσης 'Ρωσίας)."[5]

The attribute *velikyi* was gradually becoming a permanent part of the title of the ruler of Rus', but it was not fated to be of use in cementing the disintegrating Kievan state. Circumstances allowed the ruler of northeastern Rus', which was developing rapidly, to adopt the title before the Kievan senior prince, even though the latter was still recognized, at least nominally, as the supreme prince of Rus'. In building his state, the prince of Vladimir-Suzdal' strived to influence the affairs common to all the Rus' lands. This time, however, the basis of his authority was to be "seniority in the land of Rus'," rather than occupancy of the throne of Kiev.[6]

In the *Tale,* only one person — Vsevolod, the ruler of Vladimir-Suzdal' Rus' and son of Jurij Dolgorukij — is given the title of grand prince:

Великыи княже Всеволоде! Не мыслию ти прелетѣти издалеча, отня злата стола поблюсти? Ты бо можеши Волгу веслы раскропити, а Донъ шеломы выльяти![7]

/Grand Prince Vsevolod! Do you intend to come from far away to watch over your paternal golden throne? For you, with the oars [of your fleet], can scatter the river Volga into droplets. With the helmets [of your army] you empty out the river Don!/[8]

5 On Byzantine opposition to the attempted creation of a second metropolitanate in Rus', see the letter from the Constantinople patriarch to Prince Andrej Bogoljubskij, dated ca. 1168 (*Russkaja istoričeskaja biblioteka* [St. Petersburg], 6 [1880]:63, 66); and W. Vodoff, "Un 'parti théocratique' dans la Russie du XIIe siècle? Remarques sur la politique ecclésiastique d'André de Bogoljubovo," *Cahiers de Civilisation Medievale* 17, no. 3 (1974): 193–215. For the seals of the metropolitans of all Rus', see A. Soloviev, *Byzance et la formation de l'Etat russe: Recueil d'études* (reprint ed., London, 1979), pp. 292–301, 317–25.

6 He did, in fact, dispose of the Kievan throne. See *PSRL,* vol. 1 (Leningrad, 1928), cols. 413, 418, 421; and 2:683, 685–86, 688–89. Cf. S. M. Solov'ev, *Istorija Rossii s drevnejšix vremen,* vol. 1 (Moscow, 1959), pp. 569–79; M. Hruševs'kyj, *Istorija Ukrajiny-Rusy,* vol. 2 (Lviv, 1905), pp. 217–21, 225–27.

7 *Slovo o polku Igoreve* (Moscow and Leningrad, 1950), p. 21; V. L. Vinogradova, *Slovar'-spravočnik "Slova o polku Igoreve,"* 5 vols. to date (Leningrad, 1965–), 1:21.

8 The English translation is taken from *Medieval Russia's Epics, Chronicles, and Tales,* ed. by S. A. Zenkovsky (New York, 1974), pp. 181–82, with one correction.

In the apostrophe, a direct appeal to Vsevolod in the second person, the author is clearly entitling this ruler, rather than simply distinguishing him from other princes of the same name.[9] After all, the author apostrophizes other princes many times, but he never calls any of them "grand prince." At the same time, he mentions — also in a panegyrical context — the princes Svjatoslav and Rjuryk of Kiev, Roman of Volhynia, and Jaroslav of Galicia, who were given this title by later chroniclers.[10] Yet, even the most illustrious of the dynasty's ancestors — Volodimer, the baptizer of Rus', and his son, Jaroslav the Wise — were not called grand princes in the *Tale*.[11]

The absence of the grand prince title might be explained away in some cases by arguing that the epic's author was often content with names alone and used titles infrequently, for the most part only where required for aesthetic reasons, that is, the rhythm of an epic narration.[12] But in the case of the Kievan senior prince Svjatoslav, who is mentioned several times, such an explanation would be inadequate and even inadmissible. The author bestowed on him the attribute *velikyi* twice: "Святъславъ грозныи великыи киевскыи . . ." and "Тогда великыи Святъ-

---

There the text begins with the word "great," as does Nabokov's version, *The Song of Igor's Campaign* (New York, 1960), p. 54: "Great Prince Vsevolod! Do you not think of flying here from afar to safeguard the paternal golden throne? For you can with your oars scatter in drops the Volga, and with your helmets scoop dry the Don." Obviously, as the discussion here suggests, the word *velikyi* must be rendered by the English "grand."

[9] Cf. D. S. Lixačev, *"Slovo o polku Igoreve" i kul'tura ego vremeni* (Leningrad, 1978), p. 129. The *Tale* mentions four contemporary princes of the same name (cf. Vinogradova, *Slovar'-spravočnik*, 1:140–41), and Vsevolod of Vladimir-Suzdal' (born 1154) was not the oldest of them. Vsevolod, the brother of Prince Ihor (born 1151), the epic's hero, was the same age as the Suzdal' prince or even a year or two older. Cf. N. Baumgarten, *Généalogies et marriages occidentaux des Rurikides russes du Xe au XIIIe siècle* (Rome, 1927), tables 4–6; B. A. Rybakov, *"Slovo o polku Igoreve" i ego sovremenniki* (Moscow, 1971), p. 89.

[10] See *Slovo o polku Igoreve*, pp. 20–23; Cf. Vinogradova, *Slovar'-spravočnik*, 5:53–54, 70–71, 108–109; Rybakov, *"Slovo"*, pp. 87, 92–95. In historiography Rjuryk passes for Svjatoslav's coregent; they were supposed to have formed a *sui generis* diarchy, with Svjatoslav ruling Kiev, and Rjuryk, the territories surrounding it from his capital in Bilhorod.

[11] The *Tale* calls them *staryi*, in the sense of "ancient," "old-time." Cf. Vinogradova, *Slovar'-spravočnik*, 5:211. Jaroslav the Wise is also once called *velikyi*: "Тои же звонъ слыша давныи великыи Ярославъ а сынь Всеволожь Владиміръ." *Slovo o polku Igoreve*, p. 15; Vinogradova, *Slovar'-spravočnik*, 1:100. But according to a completely convincing emendation, this should be read as "тъже звонъ слыша дал'ныи вънукъ Ярославль, сынъ Всеволожь Володимѣръ." L. Müller, "Einige Bemerkungen zum Igorlied," *Welt der Slaven* 10 (1965):254.

[12] The leading character of the *Tale*, Prince Ihor, is mentioned twenty-eight times by name alone and only nine times by name and the title "prince."

славъ. . . ."[13] In the first instance, in particular, the adjective *velikyi* is not needed to distinguish the Kievan senior prince from the other Svjatoslavs who appear in the epic, because for this purpose the indication that he held Kiev would have been sufficient. Nor can it be explained as an abbreviation — for *velikyi kniaz'* — as some have supposed.[14] *Velikyi* was used here merely in the sense of "chief, elder in terms of position."[15] The term accurately reflected Svjastoslav's status as Kievan senior prince. It was this status that was noted by the Novgorod chronicler who, when recording the events of 1180–1181, titled Svjatoslav "prince," but added the attribute *velikyi* when describing his arrival in Novgorod: "и въниде Святославъ великыи Всеволодиць Новугороду."[16] It follows from the chronicle data that the attribute *velikyi* was used to describe Svjatoslav's position, that is, his seniority in occupying the throne of the Kievan capital.[17] That it was in this sense, rather than as part of the title "grand prince," that the *Tale*'s author used the adjective is evident from the apostrophe of boyars around Svjatoslav who explained their ruler's dream:

И ркоша бояре князю: "Уже, княже, туга умь полонила"[18]

/And the boyars told the prince: "O Prince, sorrow has seized your mind"/[19]

In addressing Svjatoslav, the boyars in his retinue call him simply *knjaže*. Thus, the author of the *Tale* did not think that the Kievan senior prince held the title of grand prince at that time. In this context, the single instance in the *Tale* where the "grand prince" designation is bestowed — that is, on Vsevolod, ruler of Vladimir-Suzdal' Rus' — acquires significance.

The anonymous author's knowledge of the titles of Rus' princes in the final decades of the twelfth century is clearly consistent with the actual historical situation. His accuracy on this point, however, does not allow us to draw conclusions of a more general nature. Nonetheless, since the

13 *Slovo o polku Igoreve*, pp. 18, 20. Zenkovsky's English rendering of the first phrase (p. 178) is not quite correct: ". . . Prince Sviatoslav. This stern prince of Kiev."

14 The suggestion clearly influenced Nabokov's version (p. 47): "dread Svyatoslav, the Great [Prince] of Kiev."

15 See Lixačev's commentary in *Slovo o polku Igoreve*, pp. 422–23; and idem, *"Slovo o polku Igoreve" i kul'tura ego vremeni*, pp. 128–29.

16 *Novgorodskaja pervaja letopis' staršego i mladšego izvodov*, ed. by A. Nasonov (Moscow and Leningrad, 1950), pp. 36, 226.

17 See, in particular, *PSRL*, 2:624.

18 *Slovo o polku Igoreve*, p. 19.

19 *Medieval Russia's Epics*, p. 179. Cf. Nabokov, p. 50; "And the boyars said to the Prince: 'Already, Prince, grief has enthralled the mind'. . . ."

author did discern the princely designations of the period correctly, it is important at least to try to explain how that happened.

The first and simplest explanation is that since the author was a contemporary of the events he described, his discernment of the political hierarchy was natural. Another possibility is that the writer of the thirteenth century, or even much later, had access to historically accurate information that allowed him to circumvent the confusion and anachronisms about the use of the title of grand prince that has characterized historiography since the chronicles of the thirteenth century to the present time.[20] If the proposed chronology and circumstances of the adoption of the title of "grand prince" in Rus' are accepted, then the first hypothesis makes any further argument superfluous. Confirming the second hypothesis would require argumentation of a kind that I am not yet able to provide.

[20] The accounts of the 1185 campaign in the Hypatian and Laurentian chronicles already betray later emendations in the attribution of the title of grand prince to Svjatoslav (*PSRL*, 1:357; 2:644–51). In any case, the assertion that the chronicle text influenced the *Tale* is not convincing on the point alone. That the chronicle text may represent a secondary redaction is another story. Cf. E. Goranin, "Opowieść o wyprawie Igora Światosławowicza na Połowców w 1185 r.," *Slavia Orientalis* 28 (1979): 301–310.

XI

Some observations on the bronze Doors of the St. Sophia in Novgorod

The different names of the Romanesque bronze Doors which still adorn the western façade of the Novgorod Cathedral of St. Sophia reflect their historical and legendary fate wrapped partly in mystery.

These doors are called the Magdeburg doors because they were manufactured in the Magdeburg casting workshop. And also the Płock Doors because they were ordered for the Cathedral of the Holy Virgin in the Polish town Płock on the Vistula.[1]

Fig. 1. The Cathedral of St. Sophia in Novgorod. The western façade. Photo W. Jerke, Warszawa.

[1] Three life size copies of the Doors exist (2.40 x 3.60 m): a plaster one made ca 1886 in the Historical Museum in Moscow and two made out of synthetic materials in 1971–1972 upon the initiative of the Płock Scientific Society and found in the Masovian Museum in Płock and the Archaeological Museum at Warsaw. A bronze cast for the portals of the Cathedral Basilica of Płock is planned. A. Goldschmidt, *Die Bronzetüren von Novgorod und Gnesen* (Marburg a/L, 1932), p. 1–26, tables 1–70, remains the best study on the Doors treated as a work of art. Good reproductions together with a concise and clear commentary are found in the following albums: *Die Bronzetür von Nowgorod*, 43 Abbildungen, Nachwort von W. Sauerländer (Munich, 1962) and *Die Bronzetür der Sophienkathedrale in Nowgorod*, 44 Bildtafeln, ed. H.-H. J. Krause, E. Schubert (Leipzig, 1968).

They were and still are called the Sigtuna doors because the doors found allegedly their way from Magdeburg to Novgorod through the Swedish town of Sigtuna.[2] The creator of this legend was Martin Aschaneus who 1614 stayed in Novgorod and was convinced that he discovered there the town-gate was once carried away from Sigtuna. This hypothesis was aptly criticized in 1912 by Oskar Almgren.[3]

And the doors were for centuries called the Korsun Doors according to the legend that they in 989 were brought as a trophy from Cherson by king Vladimir. Herberstein, who was the first to record this tradition about the doors, heard this legend in 1517 in Novgorod. But William Coxe, the historian and travelling tutor to the son of the Earl of Pembroke, was the first to correctly identify the pedigree of the Novgorod Doors (1784).

Here I limit myself to two questions and two methods: the paleographic and the iconographic.

1. The matter of Latin and Cyrillic inscriptions on the doors—the conclusions which could be drawn from their analysis.

2. The issue of the additions to the doors.

I

The representation of Wichmann of Magdeburg (1152—1192) on the doors can be identified by the accompanying inscription "Wicmannus megideburgensis episcopus". The fact that Wichmann is titled a bishop and not an archbishop and lacks the pallium enabled researchers to assume that the doors were manufactured between 1152 and 1154.

However, it is possible to establish the date of their execution even more precisely. Wichmann, the Bishop of Naumburg, was nominated Archbishop of Magdeburg by Frederick Barbarossa shortly after May 18, 1152, but as a result of the resistence of the majority of the cathedral chapter supported by Pope Eugene III (letters of August 1 and 17, 1152) he did not take up his office immediately. Wichmann continued to govern his Naumburg diocese and counted on obtaining the Pope's approval.

The situation changed after June the 7th 1153 when Barbarossa, having learnt that Rome continued to oppose this investiture, demonstratively emphasized the inflexibility of his decision. Apparently it was only then that Wichmann assumed his new duties but he still did not use the title of archbishop. He was able to gain his pallium and with it the dignity of an archbishop as a result of the talks held between the papal legate, Barbarossa and Wichmann himself as well as the cathedral chapter at Easter (April the 4th) 1154 in Magdeburg. Wichmann got his pallium in Rome at the very end of April or very beginning of May 1154.[4]

The fact that the Latin explanatory inscriptions are divided into two groups should be connected with the time and circumstance of the manufacture of the Doors in the

[2] I.P. Šaskol'skij, Predanije o 'Sigtunskich vratach' i jego dostovernost', *Učenyje zapiski Leningradskogo Gosudarstvennogo Universiteta*, no. 112 (1949), 120—135. Recently Šaskolskij has weaked his conclusions but he still believes that the Doors were brought to Novgorod from Sigtuna following the expedition 1187 by the Novgorod-ally karelians. See: I.P. Šaskolskij, *Bor'ba Rusi protiv krestonosnoj agressii na beregah Baltiki v XII—XIII vv.*, Leningrad 1978, p. 95—104.

[3] O. Almgren, K Legende o sigtunskich vratach, *Sbornik Novgorodskogo obščestva ljubitelej drevnosti*, 6 (1912), p. 23—26. Idem, Sägen om Sigtunaporten i Novgorod, *Upplands Fornminnesförenings Tidskrift*, 37 (1922), p. 65—71; 39 (1924), p. 399—400. Cf. also A. Goldschmidt, *op. cit.*, p. 7, note 1.

[4] For more details see: D. Claude, *Geschichte des Erzbistums Magdeburg bis in das 12. Jahrhundert*, 2 (Köln, 1975), p. 71—81. A. Poppe, Die Magdeburger Frage. Versuch einer Neubewertung, in: *Festschrift Herbert Ludat*, Giessen 1980.

Fig. 2. Wichmann, the bishop of Magdeburg. Photo W. Jerke, Warszawa.

Fig. 3. The bronze doors of the western portal of St. Sophia in Novgorod. Photo of the Archaeological Museum of Warsaw (see infra note 1).

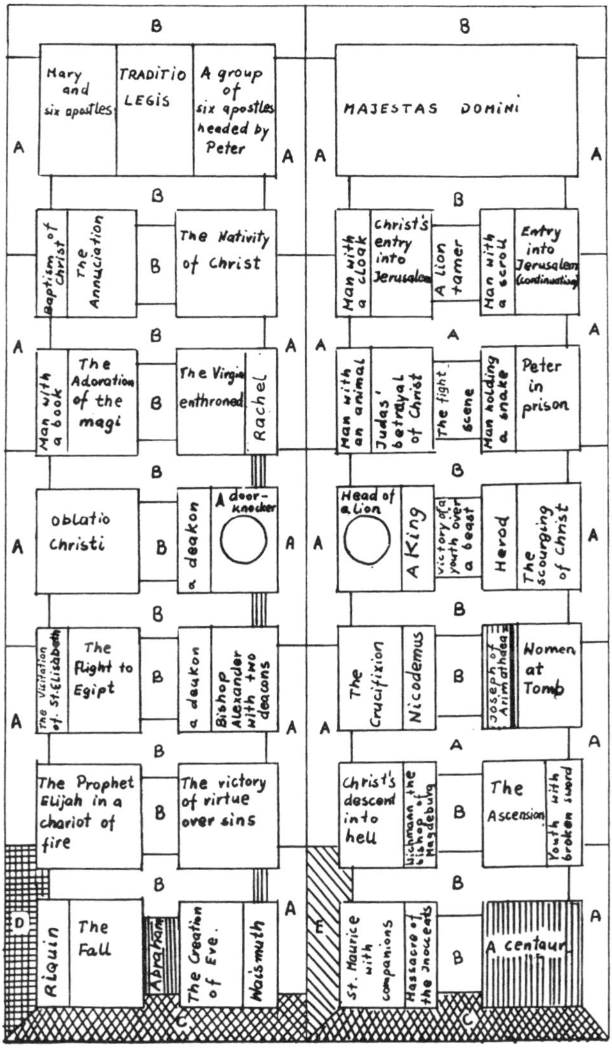

Fig. 4. A scheme of the arrangement of individual reliefs and ornamental patterns. The suggested later additions are hatched.

Magdeburg workshop. The first group contains fifteen inscriptions previously cast in bronze together with the pictures which they explain. The other seven which were etched after the casting are not so carefully drawn. Both types of writing represent a well-developed Romanesque majuscule and cannot be separated chronologically.[5] It is also

[5] A. Goldschmidt, *op. cit.*, p. 22; W. Semkowicz, *Paleografia łacińska* (Kraków, 1951), p. 547–555.

impossible to link the etching of the second group of inscriptions with a centre other than Magdeburg (for example Płock has been suggested). This is shown by the inscription WICMANNUS MEGIDEBURGENSIS EPC which belongs to those etched after the casting.

This inscription points just to a very important detail, namely that when the order was being filled and the bas-relief with the image of the Magdeburg bishop was being cast, the dispute about Wichmann's translation was still going on. This is why the inscription could not be engraved before casting. When the work was coming to an end and Wichmann still could not obtain the dignity of an archbishop, an inscription which did not conflict with the actual state of affairs was etched.[6] Simultaneously, a few inscriptions explaining the iconography were added, most certainly in accordance with the wishes of the purchaser or his plenopotentiary.

Taking all these data into consideration, the moment when our Doors were completed should be placed in the second half of 1153. In any case they were shipped to their destination before April 1154.

The fact that the execution of the order was not delayed, in spite of the uncertain situation in the Magdeburg Cathedral, is significant. It shows that the supposition that the Bishop of Płock Alexander of Malonne did not have sufficient means to pay for the Doors and for this reason they did not reach Płock has no basis.

As shown by the reliefs representing the patron of the Magdeburg diocese, St. Maurice together with his companions and Wichmann himself, which undoubtedly were originally placed alongside each other, Wichmann negotiated the order with the Magdeburg foundry and perhaps covered a part of the costs. In this mediation one should perceive a reflection of Wichmann's close relations with Alexander. Both these Church dignitaries were connected with the movement of the Regular Canons and represented a pre-Gregorian trend in following the tradition of the imperial Church.[7]

The circumstances in which the Doors were made for Płock are so clearly reflected on the plate with Wichmann's image, that one comes to the inescapable conclusion that the whole process can have taken place only in Magdeburg itself. This reveals the weakness of the assumption that the Doors were cast in Płock itself by smelters-sculptors who were sent from the Magdeburg workshop.

II

As to the time of etching the Cyrillic inscriptions on the Doors I can refer to my paleographic investigation published in *Collected articles* dedicated to the memory of N. Voronin. Here a short summary of my conclusions:

Over sixty slavonic words etched with Cyrillic alphabet provide a sufficient basis for an analysis not only of their graphic, but also of their orthographic traits. The epigraphical dating based mostly on dated objects with old Russian inscriptions mostly from Novgorod, brings us to the XV century, and particular to the period between

[6] Actually Wichmann had the right to title himself *Magdeburgensis electus (archielectus)* or *vocatus episcopus* but in this case he utilized his particular situation considering that he already was bishop. Thus the papal ordination consisted of confirming the translation and conferring of the *ius pallii*.

[7] Cf. C. Deptuła, Krag kościelny płocki w połowie XII wieku, *Roczniki Humanistyczne*, 8 (1959), no. 2, p. 32 ff., 57 ff. *Idem*, Kosciol płocki w XII wieku, *Studia Płockie*, 3/1 (1975), p. 67–71, 75–80.

[8] For details about the Russian inscriptions on the Doors see A.V. Poppe, K istorii romanskich dverej Sofii Novgorodskoj, in *Srednevekovaja Rus'. Sbornik pamjati N.N. Voronina* (Moskva, 1976), p. 191–200.

1435–1460. The principle of applying some new rules of spelling (for instance *a* instead of *ja* after vowel, *i* instead of *u* before vowel etc.) shows the new orthographic mode which appeared in Russian countries under South Slavonic influence at the end of the 14th century and progressed during the 15th century. The new phenomena in Novgorod writing do not generally appear before 1415 but in the Novgorod Manuscripts which date from 1438 and after the new writing mode is already advanced. It seems that just around this time the bronze Romanesque Doors became—as one could say*Rus'*ified.

III

A theory persists that the Doors have not been preserved in the original form in which they emerged from the Magdeburg bronze caster's workshop and that some destroyed fragments were replaced by new ones in Novgorod. This view should be reconsidered.

The remounting of the Doors in Novgorod is connected with the 13th century by those art historians who talk of the *Rus'* origin of Master Abraham who was supposed to have carried out this task. This position has been presented most fully by A.I. Anisimov, who concluded that the self-portrait of the Russian master "appeared not later then during the first half of the 14th century and not earlier than the end of the 12th or the beginning of the 13th centuries."

This scholar also supported the Novgorod origin of two further bronze plates:
1) an exceptionally elongated male figure, where "the Russian sculptor helplessly strove to repeat the Romanesque prototype"
2) the image of a centaur designed under the influence of Novgorod iconography of the second half of the 14th century. But due to stylistic differences he did not think it possible to identify their maker with Abraham.[9]

A. Anisimov's interpretation was accepted in principle by A. Goldschmidt. He strongly supported the view concerning the elongated male figure which "is certainly not an original part of the Door and is not by the same sculptor as the others; rather it was first added in Russia in imitation of the Young Man with a jar. What was previously in its place can not be determined."[10]

This statement cannot be accepted. It is worthwhile to examine this figure once more on iconographic grounds.

In the row of the Door reliefs representing Christ's earthly life, we find the one with Christ on the Cross between the Virgin and John the Evangelist. An attempt to set also the omitted Descent from the Cross here right with the Crucifixion is obvious. Next comes the scene of the Women at the Tomb—leaving aside the two male figures who remain up to date unidentified.

The question therefore arises: what should one expect to find between these two scenes? To answer it one should turn from the object to the text. From the New Testa-

[9] A.I. Anisimov, Avtoportret russkogo skul'ptora Avraama, *Izvestija Akademii Nauk SSSR*, 7th ser. (1928), no. 3, p. 173–184. Cf. V.N. Lazarev, in: *Istorija russkogo iskusstva*, 2 (Moskva, 1954), p. 136–137. A.V. Ryndina ascribes the centaur (known now only in the copy after 1947) to a Novgorodian master of the 15th century, who completed the lost plate (also with a centaur?) of the Doors. See her, Novgorod i zapadnoevropejskoje iskusstvo XV veka, in: *Drevnerusskoje iskusstvo. Zarubiežnyje svjazi.* Moscow 1975, p. 248. While not questioning for the time being the thesis about the Russian origin of the plate with the centaur, we should, however, ask whether it did not belong to the original Magdeburg decoration of the Doors. After all, the centaurs on the Augsburg door (1050–1060) and the Trani doors (1175) are not very distant from the image found on the Novgorod doors (cf. H. Leisinger, *Romanische Bronzen*, Kirchentüren im mittelalterlichen Europa, Zürich 1956, T. 36, 63, 67, 68, 81, 143).

[10] A. Goldschmidt, *op. cit.*, p. 16.

Fig. 5. Third row from the bottom of the right wing of the Doors:
a. The Crucification; b. Nicodemus with an oil-vessel; c. Joseph of Arimathaea; d. Women at the Tomb. Photo Courtauld Institute of Art, London.

ment, that is St. John's Gospel (19, 38–42) and St. Mark's (15, 42–6), we learn that two men participated in the Descent from the Cross and the Deposition: Nikodemus the Pharisee, who obtained a large quantity of myrrh and aloes, and Joseph of Arimathaea, the Councillor, who got permission from Pilate to take the body of Jesus from the Cross and to lay it in his own as yet unused tomb.

In connection with this, we should note that this relief, which depicts a Young Man with a jar, has been identified by Goldschmidt as "presumably Nikodemus."[11]

The distinguished scholar remains, however, astonishingly perplexed over the identity of the second figure. This can hardly be anyone else but Joseph of Arimathaea. According to evangelistic tradition both these rich and noble men who gave the last sad honours to the body of Jesus were His concealed disciples. To note are the long vestments typical for noble people and the linen cloths over the hands of both figures for the purpose of enwrapping the body of Jesus. It is highly probably that Joseph, like Nikodemus, had a jar of ointment in his hands, but not impossible that he held the Grail, the Chalice in which he collected Christ's blood.

In Christian iconography in the Middle Ages Joseph of Arimathaea is mainly presented as an old man with white hair and beard, while Nikodemus is differentiated from him by being less old and having a dark beard. But other representations, specially in Ottonian miniatures, are known from X–XII centuries, where both these men present at the Deposition are seen as thin, elongated young men; e.g. in the Bamberg

[11] *Ibidem*, p. 16, 17.

a d b e c

Fig. 6. Bottom row of the left wing:
a, b, c. The makers of the Door: Riquin, Abraham, Waismuth; d. The Fall; e. The Creation of Eve. Photo W. Jerke, Warszawa.

Evangelistary of 1007; the Egbert codex from Reichenau of 980, and the Gospels of Henry the Lion of 1175.[12]

In these the mature and imposing stature of both figures is remarkable; in some representations only Joseph of Arimathaea is portrayed in this way, very suitable to his prominent role at the Descent from the Cross. Such iconography seems to have its source in Byzantine art.[13] Thus there are no grounds for doubting that this relief belongs to the original parts of the Doors. The Magdeburg Master would have presented his tall figure following well-known iconographic model, and this has nothing whatever to do with an imitation made in Novgorod or elsewhere.

A. Goldschmidt also took the position that the lower part of the Doors border fragment, including the console which serves as a pedestal for Abraham's figure, which was cast together as a whole, should be considered as a later innovation in view of the difference of ornaments and in kind of juncture.[14]

These observations open up a field of other suppositions and doubts. How can they be reconciled, for example with the fact ascertained by V.N. Lazarev that, "the splendid plastic form of these Doors with their developed artistic language of mature Romanesque sculpture did not evoke any repercussion in Novgorod"?[15] Was the sculptor-caster

[12] Erna Rampendahl, *Die Ikonographie der Kreuzabnahme vom 9. bis 16. Jh.*, Diss., Berlin 1916, p. 18–21. G. Schiller, *Ikonographie der Christlichen Kunst*, 2 (Gütersloh 1970), 177 ff., 181 ff., ill. 565–586. C. Schweicher, Grablegung Christi, in: *Lexikon der Christlichen Ikonographie* 2, 1970, p. 193.

[13] G. Millet, *Recherche sur l'iconographie de l'evangile aux XIVe, XVe et XVIe siècles.* Paris 1916, p. 596, fig. 620 (the fresco from Torschanle of the middle of the 10th century).

[14] A. Goldschmidt, *op. cit.*, p. 18–19, 21.

[15] V.N. Lazarev, L'art de la Russie médiévale et l'Occident. XIe–XVe siècles (*XIIIe Congrès International des Sciences Historiques*) (Moscow, 1970), p. 25. Cf. also idem, *Iskusstvo Novgoroda* (Moskva 1947), p. 131, where the author stressed that Novgorod was interested in sculpture to a small degree and writes: "The inhabitants of Novgorod did not ever possess a developed sense of plasticity (čuvstvo plastičnogo) which is eloquently witnessed by their painting, ornaments and embroidery".

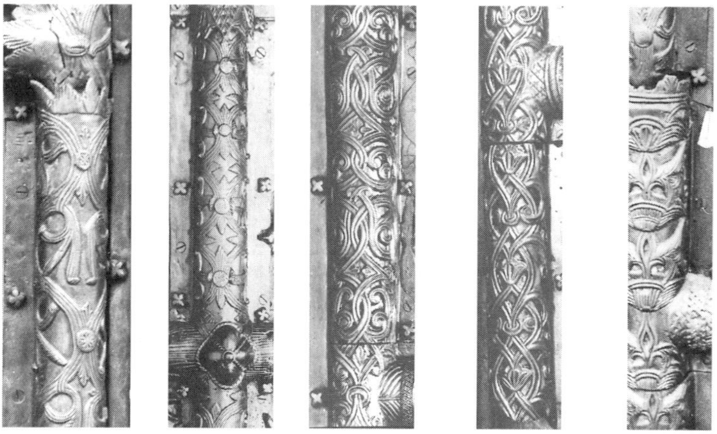

A B C D E

Fig. 7. Ornaments of the half-bolsters of the bordering: patterns *A, B, C, D, E* (description see infra note 16).

of the medieval *Rus'*, absorbed in imitating the Romanesque model, capable of achieving such distance from his own habits and artistic traditions?

Following the reasoning of Anisimov and Goldschmidt one should also suppose that faced with the task of renovating the Doors and in particular supplementing the lacking parts of the frame, the Novgorod master had not only decided to imitate stylistically but also to use patterns which are not present elsewhere in the plastic form of our Doors. Having at his disposal two different ornaments decorating the convex batten of the frame, Abraham had to provide about ten per cent of the border work and decided to decorate six half-bolsters cast by himself with as many as three new types of ornaments (patterns *C, D* and *E*).[16]

It would be premature to negate their Romanesque adherence, although it has been impossible, up to the present, to ascertain any closer analogies.[17] But it should be noted

[16] A. Goldschmidt, *op cit.*, p. 20–21. Pattern *A* reveals two wavy bands running towards each other with small rosettes at the meeting points and tendrils with three or four leaves branching off (fig. 7). Pattern *B* shows a rhythmical row of wavy half circular bands touching each other and bordering three leaved palmettes. At the meeting point of those half circles there is a rosette and four small leaves (fig. 7). Pattern *C* is made up of two rows of intertwining tendril volutes with a ring accenting the horizontal console (see ill.). Pattern *D* consists of two pairs of opposite waving tendrils which cross each other; at the meeting points they are threaded through a ring or calyx row. Pattern *E* portrays a row of climbing calices with palmettes spread out in both directions.

[17] A. Goldschmidt, *op. cit.*, p. 21, describes their style as a later one, influenced by Italian elements (esp. patterns *D* and *E*) as they appear on 14th and 15th century Russian icons. But omitting the fact of a joint Byzantine source which inspired both the Italian and Russian paintings, it should be emphasized that the analogies made by Goldschmidt including the ornaments on the 1336 Novgorod Doors, are too distant to make it possible to speak of any sort of influence. On the other hand a certain, although distant, resemblence to the tendrils of Pattern *D* can be seen in ornaments of the 12th and 13th centuries in Maastricht, Quedlingburg, Nürnberg, Denkendorf, Berg in Carinthia. See *Germania romanica*, text and photos H. Busch (Wien, 1963), Plates 6, 74, 108, 126; O. Demus *Romanische Wandmalerei* (München, 1968), plate 71. Others than in pattern *E*, but similar in a concept of tendrils of calices growing from another, are to be found in the already mentioned Berg (O. Demus, *loc. cit.*) and on the portals in Gurk also in Carinthia from ca. 1190 (*Germania romanica*, plate 158). Ten-

that it is difficult to find an exact analogy in the case of the indubitably Romanesque tendrils bordering the doors: patterns *A* and *B*.

In any case, the place of this renovation and the replacement of missing elements is more likely to be connected with an environment possessing a vivid Romanesque artistic culture or preserving such a tradition. Such a place in the 12th and 13th centuries was Romanesque Płock. But it would seem that this work, including the additions to the border, can also be linked with the casting works in Magdeburg.[18]

A. Goldschmidt had already argued convincingly that the scheme of the Doors underwent changes and additions in the course of manufacture. In particular the dimensions of the Doors were enlarged and thus precisely in the major part of the quarters a narrow plate supplements the wide one. This could also have been the result of a change in the design of the frame, revising the original division in favour of increasing the individual quarters. In such a case there could have been a lack of ornamented half-bolsters of the borderwork and perhaps this is precisely why it was supplemented by others, already at hand, with different ornaments.

The figure of Master Abraham himself with a decided Romanesque character is very akin to Masters Riquin and Waismuth, but more sharply modeled with a greater freedom and more attentive accent on detail.[19] Hence, does the figure of the master with hammer, forceps and casting spoon in his hand represent the main maker of the Doors for Płock in the Magdeburg workshop during the second, final phase? Was his name Abraham or did he intend to remain anonymous? The lack of a Latin inscription makes it possible to suppose that the plate on which the master's figure is placed, much thinner than the remaining plates, was changed. Then the question arises whether the Russian inscription МАСТЕРЪ АВРАМЪ is a translation of an unpreserved Latin inscription or whether the Novgorod artisan in remounting the Doors placed his own name here? Some of these questions would perhaps be resolved by an examination of the alloy (spectral analysis).

In one way or another the principal argument in favour of the Novgorod origin of the figure of Master Abraham remains the Slavic inscription which accompanies it. If as is generally accepted this is a self-portrait of the Russian master who remounted the Doors in Novgorod, then its execution cannot be dated differently from the Cyrillic inscriptions. And it remains to be proved that Abraham's figure was cast in the XV century. But to date I see no chance of success.

In consideration of the here presented reflections I would conclude that both reliefs, the elongated male figure presenting obviously Joseph of Arimathaea and the figure of Master Abraham and the lower parts of the border frames of the Doors, in the shape of

drils of climbing calices can also be seen in ornaments of the 10th and 11th centuries. Cf. A. Goldschmidt, *Die Elfenbeinskulpturen der romanischen Zeit* XI.–XIII. Jh., 1 (Berlin, 1914), ill. 38; 4 (Berlin, 1926), ill. 15b. It should be noted that the spired tendrils in Pattern *C* are not alien to Romanesque ornamentation (cf. H. Decker, *Italia romanica* (Wien, 1958), plate 3; *Germania romanica*, plate 29), its distinction lies in the fact that two rows of tendril volutes intertwine.

[18] A. Zarnecki (*Romanesque Art*. London 1971, p. 107, 108), emphasizing that Magdeburg "became an important center with an international reputation for the casting of bronze", conjectures that the early bronze panels of the doors of S. Zeno at Verona are a work of the Magdeburg workshop ca. 1138.

[19] H. Krohm, "Mittelalterliche Plastik in Rußland", in *Russlandbericht Excursion 1965* (Köln, 1966) p. 250, pointed to a close connection between Abraham and the Romanesque reliefs of the Doors but he did not come to any conclusion about the Romanesque origin of the figure. Ute Götz, on the other hand, in describing the Russian additions together with the figurine of master Abraham as stylistically Late-Romanesque, found it sufficient to state, that the Doors must have reached Novgorod in the Middle Ages. See U. Götz, *Die Bildungsprogramme der Kirchentüren des 11. und 12. Jahrhunderts* (Tübingen, 1971), p. 142.

six half-bolsters with three new designs of tendrils, were executed in a Romanesque workshop. The additional border fragments could have been made most probably as well in Magdeburg since the plan of the Doors underwent certain changes in the course of realization.

Fig. 8. Bottom row of the right wing:
St Maurice with his companions; centaur. Photo W. Jerke, Warszawa.

ADDENDUM

Some technological aspects

This is based on a report on the restoration of the doors (1982) produced by F.B. Arakelian, M.K. Kalish, A.V. Semechkin, N.V. Timofeeva, and A.G. Shishigin (Museum of Novgorod, Archives Nr 1544, vol. 1, spec. table 3). For a diagram of the arrangement of plates and reliefs see fig. 4 on p. 411 above. For more data, see A. Trifonova, "I restauri della Porta di Novgorod", *La Porta di Bonnano nel Duomo di Pisa e le Porte Bronzee Medioevali Europee: Arte e Tecnologia: Atti del Convegno di Studi Pisa 6–8 maggio 1993* (Pontedera 1999), 193–205; A. Poppe, "Iconografia e tecnologia della Porta di Novgorod. Riesame della questione", *ibidem*, 77–106.

A physical and chemical analysis of various parts of the doors was made in 1980 before their restoration. The aim of this examination was to determine the proper alloy to use in repairing numerous damaged points. Since only a very limited number of plates, figures and half-bolsters (about 8 %) were examined, we still do not have enough findings to draw full conclusions.

The bronze alloy of the door (26 samples) is about 75 % copper (Cu), with three supplementary metals: tin (Sn), zinc (Zn), and lead (Pb). Traces of other metals are also present. The difference in alloy content could have resulted from the use of more than one melting pot for a given form. According to the chemist who analyzed the samples in 1980, the differences could also be a result of liquefaction of the alloy during the crystallization process or merely a result of a mistake in the analysis.

The prematurity of any conclusions that can be drawn about the different times and workshops is well illustrated by the results of the 1980 examination. However, there are clear, marked differences in the makeup of the alloys used for the figures of the masters Riquin and Waismuth on the one hand and for that of Abraham on the other.

%%	*Cu*	*Sn*	*Zn*	*Pb*
Riquin (figure)	75.12	1.25	12.74	2.30
Riquin (plate)	76.64	1.43	15.52	2.41
Waismuth (plate)	79.00	1.93	15.02	1.12
Abraham (figure)	77.31	6.02	8.86	3.90
Abraham (figure, 2nd sample)	73.72	6.16	8.11	4.35
Abraham (plate)	75.02	6.89	10.24	4.50

The alloy of the Abraham figure is not far in its composition from three square plates portraying:

	Cu	*Sn*	*Zn*	*Pb*
Prophet Elijah	76.33	2.66	9.54	4.61
Victory over sins	74.27	2.61	11.36	4.29
Oblatio Christi	78.93	1.17	12.14	3.93

It is also close in composition to a rectangular plate portraying:

Three warriors: St Maurice with two companions	77.67	5.66	10.39	2.89

One can not, therefore, rule out the manufacture of the Abraham plates and the four described above by the same workshop, even by the same master. Even with our limited findings, perhaps the following tentative conclusion can be proposed: since Saint Maurice was the patron of the Magdeburg Church this image must have been cast there (unless we want to propose a different iconographic interpretation of that scene). The results of the metallurgical analysis thus provide no grounds for ruling out the production of the Abraham by the Magdeburg workshop as well.

The results of the analysis are too premature to permit any decisive conclusions about the provenance of the scenes portraying the *Traditio legis*:

	Cu	*Sn*	*Zn*	*Pb*
Christ with Peter and Paul (plate)	78.69	1.12	12.74	1.13
Mary and 6 Apostles (plate)	79.20	0.91	13.95	2.38
6 Apostles, (plate)	77.51	1.47	11.49	1.39

No sample was taken from the plate portraying Christ's Ascension. Likewise, no samples were taken from the figures of the two bishops, Alexander and Wichman. It is worth remembering that the very competent, reliable analysis described here was linked directly to the specific needs of restoration work (only Abraham seems to have been treated in any detailed way) and there are therefore no grounds to criticize the study. Nonetheless, there is clearly an urgent need for a comprehensive metallurgical analysis of every constituent bronze part of the doors (including insets and patches), one involving a few hundred samples. Even then, we will not have answers to all the questions that could be raised, since even plates manufactured in the same workshop could conceivably differ one from another. Still, having the recipes of ingredients used for the bronze alloy would clearly provide a better starting point for drawing firmer conclusions about the history of the doors.

XII

ON THE SO-CALLED CHERSONIAN ANTIQUITIES

In seventeenth- and eighteenth-century inventories, from large and small churches all over Russia as well as from private and public collections and museums, there are some cult objects of different ages and provenances, especially icons and crosses, that are described as "Korsunian." The adjective *Korsunian* suggests that these objects originated in Cherson (the Korsun' of the Old Rusian sources). It has been known for a long time, however, that most of them cannot, in fact, be Chersonian in origin. A strong conviction has evolved nevertheless that the adjective *Korsunian* originally referred to those cult objects brought to Rus' from Cherson (as we are told by the Primary Chronicle for the year 989, recording the baptism of the Rusian prince Vladimir) and was later applied to some Old Rusian precious cult objects that were distinguished by their artistic value and were archaic in origin.

The last observation, not entirely unfounded, derives from the fact that beginning in the seventeenth century, the clergy sought Korsunian cult relics for their churches. This cult was further promoted by antiquarians who found support in scientific works that assigned to Cherson an exceptional role regarding artistic influences on Rusian art of the tenth to thirteenth centuries.[1] Twentieth-century data, mainly archaeological, make it possible to ascertain that Cherson did not, in fact, exert the influences ascribed to it on the culture, the art, or even the artistic handicrafts of Kievan Rus'. It turns out that more than ten pectoral crosses with Slavonic inscriptions from excavations in Cherson, earlier regarded as proof of the production of local workshops for the market of Rus', should rather be connected with the migration of the Rusian population that fled there from the Mongol invasion in the middle of the thirteenth century.[2]

Translated from the Polish by Henrik Birnbaum.

[1] N. P. Kondakov, *Russkie klady* (St. Petersburg, 1896), 42-43, 46-47.

[2] G. F. Korzuxina, "O pamjatnikax 'korsunskogo dela' na Rusi (Po materialam mednogo lit'ja)," *VV* 14 (1958): 129-137. A. L. Jakobson, "Russko-korsunskie svjazi XI–XIV vv.," *VV* 14 (1958): 117-128, considered that in the early medieval period the cultural and economic ties of

In opposition to N. Kondakov, who linked Chersonian influences with pre-Mongolian Rus', A. Sobolevskij was prepared to date the influx of "Chersonian" objects into Rusian lands to the thirteenth and fourteenth centuries. According to Sobolevskij, after 1204, when direct contact between Rus' and Byzantium ceased, Cherson and other Crimean towns such as Sugdaia and Caffa began furnishing cult objects. The artistic products of various origins which thus found their way to Rus' began to be called "Korsunian."[3] This hypothesis is derived from the age determinations of many "Korsunian antiquities," mainly icons.

The essence of the matter rests, nonetheless, not only with the age of the relics themselves (some of which did originate in the eleventh century) but also with the circumstances under which they began to be called "Korsunian," circumstances that are so far unclear. The sources do not corroborate G. F. Korzuxina's claim that as the genuine "Korsunian" icons and other cult objects brought to Rus' from Cherson in 989 were exhausted, local ones were substituted and the old designation transferred to them.[4]

In seeking an answer to this question, one should take into account all Old Rusian references to "Chersonian" objects as well as the oldest objects referred to as "Korsunian" themselves.

The Icon of Saint Nikolaj Zarazskij "from Cherson"

Apparently one of the earliest, if not the most ancient, references to a "Korsunian" cult object is found in the cycle of Rjazan' stories about Saint Nikolaj Zarazskij, the first of which relates the story about the bringing "of the miracle-working icon of the great miracle-worker Nikolaj Korsunskij Zarazskij from the renamed city of Cherson, into the land of Rjazan'" in

---

Kievan Rus' stretched directly to Constantinople, bypassing Cherson or using it as a transition point. His suggestion that Cherson became the center of constant economic and cultural ties with Rusian lands beginning in the thirteenth century is not very convincing, especially since Nogaj's capture of the city in 1299 terminated the flourishing urban life of Cherson; see below n. 3, and J. Smedley, "Archeology and the History of Cherson: A Survey of Some Results and Problems," *Arxeion Pontou* 35 (1979): 172-192.

[3] A. I. Sobolevskij, "Dva slova o 'korsunskix predmetax,'" *Novgorodskaja cerkovnaja starina. Trudy Novgorodskogo cerkovnoarxeologičeskogo obščestva* 1 (Novgorod, 1914), 63-65. From the thirteenth century on, Surož-Sugdaia became the center of Russo-Crimean trade relations, which is indicated by the spreading of this city's name throughout the entire Crimean Peninsula (the merchants trading with the Crimea were called "Surožane"; the Sea of Azov was called "Surožean" in Rus'). See the article surveying the basic literature on the subject, D. Andrews, "Moscow and the Crimea in the 13th to 15th Centuries," *Arxeion Pontou* 35 (1979): 261-281. Following A. Sobolevskij, we would expect the imported cult objects in Rus' to be called "Surožean" and not "Chersonian."

[4] Korzuxina, "O pamjatnikax" (see n. 2), 137.

1225.[5] Nonetheless, the complicated literary history of this cycle—parts of which were formed at different times but which were copied as a single entity in the manuscript tradition known to us—does not sufficiently support the accepted fourteenth-century dating of the primary text.[6] Doubts are raised not by the fact that the two most ancient manuscripts from among the more than seventy extant copies belong to the end of the sixteenth century (since a significant hiatus between the compilation of a work and its earliest copy is quite common in the Old Rusian tradition), but by the fact that, clearly, the reconstructed history of the literary life of this text, attested in eleven versions, belongs essentially to the seventeenth to eighteenth centuries, with marks even of the second half of the sixteenth century found in the most ancient of them, the so-called basic version.[7] The year 1560, indirectly recorded in the *Lineage of the Servants of the Miracle-worker Nikola Zaraskov,*[8] probably points to the composition of the cycle of stories about Nikolaj Zarazskij as a single entity, while the question about the time of the compilation of its constituent parts remains open. Of these parts, the primary and most ancient is generally considered to be the well-known *Tale of Batu's Destruction of Rjazan'*. It opens with the report of Batu's invasion of the land of Rus' in the twelfth year after bringing the miracle-working icon of Saint Nikolaj from Cherson. The accepted dating of this tale rests on the premise that the traces of influence upon it from subsequent literary works are later insertions.[9] It is noted, in particular, that the lament of the Rjazan' prince Ingvar' over the demise of all the people close to him and the destruction of Rjazan' had as its source the lament of the widowed princess in *The Tale of the Life and Passing of Grand*

[5] *Voinskie povesti drevnej Rusi* (Moscow–Leningrad, 1949), 249.

[6] It is accepted that the two initial tales of the cycle be considered the basic ones: the previously mentioned *Transference of the Icon of Saint Nikolaj* and the military *Tale About Batu's Destruction of Rjazan'*; see *Istoki russkoj belletristiki* (Leningrad, 1970), 284-285, 287. In the opinion of the author of this section, L. A. Dmitriev, the first tale is older than the second and their merger took place in the first half of the fourteenth century. N. V. Vodovozov's attempt —in an article and subsequently in his *Istorija drevnerusskoj literatury* (Moscow, 1958), 112-116—to ascribe authorship of both tales to Evstafij, the literary participant in the transference of the icon to Rjazan' and the son of the Chersonian priest Eustaphios, must be considered odd.

[7] The literary history of the writing has been clarified thanks to the thorough textual study and publication of all its versions by D. S. Lixačev, "Povesti o Nikole Zarazskom. Teksty," *TODRL* 12 (1949): 257-406. The cycle was also published in nearly complete form (based on a few manuscripts) in *Voinskie povesti* (see n. 5), 9-29, 243-255.

[8] Lixačev, "Povesti," 302, 322; *Voinskie povesti*, 253.

[9] Lixačev, "Povesti," 258-264. Cf. J. Fennell and A. Stokes, *Early Russian Literature* (Berkeley–Los Angeles, 1974), 88-96; cf. the English translation of the *Tale* in *Medieval Russia's Epics, Chronicles and Tales*, ed. S. A. Zenkovsky (New York, 1974), 198-207.

Prince Dmitrij Ivanovič, Tsar of Rus'.[10] But as has been convincingly shown, the latter tale is a work composed in the late 1440s.[11] In the *Tale of the Destruction of Rjazan'* there also appear traces of influence from the *Tale of the Capture of Constantinople in 1453*, based on the notes of an eyewitness to the actual event and available in a reworked version from the beginning of the sixteenth century.[12] More complicated is the relationship between the *Tale of the Destruction of Rjazan'* and the Chronicle's *Tale of the Invasion of Moscow in 1382 by Toxtamyš*, found in a short version from the beginning of the fifteenth century and in an expanded one from the middle of the same century.[13] An incisive explanation of the twofold influence of the *Tale of the Destruction of Rjazan'* on the text of the story about Toxtamyš's invasion of Moscow derives from a presumption about the primacy of the first in relation to the latter.[14] However, textual parallels also render conceivable an opposite and less complicated single influence; it is therefore easier to assume that the more expanded story about the invasion by Toxtamyš (in the Fourth Novgorod Chronicle) influenced the *Tale of the Destruction of Rjazan'*. This is all the more plausible as the latter undoubtedly used a chronicle compilation in which the tale of the invasion by Toxtamyš occurs on an equal footing with the *Tale of the Life and Passing of Grand Prince Dmitrij Ivanovič*.

A conclusion about the late—no earlier than the second half of the fifteenth century—compilation of the *Tale of the Destruction of Rjazan'* would be premature. Yet the suggestion that it belongs to the first half of the fourteenth or even to the end of the thirteenth century remains an

[10] V. P. Adrianova-Peretc, "Slovo o žitii i prestavlenii velikogo knjazja Dmitrija Ivanoviča, carja rus'skago," *TODRL* 5 (1947): 94-95; D. S. Lixačev, "Literaturnaja sud'ba Povesti o razorenii Rjazani Batyem v pervoj četverti XV veka," in *Issledovanija i materialy po drevnerusskoj literature. Sbornik statej* (Moscow, 1961), 16-20; id., *Tekstologija* (Moscow–Leningrad, 1962), 254-258.

[11] M. A. Salmina, "Slovo o žitii i o prestavlenii velikogo knjazja Dmitrija Ivanoviča, carja rus'skago," *TODRL* 25 (1970): 81-104; M. F. Antonova, "Slovo o žitii i o prestavlenii velikogo knjazja Dmitrija Ivanoviča, carja rus'skago," *TODRL* 28 (1974): 140-154; W. Vodoff, "Quand a pu être composé le Panégyrique du grand-prince Dmitrii Ivanovich, tsar' russe?" *Canadian-American Slavic Studies* 13, nos. 1-2 (1979): 82-101.

[12] M. N. Speranskij, "Povesti i skazanija o vzjatii Car'grada turkami," *TODRL* 10 (1954): 136-165; Ja. S. Lur'e, *Ideologičeskaja bor'ba v russkoj publicistike konca XV–načala XVI veka* (Moscow–Leningrad, 1960), 355-356.

[13] A short account in the chronicle compilation of 1408, expanded in that of 1448. See M. A. Salmina, "Povest' o našestvii Toxtamyša," *TODRL* 34 (1979): 143-151. Cf. Ja. S. Lur'e, *Obščerusskie letopisnye svody XIV–XVI vv.* (Leningrad, 1976), 65-66.

[14] Lixačev, "Literaturnaja sud'ba" (see n. 10), 11-16; also id., *Tekstologija* (see n. 10), 249-252 (cf. the correspondences cited there).

unreliable hypothesis and requires more weighty proof.[15] The proposed attempt to reconstruct the ancient text of the *Tale* might play an important role here.[16] Such a reconstruction requires the removal of all texts recognized as insertions in the original and the exclusion of all later stylistic and linguistic phenomena, traces of Turkic influence which, incidentally, are clearly related to the fifteenth and sixteenth centuries.[17] But would these measures not violate the composition and thematic unity of the work? The *Tale of the Destruction of Rjazan'* in its present form is an artistic work, and although it deals with an important historical event, it is not very historical.[18] Moreover, the factual aspect of the event in the *Tale* is not only insufficiently illuminated but is simply confused. Attempts to make out the genealogy of the Rjazan' princes present in the *Tale* are futile since the author has simply invented several personages while indiscriminately copying others from the chronicles and then forcing them to perish at the hand of Batu's hordes, while in reality they died earlier than 1237 or continued to flourish in subsequent decades.[19] None of these genealogical distortions seem to be the "epic" inexactitudes of an artistic work that arose two to three centuries after the events described. The early dating of the *Tale* as a work of the time when the sons and grandsons of the Rjazan' princes

[15] The basis of the *Tale* is the contemporaneous chronicle account about Batu's destruction of Rjazan', which is most fully reflected in the Synodal copy of the First Novgorod Chronicle under the year 1238; see D. S. Lixačev, "K istorii složenija Povesti o razorenii Rjazani Batyem," *Arxeografičeskij ežegodnik za 1962* (Moscow, 1963), 48-51. J. L. I. Fennell, "The Tale of Batu's Invasion of Northeast Rus' and its Reflexion in the Chronicles of the Thirteenth-Fifteenth Centuries," *Russia Mediaevalis* 3 (1977): 65-66, also favors the Rjazan' chronicle as a source. In the opinion of A. G. Kuz'min, *Rjazanskoe letopisanie* (Moscow, 1965), 154-165, the particular *Story of Batu's Destruction of Rjazan'*, compiled by a contemporary of the events, appears to be the source of all the chronicle versions as well as of the *Tale*. The author's view that the *Tale of Nikolaj Zarazskij* should be dated at the beginning of the sixteenth century is undoubtedly interesting; however, his assertion that the *Story* is to be identified with the *Tale* without subsequent additions, and the attribution of the motif of the icon's transferral from Cherson to the text of the thirteenth century, reinforce the hypothetical nature of this assumption.

[16] See D. S. Lixačev, "Obščie principy rekonstrukcii literaturno-xudožestvennyx tekstov" in *Tekstologija slavjanskix literatur* (Moscow, 1973), 131-137.

[17] See A. S. Demin, "Èlementy tjurkskoj kul'tury v literature drevnej Rusi XV–XVII vv.," in *Tipologija i vzaimosvjazi srednevekovyx literatur Vostoka i Zapada* (Moscow, 1974), 321.

[18] According to the apt remark of A. S. Orlov, *Geroičeskie temy drevnej russkoj literatury* (Moscow–Leningrad, 1945), 107.

[19] Cf. Lixačev, "Povesti' (see n. 7), 261, and also his commentary in *Voinskie povesti* (see n. 5), 284ff. It should be pointed out that the genealogy of the Rjazan' princes, established in the 1540s, is based on the chronicle tradition and completely ignores the genealogical legend of the *Tale of Batu's Destruction of Rjazan'*; see the edition of family registers of the sixteenth century by A. N. Bočkareva and M. E. Byčkova in *Redkie istočniki po istorii Rossii*, vol. 2 (Moscow, 1977), 80.

lived—the princes who were contemporaries of the invasion of Batu—raises doubts that up to now have not been satisfactorily answered.

The first part of the cycle, which is dedicated specifically to the history of the miracle-working icon of Saint Nikolaj, belongs to the characteristic migrant motifs of medieval literature: transferring the sacred relics from the ancient cult site to the new. It is impossible to attribute its compilation to a time near to the imaginary event, that is, to the thirteenth century, because of the legendary quality of the main personages of this tale—including the new guardians of the icon, the Rjazan' appanage prince Fedor Jur'evič and his wife Evpraksija, "from the royal family"—who were completely unknown to the chronicles. In a completely undefined, unclear fashion, the *Tale* and the *Transference of the Icon of Saint Nikolaj* speak of the new location of the icon "within the boundaries of the Rjazan' land, in the appanage of the faithful prince, Fedor Jur'evič of Rjazan'," but the district, that is, the domain, of this prince is not named. Evpraksija, along with her infant son, was said to have thrown herself out of the church built by Prince Fedor Jur'evič (Saint Nikolaj of Cherson) when she learned that her husband had perished in a battle with the Tatars. The two hurtled (*zarazišasja*) to their deaths and therefore, "the great miracle-worker Nikolaj is called Zaraskij."[20] The author of the *Transference* indicates the old location of the icon in Cherson, in the middle of the city near the Church of the Holy Apostle James, in which the "autocrat and grand prince of all Rus', Vladimir Svjatoslavič of Kiev" was baptized. The reference to the Church of Saint James as the place of Vladimir's baptism is secondary in relation to that of the account of the Primary Chronicle and appears in the version of the *Life of Vladimir*, compiled no earlier than the second half of the fourteenth century.[21] The designation of Anastas Chersonian as bishop of Cherson seems to be a later addition. This office was assigned to Anastas only in the very latest adaptations of the expanded *Life of Saint Vladimir*, belonging already to the sixteenth century.[22] At any rate, the glorification

[20] *Voinskie povesti* (see n. 5), 10, 17, 249, 252f.; see also below, nn. 41, 42.

[21] The most ancient preserved manuscript copy of the *vita* from the 1470s (corresponding to a lost manuscript of 1414, known in a copy from the beginning of the nineteenth century) has been published by A. A. Zimin, "Pamjat' i poxvala Iakova mnixa i žitie knjazja Vladimira po drevnejšemu spisku," in *Kratkie soobščenija Instituta slavjanovedenija* 37 (1963): 72-75. From the middle of the fifteenth century, the Church of Saint James (the existence of this church in Cherson is not known) also appears in the chronicle accounts about the baptism of Rus'. See the Fourth Novgorod and First Sophia Chronicles, *PSRL* 4, pt. 1, sec. 1 (1915): 82; 5, pt. 1 (1925): 66. The Novgorodian linguistic features of the manuscripts of 1414 and the 1470s also point to the Novgorodian origin of this detail.

[22] The West Russian version according to the manuscript of the second half of the sixteenth century. See, "Sbornik Belorusskij Čudova Monastyrja. Bibliografičeskie materialy A. I.

of Anastas as bishop began no earlier than the end of the fifteenth century and in all probability was only introduced in the first half of the sixteenth century.[23] Finally, the reference to the Greek emperors—"Vasilej, Kostjantin Porfienitos, the Orthodox"—in the *Transference of the Icon of Saint Nikolaj* clearly shows the influence of the listing of Byzantine emperors, "the tsars, ruling in Constantinople, who are orthodox and heretics," a listing that appeared in Rusian chronicles and chronographs beginning with the middle of the fifteenth century.[24] The hellenized form of the record

---

Popova," ed. M. Speranskij, *ČOIDR*, 1889, bk. 3: 35-39. In the Moscow version, this *vita* is known in a manuscript copy from the seventeenth century and according to its stilted exposition is defined as a stylistic reworking of no earlier than the middle of the sixteenth century; see N. I. Serebrjanskij, "Drevnerusskie knjažeskie žitija. Obzor redakcij i teksty," *ČOIDR*, 1915, bk. 3: 62-65, nos. 7, 21-25. It seems that the advancement of the "man named Anastas" to the office of bishop of Cherson took place gradually, which is even noticeable in the inconsistency of the citations in the later reworkings of the *Life of Saint Vladimir*; the Moscow version more consistently represents Anastas as holding the office of bishop. In the Commission manuscript of the First Novgorod Chronicle (see *Novgorodskaja pervaja letopis' staršego i mladšego izvodov*, ed. A. N. Nasonov and M. N. Tixomirov [Moscow–Leningrad, 1950], 165) he is referred to as a priest for the first time. At any rate, the ascribing of the priesthood to Anastas is a fact of the fifteenth century since the Fourth Novgorod Chronicle notes it (*PSRL* 4, pt. 1, sec. 1 [1950]: 91), but in its protograph, i.e., in the chronicle compilation of 1448, judging by the First Sophia Chronicle traceable to the same protograph, Anastas was not yet a priest. Anastas' priesthood is noted by such manuscripts of the second half of the fifteenth century as the Ermolin Chronicle and the Moscow Chronicle of 1479; also some of the chronicles of the sixteenth century continue to call Anastas a priest (see the Voskresenie Chronicle, *PSRL* 7 [1856]: 313). but it is characteristic that the priesthood of Anastas is unknown to the Nikon Chronicle compilation of the 1520s and 1530s.

[23] A. A. Šaxmatov considered that Anastas was a priest, but honoring him as a bishop "seems to be in connection with the significance which this Chersonian acquired among the clergy of the Church of the Tithe" ("Korsunskaja legenda o kreščenii Vladimira," in *Sbornik posvjaščennyj ... V. I. Lamanskomu*, pt. 2 [St. Petersburg, 1908], 1109, 1064). In connection with this observation by Šaxmatov, Serebrjanskij wrote that the reports of the episcopal office of Anastas in the *Life of Saint Vladimir* "if not completely arbitrary, are in any event based on sources of dubious antiquity and extremely low value" ("Drevnerusskie knjažeskie žitija," 75ff.). In reality, Anastas was not even a cleric but a secular figure, a steward of the prince's church (the Church of the Tithe) in Kiev. See L. Müller, *Zum Problem des hierarchischen Status und der jurisdiktionellen Abhängigkeit der russischen Kirche vor 1039* (Köln–Braunsfeld, 1959), 42-47; A. Poppe, *Państwo i kościół na Rusi w XI w.* (Warsaw, 1968), 46-48; id., "The building of the Church of St. Sophia in Kiev," *Journal of Medieval History* 7 (1981): 24, 55, nn. 47-49. The groundlessness of A. Šaxmatov's attempt ("Korsunkaja legenda," 1029–1153, particularly the reconstruction, 1143ff.) to recover the ancient form (second half of the eleventh century) of the so-called Chersonian legend, i.e., the *Tale of the Life of Saint Vladimir*, by adducing later reworkings of the *Life* (where, incidentally, Anastas is named as a bishop), has been persuasively proven by Serebrjanskij, "Drevnerusskie knjažeskie žitija," 43-81. However, even Šaxmatov himself recognized the precariousness of his reconstruction: "The restoration of the *Tale of the Baptism of Vladimir* leads us into the sphere of suppositions and guesswork" ("Korsunskaja legenda," 1137).

[24] See O. V. Tvorogov, *Drevnerusskie xronografy* (Leningrad, 1975), 28, 118.

Porfienitos instead of the usual *Porfirogenit,*[25] shown along with the adapted form *Cherson* for the Old Rusian *Korsun'*, focuses attention on the attempts at erudition characteristic of Russian bookmen of the fifteenth and sixteenth centuries.

At any rate, it is absolutely impossible to recognize all these data about Vladimir's baptism in Cherson as a later insertion in the *Transference of the Icon of Saint Nikolaj.* For here lies the essence of the story: to show that the transference concerned not merely the miracle-working icon of Saint Nikolaj but an icon topographically connected with the great event that gave rise to Orthodox Rus'.

The only text of the cycle of tales about Nikolaj Zarazskij that lends itself to a more exact dating is the so-called *Kolomnian Episode*, a story about the transferral in 7021 of the miracle-working icon of Saint Nikolaj to the town of Kolomna, about the icon's later theft, and the miraculous tracking down of its frame.[26] On the basis of the mention of Prince Jurij, the brother of Vasilij III, who was considered the heir to the throne of Moscow until the birth of Ivan IV on August 25, 1530, the chronological boundaries of the compilation of the Kolomnian story have been reliably established as being between 1513 and 1530.[27] This dating can presumably be made more precise by taking into account the role ascribed in this story to Bishop Mitrofan of Kolomna, who is described as flourishing.[28] The theft of the frame apparently took place at the beginning of 1515.[29] Nothing is noted in the story about the miraculous return of the icon to its old place in the district of Rjazan'. The second Kolomnian story, which was compiled later, also relates this event to the time of Bishop Mitrofan.[30] At

[25] Cf. the list of the Byzantine emperors in the Nikon Chronicle, *PSRL* 9: 20; *PSRL* 12: 82.

[26] Lixačev, "Povesti" (see n. 7), 346-348; *Voinskie povesti* (see n. 5), 253-255. The reason for the transferral—the devastating incursion of the Tatars onto Rjazan' soil—is supported by the chronicle reports for October of 7021 (cf. *PSRL* 28 [1963]: 347), i.e., the fall of 1512, and not of 1513 as is usually recounted, disregarding September as the beginning of the year.

[27] V. L. Komarovič, "K literaturnoj istorii Povesti o Nikole Zarazskom," *TODRL* 5 (1947): 65.

[28] Mitrofan was appointed bishop on February 1, 1506, and left the post because of illness in June 1518; see *PSRL* 13: 5, 29.

[29] According to the Kolomnian story, the theft occurred two years and fifteen weeks after the icon was brought to Kolomna, and the frame was "missing" for five weeks; see *Voinskie povesti* (see n. 5), 254. At that same time (1513–14), a church was built in the name of Saint Nikolaj Zarazskij for the miracle-working icon by order of the grand prince. The existence of this church, along with its keeping by the tsar's treasury, is supported by the cadaster of 1577–78. See *Piscovye knigi XVI v.*, sec. 1, ed. N. B. Kalačev (St. Petersburg, 1872), 301, 306.

[30] Lixačev, "Povesti" (see n. 7), 348ff. The precise dating of the icon's return on the third Sunday of Lent (the Veneration of the Cross), March 9, indicates a later provenance (the middle or second half of the sixteenth century) of this story. Both of these events occurred in a

any rate, the *Kolomnian Episode* was recorded before 1528–1531—when the construction of the stone fortress and church in honor of Saint Nikolaj Zarazskij was begun and completed.[31]

Great significance must be attached to the complete absence of any reference to the Chersonian origin of the miracle-working icon of Saint Nikolaj in the *Kolomnian Episode* of 1515–1528. He is called here the miracle-worker Nikolaj Zarazskij, and never the miracle-worker Nikolaj of Cherson, although the latter appellation does appear in both of the primary tales of the cycle (it occurs in the *Tale of the Destruction of Rjazan'* and is dominant in the *Transference of the Icon of Saint Nikolaj*). This nonmention is all the more revealing since, as is clear in both Kolomnian stories, there were attempts to keep the miracle-working icon in Kolomna, not allowing it to return to its "old site," which was, after all, not within the boundaries of the Kolomnian diocese, but in the eparchy of Rjazan'. The very attempt to retain the sacred relic, additionally justified by the ever-present danger of Tatar raids, is completely understandable, but concealing the Chersonian genealogy of the miracle-working icon, thus providing more of a basis for Kolomna's ownership of the sacred relic, would be completely incomprehensible. Analysis of the Kolomnian story leads to the conclusion that the miracle-working icon of Saint Nikolaj Zarazskij was already known and worshiped in Kolomna in the second decade of the sixteenth century but that the legend about its Chersonian origin was unknown.

The challenge I have directed at the currently prevailing opinion inevitably leads to the question of when the cult of the Zarazskian miracle-working icon originated. The fact that the icon, which has been preserved to the present day, is a painting of the early sixteenth century does not answer the question, since the presumed original Zarazskian icon could have been lost and replaced. But neither is there substantiation for the assumption that the iconographic type, already known among Russian icons of the fourteenth and fifteenth centuries (which represent Saint Nikolaj standing erect in bishop's robes, the Gospels in his left hand and blessing with his right), had been called Zarazskian from the very beginning—that is, since the thirteenth century, under the influence of the cult of the Zarazskian icon of the

---

year when Easter fell on April 6. In the sixteenth century this could only have been 1539, 1550, 1561, or 1577. The icon's return occurred at the latest in 1531, when the construction of the Zarazskij fortress was completed.

[31] The Chronographic Chronicle of 1451–1551 records for the year 7036: "In the same year the grand prince founded a stone borough on the Osetr and in it the stone church of the miracle-worker Nikolaj Zarazskij," *PSRL* 22 (1911): 521; cf. S. O. Šmidt, "Prodolženie xronografa redakcii 1512 goda," *Istoričeskij Arxiv* 7 (1951): 283. For the completion of the construction in 1531, see *PSRL* 8: 278; *PSRL* 13: 58; *PSRL* 20: 412.

saint which was supposed to have begun at that time[32] The most ancient icon, which is inscribed "Nikolae Zarajski," belongs to the very end of the sixteenth century.[33] The fact that the depiction of Nikolaj with outstretched arms was in no way called "Zarazskian" in Moscow in the first quarter of the sixteenth century is verified by the extensive record of 1524 on the reverse side of the recently restored icon "of the holy and great miracle-worker Nikola," dated to the beginning of the fourteenth century.[34] It would be more correct to conclude that it was not the miracle-working icon

[32] Cf. V. I. Antonova, "Moskovskaja ikona XIV veka iz Kieva i Povesti o Nikole Zarajskom," *TODRL* 13 (1957): 375-392. Antonova's assertion about the composition of the ancient form of the *Tale About Nikolaj Zarazskij* at the end of the thirteenth or beginning of the fourteenth century forms the initial premise of her erroneous reconstructions. On the iconography of Saint Nikolaj with outstretched arms, see È. S. Smirnova, *Živopis' Velikogo Novgoroda serediny XIII—načala XV veka* (Moscow, 1976), 195-197, 201-203. It has been shown quite persuasively that the question of identifying this iconography as Zarazskian remains open; cf. G. V. Popov and A. V. Ryndina, *Živopis' i prikladnoe iskusstvo Tveri XIV–XVI v.* (Moscow, 1979), 348, no. 3. There is also reason to doubt Antonova's assertion that the original depiction of Saint Nikolaj Zarazskij, i.e., the icon which was brought to Kolomna in 1512, was *v dejanijax*, that is to say, that the depiction of Saint Nikolaj in the middle was framed by scenes from the life and miracles of the saint. From the Kolomnian stories it follows that soon after the miracle-working icon was transferred to Kolomna, a copy was made that was eventually housed in the Kolomna Church of Saint Nikolaj Zarazskij. According to V. Antonova, this icon is presently located in the Treťjakov Gallery; see V. I. Antonova and N. E. Mneva, *Katalog drevnerusskoj živopisi*, vol. 2 (Moscow, 1963), 162-64, no. 557. But is this really the same icon? In a detailed description of the icons of the Kolomna Church of Nikolaj Zarazskij from 1577–78, four icons depicting Saint Nikolaj are enumerated. The first in the description must be regarded as a copy of the miracle-working icon, distinguished by an abundance of gold and silver pendants (votive offerings), while no such ornamentation is mentioned for the second icon, described as *s dejaniem*; see *Piscovye knigi XVI v.* (see n. 29), 306.

[33] Cf. Antonova, "Moskovskaja ikona," 378, no. 3; Smirnova, *Živopis' Velikogo Novgoroda*, 196. I note the use of the new form *Zarajski(j)*, which appears only at the end of the sixteenth century, instead of the old form *Zarazski(j)*. Antonova's assertion (pp. 380-384), with reference to the Nikon Chronicle, that a church named for Saint Nikolaj Zarazskij had already existed in Moscow in 1471 must be ascribed to a pure misunderstanding, since this chronicle notes only that the metropolitan met the grand prince "with crosses near the church" (this is the way it reads in the majority of the manuscripts, but in one it reads, "near the great church," i.e., the cathedral, see *PSRL* 12: 141). Even if it is agreed that the Church of Saint Nikolaj *v sapožkax* is intended here, there is still no indication that in the fifteenth or sixteenth century it was called by the name of Nikolaj Zarazskij.

[34] Antonova, "Moskovskaja ikona," 375ff. See further, Antonova and Mneva, *Katalog drevnerusskoj živopisi*, vol. 1 (see n. 32), 78-80, no. 13. Considering that the icon represents the "Zarazskian" iconographic type of the saint, Antonova tries to prove the Kievan origin of this icon and on the same grounds to explain the national (Kievan), and not Byzantine (Chersonian) sources of the worship of the icon of Saint Nikolaj Zarazskij. Without discussing this line of thinking there, we note that Antonova's opinion that the restoration of the icon in 1524 was connected "with an intensification of interest in the *Tale About Nikolaj Zarazskij*," is completely unsubstantiated, since neither the icon-reverse inscription of 1524 nor the subsequent extensive inscriptions about the renovations in 1656 and 1691 mention that the icon depicts the miracle-worker Zarazskij.

of Nikolaj Zarazskij that gave rise to the spread of this iconographic type in Rusian lands, but the reverse: that the spread of depicting the bishop-saint standing up, blessing and teaching (the Gospels), occurred before the appearance of the local Zarazskian cult with a representation of this type.

The issue of where the cult was initially located has not been settled. As noted above, the tales of Nikolaj Zarazskij do not pinpoint the location of the miracle-working icon, referring only to the "land of Rjazan'." It is noteworthy that even from the *Kolomnian Episode* it follows only that the miracle-working icon was located in the Church of Nikolaj Zarazskij "na Rjazani," that is, on Rjazanian soil, before its transfer to Kolomna in the fall of 1512.[35] A town or population referred to as Zarazsk or Zarajsk did not yet exist at this time; claims ascribing the founding of Zarazsk to the twelfth or thirteenth century, apart from a reference to a tale about Nikolaj Zarazskij, are insufficient evidence. According to innumerable citations in the sources from the sixteenth to seventeenth centuries—including such official documents as military records, beginning with the building of the stone fortress in 1528–1531—the town continually, throughout the sixteenth and into the seventeenth century, bore the name "Nikolaj Zarazskij," sometimes with the elucidation "on the Osetr," especially in the early period.[36] That this name was derived from the fact that the fortress was built on the site of a *pogost* (i.e., a parish church with a cemetery), where the church named for Saint Nikolaj had stood, seems convincing.[37] Until

[35] Lixačev, "Povesti" (see n. 7), 346ff.; *Voinskie povesti* (see n. 5), 253 ff. Rjazan' is named in this story not in the sense of a city but in the accepted sense of the land or principality of Rjazan'. For this usage, see the Testament of Grand Prince Ivan III of 1504, in *Duxovnye i dogovornye gramoty velikix i udel'nyx knjazej XIV–XVI vv.* (Moscow–Leningrad, 1950), no. 89, pp. 357 ff.; see also p. 473 (the deed of 1539).

[36] See the index in *Razrjadnaja kniga 1475–1598*, ed. V. I. Buganov (Moscow, 1966). Here, beginning with October 1531, the fortress-town "Nikolaj Zarazskij" (by the end of the century the form "Zarajskij" also appears) is mentioned 44 times. It is interesting that in the first reference of 1531, this borough is called "on the Osetr with Nikola" (ibid., 81). In the duty-books of 1594–1597 it is named "gorod Nikoly Zarazkogo" or simply "Nikolaj Zarazskij" or "Nikolaj" (see *Piscovye knigi Rjazanskogo kraja*, vol. 1, no. 1 [Rjazan' 1898], 157-158). And in the seventeenth century, the town officially continues to be called Nikolaj Zarazskij (see *Razrjadnye knigi 1550–1636*, no. 2, [Moscow, 1976], 254); but from the end of the sixteenth to the beginning of the seventeenth century, "the Zarazskij (Zaraskov, Zarajskij) borough" comes into use; cf. *PSRL* 14: 28, 29, 89, 99, 107; 31 (1968): 152; *Pamjatniki russkoj pis'mennosti XV–XVI vv. Rjazanskij kraj* (Moscow, 1978), 80. In the 1627 source (known only from the manuscripts of the 1670s and 1680s), "the borough of Zaraesk (Zarazesk)" and "the borough Zarajskij" are mentioned; see *Kniga bol'šomu čertežu* (Moscow, 1950), 120-122.

[37] M. N. Tixomirov, *Rossija v XVI stoletii* (Moscow, 1962), 402. A. G. Kuz'min, *Rjazanskoe letopisanie* (Moscow, 1965), 87, 173, indicated with good reason a later origin of the town of Nikolaj Zarazskij but mistakenly suggested that in the 1530s the new name Nikolaj Zarazskij appeared, replacing the old name Osetr. Yet, citing the single chronicle reference to the city

1528 there had been neither fortifications nor a town there, and "none of the archaeological materials known to us from the city of Zarajsk permits us to speak about its antiquity."[38] This assertion has forced one investigator to pose the legitimate question: "Can the tale itself, closely connected by its subject matter with this town, be related to such an early time," that is, to 1225?[39] In answering this question negatively, one must, however, note that the legend in the cycle of tales about Nikolaj Zarazskij does not at all reflect an attempt to interpret the town's appellation, Zarazsk. Yet this is often proposed,[40] if only because in the sixteenth century, when this legend undoubtedly already existed, there was no town with precisely that name. The legend does attempt to interpret the church and miracle-working icon's designation "Zarazskian" as being prior to the designation "Chersonian."[41] Only a later chronographic variant (c. 1599) of the *Tale of the Destruction of Rjazan'* (a reworking of the basic version) attempts to explain the legend topographically. It mentions that the place where the church had stood, from which the princess and her son had hurled themselves, began to be called Zaraz.[42] Considering the meaning of this word as 'steep slope, precipice, ravine', it seems reasonable to assume that this attempt at an explanation was based on the topography of the site selected for the fortress "Nikolaj Zarazskij."

The Zarazskian fortress was built on a high, steep, hilly bank of the Osetr River and was, moreover, protected on all sides by gullies and ravines.[43] But before this, the wooden church of Saint Nikolaj had stood

Osetr under the year 1541 in the so-called Book of the Reign (*PSRL* 13: 434; cf. *PSRL* 34: 174), Kuz'min did not take into account the fact that the town Osetr, instead of the river Osetr, appeared here as a result of the unsuccessful abridgement of one and the same text: "the Crimean tsar came ... to the Osetr to the borough Nikolaj Zarazski," *PSRL* 13: 138.

[38] A. L. Mongajt, *Rjazanskaja zemlja* (Moscow, 1961), 238.

[39] Lixačev, *Tekstologija* (see n. 10), 544ff.

[40] Cf. Kuz'min, *Rjazanskoe letopisanie* (see n. 37), 173.

[41] The *Tale of the Destruction of Rjazan'*, reporting the burial of prince Fedor, his wife Evpraksija and son in the church "of the great miracle-worker Nikolaj of Cherson," gives the following explanation: "And because of this may the great miracle-worker Nikolaj be called Zarazskij: because the faithful princess Evpraksija, along with her son, Prince Ivan, had flung herself to her death (*sama sebe zarazi*)," *Voinskie povesti* (see n. 5), 17. The same text repeats verbatim the *Transference of the Icon,* ibid., 253. Cf. Lixačev, "Povesti" (see n. 7), 287, 300, 328, 341.

[42] *Voinskie povesti* (see n. 5), 25; Lixačev, "Povesti" (see n. 7), 353: "And whence derived the place name Zaraz: because it was there that princess Evpraksija and her son had hurtled to their death (*zarazisja*)." In an abridged chronographic redaction of about 1661, the form Zarazsk already appears; see ibid., 273, 357.

[43] V. V. Kostočkin, *Russkoe oboronitel'noe zodčestvo* (Moscow, 1962), 83-84. Settlements named Zaraz are known in the district of Moscow, Rjazan' and Tula; see V. A. Nikonov, *Kratkij toponimičeskij slovar'* (Moscow, 1966), 145. According to the cadaster of 1578–79,

there, and, because of its location either on the *zaraz* 'steep bank' of the river, or among the *zarazy* 'ravines', began to be called *Zarazskian.* The *Kolomnian Episode* of 1515–1528 has only a reference to the Church of Nikolaj Zarazskij within the Rjazan' Land. That this mention is simultaneously an indication of the site location (c. 40 km from Kolomna) becomes evident only after the building of the fortress that acquired the name Nikolaj Zarazskij. Consequently, even before the *Kolomnian Episode* of 1512, this church began to be famous for its miracle-working icon. The icon's cult had a local and limited character, which is shown by the remote placement of the parish cemetery and the wooden church. All of this also speaks in favor of the recent date of this cult. However, the first known manifestation of the icon's miracle-working power occurred in Kolomna in 1515. Hospitable Kolomna's attempt to retain the icon, and Vasilij III's attention to it—he ordered a stone church to be built in Kolomna in the name of Nikolaj Zarazskij—added a new dimension to the cult. The Muscovite grand prince continued to promote the development of the cult of the miracle-working icon. While his decision to build a stone fortress on the Osetr, protecting the southern approaches to Moscow, was dictated by military considerations, it is also true that a spiritual bulwark was purposefully raised against the Tatar threat, and thus the stone church was built along with the fortress in the name of the protector-saint, prepared to house his miracle-working icon—a palladium in the struggles with the Tatars.[44] Pilgrimages by the sovereign raised the miracle-working icon to the level of a statewide sacred relic of Muscovy: in March of 1533, Vasilij III made a

---

several toponyms are known in the neighboring Kašira district: Zaraz, Zarazy, Zarazskoe Pole; see *Piscovye knigi XVI v.*, sec. 2 (Moscow, 1877), 1389, 1404, 1406, 1411, 1416.

[44]Saint Nikolaj was widely worshiped as the patron of the Rusian land. By the fifteenth century, the cult of Saint Nikolaj of Možajsk the miracle-worker already embodied the idea of the bishop-protector. Antonova's suggestion ("Moskovskaja ikona" (see n. 32), 386) that the cult of Nikolaj Zarazskij gave birth to the iconography of the image of Nikolaj of Možajsk (with a sword and town church in his outstretched hands) is unsubstantiated, even though the Možajsk cult is older than that of Zarazskij. The description of the icons located in the churches of Kolomna in 1577—the city where, in the second decade of the sixteenth century, the miracle-working icon of Nikolaj Zarazskij was located and the Church of Saint Nikolaj Zarazskij was built—bears witness to the fact that the spread of the cult of this miracle-working icon (as attested by the practice of making copies from this icon) did not begin immediately. But of more than thirty icons of Saint Nikolaj from various churches, not one is called "Zarazskian," while four icons of Nikolaj of Možajsk are mentioned in the various churches of Kolomna; see *Piscovye knigi XVI v.* (see n. 29), sec. 1, 306, 319-320, 331. It is interesting that in Kazan', where the icons were received from all over Russia, including many donations from the tsar, the registers of 1566 make no mention of a Zarazskian copy, although they do note the icon of the saint-bishop of Možajsk among the icons of the Church of Saint Nikolaj Ratnyj; P. Zarinskij, *Očerki drevnej Kazani preimuščestvenno XVI veka* (Kazan', 1877), 106.

pilgrimage to Nikolaj Zarazskij, followed in August of 1550 and in June of 1556 by Ivan IV, and in May of 1562 by Tsarevich Fedor.[45]

The miracle-working icon of Saint Nikolaj Zarazskij had no Chersonian pedigree in the initial period of its worship. But the necessity of ascribing to it a worthy genealogy began to ripen from the moment that Vasilij III raised it to the rank of state sanctuary.[46] The origin of the legend about the Chersonian ancestry of the icon and its literary manifestation must be related to a time after 1531.[47] The addition of the icon to the sacred relics traceable to the days of the baptism of the first Christian ruler of Rus' has something in common with the ideopolitical program of the Muscovite descendants of the Rurik dynasty. But the very thought of such a genealogy could not have arisen in isolation and must be connected with the interest in the Chersonian sacred relics that began to appear in Rusian lands, primarily, as we shall see, in Novgorod. It is not by accident that the legend about the travel of the icon directed attention to that city: the icon was brought from Cherson onto the soil of Rjazan' by way of Novgorod where, remaining for "many days," it bore witness to itself "by great miracles."

[45] *Razrjadnaja kniga* (see n. 36), 129, 158; *PSRL* 8: 22; *PSRL* 13: 68, 341. But in those years the Zarazskian icon had undoubtedly not yet achieved the level of worship that the Možajsk icon, or even the miracle-working icon of Saint Nikolaj of Vjatka (Velikoreck, Vjatka) had attained. In 1555 the latter was transferred to Moscow, where it remained for more than a year and was restored by Metropolitan Makarij himself. At that same time, "many icons of him were made in his measure and likeness." The tsar even built a wooden church in honor of Nikolaj of Vjatka and established a stone side-chapel in the name of the same saint in the Church of Vasilij Blažennyj, which was being built as a monument to the Kazan' victory. See *PSRL* 13: 254–255, 273, 320.

[46] Antonova has noted that the Chersonian theme was developed in detail only in the sixteenth century during a reworking of the tales about Nikolaj Zarazskij in connection with the revival of his military cult and in keeping with the general direction of the Russian historical conception ("Moskovskaja ikona" [see n. 32], 379, 392). This quite vaguely formulated thought about a "detailed elaboration"—suggesting that in its rudimentary form, the Chersonian episode is older than the sixteenth century—was indicated by a a desire "to prove the original Rusian (Kievan) sources of the cult of the Zarazskian icon to those who have a predilection for Byzantinism." But Antonova's chronological considerations regarding the cult of Saint Nikolaj Zarazskij are unacceptable. The Zarazskian cult is actually a genuinely Russian phenomenon which, however, began at the earliest in the beginning of the sixteenth century.

[47] The dating of the Chersonian tradition of the Zarazskian icon substantiated here is consonant with the opinion of an outstanding expert on the Old Russian manuscript legacy, K. F. Kalajdovič: "The doubtful tale about its [the Zarazskian icon's—A.P.] transfer from Cherson in 1224 is not corroborated by ancient evidence: perhaps the beginning of this tale is no older than Makarij's Great Minei-Čeťi ...," i.e., the middle of the sixteenth century; K. F. Kalajdovič, *Pis'ma k A. F. Malinovskomu ob arxeologičeskix issledovanijax v Rjazanskoj gubernii* (Moscow, 1823), 73.

The "Chersonian Doors" from Magdeburg

The western façade of the Novgorod Cathedral of Saint Sophia is adorned by Romanesque bronze doors, which for centuries were referred to as Chersonian. The doors were manufactured in a Magdeburg casting workshop in 1153 by order of Alexander, bishop of Płock. No later than the first months of 1154, the doors were dispatched to their destination on the Vistula. They left Płock under unknown circumstances and at an undetermined time. However, after mysterious travels, the doors found their way to Novgorod in good condition, where, in the mid-fifteenth century, the Slavo-Cyrillic inscriptions were engraved on them.[48]

How the doors acquired the name Chersonian is one of the remaining puzzles connected with their fate. It is worthwhile investigating how the work of a twelfth-century Romanesque workshop in Magdeburg was attributed a provenance from Cherson, a Crimean possession of the Byzantine Empire.

As early as the eighteenth century, attention was drawn to the discrepancy between the name of the doors and their appearance;[49] yet, their traditional epithet continued to be maintained in the colloquial language of the Novgorodians and in Russian literature. According to one theory, the adjective *Chersonian* was applied to the doors as a definition used for Old Rusian precious cult objects, distinguished by their artistic value and archaic origin.[50] The answer that the doors received this name "either from its archaism or by misunderstanding"[51] does not seem to be satisfactory

[48] For details about the Rusian inscriptions on the doors, see A. Poppe, "K istorii romanskix dverej Sofii Novgorodskoj" in *Srednevekovaja Rus'. Sbornik pamjati N. N. Voronina* (Moscow, 1976), 191-200. On the time of manufacture and some iconographic questions, see id., "Some Observations on the Bronze Doors of St. Sophia in Novgorod," in *Acta Universitatis Upsaliensis*, 1981, fig. 19, 407-418. A major study of the doors by the present author is in preparation. The basic work on the art problems remains that of A. Goldschmidt, *Die Bronzetüren von Novgorod und Gnesen* (Marburg a/L, 1932), 1-26, tables 1-70.

[49] One of the first to mention it was the historian and traveling tutor to the son of the Earl of Pembroke, William Coxe, *Travels into Poland, Russia, Sweden and Denmark*, vol. 1 (London, 1784), 452.

[50] F. Adelung, *Die Korssunschen Türen in der Kathedralkirche zur heiligen Sophia in Novgorod* (Berlin, 1823), 99-100; Sobolevskij, "Dva slova o 'korsunskix predmetax'" (see n. 3), 59-60, 65.

[51] Kondakov, *Russkie klady* (see n. 1), 4-5. S. A. Beljaev believes that the name Chersonian was attributed to the Romanesque bronze doors because of a misunderstanding; cf. "Korsunskie dveri Novgorodskogo Sofijskogo sobora," in *Drevnjaja Rus' i Slavjane* (Moscow, 1978), 300-310. Here, the author used the name Chersonian for the doors with copper plates, whose flower cross (*crux florida*) is the central decorative element. From the seventeenth century on, these doors were set up in the arch of the cathedral that separates the side chapel of the Nativity of the Mother of God from the Porch of the Martyrs. Recognized as a monument of

either. In seeking an answer, one should follow the fate of the doors after they were already in the portal of the Novgorod Cathedral.

The Third Novgorod Chronicle under the year 1450 records: "In the year 6958 the vestibule of Saint Sophia by the Chersonian Gates (*u korsunskix vrat*) was covered with paintings by order of Archbishop Evfimij."[52] This, however, cannot be considered the oldest reference to the doors. The fresco redecoration of the western chapel was assuredly based on an older record, while the mode of localization "by the Chersonian Gates" clearly reveals a later interpolation; in all probability, it was made by the compiler of this chronicle, which was composed shortly after 1673.[53] In the thirteenth to

---

Byzantine handicraft, they were dated from the eleventh or twelfth century even at the end of the nineteenth century (I. I. Tolstoj and N. P. Kondakov). Drawing on comparative evidence, Beljaev made an artistic analysis of the doors and proposed dating them to the second half of the eighth through the first half of the ninth centuries. However, in light of known material, such precise dating of the doors seems premature, especially if we bear in mind the doors with the blossoming crosses of the eleventh century from Amalfi, Mt. Athos, Trani, and Salerno from the beginning of the twelfth century; see M. E. Frazer, "Church Doors and the Gates of Paradise: Byzantine Bronze Doors in Italy," *Dumbarton Oaks Papers* 27 (1973): 147-162, pls. 1, 4, 11, 14, 15. The doors from Novgorod seem to be closer to the doors from Italy than to those of the sixth century from the Hagia Sophia. Moreover, a certain impression of secondary accretion is produced: the simplicity of the panel composition with its blossoming crosses combines with the rich ornamentation of their borders. A more definite dating of the Byzantine doors from Novgorod is of substantial significance for the determination of their early fate. If they are a work of the eleventh century, then their appearance in Novgorod in connection with the construction of the Cathedral of Saint Sophia (1050) is tied to the prince's order in the Byzantine workshop. With the earlier dating, it would be more reasonable to propose that these doors are really a trophy from the Chersonian campaign of Vladimir in 989. But one way or another, these doors ended up in Novgorod in the eleventh or twelfth century. Even recognizing the merit of Beljaev's initial, thorough study of this artwork, I cannot, however, agree with his suggestion that these doors were called Chersonian from the very beginning; nor can I accept that they were located until the seventeenth century inside the entrance of Saint Sophia at the western vestibule, transmitting the name Chersonian to the latter. In Beljaev's opinion, the transference of these doors in the seventeenth century in connection with the liquidation of this doorway led to the Romanesque doors becoming the major doors into the cathedral, and in turn, the name Chersonian was carried over to them from the name of the vestibule (ibid., 307). Even though this is a logical explanation, in light of the data presented here, it is historically incorrect. The Byzantine, not to mention the Chersonian, origin of these doors was completely forgotten, and not to be recalled even at the height of the demand for Chersonian antiquities in the seventeenth century when a Chersonian genealogy was ascribed to clearly local wares.

[52] *Novgorodskie letopisi* (the so-called Second and Third Novogord Chronicles) (St. Petersburg, 1879), 273; ibid., 210. Under the year 1299, the reference to the Chersonian vestibule consitutes a definite interpolation in comparison with a corresponding text not only in chronicles compiled in the fourteenth and fifteenth centuries (First Novgorod Chronicle [see n. 22] 330) but also toward the end of the sixteenth century. See the Second Novgorod Chronicle in *Novgorodskie letopisi*, 24; *PSRL* 30 (1965): 188.

[53] Cf. S. N. Azbelov, *Novgorodskie letopisi XVII veka* (Novgorod, 1960), 95ff.

sixteenth centuries, the location of the western chapel was defined as follows: "to the side of the Bishop's court" or "to the west." In addition, the seventeenth-century compiler employed the term *vrata* 'gates' instead of *dveri* 'doors,' though these two terms were distinguished in the language of Old Rus' up to the sixteenth century.

In an extensive description of two processions that took place on December 8 and 15, 1499—a description rich in topographical details—the author, who undoubtedly participated, twice noted that Archbishop Gennadij stopped before the cathedral entrance at the side of his court (i.e., to the west), "sprinkled holy water on the vestibule and church doors," and blessed the participants of the procession.[54] Because of the detailed nature of this report, one can safely conclude that at the end of the fifteenth century, a more precise appellation of the doors had not become accepted, although the legend surrounding them must have already begun to take shape. The oldest trace of such a legend is contained in Herberstein's narrative. Looking at the "copper church doors," he heard that they had been brought from Greece many centuries ago as a trophy from conquered Cherson.[55] Thus, in 1517, a tradition existed in Novgorod that made it possible to call the doors Chersonian. The fact that Herberstein was shown the bronze doors manufactured in Magdeburg and was told the legend pertaining to them follows indisputably from two further testimonies: a Swedish one of 1616 and a Syrian one of 1655.

Jacob de la Gardie, the commander of the Swedish units occupying Novgorod, answered the Swedish chancellor, Count Axel Oxenstierna, on March 4, 1616, on the advisability of sending back the doors of Sigtuna, now found in Novgorod. For political reasons he advised against the confiscation of "these doors which lead to the main temple of the metropolitan, and which the Russian assure me were brought as a gift from Greece."[56] Thus, he heard the same story that the imperial ambassador had

[54] See the Second Novgorod Chronicle, *PSRL* 30: 152-154.

[55] In his autobiography (preserved in manuscript), Herberstein, describing his stay in Novgorod in April of 1517, reports: "Da liess man mich sehen ain kupferene khirchtur, die aus Griechenlanndt solte gebracht sein worden vor viell hundert Jaren, Alls man aus derselben gegenndt gezogen, unnd ain Stat, die sy Corsun nennen, belegert." See *Fontes Rerum Austriacarum, Scriptores*, vol. 1 (Vienna, 1855), 117. Cf. id., *Rerum Moscoviticarum Commentarii* (Basel, 1557), 75, and the German translation: *Beschreibung Moskaus der Hauptstadt in Russland samt des Moskowitischen Gebietes 1557*, selections translated by H. Picard (Graz, 1966), 71. In the essay, Herberstein notes that the Novgorodians brought a bell along with the doors from Cherson.

[56] A. Oxenstierna, *Skrifter och brefvexling*, vol. 1 (Stockholm, 1893), 94. The creator of the Sigtuna legend of our doors was the Swedish pastor Martin Aschaneus, who was convinced that during his stay in Novgorod in 1614 he had discovered the gates that were once carried away

been told a hundred years earlier, with the exception that his informers, most likely the cathedral clergy, omitted for good reasons the part of the tradition regarding wartime booty. When Makarios, patriarch of Antioch, visited Novgorod in 1655, however, there was no need to hide this information. His son, Archdeacon Paul of Aleppo in Syria, who accompanied him, wrote about the Novgorod Cathedral as follows: "It possesses immense wonderful doors of two wings of yellow copper; on the doors human figures and similar subtleties of art are represented. They say that the ruler of this town, around 700 years ago, led an expedition against the country of the Serbs and Greeks.... He proceeded to Cherson, conquered it, destroyed it and brought from there these doors along with other objects and great ancient, magnificent Greek icons which have survived to this day."[57]

That both Herberstein and Paul of Aleppo uncritically repeated this local tradition despite having seen the doors with their own eyes gives one food for thought. After all, Herberstein was one of few people able to read both the Latin and Slavic inscriptions on them. Paul of Aleppo, although he wrote in Arabic, knew Greek and could have observed that Greek inscriptions were lacking. One must assume that both were entertained as honored guests, surrounded, but also constrained, by their hosts' hospitality, and did not have enough time to take a closer look at the relics. The stories of the hosts must also have been extremely convincing. Even at the beginning of the nineteenth century, when the question of the doors' genealogy was better known, a German traveler saw in them "the entire Greek hierarchy from the sacristan to the patriarch in contemporary costumes of the period and the Greek court in figure bas-reliefs with inscriptions."[58]

The first source calling the doors Chersonian is the so-called Second Novgorod Chronicle, a compilation preserved in a manuscript from the end of the sixteenth century. The extensive description of the procession with the icon of "Our Lady of Vladimir" on Sunday, June 22, 1572, was the work of an eyewitness. Tsar Ivan IV (the Terrible) was staying in Novgorod and participated in this procession, which wended its way toward the

---

from Sigtuna. Aschaneus even aroused the interest of King Gustavus Adolphus in this matter. The hypothesis that the doors found their way from Magdeburg to Novgorod through the Swedish town of Sigtuna cannot be substantiated. It was aptly criticized by O. Almgren in 1912 but still finds support. Cf. recently again I. P. Šaskoľskij, *Bor'ba Rusi protiv krestonosnoj agressii na beregax Baltiki XII–XIII vv.* (Leningrad, 1978), 94-104. For details on the Sigtuna legend, see my study in preparation (see n. 48).

[57] "Putešestvie Antioxijskogo patriarxa Makarija v Rossii opisannoe ego synom arxidiakonom Pavlom Aleppskim," *ČOIDR,* 1898, bk. 4: 70.

[58] D. Raupach, *Reise von St. Petersburg nach dem Gesundbrunnen zu Lipezk am Don* (Breslau, 1809), 33.

cathedral and reached the Chersonian Doors.[59] During the ceremony in front of the cathedral entrance the tsar, surrounded by church and lay dignitaries, stood before the Romanesque doors looking at the religious scenes on them. What is noteworthy is that two years earlier, Ivan IV had taken other church doors—manufactured in 1336 by order of Archbishop Vasilij—from Novgorod to his residence near Moscow. These "gilded bronze doors," somewhat smaller than the Romanesque ones, had adorned the cathedral's southern portal until 1570; this was the southern chapel, also called "golden."[60] The evidence from 1570 and 1572 makes it possible to reject the assumption that the name "Chersonian Doors," originally ascribed to the 1336 doors, was transferred to the bronze Romanesque doors from Magdeburg. That the Chersonian Doors were considered a special ornament of the archepiscopal cathedral is shown by the fact that a proper decorational frame was provided for them in the fifteenth or sixteenth century. The western façade at that time was not covered with white plaster as it was in 1439 when Archbishop Evfimij "whitewashed the entire Sophia Church." In 1528 Makarij, then archbishop of Novgorod, "ordered the icon painters to cover the wall of Saint Sophia with frescoes above the doors through which he himself entered from the west and to paint the Holy Trinity higher up, but Saint Sophia, the Divine Wisdom, and the image of the holy face of Our Lord Jesus Christ [i.e., the Veronica—A.P.] lower down, and two archangels on both sides; and the archbishop himself entering and leaving the cathedral prayed here." We learn from this contemporary record, moreover, that "there had also been a painting on this site earlier, but only one image of the Pantocrator—a bust, occupying practically the entire site where the frescoes are painted now—however, it had been destroyed because of age."[61] The image of Christ Pantocrator placed

[59] *Novgorodskie letopisi* (see n. 52), 103; *PSRL* 30: 161. The Novgorodian Saint Sophia *Pontifical* of c. 1630 also indicates that during major church celebrations, ceremonies took place in front of the Chersonian Doors; see "Činovnik Novgorodskogo Sofijskogo sobora," ed. A. Golubcov, *ČOIDR*, 1889, bk. 2: 166, 183, 205.

[60] Beginning with the record of 1336 in the First Novgorod Chronicle, there is much that speaks for the fact that these doors, ordered by Archbishop Vasilij, were originally intended for the main (western) entrance. This possibility was not considered here because it is believed that the western portal of Saint Sophia had already been decorated with the Romanesque bronze doors in the fourteenth century. In any event, the doors that were executed in 1336 could be found in the doorposts of the southern chapel some time after 1411. See V. N. Lazarev, "Vasil'jevskie vrata 1336 g." in his book *Russkaja srednevekovaja živopis'* (Moscow, 1970), 181-183, 189-190. For illustrations of these doors, see also *Alexandrov*, ed. A. Rogov (Leningrad, 1979), 60-65, ill. 47-59.

[61] Second Sophia Chronicle, *PSRL* 6 (1853): 285, and the Novgorod Chronicle, Dubrovskij manuscript, *PSRL* 15, pt. 1, sec. 3 (1929): 546; cf. N. E. Andreev, "Mitropolit Makarij kak dejatel' religioznogo iskusstva," *Seminarium Kondakovianum* 7 (Prague, 1935), 234, reprinted in

on the external wall and hence exposed to the destructive effects of weather must have been made only after 1439, most likely around 1450, when the western chapel was decorated with paintings by order of Archbishop Evfimij. This decoration was preceded in 1439 by the renovation and gilding of the tombstones located here—those of the cathedral's founder, Prince Vladimir (d. 1052), and of his mother, connected with the inception of their cult.[62] These dates are not too remote from the time when the Cyrillic inscriptions were etched on the doors. It is therefore reasonable to assume that the installation of the Romanesque doors in the cathedral's portal was connected with the redecoration of the western chapel.

It should be emphasized here, once again, that the author of the passage from the Chronicle quoted above, writing immediately after 1528, used the description "doors ... to the west" although he must have known the legend about their Chersonian origin. It would seem that at this time the name Chersonian Doors had not yet gained acceptance. But a few decades later it came to be the colloquial name among the Novgorodians for the western gates of the cathedral.

The middle of the fifteenth century could be considered the defiinite *terminus post quem* for the rise of the tradition that was to justify the name Chersonian for the bronze doors. These new doors, unusual for Novgorodian religious art, were placed in the portal of Saint Sophia during the work of restoration on the western chapel undertaken in 1439–1450.

The decision to adorn Saint Sophia, which was the heart of the Novgorod Republic, with the Romanesque doors, betokened no lack of awareness of the doors' Western provenance, if only because of the Latin inscriptions. After all, Latin was not unknown in Novgorod;[63] the author of the

---

his *Collected Studies in Muscovy: Western Influence and Byzantine Inheritance* (London, 1970), no. 4.

[62] First Novgorod Chronicle (see n. 22), 420; *PSRL* 30: 118. A. S. Xorošev ("Iz istorii bor'by Novgoroda protiv Moskvy. Mestnye kanonizacii 30–40-x XV v.," *Vestnik Moskovskogo universiteta*, 1971, no. 6: 59ff.) considers that the establishment of the commemoration of the cofounder of Saint Sophia Cathedral—a symbol of Novgorod's independence—also had its own anti-Muscovite, political motivation.

[63] The lively trade and diplomatic relations with their frequent conflicts, particularly with the Hansa and Livonia, and their permanent representatives in Novgorod (the German and Gotland factories; the Catholie church) promoted contact between the Novgorodians and the "Latins" as well as familiarity with Western Europe. See, for example, N. A. Kazakova, *Russko-livonskie i russko-ganzejskie otnošenija. Konec XIV–načalo XVI v.* (Leningrad, 1975), 85-123; A. L. Xoroškevič, *Torgovlja Velikogo Novgoroda s Pribaltikoj i Zapadnoj Evropoj v XIV–XV vv.* (Moscow, 1963), 5-31. It should also be emphasized that the Novgorod archbishop Evfimij II (1429–1458) was known for his patronage of the arts, numerous building projects, and contacts with the West; see V. N. Lazarev, *Iskusstvo Novgoroda* (Moscow–Leningrad, 1947), 134ff. J. Raba, "Evfimij II., Erzbischof von Gross-Novgorod und Pskov. Ein Kirchen-

Rusian inscriptions was able to read and translate them, at times with an exaggerated literalness. At the end of the fifteenth century, attempts were even made to teach Latin more broadly at the archepiscopal court and in the monasteries.[64] Hence, it cannot be said that the competent church hierarchy was ignorant either at the time the doors were being put up or later when they began to be associated with Cherson. Nevertheless, from the moment the church leaders decided to expose the doors to public view, a question arose concerning how to define the nature of their iconography from the point of view of the Orthodox canon. The religious and symbolic content of the bas-reliefs did reach through Italy to Byzantine patterns. Only in the treatment of one of the subjects did they differ essentially from representations proper to Byzantine art.[65]

Before it was decided to place the Romanesque doors in the main portal of Saint Sophia, the archbishop and the cathedral clergy had to agree that their iconography accorded with the tradition of Orthodox representation. The Cyrillic inscriptions then etched on the doors were a visible expression of this *imprimatur* of the church authorities.[66]

---

fürst als Leiter einer weltlichen Republik," *Jahrbücher für Geschichte Osteuropas* 25 (1977): 166-172; also A. V. Ryndina, "Novgorod i zapadnoevropejskoe iskusstvo XV veka (o nekotoryx izdelijax xudožestvennogo remesla iz raskopok Gotskogo dvora)," in *Drevnerusskoe iskusstvo. Zarubežnye svjazi* (Moscow, 1955), 240-251. It should be noted that Raba's attempt in the above-mentioned article to divide up the activity of Evfimij II into two periods, one when he was innovative in his perception of Western art (1429–1437), and a second, when he became a traditionalist, is grossly oversimplified. The political vacillations of Evfimij did not find such an impudent and direct reflection in his cultural policy. Any reference to his commission to build a church on "the old base" as an expression of his traditionalism is entirely unfounded. In Old Rusian church architecture, the use of old foundations was normal.

[64] A. O. Sedeľnikov, "Očerki katoličeskogo vlijanija v Novgorode v konce XV–načale XVI veka," *Doklady AN SSSR*, 5th ser., 1929, no. 1: 16-19. On the "Latinism" of the Gennadij circle, see Lur'e, *Ideologičeskaja bor'ba* (see n. 12), 266-283. See also J. L. Wieczynski's summarizing survey, "Archbishop Gennadius and the West: The Impact of Catholic Ideas upon the Church of Novgorod," *Canadian-American Slavic Studies* 6 (1972): 374-389.

[65] I refer to the bas-relief of the enthroned Christ between the Apostles Peter and Paul—a composition strongly emphasizing Peter's primacy, derived from the *traditio legis.* This scene and its reinterpretation in Novgorod as a special variant of the Deësis composition, is discussed in my unpublished study (see n. 48).

[66] The decision of the Stoglav Church Council of 1551 spelling out the requirements for an icon painter and emphasizing the responsibility of church authorities, established the earlier, particularly Novgorodian, practice as a general rule. Questions dealing with denomination, i.e., the inscription of the icons, were also debated at the Council. See G. Ostrogorsky, "Les décisions du 'Stoglav' au sujet de la peinture d'images et les principes de l'icongraphie byzantine," *L'art byzantine chez les Slaves. Recueil Th. Uspensky*, vol. 1 (Paris, 1930), 393-411; Andreev, "Mitropolit Makarij" (see n. 61), 237–242. The superscripts explaining the image depicted are its essential component and were perceived as "the image of the voice" and "the soul of the icon," since only an image that is attested by name becomes an icon in the proper sense of the

Thus, once the subject of the doors was recognized as Orthodox, as being in accordance, in the terms of that time, with the "Constantinople mode" and "old Greek patterns," they began to be considered by many as a work of Greek masters, that is, as a Byzantine relic. Thanks to Herberstein, it is known that in 1517, and certainly for some time before that, the doors were perceived in Novgorod as a trophy brought from Cherson. This perception was possibly based on the reference to "four copper icons" among the loot brought from Cherson by Prince Vladimir, noted in the mid-fifteenth-century manuscript of the Novgorod Chronicle under the year 986.[67] The expression *icon* also had the broader meaning of any image, any figural representation and, hence, one should consider the Novgorod correction of the original record as very ingenious. The doors with their subject matter—a kind of iconostasis—fully deserve, in the eyes of a Christian of medieval Rus', the name of "copper icon." It was only a matter of time before the Novgorod cleric or lay person began to associate the doors, before which he prayed upon entering and leaving the cathedral, with the legend of their having been brought from Cherson: to call them Chersonian on an everyday basis, in accordance with a point of view felt to be so important then. The end of the fifteenth century saw the formation of the tradition itself, while the name Chersonian Doors became permanent during the second half of the subsequent century.

word. Without an inscription it cannot be an icon, since worship is equally related to the image and the name. The right of appellation—i.e., the assertion of the auto-identity (*samotoždestvo*) of the person depicted, and the furnishing of inscriptions on an icon—belongs to the Church and is carried out under the supervision of the bishop or even with his participation in important cases. See P. A. Florenskij, "Ikonostas," in *Bogoslovskie Trudy* (Moscow, 1972), 111ff., 137; B. Uspensky, *The Semiotics of the Russian Icon* (Lisse, 1976), 11, 24, n. 25.

[67] First Novgorod Chronicle (see n. 22), 156; this reading also occurs in some later manuscripts, ibid., 548; *PSRL* 30: 36. The original record in the Primary Chronicle refers to "four bronze horses," i.e., the *quadriga*; cf. *PSRL* 1: 116; *PSRL* 2: 101; *The Russian Primary Chronicle: Laurentian Text,* trans. and ed. S. H. Cross and O. P. Sherbowitz-Wetzor (Cambridge, Mass., 1953), 116. Evidently the text did not convey much to the person transcribing it in the middle of the fifteenth century; believing that his predecessor accidently omitted the letter *i*, he filled in the gap, changing *koni* to *ikoni*. The tendency toward this erroneous reading can be seen in the Laurentian manuscript of 1377, *PSRL* 1: 116 (*koně* to *ikoně*). It would be simpler to suggest that in Novgorod during the second half of the fifteenth century, there remained a remote recollection about the importation of Byzantine (Chersonian) doors at the dawn of Christianity (see n. 51). But such a situation should be recognized as implausible when the memory of the object is not associated with the object itself, which was not only preserved but even continued to function in full view in one of the apertures of Saint Sophia.

The "Chersonian" Shrines between Novgorod and Moscow

There is no need to examine all references to Chersonian religious artworks or every relic designated as Chersonian.[68] All those I have examined lead me to conclude that the attribution Chersonian originally appeared in Novgorod, with the oldest references belonging to the second half of the fifteenth or, rather, to the turn of the sixteenth century. Further references appear sporadically during the sixteenth century, while in the seventeenth, the number greatly increases. While sources contemporaneous with Ivan the Terrible indicate that he confiscated three icons considered to be of Chersonian origin, the seventeenth-century report of the Third Novgorod Chronicle creates the impression that at that time innumerable "valuable Greek, i.e., Chersonian icons" were carried away from Novgorod and its environs.[69]

To explain why the Chersonian shrines appeared so late and primarily in Novgorod, it is worth taking a closer look at the oldest references to these relics as well as at the objects themselves. Such a review reveals how very gradually the conviction emerged concerning their origins in Cherson, Greece, or Constantinople, and how only with time the label Chersonian became permanently connected with its object.

When recording the "peculiar signs" that foretold the fall of the Novgorod Republic in 1471, the chronicle written in Moscow in late 1490 mentions that "in the Church of Our Savior, in the Xutyn' Monastery (near Novgorod), the Chersonian bells rang by themselves."[70] This tale of a requiem for Novgorod had to appear, then, no earlier than after the final defeat (in 1478), since the record in the Stroev Manuscript of the Fourth

[68] For example, the famous *Mstislav Evangelistary* of 1115–1117 was acknowledged as a Chersonian article. Its binding, as is apparent from the colophon, was completed in Constantinople by order of the prince and has been preserved to the present day with significant changes and additions made in the sixteenth century; see I. I. Tolstoj and N. P. Kondakov, *Russkie drevnosti* 5 (St. Petersburg, 1897), 532; 6 (St. Petersburg, 1899), 159. The name Chersonian was also attributed to the Church of "Fiery Gilding" by a Russian workshop at the end of the fifteenth century; see *The Dormition Cathedral in the Moscow Kremlin*, ed. M. P. Alpatov (Moscow, 1971), 17, 50.

[69] *Novgorodskie letopisi* (see n. 52), 341, 399-400.

[70] The text about the Chersonian bells is absent from the Muscovite chronicle compilation of the early 1490s (*PSRL* 25 [1949]) but is present in the chronicle compilation from the very end of the 1490s found in the Simeon Chronicle (*PSRL* 18 [1913]: 224), Vologda–Perm' Chronicle (*PSRL* 26 [1959]: 279), Nikanor Chronicle (*PSRL* 27 [1962]: 128) and chronicle compilations of 1497 and 1518 (*PSRL* 28 [1964]: 121, 230). The Chersonian bells in Xutyn' are also mentioned in the compilations from the first half of the sixteenth century. See *Iosafovskaja letopis'* (Moscow, 1957), 62; *Nikonovskaja letopis'* (*PSRL* 12 [1901]: 124), *Voskresenskaja letopis'* (*PSRL* 8 [1859]: 158). Of later manuscripts, see *Novgorodskie letopisi* (see n. 52), 305.

Novgorod Chronicle, running through the year 1477, is satisfied with a more modest listing of these prophecies and does not mention the Chersonian bells.[71] As to their number, opinions must have differed, since in 1517 Herberstein was told of one bell that had been brought with the doors as a trophy from Cherson.

A Chersonian bell was also reported in Pskov, a center closely connected with Novgorod. In this case it is possible to determine the chronological period of the legend's origin. The Pskov Chronicle compiled in 1547 tells us that in 1518 Pskov received from the Muscovite ruler a new bell "in place of the previously removed Chersonian bell which was used to call the town assembly." The extensive *Tale of the Occupation of Pskov,* written after the events of 1510, contains a detailed description of the confiscation of the assembly bell, but the author says nothing about its genealogy or age, although he tells of the despair and tears of the Pskovians.[72] Thus, the tradition was born somewhere between 1510 and 1547.

The Chersonian icon of the Mother of God appears in the *Vision of Sacristan Aaron of Saint Sophia*: spending the night in the church, the sacristan, a monk Aaron, awoke and saw a procession from the vestibule to the altar of former Novgorodian archbishops, who then sang for a whole hour in front of the "Chersonian icon of the most pure Mother of God." When Archbishop Evfimij heard about what had happened from Aaron, he interpreted the vision as follows: "God will not leave this place thanks to the prayers of its archbishops."[73] An inscription recently discovered on the

[71] *PSRL* 4 [1848]: 128; *PSRL* 4, pt. 1, sec. 2 [1925]: 446.

[72] *Pskovskie letopisi*, vol. 1, ed. A. N. Nasonov (Moscow, 1941), 94ff., 100; ibid., vol. 2 (1955), 224, 255. On the copy of 1547, see A. Nasonov, "Iz istorii pskovskogo letopisanija," *Istoričeskie zapiski* 18 (1946): 260-268. On the history of Pskovian chronicle writing in the sixteenth century and its anti-Muscovite tendency, see N. E. Andreev, "O xaraktere Tret'ej Pskovskoj letopisi," in *The Religious World of Russian Culture. Russia and Orthodoxy: Essays in Honor of Georges Florovsky*, vol. 2 (The Hague–Paris, 1975), 117-158.

[73] *Aaron's Vision* is included in the Novgorod Chronicle, Dubrovskij MS, under the year 6966 (1458) immediately following the report of the death of Archbishop Evfimij (*PSRL* 4, pt. 1, sec. 2: 491) and in the Third Novgorod Chronicle in the version of c. 1673 (according to the manuscripts of the eighteenth century and the Pogodin MS, no. 1416 from the end of the seventeenth century; see *Novgorodskie letopisi* (see n. 52), 271; *PSRL* 3: 239). Thanks to the obliging help of I. P. Šaskol'skij, Leningrad, and Ja. N. Ščapov, Moscow, we have at our disposal the unpublished text of the "Vision" from two manuscripts: (1) one from the mid-seventeenth century belonging to the Leningrad division of the Institute of History of the Soviet Academy of Sciences, N. P. Lixačev Coll., no. 294, fol. 47v–48v; and (2) one from c. 1540, a miscellany of the Lenin Library, Volokolamsk Coll. (F. 113), no. 659, fol. 357–357v; cf. also the notes on these manuscripts by L. A. Dmitriev, *Žitijnye povesti russkogo severa kak pamjatniki literatury XIII–XVII vv.* (Leningrad, 1973), 171-174. I am also indebted to Ja. N. Ščapov for the reference to the copy made by P. Stroev in 1816 from MS no. 196 of the Savvin-Storoževskij Monastery coll. (Rumjancev 39/1, fol. 12v). Its text is very close to the

lower frame of one of the icons of the iconostasis in the Cathedral of Saint Sophia, which tells about the painting of icons by the monk Aaron in 6946 (1438) by order of Archbishop Evfimij, provides a good reason to identify the sacristan monk Aaron with the icon-painter monk Aaron.[74] The story about *Aaron's Vision* must have been composed long after his participation in icon painting had been forgotten; in order to explain Aaron's presence in the cathedral at night, he was made a sacristan, which he could, in fact, have become at a later time. But by the same token, the text has preserved an interesting detail: when he saw the archbishops' procession, Aaron, "lying on his bed, overcome by great fear, did not dare to awaken his associates." This detail, completely superfluous from the standpoint of the *Vision*, becomes understandable if we consider that the monk Aaron was an icon painter and was conducting work at that time in the cathedral along with his partners, who, like himself, were icon painters. Such artistic artels were commonplace, as was the practice of spending the night in a building of the church while working. During these years Archbishop Evfimij was in fact restoring and redocorating the Cathedral of Saint Sophia.

The observations referred to above (n. 73) regarding the composition of the Volokolamsk Collection Manuscript 659 and the indirect connection between the *Vision* and the cycle of Novgorodian legends suggest that the *Vision* was recorded in the last quarter of the fifteenth century[75] It must be added that *Aaron's Vision* remains indisputably connected with the cult of Archbishop Evfimij; evidence of his worship, apparent in the last decade of the fifteenth century, was established by Evfimij's successor, Archbishop Iona (1458–1470), when he ordered the *vita* of his predecessor to be written

---

Volokolamsk MS 659. Comparing the known manuscripts, I conclude that the Volokolamsk MS 659 has preserved the most precise, original wording. The Dubrovskij MS from the very end of the sixteenth century suffers in its characteristic mechanical omission and simultaneous addition (copied from Novgorodian chronicles of the fifteenth century), placing the vision in the year 6946 (1438). The late sixteenth-century manuscript connects the vision with the subsequent renovation of the tombstones of Prince Vladimir and his mother and the establishment of their commemoration on October 4. The text, included in the Third Novgorod Chronicle (without noticeable omission), shares a common protograph with the Dubrovskij MS. The wording of the *Vision* in Lixačev no. 294 is clearly secondary in relation to Dubrovskij's protograph, disseminated as it was in the verbose style of the end of the sixteenth and the seventeenth centuries and remade into a narration by Aaron himself (conducted in the first person) and late at night on the 3rd of October, 6846.

[74] See V. V. Filatov, "Ikonostas Novgorodskogo Sofijskogo sobora" in *Drevnerusskoe iskusstvo. Xudožestvennaja kul'tura Novgoroda* (Moscow, 1968), 65-68; È. S. Smirnova, "Ikony 1438 g. v Sofijskom sobore v Novogorode" in *Pamjatniki kul'tury. Novye otkrytija. Ežegodnik 1977* (Moscow, 1977), 215-224.

[75] V. I. Ključevskij, *Drevnerusskie žitija svjatyx kak istoričeskij istočnik* (Moscow, 1871), 161-164; Dmitriev, *Žitijnye povesti* (see n. 73), 171-173.

by Paxomij Logofet.[76] This *vita* was compiled in the 1460s.[77] The cult of Evfimij which arose thereafter undoubtedly stimulated the oral, and later written, record of the *Vision*. There are, however, no data that permit a closer determination of the time of the *Vision*'s literary treatment.[78] Perhaps it was written only in the sixteenth century: *Aaron's Vision* did not exist in

[76] E. E. Golubinskij, *Istorija kanonizacii svjatyx v russkoj cerkvi*, *ČOIDR*, 1903, bk. 2: 82.

[77] Ključevskij, *Drevnerusskie žitija svjatyx* (see n. 75), 153-156; V. Jablonskij, *Paxomij Serb i ego agiografičeskie pisanija* (St. Petersburg, 1908), 17ff., 80-83. On the *Life* with miracles added as late as the sixteenth century, see *Pamjatniki starinnoj russkoj literatury*, ed. G. Kušelev-Bezborodko (St. Petersburg, 1872), 16-26; there is, however, no allusion to *Aaron's Vision*. The *Life* is usually dated c. 1460, when Paxomij was in Novgorod; but during the term of office of Archbishop Iona (1458–1470), he could have visited this city more than once; living in Moscow, Paxomij remained in constant contact with the Novgorod prelate, and therefore it is more correct to date the *Life of Evfimij* over a broader period.

[78] A reference to the *terminus post quem* for such a literary treatment may be contained in *Aaron's Vision*. Deserving of attention is the report that "the already deceased archbishops entered the church from the vestibule through the former church doors and went to the holy altar; the church doors opened to them by themselves" (Volok. 659, fol. 357). Ascertaining which doors this passage may refer to holds a decisive significance for further conclusions. First of all, we must exclude the enticing possibility that the story was referring to the doors at the main outside entrance to the cathedral, i.e., those doors that were replaced by the Romanesque bronze doors, since the procession did not accidentally begin from the western vestibule where several burial sites of Novgorodian bishops were located. The reference may have been to the inside doors leading into the actual cathedral since such doors separating the vestibule from the church proper existed even at the beginning of the seventeenth century (cf. "Činovnik Novgorodskogo Sofijskogo sobora [see n. 59], 210, and Beljaev, "Korsunskie dveri" [see n. 51], 307). But considering the context, which indicates that the procession set off to the altar with the undoubtedly closed Royal Doors (Gates of Paradise), it is more likely that the story has in mind only these doors. Calling them "Church" (*cerkovnye*), and not "Royal" (*tsarskie*), Doors does not preclude such an interpretation of the text since a general designation of the Royal Doors as "Church" Doors was known to have existed (cf. I. I. Sreznevskij, *Materialy dlja slovarja drevnerusskogo jazyka*, vol. 1 [St. Petersburg, 1893], 648). If this is the case, then the designation of the doors as "former" acquires a special meaning in comparison with the chronicle's information that Archbishop Makarij in 1528 ordered that "Royal Doors into Saint Sophia be constructed, because the former doors had long since become dilapidated, no longer beautiful" (*PSRL* 6: 284; 4, pt. 1, sec. 3 [1929]: 545). The designation of the doors as "former" could be attributed to the author of the literary wording of the oral *Vision*, which must, then, be dated to the time shortly after 1528 when the impression of the construction of new "Royal Doors" was still fresh. The possibility of such a later dating of the written version of the *Vision* remains, however, a hypothesis that requires further verification. The later inclusion of *Aaron's Vision* in the practice of the Church is indicated by the *Pontifical* of the Novgorod Cathedral of c. 1630, thus registering a liturgical practice that arose in the sixteenth century, probably around the time of Makarij, i.e., before 1542. In the *Pontifical* under October 4 (ibid., 41), the day that coincides with the requiem in memory of *Aaron's Vision*, there is no mention of the vision although the appearance of the saintly Novgorodian Archbishop Ioann to Archbishop Evfimij is noted. As a result, October 4 was established as an annual day of requiem in memory of all the Novgorod bishops. Evfimij's vision itself, the so-called *Tale of the Tomb of Saint Ioann of Novgorod*, was compiled in the 1470s. See Dmitriev, *Žitijnye povesti* (see n. 73), 160-169.

the chronicle compiled in Novgorod shortly after 1491, but judging by the Dubrovskij manuscript, it was already included in the Archbishops' Chronicle of Novgorod, compiled between 1542 and 1548, containing information through the year 1539.[79] At any rate, by the end of the fifteenth century, at least an oral tradition about *Aaron's Vision* was alive in Novgorod, a tradition containing a reference to an icon in front of which the dead archbishops prayed. This reference must have been topographically concrete and comprehensible to every Novgorodian, since there was more than one icon of the Mother of God in Saint Sophia. Therefore, lacking other distinguishing marks, the reference to this icon of the Mother of God as Chersonian must be interpreted as being initially inherent in the tradition. Evfimij's interpretation of Aaron's vision—that God would not leave Novgorod because of the prayers of its holy archbishops—was topical after the events of 1471, on the eve of the last attempt to defend the city-state's independence at the end of the 1470s, and continued to sound encouraging and comforting even after 1478.

The icon of Our Lady of Cherson, to which *Aaron's Vision* referred, is in all probability the very same one that is located in Novgorod's Saint Sophia to this day. This huge icon (173 centimeters in height) in the basic tier of the iconostasis is painted in several coats (the uppermost coat is from the nineteenth century) and, judging by the frame, belongs to the twelfth century. It represents a type of Hodegetria, similar to other Chersonian icons, one from Toropec, dating from the twelfth or thirteenth century, and the other from the Annunciation Cathedral of the Moscow Kremlin, dating from the end of the thirteenth century. However, these oldest icons had no influence on the shaping of the iconographic type of Our Lady of Cherson; the latter was formed only in the sixteenth and seventeenth centuries on the basis of one of the variants of the Virgin Glykophilousa.[80]

[79] The Dubrovskij MS belongs to the very end of the sixteenth century, but there is no basis for suggesting that it was supplemented while being copied, i.e., after the 1540s. True, the *Vision* does not appear in the Academy MS which reflected this chronicle compilation (cf. *PSRL* 4, pt. 1, sec. 2: 463-470), which A. Šaxmatov explains through the abridgement of a text identical with the Dubrovskij MS. Nor is it contained in the MS of the Archive Collection (*CGADA* F. 181, no. 20/253); but this is for another reason, since in this MS the chronicle compilation of 1539 is represented as beginning with 1479. See A. A. Šaxmatov, "O tak nazyvaemoj Rostovskoj letopisi," *ČOIDR*, 1904, bk. 1: 50-66, 163–177. On the chronicle compilation of 1491 and 1539, see also A. N. Nasonov, *Istorija russkogo letopisanija* (Moscow, 1969), 354ff., 465-470; and Lur'e, *Obščerusskie letopisi* (see n. 13), 135, 169, 177, 190, 252ff.

[80] See Tolstoj and Kondakov, *Russkie drevnosti* 6 (see n. 68), 155; cf. N. P. Kondakov, *Ikonografija Bogorodicy*, vol. 2 (Petrograd, 1915), 207; Antonova and Mneva, *Katalog*, vol. 2 (see n. 32), 263; O. S. Popova, *Iskusstvo Novgoroda i Moskvy pervoj poloviny četyrnadcatogo veka. Ego*

Two more icons from the Novgorod Cathedral of Saint Sophia, both of which have been preserved and described as Chersonian, deserve mention: the Savior enthroned (with a finger pointing to an open Gospel) from the end of the fourteenth or the beginning of the fifteenth century; and Peter and Paul from the eleventh or twelfth century. The first of these icons inspired the author of the *Tale of the Miraculous Appearance of the Image of the Savior to Manuel, the Greek Emperor.* We find out from this tradition, which arose in Novgorod in the first quarter of the sixteenth century, that "this icon was in Constantinople before the baptism of Vladimir and was painted by Manuel, the Greek emperor."[81]

At the time this asynchronism might not have been shocking, but the reference to Manuel I Komnenos, an emperor with theological ambitions, was not accidental. A concise interpretation of the symbolic nature of the picture reveals the author's true aim: to condemn the infringement of the Church's judicial immunity by a secular ruler. Recalling the rights of the *sacerdotium* and the duties of the *imperium* was very topical in view of the increasing interference of the Muscovite ruler in Novgorod's church affairs.

The Novgorod chronicler, writing about these two icons being taken to Moscow in 1561 and their subsequent return in 1572, says nothing about their Chersonian derivation.[82] But the seventeenth-century editor clearly interpolates the text, "the icon ... of Peter and Paul ... almost entirely covered with silver," by adding "Chersonian."[83] This icon has been preserved and dates to the eleventh century; its silver frame is a local twelfth-century product, as is shown by the Old Rusian inscriptions. Both icons must have been particularly distinguished among the others of the Novgorod Cathedral since the author, writing in the 1530s, names them, stating

---

svjazi s Vizantiej (Moscow, 1980), 168ff. For a photograph of the Novgorodian icon and of Our Lady of Cherson and remarks about them, see N. Mneva and V. Filatov, "Ikona Petra i Pavla Novgorodskogo Sofijskogo Sobora," in *Iz istorii russkogo i zapadnoevropejskogo iskusstva* (Moscow, 1960), 86 n. 13, 92 n. 27, 97; and Smirnova, *Živopis' Velikogo Novgoroda* (see n. 32), 65, 153.

[81] *Novgorodskie letopisi* (see n. 52), 183; V. G. Brjusova and Ja. N. Ščapov, "Novgorodskaja legenda o Manuile care grečeskom," *VV* 32 (1971): 85-102, text 103, ill. 1. In V. Brjusova's opinion, the icon was painted in Novgorod after a model of a Greek icon of the eleventh to thirteenth centuries.

[82] Second Novgorod Chronicle, *PSRL* 30: 174-192. Here the chronicler—an eyewitness to the event—describes these icons simply as the "basic, old" ones, i.e, the icons long since belonging to the regular (basic) tier of Saint Sophia's iconostasis. On their return, it was not noticed that the icon of the Savior was a copy, but the question came to light in the seventeenth centry. At any rate, it was perhaps considered improper to doubt the tsar's gesture.

[83] Cf. *Novgorodskie letopisi* (see n. 52), 93, 117, 347. For photographs of the silver frame, see A. N. Svirin, *Juvelirnoe iskusstvo Drevnej Rusi XI–XVII vekov* (Moscow, 1972), 46-69, nos. 17, 18.

that Archbishop Makarij "recommended that the icons in Saint Sophia be arranged according to a determined order ... also the Constantinopolitan icons of Our Most Merciful Savior ... and of the Holy Apostles Peter and Paul."[84] Thus, the icons, which by the seventeenth century and perhaps a bit earlier were consistently being called "Chersonian," are here labeled "Constantinopolitan."

There is one more Chersonian icon with an interesting history. This is an Annunciation depicted in a rarely encountered iconographic version with the Child descending to the Virgin's womb. It is the so-called Ustjug Annunciation, a twelfth-century icon from the Saint George Monastery near Novgorod, at present in the Treťjakov Gallery.[85] Taken to Moscow at the turn of 1553, it was soon the object of disputes being waged at that time on the permissibility of various iconographic representations from the Orthodox point of view. Among the participants of the discussion were the former archbishop of Novgorod and, after 1542, metropolitan of Moscow, Makarij, as well as the priest Silvester, brought in from Novgorod. These two had recruited to Moscow numerous icon painters from Novgorod and Pskov who hastened the development of a new tendency in church art and aroused the opposition of conservative circles.

Both sides, however, invoked tradition. In the dispute with Chancellor Ivan Viskovatyj, who protested against certain departures from the canon in the composition of the Annunciation (among them "Latin sophistication"), Metropolitan Makarij, referring to the icon brought from Novgorod, explained that "it was painted in Cherson and brought from there 500 years ago or more." In other statements, Makarij constantly invoked the tradition of the Eastern Church, citing "Constantinopolitan" or "Greek painting" as the

[84] *PSRL* 6: 285. Cf. Mneva and Filatov, "Ikona Petra i Pavla" (see n. 80), 81-102; V. N. Lazarev, *Novgorodian Icon-Painting* (Moscow, 1969), 6, pl. 1. In the works cited here, the proposed dating of this monumental icon of Peter and Paul on a limewood panel (236 × 147 cm) from the middle of the eleventh century, which would make the painting of the icon coincide with the date of the building of Novgorod's Saint Sophia, does not sound convincing, particularly since there is no way to distinguish the palette of an eleventh-century artist from that of a twelfth-century one. Moreover, a substantial detail—the lack of traces of paint on the wide (17 cm each) borders—indicates that from the very beginning the icon was intended for framing. The silver setting of the locally executed frame has been preserved on the icon. This frame may be dated from the 1120s, although according to the paleographic characteristics one could certainly speak loosely about the twelfth century. There are no grounds for suggesting that the first frame was replaced in such a relatively short period of time, all the more since it has become clear in the course of restoration that while the faces, hands, and feet of the apostles were touched up several times (the oldest coat is from the fifteenth century), the areas covered by the frame were never retouched.

[85] Antonova and Mneva, *Katalog*, vol. 1 (see n. 32), 54-57, pl. 20; Lazarev, *Novgorodian Icon-Painting*, 9, pl. 6.

obligatory model. He expressed pride in the fact that the Novgorod Saint Sophia was adorned with paintings by "authentic Greek painters" and emphasized that he recommended "that the painting be done according to old Greek patterns." Similarly Silvester, in defending the orthodoxy of the composition of the icon of Saint Sophia—the Divine Wisdom—indicated that it was a copy of a Greek icon contemporaneous with the building of the Novgorod Cathedral, and thus from the middle of the eleventh century. And then, generalizing, he stated: "And in all Rus' what is painted on walls and on icons is Greek and Chersonian painting while the works of the local painters are also based on these models."[86]

It can be seen that in the dispute about the iconographic and theological content in religious art, the label "Chersonian" was used as an equivalent for "Constantinopolitan" or "Greek." This dispute also unambiguously stated that Rusian iconography was derived from that tradition of painting initiated by the icons brought from Cherson by Saint Vladimir, the baptizer of Rus'. They found their way to the temples of Kiev and Novgorod, and after the destruction of Kiev were preserved only in Novgorod; it becomes evident that the proper guardian of Orthodox tradition is the Novgorodian Church. Thus, it is obvious that the confiscation of the Chersonian icons in Novgorod, ordered by Ivan IV and supported and inspired by Muscovite Church circles, formed part of the program aimed at guaranteeing the spiritual primacy of Moscow.[87]

There is no doubt that the dispute taken up in the early fifties of the fifteenth century in Moscow was a continuation of the countless opposing tendencies in religious art that had already come to the surface much earlier in Novgorod. Makarij himself, as archbishop of Novgorod (1526–1542), as well as his eminent predecessors in this post such as Gennadij (1482–1503) and Evfimij II (1429–1458), did not refrain from Western influence. The Novgorodian church hierarchy tolerated the penetration of "Latin" motifs into religious

[86] See the notes on the questioning of chancellor (dumnyj d'jak) I. Viskovatyj in *ČOIDR*, 1858, bk. 2: 3, 11, 13, 21; cf. N. E. Andreev, "O dele d'jaka Viskovatogo," *Seminarium Kondakovianum* 5 (Prague, 1932), 197-241, reprinted in *Studies in Muscovy* (see n. 61); "Mitropolit Makarij" (see n. 61), 227-244. L. Ouspensky, "Rol' Moskovskix cerkovnyx soborov XVI veka v cerkovnom iskusstve," in *Messager de l'Exarchat du Patriarche Russe en Europe Occidentale* 64 (Paris, 1968), 217-250.

[87] The fashionability of Chersonian icons and other objects of church art also appeared in the Grand Duchy of Lithuania in the sixteenth century. A legend arose about the expedition of Prince Olgerd to Cherson in 1363 and the bringing back, among other numerous icons, of the icon of Our Lady of Ostra Brama. It was even claimed that the Gniezno Doors came from Cherson via Kiev. Cf. *Drzwi Gnieźnieńskie*, vol. 1 (Warsaw, 1956), 109. The interest in Chersonian objects in the Ukraine and Belorussia requires examination. It seems to be linked with the aspirations of the Orthodox Church in the Jagiellonian states.

iconography, particularly those that enriched its theological-didactic content;[88] but when disputes or doubts arose it favored the new, while simultaneously emphasizing—as was still done by the Novgorodian priest Silvester in Moscow—that Novgorodian religious art took a determined stand on the basis of the canons of Orthodox Christianity and that its origin was immaculately Byzantine.

Thus, in the case of debatable subjects of iconography, the attestation by ecclesiastical authorities that this was a "Greek," "Constantinopolitan," or "Chersonian" painting signified the assertion of Orthodox iconographic tradition. The Byzantine canon in iconography was binding to such a degree that when the Pskovian icon painter invoked "Greek patterns" c. 1502, this swayed the opinion of Gennadij, the archbishop of Novgorod and Pskov.[89]

The history of the Novgorod Republic in the fifteenth century, its political downfall in 1471–78, and the intensification of its intellectual and artistic life that subsequently followed, explain why it was precisely in Novgorod that the need arose for religious art with a Chersonian pedigree. In the fifteenth century and in the first half of the sixteenth, Novgorod, thanks to its lively contacts with Western Europe, was not only under the influence of the latter but itself undertook the initiative for assimilating the achievements of the world of Latin culture. Indeed, during the last decade of the fifteenth century, the Dominican Benjamin worked at the court of Saint Sophia on a translation and codification of the full text of the Bible.[90] In spite of obvious contacts with

[88] An informative example of the influence of Western art as well as a Latin commentary on the subject is furnished by the Apocalypsis icon of c. 1500, whose iconography transcends the framework of Byzantine tradition. Cf. Y. Christe, "Quelques remarques sur l'Icone de l'Apocalipse du maître du Kremlin à Moscow," in *Izograf* 6 (Belgrade, 1975), 54-67, and 14 plates. For the same icon in color, see M. V. Alpatov, *Early Russian Icon Painting* (Moscow, 1974), pls. 159-162. The influence of the Gothic model on the Novgorodian icon "The Mother of God with the Child Enthroned" has been convincingly shown by M. Alpatov in "Eine abendländische Komposition in altrussischer Umbildung," in *Byzantinische Zeitschrift* 30 (1929): 623-626. The author dates the icon from the second half of the 15th century, while V. Lazarev (*Iskusstvo Novgoroda* [see n. 63], 118), on the basis of the icon's coloring, dates it from the first half of the fifteenth century. The presence of Saint Sergij of Radonež among the figures on the border would contradict this dating, if not for the assumption that this figure was added later; cf. Antonova and Mneva, *Katalog*, vol. 1 (see n. 32), no. 49, 111, ill. 59.

[89] See the letter of Dmitrij Gerasimov (who had been one of the members of the Gennadij circle) to the Pskov governor M. G. Misjur'-Munexin (after 1510, in *Pribavlenija k tvorenijam sv. otcov* 17 (1859): 190 ff; cf. N. Andreev, "Inok Zinovij ob ikonopočitanii i ikonopisanii," *Seminarium Kondakovianum* 8 (1936): 272 ff., reprint in *Studies in Muscovy* (see n. 61). On the identity of the letter's author, see Lur'e, *Ideologičeskaja bor'ba* (see n. 12), 484, n. 270.

[90] On the study of the translation itself, see the works of G. Freidhof and his contribution in the present volume; cf. A. D. Sedel'nikov, "K izučeniju 'Slova kratka' i dejatel'nosti dominikanca Veniamina," *IORJaS* 30 (1925/26): 205-225. This "Slovo kratko," written at the request of Archbishop Gennadij by a Catholic author, was directed against the encroachment (of the

Catholic countries, however, Novgorod was far from "falling into the Latin heresy." Yet it was precisely this accusation that served as a pretext for the 1471 expedition that deprived Novgorod of its independence.[91] The Novgorodian Church was thrust into a stance of constantly having to prove its fidelity to the principles of Orthodoxy and of defending its position, including property, against the secularization attempts of the Muscovite authorities.[92] In losing the political struggle with Moscow, Novgorod did not neglect the ideological confrontation, justifying its rights to spiritual supremacy. An entire cycle of tales that arose during the last decades of the fifteenth century and the first half of the sixteenth served this purpose.[93] These tales stressed that for

Muscovite authorities) on church property; see also Lur'e, *Ideologičeskaja bor'ba* (see n. 12), 225-228. On the variety of cultural relations, see the article dedicated essentially to Novgorod by N. Angermann, "Kulturbeziehungen zwischen dem Hanseraum und dem Moskauer Russland um 1500, *Hansische Geschichtsblätter* 84 (1966): 20-48. See also H. Birnbaum, "Die Hanse in Novgorod," in *Festschrift für Dietrich Gerhardt* (Marburg, 1977), 28-35; id., "Lord Novgorod the Great: Its Place in Medieval Culture," *Viator* 8 (1977): 249-254.

[91] In M. N. Pokrovskij's apt estimation (*Izbrannye proizvedenija*, vol. 1 [Moscow, 1966], 226), the subjugation of Novgorod was perceived by Moscow as a crusade against apostates from Orthodoxy. On the history of the fall of the Novgorod state, see L. V. Čerepnin, *Obrazovanie russkogo centralizovannogo gosudarstva v XIV–XV vv.* (Moscow, 1960), 855-874; J. Raba, "The Fate of the Novgorodian Republic," *The Slavonic and East European Review* 45, no. 105 (1967): 307-323. The most thorough research in recent times—by V. N. Bernadskij, *Novgorod i Novgorodskaja zemlja v XV veke* (Moscow-Leningrad, 1961), 265-313—is not always sufficiently critical regarding the pro-Muscovite sources. This is undoubtedly due to the influence of a conscious interpretation of the subjugation-annexation of Novgorod "in light of the main political task of the epoch—the completion of the unification of Great Russia" (ibid., 7, 9ff., 308). On the tendentiousness of the Muscovite chroniclers, see the substantive remarks on the sources by Ja. S. Lur'e, "K istorii prisoedinenija Novgoroda v 1477–1479 g..," in *Issledovanija po social'no-političeskoj istorii Rossii. Sbornik statej pamjati B. A. Romanova* (Leningrad, 1971), 89-95.

[92] On the "Slovo kratko," directed toward the defense of church property, see n. 90. It is not by accident that in the struggle with the "heretics," or rather, with those whom it was convenient to accuse of heresy (for example, the "Nonpossessors"), the church circles of Novgorod headed by Archbishop Gennadij represented themselves as the fervent champions of Orthodoxy, assuming the duty of uprooting any type of "heresy," not only among their own but in Moscow as well, in the environment of the sovereign himself. The relationship to tradition (and the perception of innovations in the spirit of truly Orthodox tradition), including icon painting, undoubtedly formed a substantial part of the ideological battle around the vital issues of that time. On the role of Novgorod in the struggle with the Novgorod–Moscow "heresy," see Lur'e, *Ideologičeskaja bor'ba* (see n. 12), 75-203; E. Hösch, *Orthodoxie und Häresie im alten Russland* (Wiesbaden, 1975), 68-72; cf. also F.v. Lilienfeld, "Die 'Häresie' des Fedor Kuricyn," *Forschungen zur osteuropäischen Geschichte* 24 (1978): 39-60.

[93] In *Drevnerusskie žitija svjatyx* (see n. 75), 162, V. Ključevskij writes: "In our history there are not many epochs which would have been as surrounded by a swarm of poetic tales as the fall of Novgorodian liberty. It seemed that 'Lord Novgorod the Great,' feeling its life's pulse weakening, transferred its thoughts from Jaroslav's Court, where its voice had fallen silent, to Saint Sophia and other local shrines, calling forth from them the legends of olden times." On

centuries Novgorod, after Kiev, had occupied the first place in Rus'. The "Muscovites" were scoffed at because they had accepted the faith of Christ later, and they were reminded of the blows they had suffered in 1170 from the Novgorodians, supported by the Holy Virgin.[94] Material and written proofs were invoked as testimony that Novgorod was the legitimate heir to the heritage of Constantinople-Cherson-Kiev. For this purpose, some of the icons and other cult objects were now given a Chersonian origin, that is, were associated with the beginnings of Christianity in Rus'. The premise for this was furnished by the well-known record of the Primary Chronicle of 988 concerning the icons and other church objects transported from Cherson to Kiev. The interpretation that something of this fell to Novgorod's lot was facilitated by the list of the Novgorodian bishops, composed only at the beginning of the fifteenth century, naming Joachim of Cherson as the first archbishop of Novgorod. This was then interpolated by the Novgorod Chronicle into the story about the baptism of Rus'.[95] The chronicler gave

---

Novgorod's literature of the second half of the fifteenth through the first half of the sixteenth century, see the comprehensive section by D. S. Lixačev in *Istorija russkoj literatury*, vol. 2, pt. 1 (Moscow–Leningrad, 1946), 368-389. In recent times there has been a tendency to avoid an isolated treatment of Novgorod's literature from the time when Novgorod lost its independence. The story about the miracle "in the city of Cherson" during the harvest feast on the occasion of the holiday of Saints Koz'ma and Damian, compiled in Novgorod (the oldest MS is from the threshold of the sixteenth century), must be attributed to the time when Cherson became fashionable and the notion of it became, to a certain degree, an epic designation. See M. N. Speranskij, "'Korsunskoe' čudo Koz'my i Damiana," in *IORJaS* 1, no. 1 (1928): 358-375. The author's attribution of the compilation of this story to the fourteenth century seems too early in light of the considerations expressed in the present paper.

[94] A literary rewriting of the *Tale about the Sign from the Icon of the Mother of God* from the middle of the fourteenth century is attributed to the middle or second half of the fifteenth century. This legend acquired a clearly anti-Muscovite character during the period of the fall of Novgorod. For the manuscript tradition, see Dmitriev, *Žitijnye povesti* (see n. 73), 95-148. The icon known in several copies from the second half of the fifteenth through sixteenth centuries, depicting the "Battle of the Novgorodians with the Suzdalians," appears to be a representation of this struggle; see Lazarev, *Novgorodian Icon-Painting* (see n. 84), 35ff., pls. 51-53. Cf. also A. Florow, "Le 'Znamenie' de Novgorod. Évolution de la légende," *Revue des études slaves* 24 (1948): 67-81; 25 (1949): 45-72; D. S. Lixačev, "Ideologičeskaja bor'ba Moskvy i Novgoroda v XIV–XV vekax," in *Istoričeskij Žurnal*, 1941, no. 6: 43-56.

[95] First Novgorod Chronicle (see n. 22), 160, 163, 473, 551. The date of the listing of the Novgorodian bishops and archbishops is based on the results of the study of the listing of *posadniks* by V. L. Janin, *Novgorodskie posadniki* (Moscow, 1962), 14-44. On the first Novgorodian bishop, see A. Poppe, *Państwo i kościół na Rusi w XI w.* (Warsaw, 1968), 162ff. V. G. Brjusova ("Russko-vizantijskie otnošenija serediny XI veka," *Voprosy istorii*, 1972, no. 3: 51-62) has tried to prove that the "Chersonian antiquities" appeared in Novgorod as the result of the campaign and capture of Cherson in 1044. She cites, among other things, the evidence of the Primary Chronicle that all the icons, crosses, and church vessels taken from Cherson were handed over by Vladimir to the Kievan Tithe-Church of the Mother of God. But the hypothesis about the campaign of 1044 is based merely on an uncritical interpretation of legendary

Joachim the cognomen "of Cherson," concluding that the first Novgorodian bishop must have descended from those "Chersonian priests" who were brought into Rus' by Vladimir as mentioned in the Primary Chronicle. It is no wonder, then, that when during the last decades of the fifteenth and the beginning of the sixteenth centuries, material proofs had been gathered and enumerated regarding Novgorod's role as the second spiritual capital of Rusian Christianity after Kiev, the doors of Novgorod's Saint Sophia, considered a Byzantine work, found their way to this list as one of the first items.

The first tradition about the Chersonian sacred shrine preserved beyond the confines of Novgorod—namely, the miracle-working icon of Saint Nikolaj Zarazskij—undoubtedly arose under the influence of the legend about the Chersonian heritage of several Novgorodian "antiquities." It may have been one of the last attempts by the Rjazan' princes who had lost all their independence,[96] to furnish evidence following Novgorod's example, of a direct God-given connection, without Moscow's mediation, between Rjazan' Christianity (and the Rjazan' princes) and the sources of the Christian statehood in Rus'. But even if the cult of the miracle-working icon had been conceived in this fashion, *in statu nascendi* it was imitated and included in the service of all-Russian ideas as a spiritual bulwark on the southern border of the Muscovite state, which was endangered by the Tatar invasions.

In the end, a simple conclusion can be drawn: the tradition about the sacred "Chersonian antiquities," preserved through the centuries in Russia, appeared no earlier than the second half of the fifteenth century during an ideological confrontation with Moscow, when Novgorod invoked its famous past and its right to be the guardian of Orthodoxy in Russian Christendom. Thus, all the "authentic" Chersonian antiquities received their pedigree beginning at that time.

In Russian ecclesiastic circles of the sixteenth century, the definition of a religious iconographical object as "Chersonian" became synonymous with "Greek" or "Constantinopolitan," that is, as being in accordance with the Orthodox canon. At the same time, the designation "Chersonian" gave concrete historical expression to the Byzantine tradition that began for Rus', according to the Primary Chronicle, with the baptism of its ruler—*isoapostolos* Vladimir—in Cherson.

---

material from the sixteenth and seventeenth centuries. Also highly uncritical is the attempt to ascribe to the trophies of 1044 those Novgorodian objects of church art, for which the appellation "Chersonian" had become established.

[96] At any rate, before 1521, when the last Rjazan' prince fled to Lithuania; see A. A. Zimin, "Feodal'naja znat' Tverskogo i Rjazanskogo velikix knjažestv i Moskovskoe bojarstvo konca XV–pervoj treti XVI veka," *Istorija SSSR*, 1973, no. 3: 134-42.

ADDENDUM

Bibliographic notes

1. The section of the Catalogue of Christian Relics in the Kremlin Museum listing about 30 icons, crosses, reliquaries from the 11th to the 18th centuries, of varied style and known collectively as the "Chersonian Antiquities", with a competent introduction and added English-language description of 11 items, is heartily recommended. See T.V. Tolstaya and E.V. Ukhnanova, "The 'Korsun Relics' and the Baptism of Rus'", *Христианские реликвии в Московском Кремле* (Moscow, 2000): 147–186

2. The two last papers of D.S. Likhačov, recapitulating an earlier, preliminary study begun in 1949, one of an encyclopedic nature, and another, written slightly earlier, emphasize that the priest "Eustathius the second", son of Eustathius of Cherson, authored the "Translation of the icon of Saint Nicholas from Cherson" during his mid-13th c. sojourn in Novgorod, and in this indirect way digress from the question of revision of his hypothesis. See Д.С. Лихачев, "Повести о Николе Заразском", *Словарь книжников и книжности древней Руси X – перв. пол. XIV в.* (Leningrad, 1987): 332–337; idem, "Авторы рязанского цикла 'Повестей о Николе Заразском'", *Россия на пути централизации* (Moscow, 1982): 201–205. A study of the manuscript tradition of the St Nikolas Zarazskij cycle, made by B.M. Kloss, dated its origins to around 1560. My remarks about the circumstances of the composition of the aforementioned "Tale of the Translation" and my chronological conclusions (see pp. 72–84 above) are corroborated by those manuscript studies. See: Б.М. Клосс, *Избранные труды*, vol. 2 (Moscow, 2001): 409–463 (chap. 8: "Повести о Николе Заразском").

Ad fn. 36 above: For a recent treatment of the early 16th-century history of the borough of Zarazsk (from 17th-century Zarajsk), see: В.А. Кучкин, "Ранняя история города Зарайска и проблема ее источников", *Зарайск т. 1: Исторические реалии и легенды* (Moscow, 2002): 40–113.

*Woytowich*Ad to fn. 41: A curious interpretation of St Nikolas's epithet "*zarazski*" (i.e., that it derives from *zarasiti* "to hit", – cf. above pp. 82–83) recalls the tale of ancient vintage whereby the holy archbishop received his omophorion (pallium) from Our Lady as a reward for having slapped the heresiarch Arius in the face. In this way, a Slavist from Münster suggests, an ancient epithet of St Nicholas came from Cherson to Rus'. See G. Birkfellner, "Sv. Nikola Zarazskij. Literaturgeschichtlich-philologische Überlegungen und Deutung des Epithetons", *Sprache und Literatur Altrusslands* (Münster, 1987): 253–272.

INDEX

Note: The articles in this volume use a whole variety of name forms and transliterations. For this index they have mostly been standardized.

Aaron, sacristan of St Sophia in Novgorod: XII 94–5
Abramovič, D.: III 297; VII 138, 147, 164; VIII 11; IX 172
Abū Shujā: III 292
Abydos: I 5; III 288; V 321, 327
acculturation: III 290
Adalbert, of Trier, missionary bishop to Rus', archbishop of Magdeburg: II 273–6; V 319, 369
  Continuatio Reginonis II 273, 274; V 315–17
Adam of Bremen: II 275; III 298; V 347, 382
Adelung, F.: XII 85
Adrianova-Peretz, V.P.: XII 74
aemula (imitation): III 298, 299
aer (embroidered cloth): VIII 34
Ahrweiler, H.: III 288; V 378
Akent'ev, K.K.: V 380; VIII 13, 15, 41
Akindin of Tver', monk: I 13
Aleppo (in Syria); XII 88
Alexander of Malonne, bishop of Plock: XI 412; XII 85
Alexander Mikhailovich, prince of Tver': VIII 31
Alexander, grand prince of Lithuania I 18
Alexander Nevskii, grand prince: I 12, 14, 22; V 361, 362, 390, 391; VIII 33
  Life of :VIII 22, 27, 28
Allsen, T.T.: V 391
Almgren, O.: XI 408
Alpatov, M.V.: XII 101
Amalfi: XII 86
Anastasia Romanova, wife of Ivan IV: I 21, 23
Anastasios of Cherson: XII 76, 77
Andreev, N.E.: XII 89, 94, 101
Andrew the Apostle: III 301; IV 493, 498–500; V 336, 377; VIII 25, 50, 51
Andrews, D.: XII 72
Andrei Alexandrovich, prince: VIII 27, 28
Andrei Bogolubskii, prince of Vladimir in Suzdalia: I 10; V 353, 381, 386; VI 9, 10; VIII 30; IX 177, 180–82; X 686
Andrei Ivanovich, son of Ivan Kalita: VIII 33
Andrei, brother of Alexander Nevskii: I 22
Andrei, son of Vladimir Monomakh, prince of Pereiaslav: VII 166, 167
Andronikos, disciple of the Apostle Paul: IV 493; VIII 50
Andronikos Kamateros, *megas droungarios*: VI 6–8, 10
Andronikos I Komnenos, emperor: VI 11
Angelov, B.S.: IX 170
Angermann, N.: XII 102
Angold, M.: IV 495
Anisimov, A.I.: XI 416
Anna *porphyrogenita*, wife of Vladimir I: I 5, 6; II 273; III 289, 294, 300, 301; IV 489, 497; V 320, 324, 325, 327, 331, 337, 338, 340, 344, 345, 372, 375, 379, 383; VII 133, 134, 137, 138, 140–43; VIII 6, 9, 10, 13, 29, 39–42
Anna, Iaroslavna, queen of France: V 383
Anna, second wife of Olgerd, grand prince of Lithuania: VIII 32
anointment: V 384
Anthony, bishop of Peremyshl: V 360
Anthony, St, of the Caves Monastery: V 382
Antioch: III 291; VII 133; VIII 41, 51; XII 88
antiphon: VIII 20
Antonopoulos, P.T.: V 369
Antonova, V.I.: XII 80, 84, 97, 99, 101
Apocalypsis icon: XII 101
apostasy: V 344

Arian: IV 492
Arius, heresiarch: XII add. 105a
Armenians: V 322, 325, 338; VI 7
Arpad, Magyar ruler: IX 164
Arpads, Hungarian dynasty: I 5
Arranz, M.: V 375; VIII 12, 51
Arrignon, J.P.: V 369; IX 159, 176
Arsenios Autoreianos, patriarch of Constantinople: V 389
Aschaneus Martin, creator of legend of Sigtuna doors: XI 408
Asia Minor: IV 499; V 321; VIII 51
Asoghik *see* Stephen of Taron
Asseev, Iu.: VIII 39
Astronomus, author of *Vita Hludovici imperatoris*: VII 139
Athos, Mount: V 355, 382, 387; XII 86
Attalea: V 386
Averintsev, S.S.: V 380; VIII 13, 15
Azbelov, S.N.: XII 86
azyma: IV 496; VIII 4

Bahalija, D.J.: III 292
Baldwin I, king of Jerusalem: IX 170
Bamberg: I 10; XI 414
Bank, A.V.: VIII 15
baptism, compulsory: V 344
Bardach, J.: IX 161
Bardas Phokas: III 291, 292, 294, 301; IV 489; V 321, 324, 325, 329, 372
Bardas Skleros: III 294; IV 489; V 322
Baronius, historian: II 276
Basil, chamberlain: VII 142
Basil, St, "the Great": VIII 35, 49
  Christian name of Vladimir: I I 5; V 331; VII 156
  church of: VII 154, 157
Basil I emperor: III 291, 300; V 327, 329, 358, 372, 373; VII 139–41, 142; IX 164
  Life by Constantine Porphyrogennetos V 324
Basil II emperor: I 4, 5; II 274, 277; III 287–90, 301; IV 490; V 320, 321, 322, 325–8, 330, 331, 337, 371, 374, 377, 378; VII 137, 138, 142; VIII 13, 40
  Menologion: IV 499
Basileion, metropolitanate: V 385
Batu-Khan: I 11; V 361; XII 75, 76
Bauer, A.: II 273
Baumgarten, N.: VII 154, 155, 157; VIII 23, 31, 33, 34
Beck, H.G.: IV 495, 496; V 378; VI 6, 11; VIII 43
Begunov, I.K.: VIII 22
Belarus, Belarusians: I 1, 17; V 311
Belgorod: V 341, 380; VIII 17
  cathedral of the Holy Apostles: V 341
Beliaev, S.A.: XII 85, 96
Beneševič, V.N.: IX 167
Benjamin, Dominican: XII 101
Berger, A.: V 374
Bernadskij, V.N.: XII 102
Bertha-Eudokia († 949): II 272
Bibikov, M.V.: VI 8
Birkfellner, G.: XII add. 105a
Birnbaum, H.: IV 488; V 373; IX 159; XII 71, 102
Black Sea: I 4; V 321, 324
Bočkareva, A.N.: XII 75
Bogdanova, N.M.: V 371, 375
Bohemia: V 361
Bohemian Forest: I 1
boiari: IX 165, 167, 168
  boiarskij čin: IX 167
  boiarskij sbor: IX 167
  menšie: IX 166
  veliči: IX 166, 167
Boleslav the Bold, king of Poland (d. 1082): IX 173
Boleslav the Brave, king of Poland (d. 1025): I 8, 10; VII 143, 144; VIII 4, 5, 19, 38; IX 173
Boleslav-Yurii of Mazowia: I 12
booty: V 381
Boris Andreevich, prince: VIII 28
Boris and Gleb (Roman and David), sons of Vladimir I and Anna: I 8; VII 138, 154–6
Boris and Gleb, saints: IV 492; V 335, 346; VII 134, 136, 137, 141, 143, 144–7, 149, 153, 154–6, 160, 161; VIII 10, 22, 25, 26 31, 35, 36, 48, 49
  assassination of: IV 502; V 345; VII 133, 167, 168
  ceremonies of: I 15; VII 164
  church dedicated to: VII 159
  Lives: I 8; III 297
  Nestor, The Lesson of the Life and Murder: VII 136
  Office for the Holy Martyrs: VII 136, 138, 164; VII 162
  relics: V 351; VII 153, 154, 159
  Tale of the Miracles: VII 136, 157, 159, 161–3, 164
  Tale of the Passion of Holy Martyrs: IV 501; VII 136, 154 , 160, 161–3
  veneration of: VI 157, 161, 165, 166
Boris-Michael, baptizer of Bulgaria:

VII 138
Boris II son of Bulgarian tsar Peter: VII 138, 142
Boris Godunov, tsar: I 21, 22
Borisov, N.S.: VIII 33
Borzakovskii, V.: V 390
Bosphorus: I 5; V 324, 373; VI 2
Braichevskiyj, M. Iu.: III 298
Brandes, W.: VIII 7
BriacheslaV son of Iziaslav, prince of Polotsk: VII 148, 151, 156
Briusova, V.G.: XII 98
Brubaker, L.: VII 139
Bruno of Querfurt: II 275, III 292, 293; V 317, 334, 340, 346, 350, 377, 379; VII 133; VIII 7, 15, 16, 17–21, 40, 45, 50
Budilovich, A.: IX 167, 169
Bugoslavskii, S.A.: VII 163; VIII 47
Bührer, P.: IX 161
Bulanina, T.: IV 496
Bulcsu, Hungarian prince: II 272; V 368
Bulgaria, Bulgarians: I 5; II 273; V 315, 318, 336, 343, 347, 371, 381; VI 3, VII 140, 142; VIII 3, 13; IX 169
  battle on 17 August 986: V 322
  conquest and hellenization of the Church: V 344; VIII 13
  oldest manuscripts: V 343
Bulgars on Volga: I 4, 11
Burckhardt, A.: III 292
Bychkova, M.E.: XII 75
Byzantion, Byzantium: I 3–5, 18; III 297; IV 496; V 320, 376; VI 4; VIII 39; IX 177; XII 85, 91, 103 (*see also* Constantinople)
  agreement with Rus': II 271; V 327
  expeditionary corps against Rus' in 988–9: V 328

Caesarea in Cappadocia: V 389
cap, princely: VIII 35
capella regia: VII 150
Capetian dynasty: I 5
Carolingians: I 1; V 337; VIII 14
Casimir IV, ruler of Lithuania and Poland: I 17
catechumenate, ritual of: V 375
Charlemagne: VII 133; VIII 8, 19
Charles the Bold: VII 139
Chekin, L.S.: V 384
Chelcov, M.: IV 496
Cherepnin, L.V.: VIII 27; IX 160
Chernetsov, A.: V 368
Chernigov: I 10, 11, 12; V 351, 359, 383, 385, 386; VII 148, 153; VIII 10; IX 176
  bishopric:V 341
  cathedral of Transfiguration: V 341
  church of saints Boris and Gleb: VII 166
  titular metropolitanate: V 350
Cherson (Korsun'): III 300, 301, 302; IV 498, 500; V 320, 329, 343, 370, 372 373, 377; VIII 4, 14; XI 408; XII 71, 72, 76–8, 84, 85, 87, 103, 104
  antiquities: XII 103, add 1, 71–104
  capture by Tauroscythians: V 321, 327, 371, 375; XII 72
  church of St James the Apostle: XII 76
  coins: V 375
  doors: XI 408; XII 89, 94
  four bronze horses (*quadriga*): XII 92
  gates and bells: XII 86, 87, 93, 94
  icons XII 93, 99, 100
    icon of Annunciation XII 99
    icon of the Holy Apostles Peter and Paul called Chersonian: XII 99
    icon of the Mother of God: XII 94, 97
    icon of Our most Merciful Saviour called Chersonian: XII 99
    icon from Toropec called "Cherson-ian": XII 97
  legend: III 299, 300; V320, 326, 329, 332
  relics: XII 93, add. 105a,
  revolt in: 1016: V 322
  war: 986–9: V 321; XII 86
Chichurov, I.S.: V 384; VIII 50
Chistiakov, O.: IX 160
Chizhevskii, D.: IX 179
Christe, Y.: XII 101
Christian clergy, prayer name: I 7, 19; V 347; VIII 12
Chronicles (Rus'ian):
  of Ermolin: XII 77
  Hypatian: IV 492; VIII 24; IX 165, 172; X 689
  Iosifvskaia letopis: IX 173, XII 93
  Laurentian: IV 492; VIII 22; IX 163, 165, 166, 172; X 689
  of Moscow: XII 77
  Nikonian: IV 489; V 388; XII 77, 93, 143
  Novgorod first: IX 173, 179; XII 75, 77, 86, 89, 90, 103
    Commission ms.: VIII 26
  Novgorod second: XII 86, 87

Novgorod third: XII 86, 93, 94, 95
Novgorod fourth: XII 74, 77
Novgorod, Dubrovskii MS: XII 89, 94, 95, 97
Primary (*Povest vremennych let*): I 2; II 271, 272; III 289, 296, 297, 299, 300, 302; IV 492, 493–5, 498, 500, 502, 503; V 314, 320, 329, 330, 332, 340, 348, 377, 379, 382, 383, 385; VII 134, 137, 145, 147–9, 151, 153, 155, 159, 162, 164, 165, 168; VIII 1, 4, 11, 13, 15, 44, 45, 50; IX 161, 163, 168, 173, 178; XII 71, 76, 103, 104
Pskovian: XII 94
Sophian of Novgorod:
first: XII 77
second XII 89
Vologda-Perm: XII 93
Voskresenskaia: XII 77
Chronicle compilation of 1539: XII 97
chronography: III 287; XII 79
Chrysokephalas, M.: VI 3
Chrysopolis, battle: I 5; V 379
Chud′: I 2
Cividale Codex: V 354
Claude, D.: XI 408
Clement, St, relics brought to Kiev: III 300
Clement (Kliment) Smoliatich: V 341, 359; VI 8
Clovis: VII 151
colophon of 1076 miscellany: IX 171
commemoration of the deceased: V 345
compellere intrare (Luke 14:23): V 317, 377
Constantine the Great: I 8; III 297; IV 497; V 332, 334, 339; VII 133, 134; IX 172
Constantine VII Porphyrogennetos: I 4; II 271–4, 276, add. 279a; V 314–17, 320, 321, 365, 368, 370, 372, 374; VIII 11; IX 162, 164, 166, 168
De administrando imperio: II 272, 275 V 318
De cerimoniis aulae byzantine: II 272, 273, add. 278a; V 314, 315, 369; IX 162
Life of Basil I: V 324
Constantine VIII, emperor: VII 142; VIII 1, 36–8, 49, 50
Constantine IX Monomachos, emperor: I 7, 10; VII 141, 150
Constantine, prince of Rostov: VIII 23, 31
Constantine, son of Vsevolod, prince: V 384; IX 175
Constantine I, metropolitan of Kiev: V 359, 379; VI 4, 8, 12
Constantine II, metropolitan of Kiev: VI 8–10, 12
Constantine-Cyril, apostle of the Slavs, *Vita*: IX 168
Constantinople: I 3, 11; II 271–3, 275, add. 278a, 279a; III 298, 299; IV 497, 501, 503; V 312, 314, 315, 317–19, 327, 336, 338, 340, 351, 359; VI 4, 6, 8, 10, 11; VII 140, 149, 150; 180, 181; VIII 3, 11, 14, 18; XII 72, 77, 93, 98, 103
Hagia Sophia: II 276; V 341, 371
monastery of St Mamas: V 313
patriarch and patriarchate: IV 498, 499; VI 1, 4, 7, 12, 13
Patria Constantinopoleos: IV 490, 499; V 328
Tale of the Capture of Constantinople in 1453: XII 74
coronation of rulers of Kiev: I 7
Cosmas and Damian, Sts: XII 103
Coxe, William: XI 408; XII 85
Cramer, I.A.: V 374
Credo: III 300
Crete: VI 6, 10
Crimea, Crimean Peninsula: III 300; V 350, XII 72
Croats: II 272
Cross, S.H.: III 289–301; IV 492–4, 497; V 367; VII 134; IVIII 45; X 163
Crostini, B.: V 378; VIII 40
Crown, imperial: VIII.35
crowning with a stemma: VII 140
Cumans (Polovcians): X 684
Cyprus, Cyprians: V 356, 357; 387; VI 6, 7, 10
Cyriacus, martyr: VIII 22, 31
Cyril II metropolitan of Kiev: V 341, 360–65, 389; V 391; VI 11
Cyrillic inscriptions: XII 90, 91
Czech land: VIII 24

Dąbrowski D.: VIII 23
Danes: VIII 28
Daniel, Danilovichi, princes of Moscow: I 7, 13, 14
Daniel, hegumen and pilgrim to the Holy Places: V 356, 357, 387
Daniel, prince of Halich: VIII 23
Daniel, prophet: VIII 8
Daniel Romanovich, prince: VIII 24
Danube, Danubian territories: V 350; VII138
Danylo, son of Roman (d. 1264):

grand prince of Kiev (1246–9): V 362
king (rex coronatus) of Halych-Volhynia: V 360, 366, 368
Darrouzès, J.: V 380
David, archbishop of Novgorod: VIII 26
David Igorevich, prince: VII 155, 156
David, king (in the Old Testament): I 5; V 349; VII 139, 155, 161; VIII 36
David, prince of Chernigov: VIII 10
Deesis composition: XII 91
Delehaye, H.: VIII 43
Demetrios, St, of Thessalonica: VIII 34
Demin, A.S.: XII 75
Demus, O.: XI 416
Denmark: VIII 27
Deptuła, C.: XII 412
Desna-Bryansk forest: I 12
Diehl, A.: IV 490; V 374
Dimnik, M.: VII 154; IX add.185a
Dionisii of Suzdal, metropolitan of Rus′: VIII 37
Dmitriev, L.A.: XII 73, 94–6, 103
Dmitrii Donskoi son of Ivan Kalita (b. 1350, d. 1389): I 15, 16; VIII 33, 34, 50, 51
Dmitrii, son of Ivan: IV I 1921, 22; XII 74
Dmitrii, False: I 22
Dmitrov: VIII 36
Dniepr, river, basin: I 4, 12, 14; II 275; V 312, 317, 324, 331, 332, 336, 337, 340, 343, 356, 365; VII 137, 148, 153
Dniester, river, basin: I 12; V 358, 360; VII 156
Dobrava, Czech princes: III 293
Dobrynia: V 333, 342
Dölger, F.: II 274; III 288; V 369; IX 164
Dölker, A.: IX 172
Domentian, Serbian monk, author of the *Life* of Stefan (Simeon) Nemanja: VIII 42
Don, river: I 15; V 362; X 686
Dostal, A.: VIII 20
Downey, G.: V 371
Drevlians: I 3; IX 169
druzhina (retinue of warriors): I 2
Druzhinin, V.G.: VIII 50
Duby, G.: IV 490; VIII 8
Du Cange, Ch.: V 389
Dümmler, E.: V 373
Dulaurier, E.: III 292;
Dunn, M.: VIII 18
Dvornik, F.: IV 495, 498, 499

East Slavs: III 290; IV 503; V 311, 342; VIII 2; IX 159
Ecclesia, privata; publica (katholikii, sobornaia):V 346, 367
Egbert, archbishop of Trier: VII 139
Egypt: V 329; VIII 51
Fatimid caliph: V 329
Ehrhardt, H.: VII 151
Einhard: VIII 8
Eksempliarskii, A.V.: VIII 31–3
Emin, N.: III 292
encomium: VII 162, 164
enthronement: I 5, 6; VI 1; VII 140, 141
Ephesus, bishopric: IV 499
Ephrem, of the Caves Monastery, titular metropolitan of Pereiaslav: V 351, 352, 357, 386; VII 162; IX 167
Epiphanius "the Wise":
epitheta ornantia IX 162, 164, 166, 172, 182
eugenestatos: IX 163
lamprotatoi (*clarissimi illustrissimi*): IX 167
Life of St Stephan of Perm: VIII 37, 50
maiores: IX 168
megaloprepestatoi (*magnificentissimi)*: IX 167
megas- velikii: IX 161, 164, 170, 171, 172, 173, 176, 174, 177, 179, 180, 181; X 684
former, old, elder: IX 172
megistanes: IX 168
meliores: IX 168
optimates: IX 168
peribleptotatoi (*spectabilissimi*): IX 167
primates: IX 168
splendidissimi: IX 167
Eupraksiia, wife of Fedor Jurevich, prince of Riazan′: XII 76, 82
Eusebius of Caesarea: IV 499
Eustathius of Cherson and his son:
"Translation of the icon of St Nicolas from Cherson": XII add. 105a
Evfimii (Euthemius), archbishop of Novgorod and Pskov: VIII 44; XII 86, 89, 90, 94, 95–7, 100
Ezekiel, prophecies of :V 327

Featherstone, J.: II 277, add. 278a
Fennell, J.: III 295; IV 500; V 371, 390, 391; VIII 11, 22, 29
Feodor, son of Iaroslav-Dmitrii, prince of Viaz′ma (d.1344): VIII 32
Feodor, son of Ivan IV the Terrible: I 21, 23
Feodor Iurevich, prince of Riazan′: XI 74, 82

Feodotov, G.P.: IV 502; VII 167, VIII 22
Ferluga, J.: IX 162, 168
Fet, E:. II 272; VIII 47
Fichtenau, H.: II 276
Filaret (Feodor Nikitich Romanov), patriarch of all Rus′: I 23
Filatov, V.V.; XII 95, 98, 99
filia sancti imperii: III 293; IV 489
Finno-Ugric tribes: I 11
Fleckenstein, J.: II 276
Florence:
  Council of VIII 37
  Union of (1439): I 16
Florenskii, P.A.: XII 92
Florov, A. XII 103
Florovsky, G.: XII 94
Forsyth, J.H.: III 291
Frankfurt: I 4; II 274
Franklin, S.: III 290; V 368, 370, 377, 380, 382, 383; VI 12; VII 138; VIII 8, 40, 41; IX 159
Frazer, M.E.: XII 86
Freidhof, G.: XII 101
Freydan, D.: V 381
Fried, J.: V 369, 374; VIII 7
Froianov, J.: V 382; IX 160

Gaiffier, B. de: III 300
Galilee: VIII 21
Gdansk: I 19
Geary, P.: VII 153
Gedymin, Gedyminids: I 11, 12, 14, 17, 18
Gelzer, H. II 292
Gennadii, archbishop of Novgorod and Pskov: XII 91, 100, 101, 102
Gens′ors′kii, A.I.: VIII 25
George, metropolitan of Kiev: IV 495; V 351, 385; VII 160
George Hamartolos: IX 167, 169
George Maniakes: I 9; VII 150
Georgi, W.: V 373
Georgia: IV 500
Gerbert of Aurillac: VII 139
Gerbert of Reims: II 274
Germans: IV 495
Gertrude, daughter of Mieszko II and Richeza: I 10; V 354, 387
Giedroyc′, M.: V 392; VIII 37
Gieysztor, A.: III 290; V 381; VIII 32
Glaber Rodulphus, *Historiarum libri quinque*: VII 139
Gleb *see* Boris and Gleb, Saints
Goetz, L.K.: V 383; IX 160, 161, 163, 174, 181; X 685
Goldblatt, H.: VII 163
Golden Horde: I 13, 15, 16, 18; V 362, 364
Goldschmidt, A.: XI 407, 408, 413–17
Goliath: VII 139
Golubev, S.T.: VIII 29
Golubinski, E.E.: V 387, 388; VII 167; VIII 12, 22; XII 96
Goranin, E.: X 689
Gordenko, E.A.: VIII 35
Gorski, A.: III 294
Götz, U.: XI 417
Gouillard, J.: VI 6
Grala, H.: VI 8
Granstrem, E.E.: V 386
Greece, Greeks: VIII 12, 51; XII 87, 88, 93
Greek patterns in iconography: XII 101
Greek philosopher: IV 493, 495, 496
Gregorovius, F.: II 276; IV 489
Gregory of Nazianzus: IX 169
Grekov, B.D.: IX 160
Gribanova, N.: VIII 39
Grierson, Ph.: VIII 9
Grumel, V.: VI 6, 7, 9–11
Gudelis family: VI 4
Guida, wife of Vladimir Monomach: I 10
Guilland, R.: V 369
Gustavus Adolphus, king: XII 88
Györffy, G.: II 272
Gyula, Hungarian prince: II 272; V 368, 369

Habsburg eagle: I 19
Halich-Volhynia: I 11, 12; V 359, 360, 365; VII 157
  bishopric: V 358
  metropolitanate: V 366
Halperin, Ch.J.: V 390
Hamdani, A.:V 374
Hamilton, B.: VIII 18
Hansa: XII 90
Hauck, K.: II 274
Heider, S.: II 274
Helena, *see* Olga
Helena, daughter of Romanos II: II 294
Helena, mother of Constantine the Great: V 339
Helena, wife of Constantine VII: I 4; II 271; V 314
Helena, wife of Alexander of Lithuania: I 18
Helena Lekapena, empress: III 294
Hellman, M.: III 292, 294, 181; VIII 7
Henry, Graf von Stade: III 293
Henry II, German king: III 292, 294; V 377, 334, 379; VIII 6, 7, 15, 18, 19
Henry IV, emperor: I 10

Herberstein: XI 408; XII 87, 94
Herman of Meissen, margrave: VII 14; VIII 38
Hierotheos, missionary bishop: V 369
Hierotheus, martyr: VIII 44
Hilal as Sabi (970–1056), *Chronicle*: III 292
Hilarion: III 296, 297, 299, 300, 301, 302; IV 491, 494, 495, 497, 499, 500, 502; V 311, 333, 334, 339, 340, 341, 348, 377; VII 134, 137, 157, 158; VIII 8–10, 12, 13, 40, 50
  Encomion to Vladimir: VIII 19, 48
  History of Salvation: IV 503
  Sermon on Divine Law and Grace: III 295; IV 491, 502, 503; V 339; VII 134; VIII 1, 8, 10, 24, 25, 30, 41–3, 45, 46
Hlawitschka, E.: II 275, 276; IV 489
Hludovici imperatoris Vita: VII 139
Hösch, E.: XII 102
Hollingsworth, P.: V 368; VII 135, 168; VIII 11, 47
Holtzmann, R.: III 293; VIII 4
Holy Cross: IV 497
Holy Land: V 356, 357; VI 5, 7, 11
Holy Sepulchre, cathedral of: VI 11
Holy Trinity: XII 89
Howard-Johnston, J.D.: VIII 18
Hrushevsky, M.: V 367, 383, 385, 388, 390, 392; VII 143; IX 174; X 686
Hucke, H.: VIII 20
Hugo Capet, king of France: IV 489; V 327
Hungary, Hungarians: I 4; V 359, 361
  Princes: II 273
Hunger, H.: VII 139
Hurwitz, E.: IV 491

Iakov-Svietoslav Bulgarian despot: V 389
Ianin, V.L.: V 385, 387; VII 140, 155; VIII 29 IX 160, 162; IX 171, 178; XII 103
Iaropolk (d.980): II 277; V 345; VII 150, 151
  transfer of remains VII 153, 154
Iaropolk-Peter, son of Iziaslav, prince of Vlodimir-in-Volhynia (d. 1086): V 354 355; VII 151
Iaropolk, son of Vladimir Monomach, prince of Pereiaslav: V 358
Iaroslav the Wise: I 7–9; IV 492; V 334, 342, 346, 347, 349, 351, 358, 383; VII 134, 137, 138, 140, 141, 144, 148–51, 153–5, 158, 160; VIII 13, 23, 34, 40–42; IX 167, 171, 178, 179; X 687
Iaroslav, son of Vladimir, grandson of Mstislav: IX 180
Iaroslav, son of Vsevolod "the Great Nest": V 361; VIII 33; IX 176, 180
Iaroslav of Tver, brother of Alexander Nevskii: V 362
Iaroslav-Afanasii, son of Vladimir the prince of Serpukhov (b.1388): VIII 34
Iaroslav-Dmitrii, prince of Riazan′: VIII 32
Iberians: V 322, 325
Ibn Khurdadbeh, Arab writer: V 312
Ignatius, bishop of Rostov: V 363
Ignatius, patriarch of Constantinople: IV 498, 499
Igor, son of Iaroslav the Wise: VII 155; IX 178, 179
Igor, son of Rurik, prince of Kiev: I 3, 4; II 271; III 296; V 314, 336; VII 137, 152; VIII 24; IX 162, 163, 170
Igor, prince, hero of campaign 1185: IX 173; X 684–9
Ingelheim: I 4
Ingigerd-Irene, wife of Iaroslav the Wise: III 295; VI 387, VII 137
insignia, royal: I 6
Iona, archbishop of Novgorod (1458–70): XII 95, 96
Ionah, metropolitan of Moscow: VIII 37
Irina, wife of Feodor: I 21
Isaiah, of Caves Monastery, bishop of Rostov: V 352
Istrin, V.M.: IX 167
Italy: VIII 18; XII 91
Iury, son of Daniel, prince of Moscow: I 17
Iury Dolgorukii: I 10; V 352, 359; VI 8; VIII 23; IX 173, 174
Iury, brother of Vasilii III, prince: XII 78
Ivakin, G.: V 390
Ivan, son of Andrei Ivanovich (b. about 1350): VIII 33
Ivan, son of Fedor prince of Riazan: XII 182
Ivan II son of Ivan Kalita: I 19
Ivan III son of Vasily: II I 7, 18, 19; XII 81
Ivan IV the Terrible (b.1530, d.1584): I 18–22; XII 78, 93, 100
Ivan Kalita: I 12, 15, 16; VIII 24, 25, 31, 33, 37
Ivan Viskovatyj, chancellor: XII 99
Ivanov, S.A.: III 287
Iziaslav, son of Vladimir I prince of Polotsk (d.1001): VII 151, 155, 156; IX 171
Iziaslav, son of Iaroslav the Wise: I 9;

V 350, 352, 354, 355; VII 138, 151–3; VIII 21
Iziaslav, son of Mstislav, grand prince of Kiev (1146–54): V 359; IX 178

Jablonskij, V.: XII 96
Jacob de la Gardie, commander of the Swedish units: XII 87
Jagiello, king of Poland: IX 180
Jakobson, A.L.: V 375; XII 71
Jeremy, of the Caves Monastery: V 340
Jerusalem: VI 6, 7; IX 170 ; VIII 15
patriarch: VI 7
Joachim of Cherson, archbishop of Novgorod: XII 103, 104
John the Evangelist
as founder of the bishopric of Ephesus: IV 499
Epistle: VII 165
John II Prodromos, metropolitan of Kiev: III 289; IV 495; V 352, 354, 356, 379, 385; VI 12; VII 160, 163; IX 163
John IV metropolitan of Kiev: VI 8, 9
John XV pope (985–996): IV 489
John Geometres, metropolitan of Melitene: V 328, 374
John de Plano Carpini: IX 176
John the Theologian: IV 499;
apostle of Asia: VIII 51
John Tzimisces, emperor: I 4; V 321, 322, 325, 327, 373; VII 142; IX 163, 164
Joseph of Arimathea: XI 414, 417
Judith (Constance), wife of Robert the Pious: VII 139
Juliana Aleksandrovna, wife of Olgerd: VIII 32
Julitta martyr, mother of St Cyriacus: VIII 22, 31
jus spolii: V 344

Kahl, D.H.: III 292
Kalachev, N.B.: XII 7
Kalajdovich, K. IV 495
Kalisz, Polish city: VIII 24
Kalokyros, patrikios, a member of Cherson's nobility: V 321, 372
Kämpfer, F.: V 375, 387; VII 133, 149, 154
Karakorum, capital of Mongolia: I 11
Karamzin, N.M.: VIII 17
Karayannopulos, J.: III 287, 289
Karelian isthmus: VIII 27
Karger, M.K.: VIII 29, 35
Karskij, E.F.: IX 170
Karwasinska, J.: III 292; V 377
Kashira, district: XII 83
Trinity Monastery: VIII 33
Kashtanov, S.M.: IX 161, 162
Kassim khan: I 16
Kazakova, N.A.: XII 90
Kazan′: I 18; XII 84
Kazhdan, A.P.: V 371, 384; VI 7
Kezma, T.: III 292
Khaburgaev, G.A.: V 381
Khazars: I 4; V 312, 318
Kholm (Chełm): V 360, 361, 365
Khopor, river: V 362
Khoroshev, A.S.: VIII 30; XII 90
Khoroshkevich, A.L.: V 391; XII 90
Kienast, W.: IX 161
Kiev: I 1, 11, 12, 18; II 276, 277; III 298; IV 495, 496, 501; V 316, 319, 323, 324, 326, 328, 329, 334, 336, 347, 351, 363, 381; VI 4; VII 134, 138, 140, 142, 149, 153, 166; VIII 7, 10, 11, 15, 17–20, 29, 40; IX 173, 174, 159, 166, 171, 172, 176, 180, 181; XII 76, 100, 103
boyar's residences: V 346
cathedral of St Sophia: V 319, 340, 347, 379, 380; VI 1; VII 149; VIII 9, 13, 14, 41
frescoes: I 9 church of the Annunciation: VIII 41
church of the Tithe (*capella palatina*): III 295; VII 150, 154; VIII 8, 9, 29, 39, 41, 46; XII 103
cross on the hills: IV 500
Golden Gate: V 347; VIII 41
journey Kiev-to-Constantinople: V 325
Kievan's mass baptism: V 332
metropolitan see: I 14:V 341, 357, 362
Monastery of the Caves: III 300; V 320, 340, 348, 352, 354, 355, 356, 357, 360, 364, 382, 387; VI 9, 12; VII 134, 147, 165, 168; VIII 46–7; IX 179
Paterikon: V 386, 387 VII 168
monastery of St Demetrius: VIII 21

synod in 1273: V 364, 391
throne: I 9; V 335, 345; VI 1, 10; VII 141, 145, 148, 155, 159, IX 183
wooden cathedral: V 379
Kiev-Volhynians line of descendants from Vladimir Monomach: I 12
Kliazma, river: I 13; V 359
kliros: V 353, 358, 387
Kliuchevskii,V.O.: IX 159; XII 95, 96, 102
Kloss, B.M.: IV 489; XII add.105a

Kmietowicz, Fr.: IX 166
Kołakowski, L.: III 290; IV 491
Kolomna: XII 78, 81
  church and icon of St Nicolas Zarazskii: VIII 35; XII 80
Komarovič, V.L.: XII 78
Komech, A.I.: III 298; VIII 9, 39
Komnenoi, dynasty: IX 171
Kondakov, N.P.: XII 85, 86, 93, 97
Korzukhina, G.F.: XII 71, 72
Kosmas, bishop of Halych: V 359
Kostočkin, V.V.: XII 82
Kostomarov, N.I.: I 24
Kotkov, S.I.: V 38
Kotliar, M.: V 373
Kovalchik, E.: VIII 19
Krasimir, prince of the Croats: II 272
Kratchkovsky, I.: III 291; V 379; VII 133; VIII 42
Krause, H. XI 407
Kresten, O.: II add. 278a; VII 139
Krohm, H.: XI 417
Krüger, K.H.: VIII 9
Kruszwica: IX 171
Krymsky, A.: III 292
Kucharek, C.: VIII 20
Kuchera, M.: VIII 19
Kuchkin, V.A.: V 386, 388, 390; VIII 33; IX 181; XII add.105a
Kulikovo Pole, battle in 1380: I 15; VIII 31, 32
Kuno, graf of Ohningen: II 277
Kursk: VII 166
Kuz'min, A.G.: V 383; IX 161; XII 75, 81, 82

Labuda, G.: II 275
Labunka, M.: II 271, 275; IV 488
Ladoga: I 2
Laiou, A.: VIII 6
Lakedaimon, metropolitanate: V 385
Latin inscriptions: XII 90
Latin heresy: XII 102
Latin motifs in religious iconography: XII 100
Latins: IV 494, 495; VI 7; VII 147
Lauer, H.H.: VIII 15
Laurina, V.K.: VIII 35
Lavrov, P.: IX 168
Lavrovskij, N.: IX 162, 163, 166
Lazarev, V.N.: VIII 35; XI 413, 415; XII 90, 99, 103
Lechner, K.: III 288
Leisinger, H.: XI 413
Leitsch, W.: V 391
Lemerle, P.: IV 495
Lenhoff, G.: VII 136
Leo, brother of Nikephoros Phokas: V 372
Leo, titular metropolitan of Pereiaslav: V 351, 352, 386
Leo the Deacon: I 3; III 287, 288; V 321, 327, 374
Leontii, bishop of Rostov: VII 168
Leontios of Patmos: V 379, VI 2–6, 10, 11
Lewicki, T.: V 367
Liakh, Liashko: VII 146
Libutius, monk from St Alban in Trier: II 273, 274, 275; V 316, 317
Likhachev, D.S.: IV 492; V 370, 383; VIII 22, 23, 45; X 687; XII 73–5, 78, 81, 82, 103, add. 105a
Likhacheva, O.P.: VIII 25
Lilienfeld, F. von: V 383; VI 19; VIII 13; XII 102
Limonov, Ju.: IX 160, 174
Lind, J.: VII 158; VIII 44
Lintzel, M.: II 274; V 369
Listven', battle: VII 148
Litavrin, G.G.: II 271–3, add. 278a; III 287; V 368, 369, 374; VI 3; XII 140
Lithuania: I 15–19, 21; VIII 32, 37; XII 104
  metropolitanate: V 392
  grand princes: I 16, 17
Liutprand, bishop of Cremona: V 325, 367, 373; VII 142
Livonia: I 20; XII 90
  Livonian order: I 19
loros, imperial garment: V 168, 369
Loseva, O.: VIII 25
Łowmiański, H.: IX 165, 168, 169
Lta (Alta), river, church on the: VII 162
Lucas Chrysoberges, patriarch of Constantinople: IX 180
Ludat, H.: XI 408
Lukas, A.T.: V 381
Luke, Apostle: VIII 51
Lur'e, J.S.: V 383; XII 74, 91, 97, 101
Lutsk (Luchesk): V 361, 365
  bishopric: V 388
Lvov: IV 496

Macedonian dynasty: V 326; VII 142
Macler, F.: III 292; VII 142
Macrides, R.: V 375; IX 161
Magdalino, P.: VI 2, 5
Magdeburg: VII 142; VIII 6; XII 85, 87, 88
  cathedral of St Maurice: XI add. 420a
  doors: XII 407
  masters: XI 415
  romanesque workshop: XII 85

Maiasova, N.A.: VIII 34
Makarii, archbishop of Novgorod: XII 96, 99, 100
Makarii, metropolitan of Moscow: XII 84, 99
Great Minei-Četii XII 84
Makarios, patriarch of Antioch: XII 88
Mal, prince of Drevliane: IX 169
Malakhias, vicar of the Moscow metropolitan in Vladimir in Suzdalia: V 386
Malamut, E.: V 384
Malbork: I 19
Malusha, mother of Vladimir the Great: II 277; V 333, VII 143; VIII 11
Mango, C.: III 298; V 371, 378; VIII 9
Manuel I Komnenos, emperor: V 379 VI 2, 3, 6, 8, 9, 11; XII 98
Manuel, bishop: V 358, 387
Manzikert, battle in 1077: V 350
Margoliouth, D.S.: III 292
Maria "the Alan", Byzantine empress: VII 141
Maria Skleraina, concubine of Constantine: IX: I 10
Maria, daughter of Ivan Kalita, wife of Constantine of Riazan′: VIII 31
Maria, widow of Simeon the Haughty: VIII 34
Mark, Apostle of Egypt: VIII 51
Mark, bishop of Pereiaslav: V 358
Markopoulos, A.: V 374
marriage, sacrament: V 345
Martysevič, I.: IX 160
Matthew, metropolitan: V 360
Matthew Paris, *Chronica maiora*: V 389
Maurokastron, *see* Chernigov
Maxim, metropolitan of Kiev (1283–1305): V 365; VIII 29
Menaion service (office): VIII 30
Merovingians: VIII 14
Mestisthlabos megas archon Rhosias, (inscription on seal): IX 178
Metropolitanates, titular: V 354
Meyendorff, J.: IV 495, VIII 13, 21, 37
Meysztowicz, W.: VIII 7
Michael, son of Alexander grand prince of Tver and Vladimir: I 13
Michael Feodorvich (*see* Filaret), tsar: I 23
Michael-Boris, Bulgarian ruler: II 272
Michael of Anchialos, patriarch of Constantinople: VI 7
Michael II metropolitan of Kiev V 358; VI 8, 10
Michael Kerularios, patriarch: IV 495
Michael Skopin-Shuisky: I 22
Michael synkellos, *Confession of faith*: III 299; IV 494, 495
Mieszko I, prince of Poland: III 293
Migne, J.P.: V 367
Mikhail, son of the prince of Tver′ (b.1333): VIII 31
Mikhalko, prince: IX 174
Millet, G.: XI 415
Mineia Prazdnichnaia: VIII 31
miniatures:
of Radziwiłł chronicle: VIII 25
of the pictorial Tale(Sylvestrian collection) of Sts Boris and Gleb: VIII 35
Minsk: I 17
Miroslav, prince of the Croats: II 272
Misjur′-Munekhin, M.G., governor of Pskov: XII 101
Mitrofan, archbishop of Novgorod: V 360
Mitrofan, bishop of Sarai: V 362
Mitrofan, bishop of Kolomna: XII 78
Mneva, N.E.: XII 80, 97, 98, 99, 101
Moisei of Vydubiči, *Kievan chronicle*: IX 173
Mojmir dynasty: IX 169
Moldovan, A.M.: II 294, 296, 297; IV 491, 493, 494, 497–500, 502, 503; V 377, 379, 382; VIII 12, 24, 40, 50
Mongait, A.L.: XII 82
Möngke Temür, khan: V 362
Mongolia, Mongols: I 4, 11, 13; V 365–4, 389; VIII 51; XII 71
Moravia: IX 169
Moravcsik, G.: II 272; V 368, 372; IX 164
Mordvinians: I 11
Moscow: I 7, 10–19, 21; 489; VIII 27, 37; XII 74, 82, 84, 93, 104
Cathedral of the Annunciation: XII 97
chroniclers: I 18, 77
metropolitanate: I 16
as "third Rome": I 19
throne, rulers: I 2, 3, 16
Motsia, A.P.: V 368
Mstislav, son of Iziaslav (d.1061): IX 179
Mstislav, son of Vladimir the Great: VII 144, 148, 160
Mstislav, son of Vladimir Monomakh: V 358; IX 173, 180, 182
Evangelistary 1117: XII 93
Mstislav Danilovich: VIII 24
Müller, L.: II 271, 274; III 289, 295–9, 301; IV 490, 493, 494, 497–500, 502, 503; V 382; VII 136, 139; VIII 15, 17, 24; IX 172; X 687; XII 77
Murom: V 359, 388

Mysia (Bulgaria): VI 3

Nabokov, W.: X 688
Nasonov, A.N.: V 388, 390, 391; VIII 26; IX 173; X 688; XII 77, 94, 97
Nazarenko, A.V.: II 271, 274–7, add. 278a; V 385; VII 142; VIII 16, 17
Nazianzus, metropolitanate: V 385
Nebuchadnezzar, king: VIII 8
Nelson, J.L.: V 384; VII 139
Neofit, titular metropolitan of Chernigov: V 351, 385, 386
Neredica, church of the Saviour: IX 180
Nestor, bishop of Rostov: V 352
Nestor, hagiographer: III 297; IV 498; VII 135, 160, 163–5, 168; VIII 11
  Life of Boris and Gleb: III 299; VII 136
  Life of Feodosii: VII 165
Neva: VIII 27, 28
  battle in 1240: I 11
"neveglas": VIII 14
New Jerusalem: III 299; IV 497
  Cross from: III 298; V 339
  see Constantinople
Nicea, in Bithynia: V 340, 361, 389
Nicetas, metropolitan: V 358
Nicol, D.M.: IV 495
Nicolas of Mozhaisk , St.: XII 83
Nicolas Zarazskii, St.: XII 73, 80–82, add. 104a, 105a
  church and icon: XII 72, 76–84, 104a, 105a
  omophorion (pallium) received from Our Lady: XII add. 104a
Nieman, river: I 19
Nikephoros I metropolitan of Kiev: I 5, IV 495:VI 11; IX 172
Nikephoros II, metropolitan of Kiev: V 359; VI 8, 11
Nikephoros II, patriarch of Jerusalem: VI 7
Nikephoros Phokas, emperor: I 4; V 321 326, 327, 328, 372, 374; VII 142
Nikitenko, I.H.: VIII 15
Nikolskaia, A.V.: VIII 24
Nikolskii, N.K.: VIII 30, 42
Nikonov, V.A.: XII 82
Nilos Doxopatros: IV 501; VI 12, 13
Nomokanon (*Kormchaia*): VIII 25; IX 167
  Novgorod redaction of 1282: VIII 26
  Rostov-Vladimir redaction: VIII 26
  Volhynian redaction: VIII 26
Noonan, T.S.: V 367
Norse I.: V 336
Notitia episcopatuum Ecclesiae Constantinopolitanae: V 338, 352, 385, 389, 392
Novgorod: I 2, 11, 19; V 333, 355, 360, 380, 381, 383, 384; VII 144, 151, 152, 153; VIII 27, 31, 43, 44; IX 173, 175, 178, 180; XII 84, 87, 88, 89, 90, 93, 97, 103, 104
  annual day of 4 Oct. in memory of all Novgorodian bishops: XII 96
  cathedral of St Sophia: V 342 VIII 13; XII 85, 86, 89, 90, 92, 95, 97, 98, 100, 101; frescoes: XII 89; icons: XII 97–9; of the Saviour enthroned: XII 98; iconostasis: XII 95, 98; Doors: XI 407–18; XII 104; Cyrillic inscriptions: XI 412; plates: master Abraham: XI 413, 415–417, add. 419a; master Riquin: XI 415; add. 419; master Waismuth: XI 415, 417, add. 419a; crucifixion: XI 413; descent from the Cross: XI 415; Nicodemus: XI 414; women at the Tomb: XI 413, 414; St Maurice: XI add. 420a; centaur: XI 413; half-bolsters XI 416; Chersonian Gates: XII 86, 87; western chapel: XII 86–90; *Pontifical 1630*: XII 89
  church of St Vladimir: VIII 36
  Chutyn' Monastery and church of our Saviour: XII 93
  cycle of legends: XII 95
  fall in 1471: XII 93, 102
  icon of battle of the Novgorodians with the Suzdalians: XII 103
  manuscripts: XI 413
  monastery of St George: IX 178; XII 99
    icon of Annunciation XII 99
  monastery of St Panteleimon: IX 178
  Tale of the Tomb of St Ioann: XII 96

Obolensky, D.: II 271, 273; III 288, 290, 299; IV 491; V 370, 371, 372, 373, 378
Ochrid: V 344; VI 12
Odalrici praepositi Remensis ecclesiae psalter: III 300
Ohnsorge, W.: II 274, 291; V 373
Oka, river: I 10, 12; V 356, 359; IX 184
Okhotina, N.A.: V 391
Okhotnikova, V.I.: VIII 22
Okunev, I.; VIII 35, 36
Oleg the Seer, ruler of Kiev: I 3; IX 163, 165, 166
Oleg, brother of Vladimir the Great (d.977): V 345
  transfer of remains in 1044: VII 150,

151, 153, 154
Oleg-Michael, son of Sviatoslav, prince of Chernigov: V 384: VII 151; VIII 10, 44
Olga-Helena, archontissa of Rus': I 3, 4; II 271, 272, 274, 277, add. 278a; III 283, 299, 300; IV 492, 497, 502; V 311–16 319, 320, 333–338, 368; VII 137, 143, 151; VIII 4, 11, 18; IX 162, 170
  baptism: II 271; V 317, 368
  visits to Constantinople: II 275, 318
  embassy to Otto: I II 276; V 319
Olga-Helena of Brian'sk: VIII 23
Olgerd, grand prince of Lithuania: I 17; VIII 32, 37
orbis romanus: III 288
Origen: IV 499
Orlov, A.S.: XII 75
Orthodoxy: I 5, 18, 19; XII 91
Osetr, river: XII 79, 81, 82
ospodar, host, lord of the house: IX 177
Ostrogorsky, G.: II 271, 276; V 368, 374, 384; VII 138; IX 162, 164
Ostromir, governor of Novgorod: V 343; VII 138
Ostrowski, D.: V 391; VIII 4
Oswald, F.: VIII 9, 39
Otto I: I 4; II 274–6; III 293, 312, 316, 318, 325, 327, 369, 373; VII 142; VIII 18
Otto II: III 293, 294; V 325, 369, 373; VII 151
Otto III: II 273; III 294; IV 489; V 325; VIII 5, 6
Ottonian empire: II add. 279a
  chancellery: V 316
  mission: V 315
Oxenstierna, Axel, Swedish chancellor: XII 87

Pakhomii Logofet: XII 96
Palestine: V 356
pallium: VIII 17
Panova, T.: V 368
Parthey, G.: VI 13
Pashuto, V.T.: IX 160
Patlagean, E.: V 375
Paul of Aleppo, archdeacon: XII 88
Paul, Apostle: III 302; IV 493, 494; VIII 50, 51; XII 91, 98 Pechenegs: I 4; III 292; V 318, 334, 340, 346, 349, 350, 351, 370, 379; VII 143, 144, 145, 148; VIII 7, 15, 16, 17, 19, 21, 36; IX 164
Peipus Lake, battle in 1242: I 11
Pelenski, J.: V 386
Pereiaslav: I 10; V 351, 357, 358, 385, 386, 388; VII 153, 166, 167
  bishopric; V 352, 358, 387
  titular metropolitanate: V 350, 385
  cathedral of the Archangel Michael: V 349
Peremyshl: V 359, 361, 365, 389
  vicariate of the bishopric of Vladimir-in-Volhynia: V 360
  church of St John the Baptist: V 360, 388
  stone rotunda: V 368
Peretz, V.: IX 179
Perfecky, G.: VIII 24
Peter, Apostle: IV 494; VII 140; VIII 7, 189, 21, 51; XII 91, 98
Peter Akerovych, hegumen from Kiev: V 389
Peter of Antioch, patriarch: IV 495
Peter, bishop of Pereiaslav: V 351, 352
Peter, ruler of Bulgaria: VII 140, 142
Peter Damiani: VIII 16
Peter Mohila: VIII 35
Petit, L.: VI 3
Petrovskii, M.: VIII 43
Phebus, St, relics brought to Kiev: III 300
Philip of Swabia: IX 182
Philipp, W.: V 391; VIII 15
Photios, patriarch: I 18; IV 498, 499; V 312
Piast dynasty: I 5, 12
Pickhan, G.: VII 149
Pinsk: VII 143
Pliguzov, A.I.: V 391
Płock on the Vistula: XI 407, XII 85
  cathedral of the Holy Virgin: XI 407
  doors: XI 412
Plykhanova, M.: VIII 35
Podskalsky, G.: III 289, 290, 295, 299, 300 301; IV 490, 491, 496, 498; V 367, 370 377–81, 383, 386–9, 391; VI 2, 12; VIII 22, 47 50
Pokrovskii, F.I.: VIII 42
Pokrovskii, M.N.: XII 102
Poland: I 17, 21, 22; V 361; VIII 18, 24
Polesie: V 354
Polotsk: V 346, 381; VII 134, 141, 143, 148, 151, 152, 155, 156, IX 169
  episcopal see: V 341
  cathedral of St Sophia: V 341, 342, 346; VIII 13
Polovtians (Cumans): I 4, 11; V 350
Polyeuktos, patriarch: II 276; V 319
Pompeiupolis: V 338
Ponomariev, A.L.: V 371

Ponyrko, N.V.: V 38
Pontus, diocese: IV 299
Popov, A.: VIII 37
Popova, O.S.: XII 97
Poppe, D.: III 294
Preger, T.: V 374
Premyslids, royal family: I 5
presbyterion, capitulum, kliros: V 353
Preslav manuscripts: V 381
Presniakov, A.: V 385; IX 168
Priselkov, M.D.: III 298; V 386; IX 174; X 685
Pritsak, O.: II 271; V 367; X 684
Prokhorov, G.M.: VIII 37
Pronsk: IX 175
proskynesis: I 6; II 277; V 368, 369
Prus, legendary ancestor of Rurik: I 19
Prussian land: I 19; VIII 16, 19
Prypiat′, river: I 3; V 354
Psellos, Michael: III 287, 288, 289, 295; V 324, 373
Pskov, Pskovian: I 19; VII 148; VIII 31, 36; XII 94
  icon painter: XII 101
Ptashycki, S.: IX 180
Pushkareva, N.L.: VIII 6
Put′sha, a princely agent: VII 146

Raba, J.: XII 90
Radonezh, monastery of the Holy Trinity and St Sergius: I 14
Rampendahl, E.: XI 415
Rapov, O.M.: V 375
Rappaport, P.A.: III 298; V 382
Rau, R.: II 273
Raupach, D.: XII 88
regalia, imperial: I 7; VII 141
Regelindis: VII 144
Regino of Prüm, abbot, *Continuatio Reginonis Chronicon*: V 315, 369
Reinbern, bishop of Kolberg: III 293; VII 144; VIII 4
Reisman, E.: VII 168
responsorium (antiphon): VIII 20
Reutov, A. VIII 39
Revel: VIII 27
Revelli, G.: VII 163
Riazan′: I 19; V 359, 362; XII 73–5, 76, 78, 79, 81, 82, 84, 104
  bishopric: V 388; XII 79
Riché, P.: IV 489, 490
Richeza, wife of Mieszko: II I 10
Richtlint, daughter of graf Kuno of Ohningen: II 277
Ritzer, K.: VIII 6
Robert the Pious, son of Hugh Capet: IV 489; V 327; VII 139; VIII 7
Rogneda , wife of Vladimir the Great: VII 141, 142, 155
Rogovold, prince of Polotsk: VII 155, 156; IX 169
Roman Empire: I 19
Roman Mstislavich, prince of Halych in Volhynia (d. 1205): I 12; V 366; IX 176, X 687
Romanos I Lekapenos, emperor: II 272, 273, 276; V 318; VII 142
Romanos II, emperor: II 272, 274, 277; III 294; V 315, 316, 317, 320; VII 138
Romanos the Melode, St: VII 161
Romanovs, dynasty: I 23
Romanus, son of Bulgarian tsar Peter: VII 142
Rome: II 275; IV 499; V 317; VIII 3, 7, 18
  papal court: V 354
Rostislav (b. 1070), son of Vsevlod: I 7; VII 152
Rostislav, son of Mstislav, prince of Smolensk: V 358
Rostislav, son of Vladimir, prince of Novgorod (d. 1067): I 12
Rostislav, Moravian prince: IX 168
Rostov: I 13; V 352, 358, 363, 386
  bishopric and cathedral: V 353, 355; VII 168
Rostov-Suzdal land: I 10; V 357, 359; IX 174
Royal doors as "church" doors: XII 96
Rozen, V.R.: III 291; V 379
Rozov, N.N.: III 295; IV 491; V 383; VIII 43
Rurik (Hrorikr), founder of dynasty: I 2, 13, 19; VII 152
Rurik, ruler of Kiev (1180–1181): IX 173; X 687
Rurik, son of Rostislav: VII 156; IX 174, 176; X 685
Rurikid dynasty I 1–25; V 326, 341, 384; VII 141, 156, 168; VIII 23, 29; IX 162, 169; XII 84
Rurikid lineages:
  of Halych-Volhynia: V 366; VII 157; VIII 43
  of Moscow: I 14
  of Suzdal-Nizhny Novgorod: I 22
Rus′ (Russia, Rhōs, Rhōsia), terminology: I 1, 2, 13, 14, 17; II 275; IV 500; V 312, 365, 367, 385; VI 8; VIII 1; IX 159, 170

baptism: V 324; XII 103
Christianity: IV 501, V 319; VII 134
conversion: III 287–302; IV 488–504; V 320
embassy to Constantinople: V 316, 327
great (*megale, pases, vseia*): V 65, 366
little (*mikra*) Ukraine: I 12; V 360, 362, 366; metropolitanate V 361
metropolitanate: I 5; V 338, 340, 366, VI 2
presence at Chrysopolis: V 327
treaties with Byzantium: IX 161; of 911 VII 313; IX 163–5, 170; of 944: V 315, 322, 372; X 163, 164, 166, 170; of 971: V 322; IX 163
Rus'ian Church: I 16
Ru'sian nation: I 13
Russians: I 1; V 311
Ruthenians: I 1, 12
Rybakov, B.A.: VII 168; VIII 3; IX 160, 166, 177; X 687
Ryndina, A.V.: XI 413, XII 91
Rynne, E.: V 381
Ržiga, V.F.: IX 177

sainthood, political: VII 168
Sakharov, A.N.: IX 161
Salerno: XII 86
Salians, royal house: I 5
Salmina, M.A.: XII 74
Samuel, Bulgarian tsar: V 381
Macedonian gospel; V 343, 381
San, river: V 358
sanovniki (dignitaries): IV 497
Sansterre, J.M.: VIII 18
as-Saqāliba, people: V 313
Saracens: II 277
Sarai: V 362

Sauerländer, W.: XI 407
Saxons: VII 144, 146, VIII 16, 38
Scandinavia: I 2, 5, 19; V 311, 324
Scheideweiler, F.: V 374
Schiller, G.: XI 415
Schmidt, K.R.: IX 160, 178
Schmidt, S.O.: XII 79
Schneider, N.: III 298; VIII 15
Schramm, P.E.: IV 489
Schreiner, P.: II add., 278a; IX 161, 164, 171
Schubert, E.: XI 407
Schweicher, C.: XI 415
Sclavonia: II 275
Scott, R.: VIII 1
Scythia: IV 499
Sedelnikov, A.D.: XII 91, 101
Sedov, V.V.: V 368
Seemann, K.: IX 170
Senderovich, S.: VIII 50
Senyk, S.: V 375
Serapion, bishop of Vladimir in Suzdalia: V 364
sermons: V 391
Serbs: XII 88
Serebrianskii, N.I.: VIII 22, 46, 49, 50, 51; XII 77
Sergiei of Radoneh, St.: XII 101
Serikov, N.I.: V 371, 375
Ševčenko, I.: III 290; IV 488; V 367, 370; VII 134; VIII 9
Shakhmatov, A.A.: V 370, 383; IV 492; IX 165, 174; X 685; XII 77, 97
Shaskolskii, I.P.: VIII 27 XI 408; XII 88, 94
Shboul, A.M.H.: VII 141
Shchapov, Ia.N.: VI 1; V 382, 385, 386–9; VIII 3, 26; IX 167; XII 94, 98
Shepard, J.: V 368, 370, 383; VII 133, 142 150
Sherbowitz-Wetzor, O.P.: III 289; IV 492 V 367; VII 134; IX 163
Shusharin, V.P.: IX 160
Sicily, royal court: VI 13
Sigismund Vasa, king of Poland: I 22
Sigtuna, Swedish town, doors: XI 408; XII 87, 88
Silvester II, pope: IV 489; VII 137
Silvester, priest: XII 99, 100
Simeon, bishop of Pereiaslav: V 357, 358
Simeon the Haughty (d.1313), son of Ivan Kalita: I 15; VIII 33, 34
Simeon Metaphrastes, *Menologion* of Basil II: IV 499
Simeon, ruler of Bulgaria (893–927): VII 140; IX 170
Codex: V 343, 381
Simeon of Suzdal, polemic with the supporters of Florence Union: VIII 37
Simeonian chronicle: XII 93
Simon, a Varangian Christian: VII 147
Siuziumov, M.J.: III 287
Skylitzes, John (*Synopsis historiarum*): II 272, 273, 276, 277, add. 279a; III 289; V 368, 369, 370, 374, 381
slaves (kholopy): I 14
Slavic language: V 336
Slavs: IV 500; VIII 14, 16
Slavs on the Danube: IV 493, 500; V 336
Sluch, river: I 3
Smedley J.: VIII 1; XII 72
Smiadin', church on: VII 162

Smirnova, E.S.: VII 164; VIII 34, 35; XII 80, 98
Smolensk: I 19, 23; VII 155, VIII 32
bishopric: V 354, 357, 387
stone church of the Dormition: V 357–8
Smorgunova, E.M.: VIII 25
Soboleva, N.A.: VIII 37
Sobolevskii: IX 180; XII 72
Sokolov, P.: V 386; VIII 37; IX 181
Sokolova, I.V.: V 375
Solomon, King of Israel in OT: VIII 3
Soloviev, A.V.: IV 491; V 385; VIII 41; IX 162, 163, 167, 170, 171; X 686
Soloviev, S.M.: VII 138, 144
Sophia (Zoe) Palaiologina, wife of Ivan: III I 18, 19
Sophia, wife of Vasilii: I I 15
Sotnikova, M.P.: VII 140
Spasskii, I.G.: VII 140
Speranskii, M.N.: XII 103; XII 74, 77
Spinoza, B.: III 290; IV 490
Spuler, B.: V 390
Sreznevskii, I.I.: IV 497; VIII 44; IX 177; XII 96
Stadtmüller, G.: VI 7
Stefan Nemanja, Life of: VIII 42
Steindorff, L.: VII 158; VIII 44
Stephan, St, bishop of Perm, his *Vita*: VIII 27, 50
Stephen of Taron (Asoghik): III 291, 292; V 321, 371
Stephen of the Caves Monastery, bishop of Vladimir in Volhynia: V 355
Stiernon, D.: VI 3
Stoekl, G.: V 389; IX 160, 161, 177
Stoglav, church council of 1551: XII 91
Stokes, A.: III 295
Stoudios, St John monastery: V 382;
church statute: VIII 31
Stroev, P.: XII 94
Strumnitsa, region in northern Macedonia: VI 3
Strzelczyk, J.: III 295
Sudislav: VII 135, 148, 149
Sukhomlinov, M.: IV 494
Surohz-Sugdaia: XII 72
Suzdal, Suzdalia (land): I 13; V 357, 358; VI 10; X 175, 180, 181; IX 174
Sventopolk, prince of Moravia: II 272
Sverdlov, M.B.: V 382; IX 160
Svet (-malik), ruler of the Slavs: IX 166
Sviatopolk, son of Vladimir the Great: I 6, 8; III 293; VII 143–8, 166; VIII 17, 38, 42
coins: VII 140
Sviatopolk, son of IziaslaV prince of Kiev: V 355
Sviatoslav the Glorious, son of Igor and Olga (b.c.938–d.972): I 4; II 271, 275, 277; III 296; V 319, 322, 326, 327, 333, 336; VII 135, 137, 143, 150, 152, 154; VIII 11, 15; IX 163, 165
Sviatoslav, son of Iaroslav, prince of Chernigov (d.1076): I 7, 10; V 350, 381, 383; VII 153, 155, 159, 165; IX 170
Izbornik of 1073: V 343; IX 170
Sviatoslav, son of Vsevolod, prince of Kiev (1176–1184): IX 173, 174; X 685, 687, 688
Svirin, A.N.: XII 98
Svoboda, W.: VI 3
Swedes: VIII 22, 27
Synaxaria: VIII 30
syncretism (*dvoeverie)*: V 380; VII 142
synkellos (member of the Byzantine imperial senate): V 351
synkletos/*boljarskij sobor*: IX 167
synods: V 340, 362, 389; VI 1
Synodal manuscript of the first half of 14 c.: VIII 26
Syria: V 374; XII 87, 88

Tachiaos, A.: V 370; VIII 20
Tale about the Sign from the icon of the Mother of God: XII 103
Tale of the Spread of Christianity in Rus': IV 492, 503
talets'-a captive: VII 146;
Tatars: I 4, 14–16; XII 76, 78, 79, 83
princelings and mirzas: I 14
tribute: I 15, 16; VIII 51
yoke thrown off: I 18
Tatishchev, V.N. V 383, 388
Tauroscythians: IV 489; V 327
Taurus, forum: V 328
Temp, E.: VII 139
Terpimir, prince of the Croats: II 272
Teutonic Order: I 17
Teutonic Prussia: I 19
Theodora, empress: V 375
Theodore, metropolitan of Kiev: VI 9
Theodosius (Feodosii), St, of the Kievan Caves monastery: IV 496; V 348, 354, 382, 383; VII 159, 165
Theodosius I Boradiotes, patriarch of Constantinople: VI 11
Theodosius Gudelis VI 2
Theognostos, bishop of Sarai and

Pereiaslav:V 362
Theognostos, metropolitan of Moscow: VIII 33
Theoktist, archbishop-elect: VIII 28
Theoktistos, abbot of monastery of St John the Theologian: VI 5
Theophana, wife of Ostromir: VII 138
Theophanes Continuatus, *Chronografia*: II 272; III 289
Theophanō, wife of Romanos II, empress: II 272, 277, 294
Theophanū, wife of Otto II: III 293; IV 489; V 325, 326, 373, 367, 375
Theophylaktos, patriarch of Constantinople (d. 956): II 272, 276; V 318
Theophylaktos of Sebaste, metropolitan (after 988) of Kiev: III 290
Thietmar of Merseburg, chronicler (975–1018): III 293, 294; IV 491; V 340, 379, 382; VII 137, 144, 145; VIII 4, 5–7, 9–11, 39, 40, 41
Thomson, F.J.: III 290; V 381, 382; VII 163
Thurn, I.: V 368
Tikhomirov, M.N.: XII 77, 81
Tinnefeld, F.: II add. 278a, V 371
Titles:
  archon: IX 169, 162, 168
    archontes periphanestatoi: IX 167
    megas archon: IX 177; X 685
    archon Rhosias: I 3; IX 162, 164, 177
    archontissa: V 315, VII 140
  basileus: I 13; VII 140; IX 169
    megas basileus: IX 164
    basilissa: VII 137, 139, 140, 151
  caesar: I 13
    cěsar': IX 164, 169, 170
    velikii cěsar': IX 164
  edinoderžec, edinovlastec, samoderžec: IX 183
  hegemon: IX 170
  kniaz': I 2, 3; VIII 2; IX 162, 164, 168, 169, 170; 172, 174, 175, 180
    blagovernyi kniaz': IX 163
    velikii (yfirkonungr) kniaz': IX 161, 170, 175; X 688
    smalkonungar kniazi: IX 170
    velepotnii i slavni kniazi: IX 167
  kagan: VII 134
  king: I 2
    great king I 11
  kuning, kuningaz: I 2
  metropolitan: X 686
    titular V 351
  prince, princess: V 340; IX 164, 168;
    subordinates: IX 166
    grand prince: IX 159–4
  rex: I 2; VIII 2; IX 170, 180
    rex coronatus VII 141
    rex Russiae: I 3; IX 170
    magnus (megas) rex: I 11; IX 174
  tsesar, tsar: I 10, 13, 14, 18, 19; IX 183
    tsar's regalia: I 22;
  *velikii-staryi (*great, old): VIII 24
  zōsta, patrikia: I 4; II 272, 273
Tmutarakan'(Tamatarkha): IV 500; V 320; VII 144, 148, 152; IX 178
Tobias, N.: VII 141
Tokhtamysh, Mongol (Tatar) khan, *(Invasion of Moscow in 1382)*: XII 74
Tolochko, O.P.: V 389; IX 160
Tolochko, P.P.: IX 160, VIII 4
Tolstaia, T.V.: XII add.105a
Tolstoi, I.I.: XII 86, 93
Tolstoi, N.I.: V 380
Toporov, V.N.: V 391; VIII 14
Torchin, killer of Gleb: VII 146
Torschanle, fresco from: XI 415
Trani (in Apulia): XII 86
translatio regni: V 353
Trillmich, W.: III 293; V 382; VIII 4
Troitskii, I.: VI 3
Tsougarakis, D.: VI 3, 5
Tula, district of: XII 82
Turov (Turau): V 365; VII 143
  bishopric and cathedral of Dormition: V 354, 355
Turov-Pinsk: VII 148, 152
Tver: I 13, 15
Tvorogov, O.V.: IV 492, 496; VIII 47; XII 77

Uhrliz, M.: IV 489
Uhrusk, on the Bug: V 360
Ukhnanovova, E.V.: XII add.105a
Ukraine, Ukrainians: I 1, 12, 17
Uliana, wife of Olgerd: I 17
Uspensky, F.B.: VII 6; VII 134; VIII 47, 48, 49; XII 92
Uspensky Sbornik XII–XIII c.: V 387
Uzes: V350, 351

Van den Baar, A.H.: VIII 31
Varangians: I 1, 2; V 386; VII 147, 162
  "road from the Varangians to the Greeks": V 341
Vasilevsky, V.G.: V 371, 373, 374
Vasiliev, A.: III 291; V 379; VII 133
Vasilii, archbishop of Novgorod: XII 89

Vasilii I, son of Dmitrii Donskoi (d.1425): I 15
Vasilii II the Blind: I 15, 16, 18; VIII 37
Vasilii III (1505–1533), son of Ivan: II I 18, 19; XII 78, 83, 84
Vasilii Shuisky, tsar: I 22
Vasilii Vasileevich, grand prince: VIII 37
Vasilissa of Rostov, wife of Andrei Alexandrovich: VIII 28
Vasilko, son of Rostislav: VII 156
Vasmer, M.: VIII 15
Vavřinek, V.: V 378; VIII 20
Vernandsky, G.: IX 161
Verona, doors of St Zeno church: XI 417
Vesterfeld, A.: VIII 35
Viacheslav , prince of Smolensk: VII 155
Viatka, icon of St Nicolas: XII 84
vicar (*namestnik*), vicariates: V 353, 356, 363,
Vilnius: I 17
Vinogradova, V.L.: VIII 24; X 686, 687
Virgin Glykophilousa, iconographic type: XII 97
Viskovatyi, K.: IV 496
Vismara, G.: III 288
Vitovt, grand prince of Lithuania: I 15–17
Vladimir, abbot of the Trinity Monastery in Kashira: VIII 33
Vladimir the Great, St, son of Sviatoslav: I 4–6, 9, 13, 18, 19; II 277, 296; III 287, 289, 296, 298, 301; IV 492, 495, 497, 500, 501, 503; V 315, 320, 321, 327, 329, 331, 334, 335, 338–40, 342, 347, 349, 375; VII 133, 134, 137, 138–45, 149, 150, 152, 155, 157; VIII 1, 11, 49; IX 172, 180, 181, 182; X 687; XII 71, 76, 90, 95, 98, 100, 103, 104
  baptism: I 8; V 320, 324, 330, 332, 333, 370; VII 137; XII 78
  church dedicated in 1311: VIII 34
  coins: VII 140
  conversion: III 299; VII 134;
  cult: I 16; VII167
  icon: VIII 36
  Life: VIII 46, 50; XII 76, 77
  Memory and Eulogy: II 272, 299; VIII 46, 47; V 314, 330–32
  sarcophagus: VII 37
Vladimir, prince of Halych: V 359
Vladimir, prince of Pereiaslav (b.1194): VIII 23
Vladimir, son of Alexander, prince of Tver: VIII 31
Vladimir, son of Constantine, prince of Rostov: VIII 31
Vladimir, son of David, prince of Chernigov (d. 1151): IX 176
Vladimir, son of Iaroslav, prince of Novgorod: V 383
Vladimir, son of Olgerd grand prince of Lithuania: VIII 32, 37
Vladimir-Boris(?)Andreevich, grandson of Alexander Nevskii: VIII 27
Vladimir Andreevich "the Brave", prince of Serpukhov: VIII 33
  descendants: VIII 34
Vladimir-Ioann Vasylkovich, prince of Vladimir in Volhynia: VIII 23–6
Vladimir Monomakh, son of Vsevolod (b. 1053, d. 1125): I 7, 10; IV 495; V 357, 358, 383, 384, 387; VII 141, 150, 166; VIII 10, 23, 44; IX 171, 172, 179, 182
  legend about Byzantine regalia: I 13; "the cap of..." as a crown: I 18
  Volhynian line, descendants: I 12, 13; V 366; IX 172, 173
Vladimir Golokhvastov: VIII 36
Vladimir Vsevolodovich, Muscovite commander in 1380: VIII 32
Vladimir-in-Volhynia, city and principality: V 359, 360, 365; VII 156;
  bishopric: V 354, 355
  cathedral of the Dormition; V 355
Vladimir-in-Suzdalia, city and principality: I 10, 11, 13–15, 17; V 352, 353, 359, 362, 365, 386; VIII 29; IX 174, 175, 176; X 685, 686
  Golden Gates: VIII 30
  bishopric: V 359; IX 180
  Chronicle: IX 176
Vlasto, A.P. III 289
Vodoff, V.: III 299; IV 490, 500; V 386; VII 134; VIII 20, 22, 37; IX 159, 174, 175, 177, 183, 184; X 686
Volga, river: I 10, 12; V 362; IX 184
Volhynia: V 361, 362
Volhynian chronicler: VIII 25
Volkhov: VIII 27
Volodar, prince: V 388
Volodia, diminutive of Vladimir: VIII 32
Volokolamsk Collection, Manuscript 659: XII 95
Vorona, river: V 362
Voronin, N.N.: IX 178, 181; XI 412
votchina, patrimonial landholding: I 18
Vseslav, prince of Polotsk V 346, 381; VII 134, 155, 162
Vsevolod-Andrew, son of Iaroslav, prince

of Pereiaslav, senior prince of Kiev (1078–1093): I 7, 10; V 354, 350, 355; VII 152, 153; IX 171
Vsevolod, son of Gleb, prince of Pronsk: IX 175
Vsevolod, brother of Ihor (b. 1151): X 687
Vsevolod "Big Nest", grand prince of Vladimir-Suzdalia: I 10, 11, 12; V 350, 359; VIII 323; IX 174–7, 180; X 685, 686, 687, 688
Vysheslav, son of Vladimir Monomakh: VII 143
Vyshgorod: VII 145, 147, 154, 158, 159; VIII 10
church of Sts Boris and Gleb: VII 166
translation of relics in: 1072 V 385; VII 155, 160–62
to the new church in 1115: VII 163, 165
Vysockii, S.A.: IX 171

Wasilewski, T.: V 374; VII 141; VIII 32; IX 169
Weiss, G.: III 287, 289
Wenskus, R.: VIII 19
Wepsians, Finnish people: I 2
Westerink, L.G.: V 371
Wichman, bishop of Magdeburg: XI 408, 412
Wieczynski, J.L.: XII 91
Wilhelm, archbishop of Mainz: II 274; V 317
Wörn, D.: IX 182
Wojtowicz, M.: VIII 32
Wollasch, J.: VII 153
Wozniak, E.E.: V 372
wizards: VII 134
Yahyā of Antioch: III 291; IV 491; V 321, 375, VIII 41

Zamaliev, A.: IV 492
Zarazsk (Zaraisk), fortress on the Osetr: XII 81, 82; 83, add. 104a
see also Nicolas Zaraskii
Zarnecki, A.: XI 417
Zarinski, P.: XII 83
Zavadskaia, S.: IX 167
Zenkovsky, S.A.: III 295; V 391; VII 143; X 686, 688; XII 73
Zhivov, V.M.: V 380
Zimin, A.A.: II 272; V 368, 375; IX 163, 166; XII 76, 104
Zimmerman, H.: II 276
Zoc, V.: IV 492
Zuckerman, H.: II add. 278a